About the author

Robin Jenner was born in 1946 and grew up in Newhaven, Sussex, a few miles east of Brighton. He and his late brother Martin both played the guitar and they formed their first band in 1960 and for the next few years, enjoyed some success. In 1963, they went their separate musical ways, Martin enjoying huge success during a lengthy career which included playing with the likes of Cliff Richard and the Everly Brothers. Robin took a lengthy break from live playing and went to teachers training college in 1971 to train as a history teacher, but the pull of the music business brought him back and history took a back seat for many years. After a period teaching guitar and playing in a London based band, he decided to retire from live playing and return to spend more time studying history, the 18th century being his main passion.

Robin's other interest is writing, and during his career in music, has written many songs including two musicals. The twin passions of writing and history led Robin down the inevitable path of writing this book which he hopes will be read and enjoyed by students, academics, or just about anybody who is interested in history and wants to know more about this fascinating period and the people who shaped it. When not writing, Robin works in the antiques trade and as a volunteer at Gloucester Cathedral.

Dear Margaret
Happy reading
(I hope!)
Love Robin
x

Dedication

This book is dedicated to the memory of Jim Read and Sue Lind, two great friends who I miss so much, but who both changed my life in different ways. I will never forget either of them and I have so much to thank them both for.

Robin Jenner

EIGHTEEN LIVES FROM THE EIGHTEENTH CENTURY

AUSTIN MACAULEY
PUBLISHERS LTD.

A CIP catalogue record for this title is available from the British Library.

ISBN 978 1 84963 881 4

www.austinmacauley.com

First Published (2015)
Austin Macauley Publishers Ltd.
25 Canada Square
Canary Wharf
London
E14 5LB

Printed and bound in Great Britain

Acknowledgments

There are many people who have given me great support whilst I have been researching and writing this book, but I must especially thank the following

Lynne Lee is the manager of the gift shop at Gloucester Cathedral and listened patiently over a lengthy period of time whilst I talked about writing it but never actually did anything about doing it. One day, whilst listening once again to my ideas she told me in the nicest possible way to stop talking about it and get on and do it. If it wasn't for that comment one morning in 2007, I might well still be droning on about it now. As it was, after my shift at the cathedral, I went home that afternoon and started work on it.

I'd like to thank Kate Saidi who was working at the Gloucester branch of Waterstones Bookshop at the research stage of the book and spent several years looking up what Miv, another worker who was there at that time, called 'Robin's obscure books'! Always done with patience and a smile thrown in, I'm very grateful to Kate for her enormous help.

My long standing friends Pete and Linda Base deserve my thanks for helping me out in so many ways when I first came to Gloucester in February, 2002. They gave me a home for several months when I moved up from Brighton and did so much to help me settle in to a place where initially I knew nobody. I would not have been able to settle here without their support and if I hadn't settled in Gloucester the way that I have, this book would almost certainly have never been written.

I'd like to thank my friends, Jeff and Pam Gray for their support whilst I was working on the book. Like me, they have a great interest in the 18th century and it has helped me enormously to have someone around to share that interest with.

Caroline Green has been a great friend for many years and has always supported my creative efforts, be they music or this book. After I had spent eighteen months writing to publishers and getting nowhere, she was there encouraging me and gave me the final push to 'sign on the dotted line' when I was about to give up even though I had secured an offer. I have always valued her friendship and without her encouragement at a crucial time, the manuscript of this book might well have ended up gathering dust in a cupboard somewhere in my study.

I owe a great debt of gratitude to a very good friend of many years, Gavin Bourne. Gavin and I have worked together as musicians and not only is he a fine musician, he is an expert on computers whilst everybody who knows me knows that the sum total of my knowledge of computers can be written in block capitals on the back of a postage stamp and there would still be space left to write Tolstoy's 'War and Peace'. He has helped me out on numerous occasions and done it from Sydney, Australia where he now lives with his wife, Maria and young son, Ethan. I owe him a great deal for his knowledge and patience.

I should like to thank Professor Lucy Delap, Lecturer in Modern British History, University of Cambridge. The remarkable thing about Lucy's contribution is that at the time of writing, we had yet to meet and our communications have been by letter or e-mail. I saw Lucy on television talking to Julian Fellowes and the combination of her being a published author and a historian made me wonder if she would be able to help me. She also seemed eminently approachable and so I took a chance and wrote to her. I don't know how she felt at receiving a letter from a complete stranger asking for advice as to how to get a publisher, but three weeks later, I received a lengthy hand written letter which she had clearly put a lot of thought into, and I shall always be grateful for her comments.

Finally, I'd like to thank all at Austin/Macauley, the publishers, for having faith in me and giving me the chance to get this, my first book, into print. It is difficult in these economic times to spend money and time on an unknown writer, and I'm very grateful to them.

There are others too many to mention, but they know who they are, and along with those mentioned above, must know that I am deeply grateful to them all.

Robin Jenner
Gloucester, March, 2015.

Contents

Introduction

This book contains an introduction to the lives and careers of eighteen people who made their mark in the eighteenth century – hence the title of the book. I have written this book with the hope that people will read it and if they find they are interested in some of the people contained therein, could be tempted to find out more about that person by buying a full biography. I hope also that readers approaching the 18th century for the first time will gain some knowledge of this period which contained many changes in the way people led their lives and also gain an interest in finding out more about this fascinating period in our history that produced so many great people.

I am starting this book with this brief introduction by giving a simple outline of life in the 18th century from different angles and in my choice of people, I have tried to cover the main aspects of life such as politics, religion, war, the slave trade, navigation, exploration, feminism, medicine, botany, and most of the parts of life I have featured in the various chapters. There are eighteen main people featured here but I have sometimes given a brief outline of other people within the main chapter that I am writing about in case they too, will interest the reader. For instance, in the chapter on Edward Jenner, I have included some information on Dr. John Hunter (1728-93) who tutored Jenner from 1770 until 1773 and had such a profound effect on Jenner's life and work. I have deliberately kept away from using endless notes at the bottom of each page which some writers use but which I think interrupts the flow that the reader is hopefully experiencing. Instead I have woven other names such as Hunter into the text of the chapter.

Each chapter has a specific purpose:- for instance, I have written about Admiral William Bligh because the man has been treated badly by history and many untruths have been written which I have tried to put into perspective. Admiral Arthur Phillip (1738-1814) is included because he was in charge of the first settlement in New South Wales which grew into the great country of Australia that we know today. William Pitt the Younger (1759-1806) has a chapter because this extraordinary man became Prime Minister at the age of twenty-four and served in this post for twenty out of the next twenty-three years from his appointment. The youthful age in which he became Prime Minister and the length of time that he served in that position will never happen again. I have included a chapter on King George III (1738-1820) as he reigned for the second half of the century, but I have also included Mary Wollstoncraft (1759-97) and Thomas Paine (1737-1809), both of whom would have preferred Britain to be a republic. I have also written a chapter on Admiral Cuthbert Collingwood (1748-1810), the forgotten hero of the Battle of Trafalgar. When Nelson was fatally shot by a French sniper, it was Collingwood who took command of the fleet although he is barely known about by the public and was certainly badly treated by the Admiralty at the time. The biography on Collingwood by Max Adams goes a long way towards setting the record straight and I hope that my small effort will be of some help as well. Medicine is touched on with the discovery of vaccination being covered in the chapter on Edward Jenner (1749-1823). This brilliant man cured the world of the dreaded disease of smallpox which killed millions and he did it with no thought of either fame or financial gain which is why he turned down a chance to go on Captain Cook's second great voyage of discovery in 1772. He also turned down the chance to have a lucrative practice in London to return to the country and work in his beloved village of Berkeley, Gloucestershire. I claim the right to praise Jenner to the skies as he is not a relation of mine – would that he were! I haven't covered everybody who made their mark in the eighteenth century, in fact, I've barely scratched the surface, but I hope that this book will be a start. What follows then is a very brief outline on some aspects of 18th century life for the reader to look at which I hope will whet the appetite and encourage the same reader to learn more about the people who lived during that time. The 18th century was a fascinating period in which great inventions took place and the industrial revolution which happened during this period changed the way people lived.

Speaking in more general terms, farming was important and many people lived on the land, although farming methods changed during this period. For hundreds of years, villages were surrounded by open fields and the inhabitants had rented strips of land to grow their crops and feed any animals they had. Gradually from the middle of the century, more and more land was enclosed and whole fields were fenced in.

Attitudes also changed as women writers such as novelists Fanny Burney (1752-1840) and Jane Austen (1775-1817) became accepted, along with political writers such as Mary Wollstonecraft (1759-97), a feminist before the term had been coined. Before these and other women writers, women often published their books anonymously.

The 18th century is known as the Georgian period due to the names of the Kings who ruled. George I ruled between 1714 and 1727, George II between 1727 and 1760 whilst George III ruled between 1760 and 1820 although illness meant that his son George ruled as Regent between 1811 and his father's death in 1820, when he became King George IV in his own right, ruling until his own death in 1830.

The position of Prime Minister was effectively created by King George I. The King was German and only distantly related to the English Royal Family, but was made King as the Act of Settlement of 1701 stipulated that the Monarch should be a Protestant. George I was the first of the Hanoverians to rule because there was no direct Protestant successor to Queen Anne who ruled from 1702 until 1714. Because George I refused to learn English, he took virtually no part in the affairs of state, refusing to attend Parliament and leaving the business of government to a small group of members who eventually became what is now the Cabinet. The Cabinet needed a Chairman to keep the policy meetings in order and to feed the results back to the King and this job went to Robert Walpole (1676-1745), who by definition became the first Prime Minister serving in the post between 1721 and 1742. The century not only brought the first ever Prime Minister but as mentioned earlier the youngest ever Prime Minister in William Pitt the Younger (1759-1806) who took office when he was just 24 years of age. He served almost as long as Walpole being Prime Minister from 1783 until 1801, and then again from 1804 until his death in 1806.

William Wilberforce (1759-1833), a friend and parliamentary colleague of Pitt's, headed a lengthy campaign to get rid of the slave trade which was abolished in 1807 with slavery itself finally being abolished in 1833. The British economy relied on the slave trade which is why it took so long to abolish it. The so-called 'triangular' trade worked by Britain shipping goods such as cotton, cloth and iron from ports such as Bristol and Liverpool to Africa where it was used to buy slaves. These slaves had often been dragged away from their families and many were children who would never see their parents again. They were put on board ship in the most appalling conditions and carried across the Atlantic to the West Indies where they were sold to work on the plantations there. The slave traders would then load their ships with sugar, tobacco and various raw materials before returning to Britain. Huge profits were made by the ship owners, along with the plantation and cotton factory owners. The slaves suffered dreadfully and many died on route which sometimes was considered a merciful release for them, so appalling were the conditions in which they were kept. The campaign to end this barbaric trade took nearly twenty years and took a toll on Wilberforce's health along with those of people like Thomas Clarkson (1760-1846) who was also in the forefront of the fight to abolish the trade. During most of the century the trafficking of slaves was considered perfectly acceptable and much of the country's wealth was built on this appalling trade. Wilberforce lived just long enough to hear that it had finally been abolished in 1833.

Britain had been at war with France both in 1756 until 1763, and again in 1793 until 1815. The war with France between 1756 and 1763 was known as the seven years war and was fought over who controlled Canada and North America. Up until that time, Britain governed thirteen states on the east coast of America whilst France held the rest. In 1759, the Prime Minister of Britain was Thomas Pelham-Holles (1693-1768), who had held the office from 1754 until 1756 and then again from 1757 until 1762. However, the dominant person in his second administration was William Pitt the Elder (1708-78), later Lord Chatham, who prosecuted the war and it was he who sent General Wolfe (1727-59) to attack Quebec which was held by the French which he successfully did although Wolfe was killed in the fight. However, the British carried on and by September, 1760, had captured Montreal and eventually took control of Canada in its entirety. Britain now had control over Canada as well as virtually all of North America, which added to the thirteen colonies on the east coast, meant that the entire nation was governed by Britain.

It was this situation that America was in when in 1775, the thirteen colonies rose up in revolt over the taxes imposed on them by Britain. In 1773, the Tea Act enabled Britain to sell the colonies tea via the East India Company but imposed tax on them which they refused to pay resulting in the consignment of tea being thrown overboard during a mass demonstration known as the Boston Tea Party. The British retaliated by closing the harbour and then stationing troops in Boston. The first clash between the British and the American soldiers happened in April 1775 at Lexington. The famous 'Declaration of Independence' was written by Thomas Jefferson (1743-1826) in 1776 and after that had been approved, there was no going back – the colonies would fight to the death for their independence. At first, it was felt that the colonies could not possibly win a war against Britain who had a well-trained army which was fighting against a bunch of New England farmers and mechanics that the so-called troops of America consisted of. However, America had a brilliant Commander-in-Chief in George Washington (1732-99) and gradually the tide turned and Britain for all its troops, begun to realise that it was difficult to run the war from the mother country which was thousands of miles away, and with France and Spain coming in to support the colonies, there was only going to be one winner. King George III would not face reality and refused to make a deal with America but after the 1781 surrender of General Cornwallis (1738-1805) at Yorktown, Virginia, the war was all but over and America became an independent country in 1783 with George Washington becoming the first ever President of the new nation. The defeat cost Lord North, (1732-92), the British Prime Minister who had held office between 1770 and 1782 and therefore throughout the war with the colonies, his job in March 1782. After three short-lived Prime Ministers, North's defeat led the way for William Pitt the Younger (1759-1806) to take the job at the age of twenty-four years in December, 1783 and bring some much needed stability to the country.

In 1789, the French Revolution began and King Louis XVl was executed on 21st January, 1793. European countries with a Monarch were horrified at this barbarity and were worried that the same thing would happen to them. Just over a week later, France declared war on Britain on 1st February, 1793 and from 1799 were led by a young Corsican General by the name of Napoleon Bonaparte (1769-1821) who rampaged his way through Europe. The war with France produced the greatest British naval hero of his time, Admiral Lord Horatio Nelson (1758-1805), who defeated the combined Spanish and French fleet at Trafalgar on 21st October, 1805, the battle in which Nelson was killed. Nelson's victory did not end the war, but it did prove that Britain had the superior navy, which ensured that the French would not be able to invade Britain. The war with France was finally won after the Duke of Wellington (1769-1852) defeated the French at the Battle of Waterloo in June, 1815.

After losing the American War of Independence which was fought between 1775 until 1783, Britain had no place to send its prisoners to, the prisons in Britain being massively overcrowded and instead colonised the country which is the present day Australia, making it the great country it is today. Arthur Phillip (1738-1814) was the first Governor-General initially landing troops and settlers in Botany Bay in January 1788, which resulted in the great city of Sydney being named after Thomas Townshend (1733-1800), who as Lord Sydney was the British Home Secretary of the day. Botany Bay had been suggested as a place for criminals to settle by the botanist Joseph Banks (1743-1820) who had been on the first of the three great voyages carried out by Captain James Cook (1728-79) on his ship the *Endeavour* between 1768 and 1771. They had landed at Botany Bay in 1770 and Banks had remembered it. Banks went on to be one of the eminent botanists of his time, was knighted and was President of the Royal Society for forty-one years until his death in 1820.

Back at home, inventions were changing the way people lived. Up until the 17th century most cloth was made from wool, but after that cotton became popular and initially it was imported cheaply from India. However, in 1765, things were about to change. King George III (1738-1820), the great grandson of King George I, had ruled for five years. It was in 1765 that James Hargreaves (c1720-78) built a machine called the Spinning Jenny that enabled not one but sixteen threads to be made at the same time. Four years later, in 1769, Richard Arkwright (1732-92) invented a water frame for spinning which was powered by a water mill and then in 1785, Edmund Cartwright (1743-1823) made the first power looms for weaving. At first they were powered by water but later by steam. Steam engines were also being invented and in 1769 James Watt (1736-1819) built one as did Matthew Boulton (1728-1809). Improved roads were built along with canals that made internal transport better and enabled goods to be transported round the country more easily. Because more machines were being built, so was there a demand for more factories, more so in the north country. People left the countryside in droves to work in the factories, and whilst there was plenty of work, the conditions were extremely harsh. Workers would start at 6 or 7am and carry on with a short break for breakfast and a one hour break for lunch. They would then carry on until 8 o'clock in the evening. They would keep this exhausting schedule up for six days a week with just Sunday off before starting work again on Monday. Some mill owners were humane men and fed the workers properly and even organised schools for the children, but the majority of them mistreated their workers disgracefully. Exhausted children who fell asleep at work were often beaten but there was nothing to be done as there were no trades union at the time.

This introduction barely scratches the surface in terms of outlining the changes that occurred in the 18th century and neither does it go very far in naming all the people that were involved in the great changes that were made, but it is a start. Hopefully, what it does do is to give a small outline as to the events that were happening and some of the people involved in these events. This period in history was fascinating and whilst life in the 18th century was good if you were wealthy, without any social security back up that we take for granted today, life was very hard if you were poor. Whilst the rich enjoyed living in elegant town houses employing servants, the poor often consisted of large semi-starving families living in one room. There is no doubt however, that the century produced some brilliant people such as those already mentioned along with other greats such as John Harrison (1693-1776), the carpenter who became a self taught clockmaker who spent his lifetime working to solve the problem of calculating longitude at sea. After the death of George IV in 1830, his brother, the Duke of Clarence (1765-1837) took the throne as William IV until his own death in 1837 which marked the end of the reigns of the various Hanoverian kings. William IV was a Whig when younger, but in later life became a Tory and he did as much as he could to obstruct the Great Reform Act of 1832 which the then Prime Minister, Earl Grey (1764-1845) brought in which ushered in many constitutional changes. The 1832 Act and the young Queen Victoria taking the throne on the death of her uncle, King William IV in 1837 brought to an end a fascinating period in our history. After 1837, life would never be the same and the Georgian period had finally come to an end – the period known as the Victorian Age had now begun.

Robin G. Jenner
March, 2015.

1
William Pitt the Younger
(1759 - 1806)

At twenty four years of age, the youngest person ever to become Prime Minister, the post which he held between 1783 and 1801, and again from 1804 until his death in 1806.

For many years, the name William Pitt meant William Pitt, the 1st Earl of Chatham, born on 15th November, 1708 and who died a month after dramatically collapsing in the House of Lords on 7th April 1778 during an impassioned speech he was making criticising the government's handling of the war with America.

Exceedingly ill, he had nonetheless struggled into the House aided by his son William, and his son-in-law, Charles Viscount Mahon, who was married to Pitt's daughter, Hester. Pitt died one month later in May, and was buried in the North Transept of Westminster Abbey on Tuesday, 9th June, 1778 after his body had lain in state in Westminster Hall. It was thought that no less than one hundred thousand people had filed past his coffin the previous day to pay their tribute to 'The Great Commoner' as he was once known, although he had been created the 1st Earl of Chatham on 28th July, 1766 when he became Lord Privy Seal and de facto Prime Minister.

Pitt had been educated at Eton and Trinity College, Oxford although his time at Eton would appear to have been unhappy as he vowed in later life to educate his children at home rather than send them away. Although he was forty-six years old when he did eventually marry, he and his wife, Hester Grenville, had five children and Pitt was as good as his word, educating them all himself with the help of a tutor, Mr. Edward Wilson.

He first entered Parliament in 1735 for the family borough, Old Sarum. He held a variety of posts but it was 1759, the year of his son William's birth that his career approached its height. The Prime Minister was the Whig, Thomas Pelham-Holles, (1693-1768) the Duke of Newcastle, who had previously been Prime Minister from 1754, when he succeeded his brother, Henry Pelham, but resigned in 1756. However, in July 1757, he was again Prime Minister whereby he appointed William Pitt to his cabinet as the chief prosecutor of the war that eventually became known as the seven years war that lasted from 1756 to 1763. The war was conducted between Prussia, with Britain as it's only ally, against the combined forces of France, Austria, Russia, Saxony and Sweden under the Hanoverian King George ll who reigned as the British Monarch between the years 1727 and 1760.

Pitt was not always held in high regard but a number of military successes enhanced his reputation considerably. Coupled with his management of the military campaigns, was a natural eloquence at a time when it was important for politicians. Although there were the Whigs and the Tories, party politics was not so entrenched as it is today, and a good speech in parliament could and often did, sway someone's opinion, and Pitt was very highly regarded as an orator.

But it was not just his father, the Earl of Chatham, who the young William Pitt had for a role model. William Pitt the Younger came from a highly political family – his pedigree for later becoming Prime Minister at the extraordinarily young age of twenty-four was impeccable. As well as his father, his uncle, his grandfather, and great grandfather had all been members of Parliament and on his mother's side, the Grenville family were equally famous, two uncles were in the House of Commons, and one was in the House of Lords. William Pitt the Elder married Hester Grenville (1721-1803) when he was forty-six years old and she was thirty-three. It was almost a match made in heaven as the two families not only had great political pedigrees, but Pitt was hopeless at managing his finances even though he had been left £10,000 by the Duchess of Marlborough in 1744. Sir William Pynset left him £3,000 a year along with his Somerset estate which then became Pitt's family seat.

William Pitt the Younger's great grandfather was Thomas Pitt of Boconnic (1653-1726). Known as 'Diamond' Pitt, he had a buccaneering spirit that took him to India where he made a fortune trading against the East India Company before returning home and purchasing property including the ancient borough of Old Sarum which was near Salisbury. Parliament did not have contests for seats in the way we have today as there was no universal suffrage, and Old Sarum was eventually to become notorious in the nineteenth century for returning two members of Parliament without having any voters at all. Thomas Pitt returned to India on behalf of the Company as Governor of Madras and it was there that he purchased a 130-carat diamond for £25,000 and sold it on to the Regent of France for a healthy profit. He returned once more to purchase more estates and secure the future finances of his children.

One of these was Robert Pitt (c1680-1727) who was Pitt the Younger's grandfather. In 1705, he was also put into Parliament as a member for Old Sarum alongside his father. His career was undistinguished and the only achievement that he had of any note was that he fathered five children. The eldest, Thomas Pitt (c1705-1761) was Pitt the Younger's uncle, and he inherited most of the family wealth, but it was Thomas' younger brother, William (1708-1778) who was to achieve fame and become known as William Pitt the Elder and who also became the 1st Earl of Chatham.

At the age of forty-six, William Pitt the Elder had the great good fortune to marry Hester Grenville (1721-1803), whose brothers included the famous George (1712-1770), Richard (1711-1779), who was to become Earl Temple, James (1715-1783), and Henry (1717-1784). These were all Pitt the Younger's uncles by marriage.

Hester Grenville was a wonderful choice for a wife by Pitt the Elder. He was very badly in debt when they married, but Hester took over the running of his financial affairs, and whilst not able to put him in a position whereby he could repay them, she put them in some sort of order and stopped them getting worse. Pitt was forty-six years old when they married, and Hester was thirty-three. In the normal run of things, this was quite an age difference, but in this case it seemed even bigger due to the fact that Pitt was often very ill and Hester nursed him without seeming to complain. Indeed, she was devoted to him, and in one of her early letters to her husband, described herself as: "ever unalterably your most passionately loving wife". A great many of Pitt's illnesses seemed to be associated with gout and the sight of him making a speech in the House of Commons supported by a walking stick and wrapped in flannels was a normal sight but presumably an unedifying one for most eligible young women of the day with the sort of family background that Hester enjoyed. Still, she loved him and remained loyal to him.

In 1755, the year after William and Hester married, he purchased Hayes Place in South London, near the then village of Bromley. It must have seemed sumptuous at the time, having as it did twenty-four bedrooms along with elegant gardens and several hundred acres of pasture and woodland. However, ten years later, we have firm evidence just how hopeless Pitt the Elder was at managing his finances. In 1765, he inherited Burton Pynsent, a large estate in Somerset from Sir William Pynsent, who not only was unrelated to Pitt, but was merely an admirer who hadn't even met Pitt. Naturally, the family of Sir William were none too pleased and challenged the will but to no avail, and Pitt set about spending a fortune in huge alterations along with landscaping. He could not afford the alterations that he was planning to make, so he sold Hayes Place to finance the work but repurchased it at a price that was higher than that which he sold it for. Apparently after selling it, he decided that he needed a large house near London to help him run his affairs, and it was these transactions that started the debts that would remain with him all his life. Bad though they were, he had Hester to thank for them not getting even more out of control, as she more or less took over the running of his financial affairs from then on and stopped a bad situation from getting worse. Even so, he died heavily in debt and a grateful Parliament voted for £20,000 to clear those debts after his death. This was a huge amount and is the equivalent of well over £1 million today – a scenario which simply would not happen in this day and age however high the deceased person was esteemed. Parliament also voted for an annual sum of £4,000, nearly a quarter of a million pounds today, to the Earldom of Chatham, which had been inherited by William's elder brother John.

William and Hester Pitt produced five children, John, the 2nd Earl of Chatham, (1756-1835), James (1761-1780), Harriot (1758-1786), Hester (1755-1780), and the most famous of them all, William (1759-1806), who would one day become known as William Pitt the Younger and eventually eclipse the fame of his father, although such was the standing of the Earl of Chatham, no-one would have believed it at the time. Apart from the eldest child, John, all the siblings were to die relatively young, even for those days, but such were the achievements of father and son, William the Elder, and William the Younger, the Pitt family name is unlikely ever to be forgotten when the future history books are written.

William was born on 28th May, 1759 in Bromley after a difficult birth. William Pitt the Younger was always old for his age and whilst his father undoubtedly loved all of his children, it must be said that William junior was his favourite. All the children spent a great deal of time at home, because it was there that Pitt the Elder and the tutor, Mr. Edward Wilson, taught them. There were always visitors at the home but all the stories that these visitors told would more often than not concern young William. Lady Caroline Holland (nee Lennox), wife of Lord Holland and the mother of the famous Charles James Fox (1749-1806), the future Whig politician, was supposed to have said when both William and Charles were young boys: "I have been this morning with Lady Hester Pitt, and there is little William Pitt, not eight years old and really the cleverest child I ever saw; and brought up so strictly and proper in his behaviour, that, mark my words, that little boy will be a thorn in Charles's side as long as he lives". That comment if true, would turn out to be incredibly prophetic as that is exactly what happened. He seemed to be interested in politics and philosophy at a very young age, and this was undoubtedly due to not only the influence of his famous father, but also his mother. Although they lived in an era where women were light years away from getting the vote or being able to stand for parliament, it has to be remembered that Hester was a very clever woman whose own family were steeped in politics. Letters that the family wrote when talking about William, would refer to him as 'The Philosopher', 'The Young Senator, and 'Eager Mr William'. In 1766, when William was seven years old, his tutor Mr. Wilson, wrote about him: "...Mr. Pitt, if it is anything he may attend to, constantly places himself by me, where his steady attention and sage remarks are not only entertaining but useful; as they frequently throw a light upon the subject, and strongly impress it upon my memory". William was entertaining and witty, but he was certainly old for his time, and this characteristic continued throughout his life when it is seen how young he was when he became Prime Minister, and also the fact that his body was worn out through work when he died at the age of 46 in 1806. He would write letters to his father in Latin and English, the latter tending to be rather pompous and wordy and in this he was merely copying his elders, because letters tended to be wordy during the eighteenth century.

Father and son were extremely close. This was partly William's aptitude for the written and the spoken word, but also because he was a child who suffered from ill health all his life, which meant that he was tutored from home, although his father, hating his own experiences at Eton, determined to do this anyway for all his children. In years to come, Pitt the Elder described his son as: "the hope and comfort of my life". In 1772, Hester took William's older brother John, and his two sisters, Harriot and Hester, to Hayes and William and his younger brother James were left in the care of their father in Burton Pynsent. Pitt the Elder wrote to his wife: "My dearest wife will read with joy that the boys go on well. I believe William's sequestration, as he learnedly terms it, agrees better with his contemplative constitution than more talk and more romps. Airing, literature, the arts, tea table, sober whist and lecturing Papa for staying out too late, together with the small amusement of devouring a joint of mutton, or so, before I can look about, make up our daily occupations". His wife Hester wrote back: "I do not in the least wonder that the style of William's present life agrees with him. It is certainly not better suited to the state of his constitution, than to the fineness of his mind, which makes him enjoy with the highest pleasure what would be above the reach of any other creature of his small age".

Pitt the Elder loved all his children, of that there is no doubt, but it is equally certain that he had a special bond with young William, seeing as other people saw later, something of himself in his son. Each day, young William would recite passages from the great writers and poets, such as Shakespeare and Milton. Lord Stanhope, (1805-1875) was a biographer of Pitt the Younger. Stanhope was the 5th Earl and an English historian and after entering Parliament in 1830, was instrumental in the passing of the Copyright Act of 1842. Although Stanhope was born only a year before Pitt had died, and therefore could have had no direct recollection of Pitt himself, Stanhope's father had actually been in Parliament with Pitt and in his work on Pitt the Younger, Lord Stanhope wrote: "My father had the honour to be connected in relationship with that great man – and, as such, he had the privilege of being in the house with him sometimes for many weeks together. Presuming on that familiar intercourse, he told me, he ventured on one occasion to ask Mr. Pitt by what means – by what course of study – he had acquired that admirable readiness of speech – that aptness of finding the right word without pause or hesitation. Mr. Pitt replied that whatever readiness he might be thought to possess in that respect, he believed that he derived it very much from a practice his father – the great Lord Chatham – had recommended to him. Lord Chatham had bid him take up any book in some foreign language with which he was well acquainted, in Latin, Greek, or French for example. Lord Chatham then enjoined him to read out of this work into English, stopping where he was not sure of the word to be used in English, until the right word came to his mind, and then proceed. Mr. Pitt states that he had assiduously followed this practice. At first he had often to stop for a while before he could recollect the proper word, but he found the difficulties gradually disappear, until what was a toil to him at first became at last an easy and familiar task".

In 1773, when his father decided that his home education had been more or less completed, he sent William to Cambridge at the extraordinarily early age of fourteen. At this time, William could read up to seven pages of Thucydides without having previously seen it and barely making a mistake in the process. Thucydides (c460-c400BC) was born near Athens and was a Greek historian of the Peloponnesian war and who suffered in the Athenian plague of 430BC but managed to survive. As William was only fourteen years old, such a talent was amazing.

For a boy of William's age to be entering Cambridge was an extraordinary achievement and was no less unusual then as it would be today. Also, just as if that happened today, there would be concern as to how he would mix with his fellow undergraduates for two reasons: the first because of the age difference between William and his fellow students, the second because up until this time, he had been educated at home and had rarely mixed with boys of even his own age. He had also had various illnesses but his tutor, Mr. Wilson, and his father obviously thought that he was ready and his name was entered into the college admissions on 26th April, 1773, one month before his fourteenth birthday. Despite his age, Mr. Wilson had no concerns about the new student. Wilson wrote: "He will go to Pembroke not a weak boy to be made property of, but to be admired as a prodigy; not to hear lectures, but to spread light".

Wilson and William travelled from Somerset to Cambridge, a journey that took five days, in October, 1773. William was obviously looking forward to his entrance in to the big wide world as Cambridge must have seemed to him, and on arrival wrote to his father:

"I have the pleasure of writing to my dear father, after having breakfasted upon College rolls, and made some acquaintance with my new quarters which seem, on the short examination I have given, neat and convenient.....To make out our five days, we took the road by Binfield, and called in upon Mr. Wilson's curate there; who soon engaged with his rector in a most vehement controversy, and supported his opinions with Ciceronian action and flaming eyes.....We slept last night at Barkway, where we learnt that Pembroke was a sober, staid college, and nothing but solid study there. I find indeed, we are to be grave in apparel, as even a silver button is not allowed to sparkle along our quadrangles, &c.; so that my hat is soon to be stripped of its glories, in exchange for a plain loop and button".

The quarters that he described were previously lived in by Thomas Gray, the poet, who had said of William Pitt the Elder's decision to accept a peerage in July, 1766, "the weakest thing ever done by so great a man". This was when Pitt became in effect, Prime Minister and it was the loss of his great speeches in the Commons that caused Gray's remark. After Gray, the quarters at Cambridge were occupied by Mr. Wilson's brother who vacated them to travel the world. Now young William Pitt was to occupy them.

William was interested in world events, and coming to Cambridge must have seemed like quite an adventure for a boy of just fourteen, but in fact he was entering into a small, enclosed world. At this time, there were approximately fifty undergraduates at Pembroke College and less than a thousand in the whole university. Pitt was only at Cambridge a week when he wrote to his father telling him that he was studying Quintilian and that Dr. Brown, who was the Master of the College had taken an interest in him, which given his age and abilities, was not surprising. Quintilian, or Marcus Fabius Quintilianus (c35-c100) was a Roman rhetorician born in Calagurris in Spain. He studied oratory in Rome, and eventually became a state teacher of the oratorical art. His pupils included Pliny the Younger (62-113), the Roman writer and orator, and the two grand nephews of Domitianus (51-96), the Roman Emperor.

William had made an outstanding beginning to his studies at Cambridge, but sadly, it was not to last. Illness caught up with him and Mrs. Sparry, the family nurse, stayed with William in order to look after him which she did for two months, two months in which he was confined to his rooms. After that, it was decided to take him home which they did until the summer of the following year. It was a massive blow, but his father was encouraged by a letter that arrived from Dr. Brown even before William had arrived back with his family. Brown wrote:- "not withstanding his illness, I have myself seen, and have heard enough from his tutors, to be convinced both of his extraordinary genius and most amiable disposition.....I hope he will return safe to his parents, and that we shall receive him again in a better and more confirmed state of health."

The family physician was Dr. Addington (1713-90), who was the father of Henry Addington (1757-1844) who took over as Prime Minister from William in 1801 until 1804 when Pitt the Younger again took on the job. Dr. Addington was also a friend and adviser to William's father, Lord Chatham. Addington Senior had been educated at Trinity College, Oxford, where he gained an M.A. in May, 1740, and a M.D. in January, 1744. He was highly thought of by his peers and was one of the doctors called in to treat King George III during the latter's illness in 1788. In the 18th century, medicine was slightly hit and miss to say the least, and whilst there were certain areas of medicine that doctors were highly skilled in, there were other areas that they simply got completely wrong. At this time, whilst William was still young, he received medical advice from Dr. Addington that however well intentioned, almost certainly did the young Pitt great harm in the long term and along with his massive workload, could possibly have eventually lead to Pitt's early death. Amongst some things that were harmless, such as getting to bed early, and regular horse riding, Addington advised William to drink a daily quantity of port wine, possibly as much as a bottle a day which was advice that was anything but harmless. This was quite standard advice at the time as it was felt that an intake of alcohol would cause other toxins in the body to disperse and eventually disappear altogether. If a doctor were to advise a patient to drink a bottle of port in such quantity in this day and age, people would be astonished, but it has to be remembered that as recently as 1893, a Dr. Thomas Richard Allinson (1858-1918) was struck off and not allowed to practice medicine any more by the General Medical Council because he had suggested that smoking was bad for people. At that time, it was felt that cigarette smoke actually cleared the lungs. Dr. Allinson had also advocated three hours of walking a day, advised people not to work too hard, to cut down on salt, eat fruit and vegetables, avoid tea and coffee and to refrain from drinking alcohol. However, during Pitt the Younger's life, the medical advice he was given by Dr. Addington was fairly standard and this, along with the fact that from that time onwards, William's fragile health had started to improve, certainly in the short term at any rate, made him think the advice was good.

Eventually William returned to Cambridge in July 1774 and his tutor was Dr. George Pretyman, a junior Fellow at Pembroke who was only eight years older than William. The working relationship between the two was good and eventually they became firm friends that lasted into a lifelong friendship. When Pitt became Prime Minister, Dr. Pretyman was on hand as an adviser in his early years in the job and was with Pitt when he died in 1806. When he was Pitt's tutor, he became very impressed with his talents, and Pitt, having gone through as many Latin and Greek texts as he was able, was always asking Pretyman to stretch him more – he was a very willing pupil. Dr. Pretyman actually wrote a biography of William in later life entitled *Life of Pitt*, but despite knowing his subject well, the book gave little insight into Pitt's character. However, it would appear that although William was always regarded as an amiable person, he continued to be rather old for his age and seemed to spend more time with

Pretyman than his fellow students. Pretyman wrote in his biography of Pitt:-
"While Mr. Pitt was under-graduate, he never omitted attending chapel morning
and evening, or dining in the public hall, except when prevented by
indisposition. Nor did he pass a single evening out of the college walls. Indeed,
most of his time was spent with me." Pretyman also wrote:- "I never knew him
spend an idle day; nor did he ever fail to attend me at the appointed hour". This
was written about a person in their mid teens so there was clearly none of the
high living that one would expect from a young man away from home for the
first time. Even in his youth, William Pitt was clearly focused and destined for
great things in years to come. He studied Classics and Mathematics from Dr.
Pretyman and had little interest in any other subjects, even that of theology. This
was despite the fact that Pretyman himself was considering a future career in the
church, along with a great many of Pitt's fellow undergraduates, but Pitt simply
wasn't interested.

In 1776 onwards, William took his Master of Arts degree and from that
point, did in fact make friends more akin to his own age. Some life long
friendships were formed including that of Edward Eliott who became his
brother-in-law in years to come, marrying Pitt's sister Harriot. Harriot and
Edward eventually lived with him in Downing Street and Edward became a
member of the Board of the Treasury in Pitt's administration. Several other
friends made at Cambridge were eventually members of his future government
and while they were undergraduates, the lighter side of Pitt's character
blossomed as he became part of this clever and politically minded group of
young men. Pitt would never do anything that would embarrass the family name,
but he did make friends with William Wilberforce (1759-1833), who, although
being part of a different and more racy set than Pitt, eventually became an
evangelical Christian in the mid 1780's, and who was to take such an active role
in the abolition of the slave trade, the trafficking of which became illegal in
1807, an achievement which Wilberforce took a leading part in bringing about.

Pitt's friends were a lively crowd, intellectually stimulating, and whilst they
drank a great deal of port together, did not get involved in any of the vices
usually undertaken by undergraduates. They were all the sons of noblemen and
that coupled with the fact that he came into contact with very few women, meant
that although he was away from the cloistered upbringing of being tutored at
home, he still operated in a limited circle in terms of the type of people he met.
This may have caused some people in his later life who did not know him to
consider him aloof and haughty. In company that he was comfortable with
however, he was relaxed and friendly and on a determined path to high political
office via the law.

In later years it would be seen that both Pitt the Elder and Pitt the Younger
were exceedingly careful with the nation's finances, but hopeless with their
own. Pitt the Elder had died in 1778 leaving William £3,500 (£200,000+ in
today's terms) but he never received it. The money that Parliament had voted for
in order to clear his father's debts had done just that, cleared his debts, but they
left nothing for young William to inherit. He did not receive any of the legacy
until the property at Hayes was sold, and by this time Pitt the Younger was
Prime Minister. When he left Cambridge, his total income was £600 (£36,000)

per year, an enormous sum by most people's standards for a person leaving university, but not apparently enough for Pitt the Younger, although it must be borne in mind that MP's were not paid in those days, so it was considered necessary to earn more in order to launch a career in politics. This £600 was paid to him by his elder brother John Pitt (1756-1835) who had become the 2nd Earl Chatham on the death of their father in 1778. However, this income still did not stop William writing to his mother from time to time requesting further funds. Lady Hester continued to worry about her son's health, and William wrote to her in January, 1780:- "The Charge of looking slender and thin when the doctor saw me, I do not entirely deny; but if it was in a greater degree than usual, it may fairly be attributed to the hurry of London, and an accidental cold at the Time......The use of the horse I assure you I do not neglect, in the properest medium; and a sufficient number of idle avocations secure me quite enough from the danger of too much study......... Among the Principal Occupations of Cambridge at this Season of Christmas are perpetual College Feasts, a species of Exercise in which, above all others, I shall not forget your rule of moderation."

His mother's situation meant that she had not been able to give William substantial financial help, so he had borrowed £1,000 from Thomas Coutts, the banker at five percent interest but in order to carve a career for himself in the law, he needed an address in Lincoln's Inn Fields and felt that he needed even more financial backing. He wrote to his mother asking for help saying:- "It will very soon be necessary for me to have rooms at Lincoln's Inn......The whole expense of these will be Eleven Hundred Pounds, which sounds to me a frightful sum......and whether there are any means of advancing the money out of my fortune before I am of age." Much as she wanted to however, his mother simply did not have the necessary funds to help William in the way he needed but help came from his Uncle Richard Grenville, the 2nd Earl Temple (1711-1779), and elder brother of George Grenville (1712-1770). George Grenville had become First Lord of the Admiralty in 1762 and Prime Minister in 1763 whilst Richard himself had been First Lord of the Admiralty between 1756 and 1761. Richard had previously said that he would advance Pitt the money that he needed but after paying the first instalment, Earl Temple died. Pitt was able to secure the chambers on the promise of Temple's obligation, only to mortgage them the following year in order to raise more cash. William Pitt was but twenty-one years old, his career had barely begun, and already his finances were beginning to spiral out of control. Nothing much changed for the better in that direction and when he died twenty-five years later he left substantial debts just as his father had done before him.

Pitt had spent his late teens busily moving between the life he knew at Cambridge, and moving between family homes, although the one he preferred to stay at most of all was that of his sister Hester, who had married Lord Charles Mahon (1753-1816), and who in 1786 would become the 3rd Earl Stanhope on the death of his father, Philip, the 2nd Earl (1714-1786). James, the 2nd Earl Stanhope's father (1673-1721) was the 1st Earl Stanhope and was married to William's great aunt, Lucy Pitt (1693-722) making William and his brother-in-law distant cousins. There was a great deal of inter marrying amongst families in those days, even amongst the aristocracy. Although William attended the opera from time to time and enjoyed music, it was really the intellectual evenings that he preferred and there was one well documented occasion during a dinner at Lincoln's Inn Fields when he had an argument with the famous historian, Edward Gibbon (1737-1794), who was having the second and third volumes of the *Decline and Fall of the Roman Empire* published. Not only an historian, Gibbon had entered Parliament in 1774 and had served as Commissioner of Trade and Plantations under the man he worshipped, Lord North (1732-92) who was Prime Minister from 1770 until 1782.

A young lawyer present by the name of James Bland Burges described how Gibbon had finished one of his many anecdotes and was expecting the usual polite appreciation from those present. On this occasion however, he was surprised to find some of his views questioned in a calm confident manner by a twenty-one-year-old William Pitt. Gibbon, not used to having his views challenged, and certainly not by a man twenty-two years his junior and not long out of university, hit back, and an exchange of views between the two men took place that on both sides, bordered on brilliance. Burges describes the outcome:- "...at length the genius of the young man prevailed over that of his senior, who, finding himself driven into a corner from which there was no escape, made some excuse arising from the table and walked out of the room". Burges went on to explain that Pitt continued to expand on the subject that had caused Gibbon to leave the room and gained admiration with his grasp of the subject in hand and his ability to articulate it. Pitt was beginning to make a name for himself.

Pitt was called to the bar in 1780 and doubtless would have made a brilliant lawyer, but it was in fact inevitably politics that he was being drawn to. During the summer of 1779, the war with America was not going well and Lord North, the Prime Minister, was being criticised. In those days, Parliaments ran for seven years but it looked at this time as if it might not run its full course, and so William Pitt looked to see if there would be any chance of his gaining a seat.

From an early age, William Pitt was a driven man. He not only knew that he wanted to go into politics, but he knew exactly which constituency he wanted to represent, which was Cambridge University, in those days represented by two members. There was no universal suffrage in those days, and the only people who were allowed to vote at Cambridge were academics who were members of the university senate. The whole voting system in the 18th century seems undemocratic and chaotic to us today, as indeed it was, but it seems to have worked at the time.

Some constituencies had barely any voters at all, whilst others could number up to 20,000 who were entitled to vote. With no party funds behind them, would be Members of Parliament needed a great deal of money to fight an election, so that not only was the voting population limited, but so was the number of people that could actually put themselves forward for election. Pitt had no money to speak of, and so Cambridge would be an ideal seat to fight. In July 1779, he wrote to his mother:- "It is a seat of all others, the most desirable, as being free from expense, perfectly independent, and I think in every respect extremely honourable.....You will perhaps think the idea hastily taken up, when I tell you that six Candidates have declared already; but I assure you that I shall not flatter myself with any vain hopes".

Pitt set about canvassing views about the possibility of standing for Cambridge but received little encouragement from neither the Marquis of Rockingham nor Earl Temple. However, this did little to deter Pitt's determination but in the event, he was beaten temporarily at any rate, by events that were out of his control. Much to people's surprise, the government of Lord North, the Tory Prime Minister, didn't fall, and there was no election in 1779. William had to content himself by playing a waiting game and to watch the debates in Parliament as a bystander. He did not have to wait long however. On 1st September 1780, Lord North asked King George III permission for Parliament to be dissolved and a general election was announced. This took everyone by surprise and there was no time for opposition forces to be organised, and so Lord North was confident of staying in office which he succeeded in doing, not losing power until 1782. Pitt fared much worse than North in this 1780 election. Despite there being no time to prepare, he stood for Cambridge but finished bottom of the poll of five candidates, one seat being won by a sitting member and the other by someone who had been a candidate in a previous election and who was a follower of Charles Watson Wentworth (1730-1782), who became the second Marquis of Rockingham on the death of his father. Rockingham had previously been Prime Minister in 1765 to 1766 and had always opposed Lord North's policies on the war with America. He eventually became Whig Prime Minister again in March 1782 after Lord North resigned but died four months later.

Pitt had youth on his side but was more philosophical about his defeat than one might imagine given his ambition. Straight after his defeat was announced he wrote to his mother:

"Pemb. Hall, Sept. 16, 1780

My dear Mother,

Mansfield and Townshend have run away with the Prize, but my struggle has not been dishonourable.
I am just going to Cheveley (the seat of the Duke of Rutland) for a day or two, and shall soon return to you for as long as the law will permit, which will now be probably the sole object with me. I hope you are all well. Your ever dutiful and affectionate,

W. Pitt"

It was a difficult time for William and his mother. Pitt's sister Hester had had a third child, Lucy, in February of that year, 1780, but had not recovered properly from the birth and died in July aged just twenty-five. Another tragedy hit the family when James, Pitt's youngest brother, died on active service in the navy in the West Indies at the end of 1780 although they did not receive the news until the new year.

James, born in 1761, was like Hester, very young, being only nineteen years old when he died, and had been much loved by William. The previous year, 1779, had seen the death of Richard Grenville, the second Earl Temple, who was William's mother's brother, and therefore his uncle. The previous year to that of course, 1778, had seen the dramatic collapse in Parliament of Pitt's father, Lord Chatham, and his subsequent death a month later, so in the course of two years, William's mother had lost her husband, brother, and two children who were relatively young adults.

It was a terrible series of blows to the family, but the young William Pitt was determined to carry on with his ambition to enter Parliament. Although beaten in September 1780 in his attempt to become a member, his chance came when a friend of a friend, Sir James Lowther, who controlled a number of so called pocket boroughs in the north of England, found that his cousin William had been elected for both Appleby and Carlisle and decided that he would sit for Carlisle. Pocket boroughs were sometimes known as rotten boroughs, as they had virtually no electorate and were usually owned and controlled by one man who could put a person of his choice into parliament, and in return, exercise some influence. This meant that a member had to be found for Appleby and due to his connections with Lowther, Appleby found that they had a new Member of Parliament, William Pitt, son of the great Lord Chatham. It was not achieved in the manner in which he had hoped, but at the age of twenty-one, he had got his wish, and his Parliamentary career could begin which it duly did, on the 23rd January 1781, which is the day he first entered the House of Commons as a fully fledged Member of Parliament.

The House had not sat since early December the previous year because of the Christmas break, so the day that Pitt took his seat was the first day available to him after the holiday. There were no women MPs in those days and the average age of the all male establishment was younger then than it is today, so the atmosphere could be fairly rumbustious. There would have been a large number of young men from aristocratic families, as well as lawyers along with some military men. The industrial revolution was taking place and eventually there would be an increase in the number of businessmen and merchants in the House. The makeup of the House was necessarily limited as there were no salaries or pensions paid so members had to be financially independent. Although then, as now, there was a Speaker to keep order, he wasn't always very successful and the House was a lot more noisy and boisterous than it is now. In an age where we think of people having good manners, there was often a complete lack of decorum and if members were bored with a speech that they were listening to, no pretence at politeness was observed and members would simply talk loudly amongst themselves making it impossible for the member speaking at the time to even hear himself, let alone enable others to hear him.

This was the atmosphere that the twenty-one–year-old William Pitt found himself in on 23rd January, 1781. Although party politics did not hold the same sway as they do now in terms of discipline, there were two main parties, the Tories and the Whigs. Put in simplistic terms, the Tories were rather like today's Conservatives and believed in the old systems of authority. They supported the Stuart line of Kings and felt that the Monarchy had a divine right to rule and that the King's views should hold sway over Parliament. The Whigs on the other hand supported the Hanoverian line of Monarchs but wanted to limit their powers in favour of parliamentary rule. They were almost the forerunners of today's Liberal Democrat party, the Labour Party being over a hundred years away from being formed. Two years before entering Parliament, Pitt had written: "I do not wish to call myself anything but an Independent Whig which in words is hardly a distinction, as everyone alike pretends to it". When Pitt took his seat, Lord North was still Prime Minister but reluctantly so, in fact he didn't even like to be called Prime Minister as fairly or unfairly, it is perceived historical wisdom that he mismanaged the war with America and was not keen to be held accountable for it.

The main reason he stayed in office was the debt that he owed King George III who had paid off his debts of £18,000 (£1 million + in today's terms) but he soldiered on with the help of various powerful factions including John Montague (1718-92), the 4th Earl Sandwich who was also First Lord of the Admiralty from 1771 until 1782. Although basking in the glory from the achievements of Captain Cook's voyages between 1768 and 1779, Sandwich was also tainted with his inability to manage the war with the Americas properly.

Facing Lord North on the opposite side of the House was the famous Charles James Fox (1749-1806), son of Lord Holland, previously the politician Henry Fox (1705-1774) and Lady Caroline Holland (1723-1774), one of the famous Lennox sisters. Charles James Fox was an excellent debater and could persuade people in the days when debates were allowed to do exactly that, persuade Members in an age where they were not bound so rigidly to the party system as is the case today.

Although the House was often noisy during debates, there were some brilliant speakers who could command the attention of the House and who were able to be listened to in relative silence. Charles James Fox was just such a man. He was not handsome in the classical sense at all, and not particularly well dressed, but he had such a charisma about him that he was a compulsive womaniser, and in fact, was said to have had an affair with Georgiana, the Duchess of Devonshire (1757-1806), who was part of the Spencer family, still so famous today. In 1774, Georgiana had married William Cavendish, the 5th Duke (1748-1811) who was an extremely wealthy man and who was said to have had an income of £60,000 per annum by the time he was sixteen. This would amount to more than £3,500,000 in today's terms, an unthinkable amount for a boy that age. However, although considered a beauty and certainly clever, Georgiana never seemed to satisfy her husband and countered his affairs by having some herself, the 2nd Earl Grey (1764-1845) being one of her lovers, although in fairness to her, it seems she truly loved him and had a daughter by him, although she was not allowed to keep her, the daughter being taken and brought up by the Grey family. She was the undisputed queen of fashionable society and would spend a great deal of time socializing with and raising funds for the Whig party, of which Fox was a leading member. Not only was Fox a womaniser, but he was also a compulsive gambler, a habit that his father Lord Holland indulged him in when Fox was a very young man, often paying off all his debts, so it was no wonder that he never lost the habit. It was said that he and his brother once lost £32,000 in one night, which would be the equivalent of nearly £2 million in today's terms.

There were some very powerful politicians in the House in those days, but although surprising to us today, one of the men who wielded a great deal of political power was King George III, the reigning Monarch, although naturally he had no seat in the House, his power being wielded behind the scenes. When he was a young man and new to the throne in 1760, the man he looked to for guidance was the Scottish statesman, Lord Bute (1713-1792). King George III's father was in fact Prince Frederick, but he had died in 1751 before his father, King George II, so it was George II's grandson, King George III, who succeeded to the throne aged just twenty-two years old, having been born in 1738. Bute in fact became Prime Minister in 1762 although he lasted less than a year in that office. George Grenville was his successor and then Lord Rockingham before he made way for Lord Chatham (Pitt's father) in 1766. Chatham was opposed to the manner in which the war had been managed, which as everybody knew, was influenced by the King, but when Lord North became Prime Minister in 1770, George III had eventually found someone to do his bidding as North was far easier to manipulate than Chatham. North was still hanging on to the job of Prime Minister and that was the political situation that William Pitt the Younger found himself in when he made his entrance to the House of Commons that January day in 1781.

It was a whole month before Pitt made his maiden speech after entering the House. A maiden speech in those days was much as it is now. New members were expected to know their place and the result was usually a rather bland, non-controversial speech delivered by a new, rather nervous member. Pitt's was nothing like that.

The day he spoke, the 26th February, 1781, was during a debate on economic reform that was being proposed by Edmund Burke (1729-1797), the Irish statesman and philosopher. Burke was a powerful man who served as Paymaster of the Forces in 1782 and 1783 but the government under North was determined to vote down the bill that Burke brought to the House. Lord Nugent was finishing off a speech attacking the bill, and although Pitt supported Burke, there was no certainty that he would speak. Several members cried:- "Mr. Pitt, Mr. Pitt". Although Pitt had not necessarily planned to say anything, it was a subject that he knew a great deal about, and so, although when he did get up, he probably had a good idea what he was going to say, it probably sounded as if it had been delivered off the cuff.

Whatever preparation he did or did not do, the speech that he made was electrifying. Delivered without any notes in a calm confident manner, he demolished Nugent's speech in a way that drew admiration throughout the whole House. Pitt's speech was brilliant, although it was not enough to win the debate on that occasion, North defeating Burke's proposal by 233 votes to 190. However, Pitt's speech delivered with no notes and seemingly delivered with no prior planning had held Members spellbound and sealed his reputation from that moment on – the young Mr. Pitt had made his mark in the most spectacular fashion.

Members from both sides of the House were impressed. The Prime Minister, Lord North described it as, 'the best *first* speech he ever heard', whilst Edmund Burke, who had been in Parliament since 1765 and had heard many of Lord Chatham's speeches first hand, said that Pitt, 'was not merely a chip off the old block, but the old block itself'. Charles James Fox was delighted and also lavished praise on Pitt.

The two men were very different but both appreciated the others skills. Whilst Fox was more emotional, his speeches going off in different directions but always returning to the main point, Pitt built his speeches up in a more measured, logical and constructed way. Both men were brilliant however and both were admired by all.

Meanwhile, the war in America was not going well. Up to the end of 1779, the war had been fought mainly in the North American states, but the Commander-in-Chief of the British forces, Sir Henry Clinton, decided on a new tactic, planning an attack in the Deep South. He captured Charleston in May of 1780, which did great damage to the American cause, and then left four thousand troops under the command of Lord Cornwallis, another British General. For almost the whole of the following year, 1781, there appeared to be a kind of stalemate going on and no territory of any significance was either gained or lost on either side. The British troops were superior to those of the so-called rebels in every way, but the Americans had one advantage over the British that they were unaware of – Clinton and Cornwallis simply didn't get on and this was to lead to the eventual downfall of the British. Clinton thought that the bulk of the American troops along with their allies the French, would attack him in New York and was therefore unwilling to send re-enforcements to Cornwallis in Virginia. Tragically, Clinton got it all wrong, and the combined American and French troops attacked Cornwallis as he and his troops were marching northwards through Virginia. Clinton eventually sent troops to help as Cornwallis with an army of 9,000 was facing an enemy numbering 16,000, but it was too late. Cornwallis had no option other than to surrender, which he did on 17th October, 1781 at Yorktown. The war with the Americas was effectively lost that day.

Communications were incredibly slow in those days and it was another five weeks before news reached the British government. On Sunday, 25th November, the first news of the defeat reached London. A messenger was sent from Falmouth to Pall Mall where Lord George Germain lived. Germain (1716-85) was Colonial Secretary holding the post from 1775 until 1782, the year that North resigned. As well as being a British statesman he had also previously been an army general but had been dismissed from the service after questionable conduct at the Battle of Minden in 1759. He was often blamed for the loss of the war with America but in fact was a very competent minister showing energy and resolution and although his strategic skills were recognised later on, he was removed from his post and was created Viscount Sackville in 1782. If he was upset at the news of Cornwallis's surrender then Lord North was doubly so. North was said to have reacted 'as he would have taken a ball in his breast. He opened his arms, exclaiming wildly, as he paced up and down the apartment a few minutes, "Oh God! It is all over!" Words which he repeated many times under emotions of the deepest consternation and distress'.

Lord North was quite correct. It *was* all over, not only in terms of losing the war, but also him losing office, although that didn't happen straight away. The main reason for this was the fact that the opposition were not prepared and lacked the cohesion needed to turf the government out of office. On 12th December, they beat the opposition by 220 votes to 179 in a motion of censure, a majority of forty-one votes but there was uncertainty amongst ministers as to how to conduct the war if indeed it was to be continued. Pitt, like others, wanted to exploit that disunity, but he had a slight problem. He wanted to criticise Lord North for his handling of the war, but didn't want to criticise the King, even though it was well known that the King's handprints were all over the policy. When Pitt got up to speak in the House, Sir Nathaniel Wraxall, the great parliamentary diarist at the time, wrote the following:-

'In a speech of extraordinary energy (throughout the course of which he contrived with great ability to blend professions of devoted attachment to the person of the King with the severest accusation of his Ministers), he fully confirmed the high opinion of his judgement and parliamentary talents already entertained throughout the country......... He concluded by calling on Ministers to state without circumlocution or deception what were their intentions as to the further prosecution of the American war, and to give some general idea of the manner in which it was henceforward to be pursued. A sort of pause took place when he resumed his seat, while the eyes of all present were directed towards the Treasury bench.........'

Lord North and George Germain didn't even rise to attempt an argument against Pitt's speech, and Pitt, sensing discontentment and disunity amongst the cabinet, had won a victory.

Two days later, on the 14th December, 1781, Pitt rose again to speak and this time it was clear that there was definitely disunity on the government benches. Seizing his chance, he said:- "I shall wait till the unanimity is better settled, and until the sage Nestor of the Treasury Bench has brought to an agreement the Agamemnon and the Achilles of the American War". A great many members had no clue as to the extent of Pitt's classical education, and the atmosphere in the House was electric.

Pitt's reputation was soaring once again. Horace Walpole, the 4th Earl of Orford (1717-97) wrote:- 'Another remarkable day; the army was to be voted. William Pitt took to pieces Lord North's pretended declarations and exposed them with the most amazing logical abilities, exceeding all the abilities he had already shown and making men doubt whether he would not prove superior even to Charles fox'.

Pitt's speeches were helping to destroy the government, and Lord North began to realise that he had to make peace, although George Germain was resolutely against this, as was Lord Sandwich, the First Lord of the Admiralty. Henry Dundas (1742-1811), a strong supporter of North, urged him to get rid of Germain as he thought that the government could then re-unite, but unfortunately, North hesitated and the moment was initially lost only to return when once again, Dundas, this time with the support of Richard Rigby, the

Paymaster General, forced North to sack Germain which is when he went to the Lords as Viscount Sackville. The opposition then turned their fire on Lord Sandwich, with both Pitt and Fox pitching in. Although they were on the same side, their approach was very different. Pitt supported the King and made clear that any speech attacking Sandwich was purely concerned with policy not personality, whilst Fox was the complete opposite. He referred to the King in private as 'a blockhead' and likened his conduct of the war as the actions of a tyrant and an oppressor. Pitt agreed with Fox that the power of the monarch was too great, but he disagreed with Fox who wanted the sovereign's power to be transferred to the Whig aristocracy. On 27th February, 1782, the North government were defeated in the House by 234 votes to 215 on a motion which demanded the end of the war with America. On the 8th of March, there was a vote of no confidence taken, which the government narrowly won by 236 votes to 227. Although the motion was defeated, the North administration was in its death throes as in those days, a motion of confidence won so narrowly was seen as a defeat.

Lord North was set to resign and advised the King to send for Rockingham and Shelburne. Both men had experience and talent but unfortunately neither man appealed to the King at all. Charles Watson Wentworth, Marquis of Rockingham (1730-82) had been the leader of the Whig opposition when he was appointed Prime Minister in 1765 but only lasted a year before giving way to Lord Chatham, Pitt the Younger's father. William Petty-Fitzmaurice, Second Earl of Shelburne (1737-1805) like Rockingham, was a Whig and had served in the army before entering parliament, succeeding to his father's earldom in 1761. He had been President of the Board of Trade in 1763 and also served as Secretary of State in 1766 during Chatham's administration but the King was opposed to both men succeeding the outgoing Prime Minister. The King replied to North:- "My sentiments of honour will not permit me to send for any of the Leaders of Opposition and personally treat with them". However, Lord North knew that his time as Prime Minister was finished. On the 20th March, 1782, he rose in the House and before the opposition had time to table a vote of no confidence, announced amongst a great deal of noise that he and his government were resigning and with that, bade his fellow members a cheery good night before getting into his cab, driving away into the snowy night, and giving up the reins of office, something that he had wanted to do for a very long time.

The King was furious with North for resigning, but could do little about it. He initially refused to ask Rockingham to form an administration and asked Shelburne to form a government instead but Shelburne declined, so it was Rockingham who formed the first administration whilst Shelburne served under Rockingham as Secretary of State for Home and Colonial Affairs and Charles James Fox was made Secretary of State for Foreign Affairs.

The new government met on 8th April, 1782 and immediately made their views on America clear – they wanted peace and to accept America as an independent country which must have been hard for the King to accept. Pitt, although now crossing over to the government side of the House, and despite his obvious brilliance, was not initially offered a post in the new administration. At the age of twenty-two, he had time on his side, but it is possible that his cause was not helped by an extraordinary statement he made in the Commons in March:- "For myself, I could not expect to form part of a new administration; but were my doing so more within my reach, I feel myself bound to declare that I never would accept a subordinate situation".

Perhaps the praise that had been heaped on him since his very first speech had gone to his head, or perhaps he genuinely thought that his talents would be wasted in a junior position, because in effect, he was saying he would not accept anything less than being a senior Minister in the Cabinet. Whatever his motives for saying that were, it was ill considered. Horace Walpole declared it:- "so arrogant a declaration from a boy who had gained no experience from, nor ever enjoyed even the lowest post in any office, and who for half a dozen orations, extraordinary indeed, but no evidence of capacity for business, presumed himself fit for command, proved that he was a boy, and a very ambitious and a very vain one. The moment he sat down he was aware of his folly, and said he could bite his tongue out for what he had uttered." It had been only three months since Walpole had lavished praise on Pitt's speech of the 14th December, 1781 denouncing Lord North's handling of the war with America and the resulting disunity in the then government, so that Walpole clearly thought that Pitt had become rather above himself. The fact that Pitt was the son of the great Lord Chatham cut no ice with Walpole at all.

Walpole's assertion that Pitt instantly regretted his speech is debatable. Pitt usually thought long and hard before saying anything. He had an independent nature and did not wish to be reliant on anybody for preferment. It therefore made sense that rather than be a junior minister and be dependent on someone more senior for promotion, he would rather have the independence of being a senior Minister or a back bencher, both roles making it easy for him to speak his mind. Also, had he regretted making the speech in March 1782, it is unlikely that he would have turned down the position of Vice-Treasurership of Ireland and with it the salary of £5,000 per annum (approximately £300,000 in today's terms) which Rockingham offered him a few weeks later. Pitt, it would appear, was supremely confident of his own abilities and was prepared to wait for something better.

It was not that long in coming. Rockingham held his government together but that was about all. Although he was not a strong leader, in opposition he had held the Whigs together as a credible alternative government throughout the 1770's, but once Prime Minister, he was ineffective. He was forgetful, indecisive and unlike many other politicians who were criticised for not having interests outside politics, Rockingham had so many that it was a wonder that he had time to be Prime Minister at all. He seemed more interested in racing, farming and horse breeding and George III once remarked that he:- "never appeared to him to have a decided opinion about things". As it turned out, he was only Prime Minister for four months before dying on 1st July 1782, and as is usual in politics, there was an unseemly haste in looking round for someone to replace him.

Charles James Fox immediately nominated the Duke of Portland for the job. Portland was an Aristocratic Whig who Fox could control. Fox knew that he would never be accepted by George III as Prime Minister, and thought that this was the clever route to being in control himself. The King had already out-witted Fox however, because he sent for Shelburne and offered him the job which took the Rockingham Whigs completely by surprise as the doctors had not forecast the Prime Minister dying. Fox immediately resigned being totally unwilling to serve under Shelburne and it was at this point that the young William Pitt got what he wanted:- he was appointed Chancellor of the Exchequer. Fox not only refused to serve under Shelburne, but he continually attacked him, causing great offence to many other members, including William Pitt. Apart from Burke who also resigned, Fox was the only member of the previous administration to prove unwilling to serve under the new Prime Minister. Pitt went on the attack against his erstwhile friend and colleague:- "The Right Honourable Secretary assures us, that it was with the sole view of preventing dissentions in the Cabinet he retired from office. I believe him, because he solemnly declares it; otherwise I should have attributed his resignation to a baulk in struggling for power. If, however, he so much disliked Lord Shelburne's political principles or opinions, why did he ever consent to act with that nobleman as a colleague? And if he only suspected Lord Shelburne of feeling averse to the measures which he thought necessary to be adopted, it was his duty to have called a Cabinet Council, and there to have ascertained the fact before he took the hasty resolution of throwing up his employment?"

Like many brilliant men before him and after him, Charles James Fox was flawed and prone to impulsive outbursts as the events of July 1782 showed. Pitt becoming Chancellor of the Exchequer at the age of just twenty-three years at the same time as Fox resigning, leading to these two men, friends and colleagues over many years, never speaking from the same side of the House again. Lady Caroline Holland's prediction made many years before when Pitt was just a child, that the young William Pitt "would be a thorn in Charles's side as long as he lives" seemed to be coming true.

Although Pitt becoming Chancellor of the Exchequer at such a young age was a remarkable achievement, it has to be pointed out that he was not first choice; in fact it had been offered to three other people before him, each of whom turned it down.

He was still second in line behind the Prime Minister in terms of government seniority however which is still the case today with that post. However, in Pitt's time, the position of Chancellor did not have quite the same power as it does today because the position of Prime Minister was at that time an informal title, the formal title being The First Lord of the Treasury, and was therefore more involved in fiscal matters than a Prime Minister would be today. Pitt's rise to his position, although extraordinary even at that time, could not happen today. In the 18th century, there were more young people in Parliament than today, a great many of them merely being there due to family connections. There were others besides Pitt who reached high office at an early age, Charles James Fox being one. He had become an MP at the age of just nineteen and a Lord of the Admiralty at the age of twenty-four.

The country even had a young monarch, George III becoming King in 1760 at the age of twenty-two, although that was only because his father, Prince

Frederick had died in 1751, before *his* father, George II, so the monarchy had skipped a generation out of necessity.

It was usual then, as it is today, that the First Lord of the Treasury (Prime Minister) resides in 10, Downing Street. Sir Robert Walpole (1676-1745) was the first Prime Minister serving as he did from 1721 until 1742 making him not only the first Prime Minister but also the longest serving one with the result that in 1732, the then grateful Monarch, George II presented the house to him. Walpole only accepted the gift on the condition that it was given to the nation rather than himself, and since that time, it has been the official residence of the First Minister, although not all of them have lived there.

One of these was Lord Shelburne who preferred his house in Berkeley Square so that in August 1782, William Pitt moved in. When he later became Prime Minister, he would end up living in 10, Downing Street for more years than any other person. The Street was named after Sir George Downing (c1623-1684), an English soldier and diplomat, who was born in Ireland but as a fifteen year old, emigrated to New England with his parents. On returning to England he fought for parliament and undertook several diplomatic missions for Oliver Cromwell. He doesn't enjoy the posthumous fame that many of his contemporaries have, but his legacy to the nation is the house, number 10, Downing Street, which is now one of the most famous addresses in the world.

Pitt worked hard in his new job, and many of his ideas were similar to those of Shelburne, but Shelburne was not easy to work with or for, and the two men, although achieving a working relationship, never got close. Shelburne also worked hard, but he wasn't a particular clever Parliamentarian and misread the strength of his government. When the House went into recess people expected Shelburne to bring some opposition members such as Fox into the government to make it stronger, but Shelburne did nothing. Negotiations were under way in order for peace to be made with America, and Shelburne had to accept the fact that America had to be accepted as a fully independent country. His government, with both Fox and North on the opposition benches looked weak, and he had overestimated the support that he would receive in the House generally. Eventually Fox and North put aside their differences and colluded to bring Shelburne down putting forward a motion on 21st February 1783 saying that the concessions to Britain's enemies were too great. Pitt, although ill, made a two and three quarter hour speech that was one of the finest he ever made. He was fighting a rearguard action however because the Shelburne administration was doomed and he knew it, but he put everything into the speech denouncing the Fox-North coalition in the process.

Pitt knew that he was almost certain to lose office and as well as railing against Fox and North for their behaviour whilst in opposition, provided the House with a lengthy description as to how he would conduct himself in opposition. It couldn't save the government and wasn't designed to, but according to Thomas Pelham, an opposition MP, it was "the finest speech that ever was made in Parliament". The government duly lost the vote by 207 to 190 and on 23rd February 1783, Lord Shelburne announced his resignation. In so doing, he asked that the King send Thomas Townshend to the Lords which he duly did. Townshend (1732-1800) became Lord Sydney and as Home Secretary in 1787 when the first convict fleet was sent out to Australia, gave his name to the huge city of Sydney that we know today.

Shelburne was determined that the Fox/North coalition would not gain power, and instead asked the King to send for the twenty-three-year-old William Pitt and invite him to be First Lord of the Treasury. Pitt's speech on the 21st February had sealed his reputation. Shelburne was defeated and Townshend had gone to the Upper House as Lord Sydney. People therefore started to look to Pitt as Shelburne's successor despite the fact that he was only twenty-three-years-old. One of his biggest champions was Henry Dundas (1742-1811). The son of Robert Dundas, Lord Arniston (1685-1753), Henry Dundas was called to the Scottish Bar in 1763. He had been elected to Parliament in 1774, when he became MP for Midlothian. In 1775 he had been made Lord Advocate and 1777 saw him as Keeper of the Signet for Scotland. He was a firm supporter of Lord North and his policies during the war with America, and without actually wishing the top job for himself, nevertheless wanted to wield influence. Dundas was a wily operator, and he felt that he, Dundas, with his Parliamentary skills coupled with Pitt's intellect and oratory would be an ideal partnership.

On Monday, 24th February 1783, William Pitt, with three months to wait before his twenty-fourth birthday, was summoned by the King and asked to be First Lord of the Treasury and de facto, Prime Minister. Lesser men than Pitt would have been flattered enough to accept on the spot, but Pitt did not and took several days to think it over. On the 27th, after three days thinking about it, he decided to decline and reluctantly wrote to a disappointed Dundas telling him so. He felt that he could not guarantee having a majority in the House and refused to entertain the notion of working with North. Pitt then had a long audience with the King who tried in vain to change Pitt's mind – even at such a young age and with time to return to office if he was ousted, he said that he had no wish to be Prime Minister for a week. Pitt's refusal sent everybody into confusion – Rockingham had held the top job from April 1782 until dying three months later on 1st July, and Shelburne had been in post from July 1782 before resigning in late February 1783 meaning that a third First Lord in less than a year would have to be appointed and no-one was clear as to who it was going to be. At this time, all was confusion and the King was even talking of abdicating. He even turned to Pitt's cousin, Thomas Pitt (1737-93), the member for Old Sarum, who was later to become the 1st Lord Camelford, but Thomas wisely turned it down realising that he was not up to the job.

George III became desperate and William Pitt wavered, giving Dundas the idea that he would take the job after all and on 24th March Pitt made a speech in the House expecting support but all he succeeded in doing was to confuse members who thought that he would give them a lead. Although he didn't receive the support he craved however, the speech was well received and he wasn't damaged by the confusion that had now been going on for a month because most members were unaware of the protracted negotiations that he had had with the King. In the end, the King got what he did not want, a Fox/North coalition. On the 2nd of April 1783, Fox came back as Secretary of State for Foreign Affairs, whilst Lord North was Secretary of State for the Home Department. William Henry Cavendish-Bentick, (1738-1809), the 3rd Duke of

Portland, became First Lord of the Treasury and therefore Prime Minister. Portland had been elected to Parliament in 1761 before taking his father's title the following year and was generally associated with the aristocratic Whig party of Rockingham. He had served under Rockingham twice – the first time as Lord Chamberlain of the Household in Rockingham's first administration in 1765 to 1766 and as Lord Lieutenant of Ireland in Rockingham's second and short - lived government of 1782. Portland resigned the post after the death of Rockingham. Now he found himself to be the third Prime Minister to be appointed in the two years since Lord North left office and after the stability that North gave the country by remaining in post twelve years, from 1770 until 1782, there was now instability with little confidence that he was the man to restore it.

This was due to the fact that Portland was really just a titular head of a coalition government that was really being led by Charles James Fox and Lord North, so much so that it was often referred to as the Fox/North coalition. It was highly unlikely that George III would want to put up with Fox for longer than was necessary but for the short term anyway, he had little choice.

Pitt was now no longer Chancellor, and had to vacate Downing Street. If he was bothered about it, he hid it well from everyone probably because he knew that the King was unhappy with the present arrangement and thought that his chance would come sooner rather than later. In fact the King was to spend many months plotting to remove the present administration which he hated, and eventually he succeeded using the vehicle of the East India Company to bring this about.

There was a great deal of agreement between many Members that the way that India was governed had to be reformed. In 1781, a Select Committee had been set up to look at this and in the Commons on the 18th November, 1783, Charles James Fox presented the East India Bill which would severely limit the influence of the Crown over the financial affairs of the East India Company. Fox wanted a system whereby Commissioners appointed by him would take more financial control and there were debates in the House on 18th and 27th November. Pitt attacked the proposals but Fox got them through the Commons with little trouble and he was now supremely confident. However, although the East India Company had been initially surprised, they now, realising what would happen, petitioned Parliament saying that the finances were in a better position than originally thought.

Newspapers joined in the arguments against the Bill, and wrote that they were concerned that even if he lost office, Fox's appointees would stay in post, giving him too much power. Pitt's cousin George Grenville, the 3rd Earl Temple who was also the 1st Marquis of Buckingham, and Baron Edward Thurlow, the Lord Chancellor, colluded with the King and Pitt gave the King the impression that he was now ready to take office if required. Before the Lords were due to debate the matter, George III did an extraordinary thing – he gave Temple a card which read:- "His Majesty allowed Earl Temple to say, that whoever voted for the India Bill was not only not his friend, but would be considered by him as an enemy; and if these words were not strong enough, Earl Temple might use whatever words he might deem stronger and more to the purpose".

On the 15th December, 1783, the Lords debated the Bill, and Fox, unaware of exactly what had been going on behind his back was still very optimistic. The King's tactic had worked however and twenty-seven Members changed their voting pattern as a result of his intervention culminating in the Bill being defeated by 87 votes to 79. On the 17th December, both Houses met for the final debates and the Bill was finally beaten in the Lords by a majority of nineteen. Accusations of treachery were bandied about but Pitt, sensing power in his grasp, simply lied and said that he knew of no dealing behind the scenes. The following day, Pitt had an audience with the King and confirmed that he would be prepared to take office.

Later that night, Portland, Fox and North were asked to surrender their seals of office, and although furious, they had no option other than to comply.

On Friday, 19th December, 1783, at the age of twenty-four years, William Pitt entered the House of Commons as First Lord of the Treasury (Prime Minister) and Chancellor of the Exchequer. The supporters of the Fox/North coalition roared with laughter at someone so young taking on the job thinking he would be forced out in weeks. Pitt allowed them plenty of time to laugh – he was Prime Minister for the next eighteen years until 1801 and again from 1804 to 1806. Apart from Robert Walpole, the first Prime Minister, no-one in the history of British politics had held the post for so long, and none will ever do so in the future.

Pitt did not have a majority in the House but he was always clear what he wanted to achieve. One of these was harmonious relations with America, an idea that appalled King George III, who could barely bring himself to say the name, much less accept the fact that America was an independent country. Pitt also wanted union with Ireland which he achieved in 1800.

The situation in the House was far from ideal for Pitt. Although he was First Minister, he did not command a majority and when Pitt's own India Bill had it's second reading in the House on 23rd January, 1784, it was defeated by 222 votes to 214, a small majority of just eight votes, but a majority just the same. Basically Pitt wanted a Board of Control, appointed by the government of the day, along with Directors of the Company, and together they would govern India, but it was Fox, in no mood to be helpful to Pitt, who had managed to get Pitt's Bill so narrowly defeated.

Despite the defeat in the House, Pitt felt the tide of public opinion turning towards him – his sober manner contrasted sharply with that of Fox's gambling and womanising, and Pitt felt that he could obtain his majority with a general election. The King announced the Dissolution of Parliament in the Lords on 24th March 1784 and the election took place over a five week period which started days after the Dissolution was announced. The House of Commons was to meet on 18th May and it was announced that Fox had been defeated in the Westminster seat that he wanted. Despite being helped by the fashionable Duchess of Devonshire, Fox was beaten by Lord Hood although he returned to the House as the Member for Orkney – disgruntled, but still a member. Many of the supporters of the Fox/North coalition were missing and Pitt had his huge majority. Pitt also achieved something else that he had always wanted – he was returned as member for Cambridge University allowing him to give up the pocket borough of Appleby.

Pitt had left the India Bill on the back burner while he presented his first budget which he did on 30th June, 1784. He had inherited a very difficult financial situation partly being due to the enormous cost of waging war with the Americas. The country had annual tax revenues of £13 million but was paying £8 million in interest charges. Despite this, Pitt delivered the budget in a manner that astonished onlookers - his mastery of financial detail and his maturity impressed everybody, supporters and opposition alike. He set up a sinking fund, which was basically money put aside to pay debts at a later date, along with the sale of government stock. Despite this, he felt that he also needed to raise taxes which he did by spreading it over a number of items such as bricks, candles, linens, coal, gold and silver plate, hats, ribbons and other items. It would have been similar to Purchase Tax of the 20th century that evolved into VAT that we have today.

With these measures up and running, and with his reputation further enhanced, Pitt set about trying to get his India Bill through, which he did on the 6th July, 1784 with a majority of 271 votes to 60, an extraordinary turn in his fortunes given that there wasn't a great deal of difference between his new Bill and the one that had been defeated only six months before.

So started a period whereby Pitt was Prime minister for a period of nineteen years out of the next twenty-two, an achievement that will almost certainly never be equalled. Those nineteen years were to throw up monumental problems and one of the most difficult of these he had to deal with was the illness of King George III which started in 1788.

In October 1788, the King became ill and in early November, it seemed that he had literally gone mad. It seemed to start the previous summer when he suffered from stomach cramps and severe bilious attacks, but the condition seemed to improve after the King and Queen had visited the spa town of Cheltenham to take the waters. However, a little later on when he visited the west of England to celebrate his recovery, his behaviour seemed eccentric, and on one occasion he pretended to conduct an orchestra in Worcester Cathedral as they were playing Handel's Messiah, although at the time, his courtiers were not unduly alarmed. However, on his arrival back at Windsor he became very ill indeed, was very angry with his doctor, and seemed to understand what was happening to him. There were times when his behaviour was uncontrollable but at other times lucid. It was on one such occasion that he told the Duke of York:- "I wish to God I may die, for I am going to be mad".

Pitt was faced with a real dilemma which concerned him in two ways:- firstly, the good of the country as a whole, but secondly, also for him personally, although it's fair to surmise that he probably thought the two were intertwined. Charles James Fox was very friendly with the Prince of Wales, and if the King became incapable of fulfilling his duties, then the Prince would be made Regent, in other words, King in all but name. It would be almost certain that the Prince would dismiss Pitt and send for Fox to form an administration. The same thing would happen if the King were to die and the Prince then became George IV – again Fox would be sent for.

Pitt had to fight for his political life because many of his colleagues, firmly believing the King's reign to be drawing to a close, began drifting to the Fox camp. It took all of Pitt's considerable parliamentary skills to stay in office, but by clever use of delaying tactics, he succeeded in keeping the opposition at bay. He brought in two doctors, Dr. Anthony Addington, the doctor who had given him the advice fifteen years before to drink plenty of port and which probably turned him into an alcoholic, but possibly the most significant, Dr. Francis Willis (1717-1807), who had had a long, and he claimed, successful career in treating mental disorders.

Willis lived in and ran a private asylum at Greatford Hall, Lincolnshire and was very confident of his own ability. On 4th December, a Commons Committee questioned several doctors on the King's condition with Willis insisting that he would recover. On the 10th December, 1788, in a masterful speech, Pitt once again bought himself time by requesting the formation of another committee to look into any precedents that may have happened in a similar situation – once again the impatient Whigs were left fuming. Against all odds, fortune seemed to be favouring Pitt as one of the things in his favour was that he and the King were very popular whilst Fox and the lazy, debt-ridden Prince of Wales were not. In all the twenty plus years of rivalry between the two men, this debate between them was seen as a classic and during it, Fox fell right into Pitt's hands by expressing the opinion that the Prince of Wales had the right to claim the throne as Regent. On hearing that, Pitt gleefully responded by slapping his thigh, saying to those around him:- "I'll unwhig him for the rest of his life", and then got up from his seat to point out that since 1688, the will of Parliament had taken precedence over that of the Monarchy, so the Regent had no such right. The Parliamentary battles between Pitt and Fox continued throughout December and whilst Pitt always seemed to be one step ahead, he still had no option other than to prepare a Regency Bill which he duly presented to the House of Commons on 5th February, 1789, and again to the House of Lords on the 16th. By this time, Fox was convinced that at long last, the chance to make the Prince of Wales Prince Regent in the very near future, was his for the taking, but the very next day, the 17th, a bulletin was given out by the King's physicians saying that the King had in fact, recovered. Pitt had been days away from almost certainly losing power but the combination of his political skills and the amazing timing of the King's recovery had saved him. At the time, Dr. Willis was given the credit, along with a great deal of money for curing the King, but we now know that the King was almost certainly suffering from Porphyria, a genetic illness which has all the symptoms that the King was suffering from but was unheard of in the 18th century. With or without the treatment that Willis had meted out, King George III would almost certainly have recovered anyway.

Festivities celebrating the King's recovery started in March culminating in a Thanksgiving Service held in St. Paul's Cathedral on the 23rd April 1789, St. George's Day. At the age of barely thirty, Pitt was at the peak of his power, but he would need to be, as the even bigger challenge of the war with France was looming.

Huge problems were looming with France that commenced soon after they started the revolution in 1789. The King, Louis XVI, was born in 1754 and married Marie Antoinette in 1770. He was popular for a while in the 1770's but things became worse a decade later. He dissolved all parliaments in May 1788 but things became even more dangerous when in August of the same year, he said that all cash payments should cease apart from those to his troops. The National Assembly was formed, and undertook to devise a new constitution, and they called themselves the Constituent Assembly. There were outbreaks of violence in Paris on 12th July, 1789 and two days later the people stormed the Bastille. The Assembly dissolved itself in December 1792 by which time the Royal Family had been imprisoned. The National Convention took the place of the Assembly and the Republic was born. Louis XVI was brought to trial on charges of treason and on the 21st January, 1793 he was executed. Prior to this the French Royal Family had been all-powerful over the centuries and the shockwaves of this terrible event spread far and wide. Spain and Portugal joined France in a coalition and on 1st February, 1793, they declared war on Great Britain and the Netherlands.

It had only been ten years since the war with America had all but bankrupted the nation, and now William Pitt, not quite thirty-four years old, was Prime Minister of a country at war again, with the added problem that there would be people sympathetic to the idea of getting rid of the monarchy and creating a republic, although most people were horrified at the violence and bloodshed that had occurred in France.

Pitt had to raise money to pay for the war which was financially crippling for the country, and he did it with the then completely novel idea of another form of tax, quite different from the taxes he had previously placed on purchases – this was income tax. Pitt calculated that he wanted to raise £10 million a year. He wanted it to be fair and based on the ability to pay and with this in mind he set his ideas out on 3rd December, 1798 in a speech to the House lasting two and a half hours. Calculated on a sliding scale, he said that anyone on an income of £60 per annum would pay nothing, those on an income exceeding £60 would pay one twentieth, whilst people receiving £200 or over would pay one tenth. Naturally, this was initially greeted with horror, not only because part of people's income was being taken away, but also because it would mean that the state would be entitled to look into people's hitherto private financial affairs. However, the reality of the situation soon set in and Pitt got the policy through Parliament as quickly as January, 1799 with a comfortable majority. He was also able to persuade Members that the tax would just be a temporary measure which initially it was, but it was to become a permanent fact of life fifty years later under Sir Robert Peel. However, as it stood at the end of the eighteenth century, it was a short term measure created to pay for the war with France.

For the rest of his life until he died in 1806, William Pitt the Younger fought the French, being Prime Minister for all but the three years between 1801 and 1804. He returned to office in 1804 and formed a coalition with Russia, Austria and Sweden. His finest hour in the war was delivered to him on 21st October 1805 when Nelson in the flagship *Victory* along with his British fleet beat the combined forces of the French and Spanish ships in the Battle of Trafalgar where Nelson lost his life. Pitt was called the 'Saviour of Europe' as it stopped the brilliant Napoleon Bonaparte's plans of invading Britain by sea although the war was to last another ten years and Bonaparte was not completely beaten until the Duke of Wellington beat the French troops at the Battle of Waterloo on 18th June, 1815. Bonaparte (1769-1821) was a brilliant Corsican General whose troops had rampaged their way through Europe and it had seemed that no-one was capable of stopping him until Wellington. However, as previously mentioned, Pitt's finest hour was the 21st October, 1805 and the victory at Trafalgar which pleased the whole country, although none more so than Admiral John Jervis, the Earl St. Vincent (1735-1823) and First Lord of the Admiralty between 1801 and 1804. The Earl St. Vincent was supremely confident of the power and skill of the British fleet and before Trafalgar had said of the French:- "I do not say the French cannot come. I only say they cannot come by sea".

All through the traumatic times of the war with France, Pitt had another battle to contend with – that of the abolition of slavery and it is there that the name of William Wilberforce joins that of William Pitt.

William Wilberforce was born in 1759, the same year as Pitt, but lived longer, dying in 1833. He was elected MP for Hull in 1784, and became a lifelong friend of Pitt's, although they were independent of each other politically. Soon after that Wilberforce was converted to evangelical Christianity and with the support of amongst others, Granville Sharp (1735-1813), Thomas Clarkson (1760-1846), two famous abolitionists, and Hannah More (1745-1833), a playwright, religious writer and member of the famous Blue Stocking Club, he started a relentless nineteen year campaign for the abolition of slavery. Pitt was always encouraging, and when Wilberforce was unable to present his motion for the Abolition of the Slave Trade to the House in May, 1788 due to severe illness, Pitt agreed to present it for him. He did so on 9th May, moving for an Inquiry into the Slave Trade. Pitt had to be cautious when presenting it, as he was unable to commit his government to it as many members were opposed to the abolition. Things were stepped up when in the summer of that year, 1788, the Member for Oxford University, a senior MP by the name of Sir William Dolben had inspected a slave ship moored in the Thames. He was horrified by what he had witnessed and Pitt brought a Bill through Parliament limiting the number of slaves that could be transported at any one time. It went through the Commons easily, but Pitt only just got it through the Lords after a great deal of opposition. It was going to be a long hard fight. After nineteen long years, with Pitt's help and support, William Wilberforce managed to get the abolition of slavery through the House with the passing of The Slave Trade Act 1807, although slavery was not completely abolished worldwide until The Slavery Abolition Act was passed in 1833, the year of Wilberforce's death. In fact, Wilberforce was to die just three days after the Bill was safely passed. The achievement of 1807 was immense however, but it was a pity that William Pitt, who for so many years had supported Wilberforce, was to die the year before, in 1806. When the bill was passed the year following his death, his cousin, William Wyndham (Lord) Grenville (1759-1834), was Prime Minister, thus history deprived Pitt of much of the credit. However, it has to be said that some historians view the fact that the passing of The Slave Trade Act in 1807, happened so quickly after Pitt's death, that it constitutes a failure on Pitt's part and they accuse him of not working hard enough to get rid of this abomination. This would seem a harsh judgement as Pitt was so much involved in all the years beforehand – maybe it was simply that the time was right in 1807 for the bill to be passed and would never have happened beforehand whoever was Prime Minister.

Another problem that William Pitt had to tackle was one that has dogged politicians for centuries – that of Ireland. In 1798, the Irish Nationalists rebelled and in so doing, hoped that the French would help them overthrow the monarchy. Up until this time, there had been a parliament in London and another in Dublin. Pitt felt that the only way that the Irish problem would be solved was to have one parliament and for the two countries to be united politically. It wasn't going to be an easy task and it is thought that a great deal of bribery was used for Irish MPs to vote in the way Pitt wanted. These were the Protestant legislators and the Catholic opposition was rather muted as they were given the impression that Catholic emancipation would certainly be the result of unity although given King George III's violent opposition to it, this was never going to happen. The King felt that it was against his Coronation Oath which said that he promised to safeguard the Church of England and he would not be moved on this point. However, Pitt got the Act of Union through in 1800 and more formally on 1st January 1801 with the United Kingdom of Great Britain and Ireland Act. The question of Catholic emancipation was harder to resolve however, and a couple of months later would lead to the resignation of Pitt in favour of Henry Addington, 1st Viscount Sidmouth.

To Pitt, the emancipation of Catholics was the logical way forward after uniting Ireland with the rest of Britain, but unfortunately, George III thought very differently and would barely even discuss the subject, much less give way on it. When Pitt had previously disagreed with the King, the unity of his cabinet had helped him win the day, but it was not to be in this case. Pitt had held a cabinet meeting in September 1800 to discuss the situation and to plan the way forward in 1801. But there was one person attending this meeting who would turn out to be crucial – Lord Loughborough. Loughborough (1733-1805), was a wily character and had entered Parliament in 1762. He had been made Lord Chancellor in 1793 and whilst Pitt was arranging his cabinet meeting, Loughborough was staying with the King in Weymouth. In September, Pitt wrote to Loughborough asking him to attend the meeting and cut short his holiday. Loughborough, in a barely disguised effort to put himself in favour with the King, told the King all about the proposed meeting and asked for his views. The King was adamant – there was to be no Catholic emancipation and Pitt found himself against powerful opposition. The King had always felt that the whole idea would violate the Coronation Oath, and it was Loughborough himself who in 1794 had advised the King that this would indeed be the case. Pitt, who by now had been Prime Minister for seventeen years and who was normally a shrewd political operator, had been completely outwitted by Loughborough and the King. Even the King himself had no illusions about Loughborough who he thought untrustworthy. When Loughborough died in 1805, the King said:- "Then, he has not left a greater knave behind him in my

Dominions". On the subject of Catholic emancipation however, the King was only too happy to have Loughborough on his side. Pitt wasn't going to give this up without a fight and tried to use his own political skills to get this measure through, and he called a Cabinet meeting of 25th January 1801 with a view to sidelining Loughborough who would not be present. It didn't work. Details of the meeting got back to the King who on 28th January, whilst at a levee was heard to explode:- "What is the Question which you are all about to force upon me? ....I will tell you, that I shall look on every Man as my personal Enemy, who proposes that Question (Catholic emancipation) to me.........I hope All my Friends will not desert me". It was almost a re-run of the sentiments the King had used so effectively against members of the House of Lords eighteen years earlier which all but killed off the proposed India Bill and allowed Pitt to become Prime Minister in the first place. Now these sentiments were coming back to haunt Pitt in a way he simply hadn't foreseen.

There were letters going back and forth between Pitt and the King but no agreement could be reached and accordingly, on the 5th February 1801, Pitt resigned from the job he loved, although he carried on temporarily and even presented a budget on 18th February. The King sent for Henry Addington (1757-1844) to form an administration, which he duly did on 14th March 1801 until May, 1804. Addington's administration had not been effective however, and Pitt was asked to return to the job of Prime Minister which he did on 10th May, 1804, whilst Addington was created the 1st Viscount Sidmouth in 1805.

Pitt's second administration was not nearly so effective as his first – it couldn't be. He had already been Prime Minister nearly eighteen years when he returned to office on 10th May 1804, and whilst still only forty - five years old and therefore technically young enough to serve another eighteen years, it was clear that he was worn out and ill. In his early years, he had been advised by Dr. Addington, the father of his friend Henry Addington, the man who he had just succeeded as Prime Minister, to spend his life drinking large quantities of port, a habit that he took to only too willingly. It was now catching up with him and he gradually became more ill as these final years passed. Since 1792, Pitt had been Warden of the Cinque Ports, a position that was largely ceremonial, but allowed him the use of Walmer Castle, and it was there that he was staying for long periods of time.

Eventually, he became too ill to carry on the demanding job of Prime Minister and he died at the tragically young age of forty - six years on 23rd January 1806.

Historians cannot agree as to the actual cause of death although many believe it was cirrhosis of the liver brought on by a lifetime of heavy drinking. Another explanation is that the symptoms he exhibited at the time were more likely to be caused from a peptic ulceration of his stomach or duodenum. Whatever the cause, his whole system was unable to take any more and after a lifetime of work, had simply broken down. Like his father, the great Lord Chatham before him, Pitt was hugely in debt to the tune of £40,000 when he died but a grateful Parliament, now led by William Wyndham Grenville (1759-1834), the 1st Baron Grenville and Pitt's cousin, voted to pay that amount off. It seems a paradox that although both William Pitt the Elder and William Pitt the

Younger spent a great deal of time looking after the nation's finances, neither seemed to find the time to look after their own finances. Both of them excelled at macro-economics but sadly lacked the basic skills of micro-economics probably thinking the latter too unimportant to worry about.

The funeral was a huge occasion but obviously filled with a great sadness. Every so often, a great person dies and plunges the country into a collective mourning. In 1965 it was Winston Churchill, and in 1997, it was Lady Diana Spencer, the Princess of Wales. On the 22nd February, 1806, England was hit by a double blow, because William Pitt's funeral that day followed the funeral service of Admiral Lord Nelson's on 9th January, 1806 by just six weeks. The celebrations of Nelson winning the battle of Trafalgar on 21st October, 1805, were overshadowed by the loss of these two great men, both of whom served their country all their lives, and both of whom died in its service although neither would have had it any other way. Pitt's funeral was watched by thousands of people which followed the tens of thousands who filed slowly past the body that had lain in State in the Painted Chamber of the Palace of Westminster for two days prior to the service. There were medallions struck at the time showing a weeping Brittania each having the engraving:- "NON SIBI SED PATRIAE VIXIT" - "He lived not for himself but for his country". After the funeral service, he was laid to rest in Westminster Abbey.

Pitt had been Prime Minister for nearly twenty out of the last twenty-three years of his life. It could never happen today and it was an intolerable burden for any one person to carry. He saw through the India Bill, much of his Premiership was taken up in fighting the French: he brought in taxes on various items which related to people's expenditure, and created a sinking fund in order that the country might pay off its debts. He virtually invented Income tax which although meant as a temporary measure, is part of our system of governing today. He saw the country through King George III's illness, was Premier when his friend William Wilberforce battled for years against slavery, and had the problems of Ireland to contend with.

Pitt was often seen as aloof, but not by people who knew him who found him good company and he was actually blessed with great wit. Being a single man, he had to rely on a succession of women friends to act as hostess at No. 10 Downing Street and for a while in the 1780's, these duties were carried out by a friend called Jane, Duchess of Gordon. After a while the friendship cooled and a few years later when they met, she is supposed to have said:- "Well Mr. Pitt, do you talk as much nonsense now as when you lived with me?", to which he instantly replied:- "I do not know Madam whether I talk so much nonsense, I certainly do not hear so much".

He never married and seemed completely disinterested in women and this caused questions to be brought up about his sexuality. There was an occasion where he did have a chance to marry but in 1797 broke off an understanding with Eleanour Eden on the grounds of the debts that he had accumulated, but that reason is not believed in many circles. He seemed to be married to his job, and rather than leanings towards homosexuality, it is more likely that he was simply asexual and allowed no room in his life for marriage and the almost inevitable children that would result. He was cool and courageous, and there is

47

one famous occasion when in 1786, he had to have a cyst removed from his face. The famous Dr. John Hunter (1728-93), Surgeon-Extraordinary to King George III and the man who taught the young Edward Jenner (1749-1823) who himself was to eventually rid the world of smallpox, was designated to carry out the procedure. There were no anaesthetics in those days, and Hunter informed Pitt that the operation would take six minutes. Pitt refused to have his hands tied, the usual procedure at the time, and whilst the growth was being removed, sat motionless and stared out of the window during the entire time. Hunter said afterwards, that:- "I have never seen so much fortitude and courage in all my practise". At the end of the operation, Pitt said nothing other than:- "You have exceeded your time half a minute".

William Pitt the Younger was an extraordinary man in a century which contained extraordinary people and produced extraordinary events. He was both the youngest ever person to become Prime Minister and once there the longest serving holder of the post apart from the first Prime Minister, Sir Robert Walpole. It is safe to say that politics will never see his like again.

-oOOo-

2
Sir Joseph Banks
(1743-1820)

Famous botanist who sailed with Captain Cook from 1768-71 and was President of the Royal Society for 41 years.

Joseph Banks IV, explorer, naturalist, botanist, and considered by many to be the founding father of modern day Australia, was born on 13th February, 1743, to William and Sarah Banks (nee Bate). At the age of eighteen, he inherited the family home of Revesby Abbey due to the death of his father in 1761. Revesby Abbey had become the family home when Joseph Banks 1 (1665-1727) and his wife Mary (nee Hancock), installed their son, Joseph II, there in 1715. Joseph II was born in 1695 and married Anne Hodgkinson in 1714. Anne was the daughter of William Hodgkinson, a very wealthy merchant and mine owner of Overton in Derbyshire.

Joseph I seems to have been a kindly man with good intentions towards helping the poor of the area. He was a Member of Parliament for Grimsby and later for Totnes but he died whilst falling from the rafters of Revesby Abbey in 1727. His son, Joseph Banks II (1695-1741), inherited the estate and continued his father's good works by building almshouses for farmers who had fallen on hard times, and he also set up a foundling hospital in London. This Joseph was also a Member of Parliament representing Peterborough and became a member of the Royal Society in 1730. Joseph and Anne had six children, Joseph III, b.1715, Lettice, b.1716, William, b.1719, Elizabeth, b.1720, Robert, b.1722, and Eleanore, b.1723. Sadly, Joseph's wife Anne, died in 1730 and Joseph married again, a lady by the name of Catherine Wallis, and they were to have two more children, Collingwood, b1734, and George making a total of eight. In the normal run of things, Joseph III, as the eldest son, would have inherited the estate, but he died in 1740, the year before his father, Joseph II, who died the following year in 1741. Thus it was, that in 1741, William Banks, the second son of Joseph II, took over the family home on the death of his father and it is William (1719-61) who was the father of Joseph Banks IV. In that same year, 1741, William married Sarah Bate, a wealthy heiress in her own right, so at the age of twenty-two, William and his new wife Sarah, were a very wealthy young couple.

Joseph IV was born on 13th February 1743 and the following year, William and Sarah had a daughter, Sarah Sophia (1744-1818). There were no other children from this match, making Joseph the only son and heir.

In 1752, at the age of nine years, Joseph attended Harrow school, but he was not an academic success. He found concentration on Latin and Greek difficult and generally found anything to do with books uninteresting. He was poor at spelling and never learnt punctuation properly. However, he certainly wasn't lacking in intelligence, it's just that the academic world held no attractions for him. His father tried to rectify this by sending him to Eton in 1756 when young Joseph was thirteen. This made no difference as Joseph still couldn't bring himself to be remotely interested in books, especially if they contained Latin or Greek. However, he did find solace in the discovery of nature, which in turn led him to studying books as a way of finding out more about plant life. In short, he became a botanist at the age of fourteen, and the passion for botany was to stay with him all his life, eventually taking him round the world and to be employed by King George III. It is said that he had his portrait painted by Lemuel Francis Abbot at about this time although it is difficult to see how as Abbot wasn't born until 1760. More recently some scholars have credited Johann Zoffany with the picture, which is far more likely.

Abbott (1760-1802) was an English painter who specialised in portraits and who is best known for his painting of Lord Nelson, the picture hanging as it does in 10, Downing Street. Zoffany (1733-1810), is probably even better known – a German portrait painter, he settled in London in 1758 after studying in Rome. He founded the Royal Academy in 1768 and later travelled in Italy and India. As well as painting portraits, he also painted theatrical scenes and pictures of the Royal family when he enjoyed the patronage of King George III. Joseph Banks was obviously used to mixing with famous people from an early age.

During the remainder of his time at Eton, his love for botany grew and every moment he was escaping from his hated Latin and Greek was spent looking for and collecting plants and insects. In 1760, shortly after his seventeenth birthday, he was inoculated against the then dreaded disease of smallpox. Until Edward Jenner (1749-1823) discovered a cure for this by vaccinating patients with cowpox which effectively immunised people against the much more serious smallpox, people were inoculated with a small amount of smallpox which while stopping a larger and more lethal dose later on, still made the patients very ill, as well as still spreading the disease. In the event, after one false start, Joseph was effectively inoculated but by the time he recovered, his father decided not to return him to Eton. He was sent instead to Christ Church, Oxford where he was able to spend time studying his beloved natural history as opposed to the classical curriculum. He was determined to concentrate on botany and actually paid a Cambridge botanist by the name of Israel Lyons to deliver a series of lectures at Oxford in 1764. Israel Lyons was a brilliant young man who was only four years older than Joseph. He was well thought of by both the Professor of Botany and the Master of Trinity at Cambridge, and had published a paper "Treatise of Fluxions" at the age of only 19 and a survey of Cambridge flora a few years later. Less than a decade later, he was to be the astronomer for the 1773 voyage to the North Pole led by the Hon. Constantine Phipps, F.R.S. His position on the voyage was due to his continuing friendship with Joseph Banks, who in 1771 had returned from a three year voyage round the world with Captain Cook. Lyons was to die a tragically early death at the age of 36 in 1775, but in 1764, when he delivered the lectures to Banks and his fellow students at Cambridge, Lyons was just 24 years old.

Returning to Banks and his time at Cambridge, Joseph's father died in 1761 leaving Joseph a very wealthy young man at the age of just eighteen, although he did not actually inherit the wealth until he reached the age of twenty-one. It is to Banks' great credit that he didn't run wild as many young men in his situation would have done, but continued at Christ Church right through until 1765 when he eventually left. It was probably his love of botany and his determination to continue to study the subject that kept him on that career path.

Joseph Banks became a member of the Royal Society in 1766 at the age of just 23 years. The Royal Society had been set up a century earlier by Christopher Wren (1632-1723), the architect who designed St. Paul's Cathedral amongst many other things, and The Hon. Robert Boyle (1627-91), the Irish physicist and chemist who carried out experiments on air, vacuum, combustion and respiration with his famous assistant Robert Hooke (1635-1703), the English chemist, physicist and architect. These men, along with other Oxford intellectuals formed the Royal Society to discuss "The founding of a college for the promoting of physio-mathmatical experimental learning". Given that previous members had also included Sir Issac Newton (1642-1727) the English scientist and mathematician, and Edmond Halley (1656-1742), the Astronomer and mathematician, this was no mean achievement although it would be naïve to ignore the fact that his wealth and status almost certainly helped him. That same year, 1766, Banks had set up and financed a trip to Newfoundland with the sole purpose of bringing back as many different kinds of plants as possible which he duly did, but it was between the years of 1768 and 1771 when he really made his name having sailed round the world with James Cook on board the *Endeavour* during the first of Cook's three great voyages.

James Cook (1728-79) was a non-commissioned naval officer aged 40 who, despite being a brilliant navigator, had been turned down for promotion to commissioned rank no less than three times. The son of an agricultural labourer, he had joined the navy in 1755 and reached the rank of Sailing Master in 1759. For eight years he was involved in the surveying around the St. Lawrence and the shores of Newfoundland, but whilst generally considered brilliant at his job, was almost certainly held back in his various bids for promotion by his lowly background in an age where status carried much weight. In 1768, his luck changed however when he was promoted to Lieutenant and given command of the *Endeavour*. His brief was to sail to Tahiti and observe the transit of Venus the following year, and after that, to search for the great southern land mass which many eminent scientists believed existed. Banks hand picked an entourage of skilled people to accompany him on this same trip in order to explore the different kinds of plant life that existed in the places that they were to visit. With Banks were Daniel Solander, botanist, Hermann Sporing, naturalist, Sydney Parkinson, artist, Alexander Buchan, artist, and Charles Green, astronomer.

Daniel Solander was born in Old Pitea Town (Ojebyn) on 19th February 1733. He passed through the local school with very good grades and studied under the great Carl Linnaeus (1707-1778), the man who is generally held responsible as to the way we classify plants to this day. Two prominent English naturalists, Peter Collinson (1694-1768) and John Ellis (1710-1776) asked

Linnaeus if he would send one of his best pupils to England to spread the word of this classification method known as the *Systema Naturae* and Solander was chosen. He was a friendly, gifted man and learned English quickly and was quick to make friends. He became a member of the Royal Society in 1764 and it is thought that he became friends with Joseph Banks in that same year – it was a friendship that was to last all his life until he died of a cerebral haemorrhage on 13th May, 1782. At his bedside was Carl the Younger, the son of his mentor Carl Linnaeus.

Virtually nothing is known of Hermann Sporing other than he was Swedish but he lived in London as a watchmaker and for the two years prior to joining the *Endeavour*, assisted Daniel Solander as his clerk, secretary and draughtsman before joining the *Endeavour* in 1768. He died on 25th January, 1771 as a result of dysentery which the crew picked up during their stay at Batavia, where they docked in order to repair the ship after the damage caused when they struck a barrier reef off the north-east coast of Australia on their way home.

Sydney Parkinson was the artist on the trip, and a very talented one. We do not know his exact date of birth, but it is believed to be around 1745 in Edinburgh. When he finished his schooling, he was apprenticed to a Boolean draper but being a Quaker, he believed in hard work, and he also studied draughtsmanship under William de la Cour to refine his skills. He became very proficient at drawing plants and flowers and so his studies changed direction. In 1766, he travelled to London and spent a great deal of his time drawing plants at 'The Vinyard', which was the nursery of two men by the names of James Lee and Lewis Kennedy. Lee had written a book *An Introduction to Botany* which described the Linnaeus system and made him and the Vinyard famous. Consequently, many botanists visited the nursery and it was on one such an occasion that Joseph Banks went there and met Parkinson. Impressed with both Parkinson and his work, he had no hesitation in asking Parkinson to accompany him on his proposed trip with James Cook. Parkinson, the gentle, mild mannered Quaker, was to die on the 26th January, 1771, like so many others, the victim of dysentery caught at Batavia.

Alexander Buchan, like Sporing, is another virtual unknown before he joined the *Endeavour* in 1768. He suffered from a severe form of epilepsy which sadly killed him on 17th April, 1769 after a seizure the previous day. Although on the *Endeavour* for less than a year, he produced several important drawings. One of these was of the people of the Bay of Success, and was inscribed *An Indian Town at Terra del Fuego*. It was engraved by a J. Newton as plate II in Sydney Parkinson's *Journal of a Voyage to the South Seas (1773)*. There were several other drawings, another one being *Inhabitants of the Island of Terra Del Fuego* which was used by Giovanni Battista Cipriani (1727-85) as the basis of a wash and water colour drawing for Francesco Bartolozzi's engraving in Hawkesworth's *Account of the Voyages...to the Southern Hemisphere (1773)*. Cipriani was an Italian historical painter who had come to London and in 1768 had been made a member of the Royal Academy, whilst Bartolozzi (1727-1815) was an engraver and enjoyed the patronage of King George III. Bartolozzi was also Italian, and like Capriani had been born in Florence. After Alexander

Buchan's death, his drawings were taken into the possession of Joseph Banks, along with Parkinsons, when the latter died after the Batavia trip.

The Astronomer, Charles Green was born in 1735 in Yorkshire. In 1761, he was appointed Assistant to the third Astronomer Royal, the Rev. James Bradley, at the Royal Observatory, Greenwich. In November 1763, "Two gentlemen well skilled in astronomy" were required to sail to Barbados to test John Harrison's fourth timekeeper. John Harrison (1693-1776) was an English inventor who had spent his adult life since 1730 building a succession of timekeepers in order to solve the problem of calculating longitude at sea. Charles Green was to be one of those men and Nevil Maskelyne was appointed Chaplain to the *Princes Louisa* in order that he may help Green with the tests. Maskelyne (1732-1811) was an English astronomer and a seasoned traveller, having already been to St. Helena in 1761 to observe the transit of Venus but the two men fell out on their return in 1764 when Maskelyne became the Astronomer Royal, and Green left him to become a purser in the navy. It was from this position that he joined the *Endeavour* in 1768. Green died on 29th January, 1771, three days after Sydney Parkinson.

Added to these eminent men were four servants, Peter Briscoe, John Roberts, both of whom had worked for Banks at the Revesby Estate, and a further two, Thomas Richmond and George Dorlton. There is a story often repeated and generally assumed to be true, that Banks was engaged at the time of his departure, and the night before he was due to leave for the *Endeavour*, was at the opera with his fiancée, Miss Harriet Blosset. Apparently, Banks made no mention of his proposed trip and simply left without saying anything to her or her family. On his return he failed to visit Miss Blosset but after receiving a letter from her requiring a meeting or explanation, wrote a letter back professing love, but, "That he found that he was of too volatile a temper to marry". There was a meeting between the couple, but no marriage took place, although Banks was rumoured to have given the Blosset family a considerable amount of money, "To console her for all the knitted waistcoats with which she had sought to enmesh him".

The *Endeavour* set sail from Plymouth on 26th August, 1768. She was a shallow draft Whitby cat, much loved by Cook, but frowned upon by Banks who thought her too small for his needs. However, he had no choice and the officers and Banks' entourage had to make the best of the confined space. Banks not only had his people on board, but a great number of scientific instruments which he insisted were essential. Cook, despite his humble beginnings was a stubborn man, and there were tensions between himself and the upper crust Banks who possibly had to be reminded from time to time as to who the actual captain of the ship was. Banks too could be stubborn, and when the *Endeavour* reached Tierra Del Feugo, he ill-advisedly went ashore with the ship's surgeon William Monkhouse, along with Daniel Solander, Charles Green, and his servants to go deep in to the country and collect as much plant life as was possible. The weather turned against them however and became exceedingly cold, and the long and short of it was that after two of the servants lagged behind, they were found dead from the intense cold. They had taken some of the drink, had drunk themselves insensible and laid down and simply frozen to death. The next day, the rest of the party returned to the ship after spending hours walking through the freezing weather. They were all lucky to be alive and Cook was relieved more than angry as he was using this trip to make a name for himself. Being of humble origins, he had nothing but his abilities as a seaman and leader of men with which to further his career and he must have pondered as to what would have happened to him if he had lost the great Joseph Banks so early in the voyage.

Another problem was to hit them however and again it concerned Joseph Banks. It is a commonly held belief that there was no scurvy at all on board the *Endeavour* but there were in fact five cases of the disease breaking out. One of these who suffered was Joseph Banks himself and on the 11th April, 1769, two days before they arrived at Tahiti, Banks recorded in his journal:-

"About a fortnight ago my gums swelled and some small pimples rose in the inside of my mouth which threatened to become ulcers. I then flew to the lemon juice which had been put up for me according to Dr. Hulmes method described in his book and in his letter which is inserted here: every kind of liqour which I used was made sour with the lemon juice No. 3 so that I took near six ounces a day of it. The effect of this was surprising, in less than a week my gums became as firm as ever and at this time I am troubled with nothing but a few pimples on my face which have not deterred me from leaving off the juice entirely".

So there it is. The ship has not yet reached Tahiti to undertake the first part of the Admiralty's orders, the transit of Venus, and Cook had been in danger of losing Joseph Banks twice. On this first trip at least, Captain James Cook's luck was holding up well.

However, after the mistakes made by Banks' party at Tierra del Feugo, the *Endeavour* continued its journey without any further misfortune, rounded the Horn and eventually sailed into Matavai Bay, Tahiti, also known as Otaheiti on 13th April, 1769. Apart from the outbreak of scurvy of the five men, there had been hardly any sickness on board, and this was largely due to the skill and forward thinking of James Cook, the captain. The biggest killer of sailors was the disease of scurvy, and this killed far more men than wars had ever done. By getting the men to eat Saukraut, portable soup, lemon juice and malt, Cook had virtually eliminated scurvy from his crew, although there was an eminent Scottish surgeon by the name of James Lind (1716-1794) who also deserves credit. His book *A Treatise Of The Scurvy* published in 1753 was largely ignored when it first came out but many years later, it was recognised as a medical classic, although it wasn't until 1795, the year following Lind's death, that the Admiralty finally issued instructions for ships to carry lemon juice. The doctor Nataniel Hulme (1732-1807) who Banks mentions in his journals relating to his own illness, supported the ideas of James Lind during the time the *Endeavour* was on this voyage, but for some reason changed his mind about the effectiveness of lemon juice a few years later, recommending other methods entirely. It was these confusing opinions held by different doctors that caused the delay in the carrying of lemon juice and explains why it did not become compulsory until years later in 1795.

Meanwhile, the ship had anchored in Matavai Bay, Tahiti. Otaheiti, as it was also called, was discovered in 1767 by Samuel Wallis in the *Dolphin*, only a year before the departure of Cook's expedition. There had been initial trouble between the *Dolphin's* sailors and the local people, but by the time Banks and the *Endeavour* arrived, all memories of this had been forgotten and the ship received a rapturous welcome. Hundreds of canoes paddled out to the ship to greet them and they were literally welcomed with open arms. All the people were very friendly and the women were very free with their sexual favours. John Gore, one of the *Endeavour's* Lieutenants, had been on the *Dolphin* with Samuel Wallis, the then captain three years before as a petty officer. He was also on the *Dolphin* under Commodore Byron (the poet's grandfather) when he had sailed across the Pacific in 1765. Apart from the fact that he had already been to the Pacific twice before, John Gore was considered to have outstanding abilities which is why he had been promoted to Lieutenant for Cook's trip and he was aware of the local customs.

All the women required for the price of their love was a ship's nail or something else made of iron which the men of the *Endeavour* were only too pleased to produce. Joseph Banks was a healthy 25-year-old man and was only too eager to take full advantage of the local customs and was an all too willing participant.

It is all too easy to understand the cause of the famous mutiny that occurred on the *Bounty* two decades later. To the European crews, Tahiti was paradise on earth. The men from whatever ship that visited would have spent months at sea in cramped, wet conditions. For the most part, the food was poor and they had to spend a lot of time below deck in foul smelling conditions. Here, they found a race of people that wanted no possessions, and therefore had no work ethic. They simply hunted to eat. The meat and fish they ate was fresh, and there was an abundance of fresh fruit available. Because of the lack of work ethic, they would spend their days sitting around on this beautiful island doing little but making love. Sex was important to the Tahitian people and they initiated children into the art of love at an early age and were therefore without the inhibitions that the Europeans had. They were also exceptionally clean, and would wash several times a day and their teeth, unlike the often rotting mouths of the sailors, were also beautifully white and clean. However, despite enjoying all these advantages, Banks' time on the island was well spent and he didn't forget why he was there, working very hard with Solander collecting plants of all descriptions and also spending time learning the Tahitian language and customs.

The welcome they received was rapturous at first, and Cook, Banks and Solander were treated with great friendship by the local people. One chief had given them presents of cloth and poultry and Banks had returned the compliment by giving them:- "A large laced silk neckcloth I had on and a linen pocket handkerchief". All was well at that point but unfortunately events turned sour only two days after their arrival. The Tahitians were generous with love and gifts, but stole anything that they could lay their hands on and were skilful at it. On 15th April they stole a marine's musket and the marines ran after the man, shooting and killing him. Other items were stolen and Banks recorded in his journal:-

"The adventures of this entertainment I must wish to record particularly, but I am so much hurried by attending the Indians ashore almost all day long that I fear that I shall scarce understand my own language when I read it again. Our Chief's own wife (ugly enough in conscience) did me the honour with very little invitation to squat down on the mats close by me: no sooner had she done so than I espied among the common crowd a very pretty girl with a fire in her eyes that I had not before seen in the country. Unconscious of the dignity of my companion I beckoned to the other who after some entreaties came and sat on the other side of me: I was then desirous of getting rid of my former companion so I ceased to attend to her and loaded my pretty girl with beads and every present I could think pleasing to her: the other showed much disgust but did not quit her place and continued to supply me with fish and cocoa nut milk. How this would have ended is hard to say, it was interrupted by an accident which gave us the opportunity of seeing much of the peoples manners. Dr. Solander and another gentleman who had not been in as good company as myself found that their pockets had been picked, one had lost a snuff box, the other an opera glass".

The items were recovered eventually, but the incident involving the musket the next day was not so easily resolved, and the crew retired to the ship not best pleased with themselves, believing that the punishment did not fit the crime.

The day after that, the 16th April 1769, Alexander Buchan, the landscape painter, had an epileptic fit and the following day died. Because of the tensions on shore and their as yet lack of knowledge of the Tahitians religious beliefs, Banks and Cook decided that Buchan was to be buried at sea which was duly carried out.

Banks and his entourage were worried about the atmosphere, but the Tahitians were forgiving people. Two chiefs, Tubourai and Dootahah, came with presents of breadfruit and a pig and were made very welcome. It seems that the Tahitians felt that the man who had stolen the musket had been at fault and very soon, the friendly relations were restored.

An incident occurred that showed one of the many differences between the two cultures. One of the ship's crew had attempted to buy a stone axe from Tubourai's wife, Tomio, with a ship's nail, but she was an unwilling partner to this transaction. The crewman threatened to cut her throat and take it by force but fortunately was stopped by others responding to the commotion. Cook took the man back on board the *Endeavour* and also took Tubourai and Tomio on board to witness the punishment, in this case the standard practice of flogging. The chief and his wife had no idea what to expect and after the first blow was unleashed, became very upset and begged Cook to stop. He tried to explain that he was punishing the man for what he had inflicted on them, but they were too upset to watch, and Cook, being neither able nor willing to back down, had to have them taken off the ship before the punishment could be concluded. Despite the fact that the member of the crew had wronged them, the sheer physical force of the punishment seemed barbaric to them.

It was at this time that Queen Oberea appeared. Samuel Wallis of the *Dolphin* had incorrectly described her as the Queen of the whole island, and at first, that became perceived wisdom but as time wore on, the crew realised that she was but one of the rulers of Tahiti. Her chief counsellor was Tupai and her husband Oamo. Banks described her in his journal:-

"Our attention was now entirely diverted from every other object to the examination of a personage we had heard so much spoken of in Europe: she appeared to be about 40, tall and very lusty, her skin white and her eyes full of meaning, she might have been handsome when young but now few or no traces of it were left. As soon as her Majesty's quality was known to us she was invited to go on board the ship, where no presents were spared that were thought to be agreeable to her in consideration of the service she had been of to the *Dolphin*".

At this point in time, relations between the islanders and the Europeans were good, but an incident occurred that could have spelt disaster for both the relationship between the two sets of people, and the whole expedition itself. The astronomical quadrant had been brought ashore on 1st May, but was stolen by the local people the following day. Cook was furious because he knew that if they couldn't find the instrument, the whole purpose of sailing to Tahiti was pointless and he would return home a laughing stock. Luckily, Joseph Banks was of a more placid disposition, and along with Charles Green, a midshipman, and Tubourai, set out on an easterly direction to attempt to find it. They walked and half ran for some four miles in the baking temperatures, only to be told that they would have to expect to walk a further three miles before they could have any hope of retrieving the quadrant. Banks and the others pondered over their predicament. They could be as many as seven miles away from their base, were without proper arms, and could not be sure that the local people in the middle of the island would be so friendly as those that had greeted them and who they had befriended. Banks sent the midshipman back to tell Cook and to ask for back up, whilst he, Green and Tubourai continued their search. Eventually, they found the quadrant and managed to retrieve it intact and on walking back about two miles, eventually met Captain Cook with a party of Marines coming to look for them. Banks had courage and a cool head. He had taken a huge risk in going after the quadrant as his small party would have been heavily outnumbered by the local people and it is probably just as well that it was him and not the volatile Cook that recovered the quadrant. Cook was a humane man, but in this instance, his mood might not have been so forgiving as the more amiable Joseph Banks' was.

Life settled down to some sort of normality until the readings of the transit of Venus were taken a month later, on 3rd June, 1769. Although the relations were good, there was still some tension due to the islanders continuing to steal and it was with some relief mixed with a certain sadness that the *Endeavour* left Tahiti on 11th July. They had been there three months and many of the crew had formed relationships with the local women so whilst they did not want to leave, Cook knew that he had to go to avoid the almost inevitable mass desertion that would happen if they were to stay much longer. It was those feelings that provoked the *Bounty* mutiny two decades later although Cook did initially lose two marines, Gibson and Webb just before the *Endeavour* was about to sail. Sadly, this incident caused problems as Cook didn't think that he had much chance of catching the marines and was worried about the almost inevitable wholesale desertion by the men if they were allowed to get away with it. In order to guard against this, he took Queen Oberea and several other islanders hostage and refused to return them until the marines were caught. This was unfortunate to say the least as it caused bad blood just as Cook and his crew were about to depart, but luckily, the marines were caught and harmonious relations were resumed - once again the islanders showed that they were very forgiving people. Cook now had to proceed with the second part of the orders from the Admiralty that had remained sealed until they were on the point of departure, which required them to sail as far as latitude 40 degrees south, and if he found no land, to proceed to the west until he found New Zealand. He was to explore that region and return to England when he felt that the time was right and that they had accomplished all that they could.

Tupai had been the only islander who hadn't shown resentment at being held hostage on the ship, and had long expressed a desire to stay with the *Endeavour*. Of course, he could have had no inkling what life would be like when back in England or whether he could cope with it, but Banks was only too happy to oblige. Cook was against it but Banks promised that he would look after him when back home. In this day and age, Banks' motives may look questionable, even unkind, but in 1770, and given Banks' youth and position, we can afford to be more charitable, although read today, his journal looks a little suspect – "Thank heaven I have a sufficiency and I do not know why I may not keep him as a curiosity, as well as some of my neighbours do lions and tigers at a larger expense than he will probably ever put me to; the amusement I shall have in his future conversation and the benefit he will be to this ship, as well as what he may be if another should be sent into these seas, will I think, fully repay me."

This must look bad to the present day reader, but Banks' treatment of Tupai seemed to contradict all this, and was full of kindness and respect.

They sailed south and searched but failed to find the elusive southern continent before eventually giving up and deciding to make their way home via New Zealand and the eastern coast of Australia. Australia was an unknown quantity at this time and Cook eventually made sight of it and travelled up via the east coast with the intention of sailing west at the northern tip before heading home via Batavia, across the Indian Ocean and eventually rounding the Cape of Good Hope and back to England. After landing at the south-eastern part of Australia, in April 1770, they took possession of the whole country in the name of King George III, and named that part Botany Bay, a place that Banks was to make famous eighteen years later when the first immigrants landed there at his suggestion. Cook named it so, but it was named Botany Bay because of the huge number of new plants that Banks and Dr. Solander had collected. They continued their journey up the east coast of New Holland as Australia was called then, but disaster hit them when the *Endeavour* struck the great barrier reef on the 11th June. It was a dire situation and not only was the ship leaking badly, the hull could be ripped to shreds if they tried to heave her off. Their perilous situation was shown graphically from this short excerpt from Cook's log of that day:-

"This was an alarming and I may say terrible Circumstance and threatened immediate destruction to us as soon as the Ship was afloat. However, I resolved to risk all and heave her off in case it was practical and accordingly turned as many hands to the Capstan & windlass as could be spared from the Pumps and about 20' past 10 o'clock the Ship floated and we hove her off...".

Cook was very proud of the way that the crew behaved and again entered in his log:- "In justice to the Ships Company I must say that no men ever behaved better than they have done on this occasion, animated by the behaviour of every gentleman on board, every man seem'd to have a just sence of the danger we were in and exerted himself to the very utmost".

They tried to lighten the ship by jettisoning anything that was heavy, including the cannons, and the next day they managed to float her and make temporary repairs to the hull, although they knew that they weren't sound enough to get her all the way home. With his life in mortal danger, Banks must have wondered about the wisdom of being on the trip given the comfortable life he had back in England, but Banks seemed to know no fear and his thirst for adventure overcame any wish for a comfortable existence at this time of his life.

The *Endeavour* continued her journey round the northern coast of Australia and on 9th October, 1770, she eventually reached Dutch Batavia in order to rest and carry out repairs. By this time, not knowing what was in store for them here and thinking that they were safe, the men began to feel homesick. Banks has been credited with coining a new word for it – nostalgia, although there are others who claim it was in use years before, invented by a Swiss doctor in the 17th century, although they cannot name the man. Returning to the plight of the *Endeavour*, had she not stopped off at Batavia, the *Endeavour* would almost certainly not have reached England, so in one way, Batavia was a lifeline as the ship was repaired properly, but tragically, the place was rife with dysentery. Up until this time, Cook had barely lost a man through sickness, but here, disaster was to strike, and this was to be the third occasion on the voyage that Cook could have lost Joseph Banks.

Many of the crew and botanists went down with the disease, including Banks and Solander. Fortunately, they both survived, but surgeon Monkhouse wasn't so lucky. It was ironic that it was he who was the first to die, which he did on the 5th November. Tupia and Tayeto (Tupai's follower) were next and naturally Banks was grief stricken at this as they were on the trip because of him. Hermann Sporing died, along with the talented Sydney Parkinson, Charles Green and Midshipman Monkhouse, the clever brother of the surgeon. It was midshipman Jonathan Monkhouse who had patched up the hull temporarily while they were still at sea with a procedure known as fothering. This was a process whereby a sail full of oakum, which was loose fibre from an unravelled rope, was used to plug a gap in a ship's hull whilst still at sea. This allowed them to reach Batavia and Monkhouse had been asked to carry out this repair as he had once been on a ship which had been saved in this manner. By the time they reached England on 12th July 1771, a total of thirty-nine men had died – a real blow to Cook's pride as he had wanted to keep his crew healthy.

Much of the detail of Cook's first trip belongs in the chapter relating to Cook, but it is also relevant to Banks as it helped form his character and shape the rest of his life. It also gives an insight into his character as a young man. Adventurous, kindly and courteous, he was prepared to leave the comfort of his estates and risk his life and fortune in search of knowledge that would help his country, and help him make his name. He certainly made his name, but in so doing, certainly risked his life on a number of occasions along the way. First of all, there was the reckless landing at Tierra del Feugo when two of his servants died of the cold, and so too could he, all too easily. However, he survived, but in March 1769, there was the scurvy scare. This cannot be overestimated as scurvy was a dreadful killer of sailors – it certainly killed far more sailors than war ever did and on most lengthy trips by sea, ships started with twice the number of crew that they actually needed, knowing that by the end of the voyage, half the crew would have died of the disease. Then there was the dreadful moment when the *Endeavour* hit the Great Barrier Reef because when heaving her off, it would have been quite possible that the ship would have been ripped to pieces with the loss of all hands, and finally catching dysentery at Batavia on the journey home. It went through the crew like wildfire, killing a third of them, but again, Banks survived.

Whatever characteristics Banks may or may not have had, he and Cook were certainly treated differently when they arrived back in England because Banks was certainly the star. Maybe the number of men that had been lost was a factor in the different way that Cook and Banks were perceived on their return. This was Cook's great chance to make a name for himself, and had he returned home after three years with virtually a full crew, no doubt that would have seemed a great breakthrough in health at sea. As it was, through no fault of Cook's, Batavia ruined that and it was Banks and to a slightly lesser degree, Daniel Solander, who were feted on their return. They had brought back many hundreds of rare plants, fish, reptiles, birds and mammals, along with the hundreds of fine drawings by Sydney Parkinson. Banks was lauded by the King, George III, and many famous people of the day including Dr. Johnson (1709-84), the great English writer and lexicographer. Banks also had his portrait painted by the renowned Sir Joshua Reynolds (1723-92). Banks was only twenty-eight years old and Reynolds was at the height of his fame. In 1749 Reynolds had gone to Rome for three years to study Raphael and Michelangelo. Raphael (1483-1520) was the great Italian painter while Michelangelo (1475-1564) was the famous Italian sculptor, painter and poet whose most famous work was the painting of the Sistine Chapel between 1508 and 1512. The extraordinary thing about this is that Michelangelo pleaded with Pope Julius II that his main skill was that of a sculptor and that Raphael was better qualified, but the Pope insisted that Michelangelo carry out the work and it is known throughout the world as a masterpiece.

In 1764, whilst living in London, Reynolds founded the Literary Club which included members such as Dr. Johnson (1709-84), the English writer and critic mentioned in the previous paragraph and who wrote the great English dictionary in 1755, David Garrick (1717-79), the dramatist and writer, James Boswell (1740-95) the Scottish man of letters and biographer of Dr. Johnson, and Richard Brinsley Sheridan (1751-1816), the Irish dramatist. For Banks to have been painted by such a man as Reynolds at such an early age spoke volumes as to how he was seen by the public.

Banks had brought back a huge amount of plant specimens, and now he needed someone reliable to catalogue them all – a huge task. The famous Dr.

John Hunter (1728-93), who tutored the young Edward Jenner (1749-1823), famous in later years for his work that would eventually lead to smallpox being cured, was asked if he would recommend anyone who could carry out this huge undertaking. Hunter had no hesitation in recommending Jenner who accepted the challenge and carried out the work extremely diligently. For Banks to be associating with the likes of Reynolds and Hunter, two exceptionally gifted and famous men, said a great deal about the fame that he himself had now acquired.

Another factor in how Banks was perceived would have come in the form of John Montague, 4th Earl of Sandwich (1718-92) who had succeeded Sir Edward Hawke (1705-81) as First Lord of the Admiralty in 1771 before the *Endeavour* returned. Quite why Sandwich had taken over from a man like Hawke remains unclear, as Hawke had had a brilliant record in his naval career because as well as being First Lord, he had also been Admiral of the Fleet in 1768. However, the fact remains that he *was* replaced and it did no harm to Banks having Sandwich as First Lord. Although considerably older, Sandwich was a great friend of Banks – they had adjoining estates in Lincolnshire and socialised with each other there and in London. Sandwich and Cook barely knew each other as it was Sir Edward Hawke who had sent Cook away on the first voyage and their different backgrounds meant that they could not relate to each other at all. However, during the year between the first and second voyage, Sandwich began to appreciate Cook's achievements more as Banks was to find out to his cost when preparing for the second voyage, which he, Banks, had every intention of leading. It wasn't long before people judged that Cook had been unfairly treated after the first voyage but there is no doubt that Banks' achievements were immense.

As a result of his fame, Banks wanted to set out on another journey with Cook. Cook had been asked to look again to see if the great southern continent existed, but instead of being content to sail with Cook, it seems that Banks saw it as *his* trip and there was conflict about the type of ship and accommodation that they were to sail in. Banks demanded two ships rather than one, a concept that Cook had no problem with given the horror of the great barrier reef, but his insistence that he, Banks, be in command of the expedition as opposed to Cook was ridiculous and was never going to be agreed to by the Admiralty. Another problem was the type of ship. Cook felt that the Whitby Cat had proved her worth and was insistent that that was the vessel to be used, whilst Banks wanted a much larger ship such as a frigate. Two ships were found that that the navy deemed suitable and were initially named Drake and Raleigh but it was decided that naming the ships after two great English heroes would probably upset the Spanish, so they were re-named Resolution and Adventure. However, whilst these two ships were deemed suitable by the navy, Banks strongly disagreed and again demanded much larger vessels. He argued that he was putting up a large sum of his own money to finance the expedition, and felt that the two ships on offer were far too cramped to suit his needs as he would be taking a large amount of equipment and a great number of men to suit his purpose.

Banks was a wealthy young man, used to his creature comforts and also used to getting his own way and a second three year voyage in small quarters held no attraction for him. The Admiralty would not budge however, but a compromise was reached which meant that Banks could have the *Resolution* modified to suit his needs. He designed the alterations himself but in the end, they made the ship so top heavy that she was completely unseaworthy and they had to be pulled down and the ship restored to its original condition. When he found out what was happening, Banks blew his top and was by now expecting the ships and Cook to be replaced, especially as he was very friendly with Lord Sandwich, the First Lord of the Admiralty. Banks had pushed his luck too far however. He made the mistake of believing himself irreplaceable, and this, coupled with his friendship with Lord Sandwich, lulled him into thinking that it would be Cook who would be replaced.

Sandwich had many faults but he was no fool, and it was never really in doubt that if pushed, he would choose Cook to take the ships out despite his friendship with Banks. After Lord Sandwich's initial reluctance to use Cook on the first trip due mainly to Cook's humble birth, Sandwich realised that Cook was one of the greatest seamen he had come into contact with, and Banks, humiliated, had no option other than to withdraw from the voyage.

It was all very unsatisfactory. Banks was very popular with the public who had gone along with the idea that it was Banks's trip and not knowing the technical facts behind the choice of ships, thought that Banks had been treated badly by the navy. Banks however, had realised that he had behaved stupidly and due to that, and the fact that he did not want to put at risk his close friendship with Lord Sandwich, wrote a letter to the First Lord attempting to explain his reasons for pulling out of Cook's second voyage. The letter was dated 30th May, 1772 and was sent from New Burlington Street. It was a very long letter but despite its length, it didn't really tell Sandwich any more than the First Lord knew already, but it was surely Banks' attempt to put his behaviour into some sort of context. He just about succeeded, but one of the other reasons for writing it must have been an attempt to heal the breach in the long standing friendship that he had with Sandwich. In the event, he needn't have worried, as the rift was short lived, and the two men remained friends until Sandwich's death in 1792. With regard to explaining his behaviour, it also probably succeeds, although it doesn't excuse his petulance at the time. The basic premise of the letter was that he, Banks, was quite happy to have small personal quarters, in fact one part of the letter says:-

"For my own part my Lord, I am able and willing to put up with as small Accommodations as any Man living can be content with, Six Feet square is more than sufficient for all my personal conveniences ..."

What Banks went on to say however, was that his workspace as opposed to his private space was insufficient. Given the number of men that he wanted to take along as well as the inevitable equipment, he must have had a strong case. Banks had intended to take sixteen people in all, including Dr. Solander, four artists, two secretaries along with eight servants and assistants. There is another part of the letter that in order to be fair to Banks, should be quoted:-

"To explore is my Wish, but the Place to which I may be sent almost indifferent to me. Whether the sources of the Nile or the South Pole are to be visited, I am equally ready to embark in the undertaking when ever the Public will furnish me with the means of doing it properly; but to undertake so extensive a pursuit without any prospect but Distress and disappointment is neither consistent with Prudence nor Public Spirit."

Reading this paragraph, there can be no doubt as to his genuine desire to serve his country, even though his life could well be put in danger, as was demonstrated so clearly on several occasions on the first trip.

However, with no Joseph Banks on board, a replacement had to be found, and this came in the form of a German botanist, Johann Reinhold Forster (1729-98) and his son Georg (1754-94). Forster senior was a talented man but extremely difficult to get on with, and it is not clear as to who became ultimately sadder that this whole affair had happened, Cook, because he had to put up with Forster's difficult ways for the next three years, or Banks himself, who ended up missing out on a great trip. Certainly Cook regretted that Banks was not with him because despite the fact that they had quarrelled over the type of ships that were to be used, Banks was an affable man and good company, and no-one on board ship would ever have said that about Johann Reinhold Forster who was a thoroughly difficult man to contend with. Over the years, public opinion has swung away from Banks over this incident, but his letter to Sandwich clearly demonstrates his desire to serve his country, hazarding his life and his fortune in the process. However, he consoled himself by chartering a 190-ton brig *Sir Lawrence*, and taking many of the same members of his original party, sailing from Gravesend for the Hebrides and Iceland on 12th July, 1772, the same day that Cook and his ships left Plymouth Sound. It is often thought that one of the people in Banks's party was a Dr. James Lind (1716-94), the Scottish surgeon who had done so much work researching methods to eliminate the dreaded disease of scurvy, but it was in fact Lind's cousin of the same name who was on board. The trip that Banks undertook to Iceland was considered a success and he collected a large amount of new plants and specimens. However, although a success, it was overshadowed by the massive second voyage that Cook undertook between 1772 and 1775, and there is no doubt that Banks later had regrets that he had not been with Cook.

There was a spin off from the second trip that came Banks' way however, and this came in the form of a young Tahitian islander named Omai who was brought back by Tobias Furneaux, the Captain of the *Adventure*. The *Resolution* commanded by Cook, and the *Adventure* had set off in July, 1772, but after traversing a huge amount of ocean and even going beyond the Antartic Circle, Cook decided to return to Tahiti in August, 1773 and replenish his stocks of food, because although Cook's men were healthy, Furneaux's men were not and an outbreak of scurvy occurred on the *Adventure*. Whilst they were at Tahiti, they met Omai who like Tupia on Cook's first trip, asked to be taken on board the *Adventure* and go to England. Omai had originally lived on Raiatea but the people of this land were invaded by those of Bora Bora and Omai's father was killed and Omai lost his home. Omai went to Tahiti and when Cook's ships arrived, was in effect, a refugee there. Furneaux agreed to take Omai and he was duly signed on as an Able Seaman, although it is doubtful whether he actually did any work. It was just a formality to allow him to stay on board. They left the Society Islands on 18th September, 1773 with their new passenger on board.

The ships had twice been separated in their search for the great southern land and in the event of any such separation, Cook had arranged for the two ships to rendezvous at Queen Charlotte Sound. This they managed to do the first time, but the second time the *Adventure* arrived on the 30th November, 1773 and found a message from Cook in a bottle saying that he had waited from the 2nd to the 24th November but would be sailing south again. They had missed each other by a mere six days. Furneaux repaired his ship and on 23rd December, 1773 sailed eastwards but he had a depleted crew due to the horrific killing of ten of his crew just before they sailed. Apparently, Furneaux had sent a Midshipman, Master's Mate, and eight crew ashore to gather food, but they had been attacked and killed by the local New Zealand natives. When they had not arrived back on board, Lieutenant James Burney and some crewmen went to search for them and to their horror, found that not only had they been killed, but there was clear evidence of cannibalism. With the crew thus reduced, Furneaux decided to head home. The *Adventure* reached the Cape of Good Hope on the 19th January, 1774, rested for three months, and sailed for England on 16th April. The *Adventure* arrived at Spithead on 14th July, 1774, and by this time, Omai, an intelligent man, had picked up some of the English manners and mannerisms.

It is not difficult to understand why Furneaux agreed to let Omai sail with him on the *Adventure*. When Cook's men had arrived home from the *Endeavour* after the first voyage, they had brought home stories of this paradise island in the south Pacific called Tahiti. Furneaux had worked out that by bringing back a native from these islands that no-one in England would have seen before, he would make a name for himself. Whether he gave much thought as to who was going to look after Omai in England is another matter as being a serving naval officer, he must have known that he would be likely to receive another command soon after returning home, and would therefore be unable to look after Omai. Maybe there was some prior agreement with Joseph Banks before the second trip started, although at the time of their departure, Banks was in no mood to negotiate anything with anybody. However, as it turned out, just as he had hoped to do with Tupia, Banks, along with his friends Daniel Solander and Lord Sandwich, took over the welfare of Omai and proceeded to look after him, showing him off to all and sundry in the process. Not that Omai needed coaxing – he was only too keen to be introduced to all the eminent people of the day and eventually became something of a snob.

Banks was the first important person to be introduced to Omai and then straight away took him to meet Lord Sandwich. Sandwich and Banks had long since resolved the disagreements that had arisen between them at the beginning of Cook's second voyage. After grooming Omai at Banks' house in New Burlington Street, Sandwich arranged for him to be presented to King George III at Kew. Omai was suitably dressed in the English manner, and wore a brown velvet coat, white waistcoat and grey satin breeches, and was schooled in the correct way of addressing the King. It has passed into folklore that Omai addressed the King with the words:- "How do, King Tosh?" because Polynesian people were unable to say King George's name properly, but this is by no means certain. Sarah Sophia Banks herself, records that:- 'he dropped upon one knee and said "How do you do King George, I hope you are very well"'. The King was actually very kind to Omai, and promised him that a ship would take him home at some stage, but in the meantime, he was granted an allowance, presented with a handsome sword, and recommended that he be inoculated against smallpox. Whether the latter was such a good thing was open to debate, as it was to be well over twenty years before Dr. Edward Jenner (who had catalogued all of Banks's plant specimens from Cook's first trip) was to start the process of curing the world against this disease by vaccination with the less dangerous disease of cowpox. Inoculation involved giving the patient a mild form of smallpox itself, but this was always a hazardous process.

In the event, Banks himself took Omai to a Dr. Dimsdale to have the procedure carried out and although Omai was affected by it, he eventually recovered. Omai stayed with Sandwich at Huntingdon, Sandwich's vast Elizabethan house and both Banks and Sandwich were impressed by Omai's courtesy and natural good manners. Omai was introduced to many of the fashionable people of the day, including the famous Welsh writer, Hester Thrale (1741-1821) who was the wife of Henry Thrale, a wealthy Southwark brewer and with whom she had twelve children. Henry Thrale died in 1781, and Hester went on to marry the Italian musician, Gabriel Piozzi in 1784. Her Streatham home was always full of people like Dr. Johnson, David Garrick, Richard Sheridan, and Joshua Reynolds amongst others. Later on, the set also included the famous writer Fanny Burney (1752-1840), who influenced Jane Austen (1775-1817), and who was the sister of Lieutenant James Burney of the *Adventure*. Omai dined there one night when Dr. Johnson was there, and Johnson, when comparing the manners of Omai to Lord Mulgrave, another of Mrs. Thrales' distinguished guests, later remarked to his friend and future biographer, James Boswell:- "They sat with their backs to the light fronting me, so that I could not see distinctly; and there was so little of the savage in Omai, that I was afraid to speak to either, lest I should mistake the one for the other."

Omai dined with the Burneys, although Fanny had not yet published Evelina and her father, Dr. Charles Burney (1726-1814), the English musicologist, had also not yet published his famous *History of Music*. Fanny in particular, was very impressed with Omai's manners and he went on to dine at least ten times with the Royal Philosopher's Club as well as visit the House of Lords to hear King George III speak from his throne. He also had his portrait painted by none other than Sir Joshua Reynolds, William Parry and Nathaniel Dance. It was Banks who commissioned Dance to paint the famous painting of Captain Cook between the latter's second and third voyages, but although Nathaniel Dance (1735-1811) was a famous painter, it was the painting that Joshua Reynolds created of Omai that became the most famous. It was huge, and until that time, non-white people were very much seen as peripheral figures in paintings. But if Omai wanted to be famous, then Joshua Reynolds also had an eye for the main chance which is why he painted this extraordinary picture of this fashionable, famous Tahitian the way he did. For a long time Omai was the height of fashion, and all the famous people of the day wanted to meet him. He charmed society with his elegant manners, and amused them by some of his phrases. He called horses 'Big hogs', carriages he referred to as 'Moving Houses' and it is said that when offered snuff, refused saying "My nose is not hungry". During this time, that remark was seen as rather quaint and caused amusement, but viewed in today's climate, would probably be seen as nothing more than a reasonable reply from someone whose English was understandably limited. Doubtless, he spoke better English than most of his hosts spoke Tahitian with the exception of course of Joseph Banks himself who had studied the language and customs from the *Endeavour's* voyage. However, when things and/or people are the height of fashion, the inevitable happens, and eventually they go *out* of fashion. However gifted he was, Omai's conversation was inevitably limited, and people grew first accustomed, and then tired of this South Sea Island man. After all, he had always been viewed as not much more than a curiosity and Omai's invitations began to lessen and taken out of his natural environment, he started to lead a rather lonely life. He clearly could not stay, and in any event, King George III had already promised him a passage home. The chance came with Captain Cook himself, who after his second trip was virtually retired with his posting at Greenwich Hospital. Cook was bored stiff. He had spent six out of the previous seven years sailing the globe and Greenwich Hospital was not going to keep him occupied. The government was planning an expedition to search for the North West passage between the Pacific and Atlantic Oceans across the top of Canada and Alaska with prize money of £20,000 (Over a £million in 2010) for the person who found it. It was an opportunity that Cook did not want to lose out on, and it gave the government the chance to use the voyage as a cover for taking Omai home.

Placing events into the context of the period, Banks cannot be blamed for Omai's treatment. After all, it was Omai himself who had expressed a desire to travel to England, and it was Tobias Furneaux who had taken Omai from his people, not Banks, and once here, Banks looked after him well. It was just that English Society had grown bored with Omai, and it was time for him to be returned to his people. However, the question that no-one seems to have thought of when they took Omai away from the Pacific islands was whether the South Sea Islanders would still be Omai's people when he returned or would he be caught between two cultures, fitting into neither? The latter was the answer, not helped by the fact that the English gave him totally useless presents, one being a suit of armour, whilst others were a jack-in-the-box, crockery, and some fireworks. Omai simply didn't fit back in to the society he had been away from for two years, and he was often robbed and probably died very lonely. Added to this, the islanders were not impressed with his stories of English high society – in any event, it was a situation they found difficult to comprehend let alone be impressed with. A young William Bligh had been the Master of the *Resolution* on this trip that had returned Omai to what were his people. As Captain Bligh, he went back several years later and asked about Omai and was told that he had died roughly two years after his arrival home, although the manner of his death is not quite clear. Some say he died in a fight, others of illness, but he was almost certainly sad and alone, totally unable to settle back into the Tahitian way of life and neither was he able to return to England. Banks had done his best, but it had always been clear that Omai would not stay in England forever and the experiment of trying to cross the culture divide and return him to his original home simply didn't work.

When Cook set off for his third trip in July 1776, the rift he'd had with Banks four years earlier had all but healed and if Banks had wanted to go on that third trip, there is no doubt that he would have been welcomed. The three years that they had spent together on the *Endeavour* between 1768 and 1771 had formed a friendship that was not going to be ruined by one argument that both men regretted. Cook, because instead of Banks, he had to put up with Johann Reinhold Forster on the second trip, and Banks, because he missed out on yet another trip of a lifetime. The idea of the third trip was to find the elusive North-West passage through the top of the Americas that seamen had tried and failed to find for centuries. By this time however, Banks had been on dry land enjoying his creature comforts for five years and was far too settled into his life ashore advising the King on the running of Kew Gardens, and also his work with the Royal Society.

In 1774, Banks was elected to the Dilettante Society, which was an all-male dining club which sponsored artistic trips to foreign countries. There seemed to be four requirements to join this exclusive club; a love of fine antiques, a love of women, good conversation, and lastly a love of wine. Banks had no problems fitting into any of these categories and he became Secretary between the years 1778 and 1797. However, although he enjoyed the activities of this society, a much greater honour was going to come his way.

Joseph Banks had been a member of the Royal Society since 1766 and in 1778, the post of President was going to become vacant. The President of the Royal Society was a man called Sir John Pringle (1707-82), who was a distinguished Scottish physician. He had studied philosophy and classics at St. Andrews University and medicine at Leiden. Eventually he had become head of the Army Medical Service and was physician to various members of the Royal family including King George III. He had only been President since 1772 but by now was over seventy years of age and decided not to seek re-election. He was also on bad terms with the King, and all things considered, he had had enough. On 30th November, 1778, Joseph Banks was elected as President, a position he went on to hold with some distinction for 41 years, for the remainder of his life in fact. It was a great honour to be elected President, but it was not a foregone conclusion by any stretch of the imagination. Another strong candidate was Alexander Aubert, a wealthy city man. Aubert was head of the London Assurance Company but his great love was astronomy and he had made some extraordinary observations. If he was elected, it would please the Society's many mathematicians and he had a more than useful ally as Sir John Pringle himself let it be known that he favoured Aubert as his successor. However, Banks had a large number of people who wanted him to stand, and on the 11th August, 1778, his friend Dr. Solander wrote the following letter to him:-

"My Dear Sir,

This morning Mr. Planta told me that Sir John Pringle has certainly declared that he intends to resign; and Mr. Cavendish says that Sir John has mentioned it at the Mitre. It is true that he has given hints about Mr. Aubert, but all look to you. Dr. Pitcairne and others have desired me to tell you that."

Six days later, on the 17th, Solander followed this letter up with another giving further encouragement and Banks took the bait and began to canvass for votes. He relied heavily on the votes of fellow Antiquaries as many members of the Royal Society were also Fellows of the Antiquaries Society but it was not obvious that Banks would win the election that was held in November. Banks was well known and respected and came from a wealthy family, but he had published virtually nothing and at thirty-five years of age, was relatively young for such a post. However, he was liked and because he declined to get involved in politics, he had made no enemies. He got on equally well with Whigs and Tories, and that, plus his friendship with King George III, swung the voting in his favour, and in the end, he was elected quite comfortably.

His life was changing rapidly as on the 23rd of March the following year, 1779, he married Dorothea Hugessen and they settled in a large house in Soho Square, London where they lived with Banks's sister, Sarah Sophia. Dorothea was not as wealthy as her husband, but she came from a good family and brought a large amount of her own money to the marriage. She was the daughter and co-heiress of William Western Hugessen of Provender. Dorothea was a sweet natured young woman of twenty-one and she got on well with Joseph's sister, Sarah Sophia and his mother who also joined them in Soho Square where she lived with them during her final illness. The marriage was happy and provided a distant, but nonetheless real connection with the writer Jane Austen. Dorothea's younger sister Mary, had married the eighth Baronet Sir Edward Knatchbull of Mersham Hatch in Kent, and Sir Edward's and Mary's son Edward, the ninth Baronet, married Fanny Knight, Jane Austen's niece, who was the daughter of Jane's brother Edward Knight, Edward having changed his surname having been adopted by the wealthy Knight family.

Banks was made a baronet in 1781 and with his title and wealth, along with being President of The Royal Society, would have a huge influence on the future course of British science. Banks was close to King George III, and for many years advised him on aspects of science and botany as well as the running of Kew Gardens, a position that was made official in 1797. Banks was now hugely influential and arranged for many botanical voyages to different parts of the world. One of the most famous of these was in August 1787, when at Banks' recommendation, William Bligh was appointed Captain of the *Bounty*. Bligh's brief was to sail to Tahiti, to obtain large amounts of the breadfruit that grew there, and sail on to the West Indies where it would provide cheap food for the plantation slaves. Having deposited the breadfruit to the West Indies, the *Bounty* would return to England, the task having been carried out. The ship left England on 23rd December, 1787, but the expedition failed when the crew, lured by the charms of the Tahitian people, mutinied on 28th April, 1789 on the journey home, and set Bligh adrift into the middle of the Pacific in an open boat with eighteen of his followers. Bligh managed to return to England however, and after a period of recuperation, set out on a second trip in August 1791, this time better equipped and with two ships and a contingent of marines, returning in August 1793 after successfully carrying out the task. In the end, it was completely futile, as the slaves did not like the breadfruit and refused to eat it. As the navy had spent five out of the six years between 1787 and 1793 actively engaged in this expedition, it must have been one of the few failures in Banks' long and distinguished life, although none of the events were his fault.

Despite a lifetime of achievement, Banks' huge legacy must be his recommendation of a penal colony being set up in Botany Bay to solve the problem of overcrowding in England's prisons. The prisons in England were disgusting - there was no sanitation and the overcrowding was immense. There was no attempt to limit the number of people to a cell and disease was rife. Given the type of punishment at the time where people were jailed for the most trivial of offences, it was no wonder that there was a problem and the authorities had no idea as to how to solve it, especially as America had been lost and was no longer available to the government. In 1778, his first year as President of the Royal Society, Joseph Banks, remembering his trip in the *Endeavour* nearly ten years before with Cook, suggested to a Parliamentary Committee that Botany Bay should be used to house criminals. Australia was halfway round the world involving a trip of many months, and with no communication to speak of, was initially thought to be out of the question, but eventually, the idea took hold, and it was decided to set up a colony there. The first Governor-General was a man called Arthur Phillip (1738-1814). Phillip had joined the Navy at fifteen and had seen action in the seven years war. After serving for a time in the Portuguese navy, he re-joined the British Navy in 1778 and obtained his first command, that of the *Basilisk,* in 1779. He was promoted to captain in 1781 when he was given command of the *Europe*, but in 1784, he was let go again on half pay. In October, 1786, he was appointed Captain of the *Sirius*, and appointed Governor-General Designate of New South Wales.

The first fleet, which consisted of eleven ships, set sail on 13th May, 1787, and the first ship reached Botany Bay on 18th January, 1788. Phillip decided that it was not a suitable place to anchor however, plus there was no obvious water supply, so the fleet decided to go to Port Jackson. On 26th January, 1788, the marines and convicts were landed at Sydney Cove, named after the British Home Secretary, Lord Sydney, who as Thomas Townshend (1732-1800) was created Baron Sydney on 6th March, 1783. He was Home Secretary under Prime Minister William Pitt the Younger from 23rd December, 1783 until 5th June, 1789 and his background was one of wealth, unlike the beginnings of the city that was named after him, the city of Sydney we know today being born from highly inauspicious beginnings.

These beginnings were tough. The land was dry and almost impossible to farm, and because there were so few women there, there was the most terrible mass rape. It was decided that the only way to bring about a stable community was to ship out more women and try to create families. This they did, but life was unbelievably tough for many years while the new colony struggled to survive. Banks was friendly with the first governors, and encouraged them all whilst they were there. He willingly gave them botanical and agricultural advice as well as harassing the British government to send supplies out. He possibly has to share the accolade with Arthur Phillip, the first Governor-General, but Joseph Banks is seen by many if not most as the father of modern day Australia.

Although people had been settled in New South Wales since 1788, the country as a whole still had not been mapped properly and as this was a place close to Joseph Banks' heart, he was only too happy to help set up an expedition to put this right in 1801. The man chosen for this task was a young but experienced seaman, Matthew Flinders (1774-1814). Flinders had served with Captain Bligh on *HMS Providence*, which along with the *Assistant*, had carried out the successful second trip to Tahiti to obtain breadfruit and take them to the West Indies as food for the slaves. This breadfruit trip had also been set up by Joseph Banks, and probably done so with even greater determination than the first, as no doubt it was deemed by both Banks and Bligh to be unfinished business.

The ship chosen for the mapping of Australia was a three masted collier built in 1795, originally named the *Xenophon* but re-named the *Investigator*, and on 19th of January, 1801, Flinders was appointed as Lieutenant of the ship. The ship needed a captain however, and on the 16th of February, after writing to Banks on the subject, Flinders was promoted to Commander, and therefore became Captain of the ship. On the 17th April, 1801, Flinders married Ann Chappelle (1770-1852) and wanted to take her with him to Australia as they would be setting sail soon after the marriage. However, the plan was discovered and the newly married couple were forced to part from each other for what they thought would be two years.

Flinders knew that it had been against the rules, and on 21st May, 1801, a furious Banks wrote to Flinders:-

"Dear Sir,

I have but just time to tell you that the news of your marriage, which was published in the Lincoln paper, has reached me. The Lords of the Admiralty have heard also that Mrs Flinders is on board the *Investigator*, and that you have some thoughts of carrying her to sea with you. This I am very sorry to hear, and if that is the case I beg to give you my advice, by no means to venture to measures so contrary to the regulations and the discipline of the Navy; for I am convinced, by the language I have heard, that their Lordships will, if they hear of her being in New South Wales, immediately order you to be superseded, whatever may be the consequences, and in all likelihood order Mr. Grant to finish the survey."

Flinders was grief-stricken at such disapproval from Banks, but his wife, Ann, was in a worse state. She had married in the firm belief that they would travel together and she was devastated when her husband decided that on this occasion, his career must come first, and that he would leave without her. The projected two or three years was bad enough for newlyweds at the best of time, but as it turned out, the parting would last much longer.

Flinders was very successful, and between December, 1801 and June, 1803, he circumnavigated Australia but tragically, was captured in December by the French Governor of Mauritius, a General de Caen. Despite letters from Sir Joseph explaining Flinders' status, De Caen refused to release him and he did not return to England and Ann until October 1810. Even as late as the middle of June that same year, Banks had little hope of obtaining the release of Matthew Flinders, as he, Banks, had already been let down many times over the years. On 12th June, 1810, he wrote to Ann Flinders from Soho Square:-

"Madam,

I wish I could give you any Comfortable or Encouraging news respecting my worthy friend Capt. Flinders. Government can do nothing in his favour under the Capricious and insolent Government of the Tyrant of France… "
However, in the same letter Banks goes on to add a little encouragement to Ann:-
"… I am told vigorous measures are to be adopted for seizing The Island. If this Succeeds, & if it is Planned with wisdom & executed with Spirit it must succeed, we may have the happiness of seeing the Gallant Capt. return before we expect him.

I am madam,

Your Obedient Hble Servt, Jos: Banks"

However, after all his years in captivity, things were to change for Matthew Flinders because he was released on virtually the same day as Banks was writing the previous letter to Ann. Flinders sailed from Port Louis on 13th June and arrived in Spithead on 24th October, 1810. Meanwhile, one month earlier, on 25th September, Banks had written to Ann Flinders from Revesby Abbey:-

"Madam,

I have infinite Satisfaction in informing you that Capt. Flinders has at Last Obtaind his Release, & is expected in England in a few weeks, & that on his arrival he will be immediately made a Post Captain.

I am, Madam,

Your most Faithfull Servt,
Jos: Banks"

On his return, Flinders was indeed made Post Captain of *HMS Ramillies* but the years of captivity had taken their toll, and his health was poor. He started work on his book, *A Voyage to Terra Australis*, which was published on 18th July 1814. The day after publication, Matthew Flinders died aged just forty years old. It was Flinders success story, but Banks must take credit too, as he had set the project up and had appointed Robert Brown, the brilliant naturalist to the *Investigator*, and Flinders and Brown had worked well together. This project meant that another great connection had been made between Banks and the rapidly expanding country that was Australia.

In the meantime, in 1804, Banks was involved in the formation of the British Horticultural Society, still in existence today but now called the Royal Horticultural Society. It was the brainchild of John Wedgwood in 1800 but it took another four years before it actually came into existence. John Wedgwood (1766-1844) was the son of the famous Josiah Wedgwood (1730-95), who in 1763, patented a beautiful cream coloured ware (Queen's Ware) but is probably more famous for the unglazed blue Jasper ware with its raised designs in white. His son John was educated at Warrington Academy before going to Edinburgh University. After university he went into banking before going back to his father's business from 1790 until 1793, and then again from 1800 to 1812. He married Louisa Jane Allen, the younger sister of his brother Josiah Wedgwood II's wife Bessie in 1794 and they went on to have six children. John Wedgwood made a huge contribution to the family business when he came up with the idea of putting plant designs on the pottery that his father's firm produced as this design became very fashionable in the 1800's. John was a good and a gentle man, and deserves credit for the overall contribution he made to the business. Besides Joseph Banks and John Wedgwood, there were five other people present at that first historic meeting of the Horticultural Society which took place on 7th March, 1804, at a room over Hatchards bookshop in Piccadilly. Given the importance of that meeting and the fact that the society survives today, it is probably a good idea to write a few words about the other men that were present. Apart from John Wedgwood and Joseph Banks, the other five were:-

Charles Francis Greville FRS (1749-1809) – was the second son of the 1st Earl of Warwick and when his father died in 1773, his older brother became Earl of Warwick whilst Charles inherited his seat of Warwick in the House of Commons. Between 1782 and 1786 Charles had an affair with a lady named Emma Hart (c1765-1815) and took her to the studio of the great painter, George Romney (1734-1802). Greville does not come out of this relationship in a good light, as his motive for taking Emma to Romney's studio was solely to make money. Greville wanted Romney to paint a series of pictures of Emma with the idea of them selling the pictures and splitting the enormous sums they hope to make on a 50-50 basis. Quite how much Romney and Greville were going to give to Emma is not known as the plan backfired in as much as Romney was captivated by Emma's beauty and made Emma a star with a series of paintings and the situation left Greville with no money from the deal. With nothing being in it for him, Greville tired of Emma and she ended up marrying Greville's uncle, Sir William Hamilton (1730-1803), the Scottish diplomat and antiquarian. Sir William was the British Ambassador at Naples and his marriage to Emma in 1791 made her the famous Lady Hamilton who would eventually become the mistress of Lord Nelson. Meanwhile, Charles Francis Greville had a huge collection of precious stones and minerals (estimated at 14,800) that were catalogued and purchased by the British Museum. Greville was a very close friend of Joseph Banks so he was a natural person to be on the Horticultural Committee.

Richard Anthony Salisbury FRS (1761-1829) like Banks, was a British botanist. He was actually born Richard Markham but changed his name after he had supposedly made an arrangement to receive financial help from an elderly woman so that he could continue his studies. It was said that when he was 24, he had received £10,000 (not far short of a million pounds in today's terms). He married Caroline Staniforth in 1796 and they had a child called Eleanor the following year but they parted company soon after. Salisbury's reputation plummeted after that as it was thought that he had not been truthful to Caroline's family about his finances when they married because he had to file for bankruptcy shortly after their daughter was born. Quite what he had done with the £10,000 over the previous ten years is not clear but it certainly seems to have been spent. Although he was arrested for financial misrepresentation soon after being declared bankrupt, it would appear that somehow or other, his financial status took a turn for the better because he purchased a house in 1802. Salisbury was a good botanist and a member of the Linnean Society although it seems that he seemed to go out of his way to antagonise other members by taking issue with a great many of their views. He also produced a paper entitled 'On the cultivation of the plants belonging to the natural order of Proteeae' but it turned out that this was really the work of another botanist called Robert Brown, and Salisbury had simply plagiarised the main body of Brown's work from a publication of his own, 'On the Proteaceae of Jussieu'. Salisbury published his work in 1809 and unfortunately, Brown didn't publish his until the year after, so at first, it appeared that the original work was Salisbury's.

Eventually the truth came out and Salisbury was ostracised by other botanists. Robert Brown himself probably summed Salisbury's character best when he later wrote of him:- "I scarcely know what to think of him except that he stands between a rogue and a fool".

William Forsyth (1737-1804) was a Scottish horticulturalist and was a friend of John Wedgwood and for three years from 1801 was nagged by Wedgwood to form the society until at last they took part in that first historic meeting in 1804. He was born in Old Meldrum, Aberdeenshire and trained as a gardener at the Chelsea Physic Garden. In 1779, he was appointed as the chief superintendent of the Royal gardens at Kensington and St. James and in 1791, he claimed to have found a cure for diseased fruit trees and received a grant of £1,500 from the Pitt government to fund this. The government gave him the grant in the hope that it could cure the oak trees of diseases because they desperately needed all the oak they could get to build the new ships of the Royal Navy being determined to out fight the French who the country was at war with. Forsyth's cure consisted of cow manure, urine, wood ash, bone ash and lime, all of which he mixed up as a paste and treated the infected areas of the trees and it has to be said that the treatment seemed to work. He also had a group of plants named after him which were known as 'Forsythia'.

William Townshend Aiton (1766-1849), like Forsyth, was a Scottish botanist but was nearly thirty years Forsyth's junior. Aiton's father was also a botanist and also called William Aiton. Aiton Senior brought out a book entitled

'Hortus Kewensis' and during the period 1810 to 1813, the younger William Aiton brought out a second and larger edition which was a catalogue of all the plants at Kew Gardens. He followed his father as Superintendent of Kew Gardens which at that time was the private domain of King George III. This was an important post as some of the plants there were quite rare – Joseph Banks himself had a reputation for keeping rare species there. However, some of the plants started appearing in other local nurseries and Aiton accused another botanist by the name of Robert Sweet of theft and the case went right up to the Old Bailey where Sweet was accused of receiving stolen goods. Sweet was acquitted and after that, Aiton's reputation became tarnished as it was felt that he accused Sweet out of jealousy as Kew Gardens had been losing its reputation as the best nursery possibly because of Aiton's neglect in later years. This was a pity as Aiton was a talented botanist and was commissioned by King George IV to lay out the gardens at Buckingham Palace and the Pavilion at Brighton.

James Dickson (1738-1822) like other botanists, was a member of the Linnean Society which was formed and named in honour of Carl Linneaus (1707-78) the Swedish naturalist and physician. Dickson was a bit of a loner but in 1781, started to study mosses and in 1785 went to Scotland and between then and 1791, made several visits there and collected many different types of plants and fungi. In 1785, he published the first of four parts of *Fascicularis plantarum cryptogamicarum Brittanniae* (1785-1801). Dickson was unschooled in Latin and John Ziers, who was a Polish apothecary resident in London wrote the descriptions for Dickson in the first three parts but he died in 1793 and the fourth part was completed with the help of Robert Brown (1773-1858), a young Scottish botanist. This was the same Robert Brown who had had his work plagiarised by Richard Salisbury. Joseph Banks was aware of both Dickson's and Brown's abilities and it was due to Banks's influence that enabled Dickson to be appointed head gardener at the British Museum. Brown himself went with Matthew Flinders on the latter's coastal survey of Australia between the years 1801 and 1805 where he brought back nearly 4,000 species of plants for classification. In 1810, he was put in charge of Sir Joseph's library and in 1827, he became botanical keeper at the British Museum after Banks's collections were transferred there.

This then, is a brief description of the men who in 1804 formed the Horticultural Society of London which since 1861 has been known as the Royal Horticultural Society when it was granted a Royal Charter by Prince Albert, Queen Victoria's Consort.

Joseph Banks suffered from gout for the last forty years of his life. A horribly painful complaint, it affects the joints, heart, arteries, liver, and kidneys. Although suffering greatly and now in his late seventies in an age where most men were expected to live but half that time, Banks continued to chair meetings of the Royal Society even though he had virtually lost the use of his legs since 1805 and had to be carried to most meetings. He chaired them as normal in January and February 1820, and again on 20th March, although this was to be his last time. He tended his resignation, but the Council asked him to carry on which he did until dying on 19th June, 1820 aged 77 years.

Banks had a remarkable life. Given his privileged start, his life long love of botany which started at an early age almost certainly saved him from wasting his life in wealthy, useless idleness. His life was anything but. He travelled the world with James Cook, collected thousands of plants and reptile specimens, had plants and Pacific Islands named after him, he set up the breadfruit trip that involved William Bligh and the second trip that included the soon to be famous Matthew Flinders, was George the Third's advisor at Kew Gardens, organised Flinders trip where he mapped the whole of Australia in the *Investigator* between 1801 and 1803, was President of The Royal Society for 41 years and is looked upon by many as the father of modern day Australia, although that is open to question as he has to share that particular soubriquet. Banks not only suggested Botany Bay as the place to send convicts, remembering it from his time there with Cook in 1769-70, but was a friend and advisor to the first Governors there – Phillip 1788-92, Hunter 1795-1800, King 1800-1805, Bligh, 1806-1810, and one of the most famous of them all, Governor Macquarrie, 1810-1821. It is with the latter, along with Arthur Phillip, that Banks has to share the title of father of modern day Australia. Banks was always loyal to people he liked and admired, and when in 1805 he was approached by Lord Camden, the Secretary of State for War and the Colonies, to discuss the position of successor to Philip Gidley King as Governor-General, he had no hesitation in nominating his old friend William Bligh, who Banks had recommended for the ill-fated *Bounty* breadfruit trip back in 1787. Bligh subsequently accepted the job and became the fourth Governor-General of the colony from 1806 to 1810.

The years that Sir Joseph was involved with the Royal Society brought him friends who were considered brilliant in their field. People such as Lord Nelson (the brilliant naval officer who beat the French at Trafalgar), Benjamin Franklin (American Statesman and Scientist), Sir William Hamilton (Scottish diplomat and husband of the famous Lady Hamilton), Matthew Boulton (English engineer), William Pitt the Younger (apart from Robert Walpole, the longest serving Prime Minister ever), Dr. John Hunter (Scottish physiologist and surgeon), Edward Jenner (English physician who discovered the cure for smallpox), William Grenville (politician and cousin and colleague of William Pitt), John Montague, the 4th Earl of Sandwich (First Lord of the Admiralty from 1771 to 1782), and Sir Humphrey Davy (English chemist).

Even though Banks was unwell for a large part of the latter stages of his life, he still remained socially active until the very end. Apart from being the President of the Royal Society for forty-one years, he was also a trustee of the British Museum, was involved with the Royal Philosopher's Club with whom he dined on many occasions, and was an active member of the Society of Antiquaries in London. Banks was also a member of the Society of Dilettanti, a society formed to sponsor the study of ancient Greek and the creation of new work in that style and in 1773, had been elected as a foreign member of the Royal Swedish Academy of Sciences. He was also made an honorary founding member of the Wernerian Natural History Society of Edinburgh in 1808 and was one of the prime movers in the formation of the African Association which was formed in 1788 and which was dedicated to the exploration of West Africa. This list barely scratches the surface of the people and associations that Sir Joseph

Banks knew and was involved with and does not begin to do justice to their individual achievements but it does give some idea as to the influence that he wielded. Because of his earlier travel with Captain Cook, his name is also dotted around places in the Pacific – the Banks Peninsula on South Island, New Zealand, the Banks Islands in Vanuatu, and there is also a Banks Island in the North West Territories in Canada. He is also remembered in Australia where the suburb of Banks in Canberra is named after him, as is the Sydney suburb of Banks. His picture was also on Australian currency where it was found on an earlier 5$ note. He is also remembered in Lincoln, England where he inherited the family home of Revesby Abbey. Adjacent to Lincoln Castle is the Joseph Banks Conservatory and along with the castle, this attracts a great many tourists. It contains a tropical hot house which has plants such as those brought back from his voyages, and there are also samples of vegetation from around the world, some of them being from Australia. Visitors to Lincoln Cathedral can also see a window dedicated to Banks.

Joseph Banks ended his life a different man from the wilful twenty-eight year old who stamped his feet whilst throwing a tantrum at not getting his way concerning the type of ship that he wanted for Cook's second great voyage. By the end of his life which was full of achievements, he had nothing to prove, and so despite this, or perhaps because of it, Banks had become a modest man. In his will, he asked to be buried "In the most private manner in the Church or Church yard of the Parish in which I shall happen to die. I entreat my dear relatives to spare themselves the affliction of attending the ceremony and I earnestly request that they will not erect any Monument to my Memory."

His wishes were carried out. He was buried in Heston, where he died, and no gravestone was erected. There wasn't even anything saying where he lay, although in 1867, the then vicar had a tablet made stating that he was buried there. The most ordinary burial for the most extraordinary man.

-oOOo-

3

Admiral Arthur Phillip
(1738-1814)

First Governor-General of New South Wales, setting up the first colony there in 1788.

On 11th October, 1786, Captain Arthur Phillip RN, a serving naval officer, semi-retired on half pay celebrated his 48th birthday but there wasn't a great deal he had to be that happy about. His naval career had been stuttering in recent years since the war with America had finished and he was hardly expecting the call from the British government that he would receive the following day and which would change his life forever. Much more than that, it would lead to the changing of a huge barren wasteland the other side of the world into the massive country now known as Australia, and Captain Arthur Phillip would have the distinction of being the first Governor-General of New South Wales as it was called in 1788 when he and his fleet first landed there.

Phillip was born on 11th October, 1738 to Jakob Phillip, a language teacher of German birth, and his English wife, Elizabeth Breach. It was Elizabeth's second marriage: her first being to Captain Herbert of the Royal Navy and it was almost certainly due to his mother's connection with the navy that would have caused Arthur to be interested in it. On 24th June, 1751 at the age of twelve, he was enrolled in the Greenwich school for the sons of seamen which was the beginning of an apprenticeship in the merchant service, and in 1755, after two years at sea under Captain Redhead of the *Fortune,* this apprenticeship was completed. He transferred to the Royal Navy soon after, and when the seven years war started, Phillip was involved in the Battle of Minorca in 1756. This battle was fought on 20th May between the British and French fleets and was the first sea battle of the seven years war that lasted from 1756 to 1763. The British fleet were commanded by Admiral Sir John Byng (1704-57), and although the French withdrew from the action first, the British withdrew to Gibralter and by so doing, virtually handed Minorca to the French on a plate. Although Byng was cleared of cowardice, he was arrested and charged with breaching the Articles of War by not pursuing the French fleet and was tried, found guilty and executed on 14th March, 1757 aboard *HMS Monarch* in Portsmouth harbour. Given the fact that he was found not guilty of cowardice, many people thought that Byng's execution was disgraceful and desperately harsh. He clearly made his judgement to withdraw because he felt that his fleet was ill equipped and he wanted his men and ships kept safe to fight another day. If the Admiralty thought that it was an error of judgement, it would seem that a severe reprimand would have been more fitting although having said that, it is difficult to see either Admiral Sir

John Jervis (Earl St. Vincent) or Lord Nelson playing it safe in the way that Byng had done.

On 7th July, 1761, Phillip was provisionally promoted to Lieutenant on the *Sterling Castle* and this was made official a year later when he was involved in another battle that resulted in the capture of Havana. Peace came on 25th April, 1763, and Phillip found himself like many other naval officers, retired on half pay, always a frustrating as well as a financially difficult time for young officers wanting to progress in the service.

He had to do something with his time, so he turned his hand to farming by purchasing two properties, Vernals Farm and Grasshayes, both of these being at Lyndhurst in Hampshire. He also married Margaret Denison on 19th July, 1763. Margaret was the widow of John Denison, a wealthy London Merchant, but sadly, the marriage between her and Phillip was not happy and the two separated six years later in 1769. It was very unusual for people not to stay together in those days, so that life between them must have been very difficult. Phillip was restless with farming and missed the action that naval warfare could provide, so after receiving permission from the British Admiralty, he joined the Portuguese Navy during the time that the country was at war with Spain. He served with distinction between 1774 and 1778 for Portugal as a Captain in their navy, but returned to the British Navy in 1778. He was made Captain of the *Ariadne* in November 1781 and in December 1782, transferred to the 64-gun *Europe* along with a trusted fellow officer, a Lieutenant Philip Gidley King. The *Europe* was sent to India but saw no action and on 25th May, 1784, he was again retired on half pay after the peace treaties with the American colonies were signed. When on 12th October, 1786, the day after his 48th birthday, he was asked to be the first Governor-General of New South Wales, he had spent a year in southern France and was carrying out surveying work for the Admiralty.

There was a real problem in England as to what to do with people who broke the law as the prisons were full and since the American War of Independence had been fought between 1775 and 1783 and had been lost, the Americas had ceased to be an option for the British Government to send criminals to. As a result, the prisons were bursting at the seams, were cold and damp and there was no sanitation. The general public had no idea just how bad they were. There was no attempt at segregation and women and men were thrown in together. As well as no allowance for the differences in gender, there was also no allowance made for age or the gravity of the crime. Both adults who had offended for the first time and even young boys could be put in a cell with hardened criminals and would often suffer homosexual rape. Disease was rife and typhus was common and unlikely to be treated. The problem was so acute that a large proportion of prisoners were transferred to hulks that were moored in the Thames and in other ports. These were old sloop transports and men-of-war with their masts and all rigging removed and full of prisoners waiting to be transported, wherever and whenever that would be. Disease was just as prevalent in the hulks as it was in the prisons and became worse as the number of prisoners kept on increasing. John Howard (1726-1790) the son of a wealthy upholsterer, was a man who worked tirelessly for prison reform. This was as a result of him being High Sheriff of Bedfordshire in 1773 and subsequently, he became appalled at the conditions in Bedford Gaol. He travelled great distances round the country and produced his massive report *The State of the Prisons in England and Wales (1777)*. The idea that prisons could reform people was light years away and in the 18th century they were merely there to keep criminals off the street, but the inevitable result was that to survive in prison, an inmate had to be hard, and thus if they were ever released, they would remain hard – they would certainly be harder than when they went in. Howard's report was years ahead of its time. He recommended that two prisons be built in London, that the sexes be segregated, work should be carried out by inmates, and that people should be put in to single cells rather than wards. Despite all his work travelling, inspecting gaols, and preparing his report, the work recommended was never started. This was probably because the then British government led by Lord North (1732-92) who was Prime Minister between the years 1770 and 1782, thought that the American War of Independence (1775-83) would be won and prisoners would continue to be transported there and the problem would be solved. However, Britain lost the war and the problem of where to send felons loomed again.

In 1782, Lord North was no longer in office and after three short-lived Prime Ministers, the Marquess of Rockingham, the Earl of Shelburne, and the Duke of Portland who held office between March 1782 and December 1783, William Pitt the Younger (1759-1806) became Prime Minister. His friend, William Wilberforce (1759-1833), who spent so many years campaigning against slavery, pressed his friend William Pitt to build new prisons, but despite Pitt being a humane man, still nothing was done. However, Pitt did write to Wilberforce in 1788 saying that "penitentiaries shall not be forgotten", but it seemed that the government, whoever it was led by, preferred the simplistic view that people should be transported.

Virtually all historians have given the credit to Sir Joseph Banks (1743-1820) as being the first person to suggest New South Wales as an alternative home for people suffering in Britain's overcrowded jails but this may not have been the case. Another person who may have made the suggestion could have been James Mario Matra (c1745-1806), who had held minor posts in London but at the time of his putting the suggestion forward, held no official position. He had held diplomatic positions in Tenerife and Constantinople but it is almost certain that he suggested New South Wales in the hope that it would end up with him landing a job with the British government. The government took him seriously as he had been to Botany Bay in 1770 because he had served as a Midshipman during Captain Cook's first trip round the world on the *Endeavour* between 1768 and 1771. If it had simply been Matra's suggestion, then the idea may have not been acted upon, but it was at this time that Joseph Banks (1743-1820) came in to the picture. As a young botanist, he too had been on Captain Cook's first trip on the *Endeavour* and had also landed in Botany Bay with Matra in 1770. In fact, so highly was Banks thought of that Cook named Botany Bay in honour of Banks and his assistant, Daniel Solander (1733-82), who, like Banks, was also a talented botanist. Cook recorded in his log of 6th May, 1770:-

"The great quantity of New Plants Mr. Banks & Dr. Solander collected in this place occasioned my giveing it the name of Botany Bay." In the same entry,

Cook goes on to say:- "… and at Noon we were by observation… 2 or 3 Miles from the land and abreast of a Bay or Harbour wherein there appeared to be safe anchorage which I call'd Port Jackson. It lies 3 Leagues to the northward of Botany Bay."

Cook could not have known that many years later, the names of Botany Bay and Port Jackson would become so important in the future of Australia. The naming of Botany Bay was certainly a compliment to both botanists, Banks and Solander. Solander in fact had studied natural history at Uppsala University under the great Carl von Linneaeus (1707-78), and as a man ten years the senior of Banks, had not only been a knowledgeable assistant for Banks to have with him, but was also a steadying influence for the young Joseph. Nearly a decade later, in 1779, the same year that Cook was killed in Hawaii during his third voyage, a House of Commons Committee chaired by Lord Beauchamp was set up to determine where England could send its criminals to now that the Americas were no longer an option.

Joseph Banks, now 36 years old, was asked what his views on Botany Bay were as a possible place to send prisoners. It had been nine years since Banks had seen Botany Bay and even then Cook had only stayed there briefly. Banks was by nature an outgoing and optimistic man and a combination of that optimism plus the classic saying that 'Distance lends enchantment', meant that Banks painted a picture of the area which was far more attractive than the reality. He said that the climate was good and the local people were timid and that any settlement would therefore be trouble free. He also described the land as being fertile enough to allow any colony to be self sufficient within a year.

The Beauchamp Committee listened carefully to what Banks had said, and whilst they were pleased with his description of the place, did not make a decision there and then. There were other places to consider, two of these being Gibralter and the other the west coast of Africa. Australia, whilst sounding good had two major flaws; one was the huge expense that it would be to the British government bearing in mind the country was virtually bankrupt fighting the American war and the other was the distance that it was from England – it was literally the other end of the world. Any communications between the colony and England would take time and this was a major stumbling block. However, the government was eventually persuaded and Captain Arthur Phillip was chosen as the first Governor-General.

William Pitt the Younger (1759-1806) was Prime Minister when Phillip was appointed to his new post. Pitt had taken office in 1783 at the age of twenty four, and despite being laughed at for his youth, especially by his arch enemy, Charles James Fox (1749-1806) who said that he would last only a few weeks, was in fact in office for seventeen years until 1801, and then again from 1804 to 1806 when he died of illness and exhaustion. It was almost certainly Pitt who took the final decision on Phillip being made Governor-General because Lord Howe (1726-99), who Pitt had appointed First Lord of The Admiralty in 1783 when Pitt himself had taken office, was in fact against Phillip being given the job as Governor-General. Howe must have been overruled by Pitt as it is difficult to think that it was anyone other than the Prime Minister who could overrule the First Lord of the Admiralty. It is difficult to understand Lord Howe's objections because Phillip had had a good naval career and his background in farming would certainly prove vital if the new community was to survive and then flourish and in the end it was proven to be a good choice. The man who rubber stamped Phillip's appointment was Lord (Thomas Townshend) Sydney (1732-1800) who was Home Secretary at the time of Phillip's appointment. He too had been made Home Secretary in 1783, the year Pitt took office. Lord Sydney's instructions read as follows:-

"… We, reposing especial trust and confidence in your loyalty, courage and experience in military affairs, do, by these presents, constitute and appoint you to be Governor of our territory called New South Wales, extending from the northern cape or extremity of the coast called Cape York, in the latitude of 10 degrees 37' south, to the southern extremity of the said territory of New South Wales or South Cape, in the latitude 43 degrees 39' south, and all the country inland and westward as far as the one hundred and thirty fifth degree of longitude, reckoning from the meridian of Greenwich, including all the islands adjacent in the Pacific Ocean, within the latitude aforesaid of 10 degrees 37' south and 43 degrees 39' south , and of all towns, garrisons, castles, forts and all other fortifications or other military works, which now are or may be hereafter erected upon this said territory. You are therefore carefully and diligently to discharge the duty of Governor in and over our said territory by doing and performing all and all manner of things thereunto belonging, and we do hereby strictly charge and command all our officers and soldiers who shall be employed within our said territory, and all others whom it may concern, to obey you as our Governor thereof; and you are to observe and follow such orders and directions from time to time as you shall receive from us, or any other your superior officer according to the rules and discipline of war, and likewise such orders and directions as we shall send you under our signet or sign manual, or by our High Treasurer or Commissioners of our Treasury, for the time being, or one of our Principal Secretaries of State, in pursuance of the trust we hereby repose in you."

Given at our Court at St. James's, the twelfth day of October 1786, in the twenty sixth year of our reign.

By His Majesty's Command
SYDNEY

It is difficult to paint a generalised picture of the type of people that were sent to Australia as some of the crimes looked utterly trivial whilst some were far more serious. It is difficult to believe in this day and age just how savage the penalties were for some of the crimes committed. The eldest person on that first trip was a woman named Dorothy Handland who was eighty-two years old when the fleet was going to sail. She had been given a seven year sentence for committing perjury and whilst she survived the journey, once at Sydney, the poor woman could not face the prospect of living out her final days in such a place and hung herself. That was the first case of suicide that was recorded in Australia. The second eldest was Elizabeth Beckford who was aged seventy. She was transported to New South Wales because she stole twelve pounds of

Gloucester cheese. In those days there was no such thing as a safety net payment that we get today for people with no income and it is quite possible that this lady was poverty stricken and starving. However, that would have cut no ice with the judges at the time who in any case were bound by the laws on the statute book and she was transported for seven years. Given her age, this almost certainly meant that she was transported for life. The trip alone to the new penal colony must have been a nightmare for her always assuming that she survived it and was out of all proportion to her crime. Just as old people were not spared, neither were the people at the other end of the age spectrum. An eleven-year-old boy named James Grace stole ten yards of ribbon and a pair of silk stockings, and he too was transported for seven years. A lady called Elizabeth Powley was in her early twenties, had no money, no job and was starving. She broke into a kitchen and took some bacon, flour, and raisins along with some butter. For this, she was actually sentenced to hang but was reprieved but nonetheless she too was transported for seven years. The youngest recorded person was a little boy of nine who was a chimney sweep and who was called John Hudson. He had stolen some clothes and a pistol for which he also received seven years penal servitude.

It is impossible to go through them all but despite the cases of people such as Dorothy Handland and Elizabeth Beckford, by and large the people who were transported were fairly young as the Beauchamp Committee had recommended. This was requested by the committee because much of the work at the new settlement would be manual and therefore would only be able to be carried out by young settlers. However, although fitting the age criteria, the new settlers barely had the skills necessary to carry out the work that needed to be done satisfactorily. There would be the problem of growing crops in a land that they knew nothing of, and yet there was only one gardener and he was young and inexperienced. Many houses would have to be built but there were but two bricklayers, two brickmakers, and one mason. There were however six carpenters although for the amount of work that lay before them, this number was barely enough. None of this was the fault of Governor Phillip – he had no choice but to work with those he had with him. It took nearly two months of preparation before the fleet could leave to start their long voyage to Botany Bay, but eventually the ships sailed from Portsmouth on the 13th May 1787. Phillip had planned to sail the previous day but when he gave the order to weigh anchor, the order was seemingly ignored and no ship sailed. The reason for this was that some of the transports were manned by merchant seamen who claimed that they had not been paid for seven months. This turned out to be true as the crew had been on chartered vessels and their quarrel was not with Phillip and the Royal Navy, but the ship's owners. Eventually the matter was cleared up and the fleet set sail the following day at 3.00am. This first fleet consisted of eleven ships. These were two men-of-war, the *Sirius* and the *Supply*. Then there were six transports which were the *Alexander* which carried 210 male convicts, *Scarborough*, also 210 male convicts, *Charlotte*, 100 male and 24 female convicts, *Lady Penrhyn*, 102 women convicts, *Prince of Wales*, 100 women convicts, and the *Friendship*, 80 male and 24 women convicts. The final three were storeships, and were the *Fishbourn, Borrowdale*, and *Golden Grove*. The

Sirius was the flagship and was under the command of Commodore Arthur Phillip but as he was also in charge of the whole expedition, it was decided to appoint in effect, a second Captain of the *Sirius,* Captain John Hunter. Other prominent people on the voyage were David Collins who was there as he was appointed Judge-Advocate. The principal medical officer, Surgeon John White was on board the *Charlotte*, one of the transports, although there were other surgeons on board some of the other ships. On the *Golden Grove,* one of the storeships, was the Chaplain of the expedition, the Reverend Richard Johnson. Lieutenant Watkins Tench, who was to command two detachments of marines on the *Charlotte* is also worthy of mention as is Lieutenant William Dawes of the marines who built the first observatory at Dawes Point. Lieutenant King of the *Sirius* also deserves mention as an outstanding naval officer who went on to have a brilliant career which culminated in him being the third Governor-General of the colony between 1800 and 1805. However, one of the most important, but ultimately troublesome, was Major Robert Ross, who commanded the marines as well as being Lieutenant-Governor-Elect. He caused Governor Phillip problems from the beginning and in temperament and actions was everything that Phillips wasn't. Whereas Governor Phillip was kindly, amenable, and completely committed to the colony, Ross was argumentative, often in open conflict with his fellow officers, and worst of all, had no faith whatsoever in the project. It is difficult to understand exactly why he was there at all unless he was simply not given a choice and was ordered to be involved. David Collins, the Judge-Advocate, said that he held an "inexpressible hatred" for Ross. Adapting to life in this new barren land and making it work meant a willingness to be open minded and positive and Ross was never able or willing to try. Eventually he returned to England and resumed his military career there. Along with Governor Phillip, Major Ross, and all the sailors, soldiers and convicts, the number on the first voyage exceeded eleven hundred.

Lieutenant Watkins Tench wrote that the convicts were "humble, submissive and regular" on the first part of the trip. The truth is that they were scared and had every right to be. They were told in no uncertain terms that any escape attempt would be punishable by instant death and as well as that, for the most part, they were convinced that they would not see loved ones and families again. Whilst they had been anchored prior to setting sail, the ones who could read and write had sent letters home expressing these fears concerning the likelihood of never coming home but Tench was completely unsympathetic. He was charged with the task of vetting each letter and came to the conclusion that their letters were insincere and written in the way they were so as to gain sympathy which they were never going to get, not from Tench anyway. However, Tench's cynicism was extremely unfair as they almost certainly genuinely felt fear. They were setting off to a land the other side of the world which they knew nothing about, they had been taken from those that they loved and the prospect of the journey in front of them was daunting in itself.

The fear of the unknown was not limited to the convicts though. Ralph Clark, a young officer of the marines wrote in his diary:- "the *Sirius* made the signal for the whole fleet to get under way. O Gracious God send that we may put into Plymouth or Torbay on our way down channel that I may see my dear and fond affectionate Alicia and our sweet son before I leave them for this long absence". However, his hopes were dashed as the fleet did not put into Plymouth and the following day Clark wrote:- "Oh my God all my hoppes (sic) are over of seeing my beloved wife and son".

The voyage was going to be lengthy, and the amount of food needed was immense given how long it would take to reach Botany Bay as well as the huge number of people on board the ships. It was virtually impossible to keep food fresh on board for any length of time, but this problem was largely resolved by the fleet anchoring off Santa Cruz, the capital of Teneriffe, on 3rd June, 1787. The Marquis de Branceforte was the Governor of the Canary Islands, and treated Phillip and his officers with great respect. They stayed a week where the officers and crew could go ashore and stretch their legs, and due to the Governor's kindness, the members of the fleet were able to enjoy plenty of fresh water, fresh vegetables and meat as well as fresh fruit. In this port, as with others that they stayed at, the crew, marines and convicts were always given plenty of fresh food as it was very important for the crew to be well fed and rested as they needed to be in good health for the journey to be completed successfully. Once afloat, each marine was allowed a daily ration of a pound of bread, a pound of beef, and a pint of wine. The convicts were allowed three quarters of a pound of beef, and the same amount of bread but were not allowed any wine. Without the help of the Governor of the Canary Islands, the Marquis de Branceforte, whilst they were in port, the voyage to Botany Bay would not have been as successful as it turned out to be.

On the evening of 9th June, after resting for a week and re-stocking provisions, the fleet were about to leave for the next part of their journey when a convict named John Power who had been employed on the deck of the *Alexander,* cut the rope of a boat and escaped from the ship. He swam towards and clambered into a dinghy and the tide carried him towards a Dutch East Indiaman but they refused to take him on board. He then made his way to a small island and rested, his goal being to row to the Grand Canary. However, his escape had been noted and he was quickly recaptured the next morning by a search party and the fleet then weighed anchor and began the next leg of their journey. Such was the high security that the convicts were kept under that this was the only trouble the officers and crew had with the prisoners. Although it was only one prisoner who tried it, the officers felt it important to capture him in order to show the other prisoners that they would not tolerate escape bids. If they had allowed him to get away with it, there could have been many more who would have tried it, causing the journey to be delayed every time they stopped somewhere.

Their next port of call was Rio de Janeiro, which they reached and anchored in on 6th August, 1787. Rio de Janeiro translated into English means January River which was so called because it was discovered by Dias de Solis, the Spanish navigator and explorer in January, 1516 which was the feast of St. Januarius. However, it's not actually a river, although at the time of the discovery was thought to be, but an arm of the sea. Once again, the fleet was treated with kindness and a reception was given to Phillip and the officers by the Viceroy, Don Lewis de Varconcellos. Phillip was not unknown to the Viceroy as he, Phillip, had once been involved in a stand-off with the Viceroy when in command of the *Europe*. However, the Viceroy recognised that Phillip was a man of honour and merely acting in his country's best interest and the incident was forgotten. The Viceroy was very gracious and he gave orders that Governor Phillip be treated with the same honour as himself, an order that the modest Phillip tried without success to refuse. Governor Phillip and his officers were treated with great courtesy and were allowed to travel anywhere in the city and also into the country so long as it did not exceed five miles. This was freedom not given to other visitors by the Viceroy. Their stay lasted a full month, and once more they stocked up with fresh food and water, along with one hundred sacks of cassada which was a substitute for bread should that commodity become scarce. Cassada was the root of a shrub called Cassada and in its normal state is highly poisonous. However, when washed, pressed and then after evaporation had taken place, it lost its noxious qualities and became a perfectly adequate substitute for bread.

After being looked after so well for a whole month, the fleet weighed anchor on 4th September, 1787 to sail to the Cape of Good Hope, their last intended stop before sailing for Australia and their new home. When they left the harbour, the Viceroy had a twenty-one gun salute fired, the final compliment he could pay to the Governor and the rest of the fleet and this compliment was returned by the *Sirius* to acknowledge the great respect that the Viceroy and the Governor felt for each other. The fleet sailed on its way and reached the Cape on the 13th October. The Governor, Mynheer Van Graaffe was very well mannered and entertained Governor Phillip and his officers in the same way as the Viceroy had. Although food at the Cape was not so plentiful as it had been at Rio, the fleet were given all the food and water that could be spared, and the British fleet were also supplied with a great deal of live stock, five hundred animals in total before weighing anchor on 12th November for the last lap of their voyage.

On 25th November, Phillip transferred from the *Sirius* to the *Supply* because he thought that by so doing, he could reach Botany Bay before the rest of the fleet. Placing Captain Hunter in charge of the *Sirius* and the remainder of the fleet, Governor Phillip ordered three of the fastest sailing transport ships to accompany him. These were the *Alexander*, *Scarborough*, and the *Friendship* and were thought to have better sailors manning them. Captain Hunter, now in command of the *Sirius* was ordered to follow with the store-ships *Golden Grove*, *Fishburn*, and *Borrowdale* along with the remaining transports, the *Lady Penrhyn*, *Prince of Wales*, and the *Charlotte*.

The *Supply* with Governor Phillip was the first ship to reach Botany Bay on 18th January, 1788. The first task that Phillip undertook was to make himself known to the native people and this he did skilfully and with humanity. When he stepped ashore, the natives were all armed but on seeing the Governor unarmed and alone, quickly deduced that he wanted to be friendly and laid down their own arms. Governor Phillip had given his officers strict instructions that they were to treat the local people with kindness and they observed this instruction to the letter. The Governor and his officers then gave the people presents, all of which were accepted and for the few days that the ships remained at Botany Bay, there was no trouble at all.

After the *Supply* had arrived at Botany Bay, it was followed by the *Alexander*, *Scarborough,* and *Friendship* the following day whilst the *Sirius* with Captain John Hunter in command arrived the day after, on the 20th. After looking at Botany Bay it was soon decided by Phillip that this was an unsuitable place to settle the new colony. The anchorage was inadequate and no reliable water source was apparent. Captain Cook's 1770 report of Botany Bay gave a far more favourable impression of the place than Governor Phillip found it to be, but this was not surprising, as Cook and Phillip's needs were quite different. Whilst Phillip wanted to create a long term settlement with large numbers of people, Cook merely used it as a short term solution to get the men of the one vessel, the *Endeavour* rested, fed and sheltered. After a few days, Governor Phillip decided that they should look at Port Jackson which Captain Cook had mentioned and which was to the north of Botany Bay. On 26th January 1788, the marines and convicts were landed at Sydney Cove, named after the Home Secretary who had signed the original instructions for the new Governor-General. Since that historic landing, Australia has celebrated that date as Australia Day. Lieutenant Tench, commentating on the voyage, wrote the following words:- "After a passage of exactly thirty-six weeks from Portsmouth we happily effected our arduous undertaking with such a train of unexpected blessings as hardly ever intended a fleet in like predicament". The fleet had indeed had good fortune, but whether the convicts, whose travelling conditions were not comparable to those of the officers and marines, were quite so pleased, was another matter.

Once they had landed on 26th January, temporary accommodation was quickly fixed for everyone. Governor Phillip had his own building which was built from materials brought over from England, whilst everybody else lived in tents, some of which were used as hospital accommodation. In the evening of that first day, the British flag was raised and the Governor, along with his officers, drank the King's health and also to the future of the new settlement.

It did not take long for the temporary accommodation to be set up which was just as well as almost as soon as they had settled there, illness broke out in the worst possible way. The accommodation was soon needed as there was a huge outbreak of scurvy, which along with a severe form of dysentery, meant that there were many fatalities early on. This was particularly unfortunate as the health of most people during the long voyage over had been remarkably good given the conditions that people had to put up with. Surgeon White had written:- "... To see all the ships safe in their destined port... and all the people in as good health as could be expected or hoped for, after so long a voyage, was a sight truly pleasing and at which every heart must rejoice". How Surgeon White could write this is a mystery because the conditions the settlers had to put up with during the voyage were indescribably bad and in fact forty-eight people had died although by the standards of the day the figure was small. Not surprisingly the majority were convicts numbering forty in all, whilst five of the convict's children died along with one marine, a marine's wife and a marine's child. It is more of a surprise that the health of the people was good during the voyage, but less than surprising that it broke down on reaching their destination. The bilges had been disgusting in all the ships and the smell reeked of urine, faeces, sick that had not been cleared up and there had also been lice, cockroaches, fleas, and rats crawling around. It was all quite dreadful and the lack of fresh food when they landed at Sydney would have meant that the whole experience would probably have vastly reduced each person's immune system. This outbreak of illness so early on made life difficult at a time when every able bodied man was needed. Instead, the sick and those that looked after them were completely unable to carry out any work. The outbreak of scurvy must have been deeply frustrating as well as frightening as the symptoms were so appalling that if not treated quickly made death seem a merciful release. The Scottish surgeon, James Lind (1716-94) had been working on possible cures for scurvy for many years and his publication *A Treatise of the Scurvy* (1753) was considered a classic in later years but tragically was more or less ignored at the time. On his first world voyage in the *Endeavour* from 1768 to 1771, Captain Cook had taken many of Lind's ideas and had virtually eliminated scurvy because he knew that the disease could be kept at bay by having plenty of fresh vegetables and lemon juice in the sailor's diet. Scurvy was an appalling disease which killed far more sailors than wars ever did and it was almost certainly kept at bay during the voyage of the fleet to New South Wales because of the three stops that the fleet had made at Teneriffe, Rio de Janeiro, and the Cape of Good Hope. However, once at Botany Bay, all they found there was barren land and it was there that the settlers' diet was vastly reduced in both quantity and quality making illness more likely. The Admiralty were incredibly slow in using the expertise of Cook and Lind and it wasn't until 1795, the year following Lind's death, that the inclusion of lemon juice was made compulsory in the navy's ships. However, that was seven years away and was no good to the settlers who were left to fend for themselves as best as they could.

Supplies from England were naturally scarce and the settlers had to attempt to cultivate the land in order to become self-sufficient. In the early years, this was to prove difficult as the land around Sydney did not lend itself to the growing of food and most of the convicts knew next to nothing about agriculture and made reluctant farm labourers. In the early years, this would lead to a situation whereby a great many of the settlers were near to starvation. It didn't help that by and large, the marines showed little discipline or much interest in supervising the convicts, so Governor Phillip had to appoint overseers from their ranks in order to get the majority of the convicts to work. By doing this, Phillip had already realised that he could not run New South Wales as one enormous prison camp and he started a civil administration complete with Courts of Law. Part of the reason for this was the appalling scene that happened when the women stepped ashore. They had arrived later than the men, on 6th February, 1788, and their disembarkation was a dreadful affair. The longboats spent the day bringing the women from their ship, the *Lady Penrhyn* but as soon as they had arrived on shore, drunken sailors and convicts combined to effect the most appalling mass rape of the women. The Governor, his officers and marines could do nothing about it as this dreadful scene was happening whilst a hurricane was taking place. Men, filthy by lying in the muddy bogs that the land turned into continued the dreadful scene throughout the night and the whole situation was completely out of anyone's control. Arthur Bowes Smythe, the surgeon on the women's ship, the *Lady Penrhyn* wrote at length about this dreadful incident, finishing off with the words:-

"... nor do I conceive it possible in their present situation to adopt any plan to induce them to behave like rational or even Human Beings".

However, that is exactly what Governor Phillip set out to do the following morning by setting up and establishing a system of running the community. The colony was having a terrible start what with the illness that had broken out and then the events of the night of the 6th February. The system of the Courts of Law was established the following day, the 7th February 1788 and the ceremony was conducted in a very solemn atmosphere. A large area of ground was cleared at Point Maskelyne which would eventually be renamed Point Dawes after Lieutenant William Dawes of the marines who as mentioned earlier, built the first observatory there and everybody, including the convicts were summoned to hear what had been decided. It was on that date that a formal proclamation was delivered which established a form of government in New South Wales as Australia was called then. The people who were to take leading roles in the running of the community stood next to Governor Phillip. The Judge-Advocate, Mr. D. Collins read out the Royal Commission. Phillip himself was to be the Captain-General and Governor-in-Chief over the territory which was called New South Wales which covered the area already mentioned in Lord Sydney's original instructions. Major Robert Ross, the troublesome officer who was in charge of the marines became Lieutenant-Governor of the colony and once these appointments had been read out, the Act of Parliament establishing the court of judicature was read, and finally, the patents under the great seal which enabled the appropriate persons to convene and adjudicate at these courts was read by Judge Advocate Collins. Once these formalities had been completed, Governor Phillip addressed everybody present, firstly thanking the soldiers for discharging their duties in the manner in which they had and also their general conduct. Phillip then turned to the convicts and tore into them, reminding them that they were there in the first place as punishment for their activities in England. He then said that any repetition of the dreadful behaviour carried out the previous night whilst they were serving that punishment would end up with the guilty party being shot. This would also occur if any man was seen trying to enter the women's tent.

However, he then went on to say that although they were there as punishment, the building of the new settlement would give them an opportunity to start afresh and become decent members of the community that they were creating. He reminded them that they were small in number and more than likely to be caught should they carry out any unlawful acts, and expressed the view that little leniency would be offered them if they did cause trouble. Having said that, the opportunities to build a good life for themselves were there should they wish to take this second chance and he finished by declaring his aim to oversee a community that was happy under his charge.

Whilst his speech was generally well received, to his regret, Phillip had to convene a criminal court only three weeks later at the tail end of February, 1788. Some of the convicts had stolen food from their fellow settlers on a regular basis and the Governor knew that he had to be firm if he was to maintain order. Six of the criminals were sentenced to death, and one of them who happened to be the leader was executed on the same day. Having made his point, Phillip pardoned one of them and reprieved the remaining four punishing them more lightly.

The other problem that Phillip had to contend with were the local people, the Aborigines. They had been friendly towards the Governor when he first landed at Botany Bay but the language difficulty meant that there was always a chance of trouble flaring up due to misunderstandings. They were completely different from anyone most of the settlers had seen before. Men and women were totally naked, and as Joseph Banks noted in 1770 on Cook's first trip to Botany Bay, "were painted with white lines and red patches with bones across their noses". Their skin was also totally black for genetic and climatic reasons. Phillip's orders were that everybody was to treat the local people with all due kindness. This was all very well as far as it went, but the Admiralty had no thought for the land which the local people had occupied unhindered for thousands of years. The Admiralty assumed that the land belonged to everybody and so there were bound to be tensions in the long run when the settlers with their so called superior way of life, not to mention armoury, were to suddenly take large areas of the local people's land. In the short term however, although there was the inevitable language barrier and subsequent lack of communication, there wasn't a great deal of animosity between the two peoples. Indeed, the natives did not seem to be that interested in the Europeans or even surprised that they were there, and so long as the settlers did not trouble the Aborigines, they did not get trouble back. However, the peace was spoiled when the almost inevitable happened. The natives had always been trusting towards each other, and thought nothing of leaving their spears scattered under rocks on the beach. These spears were their main way of obtaining food, and when the crew of one of the transport ships stole some of their property, the trust that had developed between the indigenous people and the settlers broke down. The natives reacted by taking a shovel, spade, and a pickaxe from the crew of the *Sirius* and as a result, one of the natives was shot by one of the settlers and wounded with small-shot in the leg. By and large, the convicts treated the natives very badly and continued to steal spears from them and sell them on to the people of various ships. Judge Advocate Collins recorded many conflicts between the aborigines and the settlers, and had no hesitation in putting the blame fairly and squarely on the shoulders of the convicts. One incident which was not untypical happened when the bodies of two convicts were found "who had been employed for some time cutting rushes, pierced through in many places and the head beaten to a jelly". Although suspecting the conduct of the settlers, Governor Phillip felt that he could not ignore such actions by the local people and was anxious to discover who had committed these killings. He organised a search, and although he found some three hundred natives close to the beach, could not find who the killers were, although friendly dialogue, such as it was, took place between him and the natives. There were many incidents where the natives attacked the settlers, although not always ending up with loss of life. Sometimes, it merely consisted of the local people throwing a few spears with no-one getting hurt, but this still angered Governor Phillip. After one such incident, Phillip took an armed party to the spot where the natives had thrown the spears, and on hearing some natives in the bushes, fired upon them. Phillip was not an unkind man, but this type of action must have been the commencement of the native Australian feeling that he was being forced from his homeland, the homeland that he had happily lived in and occupied for thousands of years. There was a certain irony in this so far as Governor Phillip was concerned however, because his wish was not for the local people to feel that they were being forced out of their land, but that some of them would actually come and live with the new settlers. However, the Governor was being very optimistic if he thought that the Aborigines would willingly abandon their way of life and live with these people who had come to settle on their land, and because so few of them came anywhere near the settlers, Phillip took one by force. The thinking behind this was either to learn their language, or to get one of the local people to learn English. To this end he managed to capture a man called Arabanoo although as Phillip couldn't get the man's name from him, he called him Manly taken from Manly Cove, where he was captured.

Arabanoo didn't seem to mind his capture too much and dined with Phillip and the officers on 1st January, 1789. According to Lieutenant Tench, Manley dined heartily on fish and roasted pork and when he had finished eating, his anxieties seem to disappear and he stretched himself out and "putting his hat under his head, he fell asleep." Arabanoo lived with his captors quite happily and was thought of as a kind person by the officers. Sometimes the children of the settlers would gather round him and he would always be affectionate to them, cuddling them, and if he was eating, he would always offer them some of his best food. He adapted to his new diet soon after his capture. At first, he would not eat bread and the only drink that he took was water. Gradually, his taste in food began to broaden and writing in February 1789, Lieutenant Tench noted "Bread he began to relish; and tea he drank with avidity; strong liquors he never would taste, turning from them with disgust and abhorrence."

Governor Phillip treated Arabanoo with kindness, and felt that he was doing him a favour by teaching him some of the European ways such as drinking tea. The more used to the different ways he was learning, the more attached to Governor Phillip and his officers he became, and so it was with some shock that Phillip discovered that Arabanoo had caught smallpox. Quite how he caught it was a mystery, as none of the settlers had contracted it but in the event, his immune system couldn't cope and he died. Sadly, the world wasn't far away from finding a cure for this disease as Edward Jenner carried out the first vaccination in May 1796, but in 1789 and on the other side of the world, it might as well have been light years away. Phillip decided to capture two more aborigines, and this he did fairly quickly. They were called Baneelon and Colbee and although Colbee escaped fairly quickly, Baneelon remained and seemed to settle with the officers. Unlike Arabanoo, Baneelon quickly acquired a taste for alcohol and although he drank a fair amount, he was never seen to be drunk by his captors. He was clever and intelligent and impressed his captors by the speed in which he picked up the English language. His intelligence eventually enabled him to escape because at about 2 o'clock on the morning of the 3rd of May, 1790, he told the servant who was looking after him that he was unwell, and asked if he could go downstairs. The servant suspected nothing and once in the back yard, Baneelon nimbly jumped over the fence and ran off. He was not seen again until August of that year.

On this occasion, Surgeon White had met Baneelon by accident and Baneelon sent a piece of whale to the Governor as a mark of respect. Phillip was anxious to see Baneelon again, and along with Captain Collins and Lieutenant Waterhouse, went to see him at the place where the actual whale was lying. There were a number of natives there, and whilst the meeting was friendly, Phillips and his party, for some reason were unarmed. A native armed with a spear approached the Governor, who in an attempt to greet the man, approached him holding out his hand. The native, maybe thinking he was being threatened, set his spear ready to unleash it. Phillip, realising what could happen, called out to the man that he was wrong, and that he, Phillip, meant no harm, when the native unleashed his spear with such ferocity that it entered Phillip's right shoulder just above the collar bone and came out the other side. The man then made a dash into the woods and made his escape. Phillip was carried into a boat but he and his party had to travel six miles before they got back to Sydney, and it was a full two hours before Phillip could receive surgery to remove the spearhead which luckily was carried out successfully.

Although this was a very serious incident that could have ended in disaster, it actually helped Governor Phillip have more contact with the local people, because realising that the Governor was taking no retaliatory action, became very co-operative. Baneelon was used as a go-between and was ideal to play this role as by now he knew enough English to be able to communicate the wishes of each party to the other. Added to this was the fact that he was well disposed towards the white settlers, Governor Phillip in particular.

Phillip made a quite remarkable recovery and in the space of ten days, was fit enough to meet a number of the natives. Baneelon told Phillip that the name of the man who had attacked him was Willemering and that Colbee had severely chastised him for what he had done. Baneelon also explained that Willemering felt that he was acting in self defence as he had been afraid of the Governor and with this explanation Phillip considered the matter closed. The other natives were quite possibly sorry for what had happened, because after the incident, a closer rapport was developed between the settlers and the natives, along with a better understanding of each other's ways.

During their dealings with him, Phillip and his officers had only seen the good side of Baneelon, but unfortunately, they were soon to see another side of his character completely and one which put Baneelon in quite a different light. One day, Baneelon went to Government House to see Phillip to tell him that he was going to kill a woman but did not want the Governor to witness it. He was very angry and agitated and so Phillip removed the hatchet that Baneelon was carrying allowing him only a walking stick instead. They walked to the woman's house and Baneelon grabbed a sword and started attacking her with a ferocity that Phillip didn't think he was capable of. The woman was in fact a girl of about sixteen, and despite the fact that she was surrounded by other aborigines, they did nothing to help her and she was severely wounded. Luckily, Phillip had brought Mr. Collins and his orderly sergeant with him because the aborigines seemed to side with Baneelon and drew their spears. At this, Phillip quickly mustered a contingent of marines and stopped the attack before it could prove fatal. All the while this was going on, the woman's husband was present but made no move to help her. So badly wounded was she in fact, that Governor Phillip made the decision to remove her from the scene so that she could receive treatment at the hospital. It seems that Baneelon had been an enemy of the girl's father and the woman had sided with her father during a fight rather than with Baneelon. There is no doubt that Baneelon would have killed the girl if he had not been stopped by Phillip and the marines. It was a side to the aborigine that Phillip had not seen before and had no wish to see again, but it was but one incident that showed the many differences in culture and thinking between the native Australians and the new settlers. There would be many more over the years. However, Baneelon and Governor Phillip went on to form a friendship that lasted right up to when Phillip left the colony in December, 1792 and beyond, but it was a friendship that was to prove a disaster for Baneelon. Because Baneelon was highly intelligent and picked up the essentials of the English language so quickly, it was decided that he would go to England with Governor Phillip which he willingly did. At first he was feted as an exotic 'Noble Savage' and was treated well in England, but he had curiosity value only. English people had never seen a native Australian and Baneelon was feted wherever he was taken. However, his conversation was naturally limited and the novelty wore off so far as the so-called London elite were concerned and people lost interest in him. He was returned to his native country in 1795 when John Hunter sailed there to take up his position as the second Governor-General of New South Wales, a position he held until 1800. However, by the time he returned, Baneelon was neither an Englishman nor was he any longer a native of Australia and he simply did not fit in with his original country. He died in 1813 at the age of about 40 having become dependent on large quantities of rum and was in effect, a lonely alcoholic who didn't fit in to either country. It was a sad end to the life of an intelligent man and it should never have been allowed to happen as exactly the same thing had happened years before on Captain Cook's second voyage between 1772 and 1775. Cook's ship, the *Resolution* had become separated from her escort ship, Lieutenant Furneaux's the *Adventure* and so in 1774 Furneaux had sailed home early and taken a Tahitian man called Omaii who when in England was seen as the South Sea Island Noble Savage in exactly the same way as Baneelon was later to be viewed as. Just as with Baneelon, the novelty with Omaii had worn off and when he was returned to his native land in 1776 during Cook's third trip, Omaii simply did not fit in with the Tahitian people, and he too ended his life sad and alone, fitting in with neither culture. The experience that the navy had had with Omaii had happened fifteen years or more before they took Baneelon and the British should have learned the lesson from what had happened to Omaii.

Having touched on the relationship between the new settlers and the local people, we must return to when the settlers first arrived at New South Wales. On 15th February, 1788, after they were settled at Port Jackson, Phillip sent Lieutenant Philip Gidley King to Norfolk Island to establish a colony there. King was only thirty years old, but the Governor felt that he was by far and away the most able officer that he had with him, and indeed he ended up being the third Governor-General of the colony, serving between 1800 and 1805. However, that was over a decade away and at this time he was a relatively young lieutenant. There were no inhabitants on Norfolk Island, so King embarked with a small retinue which consisted of one subaltern officer, a midshipman, six marines, a surgeon, two men who understood farming methods, and fifteen convicts, nine of which were men and six women. There were two reasons for the setting up of this second colony. Firstly, Phillip didn't want to lose the island to the French which was a possibility at the time, as Jean-Francois de Laperouse (1741-c1788), the famous French naval officer and explorer had already been to Norfolk Island with his two ships, La Boussolle and L' Astrolabe during his famous expedition round the world. The voyage had commenced on 1st August, 1785 and had taken him to Chile, Hawaii, Alaska, California, East Asia, Japan, Russia, and the South Pacific. He went on to Australia where he arrived at Botany Bay on 26th January, 1788 which was at the same time as Governor Arthur Phillip was moving his fleet to Sydney Cove. Although Phillip and Laperouse did not actually meet, there was a great deal of assistance between the French and the British through the officers. Laperouse sailed off to carry out further explorations on 10th March, 1788 saying that he expected to return to France in May or June, 1789, but was in fact never heard of again. It is believed that he was shipwrecked on the Santa Cruz group of islands. Whilst he was still at anchor at Botany Bay, some of the English convicts escaped and made their way to the French fleet where they begged to be taken on board but the French officers refused to agree to this. The result was that the prisoners were sent back to Phillip where they were severely flogged, and although almost certainly devastated at the time, they probably felt in the long run that they had had a lucky escape. Another person who had a lucky escape was a sixteen-year-old Corsican named Napoleon Bonaparte who wanted to go on the expedition but was refused permission. His life was saved but thousands of other lives would be lost in years to come as the decision to refuse him altered European history.

The second reason that Governor Phillip wanted Lieutenant King to sail to Norfolk Island was that he needed to establish an alternative source of food for the main colony. Norfolk Island had been discovered and named by Captain Cook in 1774 and he had particularly liked the plant life there. The island was small, being approximately twenty miles in circumference and one of the advantages it had was the lack of extremes in terms of temperature. It was never excessively hot or cold due to the fact that there were continual winds coming in from the sea which stopped overheating in the summer and it was generally mild throughout the winter which meant that the vegetation grew with no seasonal interruption. Phillip had also noted that Cook had said that the soil was fertile which certainly was not the case for the main colony. Although the island was small, the appointment of Lieutenant King as Superintendent of the new community was an important one and he received lengthy and elaborate instructions from Phillip as to how it was to be managed. One of the passages taken from the original states the following:-

"You are, therefore, to proceed in his Majesty's armed tender *Supply*, whose commander has my orders to receive you, with the men and women, stores and provisions necessary for farming the intended settlement; and on your landing at Norfolk Island you are to take upon you the execution of the trust reposed in you, causing my commission appointing you Superintendent over the settlement to be publicly read". Near the end of Phillip's instructions were the words:- "You are to cause the Prayers of the Church of England to be read with all due solemnity every Sunday, and you are to enforce a due observance of religion and good order, transmitting to me, as often as opportunity offers, a full account of your particular situation and transactions". Thus did the first colony of Norfolk Island come into being in February, 1788.

The new settlement in Norfolk Island was in good hands. Philip Gidley King had been born in Cornwall on the 23rd April, 1758. He had had a good academic education and joined the navy in 1770 at the age of twelve, sailing in the *Swallow* to the East Indies where he was rated a midshipman. As well as a good academic education he also had a good naval career and met Governor Phillip in January, 1783 when the latter was Captain Phillip in the *Europe* and King was Lieutenant. They each formed a good opinion of the other and on the 25th October, 1786, King was appointed Lieutenant of the *Sirius* at the same time that the British Government was offering Phillip the post of Governor-General of the new colony.

Governor Phillip received favourable reports about the life of the settlers at Norfolk Island, and he decided to send the *Supply* back with twenty-four convicts, the idea being to unload them there and fetch supplies back for the main colony. The ship called on Lord Howe Island which had been named after the First Lord of the Admiralty when it was discovered on 17th February, 1788 by Lieutenant Henry Lidgbird Ball, the commander of the *Supply*. Lord Howe (1726-99) had had a distinguished naval career and was heavily involved in the seven years war (1756-63) and also the American War of Independence (1775-83). He went on to lead the British fleet in the battle known as the Glorious First of June, which was fought against the French on that date in 1794. The island that bears his name is halfway between Sydney and Norfolk Island, and the *Supply* called there to obtain turtle, which would be taken back to the main settlement. However, she sailed into some very bad weather resulting in hardly any turtle being caught with the result that the expedition was basically a failure and the ship returned to the main settlement on 25th May, 1788.

A few days later, on the 30th May, two men were found dead at some distance from the camp. One of the men had four spears in him, one of which had gone completely through his body and had come out the other side. The men were convicts and it was found that they had stolen a canoe from the local people and had ventured into their fishing places. The Aborigines seemed tolerant of the white settlers living on their land but their fishing was important to them and they wanted the British settlers to keep clear of these areas. Governor Phillip was very displeased that the men had clearly disobeyed orders not to antagonise the local people and he was less concerned with their deaths and more concerned that their actions had put in jeopardy his continual hope for peaceful relations with the Aborigines. He probably thought that the two men had got what they deserved because the eight survivors were taken back to the settlement and flogged with 150 lashes each and each one was placed in leg irons for a year. This harsh punishment was supposed to teach the new settlers a lesson for not treating the natives with respect, but it actually antagonised many of the convicts who felt that they were second class citizens compared to the people who they saw as 'ignorant savages' and did not like this treatment one bit.

As mentioned before, there was dreadful famine in the early years of the settlement. When the fleet left Portsmouth on 13th May 1787, they were given a quantity of food that had been calculated would last two years. As it would take less than a year to reach Australia, it was assumed that the balance of food would be more than enough until the colony had established self-sufficiency. However, the Admiralty had overlooked the blindingly obvious – the total inability in those days to keep food fresh, and long before they reached Australia, much of the food was completely inedible. If they hadn't stopped off at Teneriffe, Rio de Janeiro and the Cape of Good Hope on the way to Botany Bay, the situation, although desperate, would have been even worse. Governor Phillip wrote to Lord Sydney on 9th July, 1788 pointing out the problems and asking for a regular supply of food to be sent out. Phillip wrote:-

"… as the crops for two years to come cannot be depended on for more than what will be necessary for seed and what the *Sirius* may procure can only be to breed from. Should necessity oblige us to make use of what that ship may be able to procure, I do not apprehend that the live stock she will bring in twelve months will be more than a month's provision for the colony, and the *Supply* is totally unfit for a service of this kind."

The following day, possibly not expecting prompt action from Lord Sydney, Phillip wrote to the Admiralty in the same vein, and he spelt out very clearly just what it was that was needed:-

"1) The necessity of sending ships with provisions sufficient to victual the settlers for two years after they land.

2) That four years must elapse before a regular cultivation can be established.

3) That much more is to be expected from the *Sirius* than from the *Supply* with respect to the procuring provisions from sources outside Australia, and

4) The necessity of sending clothing, especially shoes."

In many ways, Governor Phillip had anticipated the problem and was mindful of the length of time that letters would take to reach their destination and how long it would take ships bringing supplies to reach them from England. Phillip did not leave it at that however. In a letter dated 28th September 1788, he again wrote to Lord Sydney pointing out to him the necessity of killing much of the livestock just to keep many of the people from starving and any new livestock received would also be killed for the same reason. Phillip also pointed out that bread supplies would not last a year whilst there was also a severe shortage of grain needed for sowing. Yet another letter was sent to Lord Sydney on 30th October in which Phillip wrote:-

"The same reason which makes me trouble your Lordship with tedious extracts from my former letters makes it necessary to point out in this letter that we at present depend entirely for provisions being sent from England, and I beg leave to observe that if a ship should be lost in the passage it might be a very considerable time before it could be known in England".

Phillip was all too aware of their perilous situation and was trying to cover all angles. However, although the situation looked very bleak at the present time, Phillip was able to be optimistic in the long term, as he wrote in the same letter:-

".....but my Lord, I hope a very few years will put this country in a situation to support itself, for I have the pleasure of seeing what land has been cleared in a very flourishing state."

Sadly however, Phillip's optimism was not justified as progress was hampered by severe drought, and also because the settlement failed to obtain relief from England quickly enough, and consequently, the year between the middle of 1790 to 1791 brought about mass starvation. Prior to this, Phillip had known that a famine approached, but he didn't realise quite how bad it was going to be when he ordered the *Sirius* to the Cape of Good Hope to obtain as much food as possible. She had returned on 2nd May, 1789 with supplies that would help but unfortunately did not solve the situation. Sometimes a large number of fish were caught, along with emus, kangaroos, and other game being shot which helped the settlers, and it was during these times that Phillip's rule of equal distribution of rations was sometimes relaxed.

On 4th September, 1789, a large quantity of fish were caught by both the people on the *Supply*, but also various other settlers. Had this been a normal occurrence, then the food shortages would not be so acute, but large catches like this were rare. During November, Governor Phillip ordered that the men were to receive only two thirds of the normal rations, although he refused to reduce the quantities issued to the women. 1790 was probably the hardest year that the settlers had to endure, and the period leading up to this was made worse when on 23rd December, 1789, a forty-four gun ship, the *Guardian*, hit an iceberg off the eastern coast of South America. She had recently left the Cape of Good Hope, and the only way the ship could return there in safety was to jettison most of the cargo they had on board which included the provisions that they had brought from the Cape. If the settlers had known of this catastrophe then their morale would have sunk even lower than it already was.

In 1790 the colony was hit by the terrible famine mentioned earlier and the next major voyage that Governor Phillip had organised was the sending of the *Sirius* and the *Supply* back to Norfolk Island. Although doubtless it was planned to collect some supplies for the hungry colony of New South Wales, the main reason was to relieve the pressure on the main colony by sending two hundred and eighty people including two companies of marines to Norfolk Island which was better equipped to look after them. The two men-of-war were made ready and they set sail on 6th March, 1790 to their new destination. They reached Norfolk Island a week later and with great difficulty landed the two hundred and eighty convicts at Cascade Bay on the 14th and 15th of March, these two days being needed due to the poor weather conditions.

On the following day (16th), both ships were in trouble as the already fierce wind changed direction to the north-east. The *Supply* and the *Sirius* lost sight of each other, although the *Supply* did manage to land most of the food that she had on to the island. The ships regained sight of each other but due to the weather conditions, were sailing too close to the land. Lieutenant Ball of the *Supply* tried to send a warning to Captain Hunter of the *Sirius* but was too late and the latter ship crashed against the rocks. The saving grace was that it was close to the shore, and so the crew were able to transport the provisions on to the shore for the inhabitants of Norfolk Island. Two convicts got themselves drunk and tried to wreck the plan but were stopped by a third convict, John Ascott. However, as a result of this, all the commissioned officers were mustered and they agreed that some kind of martial law should be introduced so that any repetition of this could be avoided more easily in the future.

On 5th of April, the *Supply* returned to Sydney and Phillip himself, along with Lieutenant Tench got into a boat and met the ship in the harbour. Lieutenant Tench subsequently wrote:-

"Having turned a point about half way down, we were surprised to see a boat which was known to belong to the *Supply* rowing towards us. On nearer approach I saw Captain Ball make an extraordinary motion with his hand, which too plainly indicated that something disastrous had happened; and I could not help turning to the governor, near whom I sat, and saying, 'Sir, prepare yourself for bad news' A few minutes changed doubt into certainty, and to our unspeakable consternation we learnt that the *Sirius* had been wrecked on Norfolk Island on the 19th of March (1790). Happily however, Captain Hunter and every person belonging to her were saved."

The loss of the *Sirius* was devastating news to the colony and was probably their lowest point. After a hastily convened meeting with his officers, Governor Phillip made a number of decisions in an attempt to relieve their perilous situation. Firstly, he ordered a further reduction in rations to everyone. He also ordered that there was to be an alteration in the form of justice. The civil courts of justice were to be abandoned and a military form of courts-martial was introduced. The meeting also changed the method of collecting food. Up until this time, anyone who owned a boat could fish and keep everything that they caught, but all the boats were now to be requisitioned and any fish caught were to be distributed evenly – in other words a fishing industry was to be established. It was important that as many people as possible would co-operate so that the idea would be successful, and Phillip received a promise from all the officers as well as the clergyman and surgeon of the hospital that they would go out voluntarily in the boats at night in order for this to be brought about. This was to be in addition to their normal duties. It was also ordered that as many animals which could be gathered were to be seized and distributed as evenly as possible amongst the settlers. Phillip then ordered that the *Supply* was to be prepared for sea and on 17th April, she set sail for Batavia with a view to obtaining as much food as possible for the colony. Finally, Phillip gave up three hundred-weight of flour which belonged to him but which was now to be used for the whole colony. The actual practical difference that this would make to people would be minimal, but when he declared that he wished to have nothing more in the way of provisions than anyone else had, it established an important principle of equality that helped form the nature of the new colony.

At this time it was felt that there were far too many males in the colony compared to the number of females. This fact in what was still a barren land, caused unrest and many of the women that were there had been dreadfully abused in the early days of the settlement. This situation could not go on and it was with some relief when it was realised that the human cargo on board the *Lady Juliana*, the first ship of the second fleet which had left Plymouth in July 1789 and arrived in Sydney on 3rd June, 1790, was made up entirely of women - two hundred and twenty-five in all.

The idea behind sending more women was that the best chance of the settlement surviving would be to establish families otherwise the marines would be spending all their time in keeping order in what was a potentially explosive situation. The disappointment however was the lack of provisions that it brought. The store ship that accompanied her, the *Guardian*, was lost and most of the provisions were lost with it apart from a quantity of flour that had been transferred to the *Juliana*. This had a damaging effect on the morale of everyone, but this was lifted somewhat with the unexpected arrival of the *Justinian* which arrived just seventeen days later, on 20th June, 1790. She had left Falmouth on 20th January and her passage to Sydney was remarkable for its speed, the journey being carried out in just five months as opposed to the eleven months that the *Juliana* took. The arrival of the *Justinian* probably brought more joy to the colony than all the other arrivals had done, even the *Juliana* with all its women. The *Justinian* had no passengers, but was full of provisions and Watkins Tench wrote:-

"Good fortune continued to befriend us. Before the end of the month, three more transports, having on board two companies of the New South Wales Corps, arrived to add to our society".

Quite why Tench was so delighted to see them is unclear unless as a marine, it was the arrival of military back up that cheered him. The three ships that he speaks of, the *Neptune*, *Surprise*, and the *Scarborough* were so full of sick passengers, that not only would they be unable to work, but other settlers would have to care for them, meaning that they too would be unable to work until the sick passengers recovered. The three ships had a total of 1,038 people. Of these, 273 died on the way over and 486 were sick when they landed at Port Jackson. The Admiralty back in England were either collectively stupid or cruel, for showing the same obsessive attitude to cost cutting that they had shown when fitting out the *Bounty* expedition from England to the West Indies at about the same time that caused Captain William Bligh so many problems. The three storeships that arrived in Sydney were overcrowded and suffering from an acute shortage of food. In fact, this voyage has gone down in history as the worst in the entire history of penal transport. The ships had been contracted from Camden, Calvert and King and their agent travelling with them was Thomas Shapcote. They had agreed to transport, clothe and feed all the convicts for a flat fee of £17.7s.6d (£17.38p) per head regardless of whether they were dead or alive on arrival. Camden, Calvert and King had been slaving contractors and the chains that they used to ensnare the convicts were the same as those used for the slaves. They allowed for no movement whatsoever, and the convicts were half starved and spent the journey lying in their own urine and excrement in exactly the same way that slaves had when transported. Thomas Milburn was one convict who survived and he wrote a letter to his mother describing the journey. The account was later published as a broadsheet in England. Milburn wrote:-

"We were chained two and two together and confined in the hold during the whole course of our long voyage........We were scarcely allowed a sufficient quantity of victuals to keep us alive, and scarcely any water; for my own part I could have eaten three or four of our allowances, and you know very well that I was never a great eater........When any of our comrades that were chained to us died, we kept it a secret as long as we could for the smell of the dead body, in order to get their allowance of provision, and many a time have I been glad to eat the poultice that was put to my leg for perfect hunger. I was chained to Humphrey Davies who died when we were about half way, and I lay beside his corpse about a week and got his allowance".

When news of the horrors of the second trip reached England, there was initial uproar but not much was done as the human cargo were after all, 'only convicts' and should not expect much more. No public enquiry was set up, although improvements were made in the long term, if for no other reason than the fact that it was pointless transporting people to set up a new colony if they were unfit to work when they arrived.

However, one event that was to bring happiness to the settlement was the return of the *Supply* which had left Sydney for Batavia the previous April and returned on 19th of October. The *Supply* had been considered too small to transport everything that the colony needed, so a Dutch vessel, *Waaksamheyd* had been hired and arrived two months later with further provisions on 17th December, 1790.

Early in 1791, Phillip decided that he wanted Captain Hunter back from Norfolk Island. Hunter had been at the island since the *Sirius* had been lost on 19th March the previous year. To this end, the *Supply* departed from Sydney on the 22nd of January with Lieutenant Ball in command, although as he was unwell at the commencement of the voyage, the ship's master, David Blackburn, took command until Ball had recovered. When the *Supply* returned to Sydney, Governor Phillip was told that all was not well at Norfolk Island due to the lack of food, and it was only the arrival of two ships, the *Justinian* and the *Surprise* on the 7th August 1790, that had saved the islanders from almost total starvation.

The history of the first settlement could not be complete without a mention of the famous escape from the colony of Mary Bryant, her husband William, their two children and seven other convicts. In 1786 at the age of twenty - one, Mary Broad, as she was originally known, was found guilty of stealing a cloak and was sentenced to death. This was commuted to seven year penal servitude at the new colony which was going to be formed in New South Wales. Mary left England on the first voyage in the transport ship *Charlotte* and on the way over became pregnant and gave birth to a girl who she named Charlotte, after the ship that they were on. On board was a male convict called William Bryant who she met and married on 10th February, 1788, soon after their arrival in Australia. They later had a son called Emmanuel. Mary was a spirited young woman but was beginning to despair of any hope of some sort of life in the new colony as the people were starving and she could see no way that the long term held any positive future for herself and her family. She and her husband were absolutely desperate and hungry, so they hatched a daring plan to steal the Governor's small boat with a view to sailing round the coast to Timor, a Dutch settlement just north of Australia.

On the night of 28th March, 1791, they stole the boat and sailed away, amazingly, not only arriving in Coupang on 5th June, but all of them survived, including the two young children. It was an extraordinary feat of endurance, and is on a par with Captain Bligh's famous open boat journey after the mutiny on the *Bounty* in April 1789. William and Mary told the authorities that they were survivors of a shipwreck but soon it was discovered who they really were and they were arrested. Ironically, after surviving the arduous boat journey to what they thought would be a safe land, William and their son Emmanuel died after contracting malaria which was rife in the Dutch East Indies during that time as Captain Cook found when he sailed there to make repairs to the *Endeavour* twenty years before. Cook's ship had struck the Great Barrier Reef on 11th June, 1770 and had made temporary repairs but sailed to Dutch Batavia the following October needing a place where more permanent repairs on his ship could be carried out. Whilst the ship was there, the dysentery struck the crew down and Cook was to lose a total of thirty - nine men. It was a similar situation that Mary Bryant's family found themselves in years later and which was to cause the death of her husband and son. Mary and her daughter Charlotte were sent back to England. Charlotte died on the journey but Mary arrived in England in June 1792 and was sent to Newgate prison where she was to await trial for the crimes that she had committed. However, publicity was a powerful weapon even in the eighteenth century, and after a great deal of favourable press coverage, she was pardoned and discharged from prison in May 1793 and was eventually re-united with her family in Cornwall. Despite the tragedy of losing her husband and children, it is a remarkable story of fortitude and endurance that has become part of the fokelore of the first settlement.

Back at the main colony, Governor Phillip decided that he would again have to reduce the rations to two thirds of the normal quantities which was due to both quality and quantity. The most recent purchase had been from Batavia, and as the quality had been so poor, it was decided not to purchase from there again.

Despite the lack of supplies, the Governor decided that King George lll's 53rd birthday should be celebrated, and to this end announced that the full quantity of provisions should be distributed. Added to that, he announced that anyone convicted of robbing the gardens should receive a pardon. However, on the night of the 4th of June, 1791 when the celebrations took place, six men robbed the Governor's garden and spoiled it for everyone because the decision to allow people full supplies was reversed making it a very low point for the colony.

Happily however, after that, things seemed to improve. There were several reasons for this. The farms around the main colony and at Norfolk Island seem to flourish after more than two barren years. Then a third fleet arrived and the health of the settlers carried aboard that fleet was far better than the health that previous arrivals had been in. Added to that was the fact that more provisions than had previously been brought were on board with them. This time, the convicts on board were not only better fed than before, but the Admiralty allowed for enough provisions to be transported to feed them for the first few months after their arrival at Sydney.

Finally, it was clear that the people at home were taking notice of the letters that Governor Phillip was sending to both Lord Sydney and the Admiralty as the Governor had set up a regular system of communication. The third fleet consisted of eleven ships. The first to arrive was the *Mary Ann* on 9th July, 1791. The ship brought with her ample provisions along with one hundred and forty one female passengers and six children. The *Matilda* was the next to arrive on 1st August followed by the *Atlantic* on 20th August. The following day, the *Salamander* arrived and on the 28th, the *William and Ann*. After this flurry, nothing arrived until the 21st September when the *Gorgon* anchored in the bay. The *Gorgon* carried the person of Major Grose who arrived at the colony as Lieutenant-Governor, the position which Major Ross who had commanded the marines vacated. Major Grose not only replaced Lieutenant Ross, but he formed and commanded the New South Wales Corps which replaced the marines as the controlling military presence at Sydney. Major Grose had had a distinguished career in the army. He had fought during the American War of Independence and was wounded twice which is why he had to return to England at that time. He had to stop active service and spent two years recruiting which is why his experience stood him in good stead when raising the New South Wales Corps. There were other people on board the *Gorgon* who are also worthy of mention, namely Commander King, RN, who was made superintendent of Norfolk Island, George Grimes, who was to be deputy-surveyor-general of Norfolk Island, and a Mr. Burton who was appointed superintendent of the convicts.

When the *Gorgon* anchored at the Cape of Good Hope, she took on board a great deal of livestock including sheep which were to become part of a huge industry in years to come. It was also the *Gorgon* that carried the last contingent of marines back to England, thus she was involved in some major events that helped shape the early days of the colony, making her a ship of some significance.

The next arrivals that were part of the third fleet were the *Active* and the *Queen*. Sadly, these two ships had reverted to the bad ways of previous arrivals, being overcrowded and lacking in the necessary provisions. Many of the prisoners did not even make it to the colony in bad health or otherwise, they simply died on the trip over. On the 13th of October 1791, the *Albermarle* arrived but it had been a troublesome journey. The convicts, aided by some of the seamen had rebelled and attempted to seize the ship, but the mutiny was faced down and following a court-martial, the organisers were hanged. The third fleet still had two more ships, the *Brittania* and the *Admiral Barrington* which arrived on the 14th and 16th of October respectively.

By the end of 1791, the colony consisted of one thousand, eight hundred and eighty one people, not including the military. After the arrival of the third fleet, there was no turning back. The new settlers had to become self-sufficient and to a degree, although linked to England by the monarchy, self governing if they were to survive. Eventually, the colony did settle and survive. Men and women married and with the formation of families life started to settle into some sort of normality although with still fairly primitive accommodation. Phillip could look back at the years, and despite the inevitable setbacks in a project as huge as this, he could consider that his work had been a success. It was achieved at a cost to his health however, and as early as December, 1790 he wanted to go home but he had to wait another two years before he was finally given permission to return to England. On 18th December, 1792, he set sail on the *Atlantic* and arrived in London in May the following year. He was granted honourable retirement and a pension of £500 per year. In the intervening period between Phillip leaving the colony in 1792 and the second Governor-General arriving in 1795, Major Grosse took over as Acting Governor. Unfortunately, during this three year period the settlement became chaotic and a drunken lawlessness took over. Whether Grosse colluded with this or whether he was simply not equipped to keep control is not quite clear, but during this period the officers of the New South Wales Corps gained control of trading, the main currency being rum. The New South Wales Corps became known as the Rum Corps and were eventually led by a man called John McArthur who was to become such a thorn in the side of William Bligh (1754-1817), the fourth Governor General who ruled between 1806 and 1810. This was the much maligned William Bligh who was in command of the *Bounty* when it set off from England in December, 1787 in order to sail to Tahiti, the aim of which was to collect breadfruit and take it to the West Indies where it was to be food for the slaves. Unfortunately, the crew had had to stay five months in Tahiti from the end of October 1788 until the beginning of April 1789 and they had acquired a taste for life on the paradise island with its beautiful women. Twenty-five of the crew mutinied on 28th April, 1789 and cast Bligh and eighteen of his men adrift in the *Bounty's* launch. Due to Bligh's incredible skills as a seaman and leader of men, they survived and Bligh returned to England in March 1790. Inaccurate Hollywood films have cast Bligh as a tyrant which he simply wasn't. In fact, he had a brilliant naval career before becoming Governor-General of New South Wales. He had been the Master of the *Resolution* on Captain Cook's third trip between 1776 and 1780 (although Cook was to die in Hawaii in 1779) and later fought with great distinction at the battles of Camperdown (1797) and Copenhagen (1801).

Bligh was chosen to take the *Bounty* out by none other than the great botanist, Sir Joseph Banks (1743-1820) who himself had been on Cook's first trip between 1768 and 1771 and Bligh was also recommended by Banks for the post of Governor-General in 1805. Banks was President of the Royal Society for forty-one years until his death and the fact that Bligh enjoyed the patronage of this great man speaks volumes for the calibre of Bligh.

However, Bligh's arrival at New South Wales in 1806 was fourteen years away from Phillip leaving the settlement in 1792. The troubles that happened at the new colony in New South Wales after Governor Phillip had returned to England should not detract from the work of the first Governor whose memory will always be held in affection by the people of Australia as he had left behind a settled community when he returned to England.

In 1792, whilst Phillip was still in Australia, his wife Margaret whom he married in 1763 and had been separated from since 1769, died. Consequently he was free to marry again and did so in 1794, his new wife being Isabella Whitehead and for a while, they settled into a life together in Bath, England. Phillip's health improved and he recovered sufficiently enough which enabled him to return to sea where he commanded several ships in the war against France. He was made a Rear-Admiral of the Blue on 6th January, 1799 and at the beginning of 1805, when he was in his sixty seventh year he effectively retired. As was the custom however, his journey through the ranks continued, and on 9th November, 1805, he was appointed Rear-Admiral of the Red. He was then promoted to Vice-Admiral of the White on 25th October 1809, Vice-Admiral of the Red on 31st July, 1810, and on 14th June, 1814, Admiral of the Blue. During this period, Admiral Phillip's health had declined and on 22nd February 1808, he suffered a stroke. At one stage it looked as if he might not recover, but eventually he did, although he lost the use of his entire right side including the arm and leg although his spirit and his mental capacity remained unaltered. Despite his incapacity, he retained his interest in the colony and studied the fortunes of John Hunter who had followed Admiral Phillip as Governor-General between the years 1795 and 1800, and who previously had been the second Captain of the *Sirius* when the first settlement arrived in New South Wales. Admiral Phillip also took an interest when Philip Gidley King was Governor between the years 1800 and 1805 and who had also been a serving officer on the first voyage, and Admiral William Bligh who succeeded King in 1806. Phillip continued to correspond with these and others in New South Wales before eventually dying in Bath on 31st August 1814 just over a month away from his seventy-sixth birthday. When the news eventually reached Australia, the *Sydney Gazette* inserted the following:-

"A London newspaper of a recent date announces the death of 'Vice-Admiral Phillip; at an advanced age.' This event took place at Bath, on 31st August last. To this gentleman the colony of New South Wales owes its original establishment in 1788; and in taking a retrospect of the arduous duties of such an undertaking, the many difficulties he had to struggle with, and the perils to which he was exposed, it will be only rendering a just tribute to his memory to remark that Governor Phillip manifested during the period of his administration much fortitude, zeal and integrity, and that to the wisdom of his early regulations and indefatigable exertions, the present flourishing state of the settlement bears most honourable and ample testimony. Governor Phillip died in the 77th year of his age".

It was always assumed that he died due to a mixture of age and the effects of the stroke that had felled him in February 1808, but in his biography of Phillip in 1937, the historian George Mackaness suggests that it may have been suicide. Mackaness says that in the 1930's, when he wrote the book, there were a number of elderly residents of Bath who held this view, believing that Phillip deliberately threw himself from an upstairs window to the courtyard below. The Editor of *The Bath and Wiltshire Chronicle and Herald* in the 1930's, Mr. L.B. Hewitt, said that: "There is a very definite story that Phillip took his own life." If this is true, and we do not know for sure that it is, it should not take away anything from the achievements of this great man, nor should it diminish our opinion of him in any way.

Joseph Banks is often called the father of modern day Australia, and whilst Banks was a remarkable man, he only suggested that Botany Bay could be a suitable place to land criminals, and that was only to confirm the original suggestion by James Mario Matra to the Beauchamp Committee that had been set up in 1779. The man who did all the hard work and bore all the responsibility was Arthur Phillip who was the first Governor-General and who took the first settlers to a foreign land which was completely barren. It was from that barren land that they started what is known as modern day Australia and if anyone is entitled to be known as the father of modern day Australia, it must surely be Arthur Phillip.

He was a tolerant man and a kindly one. His job was always going to be incredibly difficult even if he had received the whole hearted support from his colleagues, but he didn't. Major Ross who commanded the marines who were eventually replaced by the New South Wales Corps was one who gave him no end of trouble and adopted a negative attitude towards the colony from the outset. Another was Lieutenant Dawes, who, although unlike Ross, had redeeming features to his nature and did some good work in the colony, still went against the Governor's express wishes, and traded with the convicts. Phillip had to deal with the aborigines and it has been seen that he treated them with kindness and tolerance, befriending them collectively and individually, even after he was severely wounded in an unprovoked attack, putting the attack down as being misguided and due to a misunderstanding rather than malevolence. He also treated the convicts with kindness and fairness although often unsupported by some of the officers and marines. However, the people who gave him trouble were in the minority and apart from an odd few, when he left New South Wales to return to England in December, 1792, he was respected by just about everybody, be they military, convicts, or aborigines.

After his death, he was buried at St. Nicholas Church, Bathampton, but the treatment that he received on his death does little credit to England. Given his status and achievements, it seems extraordinary now but for many years the whereabouts of his remains were a complete mystery. Perhaps the reason was the suspicion that he committed suicide, as some clergymen of that time would deny that person a Christian burial. However, in December 1897, a slate slab was discovered under some matting at the church by the vicar at the time, the Revd. Lancelot J. Fish. The slab bore the following inscription:

"Underneath lie the Remains
of Arthur Phillip, Esq.,
Admiral of the Blue,
who died 31st August 1814,
in his 76th year.
Also of Isabella,
Relict of the Above
Admiral Phillip,
who died the 1st of March 1823,
In the 71st Year of her Age."

High upon the north wall of the church tower which can be seen only by climbing a ladder, is a small tablet bearing the inscription:-

"Near this tablet are the remains of Arthur Phillip Esq., Admiral of the Blue, first Governor and Founder of New South Wales, who died 31st August 1814, in the 76th year of his age".

There is a portrait of him in the national gallery in London, but it is in Australia where he is honoured most of all. There is a statue of him in the Botanic Gardens in Sydney, and many streets, parks and schools are named after him. His name is also kept alive in Australia by Port Phillip, and Phillip Island. In the English Chambers Biographical Dictionary the bare facts about his career are entered. In the Dictionary of Australian Biography his character is given a more just treatment:-

"Steadfast in mind, modest, without self seeking, Phillip had imagination enough to conceive what the settlement might become, and the common sense to realise what at the moment was possible and expedient. When almost everyone was complaining he never himself complained, when all feared disaster he could still hopefully go on with his work. He was sent out to found a convict settlement, he laid the foundations of a great dominion." That is a fitting tribute, but perhaps Arthur Phillip, a modest man, unwittingly composed his own tribute when in a letter to Joseph Banks many years before, he wrote:

"As to my Conduct, if ever I have erred, or Consulted my own conveniency or interest, there will soon be those at home who will not lose an opportunity of pointing it out, but I have never to my knowledge swerved from the line of Conduct which I laid down for myself the day I embarked, and which had the good of the Service on which I am employed, for it's object. I have in no one instance ever consulted my own".

In 2007, Geoffrey Robertson QC questioned whether Admiral Phillip's remains were in fact in Bathampton Church. Robertson's view which is shared by many, is that Phillip should have been buried at one of England's great cathedrals rather than a village church and he feels that the Admiral's remains should be found and should be re-interred in Australia where he is fully appreciated.

As with William Bligh and Captain Cook, it is left to Australia to properly celebrate our national heroes, but there is no doubt that Phillip shares the accolade of being a hero in two countries, Britain and Australia. There are not many people who can boast that.

-oOOo-

4
Fanny Burney
(1752-1840)

Famous writer who influenced Jane Austen.

Fanny Burney was a remarkable woman in an age where women were over a century away from achieving the vote. She was a novelist, playwright, and diarist.

She was born Frances Burney on 13th June, 1752 and was the daughter of Dr. Charles Burney (1726-1814) and Mrs. Esther Sleepe Burney (1725-1762). Charles Burney was a well known figure in his own right, eventually becoming a musical historian.

Charles was first known as MacBurney and his father was James MacBurney (1678-1749). He married an actress, Rebecca Ellis in 1697 and they had their first child in 1699 followed by fourteen more. Rebecca's exact dates of birth and death are unknown but it is thought that she was born in 1681 and must have died during or before 1720, as James married Anne Cooper (c1690-1775) in that year. Despite or possibly because of the fact that she had given birth to fifteen children, Rebecca had not yet reached the age of forty when she died. James and Anne (nee Cooper) MacBurney had five children to add to the fifteen that James had had with his first wife Rebecca. The five were:- Ann or Nancy (1722-94), Richard (1723-92), Rebecca (1724-1809), Charles, who was Fanny's father (1726-1814) and Susanna, Charles' twin (1726-c1734). Susanna, Charles' twin, died in 1734 aged just eight years. Fanny Burney's family were a closeknit group and much of this is probably due to Charles' upbringing. Along with his elder brother Richard, he was sent from the family home at the age of just three years to a Nurse Ball who lived in Condover, which was four miles from Shrewsbury, and he spent his entire childhood with her until the age of twelve when he returned to his parents. His time with Nurse Ball must have been happy however, as apparently he was grief stricken to leave her when he returned to his natural family, but the city of Chester had more opportunities for him than Condover could ever have. He began his musical training at the Free School in Chester and became assistant to the Cathedral organist when just fourteen. His half brother, James, who was organist at St. Mary's church in Shrewsbury was so impressed with his ability that he recruited him as his assistant so Charles was back to the town where he was born. This lasted two years before he went back to Chester to rejoin his parents once more. It was back in Chester that his career breakthrough happened. The composer Thomas Arne (1710-78), was an excellent violinist and famous for many compositions, amongst which was Rule Brittania, and was on his way from Dublin to take up a position as composer at the Drury Lane Theatre. During his journey he stopped off in Chester and happened to hear of this talented musician who could play the violin, harpsichord and organ and who was also composing himself.

Charles Burney was eighteen years old at this time, and Arne took him on as an apprentice. This seemed an ideal arrangement at first but eventually Burney felt that too much was being asked of him, and after two years he received a much better offer from a gentleman called Fulke Greville who wanted Burney, not as an apprentice, but as a gentleman's companion and music maker and in 1748, he eventually bought Burney out of his apprenticeship for the sum of three hundred pounds, which would be something in the region of £18,000 in today's money, an enormous sum for a twenty-two-year-old unknown musician. Burney also gave music lessons, and after composing three major pieces, Alfred, Robin Hood, and Queen Mab, he went to Kings Lynn as organist in 1751 and stayed there until 1760. After extensive travel in Europe where he was collecting material for further pieces that he was to write, Burney became Organist at Chelsea College in 1783. He had had a good career by any stretch of the imagination, but the position he longed for most, that of Master of the King's Band, eluded him which we shall look at in slightly more detail later. He mixed in exclusive circles however, and his friends included Edmund Burke (1729-97), the Irish statesman and philosopher, Dr. Johnson (1709-84), the great English writer, critic, and lexicographer, and David Garrick (1717-79), actor, actor manager and dramatist.

Despite the family originally being split, James MacBurney inspired love and affection in his family which Charles Burney was to emulate with his family years later. Although not unhappy in his childhood, Charles Burney was determined not to allow any such upheaval to happen to his own family. Fanny in fact, did not find out about the fact that her father had been removed from his parents at such a tender age until she was in her late forties, and was horrified by it.

Fanny's mother, Esther Sleepe (1725-1762), married Charles in 1749 and they had five other children besides Fanny who lived into adulthood. Esther Sleepe was a professional musician and unusually for a woman, a freeman of the Company of Musicians when she met Charles, Fanny's father. Given Charles' musical pedigree, it is not difficult to see what drew them to each other. Esther's parents were Richard Sleepe (? -1758) and Frances Dubois (who before marrying had changed her name to Wood). It is not known exactly when Frances was born or the exact year of her death, but it is thought to be pre -1775. Richard Sleepe was a musician and a member of the Lord Mayor's band which performed at various functions. Esther's mother, Frances Wood (Dubois) was the daughter of a M. Dubois who ran a shop that is thought to have had a connection with musical instrument making. Thus it was that like her parents, Fanny's maternal grandparents Richard and Frances were drawn to each other through music. Fanny's mother, Esther, was a well read woman and when the family were living in Kings Lynn, the card playing evenings adored by many of the locals bored her. She made friends with two other like-minded women, Elizabeth Allen and Dolly Young, and the three would often meet up to study rather than engage in the frivolity that she perceived in others. She became ill in 1761 after she had become pregnant for the ninth time in twelve years (three children died in infancy), and because of her coughing, was thought to have consumption. Esther's condition continued to get worse throughout 1762 and she finally died on 29th September of that year after more than a week of, "a most violent bilious complaint, which terminated, after extreme torture, in an inflammation of the bowels". She was only thirty seven years old. Besides Fanny, the children that came from the marriage were Esther (Hetty) 1749-1832, James 1750-1821, Susanna Elizabeth 1755-1800, Charles 1757-1817 and Charlotte Ann 1761-1838. Hetty was the only child present at her death as the others had been staying with Mrs Sheeles, who ran a school in Queen's Square, London where Charles, Fanny's father taught. James was away at sea in the navy, but was unable to return in time. Of all the children, Fanny who was just ten years old at the time, was the most affected and was distraught at her mother's passing, even though she had had months to prepare for it.

Charles, Fanny's father, was also completely grief stricken at his wife's death and was almost completely unable to give any words of comfort to the children. The words that he is claimed by Fanny to have written to Esther's friend Dolly Young show this only too graphically – "From an ambitious, active, enterprising being, I have become a torpid drone, a listless, desponding wretch!" Fanny wrote that it was "So ill-written and so blotted by his tears, that he must have felt himself obliged to re-write it for the post". The letter is a lengthy and emotional description of Esther's death and his resulting distress. The fact that the letter survived may mean that it was never sent and that Dr. Burney did in fact, as Fanny suggests, rewrite it, keeping the original. Another explanation that has been put forward is that the tears are from the recipient, Dolly Young herself. The reason that there is some confusion about the authenticity of this letter is the fact that Fanny doesn't mention it when going through her father's papers in 1820, complaining of the lack of written material from her father concerning her mother's death. Fanny prints the whole article that Dr. Burney wrote in her printed memoirs of 1832 but it then seems to disappear again. In her biography of Fanny, Claire Harman wonders whether it was a product of Fanny's imagination gleaned from conversations that she overheard between Dr. Burney and Fanny's sister Hetty concerning the death of Esther, and a wish that the marriage was seen as idealistic (which it almost certainly was) by the public. Whether the document existed or didn't, there is no doubt that the family were plunged into grief at Esther's death not softened by her assurances that she would be looking down on them, "from whence she was going". Up to her death, Esther was concerned that the girls' father would be looked after by them, or 'mothered' as she said. They did in fact do just that, especially Fanny, not only because she loved her father dearly, but simply on the practical basis of the fact that she didn't marry until she was forty two years of age. Meanwhile, a very brief sketch of each child of the union reads as follows:-

Esther (Hetty) was born on 24th May, 1749. Charles and Esther were unmarried at the time of her birth, and Charles was set to go abroad for what could have been many years with his then employer, Fulke Greville and his wife Frances (nee Macartney) who was not only a beautiful heiress but a gifted poet. Because of the fear that Esther had of losing Charles for number of years without the security of marriage, Charles plucked up the courage to ask the

Grevilles permission to marry which was immediately granted, and they married straight away in St. George's Chapel, Hyde Park Corner. In the event, Charles did not leave, but it meant that he had to look for work to support his young family. Meanwhile, Esther the daughter, was sent to Paris with her sister Susanna for her education with a Protestant woman in Paris who seemed to have few teaching qualifications but was cheap. All that their father Charles expected however, was that the girls would be able to learn the French language and customs. Hetty eventually married her cousin, Charles Rousseau Burney (1747-1819) in the latter part of 1770 and although they had eight children and the marriage was happy, they struggled financially. Charles Rousseau Burney was the son of Charles Burney's brother Richard, and his wife Elizabeth (nee Humphries) and Hetty's father had given both her and Charles junior music lessons when they were children. Both Hetty and her husband were talented musicians, but their talent did not translate itself into money.

James was born in 1750 and became a naval officer, sailing round the world twice with Captain James Cook on the latter's second and third voyages during the years between 1772 and 1780. He witnessed Cook's death at Hawaii on 14th February, 1779 before the two ships arrived back in England the following year. Although eventually becoming an Admiral, his naval career was largely undistinguished, although he was a popular officer on Cook's expeditions, and wrote a first hand account of the two voyages that he, Burney was on, being Cook's second and third voyages, his third between 1776 and 1780 being an unsuccessful attempt to find the North West Passage, the strip of sea across the top of the Americas that would join the Atlantic and Pacific Oceans.

Susanna (Susan) was born in 1755 and she and Fanny were very close. She married Captain Molesworth Philips who had accompanied Captain Cook on the latter's third voyage. Philips was in charge of the marines on board Cook's ship the *Resolution* and it is quite possible that Susan and Fanny's brother, James Burney, and Molesworth Philips met for the first time on Cook's third voyage, and James Burney introduced Philips to Susanna when the two men arrived home. Cook's third and final voyage ended in his untimely death during a fight between the local people of Hawaii and Cook's men on 14th February 1779. Although the sheer weight of numbers that were against them stopped Philips and the other marines being able to save Cook, Philips was reported as having fought bravely although he was perhaps not the hero he was made out to be, and certainly the marines did not exactly cover themselves with glory that day. Philips was possibly not the man that Susanna thought he was and certainly the marriage was not a happy one, with Susanna dying prematurely in 1800.

The younger Charles Burney was born in 1757 and was a classical scholar and gained a doctorate in 1808. He was a hard drinking man but a kindly person and had a huge collection of books, which were examined by experts from the British Museum and eventually purchased for the nation for the then huge sum of £13,500. His heir was Charles Parr Burney who was going to write a biography of his father, but thought better of it when he found out about his father's theft of books from Caius College, Cambridge when he went there in January 1777. When a large number of classical texts went missing soon after his being admitted to the University Library, his rooms were searched and a large number of books were found, and it was also thought that some others had been sold on. He left Cambridge in disgrace, but such was the shame felt by his family, his father refused to see him. How he left such a huge collection of books on his death from a stroke in December 1817 remained a mystery considering his limited income that he would have received on a clerical schoolmaster's salary.

Charlotte Ann was born on 3rd November, 1761. It was when her mother Esther was carrying her that she, Esther became ill and so Charlotte was put out to nurse. In the event, her mother died in the September following Charlotte's birth. In 1767, when Charlotte was just six years old, her father married a Mrs. Elizabeth Allen (1728-1796), but such was the fear that her father had of possible disharmony the union would cause, the couple continued to live apart. In July 1768 however, it was increasingly impossible to keep Mrs. Allen's pregnancy a secret although the new Mrs. Burney continued to keep her large house in Lynn spending most of her time there until she and Charles Burney moved in together. Mrs Elizabeth Burney (Allen) had three children from her marriage to Stephen Allen who had died in 1763 aged thirty-eight years. These three children were Maria Allen (1751-1820), Stephen Allen (1755-1847), and Elizabeth Allen (1761-1826). Along with Dr. Burney's six, that made a total of nine children, but two more were to come from the union of Charles and Elizabeth, making a total of eleven in all. The latter two were Richard Thomas Burney (1768-1808), and Sarah Harriet Burney (1772-1844). Eventually they would all move in together becoming one big family – whether they were happy however, is debateable, as Dr. Burney's children did not take to their stepmother and would relieve the tensions by laughing at her behind her back. It does seem however, that she made Dr. Burney happy but children do not always see that at the time, especially after the loss of their natural mother who they had clearly adored.

It had not been a straightforward courtship. Elizabeth Allen was one of the two friends that Fanny's mother Esther, had spent time with, the other being Dolly Young. It was Dolly Young that Esther, on her deathbed, had wanted Dr. Burney to marry, but although the children liked her, she was nowhere near as physically attractive as Elizabeth Allen was, and one can be sure that the fact that Mrs. Allen was a very rich widow added to her allure. However, Burney's first attempts to woo her fell on stony ground. He sent her the following poem:

"Her image by night and by day
Still haunts me, both sleeping and waking,
Steals my peace and spirits away
And my heart keeps incessantly aching."

It didn't have the effect on her that Dr. Burney hoped, and she rebuffed him to such an extent that he thought that his chances were ruined forever. It was at this time that he had decided to send two of his girls away to France to further their education. It would normally be expected to send the two eldest girls, Esther and Fanny, but Fanny was bypassed in favour of Susanna because their father thought that Fanny would not be able to cope. In light of Fanny's subsequent success in writing, it may seem extraordinary to think that her father considered her slow in learning to the point of possibly being backward. Charles, aged six years in 1764, was sent to Charterhouse whilst James had joined the navy at the age of ten, so his future was settled. Charlotte was only three so Fanny stayed at home to look after her and to act as secretary cum housekeeper to her father, a role that she seems to have settled for with little or no resentment.

It was during this time that Dr. Burney resumed his friendship with Samuel Crisp, who he had known years before in Lynn (Dr. Burney had eventually moved his family to London in 1760), and Crisp became a very influential figure in Fanny's life. Crisp was nearly twenty years older than Dr. Burney, and was single and rich, which enabled him to spend a great deal of time with the young Fanny Burney, becoming a surrogate uncle cum grandfather. He was cultured and brought the first pianoforte to England from Italy. He was also a poet, but his weakness was that he had a higher opinion of his own work than other people did. Despite his wealthy connections that enabled him to have his 'magnum opus', a tragedy in verse called *Virginia*, put on at Drury Lane by David Garrick, it was soon pulled off but Crisp came up with every excuse other than the possibility that it simply wasn't good enough, and after re-writing it, continued to pressurize Garrick to stage it again, but with little success.

Meanwhile, Fanny had already been writing what she called 'Her scribblings' since the age of ten, and being at home all the time, was largely self educated and not at all convinced that her work contained any literary merit. Fanny was a serious child, probably spending a lot of time alone with her sisters away, and her writing was extensive and took many forms; "Elegies, Odes, Plays, Songs, Stories, Farces, - nay, Tragedies, and Epic Poems, every scrap of white paper that could be seized upon without question or notice".

Fanny spent many years writing without thinking that anything she ever wrote would be good enough to be published, but eventually she wrote her first novel *Evelina* which was published anonymously in 1778. In those days, it was virtually impossible for a woman to publish her work so it was released to the public with much secrecy as to the identity of the author. It had started life many years previously as part of her jottings. Fanny had kept a diary and her first proper entry was on 30th May, 1768 and it was addressed to a 'Miss Nobody'. She had been writing before that but burned everything that she had written in 1767 as she felt that she was being pressurised into stopping as it was considered 'unladylike'. She also didn't want to upset her new stepmother. Included in the burning was her first manuscript of *The History of Caroline Evelyn,* which she had written without telling anyone. However, she continued with her diaries in which she explained why she had destroyed everything and some of the effort that she had put into *Caroline Evelyn* was used to good effect when she came to write *Evelina*.

She eventually had it published by Thomas Lowndes, but not before it had been turned down by the publisher Robert Dodsley who was unhappy at the idea of publishing an anonymous piece of work. Fanny had altered her handwriting when copying the book out because for a long time, she had acted as Dr. Burney's secretary and was afraid that her handwriting would be recognised. As she had already been turned down once, she colluded with her brother Charles, who pretended to be the author and who called himself 'Mr. King'. Fanny had not completed the manuscript when it was first delivered to Mr. Lowndes and not unnaturally, he wanted to read the complete work before committing himself. Lowndes wanted to see the complete book during the summer of 1777 but in the event, Fanny completed the work in November where she said that she stayed up: "The greatest part of many nights, in order to get it ready". Before *Evelina*, comic novels had often been rather bawdy affairs or rather cloying. Fanny was a serious and moral young lady who was not going to write anything like that, so *Evelina* actually changed the way novels were written and perceived in the future.

Fanny's two sisters, Susan and Charlotte had been in on the secret from the start, but two aunts, Ann and Rebecca Burney who were Fanny's father Charles's sisters, also had to be brought in as the proofs of the three volumes of *Evelina* had to be sent for correction to Gregg's Coffee House in York Street, Covent Garden as it was they that ran it and by this time, Fanny's brother, Charles junior, had suffered his fall from grace and had to be removed to Shinfield. *Evelina* was eventually published on 29th January, 1778. According to the story put out by Fanny many years later, she only knew that the book was ready for sale when her stepmother read aloud an advertisement of it in the newspaper at the family breakfast. It read as follows:

'This day was published *EVELINA*, or, a Young Lady's Entrance into the World. Printed for T. Lowndes, Fleet Street.'

The book was a great success but no-one was able to guess who the author was, as Fanny hadn't even allowed the words 'By A Lady' to be added to the front of the book, so there was even some debate as to the gender of the author. Fanny was still worried as to what her father would think of the book and her writing it. She was almost neurotic about it but there must have been an element of her that would want to own up to it as well as hopefully gain his approval. There was great speculation amongst the Burney set as to who the author was. Lady Hales, who was part of this circle decided that it was 'a man of great abilities' whilst another friend, a Miss Coussmaker declared that the author had to be a woman because '.......there was such a remarkable delicacy in the conversations and descriptions.......of some of the characters......' The famous Hester Thrale (1741-1821) and her friends also tried to guess who the author was. Hester Thrale was a Welsh writer, and was the wife of the wealthy Southwark brewer, Henry Thrale with whom she had twelve children before his death in 1781. She then went on to marry the Italian musician, Gabriel Piozzi in 1784. Her Streatham set consisted of such luminaries as Dr. Johnson (1709-84), the English writer, critic and lexicographer, David Garrick (1717-79), the dramatist and writer, Richard Brinsley Sheridan (1751-1816), the Irish dramatist, Joshua Reynolds (1723-92), the English portrait painter, and Warren Hastings (1732-1818), best known for being the English administrator for India and defendant in an extraordinary trial by Parliament that lasted a full seven years from February 1788 and did not finish until 23rd April, 1795 when he was acquitted. All these and more were part of Hester Thrale's set and all read *Evelina*, and all thought that Dr. Burney himself was the author. It was then that

Fanny's sister Susanna decided to come clean as she felt that if Dr. Burney read it, he would recognise some of the autobiographical elements contained within it. At this time, Fanny was ill and was staying at Chessington in order to recover, so Susanna and her sister Charlotte told Dr. Burney without letting on to Fanny, making her think that Dr. Burney had worked it out for himself. Fanny needed to have no fears over her father's reaction to the book. He loved it and was very proud of his daughter for writing it, as it must be remembered that it was not so long since he had considered Fanny a little backward, although he never loved her the less for it. Once Hester Thrale realised who the author was, Fanny started to visit her in Streatham and became part of that set. Hester Thrale was a patron of the arts whose house was a centre for her friends to discuss literary and political matters. Fanny had originally met her in March 1777 but did not become part of her circle until 1779 when she eventually owned up to being the author of *Evelina*. Hester Thrale and her circle certainly approved of her book and she wrote to Dr. Burney on 22nd July, 1779, saying that:- "Dr. Johnson returned home full of the praise of the book I had lent him, and protesting that there were passages in it which might do honour to Richardson........" Once accepted by the Streatham set, Fanny received a great deal of support from Hester and Fanny spoke very highly of her. Mrs. Thrale was not always quite so enamoured of Fanny however, thinking that she made a fuss of unimportant things and was also a hypochondriac. Hester didn't have an easy life. Her husband, Henry Thrale, was often cruel to her and her annual pregnancies coupled with the fact that she lost so many of her children at childbirth, made her less than patient with Fanny when she thought that Fanny was making a fuss over something trivial. Mrs. Thrale wrote:-

"Yet she makes me miserable too in many respects – so restlessly and apparently anxious lest I should give myself airs of patronage, or load her with the shackles of dependance – I live with her always in a degree of pain that precludes friendship – dare not ask her to buy me a ribbon, dare not desire her to touch the bell, lest she should think herself injured".

These were damning words, but Fanny seems unaware of the feelings that she is bringing out in her patron.

Evelina was a great success, and in time, Fanny came to accept that she was now generally known as the author. It was at this time that she let it be known that she was in the process of writing a play which was to be called *The Witlings*. It was to be a dramatic comedy satirizing a large segment of London society and in this she included the so-called Blue Stocking Club. Hester Thrale was often a guest at the club, but attended rather reluctantly and tended to stay on the periphery as she, and many others, felt that their literary pretentions and stilted conversations were ridiculous, and not at all relaxed such as Hester's own meetings at Streatham as well as Dr. Burney's evenings at St. Martin's Street. However, despite her misgivings over the Blue Stocking Club, Hester Thrale was keen to introduce Fanny to one of its members, Mrs. Montagu (1720-1800). Elizabeth Montagu was wealthy and was seen as the cultured author of *Essay on Shakespeare* and *Dialogues*. She had married Edward Montagu, who was the grandson of the 1st Earl of Sandwich in 1742, and established a salon in Mayfair which was at the heart of London social and literary life. However, when it took place, the meeting between her and Fanny was only a qualified success, as Mrs. Montagu seemed more keen to promote her own protégée, a one Hannah More (1745-1833), an English playwright whose work over the years was prodigious. In fact, when Mrs. Montagu finally did read *Evelina,* she was not impressed. Fanny was determined to go ahead with the play however as she was keen on being a successful playwright. *The Witlings* tells the story of two lovers, Cecilia and Beaufort, who were kept apart from each other by their respective families due to Cecilia's financial situation. She is a wealthy heiress but is seemingly bankrupted and the marriage plans founder. Eventually, the lovers get together as Cecilia's financial affairs were nowhere near as bad as first thought. However, Fanny faced two setbacks in her quest to get the play staged. Samuel Crisp, who was still a big influence on Fanny's life, advised Fanny against going ahead with the project, as ever the traditionalist, he felt that a comedy could not be achieved by a woman.

The other setback occurred when Dr. Burney read the play to a gathering that included amongst others, Crisp, Dr. Johnson, Susan, and Charlotte when Fanny was not present. It was not as well received as Fanny had hoped. She wanted a general impression of the play but was dismayed when both Crisp and her father picked the play to pieces ruling out small changes being made that would be enough to improve it. The play was never staged in Fanny's life-time, and indeed was only first published in 1995. Fanny wrote other plays including *Edwy and Elgiva*, but although that was staged, it was for one night only, and her career as a playwright simply never took off.

Whilst all this was going on, Fanny's brother, James, was away in the Pacific with Captain Cook between the years 1776-80 searching for the famous North West Passage linking the Pacific and Atlantic oceans across the top of the Americas. James was a Lieutenant on the *Discovery* commanded by Captain Charles Clerke who had sailed with Cook twice before. James had also been on Cook's previous trip between 1772 and 1775 when they searched for the southern continent that many people thought existed. On this third trip, Cook was commanding the *Resolution* as well as being in command of the whole expedition. On 10th January, 1780, a letter arrived in London from Clerke detailing the horrific death of Captain Cook at Hawaii on 14th February, 1779. By the time the letter reached London, Clerke himself was dead having contracted consumption before the ships had left England. James arrived home in October 1780 and relayed the account of Cook's death in more detail. Four marines had also died in the fracas that day, but one of the survivors of the fight was the Captain of the marines, Lieutenant Molesworth Philips. Molesworth Philips had fought bravely enough, but his reputation as the hero of the hour was perhaps a trifle undeserved, although set against the behaviour of most of his marines who simply cut and run, his conduct did stand out. James and Molesworth Philips had spent years going round the world together and had shared experiences that those at home would never understand, and they subsequently became firm friends which lasted for their lifetimes. James introduced Philips to the Burney family just as soon as he was able, and it was clear that Molesworth Philips was instantly attracted to Susan. The courtship was swift, and they were engaged within two months of meeting each other. The marriage took place in January 1782, and whilst Fanny was happy for Susan, she was bereft for herself. Susan was her best friend and they confided in each other on everything – there was simply no-one else who could take her place. Charlotte was nine years younger than Fanny and couldn't be expected to fulfil the role in Fanny's life that Susan had. Had Fanny known in advance of Molesworth Philips' treatment of her beloved sister, she would not even have had the initial feeling of happiness for her as it was soon clear that Susan was very unhappy in the marriage.

In 1782, Fanny published her second novel, *Cecilia* and her father arranged for it to be published by a friend of his, Mr. Thomas Payne. When hearing of this, Mr. Lowndes, the publisher of her first novel, *Evelina* wrote to Dr. Burney demanding to know why he, Mr. Lowndes, was not going to publish *Cecilia*. Burney wrote back a curt letter explaining to him that the author felt under no obligation to use the same publisher, at the same time pointing out that whilst the author had received only 30 guineas (£31.50p) for her work, the artist who had illustrated the book received the sum of £73.00p.

Fanny had hoped to tell her story within three volumes, but in the end, she had to write five volumes to say everything that she wanted. Dr. Burney was very proud of his daughter and very supportive, but he wrote to Fanny and suggested quite strongly that he disapproved of the story's ending – he wanted a happier one. Fanny however, knew exactly what it was that she wanted to say, and wrote back a spirited letter saying quite firmly that the ending was to stay exactly as it was. In retrospect, the words that she used to describe the disagreement with her father were interesting – she wrote that:- "it was caused by pride and prejudice – my pride and your prejudice". It was almost certainly these words in *Cecilia* that Jane Austen used as the title for her masterpiece that appeared in 1813. However, 1781 was a harrowing time for Fanny as Dr. Burney was a hard taskmaster. He could work night and day, but Fanny could not and she was making herself ill with lack of sleep. She wrote:- ".......I cannot sleep half the night for planning what to write next day, and then next day am half dead for want of rest". However, despite all this, the novel was completed and *Cecilia* was an outstanding success. There were 2,000 copies of the first edition that sold out within three months, and from the money that was invested from it, Fanny would receive £20 per annum for the rest of her life. She had received £250, considerably more than for *Evelina*, but probably still less than she should have received for it given the sales it generated. Samuel Crisp noted with some satisfaction that the publishers, Payne and Cadell, were intending to present Fanny with a 'handsome pair of gloves' over and above the £250 she received from them for the copyright. Crisp also had his own present lined up for Fanny – a portrait of himself by her very talented cousin Edward. Crisp was not well at this point of his life and in the early months of 1783, his health, already delicate, declined rapidly. He died in April of that year and the whole Burney family mourned his passing – they felt that they had lost a true friend.

Meanwhile, in 1781, Henry Thrale suddenly dropped dead in the house in Grosvenor Square. Mrs Thrale was forced to sell the brewery business and she retired exhausted to Streatham with Dr. Johnson, Fanny, and others in their circle for company. It was felt however, that the old days of entertaining were over and this was brought home to them when she fell in love with the Italian singer, Gabriel Piozzi. She had known him since 1780 when he became Mrs. Thrale's daughter Queeney's singing master. It was almost certainly this fact that caused Mrs. Thrale to think about giving up the London house that she and her husband had been renting, let the Streatham house to Lord Shelburne (1737-1805) the English statesman who was briefly Prime Minister from July 1782 to February, 1783, and to go and live in Italy with her daughters. This caused natural dismay to Fanny who had long since regarded the Streatham house as an extension of her own home, and Dr. Johnson, who was by this time very unwell, took it very badly indeed and a falling out occurred between himself and Hester Thrale that was never completely resolved to his dying day.

The decision to do all this was finally made by Mrs. Thrale in the autumn of 1782. There were two reasons for these decisions, her love for Gabriel Piozzi being one, and the other was the difficulty of looking after Dr. Johnson, who by this time was old and his frailties made him a liability to Mrs. Thrale. This made Johnson even more bitter and Fanny was devastated too as she realised that this was the end of the get togethers at Streatham Park, the place she had seen as almost a second home. However, the timing could not have been worse for Johnson. Whilst Fanny had known the Thrales for a relatively short time, Johnson had been visiting Hester for fifteen years and was beginning to be unable to fend for himself properly, so he felt the loss of the Streatham base most of all. However, it wasn't only Johnson who was upset because most of Hester's friends were also against the marriage, as was her daughter, Queeney, and Fanny, being fond of both Hester Thrale and Queeney, was stuck in the middle of it all, but loyally supported Mrs. Thrale. Before the marriage could take place however, disaster struck. In the spring of 1783, Hester's daughter, four-year-old Harriet died of measles, and Cecilia, who was two years older, contracted whooping cough. Hester was devastated, but instead of supporting her, Piozzi would not see her but instead, left the country, much to Hester's friends' relief, but certainly not to Hester's. Hester, in a very low emotional state, left to stay in Bath where she desperately craved Fanny's company, but Dr. Burney refused to let Fanny see her. It is difficult in this day and age to accept that a father could have so much influence on a thirty-year-old woman, but such were the times along with Fanny's love and respect for her father.

Things came to a head when Mrs. Thrale finished nursing her daughter Sophia through a serious illness and then had a breakdown. Her friends were concerned for her, and when it was made clear that she was determined to marry Piozzi, they relented and he eventually left Italy to come to England to marry Hester. He seemed in no hurry however, and his delay and threadbare excuses for the delay disgusted her friends. They eventually married at the end of July, 1784, but then, despite the fact that Fanny had been one of the few people to support her, Hester Thrale even describing Fanny as 'Her sweet friend', Hester was to deliver a body blow to Fanny. In a letter Fanny wrote to Queeney fourteen years later, she said:-

"Mrs. Thrale bore all my opposition – which was regularly the strongest the upmost efforts of my stretched faculties could give – with a gentleness, nay a deference the most touching to me – till the marriage was over – and then – to my never ending astonishment, in return to the constrained and painful letter I forced myself to write of my good wishes – she sent me a cold, frigid reproachful answer, in entirely a new style to any I had ever received from her, to upbraid me that 'my congratulations were not hearty!' As if I could write 'congratulations' at all! Or meant to write! How gross must have been such hypocrisy!"

Dr. Johnson had raged against the marriage while Dr. Burney, although more constrained, was also against it. Some of Mrs. Thrale's other friends did far less than Fanny in supporting the marriage, but it seemed that Fanny's inability to write a hypocritical and insincere letter of total support cost her her friendship with Hester Thrale. This lack of support from Hester came at a difficult time for Fanny. She was still mourning the loss of Crisp, was worried about her beloved sister Susan, and trying to support the ailing Dr. Johnson, who nevertheless, felt neglected by his friends. In the end, Dr. Johnson refused to see Hester Thrale, even when he was close to death although Fanny tried to bring them together. Johnson eventually died on 13th December, 1784.

Whilst Hester Thrale was suffering her emotional turmoil through her relationship with Piozzi, Fanny herself was going through an emotionally difficult time as well. She had fallen in love with a cleric, a one George Cambridge. She met him at the so-called Blue Stocking Club, which consisted of meetings run by Elizabeth Vesey, who was the wife of the rather eccentric MP, Agmondesham Vesey. People who attended on a regular basis were Mrs. Garrick, Edmund Burke, Joshua Reynolds, and Horace Walpole. Mrs. Vesey attempted to make these gatherings informal, and instead of the chairs being arranged in one circle, they were placed in different groupings so there was always more than one discussion group in progress at any one time. Richard Owen Cambridge and George Cambridge were father and son, and were often at the Blue Stocking meetings when Fanny was there. It was this club that Hester Thrale attended from time to time but had found its discussions tedious and pretentious. One of the things that Fanny admired about George Cambridge was the fact that he never spoke to Fanny about her novels - she was still very private about her work. A complication set in however, when Fanny and her parents were invited to the Twickenham home of Richard Owen Cambridge who monopolised Fanny in conversation about her book *Cecilia*, and many of her friends began to think that a romance was actually beginning to happen between Fanny and the elder Cambridge. Eventually however, events proved otherwise and the slow courtship of Fanny by George took place over a period of time. Rather a long period of time as it happened. Months turned into years although Fanny was still convinced that a proposal of marriage would eventually be forthcoming.

They got on well, laughed at the same things and even finished each other's sentences like a couple who'd been married for years. Time went on and on without a proposal however, and Fanny hung on to the belief or possibly kidded herself that it was his sensitivity that was holding him back. However, Fanny felt that she could not bring matters to a head and so the situation continued. Over the years Fanny became totally confused as to what his feelings exactly were. Sometimes she thought him highly insensitive and was perhaps being cynical and deceitful towards her, other times she chided herself for thinking that and decided that the fault was perhaps hers, and that she had misinterpreted his politeness. Eventually, Fanny bowed to the inevitable, and realising that no proposal would ever take place, accepted the situation and tried to keep out of George Cambridge's way, although this wasn't always possible.

It was about this time that Fanny became friendly with Mrs. Delaney. Mrs. Delaney was from another age, she had been born in 1700 and was therefore more than fifty years older than Fanny. She was the widow of Jonathan Swift's friend, Dr. Patrick Delaney. Mrs. Delaney reminded Fanny of her own grandmother, Frances Sleepe, and a deep friendship blossomed between the pair. Mrs. Delaney was an amateur artist, and she specialised in decoupage, embroidery, and shell work. Edmund Burke once described her as: "a pattern of a perfect fine lady, a real fine lady, of other days". Mrs. Delaney's friend, the Duchess of Portland, died soon after Fanny got to know Mrs. Delaney, and this drew them ever closer. It was Mrs. Delaney who gave Fanny her first introduction to the Royal family, because when Mrs. Delaney became ill, the Queen offered her a pension of £300 per year plus a grace-and-favour house in St. Alban's Street in Windsor which was opposite the main gate of the castle which she shared with her great niece, Miss Mary Ann Port. The Queen visited Mrs. Delaney at her Windsor house on a regular basis and Mrs. Delaney never let the opportunity go by without praising Fanny's talents to the Queen, the obvious intention being that she was hoping the Queen would grant Fanny an audience although Fanny was very nervous at the prospect. Despite, or perhaps because she was a great royalist, Fanny's meeting with the King and Queen nearly didn't take place. Once, when Fanny was visiting Mrs. Delaney at Windsor, the Queen made an unscheduled appearance, and instead of seizing her chance, Fanny simply fled the room. She ran to her own room where she was staying and wrote later that she was:- "Quite breathless between the race I ran with Miss Port and the joy of escaping". She did not escape for long however, as on another occasion, Fanny was visiting along with a Mr. Dewes who was Mrs. Delaney's nephew, and Miss Port, when a figure walked in who Fanny initially didn't recognise. It was the King and this time a terrified Fanny simply couldn't escape. Over the coming months, Fanny met the Royal couple on a regular basis and began to relax in their company as the meetings were always informal and took place at Mrs. Delaney's apartments. Fanny liked the Royal couple and knowing how pleased her family would be at such a connection, she would write regular reports to them. On one occasion she wrote of the King:-

"He speaks his opinions without reserve, and seems to trust them intuitively to his hearers, from a belief they will make no ill use of them. His countenance is full of inquiry, to gain information without asking it, probably from believing that to be the nearest road to truth".

There was one strange encounter with the King however, when he wished to question Fanny on how *Evelina* was written. His speech was disjointed and quick and Fanny had a job of both keeping a straight face and understanding what on earth it was that he was talking about. When he was animated his questions would be delivered in quick fire succession and he would keep saying "What what?" which would confuse and sometime almost frighten the person to whom the questions were addressed, and Fanny was no exception. However, she managed to cope on this occasion and the King did not seem to notice her extreme nervousness.

Fanny's contacts with the Royal family were not lost on Dr. Burney. At the age of sixty he was still ambitious, and although he had been organist of Chelsea College since 1783, the position that he really coveted was that of Master of the King's Band. The most recent holder of the post, John Stanley, died in 1785 and Burney was certain that he was a front-runner for the job. He had already presented the King with a beautifully bound copy of the 1784 Commemoration of Handel knowing full well that Handel was the King's favourite composer, and he thought that this would help his cause. In May 1786, Lemuel Smelt, who was once deputy-governor to the royal princes, advised Dr. Burney to make sure that he was seen by the Royal couple by appearing on The Terrace at Windsor – it was where the royal couple would often walk. However, on the occasion that he walked there with Fanny, he was utterly demoralised when it was Fanny that the King and Queen favoured with conversation, Dr. Burney himself was largely ignored much to Fanny's embarrassment and he was devastated when a few weeks later, Smelt asked for a private interview with Fanny. The Queen had formed a favourable opinion of Fanny and was offering her a place at Court, with apartments and a salary of £200 per annum. These positions were sought after by thousands of people and Smelt was astonished when Fanny's face fell – she simply did not want to do it. It meant the loss of her independence that meant so much to her and she wasn't sure whether she would have time to write any more. Smelt made it plain that it was just possible to refuse but she was worried about how it would affect her father and whether it would hinder any possible future preferment for him. She wrote to Charlotte Cambridge for advice, no doubt in a roundabout way of letting George Cambridge know of her dilemma in the hope that he may yet propose marriage, thus giving her a get out from the royal offer. However, it was the possible adverse affect on her father that made her, very reluctantly, accept the post. She was to be the Second Keeper of the Robes, and the appointment was carried out with the greatest speed – she was in the post within a month. Both Mrs. Delaney and Dr. Burney were delighted at Fanny's new status but both were totally unaware of the misery that it would cause her. Mrs. Delaney's delight was probably the more honourable of the two as she thought Fanny would genuinely be pleased, but Dr. Burney, a committed monarchist, was probably more pleased for himself and any future advantage it may hold for him. When Thomas Babington Macaulay (1800-59), the noted author, historian and parliamentarian, wrote his essay on Fanny many years later, he was scathing about Dr. Burney and found his love of monarchy left him lacking as a parent. Macaulay wrote:-

"Charles Burney seems to have thought that going to Court was like going to heaven; that to see the princes and princesses was a kind of beatific vision; that the exquisite felicity enjoyed by royal persons was not confined to themselves, but was communicated by some mysterious efflux or reflection to all who were suffered to stand at their toilettes, or to bear their trains".

Macaulay, whose political leanings were towards the Whig party, was never going to be a great monarchist at the best of times, but regardless of that, he was clearly not a great admirer of Dr. Burney as a parent. He was also to write that Charles Burney was:- "as bad a father as a very honest, affectionate, and sweet-tempered man can well be".

Damning opinions indeed, but Fanny was always blind to her father's faults, and would do anything to please him and was prepared to put up with the inevitable misery that was to follow for the sake of his happiness.

At this time, she still harboured feelings for George Cambridge and hoped that he would yet save her from what was to lie ahead, but nothing was heard from him, and she had to bow to the inevitable, that he didn't care for her in the way that she hoped and that a life of drudgery at Court lay ahead of her. Although it was small, the one consolation of not hearing from George Cambridge did mean that it saved her the inevitable feelings of guilt that she would have had concerning her father if she had turned the royal offer down, but it did mean that not only was she heading for a life that would hold no joy for her, but her feelings of rejection from Cambridge surfaced once more.

As Second Keeper of The Queens's Robes, Fanny was required to wait on the Queen three times daily starting at 6am. Half the time she had nothing to do, and the boredom was exceeded only by her intense dislike of her immediate superior, Mrs. Schwellenberg. Mrs. Schwellenberg had spent all her life at Court and was a powerful figure, even though many of the equerries lampooned her behind her back. Although Fanny was given a drawing room and bedroom, she had little privacy and time to herself as Mrs. Schwellenberg expected her to act as a companion to her when they were not working. Apart from being in the company of someone who she detested and who so obviously detested her, it meant that she had no time to write. Added to the fact that she was hardly allowed out of Court, and then only with the permission of the Queen, a more miserable existence could hardly be imagined for an independently minded woman such as Fanny. The occasional visit to Mrs. Delaney provided a welcome but limited respite from her misery. Welcome because she loved Mrs. Delaney but limited because she couldn't express her feelings to Mrs. Delaney as she had been so pleased at Fanny's appointment. However, even Mrs. Delaney expressed her anger and concern at Mrs. Schwellenberg's rudeness to Fanny but was powerless to act on her feelings. It did not help that the household was an unhappy one. George III and Queen Charlotte ran a strict house and the princesses feared their mother and resented the restrictions imposed upon them. The sons, the Prince of Wales (the future George IV) and the Duke of York, simply ran amok and caused their parents much heartache with their fast living, gambling, and their alignment to Whig politics.

Fanny was there on sufferance and simply didn't fit in at all. The equerries and the ladies-in-waiting were all recruited from the aristocracy and Fanny had nothing whatsoever in common with any of them. Not only that, but she made no secret of the fact that she had no interest in anything they had to say when she was forced to take tea with them, and they found her dull company. After six months of this torture, she was told by the princesses reader, Monsieur de Guiffardiere, that she had seen virtually all there was to see at Court, and whilst this was meant to put Fanny at her ease, it had quite the opposite effect and made her realise just what tedium lay ahead for her in the years to come. There was some light relief when in 1787, Mrs. Schwellenberg who suffered from asthma, stayed in London for some months, and the relations between Fanny and the equerries eased and she began to feel more relaxed in their company. However, although she was now more relaxed at Court, a big blow for Fanny was to happen in the spring of 1788 when Mrs. Delaney died. She was 87 years old and had lived a long life, but this was no consolation to Fanny who dreaded Court life without her company to ease it. Added to this, the King showed the first signs of the mental illness that was to dog him for the rest of his life. Fanny started writing to try and escape the stress of it all, and began to write a tragic drama which was to become *Edwy and Elgiva*. She wrote with little enthusiasm however and this was reflected in the quality of the work. When it was finally produced at the Drury Lane Theatre in March, 1795, it was taken off after one night only although much of this was due to the poor quality of the acting rather than Fanny's writing.

The pain of losing Mrs. Delaney along with suffering the consequences of the King's illness drew Fanny closer to one of the equerries, Colonel Stephen Digby who had left Court for some while to help nurse his wife through her last fatal illness. As chance would have it, his late wife was Lady Lucy Fox Strangeways who had taken the young Fanny under her wing when Fanny's mother had died. This drew Colonel Digby and Fanny closer together and they shared a great deal of time in each other's company. When the Royal party left for Kew where it was felt that the King would have a better chance of recovery, Digby's presence gave Fanny a great deal of comfort through this phase and he spent a great deal of time in Fanny's room reading her poetry whilst she carried on with her needlework. They were noticed by people and were seen by some as almost behaving like a couple who had been married for years.

The King was attended by many doctors, none of whom had the first clue as to what was wrong with him and were therefore unable to treat him successfully. Eventually, a Dr. Francis Willis was brought down from Lincoln to effect a cure. Willis had specialised in mental illness before with some success and was confident he could cure the King and make the probability of a Regency that Pitt, the Prime Minister was desperate to avoid, unnecessary. Apart from anything else, if the Prince of Wales was given the power of Regent, it was pretty clear that he would get rid of Pitt and bring in Charles James Fox to be Prime Minister, and that there would be a Whig administration. In the event, this was proven to be unnecessary - just. Willis's treatments were hard and brutal, and whilst we now know that the King would probably have recovered despite Willis, he was given the credit along with a great deal of money and the crisis was averted for the moment. Knowledge acquired in recent years tells us that the King was almost certainly suffering from porphyria, a rare hereditary disorder that brings on severe abdominal pains, discoloured urine and a temporary mental derangement which certainly would have made 18th century doctors think the King was mad. The only person who gained out of this very sad episode was Dr. Willis, who earned a great deal of money for treatment given that was almost certainly completely useless. However, porphyria was not known about at the time and the illness came back to haunt the Royal Family over the years, and eventually the Prince of Wales became Regent in 1811 before finally taking the throne as George IV in 1820 when the King died.

Eventually, in 1791, Fanny's five years of torture ended when she finally plucked up the courage to first tell her father that she was unhappy, and then tell the Queen that she wanted to leave. She had also confided her feelings to her beloved Susan, and several of her friends had begun to notice how frail and ill she looked. Another blow that made her ill was Colonel Digby's lack of interest in her and subsequent proposal of marriage to Charlotte Gunning, one of the maids of honour, who was also extremely rich. After rejection by George Cambridge, for the thirty-nine-year-old Fanny, this second rejection was the final humiliation.

Although she had been terrified at the thought of telling her father, he was in fact very sympathetic and understanding when she finally told him at the annual Handel Commemoration in May 1790, and he was in fact quite upset as he had long suspected that all was not well, but had not said anything to Fanny. He had begun to realise, that although unwittingly, he had been a major part of the cause of her unhappiness. It was many months before Fanny plucked up courage to tell the Queen but in the event, the Queen didn't seem to take it seriously and nothing was done. In June, 1791, Fanny was still at Court, but becoming increasingly unwell, and resorted to taking hartshorn, opium, and some unspecified medicine concocted by Dr. Willis. She was weak and debilitated and had difficulty breathing. On 7th July, 1791, the Queen finally accepted her resignation and she left court almost five years to the day that she had started. Although very relieved at the huge weight that had been lifted from her shoulders, she was still a little sad, although that sadness soon receded as her health began to improve. She returned to Chelsea College and her father set up a desk for her in his study. He had finished his lengthy *History of Music* and he was more relaxed about sharing his space.

Meanwhile, the revolution in France had taken place in 1789 and it was in the summer of 1792 that she met a group of French aristocrats who were living in a large rented house which was called Juniper Hall at the foot of Box Hill near Mickleham, where Susan lived. Amongst those staying at Juniper Hall was a thirty-eight-year-old soldier called Alexandre dArblay who had served in the army as an adjutant-general to La Fayette, a hero of the revolution. D'Arblay had made his way to London via Holland and then Harwich. He'd had a long career in the army although it has to be said that it was largely undistinguished. He lacked the drive needed to get on but was sensitive and had a charm about him. Although it's probable that Fanny fell in love with him from the beginning, Dr. Burney was less willing to show any sympathy whatsoever towards the Frenchman, especially as war was likely to break out at any minute. Despite opposition from Dr. Burney however, the couple were married on 28th July 1793 and on 18th December 1794, Fanny gave birth to their one and only son, a boy that they christened Alexander, although he was always referred to as Alex.

D'Arblay was a nice man but the possibility of his earning a living in England were virtually nil. It was left to Fanny to bring in some money and it was to this end that she finished off writing the novel *Camilla* in 1794 which was finally published in 1796. She made £1,000 from the sale of the first edition and sold the copyright for another £1,000 and this staved off their immediate financial problems. In that year they had a house built in West Humble which was fairly near Norbury Park. They moved in during October 1797 – the house was built but they had no furniture except a bench left by the carpenters. D'Arblay was hopeless with the management of money, and his estimate of £1,300 as being the cost of building was exceeded. In fact, for that sum they could have purchased the freehold of a larger house.

Fanny was always concerned about her husband's ideas or rather the lack of them concerning the management of money, and so she started writing again, this time producing a comedy play entitled *Love and Fashion*. She was to write a further two by 1801, the first entitled *A Busy Day* and the second, *A Woman Hater*.

Before these latter two pieces of work however, the Burney family were to go through two traumas, the death of their stepmother, Elizabeth Allen Burney, in late 1796, and a scandal caused by her brother James and their half sister Sarah Harriet.

Already concerned about the state of Susan's marriage to Molesworth Philips and what it was doing to Susan's health, the stepmother that none of them liked took a turn for the worse in the summer of 1796, suffering a lung haemorrhage. In September she was confined to her bed, and she died on 20th October aged seventy-one. Fanny had very mixed emotions on the matter. On the one hand, she almost saw it as a matter of rejoicing so little did she care about her step mother, but on seeing how it affected her father who was devastated, she had to face up to the fact that her stepmother had in fact made Dr. Burney happy for nearly thirty years, marrying as they did in 1767. Worried sick though she was about her father who she worshipped, she could not bring herself to feel any sorrow about the passing of Mrs. Elizabeth Allen Burney.

During all this time, James was becoming more and more estranged from his wife Sally and in September, 1798, asked his father if he could live with him. This was met with an immediate refusal and the next day James left his wife to run away with his half sister, Sarah Harriet, the daughter of Charles, James's father, and his step mother, Elizabeth Allen Burney who had recently died. The assumption was of course, that they were lovers and therefore committing incest which naturally horrified the family, none more so than the prim and proper Fanny. This assumption lasted for many years until it was called into question by a Lorna J. Clark who edited Sarah Harriet's letters. Clark put forward a less sensational theory – that the two were simply soul mates and drawn together by James's feeling of being suffocated and restricted by family life, along with Sarah Harriet's need to escape from her tedious life at Chelsea. Whatever the truth of the matter, Sally Burney, James's wife, took him back happily in 1804 and both Sally and Sarah Harriet got on well afterwards. James and Sarah Harriet continued to get on well also, which lends credence to the theory that there was no passion there, but merely a meeting of minds. It is unlikely that we shall ever know for certain however.

Meanwhile, d'Arblay continued to dream his dreams. He harboured a desire to return to France with a view to serving in the army and receiving a pension followed by an honourable discharge. Prior to d'Arblay leaving for France however, Fanny's beloved sister Susan died, on 6th January 1800. Susan had been living in Ireland with her husband and seventeen-year-old daughter Fanny, and their eight-year-old son William. The elder Fanny and the rest of her family knew that the marriage of Susan and Molesworth Philips was unhappy and that Susan's health was very poor. They were desperate for her to come back to London so that they could look after her but Philips always prevaricated. Eventually, in the autumn of 1799, he relented and Susan started her journey from Ireland in December. Fanny's brother Charles and his son, Charles Parr Burney set out to meet Susan, and after a mix-up of where they were to meet, eventually found her in Parkgate on 2nd January, 1800. Charles was shocked at her appearance – the family had no idea as to just how ill Susan was. She died on 6th January, the day after her 45th birthday and before Fanny could reach her. In fact, the funeral took place on the 10th before Fanny knew of the death, and Charles was the only family mourner there. Fanny had written to her father on the 9th on the assumption that she would see Susan in the near future so it was a note full of happiness. She was devastated, and she later described the note to her father thus:-

"These were the last written lines of the last period – unsuspected as such! – of my perfect happiness on earth."

So the new century started with great sadness for Fanny, but her one consolation was that she was in a truly happy marriage to Alexandre d'Arblay, a man who daydreamed his way through life which meant that Fanny had to be the practical one, but a man who made her happy nonetheless.

In 1801, d'Arblay travelled to France and after many requests, was offered a post by Napoleon, which was to lead a force to Haiti to quash the rebellion of the Negro slave leader, Touissant-L'Ouveture. This did not please Fanny as she was concerned that her husband would come to harm, but she also had sympathy with the cause of the slaves. Nonetheless, d'Arblay was determined to do it and came home to England at the beginning of 1802 and spent a small fortune kitting himself out with a lavish uniform. He returned to France, but when he informed Napoleon that despite being in the army, he would never fight against his wife's country, Napoleon immediately cancelled his commission. D'Arblay felt that he had been disgraced, but there was nothing that he could do about it. He lost out all ways, as his passport had been issued with the assumption that he would be a serving army officer, and it meant that he couldn't return to England and his wife and child for another year. Despairing of such a separation, Fanny packed some of her belongings, and with their eight-year-old son Alex, bade a sad farewell to her family and left to join her husband in France. She was expecting the separation to be no more than eighteen months at the most, and expected to return to England in October 1803. However, in May 1803, the decision was taken out of her hands when war was declared again on England on 16th May, 1803 after the short lived peace Treaty of Amiens. Napoleon decreed that all English adults between the ages of eighteen and sixty-years-old were to be considered prisoners of war, and therefore unable to leave the country. In the event, Fanny and Alex were to stay in France for a total of ten years.

Fanny was desperately homesick, and news was always difficult, both to send to her family, and to receive any from them. It seems extraordinary, but she didn't hear about Nelson's victory at Trafalgar until 1812, seven years after the battle. However, they settled down to a life in France and enjoyed a varied social circle whilst they were there. In fact, d'Arblay was so pleased with his wife's ability to make friends, that he foresaw a future whereby they would spend part of the year in France, and part in England. However, before any decision concerning where they were going to live could take place, something horrific was to develop in Fanny's eventful life that was quite shocking. She had had a large lump in her right breast that over the years had grown into the size of a fist. The doctors, without any examination of the breast, decided that it was cancer, and that the only cure was a mastectomy which would have to be carried out without an anaesthetic which was not available in the early 19th century. The operation was carried out on 30th September, 1811 and Fanny records it in her diary with the most excruciating detail – to this day it makes difficult reading. There were two mattresses to soak up the blood and she was attended by no less than seven doctors. From the first agonising cut, to the end whereby the scraping of the breast-bone is described, Fanny leaves nothing out. Given her delicate state of health generally, it seems a miracle that she survived the operation at all. Given also, that she'd endured the lump for several years before the mastectomy, and lived another twenty-nine years after it, one must wonder if in fact, she'd ever had cancer in the first place.

Fanny was keen to go home to England for a holiday, and as soon as she started to recover from her horrific operation, she and her son Alex set off on 14th August, 1812, and despite some difficulty caused by the calm weather in the channel, reached Deal in Kent two days later. Eventually, she was re-united with her family and she was overjoyed at seeing them. She became very friendly with William Wilberforce (1759-1833), who along with others, had worked so hard over so many years to get the traffic in slavery stopped, which he succeeded in doing in 1807. She enjoyed her chats with Wilberforce and realised that she had been missing this intellectual stimulation all the while she had been in France. After all the years spent in that country, the only thing of any worth that she felt she had was the partly finished manuscript of *The Wanderer* and she made it a priority to finish the work almost as soon as she returned to England.

Fanny stayed in England a lot longer than she originally planned. Alex, her son, who for so long had excelled in his studies seemed to alter and became lazy and sloppy in his work. Fanny was also worried about Dr. Burney's failing health. There was also the fate of her husband to worry about. There was an armistice between France and England and her allies in June 1813, but as it was, this lasted only two months. However, in February 1814, the allies were rapidly reaching Paris, and two months later the joyful news reached London that Napoleon had abdicated on 11th April and was banished to Elba. Napoleon's surrender brought relief to millions, although amongst this joy was sadness for Fanny as her father died two days later – if he had lived another two weeks, he would have reached the age of eighty-eight years. Fanny was devastated – she worshipped her father and many years later in 1832, had her *Memoirs of Dr. Burney* published, although due to what many people thought was the hyperbolic praise lavished on him, they were greeted with almost universal scorn.

Dr. Burney's will did not share everything equally between his children, indeed, there were such differences in the amounts left that it caused arguments between them all, the last thing that Fanny had wanted to happen after not seeing her family for so long. James in particular, felt very hard done by and wondered whether it was some sort of punishment for his rather stuttering naval career, and probably more importantly, the relationship that he had once had with his half sister, Sarah Harriet.

D'Arblay, on hearing of Dr. Burney's death, travelled back to England as quickly as he could. Peace had been officially declared on 30th May, 1814 and Napoleon had been banished, seemingly for ever to Elba. D'Arblay who was continually asking for work returned to France in June after just one month in England and was finally made an officer in The Garde du Corps by Louis XVIII, who was the brother of the murdered Louis XVI. D'Arblay was delighted, but his rank of Sub-Lieutenant was rather low, his pay was small, and The Garde du Corps were not rated highly by their brother officers. D'Arblay returned to England again in October 1814, and the following month, he and Fanny returned to France whilst Alex was left in England. They were expecting a future together of peace and happiness, but two things went wrong from the word go. D'Arblay was involved in an accident that had far reaching effects on his health – when approaching a horse that was eating oats in the stables, he received a kick in the right leg that was so severe it caused the leg to become infected. D'Arblay contracted a fever but fortunately recovered although his leg was never quite the same for the rest of his life. Much more seriously than that however, news came through that Napoleon had escaped from Elba and had re-entered France with a small army. D'Arblay expected to be called to fight Napoleon and Fanny was shocked at the change of character that d'Arblay exhibited once he was in uniform. This gentle, mild mannered man seemed to turn into a monster who would seemingly stop at nothing in terms of cruelty once he stepped out of his civilian clothes. As it happened, on 18th June, 1815, The Duke of Wellington beat the French forces on the fields of Waterloo, and Napoleon was finished, the war now finally over.

Napoleon abdicated on 22nd June, four days after Waterloo, and decided to put himself at the mercy of the British. He surrendered to Captain Maitland of *The Bellerophon* on 15th July, and was taken to England where for some reason best known to himself, fondly believed that the British would welcome him with open arms and allow him to live the life of a country gentleman. Given the millions of deaths that he had caused, this seemed an extraordinary hope during an era that had hung people for stealing a sheep. In the event, he was banished to St. Helena, where he lived until his death on 5th May 1821, either from stomach cancer or liver disease.

Meanwhile, with the war over, Fanny and her husband decided to return to England which they did on 17th October, 1815, arriving at Deal. They set up home in Great Stanhope Street in fashionable Bath and found that there were old friends living in the city. Mrs. Piozzi (Mrs. Thrale), by now a widow, was living close by, but when she and Fanny met, she was still unfriendly to Fanny. Mrs. Piozzi sold off the contents of Streatham Park in 1816, and included in the sale were copies of *Evelina* and *Cecilia* that Fanny had given to her. All the portraits by Joshua Reynolds that she had, including the picture of Dr. Burney, were also sold off. It must have been a hurtful time for Fanny and killed the friendship off completely, something that Fanny had hoped to avoid.

D'Arblay returned to France in the summer of 1817 for what he hoped would be an annual visit. Fanny had a great excuse to stay in England, although she hated being parted from her husband because she felt that she needed to keep an eye on their son Alex, who was approaching his finals, but was doing virtually nothing in terms of study. He wasn't doing anything at all in fact as his behaviour was very lethargic and he seemed very depressed all the time. His symptoms suggested some sort of drug addiction and this is quite possible as his father was almost certainly taking some sort of opiate for his by now chronic bowel pain and so there would have been some available in the household. Fanny too had been taking laudanum at different times, notably when she was recovering from her mastectomy and also when she was sickly at Court. Another feasible explanation for Alex's behaviour is that he was possibly an alcoholic which could also explain his listlessness and lack of interest in study. 1817 wasn't a good period for Fanny. There began a death in the family that was to precede other family deaths that made life hard for her. Her sister Charlotte who had married Ralph Broome in 1798 lost her son, also called Ralph at the age of fifteen. Ralph senior had been her second husband and she had lost him in 1805. People were struck by the seemingly calm way she handled the loss of the younger Ralph and it can only be put down to the fact that she was deeply religious and simply saw it as God's will. There were also differences in the family. In 1816, Fanny had composed the epitaph that was to go on Dr. Burney's memorial in Westminster Abbey. Charlotte's daughters, Marianne Francis and Charlotte Barrett were deeply religious like their mother and Marianne in particular objected to the wording which she felt put too much emphasis on his worldly achievements which were to be carved on what she saw was a sacred memorial. Marianne and Charlotte were Fanny's nieces, but her brothers, Charles junior and James also had strong reservations about what they saw as gross hyperbole when describing Dr. Burney's principles and achievements. Fanny was shocked at such criticism as she had not been subject to it from her own family before, but she defended herself vigorously although in the end she had to agree to some changes. Charles himself was the next family member to die. For many years, he had been a hard drinker, and after complaining for some time of pains in the head, finally died of a stroke just after Christmas, 1817. He left a huge collection of classical books, and his son, Charles Parr Burney, had intended to write a memoir about his father, but scrapped the idea when for the first time, he found out about the extent of the books that his father had stolen in his youth from Cambridge. The collection was sold for £13,500, an enormous sum in those days, and questions were certainly asked as to how a clerical schoolmaster on a relatively low income could amass 'probably the most complete (classical library) ever assembled by any man'.

That same year, 1817, d'Arblay had returned to England from France and his appearance shocked Fanny. He was thin, clearly unwell, was depressed and in a lot of pain. Along with Fanny, he had an audience with Queen Charlotte in December of that year but could barely stand. As soon as the audience with the

Queen had finished, he slumped into a chair, exhausted, in pain, and was unable to do virtually anything for the rest of the day. At a later date, Fanny wrote the experience up as if she had never seen inside the Court before and it does her little credit that she wrote more about the 'graciousness of the Queen' than she did of d'Arblay, who was in dreadful agony throughout the audience. Fanny hadn't meant to be unkind about her husband who she had always loved dearly, but like her father before her, she simply believed in 'The Divine Right of Kings' – nothing else could explain her behaviour. She was also refusing to believe just how ill d'Arblay was but eventually believed him in January, 1818, when he insisted on seeing a surgeon, but by now there was nothing to be done. He received the last rites and died on 3rd May, 1818 with Fanny and their son Alex by his side. Even then, it was only when the death was confirmed by the doctor, Mr. Tudor, that she finally accepted it. So it was that in a short space of time, Fanny lost her nephew, Ralph Broome, her brother Charles, and now, and worst of all for her, her beloved husband, the kind gentle Alexandre d'Arblay.

Fanny remained in Bath only a few months after d'Arblay's death and in September 1818 she and her son Alex moved to London to 11, Bolton Street, a quiet street off Piccadilly. Fanny's life went into a decline after her husband's death and her life was limited to visiting close friends who lived within easy travelling distance. She also visited her sisters, Charlotte and Hetty who also lived within a reasonable distance, but these outings were rare and she often cancelled when the slightest excuse offered itself.

In 1821, another blow was to hit Fanny. Her brother James, who had recently been promoted to Rear-Admiral, died very suddenly in November of that year. The rank had sounded good, but James had had a short and fairly undistinguished career since his two voyages with Cook, and had been retired for many years. His death meant the re-appearance of an unwelcome person in the form of Major Molesworth-Philips, the marine who had served with James on Cook's third trip and who had stayed friendly with him over the years. This showed remarkable loyalty on the part of James, given Molesworth-Philips's poor treatment of James's sister, Susan, throughout their marriage. It was in fact, Philips who organised the funeral and he was the main mourner, the sisters not attending.

Fanny was now being seen as the elder stateswoman of the family, and as she grew older, her social life quietened down. She was very worried about Alex, who was attempting a career in the church. George Cambridge, who in earlier years, Fanny thought she may marry, tried to help Alex get on, but he seemed lazy and disinterested. In 1824, he was eventually given an appointment as a curate at the new Camden Chapel and the Cambridges were with Fanny when Alex was due to preach the inaugural sermon at the consecration of the chapel. Even for a day as important as this, Alex was late and caused his mother deep distress by arriving at the last minute. This pattern followed, and he would often leave the preparation of his sermons to the very last minute, sometimes staying up the entire night before.

Despite Alex's behaviour, the 1820's were fairly happy years for Fanny, as she had the company of her sister Charlotte, and Charlotte's daughters and granddaughters. As mentioned earlier, Fanny wrote her father's memoirs as a result of her having heard that the publishers of Chalmers *General Biographical Dictionary* were intending to include an article on Dr. Burney in their next volume. Fanny wanted to be the first to write about him, and so she started work on her famous or depending on how you view it, infamous *The Memoirs of Dr. Burney*. Fanny went through her father's manuscripts, and by simply destroying what she thought would be harmful to include, produced a piece of work that was met with universal scorn by just about everybody. It made the doctor into an almost saint-like figure which he most certainly wasn't, and Fanny must have been aware of this, as she considered delaying publishing until after her death. Although Fanny must have been aware that much of this work was ridiculous, she carried on deluding herself, as in the closing pages, she apologises for the potential dullness of her father's perfection. Fanny may have convinced herself of this, but if she did, she was the only one who was. The book was published in 1832, and sadly tarnished her reputation, but although it meant that the year was not a good one for Fanny, she did find herself having a closer relationship with her sister Charlotte.

One more blow was to hit Fanny however, the death of her son Alex. His whole life seemed to be a story of wasted opportunities. We can now assume that he suffered from a severe form of depression, but there was nothing much that could be done for him in the early 19th century. He went missing from his jobs causing his parishioners to despair. He had a brief engagement to a very nice girl called Mary Ann Smith of Crooms Hill, Greenwich, and she remained very patient throughout Alex's absences. She and Fanny got on well and Mary Ann was a support to Fanny when Alex finally left his job and was appointed minister of Ely chapel, now known as St. Ethelreda's, and situated in Holborn. During Christmas, 1836, Alex went down with a high fever and a few weeks later his situation became far worse. His strange behaviour lasted until the very end, as he requested that his mother did not attend his bedside. As a result, he died alone, in his bed on 19th January, 1837, a desperately sad Fanny being in another room in the same house. She was by now eighty-four years old, and it is hard to think of a situation that could be worse for a mother to find herself in.

There was one more terrible bereavement that Fanny had to face before her own life was to come to an end. Her sister Charlotte, to whom she had become close, was visiting her from Brighton from where she had travelled in the summer of 1838. A short time later however, Charlotte was taken ill, and died on 12th September 1838 aged seventy-six years. Ill herself, suffering pain from the breast area where she had had the mastectomy, virtually blind, and very depressed, Fanny now had little to live for, and in the summer of 1839, her health relapsed and she had to stay in bed. Her family gathered round as they thought that she was going to die at any time, but although bed-ridden, she seemed to rally, and whether it was will power or co-incidence, she hung on and finally died in London on 6th January, 1840, forty years to the day since her beloved sister Susan passed away. Fanny lies buried at St. Swithin's, Walcot, Bath next to her husband and son.

It is almost impossible to sum Fanny Burney up in a few words or with phrases that have any consistency – she was many things to many people. She has been remembered first and foremost as a novelist and playwright – to many people the forerunner of today's female novelists. She certainly heavily influenced the great Jane Austen who was born twenty-three years later to the extent that Austen's most famous and best loved book, *Pride and Prejudice* almost certainly owes its very title to a phrase that crops up from time to time in Fanny's novel, *Cecilia*. Her diaries have been criticised for showing her to be self absorbed, but all diaries carry that risk if they are to correctly record the author's thoughts. Although criticised for being self absorbed and for not listening to others in conversation, she was loved by the younger ones in her family in later years for keeping them interested in the stories of her life. She was someone who ached for solitude and yet had to give up her independence for five years while she became Second Keeper of the Queen's Robes, a post she reluctantly accepted and held for five long years for her father's sake and which left her with almost no privacy until her health started to fail. Her writing, that was so important to her, almost disappeared during this period – certainly the quality wasn't as good. Her love and devotion to her father which in the normal run of things would be praised, rebounded on Fanny when she wrote her hopelessly biased *Memoirs of Dr. Burney* and which was heavily criticised. Despite her love of solitude, she had a need for love which resulted in her marriage to the French soldier, Alexandre d'Arblay in later life, and her role as a mother to a much troubled son. Finally, it must always be remembered the incredible bravery she showed before and during the horrifying ordeal of the mastectomy carried out in 1811 without anaesthetic – a most dreadful experience written up in all its dreadful detail in her diaries, although she has been criticised for the way that was written too.

There is a saying that the teacher is eventually bettered by the pupil, and certainly her admirer, Jane Austen, has her work performed more and is better known than the woman who influenced her, Fanny Burney. Perhaps it will always be thus, or perhaps her work will re-emerge, but whatever happens, Fanny deserves her place in history as one of the early and successful female writers.

-oOOo-

Works by Fanny Burney

Fiction:
Evelina – Published 1778
Cecilia - Published 1782
Camilla – Published 1796
The Wanderer – Published 1814

Non Fiction:
Brief Reflections Relative to the French Emigrant Clergy – Published 1793
Memoirs of Dr. Burney – Published 1832

Journals and Letters:
The Early Diary of Frances Burney 1768-1778 (2 vols)
The Diary and Letters of Madame D'Arblay 1904
The Diary of Fanny Burney 1971
The Journal and Letters of Fanny Burney (Madame D'Arblay) 1791-1840

Plays:
The Witlings 1779
Edwy and Elgiva 1790
Hubert de Vere 1778-1791
The Seige of Pevensy 1788-1791
Elberta (fragment) 1788-1791
Love and Fashion 1799
The Woman Hater 1800-1801
A Busy Day 1800-1801

5
Dr. Edward Jenner
(1749-1823)

Physician who discovered the cure for the disease of smallpox.

Visitors arriving at Gloucester Cathedral by the main south entrance, on turning immediately left, will see the tall imposing statue of Edward Jenner residing by the west window of this beautiful building.

Some people are struck by the fact that it has but one word on it – 'JENNER'. Most statues have the Christian name of the person and the dates of the birth and death, but when this statue was erected, no other information was needed other than Jenner's surname. Everyone knew that it was Edward Jenner, born in the village of Berkeley in 1749 and who amongst other things, cured the world of the dreaded disease of smallpox. The people who erected the statue clearly felt that his name would be remembered forever, but sadly this is not the case. We take the fact that there is no smallpox for granted today as the World Health Organisation declared officially that smallpox had been eliminated in 1979, but in Jenner's time, it must have been the equivalent of curing cancer today. Ironically, it was Jenner's success in curing smallpox that causes more recent visitors to the cathedral to ask the guides who Jenner was, simply because the subject of smallpox never comes up, therefore neither does his name.

Jenner was a modest man who yearned for the simple life of a country doctor in Berkeley. He was born there on 17th May, 1749 to the Rev. Stephen Jenner and Sarah Jenner (nee Head). Jenner had a friend called the Revd. Thomas Dudley Fosbroke who wrote histories of Cheltenham and Berkeley. The first Jenner that Fosbroke was able to research was Stephen Jenner (1610-1667) who was Edward's great great grandfather. He was a baker by trade and lived in Standish, which was about eight miles from Berkeley. His son was also called Stephen (1645-1727), was also a baker but moved to Slimbridge and lived there until his death in 1727. In 1669 he married a Deborah Davies (c1633-83) and they had six children, one of whom was another Stephen (1672-1728). This was Edward's grandfather and by dying in 1728, he outlived his father by just one year. In 1697, this Stephen, yet another baker, married Mary Davies (1676-1758), the daughter of Thomas and Mary Davies. We do not know whether Mary's father, Thomas, was related to her mother-in-law, Deborah Jenner (nee Davies), but it's quite possible that they were related, even possibly brother and sister which would have made her and her husband Stephen, first cousins. This happened quite often in those days as travelling outside one's immediate district was quite difficult, so it was not uncommon for husbands and wives to be related in this way. Stephen and Mary had at least three children, one of which was called Stephen and this was Edward's father who was born in 1702. This

Stephen broke with the family tradition of being a baker and went to Pembroke College, Oxford to study theology. In 1729, he married Sarah Head (1708-54) who was the daughter of the Revd. Henry and Mary Head. Henry Head was the Prebend of Bristol Cathedral and also vicar of Berkeley. In 1725, Stephen had been appointed as curate to the parish church of Coates although it would have been financially difficult for Stephen and Sarah if he had stayed in that post. In 1728, the Revd. Henry Head died and his post was given to a man called Ralph Webb. Webb however, lasted only a year, and in 1729 Stephen, the future father of Edward, was appointed as Vicar of Berkeley, the extra income enabling him to marry Sarah in that same year.

Edward was a happy young child, but his life got off to a tragic beginning when he was orphaned at the age of five years. First, his mother Sarah died on 10th October, 1754 aged forty-six having given birth to a son, Thomas, who lived just one day being christened on the 8th and buried on the 9th, and tragically, only two months later, on 9th December, his father, Stephen also died aged just fifty-two. Stephen and Sarah had had eight children, six of whom had lived into adult life. Edward's five siblings that survived were: Mary (b.1730), Stephen (b. 1732), Henry (b. 1736), Sarah (b. 1738), and Anne (b. 1741).

After the death of his parents, Edward was looked after by his brother Stephen, and his sisters, Mary, Sarah, and Anne. Even as a young child, Edward loved nature, and he seemed a happy child exploring the surrounding countryside of Berkeley but at the age of eight, he was sent away to Grammar school in Wotton-under-Edge, where he boarded with the headmaster, the Reverend Thomas Clissold. We cannot be sure how the death of his parents affected him as he was so young when they died, and he had plenty of maternal support from his three sisters, but we do know that he was badly affected by his subsequent treatment when an outbreak of smallpox occurred in Wotton-under-Edge during the year that he was sent there. Before Edward's later discovery of a cure for this disease, the standard form of treatment was the inoculation with a small amount of smallpox to a healthy person, hoping that a mild form of smallpox would prevent the patient from getting the full blown disease at a later date. This process was sometimes called 'Variolation' which was a derivation from 'Variola', the Latin word for smallpox. Lady Mary Wortley Montagu (1689-1762), the well-known English writer and society hostess, is credited with bringing the process to England in 1721 having had her first child inoculated in Constantinople a few years before. Lady Mary was born in London and was a daughter of Evelyn Pierrepoint, the 5th Earl of Kingston-upon-Hull who was the younger brother of William, the 4th Earl. She enjoyed a long standing friendship with Anne Wortley Montagu, granddaughter of the 1st Earl Sandwich, and through her, Anne's brother Edward Wortley Montagu. When Anne died in 1709, Mary and Edward became closer and wanted to marry but Lady Mary's father, the 5th Earl of Kingston-upon-Hull who was by now the 1st Marquess of Dorchester refused permission and insisted on Mary marrying another man. As a result of this, Mary and Edward eloped in 1712 and for the first few years of their married life, she spent quietly in a country house but joined her husband in London when he became a Member of Parliament in 1715. In 1716, her husband was appointed Ambassador at Istanbul where Mary joined him. When Lady

Mary was in the Ottoman Empire, she learnt of the practice of inoculation after her brother had died of the smallpox and her own beauty was marred by her catching it herself. She was enthusiastic about inoculation and brought this system of treating smallpox back to England when she returned in 1721. However, there were problems with this procedure which were twofold:- firstly, it was very risky with no guarantee that the person would not die, and secondly, the disease was still being spread leaving millions still at risk.

It was this procedure that Edward, aged just eight, was subjected to with a view to protecting him at a later date. It was not just the fact that he was given the disease that caused him harm, but the preparation period which lasted six weeks. We can quote the words of his future friend, The Reverend Thomas Dudley Fosbroke, to see just how extreme this treatment was:-

"He was bled to ascertain whether his blood was fine; was purged repeatedly, til he became emaciated and feeble; was kept on a very low diet, small in quantity, and dosed with a diet drink to sweeten the blood. After this... he was removed to one of the then inoculation stables, and haltered up with others in a terrible state of disease, although none died. By good fortune, the Doctor escaped with a mild exhibition of the disease".

It is not difficult to see how this coloured Jenner's attitude to how the disease should be treated in later years. It is difficult to understand what good the doctors thought that this dreadful preparatory procedure was doing to the patient – the best scenario is that it did no good at all, whilst the worst scenario was that it did a great deal of harm, and this was certainly the case with young Edward. It took him a long time to get over this barbaric treatment and for many years he found it difficult to sleep and was very nervous when hearing sudden noises. However, he did eventually recover and went on to become one of the most famous doctors with a name and a reputation that resonated throughout the world. However, before we look at his work at a later date, it is necessary to look briefly at the man who was to become such a huge influence on him for the rest of his life, Dr. John Hunter (1728-93).

In the autumn of 1770, Edward travelled to London to commence medical studies under the tutelage of the great John Hunter. Previously, Jenner had spent six years studying under John Ludlow, a surgeon from Chipping Sudbury. Jenner had shown no interest in a classical education at Oxford being far more interested in wildlife and fossils, and so it was decided within the family group that he would be more suited to a career in medicine whilst at the same time staying in the country, and so he was taken under the wing of Mr. Ludlow where he remained until 1769. Although suggestions as to Edward going into medicine could have come from any of his siblings, the final decision would almost certainly have been that of his brother Stephen, who at this stage of his life, was the senior Dean of Arts at Magdalen, and who was effectively Edward's guardian. It was after Edward's six year apprenticeship with John Ludlow, that he went to London to study under Dr. John Hunter (1728-93). Hunter was one of the most famous medical men of his day and to study under this great man must have been a wonderful experience. Much correspondence between the two men who were later to become friends, proved that Hunter held Jenner in high esteem. Hunter and Jenner, originally teacher and pupil, became medical colleagues, and then the best of friends not just because of the fact that Hunter held Jenner in very high regard, but their subsequent friendship was probably also helped by the fact that Hunter's wife Anne, unlike her husband, was very artistic and was a gifted poet, having had some of her words put to music by the Austrian composer, Franz Joseph Haydn (1732-1809). Anne (1742-1821) was originally Anne Home before she married Hunter – her most famous work being 'My mother bids me bind my hair'. She was also a member of the so-called 'Blue Stocking Club', set up by Mary Delany (1700-88), the English lady of letters and conversationalist, and attended by female intellectuals such as Elizabeth Montagu (1720-1800), the English writer and society leader, and Elizabeth Carter (1717-1806), the English scholar and poet. Mrs. Delany also befriended the writer Fanny Burney (1752-1840) and was to play an influential role in that writer's life after Fanny had lost both her mother and maternal grandmother. Fanny's writing was to influence that of Jane Austen in later life and her father Charles Burney (1726-1814) was a famous musician and knew many of the influential people of the day, such as Dr. Johnson (1709-84), the famous writer and creator of his extraordinary dictionary in 1755. Mary Delany was originally Mary Granville but took her name after her second marriage which took place in 1743 to the Revd. Patrick Delany (1685-1768) who was himself a writer and a friend of Jonathan Swift (1667-1745), the Anglo-Irish poet. Apart from her patronage of Fanny Burney, Mary Delany is best remembered for her 'Autobiography and Correspondence' 6 volumes 1861-62.

Anne Home then, mixed with many intellectual women of the day and was very talented herself which meant that she was in no hurry to marry and relinquish her independence to a man in an age where women did not get the vote. The result was that she and John Hunter had a long courtship, seven years in fact, but they were eventually married on 22nd July, 1771. It is not certain, but it is thought that two men who had recently become famous, the botanist, Joseph Banks (1743-1820) and James Cook (1728-79), the naval officer, both recently returned from the latter's first of three famous voyages, attended the wedding. So it was that Edward Jenner and John Hunter had the practical interest of medicine in common, but were also probably drawn closer together by the artistic talents that Edward and Anne shared, because Jenner too was a gifted poet and could also play the flute and violin. Hunter is often referred to as the father of modern surgery although his entry into the world of medicine was unusual. He left school at thirteen and after a spell working as a cabinet maker, he starting helping his brother, Dr. William Hunter (1718-83), the Scottish anatomist and obstetrician, who practiced in London. Under his brother's guidance, John Hunter learned his skills by carrying out a great deal of work on dissections. Before the brothers went into practice, people studying medicine had simply been handed down ideas that emanated from the Greeks, and were expected to accept it without question. Much of what they were taught was quite useless, and sometimes positively dangerous. John Hunter had a different attitude. He wanted statements and ideas proved and so he continually experimented. He cut open live animals during a time when there were no anaesthetics which seems barbaric today, and he also dissected dead human bodies and wasn't always too fussed as to the legality or not of obtaining them.

There were families who quite happily gave their consent to a body of a loved one who had recently died being used, but most people recoiled at the idea and so Hunter had to use other ways of obtaining bodies. The gallows was one source but as the Company of Surgeons was limited to six bodies a year for dissection, he and others had to use yet more means of getting the remains of recently deceased people. One such source would have been none too scrupulous undertakers, and there were also professional body snatchers who scoured the graveyards of London during the night in order to dig up a newly buried body before morning. It seems gruesome to us these days, but it was the only way for him at the time, and as a result, Hunter dissected thousands over the years and his knowledge of anatomy was vast. Jenner learned a great deal from Hunter, and it was during one of the dissections that were being carried out in 1772 that Jenner first discovered the causes of angina for himself. When at a later date Hunter himself began to show signs of the disease, Jenner was reluctant to pursue his ideas as he didn't want to alarm his mentor and friend, so that he tended to keep his ideas to himself in the initial stages. However, his contribution to the subject was recognised by a fellow doctor, Caleb Hillier Parry, M.D., F.R.S. (1755-1822), in his book published in 1799 – *'An Inquiry into the Symptoms and Causes of the Syncope Anginosa, Commonly call Angina Pectoris'.*

As it happened, Jenner's thinking that Hunter was unaware of what was wrong with him was well wide of the mark – Hunter knew only too well and was quoted as saying: "My life is in the hands of any fool who chooses to upset me". These words were prophetic, as after an argument with one of his colleagues at St. George's Hospital, Hunter collapsed and died on 16th October, 1793. It was very naive of Jenner to think that Hunter was unaware of his illness as a well respected English physician had already brought the condition out in the open in 1768. Well known and distinguished, his name was William Heberden (1710-1801) who originally named the condition 'Angina Pectoris' in 1768 and published a paper on it in that same year. Given that, and the fact that Hunter was a great doctor who had carried out so many dissections over the years, it is difficult to understand quite why Jenner would have thought that someone as distinguished as Hunter would not know of the condition. Heberden practiced in Cambridge and had discovered the difference between chicken pox and smallpox. Given the fact that both Heberden and Jenner worked on both angina and smallpox, it would seem natural that they should have had some sort of contact with each other, but there is no record of it. Heberden also treated Dr. Johnson (1709-84), in the latter stages of Johnson's life along with people such as William Pitt the Younger (1759-1806) and King George III during his final illness.

This then is a brief background of John Hunter, the man who took Jenner as a student in 1770. Jenner spent the next three years in London before returning to Berkeley in 1773 to set up practice as a country doctor. During the time that Jenner had been in the city, Joseph Banks (1743-1820), the great botanist who had become a member of the Royal Society in 1766 at the age of just twenty-three years, and who from 1778 went on to become President of that august body for forty-one years until his death, had spent three years from 1768 sailing round the world with Captain James Cook in the *Endeavour*. On their return in 1771, Banks had brought over thousands of plant specimens with him, and along with drawings by the ship's artist, Sydney Parkinson, these plant specimens needed to be catalogued, a huge task for any one person. Dr. Hunter knew Joseph Banks as Hunter was also a member of the Royal Society, and Hunter recommended Jenner as someone who was capable of undertaking this huge task, which Jenner duly did. Banks was obviously pleased with the resulting work and the two men remained lifelong friends. Indeed, so pleased was Banks, that he invited Jenner to join him on the second Cook voyage which was to commence the following year, 1772, but Jenner declined, preferring to remain in this country, return to Berkeley and set up practice in the village that he loved. John Coakley Lettsom (1744-1815) was a London physician and a friend of Jenner's. He was born in the Virgin Islands and sent to a Quaker school in 1750, at the age of six years. As well as being a Quaker, he was considered to be one of the best physicians in the city and had built up an established London practice. He always supported Jenner and according to Lettsom, Jenner had told him that he had turned down the chance to sail with Cook and Banks because of his "deep and grateful affection....for his elder brother....and partly by an attachment to the rural scenes and habits of his early youth". Jenner refused the chance to travel round the Pacific islands which were described by the returning seamen as a paradise on earth, and embark on a trip that not only would have allowed him to visit these islands, but would have given him lasting fame afterwards, as it had done with both Banks and Cook. However, Jenner wanted stability rather than adventure and felt he could do his work more effectively in the county of Gloucestershire that he loved so much. As it was, Joseph Banks had a huge falling out with both the Admiralty and Cook himself over the sort of vessels that would go, and withdrew from the trip, but Jenner was not to know this at the time of the offer. Jenner also made a big impact on Dr. Hunter himself, who tried to persuade Jenner to set up a lucrative practice in London, but again, the lure of Berkeley was too much for Jenner, and as he had previously done with the offer from Joseph Banks, turned Hunter down. In 1773, Jenner duly returned to his beloved Gloucestershire, and in particular, Berkeley and purchased a house called 'The Chantry' in 1785, which he lived in until he died in 1823. It houses the Edward Jenner Museum to this day.

Shortly after his return to Berkeley and long before he purchased 'The Chantry', Edward stayed at his brother Stephen's house, Stephen having returned to Berkeley a little earlier. By 1773, Stephen had become rector of Rockhampton, which is a few miles from Berkeley, but the following year he resigned the position and it was taken over by his brother Henry. It was during this time that Edward Jenner first met Edward Gardner who was to become a long lasting friend in whom Jenner confided in years to come. Edward Gardner was younger than Jenner, and earned his living as a wine merchant in the village of Frampton-upon-Severn. It was Gardner who described Jenner, then in his mid twenties, to Jenner's future friend and biographer, John Baron:-

"His height was rather under the middle size, his person was robust but active, and well formed. In dress he was particularly neat, and everything about him showed the man intent and serious, and well prepared to meet the duties of his calling. When I first saw him it was on Frampton Green… He was dressed in a blue coat and yellow buttons, buckskins, well-polished jockey boots with handsome silver spurs, and he carried a smart whip with a silver handle. His hair, after the fashion of the times, was done up in a club, and he wore a broad brimmed hat."

Ten years later Jenner was to confide in Gardner the disappointment he felt of the rejection by his first love, who it is thought, could have been Catherine Kingscote who he eventually married.

Whilst Jenner is best known for his work leading to the elimination of smallpox, his inquisitive mind led him in to other fields of activity. One of these was the launching of an unmanned hot air balloon, the idea of which first came from two Frenchmen, the Montgolfier Brothers. They were Joseph Michel (1740-1810) and Jacques Etienne (1745-99). By studying the behaviour of clouds, they came to the conclusion that a paper bag filled with smoke might fly, and after carrying out tests over many months, finally launched a version of this on 5th June, 1783. This was followed a few months later by a French physicist, Jacques Alexandre Cesar Charles (1746-1823), launching a hot air balloon filled with hydrogen in December, 1783 which reached a height of three thousand feet over Paris and managed to stay up for fifteen miles. Charles discovered what became known as Charles Law, which connected the expansion of gas with its rise in temperature and his launching of his hot air balloon was the first of its kind. Edward Jenner was intrigued by this and later the same year launched his own version of the hot air balloon with the help of the Earl of Berkeley. It was the first in this country and it travelled from Berkeley Castle to Symonds Hall. Jenner then organised a second flight which was to take off from Kingscote, almost certainly with the Kingscote family present, and it was highly likely that it was done to impress the family as Jenner was attempting to court Catherine Kingscote, but at the time the match was not looked upon favourably by her family. Everyone who launched balloons, from the Montgolfier Brothers onwards, probably owe a debt of gratitude to Henry Cavendish (1731-1810), an English natural philosopher and chemist, who having inherited a great deal of money from his uncle, devoted his life to scientific investigations. In 1760, he discovered the extreme levity of inflammable air, known in the present day as hydrogen gas and without this knowledge, no balloon flight would take place. He went on to write about astronomical instruments and The Cavendish Physical Laboratory at Cambridge is named after him and contains most of the apparatus that he used in his discoveries.

It is probably relevant to mention the Berkeley family in more detail as Jenner was their physician, lived closely by them, Berkeley Castle being very near Jenner's house, and there was quite a scandal involving the Berkeley family which called into question as to who was the rightful heir to the title on the death of the 5th Earl of Berkeley in 1810. Frederick Augustus Berkeley was born in 1745 and became the 5th Earl in 1784. On 30th March, 1785, he and his mistress, Mary Cole went through a marriage ceremony at Berkeley church. The then Vicar of Berkeley, the Revd. Augustus Thomas Hupsman was in awe of the 5th Earl and agreed to perform this ceremony which was then kept totally secret from the outside world. Berkeley was quite happy living with Mary Cole as his mistress, but the idea of someone considered to be from the lower orders to be the wife of an Earl was unthinkable. Within this marriage, Frederick and Mary had seven children, although only four lived into adulthood. The eldest of these was William Fitzhardinge (1786-1857). The marriage was perfectly legal – it was the snobbishness of the times and in particular, Earl Berkeley that had made him keep it secret because a great many questions were asked when the Berkeleys married for a second time.

Throughout the ten years of what has become known as the 'first marriage', the Earl of Berkeley had formed a genuine attachment to his wife and now with another child on the way (a fifth that would be living), he belatedly wanted to do the right thing by both his wife and children and married Mary for a second time in Lambeth Parish Church on 16th May, 1796, a highly significant date for Jenner as it turned out, for it was only two days after he had performed the first vaccination on the young James Phipps. The first child born after the Berkeley's second marriage was Thomas Moreton (1796-1882) and five more who lived into adulthood followed. The question that would one day have to be answered was who the rightful heir would be after the 5th Earl died, William Fitzhardinge, the first son after the first marriage, or Thomas Moreton, the first son born after marriage number two. William Fitzhardinge, or Viscount Dursley as he now was, had been elected MP for Gloucestershire on 18th May, 1810 but resigned the seat on the 8th of August of the same year following his father's death, in order to pursue his claim to be the 6th Earl. However, the House of Lords ruled against him and Thomas Moreton, the first son from the so-called second marriage became the 6th Earl, although he was reluctant to take the title out of respect for his elder brother, as he knew only too well that the first marriage had in fact been perfectly legal.

This affair caused a scandal at the time, but does not appear to have affected Jenner as he merely continued to go about his business, looking after the Berkeley family's health and welfare. It was to bother Catherine, by now Edward's wife however, as she was a deeply committed Christian, but in the meantime, Jenner had other things on his mind, such as the hibernation of hedgehogs, which would engage his brain more than any upper class family scandal would do.

At this time, it was known that hedgehogs hibernated in winter, but it was also thought that birds hibernated as well. It seems strange today, but many thought that they hid under mud and re-appeared in the summer. Jenner would not accept this theory however. He noted that whilst the hedgehogs finished their hibernation looking underfed and malnourished, the birds, such as swallows and house-martins that suddenly appeared were fit and healthy. Learning the lesson from Hunter that discovering facts was best achieved by observation, Jenner studied the habits of various bird species and came to the correct conclusion that birds actually migrated in the winter months which is why they returned looking healthy, fit, and well fed. Jenner produced a paper on this subject entitled 'Some Observations on the Migration of Birds' but for some reason, it was not published until 1824, the year after his death. It appeared in the 'Philosphical Transactions' of the Royal Society with an introductory letter to the President, Sir Humprey Davy from Edward's nephew, George Jenner.

Davy (1778-1829) was considered a brilliant scientist at an early age and at nineteen, became assistant to the equally brilliant but more experienced scientist Thomas Beddoes (1760-1808) at his Medical Pneumatic Institute at Bristol in 1797. Davy is famous for many works but one of his first areas of work that he was involved in was the use of nitrous oxide (laughing gas) as an anaesthetic which was not taken up at the time – in fact another forty-four years went by before it came into use, and that was only as a recreational drug for the upper classes. It was not until December, 1844, that it was used for the first time as an anaesthetic by a dentist named Horace Wells when carrying out a tooth extraction. However, due to concerns about its safety, it did not come into common use for another twenty years. It seemed that it took a long time for the concept of pain-free surgery to be accepted rather than rejected as too good to be true.

Jenner's posthumous paper that was submitted to Davy was probably delayed due to the fact that his interest in the nesting habits of cuckoos had taken over, plus the endless questions from John Hunter on the subject that Edward was only too happy to try and answer that stopped him taking the matter of the migration of birds further during his lifetime. The nesting habits of the cuckoo intrigued both Hunter and Jenner as they were unlike any other bird that they had come across at that time. After much observation and experimentation, Jenner realised that the parent cuckoo did not build her own nest, but instead laid her eggs in various bird's nests, quite often that of the hedge sparrow, and that after a while, the eggs of the host bird were pushed out of the nest, leaving the cuckoo eggs alone. At first, Jenner assumed that the foster parents threw the eggs of the host birds out although he was at a loss as to understand why, but it was this theory that he put to Joseph Banks in 1787. Because he had been so busy, Jenner had used his nephew, Henry, to help him observe the behaviour of the cuckoo, but Henry possibly was not as thorough as he should have been, which is why this incorrect conclusion was reached. However, Jenner felt that something wasn't quite right, and so he started to observe the cuckoo behaviour for himself and this eventually drew him to the extraordinary conclusion that it was the cuckoo chicks themselves who pushed the eggs out and even the tiny hedge sparrows were pushed out if their eggs had already been hatched. This idea was highly controversial, and many naturalists refused to believe Jenner. Jenner had one more surprise for them however. He said that, having pushed the hedge sparrow chicks out, should there be two cuckoo chicks left, both would feel that that was one too many. Therefore, each cuckoo chick would attempt to remove the other until after supreme effort from both, one was successful. Taking Hunter's philosophy of experimentation to prove an idea, Jenner dissected the young cuckoos, and found that there was a small indentation in the back which disappeared after a period of about twelve days, presumably as the job of getting rid of the other occupants of the nest had been achieved. With his ideas on the subject broadened, Jenner submitted a further paper, this time to John Hunter, entitled "Observations On The Natural History Of The Cuckoo" and it was this extraordinary work that enabled Jenner to be elected to the Royal Society on 25th February 1789.

Almost a year earlier, on the 6th March, 1788, Jenner had married Catherine Kingscote at Kingscote parish church. As the doubling up of the name implies, Catherine came from an eminent family and her marriage to Edward was entered in the *'Gloucester Journal'*. Edward was very nearly thirty-nine years old whilst Catherine was twenty-seven. Edward had been rejected by a lady nearly ten years before that which had plunged him into a deep depression and there has always been plenty of speculation that Catherine was the object of that first doomed love. The depression lasted years, as Jenner's letter of 1783 to his close friend Edward Gardner shows:

"I am jaded almost to death my dear Gardner, by constant fatigue: that of the body I must endure; but how long I shall be able to bear that of the mind, I know not. Still the same dead weight hangs upon my heart. Would to God it would drag it from its unhappy mansion! Then with what pleasure would I see an end of this silly dream of life."

This seems a strange letter to have written so many years after the first rejection. With so many achievements to his name already before his work on smallpox had even started, that he could write words like this which were filled with such despair spoke volumes for the depth of his misery. It is almost suicidal; certainly it is a letter from a man who seems to have given up on life. He had also written to John Hunter years before, soon after the rejection first occurred. Hunter, ever the practical man wrote back on September 25th 1778:

"I own I was at a loss to account for your silence, and I am sorry at the cause. I can easily conceive of how you must feel, for you have two passions to cope with, viz, that of being disappointed in love, and that of being defeated, but both will wear out, perhaps the first the soonest. I own that I was glad that you was moored to a woman of good fortune, 'but let her go, never mind her'. I shall employ you with hedge hogs…"

Hunter goes on to explain the experiments with hedgehogs that he wants Jenner to undertake. Regardless of whether the object of Jenner's love was Catherine, or another lady, Hunter either underestimated Jenner's feelings, or this letter simply represents Hunter's very practical nature. His "Let her go, never mind her" is always assumed to have been a quotation but the source has always remained unclear and it is possible that Hunter put it in quotations merely to emphasise it. Meanwhile, the experiments that Hunter wanted Jenner to carry out with hedgehogs concerned the fat content in a hibernating animal. In that same letter dated 25th September, 1778, he tells Jenner want he wants him to do:-

"…..I want you to get a hedge hog in the beginning of winter and weigh him, put him in your garden and let him have some leaves, hay or straw to cover himself with, which he will do; then weigh him in the spring and see what he has lost. Secondly, I want you to kill one at the beginning of winter to see how fat he is, and another in the spring to see what he has lost of his fat. Thirdly, when the weather is very cold, and about the month of January I could wish you would make a hole in one of their bellys and put the thermometer down into the pelvis, and see the height of the mercury, then turn it up toward the diaphragm and observe the heat there…"

Hunter then finished the letter by asking Edward if he would examine the stomach and intestines to see what they contain. Whilst Jenner was happy to carry out experiments for Dr. Hunter, all of which kept him busy, they did little to ease the pain of the rejection he was feeling at the time. Research from various sources do not allow us to make anything other than an educated guess as to whether the source of this misery was Catherine and her family, as even Jenner's close friend and first biographer, Dr. John Baron, is vague as to the identity of this lady who was causing so much pain. However, it is quite possible that it *was* in fact Catherine. In 1778, Edward would have been nearly thirty years old whilst Catherine would have been just seventeen. In the 18th century, class and wealth were huge obstacles to marrying if you attempted to step out of your sphere, and it is quite possible that Edward, a country doctor, whilst being a perfectly respectable gentleman in a respectable profession, was not considered a good match by Catherine's family. Given the difference in their ages, that too could have been seen as a problem. However, despite all of that, it is also feasible that if their love had lasted ten years, then Robert Kingscote, her brother and guardian, eventually if reluctantly, gave his consent. In the event, their marriage was an exceptionally happy one until Catherine's all too early death on 13th September, 1815 aged fifty-four years. They had three children; Edward (b. 1789), Catherine (b. 1794), and Robert (b. 1797).

Edward purchased Chantry Cottage in 1785, three years before he and Catherine married, and they loved the place so much that they saw it as somewhere in which they could spend the rest of their lives. Berkeley church lies to the east of the house and is separated from Chantry Cottage by a high brick wall, whilst Berkeley Castle is to the north. The house originally belonged to the Chantry Priest of St. Andrew's Alter in the parish church and had been built for him by Lady Katherine Berkeley in 1380. She also funded the Wotton-under-Edge Grammar School that Jenner attended as a boy. According to his friend, the Revd. Thomas John Fosbroke, when Jenner bought the house, he paid £600 (less than £40,000 in today's terms) from a lady called Jane Hicks. By the time that Jenner purchased it, the house had been considerably altered to reflect the period in which Jenner lived, and its Queen Anne/Georgian style remains largely unaltered to this day. It was in this house that their first son, Edward Robert was born, on 24th January, 1789. Edward and Catherine were delighted and Jenner asked his friend and mentor, Dr. John Hunter, if he would be godfather. Hunter wrote back in his inimitable style:-

"Dear Jenner, I wish you joy: it never rains but it pours. Rather than the brat should not be a Christian, I will stand Godfather, for I should be unhappy if the poor little thing should go to the devil because I would not stand Godfather. I hope Mrs. Jenner is well and that you begin to look grave now that you are a father".

Edward was always a sickly child physically and it was obvious from an early age that he had learning difficulties and would never be academically clever. There was a bond between father and son, as Edward Junior was a gentle boy who loved nature, and he and his father would spend hours together looking at bird's nests whilst his father explained how the nests were built, whilst showing his son hedgehogs and other wildlife. Edward Junior didn't live a long life, dying on 31st January, 1810, only one week after his twenty-first birthday. He was buried on 7th February in Berkeley Church and today lies with his parents, Edward and Catherine, and his paternal grandparents, Stephen and Sarah. Edward junior was deeply loved by both his parents. Three days after he was buried, his father wrote to his friend Henry Hicks:-

"I had no conception till it happened that the gash would have been so deep; but God's will be done!"

The death of his son had a lasting effect on Jenner and despite the fact that he was a committed Christian, and his wife Catherine even more so, he seemed to gain little solace from his faith. He went into a deep depression and the physical symptoms that haunted him after his smallpox variolation all those years before came back to him, and he experienced a roaring noise in the ears, an acidic stomach and along with a general heaviness, an almost uncontrollable drowsiness that would dog him for years until his sense of duty and purpose enabled him to overcome them.

The second child born was Catherine in 1794. The exact date is uncertain although she was christened on 12th August of that year so it is likely that she was born a week or so before then. Little seems to be known of Catherine other than she grew up and played with her older brother Edward in the normal way, but she seemed to be a bright child because when she was eleven years old, her father trusted her to act as his secretary, helping him with his correspondence. When her mother died, she stayed with her grief stricken father for several years until she met a Mr. John Yeend Bedford who she married in Berkeley church on 17th August, 1822. The Rev. William Davies (Edward's nephew) officiated making it a family affair. Edward's sister Anne had married the Rev. William Davies in 1766 and amongst other children, they had had a son, also called William who also entered the church like his father. It was the son William, who officiated at the wedding. He had followed Edward and Anne's father, Stephen, as Vicar of Berkeley. Jenner seems to have been a generous father to his daughter because he gave her over £13,000 when she married, to be held in trust by Colonel Robert Kingscote and the Rev. William Richard Bedford. Jenner also gave her another £1,000 on her wedding day – these were enormous sums in those days.

Catherine's new husband came from Birmingham where he had a business, and it is there that the couple lived after they were married, no doubt causing Edward more unhappiness, although he was no doubt pleased that her future was secured as his own health was failing. Sadly, Catherine died on 5th August 1833 at the age of thirty-nine whilst giving birth to her daughter, also named Catherine who survived and went on to marry and have children.

Edward and Catherine's third and final child arrived on 4th April, 1797 and he was named Robert Fitzhardinge. The first name was chosen as it was the name of Robert Kingscote, Catherine's brother, whilst the name Fitzhardinge represented a link with the Berkeley family. The birth of Robert happened at a good time as Edward was very depressed at the recent death of his elder brother, Stephen, who died a few weeks earlier, on 23rd February, 1797 at the age of sixty-four years. Stephen had been Edward's favourite brother and it was he who had more or less brought Edward up when their parents died when Edward was five years old. Robert didn't have the same learning difficulties that Edward Junior had, but they shared the same tutor, John Dawes Worgan who had been taken on in 1806 aged just sixteen to tutor Edward, and a year later tutored Robert. Worgan was a very bright young man, the son of a Bristol watchmaker and eventually he wanted to become a minister. Sadly, Worgan's health was not good and he wasn't able to tutor the children long, dying of consumption at the age of seventeen in July 1808. Robert went on to Exeter College, Oxford in 1815 but his Latin and Greek were not good and he was sent to a Mr. Joyce of Wiltshire for further tuition. The loving relationship that Edward had had with his first born son Edward junior, was very different from that of Edward Senior and son Robert. Money was a constant source of friction between them, and as an adult, Robert was always asking for more. In May 1819, Robert returned to Berkeley, but his father's hope that he would see more of his son did not materialise. Robert was made a JP and Commissioner for Turnpikes but it is thought that his motive for returning to Berkeley was not to see more of his father, but rather a lady called Mary Perrington, wife of a local tailor. Robert was very generous to Mary and her daughter Emily in his will, and it is thought, although there is no proof, that Emily was Robert's daughter and therefore Edward's grandaughter. Edward would surely have known of Emily's existence, but whether he suspected that she was his grandaughter, we do not know. Later on, Robert joined the Gloucester Militia and ended up as a Colonel, eventually dying in 1854 aged fifty-seven. He never married but it seems he had a fairly colourful life and it is not difficult to see that there would have been problems with his modest, clean living father over their lifetimes.

Despite Edward's many achievements, it is for his work leading to the elimination of the then dreaded disease of smallpox that he will be best remembered. Smallpox was an utterly dreadful disease and killed millions all over the world. It is thought that it attacked humans from about 10,000 BC and in the latter part of the 18th century, just as Jenner was embarking on finding a cure, it killed roughly 400,000 people in Europe alone every year. It was also the cause of a third of all blindness during that period and notwithstanding all that, it was thought that smallpox was responsible for the death of anything between 300 and 500 million people as recently as the 20th century.

This then was the dreadful state of affairs that Jenner set out to conquer from the little village of Berkeley, Gloucestershire as soon as he had returned from London and his studies with Dr. John Hunter. As far back as 1768, when Jenner was studying under John Ludlow, he'd heard that milkmaids who caught the very mild disease of cowpox, never seemed to catch smallpox. He would mention this to Ludlow, but Ludlow showed no interest. It would be nearly thirty years before Jenner put his theory to a practical test, and he was to find a great deal of further opposition to his theory before his ideas were accepted. In the 1780's, Jenner was part of a group of medical men who called themselves 'The Medico Convivial Society' although it was formally called 'The Medical Society'. The first title says exactly what it was – the regular meeting of like minded medical men who discussed medical matters whilst at the same time socialising with each other. Daniel Ludlow, the son of John Ludlow, Jenner's first medical tutor, was a member, along with several others. Jenner discussed his theories concerning smallpox with his friends at some length, but with no scientific proof with which to back his theories, they would tire of the subject and grow irritable with him.

On 7th July, 1792, Edward had the degree of Doctor in Medicine conferred on him by the academic senate of St. Andrews University in Scotland. In order to obtain this degree, a gift to the university was purchased along with a letter of recommendation from two doctors certifying that: "candidate for the degree of Doctor in Medicine, is a gentleman of respectable character, that he has received a liberal and classical education, that he has attended a complete course of lectures in the several branches of Medicine, and that from 'personal knowledge', we judge him worthy of the honour of a doctor's degree in Medicine". This recommendation was signed by two friends of Jenner's, John Hickes, a Gloucester doctor, and Caleb Hillier Parry who was based in Bath. Parry has been mentioned before and was a clinician who carried out a lot of work on the association of thyroid enlargement with cardiac disease. The universities of Scotland had started this practice of selling degrees during the 18th century in order to break the monopoly exercised by Oxford and Cambridge, but in 1830, a Royal Commission issued a report saying that this system should cease. Cease it did, but by this time the monopoly grip that Oxbridge had enjoyed had already been broken by the University of London and some teaching hospitals.

In 1796, four years after receiving his degree, Jenner's luck turned concerning his views on the curing of smallpox. A milkmaid called Sarah Nelmes caught cowpox from a cow called Blossom. Jenner saw his chance, and deciding to put his ideas in to practice, took a sample of pus from Sarah's hand. The next problem was to find somebody healthy to experiment on and Jenner had the idea of using James Phipps, a young boy who Jenner knew had never had smallpox. James was the son of Jenner's gardener which is how he knew the boy's medical history which was necessary if any experiment was to have meaning. On 14th May, 1796, Jenner made two scratches in James' arm and put some cowpox pus from Sarah's arm into the wounds. After four days, some redness appeared and a few days later, it was obvious that James had caught cowpox, proving for the first time that cowpox could be passed from one human being to another as opposed to merely catching it from an animal. This was a very important discovery, because if the cowpox could be transferred from one person to another, it gave scope for far more of this mild disease to be used in the vaccination of others. On 1st July, Jenner variolated James Phipps, in other words, deliberately gave him smallpox. Jenner watched for the results in a very cautious manner allowing a longer time than was felt necessary for the patient to catch smallpox before making a judgement as to whether the boy did or not. James Phipps never contracted the disease, and there finished the first and most important experiment to prove what Jenner had been saying for years, that smallpox was curable – it was a very exciting moment for Jenner. What he had done was to in effect *vaccinate* James Phipps with cowpox as opposed to the previous treatment which was to *inoculate*, or variolate with a small amount of smallpox. It will be remembered that the attempted cure for smallpox, which Lady Montagu brought to this country was to variolate, variolate being a derivation of the Latin word variola meaning smallpox whilst Jenner's technique of vaccination was from the Latin word vaccina meaning cowpox. Jenner himself later invented the Latin name Variolae Vaccinae meaning smallpox of the cow. On the 19th July, he wrote to his friend Edward Gardner:-

"As I promised to let you know how I proceeded in my Inquiry into the nature of that singular disease the cowpox and being fully satisfied how much you feel interested in its success, you will be gratified in hearing that I have at length accomplished what I have been so long waiting for, the passing of the vaccine virus from one human being to another by the ordinary mode of Innoculation. A boy of the name of Phipps was innoculated in the arm from a pustule on the hand of a young woman who was infected by her master's cows. Having never seen the disease but in its casual way before, that is, when communicated from the cow to the hand of the milker, I was astonished at the close resemblance of the pustules in some of their stages to the variolous pustules. But now listen to the most delightful part of my story. The boy has since been innoculated for the small pox which as I ventured to predict produced no effect. I shall now pursue my experiments with redoubled ardour."

Before he could do this however, there was something else that Jenner had to contend with which has been mentioned earlier – the death of his brother Stephen. At the time their parents died, Edward was just five years old, and it was Stephen who looked after him with the result that Edward was deeply fond of his brother. Stephen had also provided a home for Edward when in 1773, the younger brother had returned from studying in London under John Hunter, and this arrangement had continued for fifteen years until Edward's marriage in 1788. Stephen became ill at the end of 1796, and as they both lived in Berkeley, Edward was able to look after him. The illness lasted about two months, but sadly for Edward and the rest of the family, Stephen died on 23rd February, 1797 at the age of 64 years and was buried in Berkeley church. He never married but was much loved and missed by many people, not least his grief-stricken brother, Edward. Jenner also had a professional set back at this time. After his excitement over his successful vaccination of James Phipps in May 1796, there was no general outbreak of cowpox, so Jenner's work in this area halted for a while, although there was an outbreak of horsepox, sometimes simply called 'grease'. Men who worked with horses were asked to milk cows with the result that they caught cowpox, and this lead Jenner to believe that cowpox originated from horsepox. Eventually, another outbreak of cowpox appeared so that Jenner was again able to experiment. Henry, Jenner's nephew, helped him with these experiments, surprisingly so perhaps, as it was Henry who had misled his uncle on the nesting habits of the cuckoo. However, Henry had more success this time. He vaccinated a seven-year-old called J. Barge with cowpox and later variolated him with smallpox and the child was found to be protected. Henry then variolated another patient with the same smallpox matter and this patient did in fact develop smallpox in the usual way because the second patient had not been vaccinated. Both Edward and Henry were delighted and this was to be one of many of the cases quoted in Jenner's pamphlet, *'An Inquiry Into The Causes And Effects Of The Variolae Vaccinae'* that he submitted in June 1798. Jenner paid for the book to be printed himself and was helped by two artists, William Skelton and Edward Pearce who at Jenner's request, produced four hand-coloured plates which depicted the cowpox pustule, and these helped to bring about the success of the book. Jenner had received a great deal of support from Caleb Hillier Parry M.D., F.R.S. (1755-1822) on his earlier work on angina that Parry had recognised in his own book on the subject in 1799 entitled *'An Inquiry into the Symptoms and Causes of the Syncope Anginosa, Commonly called Angina Pectoris'*. As a result, Jenner had dedicated his own pamphlet to Parry as he and Jenner had been lifelong friends since they met when they were both students of the Reverend Dr. Washbourn at Cirencester. Parry later studied at Edinburgh where he received his M.D. degree and then travelled to Bath where he set up practice and stayed there for the rest of his life. Parry is the grandfather of Hubert Parry (1848-1918), the famous musician who has a memorial in the west wall of Gloucester Cathedral. Hubert Parry conposed many hymns including 'Dear Lord and Father of Mankind' and the tune of 'Jerusalem'.

A delighted Jenner then travelled to London with quills containing cowpox matter but much to his dismay, could find no-one interested enough to listen seriously to him. Eventually, he left the quills with Henry Cline (1750-1827), a surgeon at St. Thomas' Hospital and a friend from his time with John Hunter. Cline was considered to be an eminent surgeon. Born in London in 1750, he was educated at Merchant Taylor's School before being apprenticed to Thomas Smith, surgeon to St. Thomas's Hospital, London. During this apprenticeship he lectured a great deal on anatomy and obtained his diploma from Surgeon's Hall in 1774 and in the same year attended a course of John Hunter's lectures. Although Jenner had finished studying under Hunter the previous year, the two men remained in close contact as it was through Hunter that Jenner and Cline met. Cline became a master of the College of Surgeons in 1815 and Jenner could not have found a better person to leave his quills with than his friend Henry Cline.

Although not entirely convinced by his friend's views on vaccination, Cline eventually used cowpox on a patient and then successfully variolated that same patient and from then on became a convert, although the way it happened was almost by accident. Two weeks after Jenner had left the quills with him, Cline had come across a patient who had a hip infection which couldn't be cured. Cline obviously thought he had nothing to lose and with little enthusiasm inserted some cowpox into the patient's hip which as he thought had no effect on the infection whatsoever. However, some time later and with an equal lack of enthusiasm, he variolated the patient with smallpox and found that the patient didn't catch the disease. From that moment, Jenner had found himself another important convert. Jenner still had his disbelievers however and one of these was an eminent physician and botanist, Dr. William Woodville (1752-1805), physician to the London Smallpox Hospital. Woodville was born in Cockermouth and received a classical education before studying medicine at the University of Edinburgh where he received an M.D. degree in 1775. He moved to London in 1782 holding the post of Physician in the Middlesex Dispensary before being appointed to the Smallpox and Inoculation Hospital in 1791. Woodville experimented with cowpox at that establishment in 1799. He vaccinated eight patients, but waited only five days before variolating them. This was far too soon and the patients naturally developed smallpox. Woodville then used the contaminated matter to vaccinate six hundred other patients, and not unnaturally, there were many cases of patients catching smallpox and this was used by Jenner's detractors to great effect.

There were other detractors, one of these being Dr. Thomas Beddoes (1760-1808) of Bristol who has been mentioned earlier. Beddoes was a physician and writer and was considered a brilliant man who between 1798 and 1801 worked at his Medical Pneumatic Institute in Clifton and from 1797 had taken on Humphry (later Sir Humphry) Davy (1778-1829) where they discovered the beneficial effects of laughing gas as an anaesthetic. On 25th February, 1798, Beddoes told a German Medical writer that:- "the facts which I have collected are not favourable to his (Jenner's) opinion that cowpox gives complete immunity from the natural infection of smallpox".

Another critic was Dr. Benjamin Moseley who had been Physician to the Royal Medical Hospital in London for thirty years. He had practiced in Jamaica and had written important papers on the subject of tropical diseases. He was totally against humans being vaccinated with matter emanating from animals, an opinion seized upon by the satirical cartoonist James Gillray a few years later.

Jenner hit back however, and produced a further three papers in the next three years with data showing much success that he had had and giving advice on how to correctly store the vaccine matter, as well as the correct method of vaccination itself. He also gave descriptions of the various diseases that cows caught that were not cowpox as he felt that much of the criticism levelled against him was due to lack of knowledge by his detractors. Eventually, Jenner was to receive the long overdue recognition from his medical peers and one of these was Dr. John Coakley Lettsome (1744-1815), and with the opposition he was receiving from some members of the medical establishment, Lettsome was a powerful person to have on his side. John Coakley Lettsome became a physician and philanthropist when after first completing an apprenticeship in Yorkshire, he had come to London in 1766 to begin his medical training at St. Thomas' Hospital. Halfway through these studies his father died and Lettsome returned to the British Virgin Islands and freed all the slaves that had worked for his father, and having done that, provided medical care for the local people. Having accumulated considerable wealth due to the fact that he was virtually the only doctor on the islands, he returned to London where his reputation grew considerably over the years. Amongst other bodies, he founded the Medical Society of London which became the oldest medical club in England. There is a picture of a group of eminent physicians on the wall of the society's headquarters which Lettsom had commissioned in 1800 and although Jenner was not at the original gathering of the men who were included in the portrait, Lettsome's regard for Jenner was so high that he insisted Jenner be included in the picture. That was a great tribute from a very well respected physician but there was more still to come. On the 7th March, 1800, Jenner was presented to King George III at Court. Four months previously, in December, 1799, Edward had written to his friend Edward Gardner:-

"Great news from St. James. The King has sent me a very civil message, so you will produce a page to wait upon his Majesty and express the obligation".

After the audience had been arranged in early March, Edward then wrote to W. F. Shrapnell, a surgeon friend:-

"What will you give for a sight of me all in velvet, girt with a sword too? What a queer creature is a human being!"

Modest he may have been, but there is no doubt that Jenner was a very proud man when presented to the King on 7th March, 1800 by the Earl of Berkeley. The King gave Jenner permission to dedicate the next edition of the *'Inquiry'* to him, although as Jane Austen and others found out on other occasions, when it came to Royal dedications, words such as 'Permission' and 'Invited' were more like Royal Commands. Jenner was more than happy to go along with this however although it did not solve his financial problems which were beginning to bear down on him. The tide in favour of vaccination began to turn in Jenner's favour. Moseley was never going to agree to the use of vaccination, but many others did. In particular, there was a surgeon at St. Thomas' Hospital called John Ring who had studied with both John Hunter and his equally famous brother, William Hunter (1718-83), the Scottish anatomist and obstetrician. Ring was a poet and classicist as well as a medical journalist. For fifteen years from 1799 he wrote to doctors and periodicals defending Jenner's vaccination without question, which while helpful at first meant that in the long term he almost became a liability as his attitude to Jenner bordered on hero worship to an unhealthy degree. It has to be said though that he had a great deal of knowledge with which to back his assertions as he had vaccinated more people than probably anyone else in the country. However, after years of reading Ring's letters and articles, Jenner seemed to be unnerved concerning Ring's unquestioning loyalty to him and shared his feelings to John Baron, his friend and first biographer. At some future date, Ring broke off correspondence with Jenner, almost certainly very hurt after hearing about Jenner's criticism of him that he made to Baron.

Although he had received the recognition that was certainly due to him, he was facing financial ruin. In 1801, he published his pamphlet entitled *"The Origin Of The Vaccine Inoculation"*. At the end of this publication are the following words that read at the time, could have been seen as overly optimistic, but read today must be seen as phrophetic:-

"An hundred thousand persons, upon the smallest computation, have been innoculated in these realms. The numbers who have partaken of its benefits throughout Europe and other parts of the globe are incalculable: and it now becomes too manifest to admit of controversy, that the annihilation of the Small Pox, the most dreadful scourge of the human species, must be the final result of this practise".

Jenner had desperately wanted to find a cure for this disease and spread the news world wide but in doing so and sharing his knowledge, he forfeited the chance of making a great deal of money which he would have done if he had kept his knowledge a secret for a longer period of time. As a result of this, he was now facing financial ruin and there was now a groundswell of opinion that favoured some sort of payment to Jenner which started locally in

Gloucestershire and which was to spread nationally. The 5th Earl of Berkeley and some grateful residents of the county along with some of Jenner's friends, wrote a testimonial stating their appreciation of his work in eliminating smallpox and it was printed in the Glocester Journal of 21st December, 1801 which states:-

"Many of the Noblemen and most respectful Gentlemen of the County of Glocester having expressed a wish that some public Acknowledgement should be made to Dr. JENNER, for his singularly happy and ingenious Discovery of VACCINE INOCULATION: – We, the undersigned, desirous of promoting so laudable and so patriotic a Design, have commenced a Subscription for carrying the same into Effect... We trust it will only be the Prelude to a Remuneration in some Degree adequate to his Deserts, and to which he has the best-founded Claim on the Gratitude of the British Nation".

A momentum was gathering in London to support the people of Gloucester in helping Jenner and he alluded to this in his letter of 1st January, 1802 to Lady Berkeley, who was Mary Cole, prior to her marriage to the 5th Earl. In the letter to Lady Berkeley, Jenner states that he had been approached by one of his friends, "a respectable Gentleman of the Law" who had suggested placing the copy of the advertisement that was in the 'Glocester Journal' in to a London paper. Jenner felt unable to give a definitive response to this suggestion, which was partly why he sought the advice of Lady Berkeley, although at this stage after years of waiting, things started to move quickly.

Eventually Jenner was to receive financial compensation for his achievements, but it had been a long time coming, and had involved a great deal of hard work. On 12th January, 1802, he had a meeting with the Prime Minister, Henry Addington who was able to say that King George III was very much in favour of some sort of grant being given to Jenner. A petition was drawn up and presented to the House of Commons on 17th March, which was followed by a Committee of Enquiry on the 22nd. The Committee was chaired by Admiral Berkeley, the Earl of Berkeley's brother. The Revd. George Charles Jenner, Edward's nephew, attended in order to make notes of the proceedings, and he published these three years later under the title of 'The Evidence at Large as Laid Before the Committee of the House of Commons Respecting Dr. Jenner's Discovery of Vaccination'.

Admiral Berkeley himself was the first to speak, and although he suggested £10,000 be granted to Jenner by the Treasury, he felt that it would be the correct thing for the Committee to pay more and he would not vote against any larger sum being endorsed. Jenner himself spoke, presenting the wealth of evidence in favour of the effectiveness of cowpox vaccination and then there was the interminable examination by over forty physicians and surgeons, and not all of these were respected by Jenner. After several days of this, Jenner complained to his friend Henry Hicks:-

"Having been put in possession of the laws of vaccination by so great a number of the first medical men of the world - they should not have listened to every blockhead who chose to send up a supposed case of it's imperfection; but this is the plan pursued, and if they do not give up they may sit to the end of their lives".

Jenner was clearly frustrated and irritable as he obviously felt that far too many people were being called as was necessary and that too many who were against vaccination did not know what they were talking about. However, there were many people there giving evidence who were in his favour, one being the Earl of Berkeley, who although not a medical man, testified as to the fact that his own child was protected by Jenner's method. Another was the Duke of Clarence, one of the King's sons, and who would one day become King after his brother, George IV died in 1830. Clarence would rule as William IV until 1837 and immediately prior to Victoria taking the throne. He confirmed that a man called Johnson who was employed as one of the riders of his carriage horses, nearly died as a direct result of refusing vaccination. He also confirmed that prior to vaccination being introduced to his troops, there had been many deaths from smallpox amongst the regiments of light dragoons and these had now ceased since vaccination had started. There were other powerful witnesses in Jenner's favour. Sir Walter Farquhar, Surgeon-in-Ordinary to the Prince of Wales described vaccination in the following manner:-

"I think it is the greatest discovery that has been made for many years", and there were many other glowing endorsements from powerful medical figures.

However, one of the questions the Committee had to contend with was whether Jenner had actually discovered the cure for smallpox at all. There is the story of Benjamin Jesty, a farmer of Upbury Farm near Dorchester. In 1774, he had claimed that an outbreak of smallpox had occurred in the village of Yetminster and whilst many people had been inoculated, he remembered that he had had cowpox when he was young and had never contracted smallpox. He was also aware that two of his servants, Ann Notley and Mary Read, both of whom had had cowpox, had nursed relatives through smallpox without catching it themselves. Jesty took his wife and two small children, scratched their arms with a needle, and rubbed in matter from the pustules of a cow's udder, in effect, vaccinating them, although the word was not in use then. The boys had no problems at all, and although Jesty's wife became ill, she recovered and Jesty was convinced that cowpox was the answer. However, the public were not ready for such a cure at that time, and when they heard from Jesty's doctor what he had done and the effect that it had on Jesty's wife, they turned against him in anger. He had stones and mud thrown at him, and although he was a courageous man, decided that he would keep quiet about what he felt was an effective cure. This was all carried out twenty years before Jenner started work on the problem, but eventually Jesty got some recognition from the Vaccine Pock Institution, with the presentation of a Testimonial and gold mounted lancets in 1805. Had he had the resources and more medical knowledge, then maybe he would have been given even more recognition, but as it was, it was Jenner who had spent many years working on the problem and refining the cures.

Eventually, the Committee wrote its report which was duly presented to the House of Commons. The debate was set for the 2nd of June, 1802, and Admiral Berkeley proposed £10,000 be paid to Jenner, even though he felt that it should be double that. He proposed the smaller sum because the war with France was bleeding the country dry and he didn't think he could get the higher figure through. Several important figures also wanted £20,000 to be awarded, and in fact Sir Henry Mildmay put forward a motion that £20,000 should indeed be granted. After discussion concerning this amount, Sir Henry's motion was narrowly defeated by 59 votes to 56 and a motion awarding Jenner £10,000 was passed by the House. Edward's brother-in-law, William Davies, later noted:-

"June 2 1802 Dr. Jenner had a Reward from Parliament by an unanimous Vote for the most important Discovery that perhaps was ever made of preventing the Ravages of the small Pox by introducing Vaccine Inoculation. Ten thousand pounds."

At this time, the British government was headed by Henry Addington, (1757-1844), a Tory Prime Minister and later the First Viscount Sidmouth, who had recently taken over from William Pitt the Younger, (1759-1806) who had been Prime Minister from 1783 to 1801, a period of time unthinkable today. Pitt was to become Prime Minister again in 1804 before dying ill and exhausted in 1806, but in the meantime, although Addington always looked as if he was going to be a short term Prime Minister, it cannot be taken away from him that the first of Jenner's two grants from Parliament was awarded under his administration and it did him credit.

Despite this official recognition, there were still some detractors however. Some were in the medical profession and amongst these was Dr. John Birch (1744-1815), a doctor at St. Thomas' Hospital, who said that cowpox inoculation was "a subject he had not much attended to, as he did not like it." On the other hand, the majority in the medical profession approved, including as said before, the King's physician, Sir Walter Farquhar. There were many others in support. Dr. Richard Croft, who was to become the King's physician at a later date, said: "I doubt not but it will ultimately cause the smallpox to be remembered only by name." However, others still criticised the vaccination process, some for religious reasons as there were clergymen who thought it ungodly to vaccinate human beings with animal matter. As late as 1808, James Gillray (1757-1815), the satirical cartoonist, published a cartoon of people who had been vaccinated ending up with cows growing from their limbs – a quite dreadful sight. Gillray also planted the idea in people's minds that not only would their physical appearances change, but their minds would become dull and devoid of any intelligence. Unfortunately, Gillray had influence and that cartoon did Jenner no favours at all. Gillray was born in Chelsea and was the son of a Lanark trooper. He started his career as an engraver and was quite successful but eventually turned his hand to cartoons which became known for their savagery. There was no-one that escaped his lampooning, and William Pitt the Younger, Prime Minister for so many years, and the Kings George III and IV were amongst his many victims.

Meanwhile, on 3rd December, 1802, a gentleman by the name of Benjamin Travers, who was certainly related to and was quite possibly the brother of Joseph Travers, a London sugar merchant, convened a meeting at Joseph's factory in Cheapside, London. In attendance were Dr. William Hawes, who was one of the founders of the Humane Society, along with Joseph Leaper and John Addington, the latter two being surgeons. The gentlemen met: "for the purpose of considering the propiety of establishing an Institution for promoting universal Vaccination with a view to the extinction of Small Pox." Dr. John Coakly

Lettsom, the Quaker physician mentioned earlier who had a London practice was expected but in the event, could not make it. Jenner was unable to attend as he was still in Berkeley, so it was decided to hold a further meeting, but although Jenner lent his support to any organisation that came out of it, he expressed a wish to take a back seat as he wished to remain outside London for the foreseeable future. A second meeting was arranged and this was better attended. John Gurney, the banker, along with William Wilberforce wrote lending their support and after a third meeting, the Jennerian Society as it was called was born. The support of Wilberforce (1759-1833) was invaluable as he was a high profile politician who for so many years had led the campaign against slavery. The aim of the Jennerian Society was to promote the process of vaccination as a cure for smallpox and attempt to stop the use of variolation, which not only did not work effectively, but still spread the disease. Governors were appointed and these had to pay the society one guinea (£1.05p) per annum, five guineas in one lump sum or have left the society a legacy of at least £20. The regularity of meetings was specified and London was to be split in to twelve districts with an inoculation centre in each district. An Annual Festival was to be held each year on Jenner's birthday, although given the natural modesty of the man, it is not clear how he reacted to that last idea. Eventually, it was to become the National Vaccine Establishment in 1808. Meanwhile, with regard to the £10,000 that Jenner had been awarded by the Addington government, although it was a huge amount of money at the time and Jenner was careful with his spending, it was not enough to allow him to retain premises in London whilst losing his Gloucestershire patients in order to continue his research, which was forever ongoing. When it was calculated that at that time, he had possibly saved the lives of so many people that the exchequer was probably richer by something like £200,000 in extra taxation, the sum of £10,000 doesn't appear excessive. In fact it was felt by many that the situation would have to be looked at again at some stage.

After a spell in London, Dr. Jenner eventually retired to Berkeley, at least, that was his intention, but in fact he continued to work until the end of his life. A friend of his, a young man by the name of Robert Ferryman, designed a rustic hut which was erected in Jenner's garden and it was here that Edward vaccinated the poor once a week for free. He called it "His Temple of Vaccinia" and amazingly, it still stands today, exactly the same as it was in Jenner's time.

One of the patients that Jenner saw in his so-called retirement was Augustus, the Duke of Sussex (1773-1843), who he attended with Lord Berkeley on Friday 15th September, 1808. The Duke was the son of King George III and brother of the Prince of Wales. For a long time, the Duke had suffered from ongoing health problems and had spent many years abroad for that reason living in both Switzerland and Italy. However, he was homesick and had long since asked his father for permission to return to England. The permission was initially refused, especially as in 1793, when he was just twenty years old, the Duke had made what the King felt to be an illegal marriage in Rome to Lady Augusta Murray. She was the daughter of the 4th Earl of Dunmore, ten years older than Sussex, and was considered rather plain and bossy. The King eventually relented but he announced that the marriage was null and void considering that it contravened the Royal Marriages Act of 1772. Although furious with the couple, the King did agree to make financial provision for Lady Augusta and the Duke's two children. Despite the Duke not being a favourite with the King, it was still considered an honour to attend royalty at this level and although Jenner did not seek publicity of this nature, it did him no harm. By the end of the month, the Duke was well enough to leave Berkeley Castle. Jenner wrote in his notebook:- "He has been having a grain of epecacuani two or three times a day and occasionally the extract of Colocynth comp…" and "…He smokes three or four pipes of Turkish tobacco daily." Considering the fact that one of the Duke's ailments was a chest problem, it seems extraordinary for a doctor to encourage the smoking but it has to be borne in mind that most of the medical people at the time felt that smoking tobacco actually cleared the lungs and this school of thought prevailed right up until the 1940's. So strongly were these views held in fact that people who stepped out of that thinking were ridiculed at best, and if they were medical people it was worse as Dr. Thomas Richard Allinson (1858-1918) found out to his cost. The General Medical Council struck him off and banned him practicing medicine for stating that smoking was bad for people. A man before his time, he also recommended exercise, not to work too hard and to cut down salt and alcohol. In fact he said that it would be better if people were to be teetotal, follow a vegetarian diet and also not to drink tea and coffee near bedtime or at the very least, keep any intake of it to an absolute minimum at the end of each day. It was Allinson who founded the bakery that bears his name today. Bearing in mind all this happened a hundred years later than Jenner lived, it is no wonder that any doctor in Jenner's time would have encouraged smoking for chest trouble.

It was at this time, the early 1800's, when Jenner was attending the Duke of Sussex that Edward became a magistrate. On the 18th September, 1808, the Oath of Allegiance was administered by the Earl of Berkeley to both Jenner and his nephew, William Davies Junior at the White Lion, Berkeley. This position would almost certainly have been on offer to him before, but now that he was back living permanently in Berkeley with no thought of returning to London, he obviously felt that he was in a better position to accept. It was a position that carried a high degree of responsibility and was not open to anybody. Magistrates had to be communicants of the Church of England as well as either landowners or members of the clergy. They were also required to take Holy Communion after their appointments and on 1st October, George Jenner administered the sacrament to both his cousin William Davies and his uncle.

Jenner's fame had spread worldwide. Despite the war with France, the benefits of vaccination were made available to all, friend and foe alike. Napoleon thought so much of Jenner, that when Jenner wrote requesting the release of certain prisoners of war, the request was almost always granted. The story goes that after Josephine had brought Napoleon's attention to one such letter, Napoleon is supposed to have said: "Ah Jenner, je ne pius rien refuser a Jenner". During 1807, he had written to King Carlos I of Spain requesting the release of a judge's son and this too, was successful.

Given his extraordinary achievements, Jenner still wasn't wealthy, and a second petition was presented to Parliament requesting a further grant. Amongst other things, the petition pointed out that the Board of Longitude had put up prize money of £20,000 for solving the problem of calculating longitude at sea and that Parliament had supported John Harrison in his claim for this award. On 29th July 1807, Lord Henry Petty proposed that a further grant of £20,000 be awarded to Jenner and this was finally approved without a dissenting vote by the House of Commons on that date. It was felt by many that justice had been done at long last. He was also given the Freedom of the City of London, an honour given to only two other medical people, Florence Nightingale (1820-1910) the nurse who when working with soldiers in the Crimean War improved cleanliness and sanitation and by so doing, drastically reduced the mortality rate, and Joseph Lister (1827-1912), the English surgeon who was dubbed: "The father of antiseptic surgery" and whose methods revolutionised modern surgery.

Jenner could now afford to retire, although retirement and financial security didn't give him happiness, as in 1810, Edward, his first born son died of tuberculosis and in 1815, his beloved wife Catherine also died, also of tuberculosis. It is a sad but true irony that despite the fact that Jenner has saved millions of lives across the world, at the time he couldn't save the lives of the two people who mattered most to him. When Catherine died, he lived out the rest of his life at Chantry Cottage, hardly venturing away from it, and often feeling lonely.

On 24th January, 1823, he attended a gentleman by the name of Mr. Joyner Ellis, the Berkeley Coroner, who had been taken ill. Jenner saw Mr. Ellis, but felt that he could do nothing for him, pronouncing him to be terminally ill. Later that evening, Jenner retired to bed and when he failed to appear for breakfast the next morning, his ever faithful nephew, Henry, went to the bedroom to find his uncle unconscious. Despite being attended by Mr. Hickes, the Berkeley surgeon, he never regained consciousness, and died at two o'clock the following morning on the 26th January, 1823.

It would probably have been the wish of John Baron, Jenner's friend and first biographer, to have seen him have a state funeral and a burial at Westminster Abbey, and considering his achievements, it would have been no more than Jenner deserved. However, it would not have been the wish of Jenner himself and on the 3rd February, 1823, Jenner had a quiet funeral at Berkeley church and lies buried there with the people that he loved most of all – his wife Catherine, his parents, Stephen and Sarah, and his eldest son, Edward. No-one from the medical establishment came from London, but this modest man from a Gloucestershire village probably wouldn't have minded. As well as being modest, Edward was a very private religious man who had been happily married to a deeply religious woman until her death in 1815 and he felt that any gifts that he may have had were given for a reason. Knowing that his privacy would always be compromised by the unwanted fame his work would always attract, he had written the following to a long standing friend, the Rev. John Clinch on 16th August , 1805:-

"Never aim, my friend, at being a public character, if you love domestic peace. But I will not repine – Nay, I do not repine, but cheerfully submit, as I look upon myself as the instrument in the hands of that power which never errs, of doing incalculable good to my fellow creatures."

His legacy is with us today and will always be with us. In 1853, vaccination was made compulsory in England, and in 1979, the World Health Organisation formerly announced the total eradication of smallpox across the face of the earth – an extraordinary legacy for a country doctor. In 1772, Jenner turned down the chance to travel the world with the great Captain Cook, and in 1773 he refused the offer of a lucrative practice in London which was made to him by his mentor, Dr. John Hunter. He could have been more secretive about his methods and not only made more money but also been a great deal less prone to the criticisms that he endured as his ideas were practiced by people unqualified to do so. However, all Jenner wanted to do was to serve his fellow human beings and to do this effectively, wished to share his knowledge with the whole world. A letter he wrote after the 'Enquiry' was published demonstrates this beautifully. The person to whom it is addressed is unidentified, but the meaning is clear enough:-

"Shall I, who even in the morning of my days sought the lowly and sequestered paths of life, the valley and not the mountain; shall I now my evening is fast approaching, hold myself up as an object of fortune and for fame? - Admitting it as a certainty that I obtain both, what stock should I add to my little fund of happiness? … And as for the fame, what is it? A gilded butt, for ever pierced with the arrows of malignancy."

Jenner never received a knighthood which seems extraordinary to us today. Although essentially a modest man, he was very proud and would surely have accepted it if one was offered despite his 1805 letter. We cannot be sure why – perhaps it was partly due to King George III's illness that began in 1788, before Jenner carried out the first ever vaccination on James Phipps. It was this illness that was to cause so much disruption to the monarchy leading to the Prince of Wales being Regent from 1811 until 1820 when his father, George III finally died. However, we know that, like his father, the Prince of Wales was favourably disposed towards Jenner and his work and he did reign as George IV from 1820 until his own death in 1830 so there was time for him to bestow what would have been a well deserved accolade on Edward. There were statues erected in recognition of what he had achieved. The first one was sculpted in 1825 by Robert William Sievier (1794-1865), the English sculptor and engraver, and this statue stands proudly in the corner of the west and south walls of Gloucester cathedral. It is this statue that has nothing more than the one word 'JENNER' adorning it. As mentioned in the introduction to this chapter, Edward Jenner was so famous when it was being sculpted that no one felt any more information would be needed. However, the fact that smallpox is now no longer an issue has meant that his name is rarely mentioned which means in effect that he has become a victim of his own success. The second statue was fashioned by William Calder Marshall (1813-94), the Scottish sculptor and was placed on the fifth plinth in Trafalgar Square in 1858 but was moved to Kensington Gardens four years later much to the disgust of the British Medical Journal who wrote an editorial saying how wrong this was, and the following year another article was printed by them including the words:-

"...had been banished even with ignominy from those honourable neighbourhood of men esteemed great because they had killed their fellow creatures whilst he had only saved them".

Considering this was written in 1862, it has a very powerful message from the medical community that an injustice to a very great man had been carried out. We know that for a long time, the medical profession in his own country contained many who were unconvinced by the worth of what he had achieved, their attitude to him aptly being summed up by a quotation taken from Matthew 13/57 from the Bible:- "A Prophet is not without honour, save in his own country and in his own house". However, if his own country was slow in recognising his extraordinary contribution to world health, other countries were not, including most of Europe, and to Europe can be added the United States of America. Thomas Jefferson (1743-1826), the 3rd President between 1801 and 1809 of this still fledgling but established nation wrote to Jenner on 14th May, 1806 and the final part of his letter finishes with the words:-

"...Yours is the comfortable reflection that mankind can never forget that you have lived. Future nations will know by history only that the loathsome small-pox has existed and by you has been extirpated..."

This remarkable and quiet modest man never sought fame and did not complain when from his own country at least, it was a long time coming. He *was* sometimes frustrated at some of the criticism his methods attracted simply because he knew that the sooner his work was accepted, the sooner this dreadful disease would be conquered. He believed completely in his work and the knowledge that the truth would be accepted in future years. Although eventually given a financial award from a grateful Parliament that left him comfortably off, he was never after fame or fortune. He had a rustic hut erected in his garden which was designed for him by his friend, the Revd. Robert Ferryman, and Jenner called it 'The Temple of Vaccinia'. On certain days Jenner used it to vaccinate the poor of the area where there was sometimes a huge queue waiting for him. He carried out this exhausting work for free, happy knowing that he had conquered the most dreadful disease imaginable and he was contented that he had led a life that had been fulfilled. Edward Jenner loved the countryside of his beloved Berkeley and it is entirely appropriate that he rests with his loved ones quietly in the village church, just as he would be happy with the knowledge that from the little village he loved so much that was hidden away in Gloucestershire, he had saved the lives of millions. If he did not receive the knighthood that he surely deserved, the least he should receive is the everlasting gratitude of us all.

-oOOo-

6
Admiral William Bligh
(1754-1817)

Brilliant Naval Officer whose name was unfairly blackened in the Hollywood films but had a great career and went on to become the fourth Governor-General of New South Wales between 1806 and 1810.

"Just before Sun Rise the People Mutinied, seized me while asleep in my Cabbin, tied my Hands behind my back, carried me on Deck in my Shirt, put 18 of the Crew into the launch and me after them and set us adrift."

These words are taken from Bligh's log on the day of the mutiny, and they are the main reason why the world remembers William Bligh. However, William Bligh is different from any other person written about in this book by one major factor – he is the only one not only to have received much less credit than he is due, but worse than that, over the last two centuries his name has been blackened in a way that he has never deserved. Other people have not always received the praise due to them, but they have not been subject to the vilification over two centuries that Bligh has received. People certainly associate the name of William Bligh with the word mutiny, but his reputation has been unfairly blackened by one or two people who had vested interests at the time, and many years later, by the Hollywood film industry, interested only in a good story rather than the historical facts. William Bligh was a first rate naval officer and was neither a tyrant nor a flogger as has been portrayed over the years.

William Bligh was born on 9th September, 1754 to Francis and Jane Bligh. Francis was a customs officer in Plymouth whilst Jane Bligh was a widow when she married Francis Bligh as Jane Pearce in 1753 and a year later, William was born. Jane already had a daughter, Catherine Pearce (William's step-sister), who married a John Bond, who was a surgeon in the Royal Navy, and William Bligh remained close to his family, taking his nephew, Francis Godolphin Bond, the son of John and Catherine Bond, on his second breadfruit trip in *HMS Providence*. Sadly, William's mother Jane died in 1769 when William was only fifteen, although his father was to marry twice more before his own death on 27th December, 1780, the day after Boxing Day, and less than three months after William had returned from a four year voyage with the Captain Cook expedition after a failed attempt to find the North West Passage, the voyage leading to Cook's death in Hawaii on 14th February, 1779.

That Bligh was on Cook's ship was remarkable in itself. He was appointed Sailing Master of the *Resolution* on 20th March, 1776, when he was only twenty-one years old. He had been entered on the roll of *HMS Hunter* in July, 1770 and in September 1771 he transferred to *HMS Crescent*, a 36-gun frigate.

It was on this ship that he learned his considerable navigation and seamanship skills and in August 1774, he was taken on board *HMS Ranger* where he served as Midshipman until chosen by Cook to be Sailing Master of the *Resolution* two years later. Bligh was very able and hugely confident, but it must have seemed a dream come true to be holding such a responsible position on his childhood hero's ship.

The task of the *Resolution,* along with the accompanying ship, the *Discovery* was to attempt to find the elusive North West Passage between the Atlantic and Pacific Oceans across the top of the Americas, if indeed such a passage existed. They set sail from Plymouth in July 1776 and after unsuccessful attempts to find a passage through the ice, arrived at Hawaii on 26th November, 1778. On Cook's first two trips to the Pacific, he found that the people of the Polynesian Islands were very friendly and welcoming, especially at Tahiti, but the reception they received at Hawaii, whilst welcoming, was somehow different as if they worshipped Cook.

Historians are not all agreed as to why Cook received this adulation from the people of Hawaii, but many feel that they thought him to be the great god Lono, who according to their legend, was due to appear at the same time as Cook and his two ships actually arrived at the island. Cook stayed over two months, and by the time he set sail on 4th February, 1779, the atmosphere had become tense because the local chiefs had demanded sacrifices from the islanders which had resulted in food shortages. Both sides were relieved when Cook actually left, but sadly, the troubles were only just about to begin. Four days after leaving the island, Cook was forced to return to Hawaii in order to repair his foremast that had snapped and he needed the anchorage to repair it. The officers of the *Resolution* were uneasy at returning but Cook was adamant and the atmosphere was even more strained than before. By now the islanders doubted whether Cook was in fact the god Lono, and consequently felt foolish and angry. A cutter was stolen from the ship and for Cook, this was the last straw. He decided to go ashore and take the chief Terreeoboo hostage until the cutter was returned. At first the chief came willingly but changed his mind at the last minute. Cook and his marines were surrounded on the beach and whilst officers and men from the surrounding launches gave covering fire, Cook and four marines were killed in the resulting skirmish. Bligh was one of the officers in a cutter and took an active part in the fight. He poured scorn on the official version put out by Lieutenant King and was furious when his part in the fight was not mentioned. On top of that, subsequent charts that he drew were credited to Lieutenant Roberts and Bligh, like his mentor Cook, didn't suffer fools gladly and let his views be known. It was probably his outspoken manner at such a young age that caused him to be overlooked for promotion after Cook's death. It certainly wasn't any question of his ability which was considered outstanding. They spent another unsuccessful year looking for the North West Passage and both ships arrived back in England on 4th October, 1780. They had been away four years and three months.

Cook was obviously an important person in William Bligh's life. Cook had been his hero since Bligh was a young boy and it must have been traumatic for this by now twenty-four -year old to witness the slaughter of his mentor and be unable to do anything to stop it. It must have been traumatic too, to witness the series of bad judgements that Cook made on his third trip because there is no doubt that after the previous two trips, Cook was unwell and prone to rash decisions. Before the third trip, Cook had been away from home between 1768 and 1775, a period of seven years when he was only ashore with his family for one of those years, and consequently the man was tired and ill. He was clearly not the famous Captain Cook that Bligh had read about since he was a schoolboy.

Another important person in Bligh's life was Elizabeth Betham who he met in 1775 when his ship *HMS Ranger*, was at Douglas Pier, Isle of Man. Elizabeth was the daughter of Richard Betham, who was the Collector of Customs at Douglas but any courtship had to be put on hold because soon after they met, William was to go to sea with Captain Cook on the *Resolution* and did not return for another four years.

Once back however, Bligh soon resumed the courtship, and William and Elizabeth, or Betsy as he called her, were married at Onchan Parish Church on 4th February, 1781. Over the years, they were to have six daughters, Harriet, Mary, Elizabeth, Jane, Frances, and Anne. They were also to have twin boys, William and Henry, but they were to live but one day only. William adored his wife and their lengthy absences from each other over the years would be very difficult for them both to deal with, just as it was for other naval officers and their wives.

The other important person in William Bligh's life was Fletcher Christian. Fletcher was born on 25th September, 1764 to Charles and Ann Christian in the farmstead of Moreland Close near the lake district of Cumbria, which is near the town of Cockermouth. Charles, Christian's father, was the fifth son of John Christian. Fletcher had four brothers and one sister who lived into adulthood. They were John 1752-91, Edward 1758-1823, Mary 1760-86, Charles 1762-1822, and Humphrey 1767-90. The family was powerful and prosperous but bad management of the family's financial affairs by Fletcher's elder brothers forced them into bankruptcy. John and Edward would still have their Cambridge education but there was no money for Fletcher, Charles and Humphrey's future learning to be paid for. Their sister Mary would have no chance of marriage as she would have no fortune, at that time, and with that type of family, a disaster. Their Cumbrian home was sold and Ann, and her two younger sons, Fletcher and Humphrey moved to the Isle of Man in 1780. There they were to meet Richard Betham, the Collector of Customs, his daughter Elizabeth, and her fiancée, William Bligh who had just returned after his four years at sea with the Captain Cook expedition. Things were looking bleak for Christian at this time, but events were about to take a turn for the better. Like many naval officers, William Bligh had been laid off on half pay when hostilities with Europe had been curtailed in 1782.

He was beginning a young family and had to earn a living so he went to work in the Merchant Service for his wealthy uncle, Duncan Campbell, sailing to and from the West Indies. Fletcher Christian, seeing himself as a gentleman, but with no money to back his status with, saw the navy as a way out of his financial dilemma and went to work for Bligh on board one of Duncan

Campbell's ships. Bligh befriended Christian and generally took him under his wing in what was to be a close friendship but which was to end in a tragic way by the end of the decade.

If Bligh took Christian under his wing, then Bligh had been taken under the wing of the renowned botanist, Sir Joseph Banks. Banks had sailed with Captain James Cook on the latter's first great trip of 1768-1771, whilst Bligh had sailed with Cook on his third world trip, 1776-1780. Banks was well aware of Bligh's high abilities which were all too evident when he, Bligh, had carried out his duties on Cook's ship, the *Resolution*. In May 1787, Banks, who by this time was President of the Royal Society, had prevailed upon King George III to sanction an expedition to sail to Tahiti to pick up large amounts of breadfruit that grew in abundance on the island, and to ship it to the West Indies as cheap food for the slaves. The Admiralty purchased a ship, the *Berthia*, renamed her the *Bounty*, and she was fitted out for the proposed trip. Bligh was offered command in August 1787, and immediately accepted. He needed a second in command, and although he was not Bligh's choice, was given John Fryer as Ship's Master. Bligh had no hesitation in offering Christian the position of Master's Mate, and with it, the possibility of a future promotion to the rank of Lieutenant. The plan was to sail round Cape Horn to Tahiti, collect the breadfruit, and then sail round the Cape of Good Hope to the West Indies, deposit their precious cargo, and return to England. If they went by this route, they would have circumnavigated the globe. Much has been made concerning Bligh's so-called determination to circumnavigate the globe even in the most dreadful conditions, but it was Bligh himself who applied to the Admiralty for permission to travel round the Cape of Good Hope on the trip out in case the weather made the trip too risky, as indeed proved to be the case. The Admiralty were very slow in giving Bligh permission to set sail, so when at last he was allowed to depart, it almost guaranteed the weather at the Horn would make it impossible to go round it. Bligh's foresight probably saved many lives later on. However, after much delay that infuriated Bligh, at last they were given orders to set sail. Unfortunately, due to the delay they missed the good weather and after several failed attempts, finally set sail from Spithead on 23rd December, 1787.

Bligh had learned a great deal from Captain Cook about the importance of diet, because up until Cook's voyages, probably the biggest killer of sailors was the disease of scurvy. More sailors died from scurvy then from injuries received in battle, and so dreadful were the symptoms, that death was usually a merciful release. An eminent Scottish doctor, James Lind (1716-94), had worked on the problem of scurvy at sea for years and had written 'A Treatise of the Scurvy' as far back as 1753, which years later was seen to be a medical classic, but little notice was taken of it at the time. It is perceived wisdom that Cook was the first captain to really take Lind's ideas and use them so effectively. Lind had recommended lemon juice for the treatment of scurvy, and Cook insisted on his crew taking not only lemon juice, but also eating fresh meat and vegetables where possible, along with saukraut. Cook used psychology on his men by getting his officers to eat saukraut, knowing that the men would more easily follow suit. As a result of this, scurvy was all but eliminated on Cook's three voyages and he was admitted as a member of The Royal Society due to his contribution to health at sea. In fact, although James Lind and Captain Cook have received most of the credit for improving the diet of sailors and reducing the chances of outbreaks of scurvy happening, a British sea captain, Sir John Narborough (1640-88), seemingly forgotten over the years, had insisted on feeding his crews with oranges and lemons and fresh food when he was able to, but it is only in recent times that his contribution to good dietary habits at sea has been acknowledged. This oversight has been due to the fact that Sir John's journals only came to light at the beginning of 2009 after being lost for 300 years, although Lind and Cook still deserve the credit that is given to them, as they could not possibly have known of Sir John or his ideas on diets.

Bligh cared about his crew and was determined to look after them in the same way that Cook had looked after his. Bligh was also aware of the importance of exercise and he engaged a partially sighted fiddler by the name of Michael Byrne to play each evening whilst the crew danced. Seamen are a fairly conservative bunch of people and probably did not take too kindly to either new diets or dancing with each other, even though they were clearly there for the crew's own good.

The Bounty's journey continued to Cape Horn in the usual way, but in attempting to round the Horn on 20th March, 1788, they encountered ferocious seas which they battled through for 31 days before admitting defeat and giving up on 22nd April. Bligh hated giving in although many would have given up long before. The ship was being pounded without respite, was leaking badly, and half the crew could barely function they were so ill. Bligh was a proud and stubborn man, and was furious with the Admiralty for the delays in giving him his final orders as it meant that they reached the Horn in winter, the very thing Bligh had wanted to avoid. He now had to put about and head for Tahiti via the Cape of Good Hope, which would add many months, possibly even a year to the trip.

Bligh has always been referred to as Captain, but this was only a courtesy title for someone in command of a ship. Bligh was in fact, only a Lieutenant and not only that, had no commissioned officers or marines to back his authority with. Trouble was soon to rear its ugly head, and Bligh's skills as a leader were soon to be put to the test. On 20th August, 1788, the *Bounty* sighted Adventure Bay and anchored there on the following day. The day after that, everyone was allotted work to do and willingly carried out their duties; all that is, except Purcell, the carpenter, who felt it beneath his dignity to join the wooding party and carry out his tasks. Bligh admonished him and he answered back. Bligh was now in a dilemma. Normally an officer would simply flog a man for insubordination, but Purcell was a Warrant Officer and could not be given that punishment. Bligh could not arrest Purcell and confine him for the rest of the trip as they were not due back home for fifteen months, and Bligh needed every able bodied man that he could have as the ship was seriously undermanned. In the event, he sent Purcell back on the ship to be supervised by John Fryer, the ship's master, but Purcell did not co-operate with Fryer either. Bligh gave orders that Purcell was not to be given food or water until he obeyed orders, and this in the short term at any rate, seemed to solve the immediate problem. They hadn't even reached Tahiti, and Bligh was already looking isolated because apart from having no commissioned officers with him, one of his non-commissioned officers had blatantly refused an order, a very serious offence that was barely short of outright mutiny. There were further problems for Bligh. He seems to have had little confidence in John Fryer, the ship's Master, and on the 3rd March previously, Bligh had promoted Fletcher Christian, the Master's Mate, to be Acting Lieutenant, and effectively his second in command. Bligh seems to be justified in his actions, but whether Fryer's subsequent lack of competence was due to his declining morale at Bligh's decision or was there in the first place is open to debate. However, there was more worry for Bligh on the horizon. For a Captain who was determined to keep his crew healthy, it must have been galling for him to be saddled with a drunk, incompetent surgeon called Thomas Huggan. On 9th October, 1788, Able Seaman James Valentine died of blood poisoning almost certainly brought on by the surgeon's neglect. Bligh was livid, as he was continually being reassured by Huggan that Valentine was recovering. On the same day, Bligh had an altercation with John Fryer who had refused to countersign the expenses of the Boatswain and Carpenter unless Bligh sign a certificate stating that Fryer had done nothing amiss during the voyage so far. Whether this was due to Fryer's own lack of self belief or due to Christian's promotion is not clear, but in any event, it was an extraordinary request, and one that was immediately refused by Bligh. Bligh summoned the entire crew on deck, read them the Articles of War, and Fryer backed down and duly signed. If Bligh looked vulnerable, he didn't show it. He had complete confidence in his own ability and whatever obstacles were thrown in his way, was the type of man to battle through and get the job done, but he was under no illusions.

On 26th October, 1788, The Bounty sailed in to and anchored in Matavai Bay, Tahiti, ten months after leaving England. After being cooped up in a small ship for that length of time, Tahiti was paradise. It was an unspoiled island in the middle of the Pacific, the sun shone on them, the islanders were friendly having been on good terms with other European sailors, notably Captain Cook, and the beautiful Tahitian women were very free with their sexual favours. Bligh had been here before and understood the ways of the Polynesian people. They were generous with gifts but had a propensity to steal and Bligh, not wanting there to be any trouble, drew up a list of rules concerning his men's behaviour, one of which was the following, and here we can quote:-

"Every person is to study to gain the good will and esteem of the natives, to treat them with all kindness; and not to take from them, by violent means, any thing that they may have stolen; and no-one is ever to fire, but in defence of his life."

These were the words of a man who loved and respected the local people, and these feelings were reciprocated. The welcome they received was tumultuous with hundreds of canoes coming out to greet them. The Tahitians recognised David Nelson, the botanist, William Peckover, and Bligh himself from their trip ten years before with Cook.

Bligh met Chief Otoo who had now changed his name to Tinah, a fairly common occurrence amongst Tahitian Chiefs. Tinah and the local people entertained Bligh and the crew with gargantuan feasts whilst the women performed sensual exotic dances. There were celebrations of their arrival and exchange of gifts for two days before Bligh manoeuvred the situation in order that he may procure breadfruits. Bligh told Tinah that he had brought many gifts from King George and asked Tinah whether he would like to give something in return. King Tinah listed everything that he could think of and when he got round to mentioning the breadfruit plant, Bligh agreed casually that King George was very fond of breadfruit, and in that way, the first part of the agreement was brought about. Bligh had got exactly what he wanted.

David Nelson, the botanist, told Bligh that the *Bounty* would have to stay in Tahiti for six months, as once potted, the breadfruit would have to take root before being transported to the West Indies. This was good news for the crew who must have loved the idea, but it was very bad news for Bligh. Another possible reason for the *Bounty* staying so long was the delay in the original orders from the Admiralty resulting in them being unable to round The Horn and consequently having to sail round the Cape of Good Hope, arriving in Tahiti in October, 1788 as opposed to the previous April. If they now left in November, the prevailing winds would be westerly, making the journey home through the Endeavour Straits very dangerous and forcing a possible return to Tahiti. In the event, the resulting five month stay in Tahiti was to cause a disaster later on, but although Bligh sensed problems, he could do nothing to prevent them.

Fryer was put in charge of the *Bounty* although Bligh had no confidence in him and often returned to the ship to check that everything was running smoothly. Christian had the more attractive task of being in charge of the shore party, collecting and potting the breadfruit plants. Bligh, trusting him, left him to his own devices and Christian became a self styled Lord of the Manor, a role that had been denied him in England. Although he left Christian alone, Bligh did not trust his petty officers much and sometimes with good reason. One dreadful lapse was made by Fryer, the ship's Master, and to a degree, Cole, the Boatswain. On 17th January, 1789, Bligh asked for the spare sails to be taken out and aired, and when brought out were found to be mildew and completely rotten. Bligh had previously been assured by Fryer that the sails were in good condition, and to allow the one spare set to deteriorate was an appalling act of neglect. Bligh was furious and with good reason – he wrote in his log:

"If I had any officers to supercede the Master and Boatswain, or was capable of doing without them considering them as common seamen, they should no longer occupy their respective stations".

Both these men were Bligh loyalists who accompanied him in the open boat, so there is no denying the validity of his anger.

There were further problems. One month previously, on 10th December, 1788, Thomas Huggan, the surgeon died. He was found in an alcoholic coma and passed away at 9pm. His death was less of a surprise than his being on the trip in the first place. He was fat, dirty, indolent, and incompetent, and had clearly been an alcoholic from day one. Thomas Ledward was appointed Surgeon in his place; he was rated as Able Seaman but was in fact Assistant Surgeon and had been taken on specifically because Bligh had thought something like this was likely to happen.

Even more trouble was brewing however. On 4th January, three men, Churchill, Musprat, and Millward deserted. The fact that this happened hardly came as a surprise as Tahiti was paradise and Captain Cook had had the same problem when he was there when two of his marines did the same. If they thought that they could get away with it, probably even more men would have attempted it. They underestimated Bligh however, and he himself led the party of men who captured the deserters on 23rd January, nearly three weeks later. The men claimed that they were coming back already, but Bligh was not convinced. The following day, he had all three men flogged; Churchill with twelve lashes, and the other two with twenty - four each. He then clapped them in irons for one week and on 4th February, he had them flogged again with the same number of lashes and then released. By the standards of the day, this punishment was very lenient and Bligh was within his rights to hang them which many other captains would have done. The fact that he was relatively lenient with them was probably due to Bligh's anger with the Officers of the Watch whose neglect he felt had made it easy for the three men to desert in the first place. He felt that he could not punish the officers with flogging and therefore felt it unfair to punish the men more severely whilst only issuing the officers with an admonishment. Tahiti was paradise, but certainly not problem free, probably due to the fact that it *was* paradise.

Eventually the breadfruit plants were ready for transportation and it was time to leave their new friends in Tahiti. the *Bounty* weighed anchor and set sail on 5th April, 1789. The leaving caused many of the men to experience mixed emotions because whilst many of them were looking forward to seeing their families in England again, many of them had formed strong attachments to the women and simply did not want to leave. This was hardly surprising. They had a long voyage home on a cramped ship with poor food to look forward to, and a return to the discipline and regular work patterns that they had been completely free from for the last five months on this tropical paradise. It is thought that Christian, in particular, was distraught.

He was certainly very sad. He had had a wonderful five months in Tahiti as Bligh had more or less left him as his own boss. He had also formed a close attachment with a lady called Mauatea, who he subsequently re-named Isabella, presumably after his first love, Isabella Curwen, who had married his cousin John. He had little to look forward to back home, having lost his inheritance and he had thoroughly integrated into the Tahitian way of life which had included getting himself heavily tattooed, a custom which eventually became the norm for British sailors, but which was first seen in the Polynesian islands. He was in a vulnerable frame of mind when the *Bounty* set sail, and it wasn't long before he showed signs of cracking up. Bligh on the other hand, ever the perfectionist, was determined to impose discipline again and in order to do this, possibly overcompensated with his nagging. He had a temper as well and his frustration would boil on occasions. With Bligh however, once it was said, it was forgotten, but tragically for him, others on the sharp end of his tongue felt wounded and harboured resentment. Christian, possibly on the verge of some sort of breakdown, simply couldn't cope with his changed circumstances. It is widely believed that he made a makeshift raft with a view to sailing alone to Tofoa, the nearest island, but was persuaded from this suicidal mission that would surely have ended with an early lonely death. He must have been at breaking point to even consider such a foolish action. Christian felt that Bligh was needlessly picking on him, and this, on top of the depression he felt at leaving Tahiti in the first place, soon became too much for him. One particular incident happened three weeks into the journey home on 24th April at Annamooka. This was the last stop before the mutiny and Bligh landed there as he wanted wood and water for the ship. Bligh had been to this island in 1777 with Captain Cook, and he considered the islanders friendly, but with no chiefs nearby, the islanders were very undisciplined. There are differing accounts as to what actually happened, but the Boatswain's Mate, James Morrison, claims that the natives crowded round the shore party and attempted to take the casks from the watering party and axes from the wooding party. Christian was in charge of the watering party and was bitterly chastised and ridiculed by Bligh when they returned to the *Bounty* for not standing up to the natives all the while he had muskets. Christian is supposed to have replied, "The arms are of no use while your orders prevent them being used". This version of events occurs in many accounts, and whilst there was certainly an altercation of some sort, there is no mention of Christian specifically in Bligh's log of 25th April, but he merely refers to his officers in general. This seems odd, but perhaps Bligh, even at the height of his frustration and anger, still saw Christian as a friend and someone who was capable of being a good naval officer in the long term and didn't want to jeopardise his chances in the future.

Tensions were building all round, although Bligh seemed blissfully unaware. He was determined to restore the discipline which had all but disappeared in Tahiti, whilst most of the men were looking back to a life in paradise that had been snatched away from them. The crew of the *Bounty* were on an obvious collision course with their Captain but there was one more incident that whilst viewed in isolation, would seem trivial, even farcical, but it may have been the straw that broke the camel's back, the camel in this case being Fletcher Christian. It was 27th April, the day before the mutiny, and there was a row about Bligh's personal store of coconuts that were kept in a barrel on deck. There are several different versions of what happened, but the long and short of it was that Bligh accused the men of stealing some of his private store but was unable to find the culprit as no-one owned up, leaving Bligh fuming in impotent rage. Some of the versions put Christian right at the forefront of Bligh's verbal attack, and if this is accurate, it could finally have swayed Christian and driven him over the brink. According to accounts, Christian seemed very hurt by Bligh's anger towards him and his accusations of dishonesty, and by now his nerves were probably in shreds. It must be remembered too, that this incident was straight after Bligh had criticised Christian for his handling of the trouble at Annamooka. Bligh still seemed unaware of the hurt that he had caused however, and an example of this is the fact that he invited Christian to dine with him that very evening, although Christian, deeply hurt, refused, saying that he was unwell. The other extraordinary thing is that Bligh seems not to have entered the incident in his log of the 27th April. Bligh went to bed that night, completely unaware of the atmosphere in the ship and the catastrophe that was going to happen in the next few hours.

Just before sunrise on 28th April, 1789, Christian, Churchill, Mills and Burkett got into Bligh's cabin and pulled him from his bunk. They tied his hands tightly behind his back and hauled him on deck, threatening him with instant death if he made a noise. Bligh still yelled out loud to sound the alarm as he would have had no idea whether they were in the majority or not. Smith, Sumner, and Quintel were outside the cabin. Bligh was taken up on deck where all hell was breaking loose. There was total confusion as to who was a mutineer and who was not and so it was very difficult for Bligh loyalists to mount any form of co-ordinated resistance. Armed, angry, and probably fearful even then of what they were doing, the mutineers were out of control and must have been a terrifying sight. Also, the loyalists were taken completely by surprise as no-one was expecting a mutiny, and far from being a pre-planned action, this was almost certainly a completely spontaneous act of sheer madness. It must be remembered that Christian was going to abandon the ship on his own in a makeshift raft only the day before. However, it is widely thought that as he was preparing to do this, one of the men told Christian:- "That the men are prepared for anything". It is not certain who this was, but is widely believed to be George Stewart, a twenty-two year old midshipman. Whoever it was, this one remark, if made, created an extraordinary historical event, because if Christian had left on his own as he had originally intended, the *Bounty* would have sailed home as normal having satisfactorily completed the job, and William Bligh would not be known in the way he is today.

With his hands held tightly behind his back, Bligh and a hyped up Christian faced each other on the deck with the pandemonium going on around them. Bligh reminded Christian of past friendships and asked him if this was a proper return for the favours that he had shown Christian in the past. The question disturbed Christian, who answered with much emotion: "That Captain Bligh, that is the thing, I am in hell, I am in hell". Eventually, after a further two hours of threats and counter threats, Bligh and eighteen men were put in to the launch and cast adrift to fend for themselves. These eighteen men are always referred to as loyalists, although sometimes it was difficult to work out exactly who was loyal to Bligh and who was not. Among those in the launch were Purcell and Fryer who had both been consistent thorns in Bligh's side, whilst there were several men left on the *Bounty* who clearly had wanted to go with Bligh in the launch. Bligh knew who they were and yelled out that he would make sure their names were cleared should he ever reach England.

The jeering men on the *Bounty* threw bits of food down and four cutlasses, a pitiful defence for them if they were to land on an island and come across hostile natives. No muskets, two or three days worth of food, set adrift in the middle of the Pacific, Christian was sending his one time friend, William Bligh and his erstwhile shipmates, off to an almost certain death. Christian had no quarrel with anyone other than Bligh, and consequently there is a body of opinion that thinks it was an act of unspeakable cruelty. However, to be fair to Christian, it's quite obvious that he wasn't thinking clearly, and also that he may have thought that Bligh and the other men would find a safe island nearby, perhaps Tofoa, where they could wait to be picked up by a ship later on. This assumes however, that they would be allowed to settle there by the local people and that a ship would find them. The kindest thought that we can allow Fletcher Christian is that he was in the middle of a breakdown and not in complete control of his senses.

Bligh with eighteen men was cast adrift approximately 30 miles from Tofoa in the Friendly Isles, although as it happened, this turned out to be a highly inaccurate name. Bligh had no charts, but he had a compass, quadrant, sextant and navigational tables. He also kept the *Bounty's* logbook which has proved a blessing for historians. Bligh and his men landed at Tofoa in order to add food to their meagre rations, but although the natives appeared friendly at first, crowds appeared and started knocking stones together, a war-like threat in the Pacific Islands. Bligh and the men managed to escape to the launch and row away, but it must have been a terrifying experience and must have reminded Bligh of Hawaii ten years before when he was with Captain Cook when Cook was killed at Kealakekua Bay in a similar situation. All the men with Bligh survived however, apart from John Norton, who was stoned to death by the natives when he bravely tried to cut the rope which was keeping the boat attached to the shore. Although this was a dreadful tragedy, it probably saved everyone else's lives as Norton was by far and away the heaviest man and the boat would almost certainly not have reached eventual safety with all of them on board. After this experience, Bligh decided it would be too risky to land on any other islands, so he decided that the only course of action that was open to them was to make for the Dutch settlement of Timor in the East Indies, a distance of 3,600 miles.

It is almost impossible to describe the hardships that lay before them. They had food for three days and an open boat journey of six weeks before them. Torrential rains were to hit them, gales blew up, and although desperately weak, the men had to bale continuously in order to keep the launch afloat. The men were often soaked to the skin and freezing. Bligh advised them to remove their clothing, and wring it out in the sea as the salt water made it warmer. They were rarely dry, and suffered excruciating pains in the bowels, were starving and could barely use their limbs. Bligh made some makeshift scales from coconut shells and carefully measured their tiny rations out. As early as 3rd May, Bligh wrote in his log:

"Our wants are beginning to have a dreadful aspect which nothing but a firm and determined resolution can fight against, a situation particularly miserable on a commander".

This was written one week after the mutiny – there would be five more weeks of torture before they would reach their destination, but reach it they did, although not before they were reduced to killing a noddy bird which they managed to catch. The three weakest men drank the blood from the bird whilst the creature was divided into eighteen equal parts using Bligh's makeshift scales. The bird was eaten raw and everything was consumed including the beak and the entrails – they were that desperate.

Bligh not only had to battle against the elements and starvation, he sometimes had to battle against cold starving men who were at the end of their tether. Fryer, Purcell and Lamb in particular gave him trouble but he brought them through and on 12th June, 1789, they sighted Timor, and two days later on the 14th June, they entered Coupang Harbour, although Bligh, ever the perfectionist, insisted he would not land until he had run up a makeshift union jack made out of some signal flags that he had brought with him. Their dreadful ordeal was finally over. The men had put up with the most appalling conditions of deprivation for six weeks, conditions that had driven most of them to the brink of utter despair with unimaginable sufferings. It took supreme leadership as well as brilliant navigational skills to bring the men through this, and it took courage of the most extraordinary kind. Given the hardships that they had endured, many maritime historians have said that the like of this open boat voyage will never be equalled, and what is also so remarkable is the fact that throughout his dreadful journey, Bligh had charted all the islands that they had passed, even though he was so weak he could hardly write. It was an amazing achievement, and almost certainly, Bligh's finest hour. All of Bligh's courage in the face of the most dreadful hardship, amazing skills in the handling of his men through this prolonged crisis, plus his supreme navigational skills, saw him through this appalling period of his life. It was the eventual recognition of these navigational skills that were to get him elected to the Royal Society in 1801 when his friend and patron, Sir Joseph Banks was the President.

However, in the mean time, Bligh returned home on 14th March 1790 and was given hero status. He had to face a Court Martial for the loss of his ship but this was standard procedure, and Bligh was cleared of any blame. He took a year off to recuperate, and then undertook another trip to transport the breadfruit from Tahiti to the West Indies. This time the Admiralty took more notice of his needs, and he went out having been promoted to Captain, supported by commissioned officers, had two ships properly equipped, and also had Marines to back his authority with. He left Spithead as Captain of the *Providence* on 3rd August, 1791 with a small brig, the *Assistant* sailing with them. Bligh chose Nathanial Portlock to command the second vessel as he was known to him. Bligh had sailed with Portlock on Captain Cook's third trip. Portlock had been appointed Master's Mate in 1776 by Charles Clerke, the Captain of the *Discovery*, at the beginning of Cook's third trip, and transferred to Cook's ship, the *Resolution*, when Cook was killed by the local people in Hawaii on 14th February, 1779. Bligh also took Francis Godolphin Bond, the son of his half sister, Catherine as his own second-in-command. Another person that Bligh took along was a young midshipman called Matthew Flinders (1774-1814), who was later to become famous for completing the mapping of Australia. They arrived home on 7th August, 1793, almost two years to the day they set off, this time, completing the task without the traumas of the first trip. However, it was not an easy journey for Bligh as he was still clearly ill from the dreadful ordeal of the open boat journey, and the result of this was that he was confined to his cabin for long periods at a time suffering from the most appalling headaches.

There were twenty-five men on board the *Bounty* when it sailed off after the mutiny on the 28th April 1789, leaving William Bligh in the middle of the Pacific with eighteen men to fend for themselves. The men on the *Bounty* would have had no idea as to what would happen to Bligh and his men, but it is a safe assumption that they would assume that he, along with the others, would die. Equally, when Bligh returned to England in March 1790, nobody would have known what would have happened to the twenty-five men on board the *Bounty*. Originally, they sailed the *Bounty* to the island of Tubuai, arriving there four weeks after the mutiny with a view to setting up a settled community there. This was Christian's idea as he thought that the climate was suitable and it was off the shipping lanes should anyone try to find them later on. Not everyone agreed with him however and they were proved correct as Captain Cox of the *Mercury* passed within two miles of them one night and saw fires. Had he passed during the day, he might well have seen the *Bounty* itself. James Morrison, the Boatswain's Mate, who was to cause Bligh's reputation to be seriously damaged in the years ahead, was one of those who disagreed with Christian. Morrison wrote:-

"I cannot say that ever I agreed in Oppinion With Mr. Christian with respect to the plan he had formd nor did I ever form a favourable idea Of the Natives of Toobouai whose savage aspect & behaviour could not gain favour in the Eyes of any Man in his senses, but was fully capable of Creating a Distaste in any one."

The idea of settling on the island of Tubuai turned out to be a disaster. The islanders and the mutineers fought from day one, and whilst the islanders were superior in number the *Bounty's* guns were ferocious and several islanders were killed whilst many others were wounded. Despite this poor beginning, Christian was determined to settle on the island and returned to Tahiti for extra supplies and local women to set up a community back in Tubuai. The *Bounty* duly returned to Tahiti, and Christian told the chiefs there that Bligh had met Captain Cook and had decided to create a new settlement and needed their women and some provisions. The Tahitians thought highly of Cook and had no idea that he had been killed in Hawaii ten years before, and therefore agreed. On the 19th June, 1789, the *Bounty* left Tahiti and returned to Tubuai with provisions, animals, and nine Tahitian women and fifteen men and boys. Trouble brewed again on their return however, as there were not enough women for the men, and so the mutineers decided to take the local women by force thus provoking more trouble with the local people. Once more, the *Bounty* left Tubuai and returned to Tahiti on 20th September, 1789. This time there was no pretending about Bligh and Cook as the Tahitians that went with Christian and his party would tell the Tahitians chiefs anyway, so Christian had to come clean, although in the event, it didn't seem to bother anyone too much. The next decision to be made was where they were all going to go from here. Out of the twenty-five mutineers, sixteen opted to stay at Tahiti which was a dangerous gamble given that regardless of whether Bligh was dead or alive, and regardless of whether he managed to return to England or not, the navy would send a ship out to look for them, and the first place they would visit would be Tahiti. Christian and the other eight could see the dangers, and on the night of the 22nd September 1789, the *Bounty* quietly slipped its moorings and Christian, along with the eight other mutineers, six Polynesian men, and twelve women, sailed off to look for their paradise island. Four months later, they were to find their island, which was called Pitcairns Island and they settled there on 21st January, 1790, but it was to be no paradise. It took the group nearly a week to transfer all their supplies from ship to shore, but eventually this arduous task was completed and they were finally ready to start their new life. It had been nine long months since the mutiny.

They started their life at Pitcairns Island, but despite legend saying that they all lived happily ever after, the reverse is true. The Europeans caused the problems by dividing the land between themselves instead of sharing it with the Polynesian people. The long and short of it was that over the next few years, there was huge fighting amongst themselves and all the men, European as well as Tahitian were killed except Ned Young and John Adams. Ned Young eventually died of illness, and John Adams was the sole surviving member of the crew left alive along with assorted Polynesian women and mixed race children. After all this mayhem, Adams was to undergo a conversion to Christianity, and using the Bible from the *Bounty*, he conducted religious services which the whole community attended and he was acknowledged by all as the Father of the Community, and he brought them all up in the strict Christian faith.

Nothing was heard of them until February 1808, when Captain Mayhew Folger of the *Topaz* found them and heard the dreadful story of what happened from John Adams. Folger saw that although the initial mutiny was clearly a criminal act, he also saw that the second generation Pitcairns people were so polite and Adams so old, that it wasn't worth punishing anybody.

After Bligh had returned home in March 1790, it was decided to send a ship, the *Pandora*, out to search for the mutineers. At this stage, they would have had no idea that the mutineers had split up, so in August, 1790, the ship, captained by Edward Edwards, left England bound for Tahiti on the first leg of their search. The *Pandora* arrived in Tahiti on 23rd March, 1791 and found fourteen men, Thompson and Churchill having been murdered in the intervening period. Three men immediately swam out to the ship believing that they were not part of the mutiny and thinking that they could convince Captain Edwards of this. However, Edwards was told to treat everybody the same way as it was felt that only a Court Marshal in England could establish individual guilt or innocence. Edwards had a wooden prison built on deck that measured 11 by 18 feet and all the men were incarcerated in this small space and the conditions became almost unbearable – Edwards wouldn't even let them out to answer the call of nature so after two years of freedom in paradise, this must have felt like an extreme type of unnecessary torture.

The *Pandora* left Tahiti on 8th May, 1791 and decided to search for the other mutineers before heading for England, because that was the brief that Edwards had been given. The *Pandora* went from island to island searching in vain for Christian and his people but on the 28th August, 1791, disaster struck. The ship crashed into the Great Barrier Reef and sank losing thirty - four men by drowning. Four of these men were mutineers but it was a miracle even more weren't drowned given the callous treatment that they received from Captain Edwards. He had left it until the last possible moment before giving permission for the prison to be unlocked and the terrified prisoners had to jump from the stricken ship as best as they could. The 102 survivors stayed on a tiny island, and when their three boats were ready, made for Timor in the way that Bligh had done just over two years before. The journey, though long and arduous, was nowhere near as long as Bligh's, but for one of the crew, was particularly galling as this was Lieutenant Thomas Hayward who had been a Bligh loyalist on the *Bounty* and was now going through a similar experience again. Eventually they reached Timor, and from there sailed on a Dutch ship to Batavia which they reached on 7th November, 1791. They were transferred to a British ship, the *HMS Gorgon* and because they were no longer under the command of Captain Edwards, their conditions improved. They arrived home on the 18th June, 1792, nearly two years after the *Pandora* had left England, over three years since the mutiny, and four and a half years since the *Bounty* had left Spithead.

There were ten mutineers left to face trial on their return home. These were Peter Heywood, James Morrison, Thomas Ellison, Thomas Burkitt, John Millward, William Musprat, Charles Norman, Joseph Coleman, Thomas McIntosh, and Michael Byrne. The trial was held on *HMS Duke* between 12th and 18th September, 1792 and was presided over by the 1st Viscount Hood (1724-1816), the court being made up of eleven post captains. This Lord Hood was named Samuel and was the elder brother of two famous Admirals, the other being Alexander Hood (1727-1814), the 1st Viscount Bridport. Both men had had distinguished naval careers but in 1784, the year that the new Prime Minister, William Pitt the Younger (1759-1806) called his first election having taken office at the end of the previous year, Samuel challenged Charles James Fox (1749-1806), the famous Whig politician for the Parliamentary seat of Westminster and won. In 1788 Samuel became a Lord of the Admiralty and during the war against the French, he captured Toulon in 1793 and Corsica in 1794.

At the trial on *HMS Duke*, the men were charged with "Mutinously running away with the said armed vessel the *Bounty* and deserting from His Majesty's Service". When Bligh had returned to England in March 1790, he had been welcomed as a hero and had had an audience with King George III – a high honour indeed. Bligh's reputation was about to change however, and this was due to the extraordinary decision to hold the trial of the mutineers whilst Bligh was away on the second breadfruit trip between August 1791 and August 1793. There were ten men who were fighting for their lives and were free to say what they wanted about Bligh without any fear of contradiction. James Morrison, the Boatswain's Mate, a clever man, was to take full advantage of the situation whilst Peter Heywood would help finish Bligh's reputation off once the trial was over.

James Morrison did not have Heywood's connections, but he was a very able man and his journals were used to the detriment of Bligh. His journals were presented as having been kept at the time, but this was complete nonsense – they were written after the event. It would have been impossible for him to have kept any journals that he wrote as they would have been taken away from him whilst he was on the *Pandora* and even if he'd been allowed to keep them, would have been lost when the *Pandora* sank. Just about everything he said about Bligh was negative and Bligh was not able to attend the trial to challenge Morrison's version of events.

Unlike Morrison, Peter Heywood's family were well connected and they used those connections to good effect. Much has been made of two letters that

Bligh had written to Heywood's family on his return from the open boat ordeal. The letters are seen by Bligh's detractors as proof of his poor character but they must be seen in the context of when they were written and in what circumstances. The open boat journey was a dreadful ordeal and although Bligh got his men safely to Coupang, some did not survive the journey back to England. John Norton had been killed by natives at Tofua, and Bligh, and no doubt other men who did survive, were ill for probably the rest of their lives as a result. Bligh had taken Heywood on the *Bounty* as a favour to the family and claimed that there had never been a cross word between them during the whole trip. Indeed, that was part of Heywood's defence. The first letter is from Bligh to an uncle of Heywood's and was written on 26th March, 1790, soon after Bligh had returned home after his ordeal and before the *Pandora* had left England to search for the mutineers. The letter reads as follows:-

I have just this instant received your letter. With much concern I inform you that your nephew, Peter Heywood, is among the mutineers. His ingratitude to me is of the blackest dye, for I was a father to him in every respect, and he never once had an angry word from me through the whole course of the voyage, as his conduct always gave me much pleasure and satisfaction. I very much regret that so much baseness formed the character of a young man I had a real regard for, and it will give me much pleasure to hear his friends can bear the loss of him without much concern.

I am, Sir, & c.
(Signed) W.M. Bligh"

The second letter was written shortly afterwards, on the 2nd April, 1790, to Heywood's mother. It reads:-

"Madam,
I received your letter this day, and feel for you very much, being perfectly sensible of the extreme distress you must suffer from the conduct of your son Peter. His baseness is beyond all description, but I hope you will endeavour to prevent the loss of him, heavy as the misfortune is, from afflicting you too severely. I imagine he is, with the rest of the mutineers, returned to Otaheite.

I am Madam,
(Signed) W.M. Bligh"

To many people, given Bligh's ordeal and ongoing illness, along with the fact that he took Heywood on the trip as a favour, the tone of the letters are perfectly understandable and given Heywood's actions after the trial, actually prove that Bligh's opinions of Heywood are in fact, perfectly correct. Heywood's defence during the trial was lengthy to the point of utter tediousness but given his youth and the fact that he was facing death if found guilty he can be forgiven that. His statement was read out by one of his defence team and in it, he denied taking part in the mutiny, and stating that his youth and inexperience were the causes of his not taking a fuller part in defending Bligh. Neutrality was not a defence however, but one of the most damning statements that he made in his defence would deservedly come back to haunt him in years to come. He had made great play of the fact that Bligh had been kind to him and amongst other things, his deposition contained the following:-

"Indeed, from his (Bligh's) attention to and very kind treatment of me personally, I should have been a Monster of depravity to have betrayed him – the idea alone is sufficient to disturb a mind where humanity and gratitude have, I hope, ever been noticed as its characteristic features".

Be that as it may, and despite his connections, the court's decision given on the 18th September, 1792, was that:- "The Charges had been proven against the said Peter Heywood, James Morrison, Thomas Ellison, Thomas Burkitt, John Millward, and William Musprat and it did adjudge them and each of them to suffer Death by being hanged by the Neck, on board such of His Majesty's Ship or Ships of War, at such Time or Times and at such Place or Places..." The Court statement went on to recommend leniency by His Majesty for Peter Heywood and James Morrison and they duly received their Royal Pardons on 24th October, 1792. William Musprat was also eventually cleared on a technicality worked out by his clever lawyer, Stephen Barney although he did not earn his discharge until 11th February, 1793. Meanwhile, the unlucky Ellison, Burkitt and Millward, having no clever lawyers or family connections to help them were hanged on 29th October, 1792, on board *HMS Brunswick*. The four remaining men, Michael Byrne, Charles Norman, Joseph Coleman and Thomas McIntosh did not have the case proved against them and each were acquitted and instantly released.

It could have ended there, but unfortunately for Bligh who was blissfully unaware of what was happening in England as he was on the second breadfruit trip, it didn't. Morrison, not content with being freed, wrote a set of unsubstantiated journals damning Bligh, while even worse, Heywood, whose whole defence was based on the fact that it would have been impossible for him to have mutinied against Bligh given the latter's kindness to him, quickly forgot his good fortune at being pardoned by the King. Heywood contacted Fletcher Christian's lawyer brother, Edward Christian, and told him a completely different story about Bligh and the mutiny. The result was that Christian, an influential lawyer, backed by both Heywood and Morrison, wrote a paper criticising Bligh, which took hold both in the eyes of the Admiralty and the public at large. Bligh had left for the second breadfruit trip on the 3rd August, 1791 and in the eyes of the public was a hero, but when he returned almost exactly two years later, on the 7th August, 1793, things had changed, and the King, who had granted him the honour of an audience before the trip, now snubbed him. Bligh was hurt and confused, and although he printed a reply to Edward Christian's paper, it was ineffective and Bligh's reputation was never the same. Although Bligh had a good career after that, his reputation was forever tarnished, and the nickname *'The Bounty Bastard'* stayed with him for years.

William Bligh is known to the general public mainly for the mutiny and even then their knowledge of him is at best sketchy and at worst, completely distorted. What is not generally known is that at the time of the mutiny, he was only 34 years old and was barely halfway through a naval career that bordered on brilliance. There were 18 loyalists in the open boat with Bligh, whilst 25 (including Christian) remained on the *Bounty* which eventually returned to Tahiti. Of that twenty-five, the following happened:-

9 – including Christian sailed away along with Tahitian men and women to start a new life, and ended up on Pitcairn's Island. Seven of them were killed in internal fights, whilst one died of illness. The remaining mutineer, Alexander Smith (John Adams) was converted to Christianity and became leader of the community.

16 – remained at Tahiti. Of these:-

2 – were murdered at Tahiti.

14 – Were picked up by the *Pandora* captained by Edward Edwards. The ship had left England in August 1790 to search for the mutineers. Of these 14:-

4 – drowned when the *Pandora* sank off the north-east coast of Australia on 28th August, 1791.

The remaining 10 were brought back to England and court martialled in September 1792. Of the 10, 4 were acquitted and 6 found guilty. Of the six:- three were pardoned and three were hanged.

It was a sad, tragic and almost pathetic end to a project that should have been almost routine. Many people lost their lives, other lives were ruined and Bligh's reputation was damaged for the rest of his life. If all this wasn't enough, just to add insult to injury, the slaves did not like the breadfruit and refused to eat it making the whole sorry saga a complete and utter waste of time.

Although Bligh's name was tarnished, his sense of duty remained intact. He was determined to serve his country and he always had Sir Joseph Banks behind him which was to be useful later on in his career – Banks was a loyal man, he had influence and never stopped believing in Bligh. Meanwhile, Bligh was given a welcome command that would do much to rehabilitate his reputation.

In 1797, he took command of the *Director,* which was part of the English fleet led by Admiral Duncan, and on the 11th October, he fought bravely at the subsequent Battle of Camperdown. Through most of 1797, Admiral Duncan had been blockading the Dutch fleet in Den Helder and Texel. There was a plan to land French troops in Ireland to support the rebellion that was planned there, and Duncan was blockading the Dutch fleet that was intending to cover the French troops. In late September 1797, the Dutch changed their minds about invading and Duncan was instructed to withdraw his fleet and return to Yarmouth to re-fit. When the Dutch saw this, they came out of port to see if they could engage individual British ships but the British were alerted to this and returned to Textel to lie in wait for the Dutch fleet to return which they duly did. The Dutch and British fleets met eighteen miles from the Dutch coast, fairly evenly matched in terms of numbers, the Dutch having 25 ships and the British 24.

It is widely assumed that Nelson first came up with the idea of attacking the enemy with two columns which he did in October 1805 at Trafalgar when he split the English fleet into two when attacking the combined French and Spanish fleet. However, Admiral Duncan had the idea eight years before when he did a similar thing against the Dutch fleet at Camperdown. Duncan led one column in the *Venerable* whilst Vice Admiral Richard Onslow led the other column in the

Monarch. The Dutch fleet were led by Admiral De Winter, and his ship the *Vrijheid* engaged Duncan's ship the *Venerable*. Both fleets fought bravely but eventually de Winter's ship was dismasted and with over half her crew killed or wounded he was forced to strike his colours. Bligh's ship, the *Director* eventually finished her off and it was Bligh who received Admiral de Winter's sword when the Admiral surrendered. The fight was very even and both sides carried heavy casualties. This was a very proud moment for Bligh and gold medals were struck for all the captains involved and Bligh wore his at every opportunity with great pride. This is considered by some historians as Bligh's proudest achievement.

Four years later, Bligh was involved in another famous battle, the Battle of Copenhagen. The English fleet led by Admiral Hyde Parker (1739-1807) with Nelson as second in command, took on the Danish fleet in March 1801. The battle was caused by a succession of diplomatic failures during the French Revolutionary wars. Great Britain was vastly superior in terms of its naval strength than France, and the Royal navy searched any neutral ships that entered French ports, and if they decided they were trading with France, would seize their goods. The Russian Tsar, Paul, having been an ally of Britain, decided to arrange a League of Armed Neutrality between Scandinavia, Prussia, and Russia which he intended would enforce free trade with France. Britain thought differently however, and decided that the League was in the French interest and was therefore a threat.

In early 1801, the British Government assembled a fleet at Great Yarmouth with the intention of destroying the League, but then an extraordinary event occurred. Admiral Sir Hyde Parker, who by this time was 61 years old, had married an eighteen-year-old girl and didn't actually refuse, but nonetheless showed a great reluctance to leave Great Yarmouth and fight. He did not wish to leave port until he had attended a ball in his new wife's honour which was fixed for Friday 13th March and in the meantime, everything else concerning the fleet seemed to have ground to a halt. Time was of the essence as the British Navy needed to be out and attacking the Dano-Norwegian fleets before the Baltic Sea thawed and the Russian fleet could join their allies. If this had happened, then the British Navy would be facing a combined fleet of 123 ships-of-the-line. Something clearly had to be done and it was Lord Nelson, who was Hyde Parker's second in command, and furious at the situation that they found themselves in, who sorted the problem out. He sent a note to Captain Thomas Troubridge who was a Lord Commissioner of the Admiralty, and this prompted a private note from the Earl St. Vincent, the First Lord of the Admiralty, and the fleet sailed from Great Yarmouth on the 12th March, 1801.

In the meantime, Bligh was at home without a command but at the last minute, he was given the Captaincy of *HMS Glatton* and hurried to join the fleet before it set sail.

The battle commenced on the 2nd of April and it was once again left to Nelson to seize control of the events in order to alter the way that the battle was fought. Hyde Parker was no coward, but he was a cautious man and there were constant differences between himself and Nelson, who was much more of a fighting man, as to the conduct of the battle. It was certainly a bloody affray and after two hours, Bligh noted in his log:-

"At noon, the action continuing very hot, ourselves much cut up. Our opponent, the Danish Commodore, struck to us, but his seconds ahead and astern still keep up a strong fire".

He was referring to the Danish ships, the *Elven* and *Aggershuus*. The battle continued for two more hours with both sides pounding each other but neither giving up. At one point, the Danish Commander, Admiral Fischer, had to leave his flagship, *Dannebroge* when it was heavily fired on by both the *Elephant*, captained by Nelson, and the *Glatton*, captained by Bligh. He would not give up though and transferred to *Holsteen*. However, eventually the battle swung Nelson's way. It was Nelson who was in the thick of it whilst Hyde Parker was four miles away and didn't really know completely what was going on. At one point he raised Signal No. 39 which meant 'Discontinue the action' but Nelson, on seeing this was furious and ignored it, raising his own signal No. 16 (Close Action). One or two ships, seeing Hyde Parker's flag discontinued fighting, but most carried on including Bligh in the *Glatton* which at one point gave covering fire to Nelson in the *Elephant* when the latter was in trouble.

Eventually the battle finished, Nelson negotiating a cease fire to save further loss of life, but it had been a very close run thing and was the bloodiest battle of Nelson's career. A very proud moment for Bligh occurred after the battle had ceased when he was summoned and personally thanked by Nelson for his part in the action. Bligh, along with everybody else involved, had distinguished himself well, and was justly proud of his achievements during this dreadful carnage. The British had 264 killed and 689 wounded, whilst the Danish fleet had 2,215 killed and wounded along with 12 ships captured, 2 ships being sunk, and one ship exploding.

After taking an active part in the battles of Camperdown (1797) and Copenhagen (1801), the final service that Bligh performed for his country was in 1805, when his old friend and patron, Sir Joseph Banks, recommended Bligh for the post of Governor-General of the penal colony in New South Wales. The colony had been set up in 1788 on the advice of Sir Joseph Banks himself. The prisons in England were completely full and America had been lost and was now an independent country, so something had to be done about the prison problem. In 1778, Joseph Banks, in his first year as President of the Royal Society, had suggested Botany Bay to a Parliamentary Committee as an answer to the problem of prison overcrowding, remembering it from his visit there with Cook in 1770. At first, the idea was rejected as being not practical due to the distance from England and the resulting problems of communication that would result. However, with the lack of any alternative, the idea gradually took root and on the 12th October, 1786, Captain Arthur Phillip (1738-1814) was appointed the first Governor-General by Prime Minister William Pitt and Lord Sydney, the Home Secretary.

The first fleet comprising of eleven ships set sail from Portsmouth on 13th May, 1787 and arrived in Botany Bay (named by Captain Cook after Joseph Banks and Daniel Solander, the botanists on Cook's first trip) on the 18th January 1788. The place was deemed unsuitable for a new colony and so the fleet moved on and on the 26th January, 1788 they landed at Sydney Cove, named after the Home Secretary who had signed the initial orders.

Life was very hard at first but once new ships and people were brought over from England, the colony began to take shape and settle down. In 1792, an exhausted Phillip returned to England and because it was thought that Phillip might return, no official Governor-General was appointed until Captain John Hunter took over in 1795. In the intervening three years, the unofficial Governor was Major Francis Grose (1754-1814) who was Commander of the New South Wales Corps, the military who had taken over the discipline of the colony once the marines who had initially done the job had been sent back to England. Grose had been a veteran of the war with America and saw the posting in New South Wales very much as semi-retirement. He was not after any sort of action or any glory and happily handed over the day to day running to a young Lieutenant called John MacArthur. MacArthur dispensed with the services of the civilian magistrates – the meting out of justice in the future would be handed out by the military. The economy of the colony was a complete mess as money was almost no use to anybody as there was little or nothing to spend it on. The military therefore monopolised the economy by making the bartering of rum the mainstay of the economy. The labourers would use rum either as an escape from their humdrum existence or for trading themselves and MacArthur and his men controlled the situation.

Captain John Hunter (1737-1821) became the second official Governor in 1795 after three years of chaos left by Grose - the New South Wales Corps had by now become known as the Rum Corps. There had been a long delay in appointing him. He had applied for the post in October, 1793 and was appointed in January, 1794. However, the major delays took place after that and he did not sail until February, 1795, arriving in Sydney on 7th September, 1795. He knew straight away the stranglehold that the military had in New South Wales had to be broken, but for a variety of reasons, he was unable to do it. In fact the situation got worse for him when anonymous letters were sent to the English authorities accusing Hunter of complicity in the very thing that he was trying to stamp out. The effect of these letters meant that he was recalled to England in a dispatch dated the 5th November, 1799. Hunter returned home on 28th September, 1800 and eventually returned to sea, being given command of the *Venerable* in 1804.

The next Governor-General was Captain Philip Gidley King (1758-1808) whose tenure of office ran from 1800 until 1805. King was appointed on the 28th September, 1800, the day his predecessor, John Hunter, sailed for England. King had been a trusted officer under the first Governor Phillip and in January, 1788, had been chosen by Phillip to set up a small colony on Norfolk Island. When he arrived as the third Governor-General, he immediately started work trying to dismantle the control the military had over the colony but found it difficult to get the agricultural workers to labour for anything other than liquor. He did have successes however, and brought in regulations for prices, hours of work and financial deals that helped the smallholders and he also managed to get the troublemaker, John MacArthur sent home to England in 1801 for fighting a duel with Lieutenant-Colonel Paterson in which Paterson was wounded in the shoulder by MacArthur. MacArthur was actually acquitted, but it did get him out of the way for some time. However, the difficulties he had with the military eventually took their toll on King's health and he resigned in 1805, his health declining until he died on 3rd September, 1808. He left the colony better than he found it, but there was still a huge amount of work for his successor to take on, and this was to be the colony's fourth Governor-General, William Bligh.

In March 1805, Sir Joseph Banks was asked if he could recommend someone to be the next Governor-General and he wrote to Bligh offering him the post at £2,000 per annum which was twice the size of the salary that King had been receiving. At the end of his tenure, he would receive a pension of £1,000 per year. It was a generous offer and Bligh would normally have accepted on the spot, but there were two things he needed to weigh up before making a decision. Firstly, it would almost certainly mean the end of his active career at sea. He had served with Nelson at the Battle of Copenhagen in 1801 and it would have been highly likely that he would have served with him again at the Battle of Trafalgar. Also, and more importantly to him, his wife Elizabeth was unwell and decided that, devoted though they were to each other, she would not accompany her husband to New South Wales. They had already suffered long separations (they had spent five of the six years apart from 1787 to 1793 during the breadfruit expeditions) and if he accepted the Governorship, he would probably be away for another five years, and neither of them were getting any younger. As it turned out, Bligh did accept, and in February, 1806, set sail for New South Wales in the *Lady Madeleine Sinclair*, escorted by *HMS Porpoise*. There was a muddle right from the start as the convoy was to be commanded by Captain Joseph Short who was in the *Porpoise* but he was junior to Bligh in the Captain's list and on arrival in New South Wales, was to place himself under the command of Governor Bligh. However, whilst on the voyage, Short seemed to think that he was in command and furious rows broke out between himself and Bligh. At one point, Short even fired warning shots across the *Lady Madeleine Sinclair's* bows which considering the power that Bligh would be able to exert over Short once they reached new South Wales, was an extraordinary thing to do. The whole matter was ludicrous in fact, and neither man came out of the affair very well.

Captain Francis Beaufort, who had followed in *HMS Woolwich* and arrived two days after Bligh's ships, heard testimonies from both men and pronounced them both in the wrong, although he found in favour of Bligh. It was a ridiculous, farcical beginning to an extremely important job.

However, things were soon to get worse. There were two problems that would immediately confront Bligh on his arrival at the settlement. John MacArthur was back in New South Wales and would always be a thorn in Bligh's side and the first problem was that MacArthur had been granted 5,000 acres of land and wanted it to be at an area called Cowpastures, which had got its name when a large number of cattle had wandered off during the Governorship of King to a secluded area and had multiplied in number. King had ordered MacArthur to claim his 5,000 acres in a different area, and when MacArthur had complained to the new Governor Bligh, Bligh had given him short shrift and simply refused, saying, or rather shouting, that he had no interest in the affair. The second problem was the New South Wales Corps. The officers were controlling the currency which was the trading of rum rather than the exchange of money, and when Bligh challenged this which was part of his brief, he was immediately on an inevitable collision course with the military who were there to back his authority but who were now hardly likely to take his side. In 1807, Bligh wrote to England about how he perceived the Rum Corps as they were now known as:-

"... about seventy of the privates were originally convicts, and the whole are so very much ingrafted with that order of persons as in many instances have had a very evil tendency, and is to be feared may lead to serious consequences".

Bligh went on to suggest that the whole of the corps be sent home and replaced by regular troops. Bligh's attempts to stamp out the rum trade met with little success and although the laws against the trade were harsh, they were ineffective. This was because they were so often ignored. The settlers were tough, had already been taken from their homes in England and transported halfway round the world only to be met with a harsh regime, and so they would not be frightened that easily.

Bligh was on a collision course with MacArthur who wanted Bligh removed. There were several disputes between the two men, one of which was about land and another concerning a long overdue payment that MacArthur felt he was owed by the Judge-Advocate, Richard Atkins. MacArthur asked Bligh for help with the unpaid bill on the grounds that Atkins would hardly enforce the payment on himself, but Bligh refused. The disputes continued but MacArthur held the advantage as the military were against Bligh and wanted him removed from office. MacArthur staged a coup and wrote the following petition:-

"Sir, The present alarming state of this Colony, in which every man's property, liberty, and life are endangered, induces us most earnestly to implore you instantly to place Governor Bligh under an arrest and to assume the command of the colony. We pledge ourselves, at a moment of less agitation to come forward to support the measure with our fortunes and our lives."

To claim that people's property could be vulnerable was complete nonsense and was obviously a personal matter between MacArthur and Bligh. Bligh was arrested at Government House by Major George Johnston who was accompanied by the members of the Corps. This act was illegal but nonetheless, Bligh's rule as Governor-General was effectively over. He was placed on the *Porpoise* on the understanding that he would sail for England, but although promising to do just that, once on board he ignored the agreement that he had given Lieutenant-Colonel Paterson, the Corps' Commanding Officer on the grounds that he, Bligh, "Was an Officer and a Gentleman". He had no qualms about this and his reasoning was that he had no grounds to quit his post until instructed by London and in any event, the coup was illegal.

On the 9th May, 1809, the British Government in London appointed Lachlan Macquarrie as Bligh's replacement and he arrived in Sydney on 28th December 1809. Bligh, who had spent all this time sailing nearby in the *Porpo*ise came back to Sydney on 17th January, 1810 and was greeted with a guard of honour. Macquarrie and Bligh got on well at first but after a short space of time, the relationship between the two men deteriorated because Bligh felt that Macquarrie was taking advice from the wrong people. Be that as it may, Macquarrie became the new Governor-General and Bligh set sail for home on the *Hindostan* on 12th May, 1810 arriving at Spithead on 25th October the same year. Bligh did not succeed in stamping out the corruption, but he faced the situation head on, and laid the foundations for Governor Macquarrie to finish the job. Bligh had been in Australia with his daughter Mary, who was by now a widow. His beloved Betsy had been too ill to accompany him and the one consolation for him was that he would soon be re-united with her. Bligh had assumed that Mary would be returning to England with him, but at the last minute, she informed her father that she was going to marry Lieutenant-Colonel O'Connell, who was the new Governor-General Macquarrie's deputy. The news was a total surprise to Bligh and filled him with dismay, but he had no option other than to agree to the marriage before sailing home on his own.

Bligh was re-united with his wife for only eighteen months when she died on 15th April, 1812. They had been married for over thirty years and had been devoted to each other, but the life of a naval officer's wife was not an easy one and there had been many partings. James and Elizabeth Cook had spent nine of the last eleven years of their marriage apart and it was no different for Bligh and his wife, Betsy. At the time of the mutiny, Bligh was at home for only one of six years, as he had gone back on the second breadfruit trip only a year after arriving home from the first. Although he had spent a year at home recuperating from the ordeal of the open boat journey, Bligh was still clearly unwell when he set off on the second trip, and was often ill and confined to his cabin during that time. It was clearly duty that drove him on to carry out the second trip and probably his pride at wanting to clear up unfinished business. Bligh was also away from 1806 to 1810 when he was Governor-General of New South Wales. After such devoted service to his country for so many years, it does seem cruel that they had such a short time together before illness finally overcame her. Bligh never complained, seeing the separations as part of his duty, but he was desperately sad when she died.

Bligh never saw action again on his return from Australia, but was still a serving officer and was promoted twice more. In 1812, he became a Rear-Admiral of The White, and in 1814, he was promoted to Vice-Admiral of The Blue.

William Bligh has been unfairly treated by history but the last fifty years have seen books that have sought to set the record straight. Bligh was *not* a serial flogger as has been shown in some Hollywood films – in some ways he didn't flog enough. He expected perfection in himself and his officers and became frustrated when he felt he didn't get it and his frustration would boil over with his short temper. However, whatever Bligh said in the heat of the moment he quickly forgot, but sadly, he had no idea that his words had wounded and had caused offence. However, for all those that were offended by him, there were just as many who were devoted to him, as indeed Christian was at the beginning having already served with him twice before, and Bligh was an exceptionally gifted naval officer who was devoted to serving his country. When he returned home from his open boat voyage in March 1790, he was greeted as a hero and had an audience with King George III which was just about the highest honour that could have been bestowed upon him. The tragedy for William Bligh was that when the captured mutineers were tried on *HMS Duke* from 12th – 18th September, 1792, he wasn't there to defend himself, being away on the second breadfruit trip. This allowed the prisoners who were basically fighting for their lives, to say anything that they liked about Bligh without him being there to defend himself. One of the mutineers in particular, James Morrison, claimed to have kept a journal and gave the impression that it was kept up to date at the time. It was fairly clear that it was largely written after the event and all that he said seemed to remain unchallenged. Another mutineer who was found guilty but pardoned largely due to his connections, also did a great deal to blacken Bligh's character. This was the young midshipman, Peter Heywood who had been taken on the *Bounty* by Bligh as a favour to the family. Heywood's conduct during the period after the trial was morally questionable to say the least. A large part of his defence at the trial was based around the assertion that Bligh had been especially kind to him, and that he (Heywood) would have shown extreme ingratitude to his captain by being part of the mutiny and in any event had no reason to be disloyal. Heywood, despite saying fine words about Bligh's kindness at his trial, was not content with being pardoned despite being found guilty, and went to Fletcher Christian's brother Edward, a leading lawyer, and whatever Heywood said about Bligh caused Edward Christian to publish a document in 1794 which was highly critical of Bligh and which did him lasting damage. Bligh had his faults of course, but history has been unfair to him and the myth about his supposedly tyrannical ways have persisted, his poor reputation being cemented by the 1935 Hollywood film starring Charles Laughton and Clark Gable and further cemented by the 1961 film starring Trevor Howard and Marlon Brando. The fact is, that due to the penny pinching by the Admiralty, the *Bounty* mutiny was a serious incident waiting to happen as it left a young officer with no Marines and no commissioned officers either, so he was left with no-one who could help him reinforce his authority. Captain Cook could well have had the same problem in that situation, but he did have marines and commissioned officers and got away with it, although two marines did attempt to desert on his first trip. It is a matter of pure factual record that Bligh was *not* a flogger, and used this form of punishment less than both Nelson and Cook. His brilliant work with Captain Cook in the late 1770's, his second breadfruit trip, the part he played in the battles of Camperdown and Copenhagen, his Governorship of New South Wales, the fact that one of his patrons was the great Sir Joseph Banks who knew him for more than thirty years, have all but been buried by myth and twisted facts concerning one mutiny amongst many in the history of the navy.

William Bligh died on 7th December, 1817, aged 64 years, and is buried along with his wife and day old sons, William and Henry, in the family vault in St. Mary's Churchyard, Lambeth. The following inscription is carved on the tomb:

"Sacred to the Memory of William Bligh Esquire, F.R.S., Vice Admiral of the Blue, the celebrated navigator who first transported the Bread fruit tree from

Otaheite to the West Indies, bravely fought the battles of his country, and died beloved, respected and lamented on 7th day of December, 1817, aged 64."

William Bligh is remembered with respect and affection in Australia where there is a statue of him in Sydney. However, his own country that he served so faithfully over so many years continues to treat him with disdain, a fact which still affects his direct descendants to the present day. During the last fifty years or so, there have been books published that attempt to redress the balance and tell the truth but the myth of the tyrant and flogger still persists. It is to be hoped that one day, his own country will treat him with the same respect and affection that many people feel he so richly deserves.

-oOOo-

7
William Wilberforce
(1759-1833)

*Campaigned for twenty years before achieving the abolition of
the slave trade in 1807.*

William Wilberforce was a politician from the age of twenty-one, and his deep
religious beliefs meant that he was also a philanthropist, campaigning on many
issues including cruelty to animals. However, he is best remembered for his
campaign to end slavery, which he, along with others, spent many years working
for until the passing of the Slave Trade Act in March 1807, although slavery was
not finally abolished until 1833.

William Wilberforce was born on 24th August, 1759, in Hull. He was the
only son of Robert (1728-68) and Elizabeth (nee Bird) Wilberforce, Robert
being a wealthy merchant, his wealth being inherited from *his* father William
(1690-1776) who was young William's grandfather. Civic duty was rife in the
Wilberforce family and when grandfather William came to Hull he soon became
Mayor and carried on another family tradition by naming his own sons William
and Robert by his marriage to Sarah Thornton. These two names had appeared
many times over the generations in the Wilberforce family and William the
future politician and social reformer was the third child of the grandfather's
second son, Robert and his wife Elizabeth. They had four in all, and he was the
only boy, his siblings all being girls. The first born was named Elizabeth, after
her mother and died at the age of fourteen. The second daughter, Sarah, was
eighteen months old when William was born and the last born, Anne, died at the
age of only eight. William was a sickly child and was probably lucky to survive
given the high mortality rate amongst children at that time. He was very small
and fragile and he also suffered from poor eyesight. He became wealthy due to
the death of his grandfather William in 1776, and his uncle William in 1777,
William's own father Robert, having died earlier in 1768. William owed his
inheritance to the lack of males in the family, as his Uncle William and wife
Hannah (nee Thornton) had no children.

When families were rich as the Wilberforce family were, the normal practise
for educating sons was to send them to a private school such as Eton, or educate
them at home. Robert and Elizabeth did neither, and in 1767, sent the young
William to Hull Grammar School where he was fortunate to have a headmaster
by the name of Joseph Milner. Although Milner had been brought up in a poor
family, he had received a first rate education due to the foresight of his parents,
attending Leeds Grammar School where he was recognised as something of a
prodigy. After studying at Cambridge, he became Headmaster at Hull at the age
of twenty-three and his abilities were recognised by everybody including the

pupils, who loved and respected him. He brought his brother Issac to the school, where he became school usher, and although being taken out of formal education at the age of twelve due to his father's death, Issac showed great ability and helped his brother teach the younger boys at Hull. The school was successful, and William Wilberforce and Joseph Milner were to embark on a life long friendship. William did well at school and with life at home being happy, everything seemed to be going well for the young boy. However, as is so often the case when things are seemingly running smoothly, there was a sudden tragedy. In 1768, shortly before William's ninth birthday, his father Robert died at the age of thirty-nine almost at the same time as Elizabeth, the eldest daughter who also died aged just fourteen. William's mother Elizabeth simply couldn't cope, and William was sent to his Aunt Hannah and Uncle William, who was Robert's elder brother. Hannah and William were wealthy and owned houses in both St. James' Place, London, and Wimbledon, at that time, a village south west of London.

William was sent to a boarding school in Putney but the standard of teaching was nowhere near as good as it was at Hull and he was later to describe the school as "indifferent". He also said that the pupils were taught a little of everything, reading, writing, arithmetic and described the food that was given to them for breakfast as "so nasty, I could not swallow them without sickening".

However, there was consolation for young William in leaving Hull and living in Wimbledon. Besides being wealthy, his uncle William and aunt Hannah lived in a large house in Wimbledon, but most importantly, gave the young boy a loving home and it was almost certainly this period in his life which gave him his love of Wimbledon and the reason he stayed there frequently as an adult. Living with his aunt and uncle also gave him something else which would change his adult life – religion.

When he had lived with his parents, the only religion that William had encountered was not unnaturally, that which was practised by his parents, an orthodox Christianity. However, the religion practised by his aunt and uncle was completely different, was relatively new, and was more demanding of its followers than the orthodox type of worship and was known as Methodism. There were many people who practised religion at that time who thought that Christianity was in effect bland – they wanted something more. Methodism was started in 1729 by a group of students at Oxford who were influenced by the brothers John and Charles Wesley.

John Wesley (1703-1791) passed from the Charterhouse to Christ Church College, Oxford in 1720 and was ordained deacon in 1725 and priest in 1728. In the meantime, in 1726, he became a fellow of Lincoln and a lecturer in Greek. He temporarily left Oxford in 1727 but returned in 1729 as a tutor. It was at this time that he and his brother Charles started the group that were known as Methodists, but were also called Enthusiasts, Bible Moths or the Holy Club. Their creed was to: "Observe with strict formality the method of study and practise laid down in the statutes of the University".

Charles Wesley (1707-1788) was a hymnwriter, and like his brother, also studied at Christ Church, Oxford. He was Ordained in 1735 and with John, went to Georgia as secretary to Governor James Oglethorpe, returning to England the following year. He was less famous than his brother, but his contribution to religion was none the less for that and he wrote over 5,500 hymns, including *'Jesu, Lover of my Soul'*, *'Hark, the Herald Angels Sing'* and *'Love Divine, all loves excelling'*.

With them at Oxford was a preacher called George Whitefield (1714-1770). Whitefield was born in the Bell Inn in Gloucester and was originally educated at the Crypt School in that city. He was the son of a widow and the family were poor, so when at the age of eighteen years he entered Pembroke College, Oxford, it was as a servitor because the family had no money to pay for his tuition fees. This was considered at the time to be the lowest form of student and a servitor was often used as a servant to students from better off families. He took deacon's orders in 1736 and it was at the Crypt Church, Gloucester, that he preached his first sermon. Like the Wesley brothers, he also went to Georgia returning to England in 1739 and was admitted to priest's orders. He was not well received by the Orthodox Church however, and pulpits were closed to him, so he preached in the open air, and the first time this happened was at Kingswood Hill near Bristol in which he was well received. Soon after that, he returned to Georgia where he embarked on huge preaching tours. A difference of opinion over predestination in 1741 led to a separation between himself and the Wesley brothers, but in 1729, he was very much part of their Holy Club that met regularly at Oxford.

The three men, plus the Oxford students had regular meetings reading the New Testament to each other and amongst other things, believed in self examination and charitable work – a far more pro-active approach than that which the more orthodox Christians practised, and it was to their religion that William Wilberforce was led via his Aunt Hannah and Uncle William.

In the 1750's, Whitefield had converted a wealthy man by the name of John Thornton to his non-conformist style of Christianity. John Thornton owned an estate in Clapham, at that time, a village south of London and not very far from Wimbledon, where his half sister, Hannah Wilberforce lived, which made him William's uncle. In the late 1760's, William's Aunt Hannah took young William to listen to the evangelical preachers at the time, and one of these was John Newton (1725-1807). Newton was an English clergyman and writer, had been born in London and was the son of a shipmaster. He was press-ganged into the navy whilst still in his teens and eventually became master of a slave ship, writing vivid diaries of his life and how the slaves were bought off the coast of Africa. He was converted to Christianity in 1748 when he was on board the slave ship *Greyhound* on the Atlantic slave trade route. One night, a severe storm blew up and Newton prayed for survival as the ship was so buffeted it almost sank. Newton and the crew were spared however, and he began his conversion to Christianity on that night. The day they arrived in England was 10th March, 1748, and it was that date that Newton was always to remember as his conversion, although he still ran slave ships for a while. This seems strange to us today, but there were many people who ran slave ships at that time who considered themselves Christians, seeing no contradiction whatsoever in the practice. However, he renounced the slave trade in the 1760's and in 1764, he was offered and accepted the post as Curate in the village of Olney in

Buckinghamshire. He was a charismatic man and William never forgot his childhood memories of him.

It is unusual for a child to respond to evangelical preaching, but William did and willingly embraced the Methodist teachings that his Uncle William and Aunt Hannah adopted. They were very much followers of the doctrine as espoused by Messrs Wesley and Whitefield. William was later to write:-

"My uncle and aunt were truly good people, and were in fact disciples of Mr. Whitefield. At that time when the Church of England had so much declined I really believe that Mr. Whitefield and Wesley were the restorers of genuine religion".

However, this was soon to stop. In 1771, William's mother discovered what was going on and after talking the matter over with Grandfather William, decided that she would travel to Wimbledon and remove the child from his aunt and uncle. Many of the orthodox Christians were horrified at the non-conformist's creed and the Wilberforce family in Hull agreed with them. She therefore travelled to Wimbledon and removed young William from his Aunt Hannah and Uncle William. Wilberforce was later to write:- "When my poor mother heard that I was disposed to join the Methodists, she was perfectly shocked". Again, he would later write of the incident:- "After consultation with my grandfather she determined to remove me from my uncle's, fearful lest I should imbibe what she considered as little less than poison which indeed I at that time had done". There was a confrontation between William's mother and his aunt Hannah, and as young William had grown very attached to his aunt and uncle, he was deeply upset at being removed from them in such a manner. Unfortunately for the Wilberforce family, William could not return to the school and Joseph Milner, the Headmaster that he loved, as Milner had also become a Methodist. This was a disappointment to William, but was a disaster for Milner because religious beliefs ran more deeply in the 18th century then they do today, and many of the local people were so horrified at Milner's religious stance, that despite his brilliance, they removed their children from his school. William was therefore sent to board at Pocklington School under the studious eye of the headmaster, the Reverend Kingsman Baskett.

William had a fairly easy time there as the pupils were not pushed academically and his family paid the school £400 so that the boy had certain perks such as a room of his own, dining with the headmaster, and also being tutored on a one to one basis by him. When it is borne in mind that at a great many schools, £10 was considered the normal rate for a year's boarding, then £400 was an enormous sum. William stayed at the school, leaving in 1776 but it was a long time before he got over leaving his aunt and uncle, and he was also missing the Methodist teachings. William was a studious, thoughtful boy, and in 1774, aged only fifteen, he wrote the following:-

"Life is a very uncertain thing at best, therefore we ought not to rely upon any good Fortune, since perhaps this moment we may enjoy the greatest Worldly Happiness; the next be plunged into the Deepest Abyss of unutterable Misery".

If he was speaking of the despair he felt at being taken away from his aunt and uncle in the manner in which it happened, he had a different recollection, or had certainly reached a different conclusion on it all because twenty-five years later, in 1799, he would write:-

"My mother's taking me from my uncle's when about twelve or thirteen and then completely a Methodist, probably has been the means of my becoming useful in life, connected with political men. If I had staid with my uncle I should probably have become a bigoted, despised Methodist".

In his teens and early adult life, William drifted away from the Methodist religion, and whatever his beliefs were to become later in life, these years allowed him to enjoy the usual mixing with people and to enjoy a good social life. This in turn would enable him to involve himself with his good works later on because of his ability to mix with people easily.

In October, 1776 at the age of seventeen, he had left Pocklington School and entered St. John's College, Cambridge and it was about this time that he became wealthy, inheriting a fortune because of the deaths of grandfather William in 1776 and his uncle William the following year. This situation gave the younger William the best of both worlds. He had come into a fortune at an early age, but didn't have to shoulder any further responsibilities for any of it, because since the death of his father in 1768, the family business had been run by Abel Smith who was the descendent of a Nottingham Banking family and was also wealthy, or potentially wealthy, in his own right. Smith had married William's mother's sister, in effect making him William's uncle and his taking over the business meant William was able to settle into Cambridge University life with no financial worries, and no real incentive to work although he did rally himself enough to pass his exams, obtaining a B.A. in 1781 and an M.A. in 1788.

Having all this wealth and entering university life, especially Cambridge, where it was considered especially dissolute even compared to other universities, could have been very bad for William. He had also more or less left religion behind, and although he joined in the university life with gusto, he did know when to stop and not go that extra mile. He was either highly intelligent, very sensible, extremely lucky, or possibly a combination of all three, because the fact that he passed his exams is a great tribute to him as he could so easily have gone off the rails. A few years later, a sermon had been preached in the university church complaining of "The scandalous neglect of order and discipline throughout the University" and another person who had visited Cambridge said:- "It disgusts me to go through Cambridge... where one meets nothing academic or like a place of study, regularity or example". The tutors colluded with the university way of life and said to Wilberforce that he really did not need to work. Wilberforce was later to write:-

"Their object seemed to be, to make and keep me idle. If ever I appeared studious, they would say to me: 'Why in the world should a man of your fortune trouble himself with fagging?'" Like his fellow students, William joined in the card games, gambling, and the late night drinking sessions and it was a lifestyle that he was to enjoy to the full at the time, although he did manage to stop short of the womanising and the really excessive drinking. However, his companions at Cambridge found him generous and witty and he was very popular. Later on in his life when converted back to religion, he regretted this period which he considered a complete waste of time.

However, whatever he thought in later life of his lifestyle at Cambridge, he did make some good friends there who helped him grow as a person. One of these was William Cookson, uncle to the poet William Wordsworth (1770-1850) who took him to the Lake District on holiday, and amongst others, he met the lawyer Edward Christian, the brother of the notorious Fletcher Christian who led the famous mutiny against William Bligh on the *Bounty* in April, 1789. One man that he also met there and who was to become a life-long friend was William Pitt (1759-1806), who would eventually become the country's youngest ever Prime Minister and who soon become known as William Pitt the Younger to distinguish him from his father, the great Lord Chatham, otherwise known as William Pitt the Elder. Although Wilberforce and Pitt the Younger met at Cambridge, they would rarely socialise together. Pitt was at Pembroke College and was far more studious than Wilberforce; Pitt had a love of classics and mathematics whilst Wilberforce studied only just enough to pass his exams and mixed with a rather more rowdy set of friends than Pitt. However, despite their different backgrounds, once they did get to know each other, they became and remained firm friends until Pitt's early death in 1806.

When William Wilberforce eventually left Cambridge in 1779, he had to make his mind up as to what he was going to do with the rest of his life. He had no interest in running the family business which in any case was already in the capable hands of Abel Smith, and the Orthodox Church held no attraction for him. Law was a possibility but would have meant further years of study for someone who was always going to be independently wealthy, and so in the end he opted for politics. There were possibly two reasons for this. Civic duty had always been strong in the Wilberforce family, but after years at Cambridge, his mind had broadened, and he probably would have wanted to take that spirit of public duty and extend it to the national stage. Secondly, his friendship with William Pitt whose own family were steeped in politics, and Pitt himself had made no secret of his desire to enter that world.

There was also a great deal of activity in politics at that time. Lord North (1732-92) was Prime Minister and the American War of Independence which started in 1775, was being fought. There were powerful men who opposed the war and one of these was Charles James Fox (1749-1806) who was the youngest son of the 1st Baron Holland and Lady Caroline Holland (nee Lennox). A Whig politician, Fox had a reputation for being one of the finest orators in Parliament, and another who opposed the war was Edmund Burke (1729-97), an Irish statesman who also had a reputation for eloquence which gave him a position of standing in the Whig party. It was not only the North administration and its conduct of the war that was being attacked, but the whole system of government itself, as there were many Whig politicians who felt that too much power was invested in the crown, at this period being in the hands of King George III. One of those particularly strident in his views was that of Edmund Burke himself. Also, in April, 1778, Lord Chatham, Pitt's father, who had retired through illness, made a dramatic entrance to the House of Lords and in a powerful oratory, denounced Lord North's handling of the war but during his speech, collapsed and he died one month later. All these events, allied to his friendship with the younger Pitt, must have helped William make the decision to enter the political arena and during the winter of 1779-80, the two friends could often be seen watching the debates in the House of Commons from the public gallery.

The problem for both men, still only twenty-one years old, was how to go about it. Both men were inclined to stand for a seat that involved a genuine election between candidates, but both wanted to get into parliament sooner rather than later. Their chance would soon come. The much criticised Lord North held a surprise election in September, 1780 and to many people's surprise, managed to hold on to power which he did for another two years before finally leaving office in 1782. In the September 1780 election, Pitt stood for the seat at Cambridge University and although voting rights were by no means as universal as they are today, Cambridge University was reasonably democratic for the times, involving as it did an electorate of several hundred people, made up of members of the University Senate.

As it happened, Pitt finished bottom of the poll and was not elected. Wilberforce was more successful, being elected as the MP for Kingston-upon-Hull in the same election. It didn't come cheap however, as a great many of the voters were only those people who held power and property and Wilberforce had to do a great deal of wining and dining before he could be sure of being elected but at least he felt that there had been some sort of election. Pitt, coming bottom of the Cambridge University poll, had to enter parliament by another route – that is the so-called pocket borough. This was a system that was widespread at the time, although it was rotten to the core. A pocket borough barely had any voters and was owned by someone rich and powerful who could sell or give it to whoever he chose and would use the member to exercise influence. Not for nothing were they later to become known as 'rotten boroughs'. Pitt, having failed at Cambridge, reluctantly and he hoped, temporarily, took up one of these pocket boroughs, and entered parliament as the member for Appleby on the 23rd January, 1781 by courtesy of a rich friend of a friend, Sir James Lowther. Meanwhile, his friend William Wilberforce took the oath as the MP in the House of Commons on the 31st October 1780, taking his seat opposite Lord North and his ministers.

The main parties at that time were the Whigs and the Tories. The Tories favoured the Stuart line of succession with regard to the monarchy and felt that the Monarch had a divine right to rule. The Whigs on the other hand were more favoured towards the Hanoverian line of succession and felt that Parliament should take a more dominant role in the running of the country. Pitt entered the House as an 'Independent Whig' which he liked to call himself, but Wilberforce was less inclined to take a party label, making decisions on their individual merit. It was possible that this determination to plough a lone furrow cost him a ministerial role when his good friend William Pitt became Prime Minister in 1783, but it is doubtful that Wilberforce would have worried about it.

Wilberforce was a conscientious Member of Parliament and attended regularly. However, during this period in his life, he had left religion in the way it was practised by his aunt and uncle behind him and besides Parliament, he also attended gentlemen's clubs on a regular basis where gambling was de rigeur. He found accommodation in St. James' Square which allowed him easy access to both the House of Commons, but also the clubs which it seemed were almost obligatory to attend. There was Boodle's, which was usually frequented by the hunting and country squire type; Whites, which was very exclusive and used only by the aristocracy, and the most recently opened Brooks', which had become a playground for the leading Whigs. He was good company and popular with everyone. He was popular with women as well as men, and the famous French writer and socialite Madame Anne Louise Germaine Necker de Stael (1766-1817), once described him as "The wittiest man in England" whilst Georgiana, Duchess of Devonshire (1757-1806), socialite and strong supporter of the Whig party, said that the Prince of Wales (later to become George IV) would go anywhere to hear Wilberforce sing. Wilberforce not only had a good singing voice, but was also able to use his vocal talents to great effect whilst speaking in the House where his eloquence was much admired. James Boswell (1740-95), the diarist and author, and friend and future biographer of the great Doctor Samuel Johnson (1709-84), who created the famous dictionary in 1755, heard Wilberforce speak, and later wrote:- "I saw what seemed a mere shrimp mount upon the table, but as I listened, he grew and grew, until the shrimp became a whale".

Whilst he was attending the House regularly, his social life continued to flourish and he would happily join in with the gambling that took place during this time, which was the 1780's. London was at the height of its decadence with its outright immorality and whilst Wilberforce enjoyed himself at the time, he was to bitterly regret it years later, considering it a complete waste of time. It should be said however, that Wilberforce's behaviour was nowhere near as bad as that of some of his friends and colleagues. He had befriended the former Lord Chancellor, Lord Camden, and had always shown an interest in serious discussions with him, as opposed to the frivolous behaviour of some of his contemporaries. He would often listen to Camden's stories about his friend William Pitt's father, the 'Old Lord Chatham'. One of his Cambridge friends said at the time:- "I thank the Gods that I live in the age of Wilberforce and that I know one man at least who is both moral and entertaining", and so it was that the young William Wilberforce was able to cleverly bridge that gap between those of a more sober nature, and those with a more than rumbustious manner.

Although Wilberforce's behaviour and manners were fairly measured, the extreme behaviour continued to go on around him. However, where there is extreme of anything, whether it is behaviour, or fashion, there is often a backlash, and whilst this sort of behaviour continued throughout George IV's (previously the Prince of Wales) reign of 1820 to 1830 and again with his brother William IV's (previously the Duke of Clarence) reign which commenced on the death of George, things altered after Victoria ascended the throne in 1837, a reign which would last until 1901 and was known as the Victorian era. However, back in the 1780's, when William Wilberforce was a young MP, things were very different. He, his friend William Pitt, and others enjoyed themselves to the full although it is probably fair to say that the more studious Pitt was even a little more sober than the young William Wilberforce. However, whatever the young William Wilberforce's behaviour was like at that time, quite extraordinary sums of money were won and lost in a single evening at these gentlemen's clubs. Horace Walpole (1717-97), the 4th Earl of Orford, who was considered a distinguished spectator of politics rather than a participant, once wrote:- 'The young men lose five, ten, fifteen thousand pounds in an evening. Lord Stavordale, not one and twenty, lost eleven thousand last Tuesday, but recovered it by one great hand at Hazard. He swore a great oath – "Now, if I had been playing deep, I might have won millions!"' Betting seemed to be a complete addiction, because if no game was involved, they would take bets on events such as who would be Prime Minister by the end of a given period. When a man dropped down at the door of Whites, bets were immediately taken as to whether he was dead or not. Gambling however, was not the only vice that so-called gentlemen of the 18th century indulged in. Eating, drinking, and womanising were also very much on the agenda and one of the worst culprits with all these vices was the Prince of Wales, later to be George IV and son of the very sober George III, the current monarch. It is an extraordinary paradox that during a period in history where it was considered perfectly normal for a gentleman to have a mistress, the country had a monarch who was faithful to his wife, had been a loving father to his children, was frugal in the way in which he spent money and was a role model for any young gentleman at the time, but the lead that he gave was not followed. It is little wonder that there was so much friction between George III and his errant son, George, the Prince of Wales, who was to rule as George IV on the death of his father in 1820.

Wilberforce spent the summer of 1784 away from Parliament and after very brief stops in London and Brighton, decided to tour Europe and sailed from Dover to Calais. It was to prove to be the beginning of a life changing experience for William as far as his religious beliefs were concerned, although he had no idea that this was going to happen at the outset of the trip. Including Wilberforce himself, there were six in the party; along with William were his mother and sister and two female cousins who were unwell and it was hoped would improve with the change of air. Also travelling with William was Issac Milner, brother of Joseph Milner, William's former headmaster at Hull Grammar School. William wanted male company as opposed to having all female companions of his own family and although he did not know Issac that well, he asked him to accompany them on the trip. It proved to be somewhat of an inspired choice as Issac Milner proved to be a remarkably clever young man. Because of the death of their father, his brother Joseph had taken his brother out of education at the age of twelve to help him at the Hull school, but eventually Issac attended Queens College, Cambridge where his true abilities began to show. In 1776 he became a Fellow of his college, becoming a rector and tutor, and when he was thirty-two years old, became the first Jacksonian Professor of Natural Philosophy, a remarkable achievement given his start in life.

The party travelled across France heading towards Nice where the usual round of gambling, card parties and dinners took place and during these activities, there was no hint from Issac Milner of his religious beliefs. Wilberforce had long since lost all his and the subject of religion hardly ever came up, and if it did, it was skirted round fairly quickly. The party were enjoying their time in France and although Parliament was due to re-sit on 25th January 1785, Wilberforce showed no great inclination to go back. However, some time in January, he was to receive a letter from William Pitt, his friend and

Prime Minister dated 19th December, 1784, that was to change everything. The letter was asking him to return to England to help Pitt get his bill introducing parliamentary reform through the House of Commons. Pitt had wanted to remove all the pocket boroughs and introduce a more democratic voting pattern for these areas. It was agreed within the party that the women would stay in France, but that Wilberforce and Milner would return home. Wilberforce needed reading material for the journey and randomly picked up a book by Philip Doddridge called *'The Rise and Progress of Religion in the Soul'*. Doddridge (1702-51) was an English Nonconformist clergyman who as well as writing this book, wrote several hymns including *'Hark, the glad sound, the Saviour comes'* and *'Oh God of Bethel, by whose hand'*. When asked by Wilberforce if he could recommend the book, Milner replied: -"It is one of the best books ever written. Let us take it with us and read it on our journey". In the event, the trip home did not help Pitt who was unable to get his bill through, but reading the book on the journey would change Wilberforce's life forever. Doddridge's book was published in 1745 and much of it was influenced by the work of Richard Baxter (1615-91) who like Doddridge became an English Nonconformist clergyman. Once a Conformist, Baxter started to adopt some of the Nonconformist views when he was minister at Kidderminster from 1640 and in 1685 he was brought before the infamous Judge Jeffreys for alleged sedition in his *'Paraphrase on the New Testament'*. He was required to pay a hefty fine and was imprisoned for nearly eighteen months in King's Bench prison until it was paid. Baxter had always preached tolerance in religion, and had encouraged Christians of different denominations to concentrate on what united rather than divided them, and Doddridge followed his ideas. Wilberforce read the book whilst travelling home in his carriage, and took in many of the ideas of English Puritanism along with the whole framework suggested by Doddridge of how people should live. Doddridge's book, *'The Rise and Progress of Religion in the Soul'* put emphasis on self examination on a daily basis, prudence in recreation (gambling would be completely out), the importance of solitude, and the value of time. It also stressed the need for humans to be useful during their lifetime. The book had a profound effect on Wilberforce, and he made a decision that he would examine the scriptures for himself to see if they sat happily with the book.

When the house rose in June, Wilberforce and Milner travelled to Genoa to be reunited with the ladies, and then went on to Switzerland where he was captivated by the beauty of the scenery. On the 14th August, 1785, he wrote to Colonel John Pennington, later to become Lord Muncaster, who although considerably older than Wilberforce, was nonetheless a good friend:- 'I have never been in any other part of the world, for which I could quit a residence in England with so little regret'. By this time, he had thought long and hard about his religious beliefs and hated the materialism and what he saw as the futile pursuit of money. He was quoted as saying:- "That if a man had enough, then to torment himself for fresh acquisitions as delusive in this enjoyment and uncertain in their possession as these are, seems to me a perfect madness". Wilberforce was rapidly becoming an Evangelical Christian, both by what he read and also the arguments put forward by Issac Milner. His final conversion when it came was not a dramatic incident or vision experienced in a single moment or day, but after months of thoughtful contemplation and conversations with Issac Milner. Famous names such as Charles Wesley, John Wesley, John Newton, and William Huntington all had sudden conversions, or certainly experiences that would ultimately lead to their conversion, but Wilberforce's experience was different, it was very gradual, but nonetheless very real and would change his life and lifestyle forever.

Although his conversation changed his habits rather dramatically, it did not change his personality which remained outgoing and cheerful. Deep down however, he was bitterly regretting his past life and he was very self critical. Initially, he saw his role as spreading the word of God rather than changing anything politically for the better. In this way, he remained fairly conservative, believing in the current social order as ordained by God and did very little to help bring about any sort of realignment of the status and fortunes of the people. Due to this, he found himself in a dilemma. Evangelical Christianity was viewed with suspicion, almost hostility by people, and Wilberforce was considered too radical by Tories but on the other hand, too conservative by the progressive Evangelical Christians. Eventually of course, all this was to change when he became involved with the abolition of the slave trade.

However, before this was to happen, William was to go through some agonising soul searching about how he should live his life, and one of the options he considered was leaving political life altogether. Although his great friend Pitt was Prime Minister, he, Wilberforce, had become disinterested in politics because he felt that nothing had changed and he felt no particular loyalty to any one party. He had indulged in very deep conversations with Issac Milner and had read Doddridge's book, but he still didn't know in which way religion would determine how he should conduct his life. That was when he hinted that retirement from general life completely and perhaps live a life of contemplative solitude would be the way forward and he wrote to Pitt outlining his dilemma. On 2nd December, 1785, Pitt wrote a lengthy reply, and it contained the following sentence which would have a telling effect on Wilberforce:- "If a Christian may act in the several relations in life, must he seclude himself from them all to become so? Surely the principles as well as the practise of Christianity are simple, and lead not to meditation only but to action." It was a long letter, but that one brilliant sentence probably resonated with Wilberforce. The next day, the two friends met at Wilberforce's house in Wimbledon and Pitt even tried to talk Wilberforce out of Christianity, but by now Wilberforce was as immersed in religion as Pitt was in politics, so interesting though the conversation was, Wilberforce would not budge in terms of his beliefs.

There was someone else that Wilberforce wished to confide in, and that was John Newton, the Evangelical preacher that the nine-year-old William had been taken to see and hear by his aunt Hannah. Wilberforce was nervous about asking for a meeting with the man that he had revered as a child, but eventually the two men met on the 7th December 1785. Wilberforce's mind was all over the place and in a constant state of agitation as to how he was to lead his life, but Newton calmed him. He not only calmed him but encouraged him to stay in politics saying that politics and religion were not incompatible, and he introduced him to a wider circle of religious friends who could guide him and give him advice.

One of the people pleased with William's conversion was his uncle John Thornton, the half-brother of William's Aunt Hannah. Later that month, Thornton wrote to William assuring him that any conversion to Christianity took time and counselled him not to take any decisions in a hurry. Eventually, after much soul searching, he made his mind up as to his future course of action, and although he resigned from the various clubs in which he had previously spent so much time gambling, he resolved to stay in politics and wrote to his mother assuring her that he would not retire from public life. He continued to visit his friend William Pitt in Downing Street and also to attend Parliament, convinced at last that he could combine the twin involvement of politics and religion. This decision would have a profound effect on William Wilberforce and would help change the course of history forever.

Christianity would change William's life in many ways, but the thing that he is best remembered for is his involvement with the abolition of the slave trade. Slavery tragically has probably always been with us. The ancient Egyptians owned slaves and traded with them, and the Romans, who are looked upon today as ahead of their time and very civilised, certainly used them on a vast scale. Even the great adventurer and explorer, Christopher Columbus (1451-1506) was involved with slavery, which was when Britain had first become involved in the slave trade, and by the 1780's, Britain dominated it, and in fact the whole of the British economy was virtually built around it. In the 1740's, a British Merchant named Malachy Postlethwayt (1707-67) who thought slavery essential for the running of the British economy, wrote many publications in support of his views, notably 'The African Trade, the Great Pillar and Supporter of the British Plantation Trade in North America' (1745) and 'The National and Private Advantages of the African Trade Considered' in 1746. Postlethwayt wrote:- "The Negro-Trade and the natural Consequences resulting from it, may be justly esteemed an inexhaustible Fund of Wealth and Naval Power to this Nation". Postlethwayt's most famous work was his 'The Universal Dictionary of Trade and Commerce' (1757) which took him twenty years to complete. This book was well thought of by none other than Dr. Johnson (1709-84) who said that it:- "Was a huge storehouse of economic facts, laws and theory".

Wilberforce was certainly fighting huge odds, and during this period, the triangular route was well established. This consisted of taking British manufactured goods to Africa, buying slaves with the produce and shipping them to the West Indies where they were sold and slave produced goods such as cotton, sugar and tobacco were purchased and shipped back to Britain. The trade was barbaric and horrific. The slaves were taken from their families and were transported in the most dreadful conditions lying shackled next to each other in the holds of the slave ships being unable to move during the duration of the journey and lying in their own waste. Barely fed, many of them died which given their conditions, may have been a merciful release. By the 1780's, some people were coming round to the view that it was barbaric but justified it continuing because they felt that the British economy would collapse without it. Others merely felt that there was nothing wrong with the trade as they considered Africans were sub-human and felt that what was happening was perfectly justifiable.

Although William Wilberforce has been given most of the credit when the subject of the abolition of the slave trade is discussed, there were many such as Tom Clarkson and Hannah More, as well as Wilberforce's friend and Prime Minister, William Pitt himself who were very involved. Neither was he the first to express concern about it. As far back as 1671, the founder of the Quakers, George Fox, had called on slave-owners not to be cruel to their slaves, and that after a set number of years working for their masters should be set free, but it was not until 1783 that the Quakers presented their first petition to Parliament which although failing, raised public awareness to the trade. It was in this same year that William Wilberforce, whilst dining with Gerard Edwards, a land-owning friend from his Cambridge days, was introduced to the Rev. James Ramsay, a man who would change Wilberforce's life, although he didn't follow this meeting up immediately. Ramsay had served in the navy as a surgeon and had served on the British warship *Arundel* captained by Sir Charles Middleton during the seven years war. Later on, he became a clergyman on the island of St. Christopher in the Leeward Islands. He also became responsible for the medical welfare of the plantations and was deeply distressed by what he saw. Eventually he returned to England and was given the living of Teston in Kent by Sir Charles Middleton and his wife Margaret with whom he remained friends. In 1784, he was to complete and publish the famous *'Essay on the Treatment and Conversion of African Slaves in the British Sugar Colonies'*, a piece of work that had taken him a total of three years to finish, and like the Quakers petition before it, helped raise public awareness to the horrors of the human trade. He was encouraged in the writing of this essay by Sir Charles Middleton, Lady Middleton, Thomas Clarkson and Hannah More amongst others.

In November 1786, Wilberforce received a letter from Sir Charles Middleton, now an MP, and later to be the 1st Baron Barham. Middleton, like Wilberforce, was one of the few MPs who were Evangelical Christians along with his wife Margaret, also an Evangelical Christian, although not an MP as there were no women MPs at that time. They in turn were friends of Hannah More (1745-1833), an English playwright and religious writer. After having several pieces of work published, she went to London in 1774 and became a member of the famous 'Blue Stocking Club', other members being Elizabeth Montagu (1720-1800), another English writer and society leader. Elizabeth Montagu herself had set up the famous club as an outlet for women to gather together and discuss intellectual subjects which women were not normally expected to do. Eventually, men were allowed to attend, and other famous members included Fanny Burney (1752-1840) the English novelist, diarist, and forerunner of Jane Austen, Hester Thrale (1741-1821), the Welsh writer, David Garrick (1717-1779), the English actor and dramatist, and amongst many others, the great Samuel Johnson (1709-1784), the English writer, critic, and lexicographer who produced his famous English dictionary in 1755.

Thomas Clarkson (1760-1846) was to become an ardent campaigner for the abolition of slavery, and was educated at St. John's College, Cambridge. In 1785, he had gained a prize for a brilliant essay written in Latin entitled 'Is it right to make slaves of others against their will?' which was widely read after being translated into English the following year. These people became known as the Testonites after the place where Sir Charles and Lady Middleton lived and the group would meet there on a regular basis. The letter that Wilberforce received from Sir Charles in 1786 made him more acutely aware of the slave trade and also encouraged him to present a bill to Parliament urging the abolition of this degrading barbarity. Lady Margaret had originally urged her husband to undertake this role, but Sir Charles, realising he did not possess the powers of oratory that Wilberforce had, asked William to carry out the task. At first Wilberforce said that he felt unequal to the job, but also felt unable to decline it. Early the following year, 1787, Wilberforce met Thomas Clarkson which started a working relationship and friendship that would last nearly half a century until Wilberforce's death in 1833 – Clarkson himself living until 1846. The letter from Middleton and the meeting with Clarkson saw Wilberforce study the subject of slavery in great depth and amongst the authors he read were Montesquieu (1689-1755), the French philosopher, Adam Smith (1723-90), the Scottish economist and philosopher, and William Paley (1743-1805), the English theologian. Virtually everything that he read, not only by these authors, but by others as well, condemned the practice of slavery. By the end of 1787, Wilberforce became completely convinced that he was going to devote his life and Parliamentary career to ending the slave trade, although the real decision had been reached earlier in the year after a conversation with his friend and Prime Minister, William Pitt along with Pitt's cousin William Grenville under an oak tree at Pitt's estate in Holwood, Kent on 12th May of that year, 1787. All three men were exactly the same age being born in 1759, and Grenville was to be Prime Minister in 1807, the year after Pitt died in office. Pitt had brought a country house in Holwood, complete with gardens and woods, so that he could escape the stresses and strains of London, although being the person he was, no doubt most of his time there was spent working. Under the tree that later was to become known as the 'Wilberforce Oak', Pitt had challenged his friend:- "Wilberforce, why don't you give notice of a motion on the subject of the slave trade? You have already taken great pains to collect evidence, and are therefore fully entitled to the credit which doing so will ensure you. Do not lose time, or the ground will be occupied by another". Wilberforce could not refuse, nor would he have wanted to refuse William Pitt, a man who was a close friend as well as being the most powerful man in the land. Wilberforce had always been an MP with an independent nature, not attaching himself to any one party, so the loss of any ministerial rank through his work would not deter him in the slightest. He was to say:- "Let the consequences be what they would, I from this time determined that I would never rest until I had effected its Abolition".

Wilberforce certainly had plenty of support from people like the Middletons, Thomas Clarkson, Hannah More amongst others, and one of the most powerful, the Prime Minister William Pitt. Wilberforce started his campaign on an optimistic note, but we do not know whether he truly believed that he would achieve early success or whether it was merely to encourage others not to waver from the cause. It was probably the optimism of someone convinced of the justness of the cause and therefore was bound to succeed in the end. However, others knew that it would take years and there were two possible reasons for this. The first was the way Parliament worked in the 1780's. Although there were two main parties, the Whigs and the Tories, they did not operate in the same disciplined way that political parties do today. In today's Parliament, the main parties present fixed manifestos and backbenchers are told how to vote – indeed, a great many MP's do not even listen to the debates at all but merely vote in the way that the party whips tell them to when the division bell is sounded. In the 18th century, business was conducted in a more fluid manner, with Members listening to speeches, and often genuinely keeping an open mind until the speakers had finished. They then voted in the way that their conscience told them although they might be swayed by a certain person – eg, if they tended to vote with Pitt they would side with him, or if Fox, then again, they would vote with Fox. When one reads of how parliamentary seats were divided up in the 18th century, the conclusion is often understandably arrived at, that the system was fairly corrupt, but when one looks at how members were genuinely allowed to express their own opinions, the system then looks better than it does today. Therefore, the way that Parliament operated in the 18th century meant that although William Pitt was a powerful Prime Minister with a good majority, that majority simply did not carry the weight that it would today. The second reason that Wilberforce was being over optimistic about the speed in which the slave trade would be abolished, is the fact there he did not take into account the many vested interests in keeping it operating that were involved. There were far too many people in high places who were making fortunes from slavery, either directly or indirectly, and they were not going to willingly let a system be abolished that had served them so well and made them and their families rich. William Wilberforce was not to be deterred however and he was about to embark on a long political journey.

His first job was to obtain facts about the slave trade. Hardly anyone knew anything at all about the statistics concerning the number of people used as slaves, and they knew nothing about the barbaric treatment. It is assumed that people were either strongly for or strongly against slavery, but this is not in fact the case – most people did not really give it a great deal of thought. However, this would not mean that it would be easy to persuade people to reject it – if people do not know the facts, it is human nature to stick with the status quo and leave things as they are, so facts had to be marshalled and people moved to action if Wilberforce and Clarkson were to be successful. This would take time and the powerful forces against them would not give up their profitable way of life without a fight. Also, the Monarch had to be brought on board and this was impossible at first as he was no radical and felt the constitution should be left well alone. One of his sons, the Duke of Clarence, who as William IV would reign between 1830 and 1837, was also against any change. Despite the huge difference in character between father and son, the two men did agree on the issue of slavery.

On 22nd May, 1787, ten days after Wilberforce, Pitt, and Grenville had had their conversation under the oak tree in Holwood, the first meeting of the 'Society for Effecting the Abolition of the Slave Trade' was called, bringing together both Quakers and Anglicans for the first time in a common cause.

Amongst the people attending were Thomas Clarkson and Granville Sharp. They met again two days later to hear Thomas Clarkson's paper *'Enumeration of facts relative to the Inhumanity and Impolicy of the Slave Trade'*, and made the decision that two thousand copies be printed and distributed. The Chairman of the committee was Granville Sharp who for over twenty years had worked for the complete emancipation of slaves, but this was felt by those present to be too big a step to undertake and agreed instead to work towards the abolition of the trade, hoping that complete abolition would soon follow. Sharp (1735-1813) had been born in Durham and had been apprenticed to a linen draper. He became aware of the sufferings of slaves at a chance visit to his brother William's house in 1765. William was a doctor and often gave free treatment to those in London who were too poor to pay. A slave called Jonathon Strong had been beaten by his owner and was brought to William for treatment after which Granville became involved in a legal battle that decided that a slave was the legal property of his master even if they were on English soil. From then on, Granville Sharp campaigned on behalf of slaves and in a case that involved another slave, James Somerset, won a famous judgement that any slave would be free once they set foot in England. By the time of the meeting with Wilberforce, Clarkson and the others in May 1787, he was already a seasoned campaigner against slavery.

Wilberforce did not immediately join the Abolitionist Committee – it was against his nature to sign up to any one named organisation as he wanted to keep his independence, and he also felt that as an MP, it would be better if he was seen as working separately from the rest of the group. However, he kept in close touch with the members who met regularly on a weekly or fortnightly basis throughout the rest of 1787 as the group worked hard at successfully raising public awareness. During the first year, they raised £2,760.2s.7d (£2,760.13p), which would be approximately £165,500 in today's money and spent over a third of that sum on the printing and distribution of more than eighty thousand pamphlets and books. These included 11,500 accounts of the debates in Parliament and over three and a half thousand copies of *'Newton's Thoughts'* written by John Newton, the one-time slave-ship Captain who had renounced slavery in the 1760's and entered the church.

The achievements of this committee were extraordinary. One of the obvious ways of getting a message across to a wide public was through the media, and the media in those days consisted only of newspapers, but there were a great many of these, including the *Daily Universal Register* (which was to become *The Times*), the *Morning Herald*, the *Star and Evening Advertiser*, the *Sunday Chronicle* and the *Observer*. All these titles came into being between 1780 and 1791 and were used to great effect. As well as gaining press attention, the committee tried new ideas, one of which was asking people to boycott items such as sugar if it was produced by slaves, and they also used a campaign logo. In July 1787, Josiah Wedgwood (1730-95), was another great person brought in to the fold. He was a famous pottery-maker and in 1763 patented a beautiful cream coloured ware known as Queen's Ware. However, he was probably better known for manufacturing unglazed blue Jasper ware which featured raised designs in white. Wedgewood produced an image of a slave kneeling, with the words "Am I not a Man and a Brother?" engraved on medallions. These became a powerful weapon in the committee's armoury and the medallions became almost a fashion accessory amongst the wealthy. Men were having the Wedgewood slave medallion engraved on their snuff boxes in gold inlay whilst women wore them in bracelets as well as having them fitted on the pins for their hair. The motives of some of these people were possibly questionable as some might have seen them more as items of fashion rather than anything else, but they did help to spread the message to those who were to become genuinely committed to the cause. Whilst Josiah Wedgewood was no doubt in sympathy with the aims of the anti-slavery movement, he probably achieved some extremely favourable publicity as a result of his work. Another very powerful achievement was the picture of the hold of the slave-ship, the *Brookes,* which came from the Plymouth branch of the abolitionist committee in late 1788. This showed how 482 slaves were crammed into a small ship and it produced an instant reaction of horror to those who saw it, and there were a great many as more than eight thousand were printed as posters and distributed. Paintings were exhibited and the famous cartoonist, James Gillray produced a caricature of the Duke of Clarence, known to be in favour of the slave trade, with a black mistress.

Gillray was one of the most famous cartoonists of his generation and was born in Chelsea on 13th August, 1756 and lived until 1815. He first produced caricatures in 1779, although he was not to become famous until 1784. Between 1779-1811 he produced about 1,500 caricatures, many of which were savage and no-one was spared, whether they be Government Ministers or the Monarch of the day which was King George III. A particularly famous one was that which depicted Prime Minister William Pitt carving up Europe and dividing it with Napoleon, his archenemy and self appointed Emperor of France. Gillray was largely self-taught although he did study at the Royal Academy before embarking on his career. His cartoons were always right on the edge but his career was brought to a close in 1811 through insanity. Although a very sad end, no-one who saw his cartoons would have been surprised. During the period of the anti-slavery campaign however, his work was very powerful.

Another effective way that the anti-slavery message was spread was through the organisation of meetings throughout the land. Clarkson, in particular, worked very hard in travelling the country, and not only did he lecture, but he also spent time collecting more information which he would use as evidence. One of the surprising pieces of news that came out of this information gathering was the fact that many of the sailors on the slave-trade ships were badly treated themselves, and many of them were to become valuable witnesses. When they embarked on a slave run, the sailors knew that many of them would not be coming back alive, so most of them were easy converts to the cause.

Wilberforce, in conjunction with the committee, was preparing to make his first parliamentary moves when he was taken ill in January 1788. The illness was colitus and almost certainly brought on by stress because like Clarkson, he was obsessed with the subject of slavery, which had virtually become his reason for being over many years. He took large quantities of opium in order to kill the pain, in those days there being no other effective medicine for it, and it was also perfectly legal. It was quite obvious that Wilberforce would be too unwell to bring any motion before parliament, so on 11th February, 1788, Pitt started the campaign off by setting up a Privy Council investigation which would report to Parliament the following year. It was an inquiry by the Privy Council into 'the present State of the Trade to AFRICA, and particularly the Trade in SLAVES'.

Meanwhile, Wilberforce was very ill indeed. He was bed-ridden and when Clarkson went to see him, he thought that Wilberforce might well die and there were also others of the same opinion. By the end of February, he could barely function at all and on 4th March, he went to stay with John Thornton, half brother to William's aunt Hannah at Clapham. He felt a lot better only four days later, but on the same day, suddenly took a turn for the worse and was as poorly as ever, so bad was he in fact, that his mother and sister came down from London to see him, both of them fearing the worst. The prognosis of the eminent physician of the time, Doctor Richard Warren who came to see him, was not much better. He feared that Wilberforce could not 'possibly survive a twelve month' whilst others thought his condition much worse and that Wilberforce would not last two weeks. However, two weeks later, he was not only still alive but actually recovering well and by the end of April had travelled to Bath to recuperate. He wrote to the Reverend Christopher Wyvill who he had known for a long time, as he too had long since worked for parliamentary reform, and told him that although feeling better, he was still too unwell even to think of the slave trade as it was too much for him to tackle in his present state of health. He went on to say that he would trust his friend Pitt to take the problem on, although it could never be a long-term solution as Pitt was Prime Minister. However, it was by no means certain that Wilberforce would ever be fit enough to return to the campaign.

Pitt readily agreed and discussed the subject with Granville Sharp to make sure that the evidence of the Privy Council would be properly presented. Pitt himself presented the motion to the House of Commons on 9th May, 1788:- "That the House will, early in the next session, proceed to take into consideration the circumstances of the slave trade". In introducing this motion, Pitt deliberately did not put forward his own views for which he has been subsequently criticised, but he was actually employing clever tactics. If he pushed too hard from the beginning, the anti-abolitionists would mobilise themselves at an early stage, but by using a subtle approach early on, Pitt hoped to wrong foot them and lull them into a false sense of security. Pitt fully supported Wilberforce and had every intention of showing his hand later on. However, despite the mildness of the motion, it still caused opinions to be polarised and fierce discussions took place. Charles James Fox and Edmund Burke, although members of the opposition, spoke firmly in support of Pitt, but Bamber Gascoyne representing Liverpool, who certainly had a vested interest in holding on to the status quo, spoke equally firmly against it.

However, despite taking this cautious approach early on, Pitt was soon to change his tune and adopt a more aggressive role and showed the House where his true sympathies lay. This happened because Sir William Dolben, a member for Oxford University, had inspected an empty slave ship that was anchored in the Thames. Horrified by the conditions that he saw, he introduced a Bill on 1st May, 1788 to limit the transporting of slaves to one slave for each ton of the vessel. Although this Bill was passed in a sparsely attended house, there was so much opposition for it, especially from Liverpool MPs, that Pitt lost his temper and threatened to retract what he had previously said and "give his vote for the utter abolition of a Trade which was shocking to humanity, abominable to be carried on by any country, and which reflected the greatest dishonour on... the British nation". Despite Pitt's tough stance, there was a great deal of opposition in the Lords, especially from Lord Thurlow, the Lord Chancellor. Thurlow (1731-1806), was disliked by a great many people as he was considered arrogant, profane, vulgar and immoral, but he was respected as well, and Fox once said of him that:- "No man was so wise as Thurlow looked". However, Pitt was furious at the opposition the Bill was receiving from members of his own government and he told Grenville that should it be defeated in the Lords, he, Pitt, and those who voted against it, would never be able to work in the same administration together again. As it happened, the Bill went through by fourteen votes to twelve but it clearly showed that the fight for complete abolition was going to be long and hard.

While all this was going on, Wilberforce was fighting his illness and still using large amounts of opium. It was used by a great number of people in the 18th century, and just two of the effects it had on the user was to kill pain and relieve gastric problems. The very wise Issac Milner took it regularly and also took larger amounts than Wilberforce did, but he personally recommended Wilberforce to use it which he did until the end of his life. Feeling better, on 5th May, he travelled from Bath to Cambridge where he lived quietly and in June, travelled to the Lake District where he stayed with his mother and sister at Rayrigg. He also intended to live quietly there as well but it didn't quite work out that way. There was always a great many guests coming and going and he never got the rest that he needed, although it seems that he enjoyed the late night card games. This behaviour he felt clashed with his Christianity and he left Rayrigg in the autumn and returned to Bath deciding not to renew the lease on Rayrigg. He took to the waters of Bath in October that year and by this time he had had no political dealings with anyone for eight months. He was persuaded to attend the centennial celebrations of the Glorious Revolution in York on the 5th of November and he did so, travelling again, this time south to Birmingham where he arrived on 11th November. It was in Birmingham that he heard about the illness of the King and the serious affects that the King's health could have on the Government generally and his friend and Prime Minister William Pitt in particular.

It had been the King who had appointed Pitt as Prime Minister and if he, the King, died, then his eldest son, the dissolute Prince of Wales, would succeed him as George IV. However, if the King lived but was incapacitated to such a degree that he was unable to exercise his duties as Monarch, the Prince of Wales would become Regent and effectively rule the country. Either scenario would mean that Pitt would be removed as Prime Minister and the Whigs, headed by Charles James Fox, would replace him. Pitt spent the next few months using all his political skills in an effort to use delaying tactics to keep the Whigs and the Prince of Wales at bay, and in meeting after meeting at Downing Street, Wilberforce was there to support him. It was generally thought that the King was insane, his behaviour was extremely erratic and several doctors were brought in to treat him, the most notable being Doctor Francis Willis who specialised in mental illness. Willis spent a great deal of time treating the King, and sometimes his methods seemed very harsh, but he was adamant that he could cure the King. In the meantime, Wilberforce continued to support Prime Minister Pitt at great cost to his own health which started slipping again as the result of the many late night meetings at Downing Street. He also sat on all the Committees, one of which was concerned with precedents and which sat in December 1788, and another Committee which sat in January, 1789 examined the evidence of the King's physicians. Whilst no doubt necessary, these Committees helped Pitt in the use of his delaying tactics, but they did little for Wilberforce's health and in his diary he described himself as 'very much shattered' and 'too dissipated'. It looked as if the relapse in Wilberforce's health had all been in vain when Pitt having no other option open to him, had to prepare a Regency Bill which he put to the House of Commons on 5th February, 1789 and to the House of Lords on 16th. By this time, Fox and the Whigs were convinced that power was there for the taking, but on the very next day, the 17th, the King's doctors issued a bulletin saying that the King had recovered. Pitt would live to fight another day and Wilberforce, although unwell, could once again return to the problem of the slave trade. There were powerful people both for and against abolition and they were in roughly equal numbers. The success or failure of the campaign depended on who could win over the majority and it was here that the abolitionists had the harder task. People who are not committed tend to want to stay with the system that is already in place, and coupled with that, most people were totally unaware of the horrific treatment that was being inflicted on the slaves. Pitt of course was in favour of abolition, and in this he was joined by Charles James Fox and Edmund Burke, the latter two being powerful figures from the Whig opposition benches. However, the MPs from the ports of Liverpool and Bristol, although small in number, could be relied upon to vote against any reform and would work hard to muster support. Along with this were several members of the cabinet so that there could be no collective government support for any motion that would be automatically achieved in today's politics. Another person who was firmly against abolition was a man by the name of Stephen Fuller. Fuller was the agent for Jamaica but was based in London and so knew exactly what was happening with the abolitionist movement. However, taking a charitable view of him given the period of history that they lived in, Fuller was not all bad. He supported slavery because he simply could not see how Britain's economy could function without it, but he did urge the slave owners in Jamaica to improve the conditions that the slaves both worked and lived in. However, he wrote to the Home Secretary, Lord Sydney, and told him that if the slaves in the West Indies got wind that the problem was even being discussed, there would be wholesale revolt by the slaves and chaos and violence would result. Lord Sydney was sympathetic to Fuller's letter as he too was against the abolitionist cause but when he wrote to Pitt with Fuller's views he received a reply which gave the impression that Pitt was sitting on the fence regarding the matter. Pitt wrote:- "It would be well if it (abolition) could be brought about; but that there were so many points of the greatest consequence to this country involved in the question that he should never think of supporting any plan until after the fullest investigation".

One important ally that Wilberforce was to have came in the form of a Scottish lawyer, James Stephen (1758-1832) who was considered to be brilliant and who had worked in the West Indies. William met him for the first time on 31st January, 1789 and although they did not know it at the time, they were to become life long friends which only ended when Stephen died at Bath in October 1832. In 1800, he had married William's widowed sister, Sally (Sarah) Clarke so became William's brother-in-law. Stephen was a great addition to the abolitionist cause. When he had been in the West Indies, he had witnessed the horror of it all at first hand and was present at a grotesquely unfair trial where two black slaves were convicted of rape on virtually no evidence and were sentenced to be burned to death.

There was another powerful figure in the abolitionist camp and his name was Olaudah Equiano (c1745-1797). Born in Essaka, which was an Igbo village in the kingdom of Benin, he was kidnapped by native slaveholders when he was eleven years old along with his younger sister. The first night they had huddled together for comfort but to his distress, the next morning, he and his sister were separated, never to see each other again. Along with other slaves, he was shipped to the British colony in Virginia where he was purchased by Lieutenant Michael Pascal of the Royal Navy. He was not treated unkindly and learned skills of seamanship and served against the French in the Seven Years War virtually becoming a member of the crew. However, to his dismay, Equiano did not receive any prize money when the war ended and despite being one of Pascal's favourites, was let down again, when, far from getting the freedom that Pascal had promised him, was sold on to another master. This next master was Captain James Doran but eventually luck was to turn his way when he was bought by a Quaker merchant named Robert King, where he learnt to read and write with skill and was promised his freedom if he could give King forty pounds, the price King had paid for him. Along with his reading and writing skills, Equiano soon picked up the skill of trading and to Robert King's astonishment, eventually raised that sum and was duly given his freedom whereupon he returned to Britain and became very much an establishment figure. He had already converted to Christianity and been baptised in St. Margaret's Church, Westminster in February 1759 when he was under the care of Michael Pascal. Now he was a free man he married a white girl named Susannah Cullen, a girl from Soham, Cambridgeshire on 7th April, 1792 in the local church. Equiano subsequently wrote a book about his life and the cruelty that he and others had endured. Entitled 'The Interesting Narrative of the Life of Olaudah Equiano, or Gustavus Vassa, the African', it was published in 1789 and was a best seller, making Equiano very wealthy. Apart from making Equiano a rich man, it also helped the abolitionist cause because it made many people aware of the utter cruelty suffered by the slaves. Sadly, both Equiano and his wife Susannah died young, Susannah in February 1796 at the age of 34, and her husband just over a year later, on 31st March, 1797, aged 52. Neither lived to witness Wilberforce's triumph when the Bill to abolish the slave trade was passed ten years later in 1807.

With James Stephen and Olaudah Equiano supporting the campaign in February, 1789, Wilberforce felt ready to continue with his fight for abolition. The giving of evidence to the Privy Council that Pitt had set up in May of the previous year was coming to an end, and the King was convalescing after his illness so the political scene had settled down. However, the anti-abolitionists had seen the way Wilberforce was spending hours each day working on the abolition cause, and also feared the results of the Privy Council Enquiry that had been made ready in April 1789. They also realised that the abolition campaign was now well established, and now understood that they had a fight on their hands, and so both sides mustered their arguments in time for the first presentation to Parliament the reasons for ending the slave trade which would be heard by the House of Commons on 12th May, 1789.

It was the first speech that Wilberforce had made concerning the abolition of the slave trade to the House of Commons and it lasted three and a half hours. Using the wealth of information gathered by Thomas Clarkson, he told the House of the appalling conditions that the slaves were transported in during the journey from Africa to the West Indies and the dreadful shackles that were used. He stuck to the agreed tactics of not arguing for the complete abolition but merely the trafficking, saying that the conditions in which the slaves in the West Indies were kept would automatically improve and that the natural breeding amongst the slaves would produce all that were needed to keep the sugar plantations working. It was a long way from outright abolition but it was the only way that Wilberforce and his friends thought would be successful on a long term basis. A speech of this length was not uncommon for the times. In those days it was the only way that members would be able to listen to the facts so that when the member stood up to begin a speech on any given subject, it was quite possibly the first time that other members had heard anything at all relevant to the subject being discussed. There was no mass communication that we have today whereby people have a good knowledge of subjects almost as they happen, so speeches in the 18th century were longer and a great deal of weight was put not just on the content of the speech, but the quality of oratory. Wilberforce like Pitt, was a great orator, which was just as well, as he was embarking on a lengthy campaign that would test both his powers of speech making and also his physical health over the coming years.

It was too early however – there were too many MPs with vested interests who were against them, others were merely conservative and didn't want great change, and the House of Lords was even more hostile to the abolitionist cause than the Commons was. However, the speech heralded the opening shots in the long and bitter campaign that had been started by three men, Wilberforce, Pitt, and Grenville under an oak tree on Pitt's estate in Kent two years previously to the day.

There was a strong tide of opinion in favour of the abolitionists at this time and the voices turned against Wilberforce knew it, so they adopted their own tactics. They managed to get the vote delayed by successfully arguing that the evidence of the Privy Council was not enough in itself and that Parliament should be able to hear its own evidence, which would obviously take a lot longer to amass. Pitt and Fox were furious as there was an argument against having had the Privy Council set up in the first place if Parliament was not going to take on board its findings. Rather than help the abolitionist cause, all the Privy Council turned out to be was a delaying tactic which the anti-abolitionists took advantage of. However, Wilberforce felt that he had no option other than to agree to the motion that Parliament would gather further information. Even if the evidence of the Privy Council had been accepted, there would be no guarantee that an Act of Parliament would necessarily successfully follow, and even if it was passed in the Commons, it would almost certainly have been rejected in the Lords. Wilberforce has been criticised by historians over the years for agreeing to this, but recent historians, realising that hindsight is a wonderful thing have looked more kindly towards him, understanding that he was using the best tactics he could under the circumstances. However, in agreeing to the delay, he could have had no idea how long it would be, as the anti-abolitionists managed to defer the proceedings to the following year. It was not looking good in the summer of 1789 and there was another blow for Wilberforce when the Reverend James Ramsay died on 21st July of that year. It was Ramsay's first hand knowledge of slavery due to his work on the island of St. Christopher that had allowed him to return to England and be such a support to the abolitionist cause. William had known the Reverend Ramsay since 1783 and was saddened at his death. Whilst mourning his friend, William knew that he had to get on with the job and in January, 1790 moved that a small Parliamentary Select Committee be set up to sift through the huge amount of evidence that had been collected. There were inevitable protests but it succeeded in speeding up the hearing of evidence.

The Committee heard a great deal of compelling evidence as to the appalling treatment of the slaves but the committee was small and biased against the abolitionist cause. As if that wasn't enough to think about, Pitt called a general election in June 1790 and members suddenly became distracted by that and proceedings of the committee were stalled. Wilberforce had to drop everything and travel back to Yorkshire but as it happened, he easily retained his seat - the Whigs thought him unbeatable so concentrated their efforts elsewhere. It was clear now that Wilberforce would have to wait until the next parliamentary session to re-start his fight against slavery. By March, 1791, having been interrupted by the general election, the Committee finally finished obtaining evidence from witnesses and on 18th April, 1791, Wilberforce was at last able to present the first Bill to 'prevent the farther importation of Slaves into the British colonies in the West Indies'.

Wilberforce made an excellent but measured four hour speech outlining the arguments for abolition, but tragically, the tide of opinion had turned against them. People were worried about the French revolution and the slave revolts that had happened in the West Indies. They were not ready for such radicalism and there was a swing back to the idea of keeping things as they were. They had heard that there had been fighting in Saint-Dominque leading to atrocities being carried out against the white population, and there was further uprising in Martinique and Dominica. Even Thomas Paine's *'Rights of Man'* caused alarm amongst the British population. Paine (1737-1809) was an English born American revolutionary philosopher and writer who supported the French revolution and wanted the British Monarchy overthrown. Today, his *'Rights of*

Man' is considered by many to be a classic but at the time it was written, it simply frightened the establishment. It didn't help either, that the first person to speak after Wilberforce was Colonel Tarleton, the member for Liverpool, who said that the living of 5,500 sailors would be instantly taken away, along with 160 ships and a great deal of exports. With Wilberforce however, were powerful people such as Pitt himself and the great Charles James Fox who made a brilliant speech. It was not enough however, and after two evenings of debate, the Bill was fairly easily beaten by 163 votes to 88, but although desperately disappointed, Wilberforce had set out on a journey. Fully committed, he was convinced that one day the slave trade would go and he was determined never to give up. This extract from his speech shows his determination and the confidence he had of the long term success the abolitionists would have:- "Let us not despair, it is a blessed cause, and success, ere long, will crown our exertions. Already we have gained one victory; we have obtained, for these poor creatures, the recognition of their human nature, which for a while was most shamefully denied. This is the first fruits of our efforts; let us persevere and our triumph will be complete. Never, never will we desist till we have wiped away this scandel from the Christian name, released ourselves from the load of guilt, under which we at present labour, and extinguished every trace of this bloody traffic, of which our posterity, looking back to the history of these enlightened times, will scarce believe that it has been suffered to exist so long a disgrace and dishonour to this country".

His last sentence would prove very prophetic in years to come and it has to be said that Wilberforce, Henry Thornton, Hannah More, Tom Clarkson, James Stephen, William Pitt and all the others that were committed to the abolitionist cause were brave as well as being way ahead of their time. Wilberforce commenced a non-stop parliamentary campaign and his commitment never ceased despite the often hostile reaction against it. He was supported by the so-called 'Clapham Sect' who consisted amongst others, of his cousin Henry Thornton with whom he lived from 1792 until 1796 when Thornton married his cousin Marianne Thornton. The Clapham Sect were Evangelical Christians and were completely against the slave trade and all of them along with the above named helped Wilberforce in his work over the years.

Wilberforce tried again on 2nd April, 1792, bringing forward another Bill before the House of Commons calling for the abolition of the slave trade, but by doing so, he faced a huge problem. On 22nd August, 1791, there had been a huge slave revolt in the French colony of Saint-Dominque by the 450,000 slaves who by far and away had outnumbered the white population. The slaves massacred their masters and there were wholesale murders, rape and even little children weren't spared and were killed along with the adults. Along with this brutality, a thousand plantations were set ablaze and it has been described as the bloodiest slave revolt ever known. To bring a Bill before Parliament abolishing the slave trade would seem a hopeless cause at this time but Wilberforce decided to go ahead anyway. It was an excellent debate, and great speeches were made by Wilberforce, William Pitt and Charles James Fox amongst others. William Pitt, in particular, made a speech that was described by those that heard it as one of the greatest speeches he had ever made. When it is borne in mind that he had been making great speeches from the day of his maiden speech in the House, it only shows just how remarkable the speech in this debate was. Edmund Burke would later describe the whole debate as 'exhibiting the greatest eloquence ever displayed in the House'. Colonel Tarleton, representing his constituents of Liverpool, came back with the argument that he always used and said;- "If we were disposed to sacrifice our African trade, other nations would not enter into so ruinous a plan". However, despite the brilliant speeches made by Pitt, Wilberforce and others, the Bill was effectively beaten by the man whom Pitt himself had made Home Secretary, Henry Dundas (1742-1811), who put forward a motion of 'gradual abolition over a number of years'.

Dundas was respected rather than loved in Parliament. He had been admitted to the Scottish Bar in 1763 and was elected as an MP for Midlothian in 1774. He held numerous top jobs being Lord Advocate in 1775, Keeper of the Signet in 1777 and in parliament he lent his support to Lord North despite much criticism of the latter's handling of the war with America. After Pitt won his election in 1784, Dundas became President of the Board of Control before becoming Home Secretary in 1791. He eventually became Viscount Melville and Baron Dunira in 1802 during the Addington government of 1801/4.

The intervention of Dundas was devastating for Wilberforce, because although it represented voting for abolition for the first time, the inclusion of the one word 'gradual' rendered it virtually meaningless. It satisfied those who were for abolition but feared the consequences should it happen too quickly, and pleased those who were against it who saw it as a way of postponing abolition indefinitely which meant that although clearly meaningless, it was almost certainly going to get through. That is exactly what happened as the motion put forward by Dundas was passed by 230 to 85 votes.

However, there were people who would not accept that and wanted a firm date for abolition. During a debate on 23rd April, 1792, Dundas put forward a proposal that the date for abolition be 1st January 1800 but this was felt to be so far ahead as to still render the Bill to be meaningless, and after further debates on 25th and 27th April, the 1st January, 1796 was agreed, although Wilberforce was suspicious as to the sincerity of the agreement. Wilberforce then altered his tactics and in both 1793 and 1794, he brought Bills before Parliament which would make it illegal for British ships from supplying slaves to foreign colonies. However, both times he was unsuccessful, in 1793 losing it at its third reading and in 1794, it was postponed by the House of Lords, their time being now taken up by the conduct of the war with France, which had broken out in February 1793. Wilberforce was now beginning to despair. The tide was turning against him as the general population was beginning to associate the abolitionist cause with the revolution going on in France, while the politicians had their hands full with the management of the war with that same country. Something else was about to cause Wilberforce further despair however, and this too concerned the conduct of the war with France – Wilberforce was about to experience a breach in the very close friendship that he had always enjoyed with Pitt.

On 31st December, 1794, Wilberforce rose in the House and delivered a speech saying in effect that that the government should try and find a peaceful solution with France which clearly clashed with Pitt's handling of the war. Pitt was present whilst the speech was being made and was clearly hurt. It has to be said that Wilberforce did not find making the speech easy. He moved an Amendment and said that he had:- "To perform a painful act of duty... expressing... a difference with those with whom it had been the happiness of his political life so generally to agree". He also said:- "we think it advisable and expedient to endeavour to restore the blessings of peace to his Majesty's subjects, and to his allies, upon just and reasonable terms". Just as he thought, his amendment did not carry the day, but the resulting vote of 73 votes for with 246 against showed a considerable increase in the amount of opposition to the war that had previously been expressed. Pitt was very hurt that his long-standing friend could do this and the breach between the two men can not be overestimated. Wilberforce, although not holding ministerial office, was always in and out of Downing Street discussing government affairs, and this was now brought to an abrupt halt. Wilberforce was also deeply upset as he had not found it easy to make the speech. However, he stuck to his opinions and expressed them again in the House on 26th January, 1795 where he once again put forward the view that the government should negotiate a peace with France. Not content with that, he repeated his views again in May 1795 trying to soften the blow by claiming the right to have differing views of those of his friend and Prime Minister, but by this time the breach had more or less been healed because Pitt had generously spoken in favour of Wilberforce when in February, 1795, the latter had proposed another Motion to the House for general abolition. Predictably, this was beaten by 78 to 61 votes. However, the healing of the disagreement was again put to the test when in May 1795 another matter came to the fore in which Pitt and Wilberforce disagreed. Despite his views on the war with France displeasing the King, Wilberforce had a great love for George III, and as a Christian, the behaviour of the King's eldest son, the Prince of Wales was anathema to him as it was to the King himself. The Prince of Wales had run up personal debts of approximately £600,000 which in the late 18th century, was the equivalent of something like £36 million in today's terms, a sum which would cause uproar if it had happened in modern Britain. People were being asked to make personal sacrifices in order for the war with France to be financed, and when the government negotiated an annual sum of £125,000 for the Prince, with the proviso that part of it was to settle his debts, Wilberforce and others once again were forced to voice their disapproval. Again, Pitt was hurt by this, as the negotiations for this sum had been lengthy and involved the agreement of Parliament, the Prince of Wales and the King. Wilberforce once again reminded the House of the predicament of the King's subjects, who would one day be George IV's subjects, and the sacrifices that they were making.

The stance that Wilberforce took both on the war with France and the issue of the Prince of Wales certainly put a strain on the very long and close friendship that the two men had, but it is a tribute to the depth of their regard for each other plus the generous spirit of both men that the friendship remained intact. The only person unhappy with the reconciliation was Dundas, who suspected Wilberforce's views on settling with France, and feared that he would have an undue influence on Pitt's conduct of the war. However, although Wilberforce's latest defeat in the House on the slavery issue in February 1795 helped heal his friendship with Pitt, it had one very unhappy outcome – it destroyed the spirit of Thomas Clarkson who had worked for so many years on the anti-slavery cause. Clearly physically unwell after his years of endless toil on the issue, this was one defeat too many for him to take and he withdrew from the fight, permanently as it was thought at the time, and went to live in the Lake District. He wrote at the time:- "The nervous system was almost shattered to pieces. Both my memory and my hearing failed me". He was, certainly for that moment in time anyway, broken in body and spirit which given everything that he had done over the years, was not surprising. Between 1787 and 1794, he had travelled thousands of miles lecturing in different halls throughout the country and during that time had discovered another cause that he felt needed to be tackled which was the appalling treatment of the sailors who were manning the slave ships. The treatment of these men was little better than the treatment of the slaves themselves and Clarkson spent a great deal of time and energy collecting information to the extent that he had been able to find out what happened to over twenty thousand seamen, knowing each individual case history. It was no wonder that he was exhausted. It was all too much not only for Clarkson however, but for the whole 'Society for Effecting the Abolition of the Slave Trade' who decided to cease meeting. Sadly, as with Pitt, Wilberforce had a falling out with Clarkson, although Clarkson's state of mind probably had something to do with it. He chastised Wilberforce for not getting his brother promoted in the navy and told Wilberforce "that he had been treated in a very scandalous manner". Wilberforce stood his ground though, and wrote a lengthy letter to Clarkson in which he explained that many people expected patronage from him, but such behaviour sat ill with him, and he also reminded Clarkson that he was but one of many who expected favours.

In April 1792, a proposal had been put forward in the House that the slave trade would end on 1st January 1796. The original motion that Dundas had put forward had suggested 1st January 1800, but it was considered so far ahead as to be meaningless. However, as it turned out, the date of January 1796 that was agreed upon was equally meaningless because it was one thing to fix a date, but quite another to put such a decision into some sort of action, and clearly nothing had been done. When Wilberforce rose to his feet in the Commons on 18th February, 1796, he reminded the House of the date set back in April, 1792, and reminded them also of the fact that the decision was taken after an extremely well thought out discussion, and he now called upon the House "...for the execution of it's sentence". Still however, there were arguments against, but the brilliant speeches and logic of Pitt, Wilberforce and Charles James Fox won the day and Wilberforce was given leave to bring in his Bill by 93 votes to 67. Wilberforce sensed success at last, and the third reading was set for 15th March, 1796, but disaster was looming which he did not foresee. He was slightly but not unduly concerned that half a dozen of his supporters had gone to the opera to see a new work from Italy but felt that it would hardly make a difference. As it turned out, the vote was 70 for the third reading of the Abolition Bill, and 74 against. After nine solid years of campaigning, it was just about the most cruel blow that he could have received and utterly depressed, he noted in his diary:- 'Enough at the Opera to have carried it. Very much vexed and incensed at our opponents'. Although he didn't write it in his diary, he must have been just as vexed and incensed at the so-called supporters who went to the opera on the night of an important vote – they were the people who really let him down on what could have been a life changing decision for millions of people at that time and for the future. Wilberforce was absolutely shattered mentally and physically and by April he became seriously ill. So ill in fact, that on one occasion he was unable to see Pitt and Dundas when they called on him at his home. With the help of Issac Milner, he made some sort of recovery but was not really fit enough to engage in what he would have to do in the coming weeks.

When they made a trip out to Cambridge on 20th May, 1796, Pitt told him that there would be a general election very soon. After the recent defeat that he had suffered, he was realising only too well what Thomas Clarkson was going through and felt that this was the last thing that he wanted. Still, he was nothing if not strong willed, and gathering together all his reserves of energy, he set off to Hull, his constituency seat. As it turned out, the reception that he received from the voters was so good that it actually revived rather than tired him and he was duly re-elected for Yorkshire. Ironically, the other member being elected was Henry Lascelles, who although a supporter of Pitt, was the heir to the fortune of the Harewood family, the family fortune coming directly from the toil of slave labour in the sugar plantations although his election had had nothing to do with Wilberforce.

In April 1797, William Wilberforce was a contented man. He was not physically well, but he was happy in himself, and there were two reasons for this. The first was the publication of his book on the 12th April, 1797 entitled *'A Practical View of the Prevailing Religious System of Professed Christians, in the Higher and Middle Classes in this Country, Contrasted with Real Christianity'*. It took Wilberforce a long time to complete this book as there were so many demands on his time over the years. It had to be fitted in with his time consuming parliamentary duties, extensive travelling, and the huge amount of correspondence that always had to be dealt with. Wilberforce had long wanted to take time out so that he could devote his time completely to the book as he felt that the continual demands from other quarters not only made him take longer to finish the work, but that the quality of the book would also suffer. He certainly had his critics not least of which was the publisher, Mr. Thomas Cadell, who Wilberforce said treated him like 'an able enthusiast' meaning that Cadell thought he was not very good. Cadell also felt that there would be no demand for a religious book although he did reluctantly agree to publishing 500 copies. He was not alone in criticising the book. One reader wrote to Wilberforce saying that he had every intention of reading it, but found it impossible as it was so tedious whilst others felt that it was too vague:- "He has neglected to give a definition or a clear explanation of the doctrines which he so strongly inculcates...". However, from other people, there was great support. John Newton in particular was full of praise and wrote:- "What a phenomenon has Mr. Wilberforce sent abroad! Such a book, by such a man, and at such a time". Praise indeed from someone who Wilberforce used to listen to and hero worship when he was a young boy. There was much praise from other quarters including Edmund Burke who was by no means a close friend of Wilberforce but derived comfort from it when he, Burke, lay dying. The book came on the market at the right time as life was very hard for many people who were looking for explanations as to why their lives were as they were. Thomas Cadell, the publisher had been completely wrong because the 500 copies were sold in a matter of days and in the first six months, the book sold 7,500 copies, which at the time made it a best seller. In Wilberforce's lifetime, it was translated into French, Italian, Spanish, Dutch and German and there were fifteen editions printed. It was even available at the beginning of the 21st Century, which was an extraordinary achievement and one that Wilberforce could never have anticipated.

The second event that contributed greatly to William Wilberforce's happiness was marriage. Wilberforce had always dismissed the idea of getting married, because like his friend William Pitt, he had seemed married to his work and felt that the amount of time he needed for his various causes would rule the prospect of a partner out. However, sometimes he would let slip an opposite view as he did after spending a few weeks with his friend Edward Eliot and his cousin Henry Thornton.

Wilberforce wrote:- "I must beware of this sort of old bachelor's life". In the previous year, 1796, Thornton had married his cousin Marianne and this event really made Wilberforce think of marriage seriously. His book had been published on 12th April, 1797, and it was around this time that he travelled to Bath where on the 13th, he chatted to Thomas Babington, a friend from his Cambridge days, and who recommended a lady called Barbara Spooner to him as a suitable bride. Barbara Ann Spooner was twenty years old, and the third of ten children by a wealthy businessman from Birmingham. She was thought attractive by those who met her and as she was in Bath at the same time as Wilberforce, Babington wasted no time in arranging for the two to meet, introducing them to each other two days later, on Saturday the 15th. Wilberforce was instantly smitten and wrote in his diary:- "…What a blessed Sunday have I been permitted to spend, how happy at dinner and in love". By the following weekend he was deeply in love and the relationship then took an interesting and ironic turn. Wilberforce was keen to propose, but people like Henry Thornton and Hannah More who had been only too keen for them to get together, now counselled caution and advised him to wait a little longer before committing himself, but the matter was soon out of Wilberforce's control. On Sunday, 23rd 1797, having known Miss Spooner precisely eight days, he had written a letter proposing marriage to her but having taken advice from Babington, changed his mind. However, the letter had already been posted and that same evening, she accepted his proposal.

Despite the fact that he had stayed awake all night on the 23rd worrying about the letter having been sent, it does not appear that it was too long before he was happy with the situation and seemed perfectly content spending time with her in Bath. He was expecting to stay rather longer, but national events took a turn and after a letter from Pitt, Wilberforce knew that his place was in London to be with his friend. The Channel fleet had mutinied at Spithead and refused to sail. On top of that, the agreement with Austria looked like collapsing, which would have meant Britain fighting the French alone. Despite all this, and the fact that interest in the abolition of the slave trade was not top of anyone's agenda, Wilberforce still presented what had now become his annual motion concerning this to the House on 28th May, 1797. It was defeated as Wilberforce thought it would be, but it was reasonably close, the vote being 82 to 74. Wilberforce was not unduly worried on this occasion for three reasons:- firstly, he felt that in his heart of hearts it was not the right time, secondly, the vote was quite close, and thirdly, he was deeply in love and no one event, however serious, could alter the joy that came with the feelings that that love brought. However, events concerning the Spithead fleet were serious, and far from being quelled, the naval mutiny had spread. Austria had done what Pitt feared it would do and made peace with France leaving Britain isolated, and the army was rioting. Wilberforce said that he felt 'exceedingly hunted and shattered'. However, it didn't stop him leaving London for Bath the very next day, the 29th May and the day after that, the 30th May, 1797, he married the person who would be the love of his life, Barbara Ann Spooner. Barbara was criticised in some quarters for not wishing to attend parties and be seen in the social circles, but she was after a quieter life and wished to create a calm domestic atmosphere for her husband. Quite how calm it was is open to question as they had six children: William (b1798), Barbara (b1799), Elizabeth (b1801), Robert Issac (b1802), Samuel (b1805), and Henry William (b1807). William was a loving father and spent a great deal of time with his children. Indeed, it was a loving family home, and he never regretted his decision to marry Barbara. He loved the fact that she wanted to create a happy home, and he wrote in 1803:- "I find reason to thank God for my marriage which, by shutting me out more from the world, has tended to keep me from its infection".

Despite marriage, William continued to be as busy as ever, not just with the slavery question, but with causes such as cruelty to animals, the transformation of British Society through the moral behaviour of individual people, attempting to introduce Christianity to India, supporting his friend Pitt on the introduction of income tax, the regulation of newspapers and the day to day issues that involved him working closely with Pitt. However, despite the fact that the two were working closely with each other, another difference of opinion happened between them that could have come close to spoiling their deep friendship in the way that their quarrel over Pitt's handling of the war with France had done at the beginning of 1795. On Friday, 25th May, 1798, during a debate in the House, Pitt accused a leading opposition MP, Mr. George Tierney, of obstructing the defence of the country and when Pitt was asked to withdraw his comments, he refused to retract. Tierney challenged Pitt to a duel which Pitt accepted. Two days later on Sunday, 27th May on Putney Heath, there came the extraordinary and also alarming spectacle of the Prime Minister of the day and a leading Member of Parliament involved in what was potentially a life threatening situation. As was the custom in duelling, both men walked twelve paces before turning and firing at each other. To the relief of all, neither man was injured and as was the custom of the time, honour was satisfied. Despite both men surviving, Wilberforce was furious at his friend's action. Pitt was Prime Minister in one of the most dangerous periods in history - a time when it was important to have strong and experienced leadership. That alone was enough to infuriate

Wilberforce, but he also disapproved because of his strong Christian beliefs. He had even criticised the practice in his book *'A Practical View...'*, and last but not least in Wilberforce's eyes, Pitt had chosen to carry out this act on the Sabbath. He was not alone in being angry as King George III also shared Wilberforce's astonishment and anger and wrote to the Prime Minister saying he trusted that "...what has happened will never be repeated". Having voiced his disapproval to his friend Pitt, Wilberforce should really have let the matter drop because after all, the King had, but he felt that he could not. Wilberforce had heard about it on the Monday, the day after it happened and on the Wednesday following, put down a Commons motion condemning duelling and for good measure saying that it should henceforth be made illegal. It was an ill thought out and foolish act made in haste and was doubly stupid given that his long friendship with Pitt had already floundered before when they had disagreed three years earlier over both Pitt's handling of the war with France along with the financial help that the government were giving the Prince of Wales concerning the debts that he had accumulated. The motion put forward by Wilberforce criticising duelling drew an immediate response from Pitt that if the motion was carried, he, Pitt, would have no option other than to resign. In the end, Wilberforce backed down realising that an experienced Prime Minister of fifteen years standing would be lost at a critical time for the nation and that his friendship with Pitt, so close for so many years, would almost certainly be finished for good.

1798 was a mixed year for Wilberforce emotionally. He was taken ill again in the June and just as he was recovering, he found that his wife Barbara was pregnant but also unwell, but worse was to come. He received the news that his mother had died and he went to Hull for the funeral. He returned to London to find that Barbara had recovered and on the 21st June, his first child William was born. Wilberforce was naturally delighted and he was also pleased that on 1st August, Nelson had destroyed the French fleet in the Battle of the Nile. The war with France had taken a turn for the better, but it meant that the slavery issue was not so important for the general population. Undeterred, Wilberforce presented his Bills to the Commons as usual in April 1798 and March 1799. Predictably, both times they were defeated, the first by 87 votes to 83 and the second by a bigger margin, 84 votes to 54.

Wilberforce and his friends carried on the fight and eventually the tide of opinion turned for them. In recent years, there had been a strong reaction against the abolitionists as they related them to the revolution in France. However, they could now see that country for what it now was, a country being run by a dictator, Napoleon Bonaparte. On 30th May, 1804, Wilberforce presented the first reading of his Abolition Bill to the House of Commons and won an astonishing victory, having 124 votes for and only 49 against which meant that he had achieved a majority of 75. Wilberforce was elated, especially when he got the second and third readings through, but sadly, Parliament was too far advanced to actually get it through the Lords, so it could not become law. However, it did show the country's depth of feeling in the matter of slavery. A confident Wilberforce tried again the following year bringing it to the Commons on 3rd March, 1805, so that there would be plenty of time to present it to the Lords. However, since the votes had been held in the previous year, things had changed on three counts. Since the failure of the bill in 1799, a hundred Irish MPs were in the House, and most of them had supported Wilberforce in 1804. Also, Wilberforce had always enjoyed the support of his friend and Prime Minister, William Pitt. In the 1805 debate however, the first thing that went wrong was that the Irish members seemed to desert Wilberforce and did not vote for him in anything like the numbers that had supported him the previous year. Secondly, for the first time in nearly twenty years, Pitt seemed to withdraw his support. Heavily burdened with work in general and the war with France in particular, Pitt had no energy for what now seemed to him a distraction. Also, Pitt knew that he could not rely on particular members of his government to support him. Thirdly, the anti-abolitionists were much better organised with the result that a distraught Wilberforce actually lost the vote by 77 votes to 70 – not a huge defeat but a defeat all the same, and after the heady success of the previous year, he found it very hard to take.

As in 1799, 1806 was a year of mixed emotions for Wilberforce. His great friend and Prime Minister, William Pitt, had died on the 23rd of January which resulted in Pitt being succeeded by his cousin William (Lord) Grenville, with George III reluctantly bringing in Charles James Fox to work along side him. Both men were Whigs and Wilberforce had no choice other than to work more closely with them. However, although very saddened by the death of Pitt, Wilberforce was to have a great triumph with the slavery issue. The very clever lawyer, James Stephen, came up with a brilliant idea to tackle the slave trade issue from a different angle altogether. Stephen had become Wilberforce's brother-in-law since 1800 when he married William's sister Sally Clarke, her first husband, Dr. Clarke, dying suddenly in August 1797, only three months after William's own wedding. James Stephen had become a valuable member of Wilberforce's set over the years and in 1805, had published a book entitled 'The War in Disguise' which basically said that Britain's enemies were flourishing because of their being allowed to use ships of neutral countries to transport their cargoes. This meant that supplies which were destined for France could be transported unchallenged in a neutral ship and safely landed in France. Stephen came up with the ingenious plan to bring forward a Bill that would allow British ships to board ships flying a neutral flag and stop their cargo, including slaves, from being transported. This would be a real body blow to the slave trade as the French and Spanish governments would not use their own ships to transport slaves because they feared an attack from a British fleet. Also, the Caribbean colonies would lose their supplies and their manufacturing ability would collapse leading to a reduction in the need for slaves. On 23rd May, 1806, the Foreign Slave Trade Act was passed to the delight of Wilberforce, Stephens, Clarkson, who since 1804 had been back working against slavery, Fox, and everybody else who had been working so hard over the years. Sadly however, another death was to affect Wilberforce. After years in opposition, Charles James Fox was back in government with Grenville, but died on 13th September, 1806. It is extraordinary that both Pitt and Fox, political opponents over so many years, but such respected men who both worked against slavery, should die so closely together. However, their legacy was not going to be too long in coming. The Foreign Slave Trade Act was ingenious and outwitted everybody who was against the abolitionists as it was promoted as an Act that was necessary to help win the war. Wilberforce had kept very quiet during all the debates so as not to cause anyone to be suspicious and the plan worked to perfection. However, the slave trade, although reduced considerably, was not abolished completely.

The final body blow to the slave trade was to come the following year, 1807, and slightly different tactics were involved. Lord Grenville, now Prime Minister, decided to get an Abolition Bill through the Lords first which would be tougher than getting it through the Commons. He was by no means certain as to how many votes he would get but the tide of opinion had at last turned in favour of the abolitionists and it went through with a huge vote of one hundred votes to thirty-four. On the 23rd February 1807, Wilberforce was to have his dream finally fulfilled when the Bill went through the House of Commons with the extraordinary vote of 283 for and only 16 against. The slave trade had at last been abolished and the Prime Minister who helped it through was Lord Grenville, who as William Grenville, had sat under an oak tree in Holwood Kent, on 12th May, 1787, nearly twenty years before with his cousin William Pitt and William Wilberforce and pledged to do just that – end the slave trade. But this was Wilberforce's triumph and speech after speech heaped praise on him whilst he listened to it all with tears streaming down his cheeks as one of the greatest and longest campaigns in history came to a glorious end – it was without doubt his finest hour.

This chapter has concentrated on Wilberforce's campaign to end the slave trade as this is what he is best known for, and also the most exhausting in terms of his time and his mental energy. There were however, other aspects of life that he was interested in, not least of which was the promotion of Christianity, and it was these powerful beliefs that were to provoke criticism from certain quarters as to what they saw was a contradiction in his character and actions. It was felt that some Evangelical Christians were more interested in the worship of God than changing society. William Cobbett (1763-1835), an English writer who always fought for the poor, attacked Wilberforce for spending so much of his energy improving the lot of slaves whilst doing nothing for the poor in his own country. He once wrote:- "Never have you done one single act, in favour of the labourers of this country". It is impossible to deny the accuracy of this statement but in fairness to Wilberforce, it is often thought that it is better to concentrate on one thing and do it well, rather than spend a little time on various projects and get nowhere with any of them, and the slavery issue certainly took up most of his time and energy. One aspect of life that he did campaign for however, was the issue of cruelty to animals, and he was way ahead of his time on this. Along with some others, he helped set up the organisation called 'The Society for the Prevention of Cruelty to Animals' which was later to become 'The Royal Society for the Prevention of Cruelty to Animals'.

Despite his devotion to the cause of abolishing slavery, Wilberforce was quite reactionary in his views, and this is where William Cobbett had a point. Wilberforce was against the idea of workers forming themselves into a trade union – in fact he described unions as "a general disease in our country" and he was also against women who involved themselves in anti-slavery projects. This must have been galling for the likes of Hannah More and Elizabeth Heyrick

(1769-1831), both of whom supported the cause. After her husband's death in 1795, Elizabeth Heyrick became a Quaker and her life was devoted to radical causes including the abolition of slavery, so it must have seemed an insult when Wilberforce and others made the membership of the Society for the Abolition of the Slave Trade which was formed in 1783 an all male organisation. However, undeterred by Wilberforce and his other male companions, she continued to campaign against slavery until her death in 1831, two years before the practice was finally abolished.

Set against this however, Wilberforce suggested legislation to improve the working conditions of Chimney sweeps and textile workers, involved himself in prison reform, the conditions of which were scandalous, and gave his support to the campaigns to restrict the use of capital punishment, which was used for the most trivial of offences. He also realised that education helped families out of poverty and therefore helped out his friend, Hannah More, and her sister, when they established Sunday schools for the children of poor families in Somerset, and gave them financial help. Despite his rather reactionary views, there is no doubt that he was soft hearted and gave much of his money away to the poor seeing it as his Christian duty so to do. He had strong views on morality and seeing it almost as important as the slavery issue, Wilberforce campaigned for the moral reform of society. He deplored what he saw as the moral decadence of people and lobbied against:- "the torrent of profaneness that every day makes more rapid advances". He tried to involve public figures to his cause and formed the Society for Suppression of Vice, but he was not nearly so successful in this as he had been on the slavery issue. One can argue that he did make a difference, as after the reigns of George III's two morally challenged sons, George IV (1820-1830), previously the Prince of Wales, and William IV (1830-1837), previously the Duke of Clarence and a strong opponent of the abolitionist cause, it led the way to the Victorian era which commenced in 1837. Doubts must remain about this however, as it is arguable that decadence was still rife, it was just that Victorian society was better at hiding it, and also if the moral climate of this new era had improved, it may have happened anyway because of the attitudes of Victoria and her Consort, Prince Albert.

Wilberforce continued to fight for the total abolition of slavery, although as age and ill health caught up with him, he gave way to new and younger people who started to take an active part in the cause. In April, 1833, in Maidstone, Kent, frail and ill, he made what was to be his final speech against slavery and on the 14th May, Lord Stanley, the Colonial Secretary, proposed a motion for its abolition. Wilberforce was dying at this point and Stanley knew it, and he paid fulsome praise to Wilberforce for all that he had done over the years to bring this moment about. Charles (and since 1807, Lord) Grey (1764-1845), was Prime Minister at the time and can be justly proud of his record in office which went from 1830 until 1834. He took through the long awaited Reform Act of June, 1832 but much more importantly for Wilberforce, he saw through the passing of the Abolition of Slavery Bill on 26th July, 1833. Fortunately, although dreadfully ill, Wilberforce was with his cousin Lucy Smith at 44, Cadogan Place, London, and was therefore near enough to Parliament to be told the news that he had spent forty-six years waiting and fighting to hear. His condition grew worse, and at 3am on Monday 29th July, 1833, just three days after this Bill was passed, William Wilberforce, the great campaigner, his loving wife Barbara and son Henry with him, passed away, his body absolutely worn out, but he went knowing that his life's work was complete.

Wilberforce had professed a wish to be buried with his sister and daughter at Stoke Newington, slightly north of London, but this man who had devoted so much of his life in helping other people was not going to be let off so lightly. Members of both Houses of Parliament felt that he should be buried at Westminster Abbey, and after discussions with his family, he was laid to rest on 3rd August, 1833 in the north transept near his great friend William Pitt, a fitting tribute to a great and extraordinary man, who after so many years of tirelessly campaigning, changed the lives of millions, both in his own generation, and future generations. He was helped in his work by other great people such as Thomas Clarkson and James Stephen without whom he would not have succeeded, but there is a sad postscript to this amazing, lengthy and ultimately successful campaign to get slavery abolished. In 1838, five years after the Abolition of Slavery Bill was passed and Wilberforce's own death, there was a dispute between the roles that Wilberforce and Clarkson played in this lengthy drama. This was due to two of Wilberforce's sons, Robert and Samuel publishing a biography of their father claiming that Clarkson's own book, 'History of the Rise, Progress and Accomplishment of the Abolition of the Slave-Trade (1808)' had claimed that it was he, Clarkson, rather than Wilberforce who had been instrumental in arousing the interest of William Pitt to the anti-slavery cause. Wilberforce's sons also objected to the impression given by Clarkson's book that their father had been more of a mouthpiece in Parliament whilst he, Clarkson, had been the one travelling the country and undertaking all the gruelling work. No-one can take away the work put in by Clarkson but it is simply not true that he and not Wilberforce ignited the interest of Pitt to the slavery issue, and neither can it be correct that Wilberforce was a mere Parliamentary mouthpiece on the issue.

However, Clarkson was furious at what he saw was misinformation in the Wilberforce biography and answered some of the claims by writing another book, 'Strictures on a Life of William Wilberforce' that appeared in 1839.

This rift between the families was a great pity as Wilberforce was dead and Clarkson was an old man and it was a great misfortune that the credit was not allowed to be given to both men in equal measure. However, sad though this quarrel was, it will never take away from Wilberforce that day in Parliament on 23rd February, 1807, when the Bill to end the trafficking of slavery was finally passed and the House paid its many justifiable tributes to the man who helped end this barbaric practice. MP after MP rose to speak giving their fulsome praise for Wilberforce whilst the tears streamed down his face as he was unable to contain his emotions after so many years of campaigning. For his dogged determination over such a long time to end this disgusting trade, William Wilberforce thoroughly deserves the gratitude of millions along with his place in history.

-oOOo-

8

Jane Austen
(1775-1817)

Brilliant writer whose books are still dramatised on television to this day.

Jane Austen was an amazing young woman. Someone who spent most of her life in a Hampshire village, finished her formal schooling at the age of eleven, never travelled to any great extent, never married or bore children, who died at the age of forty-one years old, yet wrote six of the greatest books in the English language in an age where women writers were frowned upon.

Jane was born on the 16th December, 1775 at Steventon, Hampshire where her father, the Revd. George Austen was the vicar. Jane was the seventh of what turned out to be eight children but was one of only two daughters, the other being Cassandra, who became very close to Jane, being a best friend as well as a sister. When one sees Elizabeth and Jane, two of the Bennett girls in Austen's *Pride and Prejudice*, one wonders whether their relationship, although not necessarily their characters, were based on Jane and Cassandra. Jane's father George, was born in 1731 and lived until 1805. George's father was William Austen (Jane's grandfather), who was born in 1701 and set up in practice as a surgeon in Tonbridge and in 1727, married Rebecca Walter who was the widow of another medical practioner and who brought one son, William Walter to the marriage. William and Rebecca had three children of their own:- a girl, Philadelphia, who was born in 1730, George, Jane Austen's father, born the following year, and a second girl, Leonora, a year after that in 1732. It was that birth that killed the mother, but in 1737, William married again, a lady called Susanna Kelk, but lived only one more year himself, dying in 1738.

William's widow Susanna felt little or no affection towards her late husband's children and with both their natural parents dead and clearly unwanted by their stepmother, they were in effect orphans. Susanna promptly handed them over to their Uncle Stephen, a younger brother of their father's, but although Stephen only had one child, a son, he was only prepared to look after one of the children, in this case Leonora. Philadelphia moved in to a maternal aunt, whilst George, Jane's father, went to his aunt Elizabeth, who was his father's only sister. She was married to a Mr. Hooper and they lived in Tonbridge. George attended school in Tonbridge from 1741 to 1747, studying mathematics, Latin and Greek. At the age of sixteen, he was awarded a Fellowship which was open only to students of the Tonbridge School, and this enabled him to go to St. John's College, Oxford. He obtained his degree and stayed on to study Divinity which set him on course for his career in the church.

There is virtually nothing known of what happened to Leonora after that, but Philadelphia (1730-92) was a spirited girl, who after a spell as a trainee milliner in Covent Garden, travelled to India and married Tysoe Saul Hancock (1723-75), a surgeon with the East India Company. At first there were no children, but in December 1761, after eight years, Philadelphia gave birth to a girl who she named Elizabeth but who was sometimes known as Bess. After a while she became known as Eliza and the family were befriended by none other than Warren Hastings (1732-1818) who in 1773 became Governor-General of India having served in that country since 1750 when he was sent out to work as a writer for the East India Company. He resigned this office in 1784 and returned to England to face trial on corruption charges. The trial was extraordinary in length lasting from 13th February, 1788 to 23rd April, 1795 when he was eventually acquitted and he lived his final years in retirement as an English gentleman. The famous historian, Lord Macauley in his 'Essay on Warren Hastings' wrote that whilst he was impressed by the scale of Hastings' achievement in India, found that: "His principles were somewhat lax. His heart was somewhat hard". Hastings became Eliza's godfather and settled £10,000 on her. Because of the childless state of the marriage between Philadelphia and Tysoe Saul Hancock for the first eight years and the generosity that Hastings bestowed upon the family, there are suspicions but obviously no proof, that Warren Hastings was in fact, Eliza's father. In any event, Jane's cousin Eliza was to feature prominently in the lives of the Austen family in the future.

Meanwhile, George Austen (Jane's father) was ordained at the age of 24 years and for a while earned his living as a teacher at his old school in Tonbridge. However, he was taken on as assistant Chaplain at his old college in Oxford, and it was in Oxford that he met Cassandra Leigh (1739-1827) who he married in April 1764 in Bath, the same year that he became vicar of Steventon. He was thirty-two years old whilst his young wife was twenty-four. Jane's mother, Cassandra Leigh came of slightly different stock given the rigid class system that prevailed during that time. Her father, Thomas Leigh (1696-1764) was a parish priest at Harpsden, near Henley-on-Thames, and her uncle was Theophilus Leigh (1693-1785), the Master of Balliol for an extraordinary total of fifty years. His election was due not so much for what he did as to what he said. A witty man, he was not expected to live nearly as long as he actually did and it was said that he was elected to the post for that very reason, that his early death would lead to another election. As it turned however, he lived to over ninety years of age and it is unclear as to who was more surprised, Theophilus himself or the people who elected him. Cassandra was the third of four children and her brother James came into a fortune through the death of a great-uncle which enabled him to make his surname double barrelled, from then on calling himself James Leigh-Perrot. Although Cassandra Leigh was fairly down to earth, this was a period where the class system prevailed, and so she was proud of her aristocratic roots. The Leigh family claimed to have been descended from the Lord Mayor of London who proclaimed Elizabeth I as Queen of England. Since then, some of her descendants had become owners of Stoneleigh Abbey in Warwickshire and others had married into the aristocracy. With all this behind her, it must have been hard for her to accept that as a female, she saw no family wealth handed down to her, and she had to settle for being a clergyman's wife.

When she was twenty-four years old, her father retired, and he took Cassandra and her sister Jane to Bath but the Revd. Leigh was not to enjoy a long retirement, dying shortly after the family arriving at Bath. It was not long after that, that Cassandra Leigh married George Austen (Jane's father). Including Jane, the Revd. George Austen and his wife Cassandra had eight children in all. Jane's siblings were as follows:- James (1765-1819), George (1766-1838), Edward (1767-1852), Henry (1771-1850), Cassandra Elizabeth (1773-1845), Francis (1774-1865), and Charles (1779-1852). Jane, having been born in 1775 was the seventh out of the eight, the only one younger than her being the last born, Charles.

The upbringing that the children had seems strange to us today but was perfectly normal then. Jane's mother Cassandra breast fed her children until they were a few months old, and then sent them away to another home in the village for a period of twelve to eighteen months before bringing them back into the family. It seems almost cruel to us today but in those days, parents thought nothing of it as the idea of parent/child bonding is a fairly modern concept. It is possible that Jane's generation were the last to suffer it as her nephew James-Edward Austen-Leigh (1798-1874), the son of Jane's brother James (1765-1819) and his second wife Mary certainly thought it odd when he wrote the memoirs of his aunt in 1870, just less than a hundred years after Jane was born. In Jane's time, the writer William Cobbett (1763-1835) wrote about this way of raising children and was severely critical of it, although reading his words now merely shows that he was years ahead of his time. Born in Farnham, Surrey, he was a Tory in his early life but became more and more radical as he advanced in years. He always championed the poor, and with reference to the ideas of child-rearing that were prevalent at the time, he wrote:- "Who has not seen these banished children, when brought and put into the arms of their mother, screaming to get from them and stretching out their little hands to get back to the arms of the nurse." Be that as it may, that was the method used at the time, and there were many poor families in the district who would have found the extra income useful if not essential, although clearly it was a practise that was nearing the end of it's days.

One of the children, George (1766-1838), stayed with the village nurse. He was considered backward and suffered from fits. He was clearly not a Downs Syndrome child as he lived a long life which would have been impossible during the 18th century. At some stage, probably when George was in his early teens, it was decided that he should live elsewhere. A place was found at Monk Sherbourne, a quiet village near Basingstoke with the Culham family and he lived there never to come home on a permanent basis. As in the way that some families sent young babies away, this may seem cruel, but the Austens were a kindly family and the reasoning which was probably thought of as perfectly acceptable in those days, was the fact that Mrs. Austen already had her hands full running a house with not only her own children to look after, but also those of other families as she and Jane's father ran a school where the children lived in. This was done in order to supplement the Revd. George Austen's limited income as a clergyman.

Jane would not have escaped being handed over to another family, and she would have returned to find a house full of boys, as the Austens started the schooling three years before Jane was born. Jane and her sister Cassandra were the only girls and no doubt joined in the rough games that a houseful of boys would have played. As the school was small enough to be run along the lines of a large family, it was almost inevitable that lifelong friendships would grow, and this certainly happened with the Fowle Brothers, Fulwar-Craven, Tom, William and Charles. Tom in fact would later become engaged to Jane's only sister, Cassandra. In any event, Jane was always at ease in the company of boys and became mentally strong as a result.

When she was seven years old, Jane was sent away to boarding school. Quite why she was sent so early in life when the boys stayed at home until the age of twelve is not quite clear. There may have been a touch of family loyalty involved as her mother was attached to her sister Jane (1736-83), who was Jane Austen's aunt. In 1768 Jane Leigh married an Edward Cooper (1728-92) and they had two children, also called Edward and Jane. The younger Jane Cooper was very friendly with Cassandra Austen and Mrs. Austen sometimes sent her elder daughter Cassandra to Bath to keep the young Jane Cooper company, and so attached were the Austen sisters, that it may have been that the young Jane Austen would have preferred to go to school with Cassandra then be left at home without her.

They went to a school run by a Mrs. Cawley in Oxford. Some of the boarding schools that girls were sent to were dreadful. The children were not looked after properly and some became quite ill. The writer Fanny Burney (1752-1840), whose writing had done so much to influence Jane, had a friend, the famous Mrs. Hester Thrale (1741-1821), the Welsh writer, who was also a friend of the great Dr. Johnson (1709-84). Hester herself sent her four-year-old daughter, Harriet, and five-year-old Cecilia to a boarding school in 1783 but there was a measles epidemic and although Cecilia just survived, Harriet sadly died. The Austen girls could have met with a similar fate as Mrs. Cawley had moved her group of children from Oxford to Southampton which the Austen family were quite happy with as it was nearer their home in Steventon. However, Southampton was a port where troops returned from abroad, and in 1783, they brought a highly contagious fever which spread throughout the town. Cassandra and Jane Austen along with their cousin Jane Cooper became ill but astonishingly, Mrs. Cawley didn't bother to inform the parents. Luckily, Jane Cooper managed to get a letter home explaining the situation and the parents came and took them away. By this time Jane Austen was very ill indeed and could well have died if her condition had not been caught in time. She was nursed back to health by Mrs. Austen and then taken home. There was a tragic end to this episode however. Although Jane Cooper and Cassandra also recovered, Mrs. Cooper caught the disease and died leaving a grief-stricken husband, Edward Cooper bereft. Because he was unable to cope with bringing up his daughter without his wife, Jane Cooper spent a lot of time virtually living as part of the Austen family at Steventon and was very popular with her cousins.

The young Edward Cooper (1770-1835) also stayed at Steventon a great deal and in 1793, married Caroline Lybbe Powys where they went on to have eight children.

Edward was a clever young man and had distinguished himself at Oxford in 1791 by winning a prize for Latin hexameters on 'Hortus Anglicus'. His sister, the young Jane Cooper (1771-98) was not so lucky however. After enjoying her friendship and schooling with the Austen sisters, Cassandra and Jane, she married Captain, later Sir Thomas Williams in 1792 from the Austen's house in Steventon, but was killed in 1798 when her carriage was involved in an accident. The family connections between the Williams (Coopers) and Austens continued however when Jane's brother Charles Austen served under Captain Williams in several ships.

After a year at home, Jane and Cassandra were sent away again, this time to a school in Reading which was run by a Mrs. La Tournelle although quite why she adopted that name is not very clear as her real name was Sarah Hackitt. Not only that, she spoke no French although the proprietress of the school was a Madame St. Quintin. The school was well situated however and was a nice house standing near the ruins of Reading Abbey. Madame la Tournelle was in her forties and had a passionate interest in the theatre. She often told stories of actors and actresses but undertook no teaching herself, a task done for her by some young women teachers. The girls were taught needlework, French and spelling, along with dancing lessons and as Jane later played the piano, it is possible that she had lessons there. There are horror stories of some of the boarding schools of that period, and perhaps mindful of that, Mr. and Mrs. Austen appear to have chosen well, as this school had a much more relaxed atmosphere. Perhaps it was a little too relaxed for Mr. Austen who may have thought that the girls were not being taught enough for the money that he was paying. In the event, the Revd. and Mrs. Austen removed the girls in 1786, and at the age of eleven, Jane's formal education was all but over.

We already know of Jane's brother George, so we can look at Jane's other siblings. Her eldest brother was James (1765-1819). He was a studious boy and in 1779 at the early age of fourteen went to study at Oxford. However, he did not have to obtain his scholarship by showing particular intelligence as scholarships were awarded to potential students who could prove that they were attached in some way to Sir Thomas White who founded the college, and because James' mother's side of the family carefully kept records of the Leigh family history, he was able to gain entrance with relative ease. He eventually left Oxford and was ordained a clergyman in 1787, taking up a post in Overton, not far from the family home in Steventon. Despite being a curate, he seemed to mix in the right circles and met and married Anne Mathew, the daughter of a general and granddaughter of a duke. She was thirty-two, five years older than James when they married in 1792 and with a promised allowance of £100 a year from her father along with James' income as a curate, this meant that they could live comfortably. They only had one child, Jane-Anna-Elizabeth who was known as Anna in 1793 before her mother died in 1795.

James wasted little time before attempting to marry again, and the woman of his choice was the wealthy cousin mentioned earlier, Eliza Hancock (1761-

1813), who was the daughter of Philadelphia Hancock (1730-92) who in turn was the sister of George Austen (1731-1805), Jane's father. It was Philadelphia who had worked as a trainee milliner in Covent Garden before travelling to India for adventure and possibly to find a husband which she did when she married Tysoe Saul Hancock. In 1761, Philadelphia had given birth to Eliza. In 1781, at the age of twenty, Eliza married Count Jean Francois Capot de Feuillide and they had a little boy who they called Hastings, which some found suspicious as there was always the thought that Warren Hastings was Eliza's father given the childless state of the union between her parents for so many years. However, it may have merely been an innocent tribute to a close family friend. Events concerning the revolution in France caught up with Eliza's husband, the Count de Feuillide and he was executed on 22nd February, 1794 leaving Eliza a widow with a young son to look after.

In 1796 then, following the death of his first wife, James attempted to court Eliza, but she turned him down. Realising that he needed a wife to run his domestic affairs, his attentions went elsewhere when he courted a lady called Mary Lloyd (1771-1843), more it seems for practical rather than romantic reasons. The match seemed suitable as Mary had already lived in a parsonage with her widowed mother. In any event, they married in 1797 and had two children, James-Edward (1798-1874) and Caroline (1805-80). Mary always felt insecure however, as her face was marked with smallpox scars and she banned all visits from Eliza. James-Edward, whilst he did not choose his Christian names, seems to have developed a taste for double-barrelled names, eventually adding the name Leigh to his surname becoming Austen-Leigh. James-Edward and Caroline were Anna's half siblings and another niece and nephew for Jane Austen.

The next brother was Edward (1767-1852) who had left home permanently as he had been adopted by Thomas and Catherine Knight. A few years earlier in 1779, he had stayed with Mr. Knight who had been newly married and by now, rich but childless, the Knights adopted Edward who was happy with the arrangement. Although initially keeping his surname of Austen, he would one day change it to Knight, inherit their estates and fortune, and in 1791, eventually marry Elizabeth Bridges (1773-1808), a baronet's daughter from Goodnestone Park, Kent. Their eldest daughter, Fanny (1793-1882) along with James' daughter Anna (1793-1872) were two of Jane's favourite nieces. They went on to have ten more children in the next fifteen years before Elizabeth died in 1808. She had seemed perfectly healthy and was expecting her eleventh child and on the 28th September 1808, she gave birth to a boy. That day, Fanny, the eldest daughter, had written in her diary:- "About three this afternoon to our great joy, our beloved mother was delivered of a fine boy and is going on charmingly". There was obviously no hint of what was to come. On the Saturday, the child was named Brook-John but three days later Elizabeth was dead. She had eaten a big meal only three hours before the end and nobody, not even the doctor, could offer any explanation as to the cause of death or why it had happened so suddenly. She died at thirty-five, she had been well loved and looked after but perhaps eleven children in fifteen years had simply been too much for her constitution.

Henry (1771-1850) was the third brother and Jane's favourite. In 1788, he went to Oxford University with a view to eventually becoming a clergyman. It was he who won the heart and in 1797 the hand of cousin Eliza de Feuillide, the wealthy cousin who had turned James down the year before. Henry and Eliza's mutual attraction went back a long way even before the death of her husband. She and Henry spent time together and Eliza had confided to people that whilst her husband loved her very much, she did not love him at all, although she felt esteem and respect. Whilst there was an attraction between Henry and Eliza, it almost certainly went no further than flirting all the while her husband was alive. Henry had gone to Oxford with the idea of going into the church, but when war broke out between France and England in February 1793, he immediately gave up his studies and joined the Oxford Militia and spent the next seven years as an officer serving in various places such as Brighton, Ipswich and Dublin. In 1795, some soldiers in Henry's regiment rioted for food, along with other half starved people in Newhaven. The riots were brutally put down, and Henry had no choice other than to watch as the men were shot by firing squad in front of the entire Brighton garrison. It was during this time that Eliza was on his mind as he had been aware that she had been widowed for a year. He proposed to her that year but she turned him down. After being courted by Henry's brother James, and also turning him down, she eventually married Henry on 31st December, 1797. Henry was twenty-six and had his officer's pay of £300 per year. He achieved this amount by being a Captain and also regimental Paymaster, whilst Eliza was ten years older but still attractive and had what was left of her fortune plus the possibility of a further large inheritance depending how the political situation in France panned out.

Romantically speaking, it had been a complicated time for the Austen brothers, because apart from initially proposing to Eliza in 1795 and being turned down, only for his brother to court her, Henry was briefly engaged to a Mary Pearson, whose father was Sir Richard Pearson and who was in charge of the naval hospital at Greenwich. Eventually the engagement was terminated allowing him to marry Eliza. By all accounts, it was a happy marriage until her tragic death from cancer in 1813. Henry remained a widower for seven years, but in 1820, he married Eleanour Jackson, and although little is known of her, it *is* known that she was a loyal wife to him for thirty years until his sudden death in 1850.

Cassandra Elizabeth (1773-1845) was the only sister that Jane had – she was also her closest friend and they confided in each other on everything. Neither Cassandra nor Jane ever married, but Cassandra was engaged to a Thomas Fowle. He was one of four brothers who had attended the school run by Mr. and Mrs. Austen and subsequently became friends of the Austen children, being of similar ages. Later on, he became a clergyman who officiated when Jane Cooper, who had been living with the Austens after the death of her father, married a naval officer, Captain Thomas Williams in December 1792 and it was at this time that Fowle became engaged to Cassandra. Neither Thomas Fowle nor Cassandra had any money so it was always accepted that the engagement would be a lengthy one. In 1795, the war with France started to affect the Austen's directly when Tom Fowle accepted the post as chaplain to a regiment that was to be sent to the West Indies to fight the enemy and he duly went. The family expected him home in May 1797 but the spring of that year brought the dreadful news of his death from a fever in the preceding February. Cassandra was grief stricken of course, but so were the other members of the Austen family, especially James, who had been a close friend.

James in fact, wrote a poem about it:-

> "…where ocean ceaselessly pours
> His restless waves 'gainst Western Indian shores,
> Friend of my soull, & Brother of my heart! …
> Our friendship soon had known a dearer tie,
> Than friendship's self could ever yet supply
> And I had lived with confidence to join,
> A much loved sister's trembling hand to thine"

The Colonel of the regiment was Baron Craven who was a distant cousin of Tom's and it was he who had offered Tom the post, sweetening it with the promise of a good living in Shropshire once the regiment had returned to England. He too was devastated because although no blame could be attached to him, if he had not made Tom the original offer to go, then he would still be alive. Cassandra, although grief stricken, accepted the loss with a quiet dignity, helped by her religion that seemed to sustain her but she never at any time considered marriage to anyone else. The previous year, Jane had lost a man she had loved and although the sisters were still young, Cassandra being twenty-four, and Jane twenty-two, they settled on spinsterhood at an early age, and this helped bring them closer together, a bond that stayed with them all their lives until Jane's early death in 1817.

Francis (1774-1865), or Frank as he was sometimes known, entered the Royal Navy Academy at Portsmouth and in 1788 sailed to the East Indies in the frigate *'Perseverance'* after leaving the naval school in December of that year with a high recommendation to his name. He was still to reach the age of fifteen and he had to wait another year before he became a midshipman. Although very young when leaving in the *'Perseverance'*, he knew that it would be a long time before he saw his family again – indeed it was another five years – but he seems to have accepted it happily as part of the job. Jane managed to write to him however, and she took great pride in addressing the letters to 'Francis William Austen Esq Midshipman on board his *Majesty's Ship the Perseverance*'. She not only wrote letters, but she wrote stories as well which helped sustain him. He fought during the Napoleonic wars and became an Admiral. He married twice, the first time being in 1806 to Mary Gibson. She came from Ramsgate and brought no money to the marriage, but Frank didn't mind as he was Flag-Captain of the *Canopus* which was originally a French ship that Nelson had captured at the battle of the Nile and so he considered himself well off. Mary was born in 1785 and was twenty-one when they married in 1806. In the space of seventeen years, Mary gave birth to no less than eleven children, dying in 1823 during the birth of their last child Cholmely. Francis married again in 1828, but it was a very different relationship. His second wife, Martha Lloyd, was born in 1765, making her sixty-three when she married Francis, and she was nine years older than him. By this stage of his life, he was really looking for someone to keep house for him and to look after his children which Martha agreed to do. They were married for fifteen years before she died in 1843 aged seventy-eight, but Francis lived until he was ninety-one, dying in 1865. His career had progressed steadily – he had become a Rear-Admiral in 1830 and Knight Commander of the Bath in one of William IV's final investitures and he finished his career a Vice-Admiral, a rank he reached in 1838.

The youngest sibling was Charles (1779-1852). He, like Francis, entered the Royal Navy and also reached the rank of an Admiral. He went to the Portsmouth naval school at twelve by which time Francis was already an officer serving in the East Indies. In 1806, at the age of twenty-seven, Charles was an officer serving at the North America Station. He met a beautiful sixteen-year-old girl called Frances (Fanny) Palmer in Bermuda and they married in May 1807, she being seventeen and at twenty-eight, he was eleven years older. Naturally enough, there were no members of his family at the wedding as it was in Bermuda, and it was to be another four years until she met some of the Austen family when he was posted back to England. By now, they had two little children, Cassandra-Esten (1808-97) and Harriet-Jane (1810-65). They had another child, Frances-Palmer (1812-82) before Charles's wife died in 1814 giving birth to their fourth child Elizabeth who died herself three weeks later. Frances was just twenty-four years old. Six years later, Charles married again, this time to Harriet Palmer, his late wife's sister, and had another family with her, producing four more children, although only two lived to be adults. The four were Charles-John (1821-67), George (1822-24), Jane (1824-25), and Henry (1826-51). For several years Charles worked on shore, but in 1826, he was given another command but was injured by a falling mast and had to take a shore post until 1838 when he went to sea once more where he served in the Mediterranean and eventually was promoted to Rear-Admiral. He died of cholera in Burma in 1852 at the age of seventy-three.

It is difficult to piece together all the strands of Jane's life as she left no diaries and the deeply personal letters that she wrote to her sister Cassandra were burned by Cassandra after Jane's death in 1817. It is very frustrating for historians that Cassandra did that but the letters were written by Jane for Cassandra's eyes only and there was no-one in the world who was more close to Jane than her beloved sister and so her judgement has to be respected. It also has to be noted that the first biography of Jane was written by her nephew, James Edward Austen-Leigh in 1870 and that he harboured no thoughts that she would become anywhere near as famous as she did, and actually thought that his book would probably be the only biography of her. This being the case, another reason for Cassandra burning the letters could have been that she would have had no idea of their importance in years to come.

Steventon, the little village in Hampshire where the Austen children grew up, had no school, pub, or doctor and looks much the same today as it did in Jane's time. Sadly, the rectory that she was brought up in was knocked down in the 1850's. Firstly, Jane's brother James who had occupied the cottage died soon after Jane in 1819 and this meant that his widow, Mary, and the children, James-

Edward and Caroline had to move out. Henry moved in becoming rector of the parish and in 1823, he moved out and Edward Knight's (formerly Austen) son William Knight then moved in and it was at this point in time that Edward decided it was not worth spending the amount of money needed to make it habitable and it was knocked down and a new rectory built nearby. The only thing that remains from when the Austen family lived there is the nearby water pump that the Austen family used.

Returning to their childhood, Jane and Cassandra's education continued at home after they were brought back from school. In the eighteenth century, it was thought a waste of time to teach girls languages and academic subjects of any kind as it was felt that they were merely being prepared for the marriage market. Therefore, Jane and Cassandra were simply taught how to cook, sew, and tend the vegetable garden that the Austen's had so that the girls would make suitable wives one day. Jane also learned how to play the pianoforte. However, to the Austen parents' credit, they encouraged Jane to read as the family had an extensive library and it is from this library that Jane's education derived. It seems that no restrictions were put on the type of book that Jane read and this included 'The History of Tom Jones – a Foundling' that had been written in the 1740's by Henry Fielding (1707-1754) and published in 1749 to great acclaim. However, not everybody liked it thinking the sexual contents dubious to say the least and Samuel Johnson called it vicious. There were even those who held it responsible for two earth tremors that followed shortly after its publication. The author's own life could have been the subject of a novel in itself. In the 1740's he caused uproar in society by marrying his late wife's maid Mary Daniel and he helped his half-brother, Sir John Fielding (1721-1780) to found the Bow Street Runners who became the beginning of our present day police force.

Once Jane started to read, her imagination and creativity began to blossom and she started to write her own stories and her wit began to come through. Many of her stories were mischievous and nonsensical but she would read them to her family and they would cause great amusement. They seem to have been a happy family, as after dinner, they would often put the furniture to the side of the room and all dance together. Jane especially, seemed to love this. However, despite the parents' seemingly liberal views concerning Jane's reading matter, marriage was still deemed to be the best way of securing the children's future, and the best way to do this whether boy or girl, was to marry into money. In this, the boys did rather well but the girls, Cassandra and Jane, did not. Mrs. Austen tried to fix Jane up with a husband by making her attend local balls, but Jane felt that women were used in order to seemingly breed every eighteen months and keep house for their husbands, and it was not a life that she intended to pursue. She was not against marriage, but she felt strongly that people should marry for love and not money, a view that ran completely against the thinking of the day and the fact that she stubbornly resisted pressure and stuck to this view shows her courage and conviction. Despite that, or maybe because of that, it was interesting that marriage became such a dominant theme in her books. In 'Pride and Prejudice', both Jane and Lizzie Bennet said that they would only marry for love, especially the feisty Lizzie.

The fact that she was not against marriage unless it was for love was proven when Tom Lefroy arrived to visit his aunt. He is the man mentioned earlier that she had loved and lost a year or so before the time that Cassandra's fiancée, Tom Fowle had died in the West Indies. Lefroy had just finished studying for a degree at university in Dublin and was about to move to London to train as a barrister. Jane and Tom Lefroy were introduced in December 1795 during the time he was holidaying with his Aunt and Uncle Lefroy at the Ashe Rectory which was not far from the Austen's family house in Steventon. On 9th January 1796, Jane had written a lengthy letter to her sister Cassandra who was staying with her fiancee's family in Berkshire. A name that kept reappearing in the letter was that of Tom Lefroy. Jane was obviously taken with him, describing him at one point as:- "gentlemanlike, good looking, pleasant young man." Jane had described a ball that had taken place the night before and it was obvious that Jane and Lefroy had danced together because the break in the letter was due to the fact that Lefroy had just called to pay his respects to Jane. Jane starts her letter again by making it clear that she has read the book 'Tom Jones' by Henry Fielding, and had discussed its contents with Tom Lefroy. He stayed in the area for just two months until January 1796 when his Aunt Lefroy, realising what was happening between the couple, contrived to send him away and despite the fact that he visited the area again a few years later, they were kept apart and never saw each other again.

They clearly loved each other but in the spirit of the day, marriage between the two was deemed to be out of the question as there was no money on either side. It seems extraordinarily cruel to us today, whereby a man who is training to be a barrister, and who will presumably expect to earn a good salary in years to come, is not allowed to marry the woman he loves and likewise, she is not able to marry him simply because of the lack of money on her side, but that was how the marriage market operated in those days. The problem as the Lefroy family saw it, was that Tom's father was now retired and had a large family to look after. Tom was preceded by five sisters, and as the eldest son, he would be expected to look after his sisters when his father died. He had been dependent on a great-uncle who had put him through college in Dublin and it was the same great-uncle who would finance his law studies in London. By 1798, Tom Lefroy was settled in Ireland and complying with his family's wishes, married an Irish heiress called Mary Paul in 1799 with whom he fathered seven children and ended his career as Lord Chief Justice of Ireland. He lived a long life, being born in 1776 and dying in 1869. Speaking near the end of his life, he acknowledged the fact that he had indeed loved Jane when he was younger. Like their father, all Lefroy's children lived long lives, his and Mary's first being a boy, but their second was a daughter who was named Jane. Scholars differ as to the significance of this because some think it was honouring Lefroy's mother-in-law, Lady Jane Paul, whilst others think it was a tribute to Jane. The two month relationship between Lefroy and Jane during December 1795 and January 1796 ended painfully for Jane but the consolation must be that it may have given the heroes and heroines an edge that they may not have had had she not gone through the experience of young love herself. Having said that however, Jane always made clear that her characters were created, not reproduced. Her nephew, James-Edward Leigh-Perrot writing in his book 'A Memoir of Jane Austen,' which was first published in 1870, quotes Jane as saying:- "I am too proud of my gentlemen to admit that they were only Mr. A. or Colonel B". Her characters were like her children and not forgotten once the books that they had appeared in were finished. She seemed to have a particular affection for D'Arcy and Lizzie Bennet and would often invent little stories as to how some of her characters developed after each book had been completed. It was this interest in hanging on to the characters that she created which enabled us to know that Kitty Bennet eventually married a clergyman not far from Pemberley so we can assume that she saw a great deal of Mr. and Mrs. D'Arcy in the years that followed.

However, returning to real life, Jane was terribly sad at being separated from Lefroy, and being at home had more time to think about things than he did. In fact, she berated the general fact of life that men were away following busy careers whilst the women were at home with more time to think about their loss. "They forget us more quickly than we forget them" she was once quoted as saying.

However, sad as she was, Jane got on with her life and the next four years saw her busy with her writing and she was full of creativity. In the next four years, three novels were produced. The first one was called 'Elinor and Marianne' and the story was told in the form of a series of letters. Jane read it to the family at about the time that Lefroy was in her life but it was not finally published until 1811 under the title 'Sense and Sensibility'. The original manuscripts have not survived so it is impossible to know how close to the final version of 'Sense and Sensibility' it was.

Although Jane's creative juices were working overtime during this period, it was not going to be easy for her to get her work published. The second novel was started in 1796 and completed in the following year. This was entitled 'First Impressions', and on 1st November 1797, Jane's father, the Revd. George Austen was so impressed with it that he wrote the following letter to Thomas Cadell, a recognised publisher based in London and sent him the draft of the manuscript.

"Sir, - I have in my possession a manuscript novel, comprising 3 vols., about the length of Miss Burney's 'Evelina'. As I am well aware of what consequence it is that a work of this sort should make its first appearance under a respectable name, I apply to you. I shall be much obliged therefore if you will inform me whether you choose to be concerned in it, what will be the expense of publishing it at the author's risk, and what you will venture to advance for the property of it, if on perusal it is approved of. Should you give any encouragement, I will send you the work.

I am, Sir, your humble Servant
GEORGE AUSTEN"

Although Fanny Burney was an established writer by then and Jane admired her more than almost any other author, the mention of her name cut no ice with Mr. Cadell who returned the manuscript marked "Declined by Return of Post".

One can only assume that he lived to regret that decision as the book later became *'Pride and Prejudice'*, the best loved and most successful of Jane Austen's novels which was eventually published in 1813, two years after *'Sense and Sensibility'*.

The third book was started in the middle of 1798 and had a working title of *'Susan'*. It was a satire on the Gothic novel, which was popular at that time. It eventually became *'Northanger Abbey'* but as *'Susan'*, Henry Austen sent the manuscript to Richard Crosby, a London publisher who paid £10 for it, and although he promised to publish it sooner rather than later, for some reason he never did and this left Jane bereft as there was nothing she could do about it as Crosby now owned the copyright. He kept the manuscript until 1816 until eventually, Jane managed to buy it back for the same amount that she had sold it to him for, £10. This was only a year before Jane died, and it was published posthumously as *'Northanger Abbey'* in 1817, along with *'Persuasion'* which came out the same year. The other two novels that were published with great success while Jane was still alive were *'Mansfield Park'* in 1814 and *'Emma'* in 1815.

Although seemingly reconciled to spinsterhood at a somewhat early age, Jane was happy enough. She had Cassandra who was both sister and her closest friend with her and at the age of twenty-five, she had completed three novels that were destined to be a huge success, although she could not have imagined quite how successful they would eventually turn out to be. However, in December 1800, on returning home from a visit to her future sister-in-law, Martha Lloyd at Ibthorpe, she was given a twenty-fifth birthday present that was just about the last thing she wanted. She was told the news that her parents were leaving Steventon in order to move to Bath to retire, whilst her brother James and his wife were to take over the parsonage. This news shattered Jane and it also distressed Cassandra who had also been away at Godmersham where she helped her brother Frank and his wife Mary as their sixth child was due to be born. In fact, the entire Austen children were away and the decision was made without any of them having any knowledge of what was being planned. Jane was devastated. At a stroke she would lose her friends, neighbours, her pictures, pianoforte and probably worst of all, the entire books that she loved so much. For some inexplicable reason, in Jane's eyes at any rate, a couple who were about to retire and therefore presumably have more time to read, arranged for all their books to be sold off without any consultation with Jane who was presented with a fait accompli. It had all been decided behind her back and there was absolutely nothing that she could do about it. However, in fairness to her parents, they probably wanted to live in a city such as Bath whereby they could relax and party to their heart's content during their retirement.

However, the very last thing that Jane wanted to do was to move away from the countryside that she had been brought up in and which had an atmosphere that was so conducive to her writing, to move to noisy Bath with its smoky atmosphere and what she saw as its debauched way of life and its meaningless social round. She resented the planned move to Bath bitterly and she also resented the speed in which James wanted to move in to the parsonage that she loved so much. She wrote:- "The whole World is in a conspiracy to enrich one part of our family at the expense of another". Everything that she needed to write with was gone, including her beloved writing desk, and once in Bath, she was forced into an endless round of balls that she hated. She felt that the whole move was merely a set-up in order to parade her in the marriage market, a market that she had no interest in. The three novels that she took to Bath remained untouched and she became depressed and stopped writing overnight.

Today, we think of Bath as a beautiful Georgian city, and in the 18th century it was considered the height of fashion to either live or stay there. People came to Bath to take the waters which were reputed to cure many ills; however, although it was supposed to help people with their medical problems, it did little for Jane's mental well being. Apart from taking her away from the Hampshire countryside that she loved so much and instead propelled her into a round of meaningless balls and parties that filled her with dismay, it held a recent event that made the entire family unhappy. Jane's mother, had a brother James Leigh-Perrot (1735-1817) who had married Jane Cholmeley (1744-1836) in 1764. The Leigh-Perrots were rich and came to Bath on a regular basis so that Uncle James could take the waters for the gout that he was suffering from. They had taken No. 1 the Paragon, which like so many other places in Bath at the time, was a beautiful terraced house which confirmed their status as a rich couple. It was a terrible shock therefore to the whole family when the unthinkable happened – Jane's aunt, Mrs. Leigh-Perrot was accused of shoplifting. In August 1799, Mrs. Leigh-Perrot had gone into a linen drapers to buy some black lace which she duly purchased. The nightmare started when she left the shop with her acquisition because no sooner was she in the street when the owner of the shop came after her and accused her of stealing some white lace. Upon searching Aunt Jane's bag, a card of white lace worth about £1 *was* found although Mrs. Leigh-Perrot vigorously denied having taken it and said that the person who sold it to her must have accidently put the white lace in with the black. However, the shop owner was adamant that the white lace had been taken but allowed Mrs. Leigh-Perrot to continue home after obtaining her address. The Leigh-Perrots were wealthy and had no need to steal anything, and on their journey home, probably thought that it would all blow over and that they would hear no more.

It was not to be however. A few days later, she was arrested for theft and held in custody for no less than eight months before her trial. She was spared prison as such, and was allowed to live with the jailer of the Somerset County Gaol in Ilchester, Mr. Scadding and his family, but even that was a nightmare. There was noise from morning until night and Mrs. Scadding had little sense of hygiene, once cleaning a knife by licking the food from it. Added to that, the children were out of control, and with their bedroom being next to the Leigh-Perrots, there was no peace for them at all. There was one small crumb of comfort for Mrs. Leigh-Perrot however, as the ever-loyal Mr. Leigh-Perrot, Jane's uncle, insisted on living with his wife for the entire time until her trial was due.

What Mrs. Leigh-Perrot was being accused of was anything but trivial. The white lace that she was supposed to have stolen was valued at £1 (twenty shillings) and in the 18th century, the punishment for stealing anything worth just one shilling or more could actually carry the death sentence. Either that, or

Jane's aunt could be transported to Australia for as long as fourteen years and given that she was fifty-five years old at this time, it would be unlikely that she would ever return. Dr. Samuel Johnson (1709-84), the great writer, critic and lexicographer, had written that any law which made the sentence for stealing the same as for murder was quite ridiculous as well as cruel, but that would not help Mrs. Leigh-Perrot at this particular time.

After seven months incarceration, the trial was heard on 29th March, 1800 at Taunton Assizes. Mrs. Leigh-Perrot spoke in her own defence in a most effective way, and once both sides had had their say, the jury found her not guilty in just ten minutes. There were mixed views about this matter. There were many who thought her guilty but that she had been let off because she was the wife of a wealthy man, others also felt that she was guilty but had been let off because the jury may have felt the punishment that would result would be too harsh. The main defence argument was based on the belief that the clerk in the shop had accidently put the white lace into Mrs. Leigh-Perrot's bag and many people believed this likelihood also. Although the verdict was a not guilty one, people were by no means convinced. Two witnesses for the defence had been produced saying that the clerk had given them something by mistake in the past but they were unconvincing and two letters, again produced by the defence from the Leigh-Perrots saying that the clerk in the shop was of a bad character were dubious, given that the handwriting was the same and also some of the phrasing in the letters was similar. One more incident happened a few years later when Jane's aunt was in a gardening shop and seemingly attempted to steal a plant but was stopped by a young girl. Apparently Jane's aunt only got away with it because the girl's father took his daughter away because he did not wish for her to be involved. So far as the law was concerned however, Mrs. Leigh-Perrot was innocent of stealing any lace but many thought her guilty and it was this scenario that the Austens found when they came to Bath in 1801.

Meanwhile, Jane was very depressed about being in Bath, not particularly about her aunt, but more about the writing block that she suffered whilst living in the city. This state of affairs went on until November 1802 when Jane and Cassandra were invited to spend a few weeks with the Bigg sisters for several weeks at Manydown. The Bigg sisters were Alethea and Catherine who were both single, and Elizabeth Heathcote who along with her baby son William, had returned to the family home after the death of her husband the previous spring. Jane and Cassandra had known the Bigg sisters since 1789 when the family inherited Manydown which was a large manor house four miles beyond Deane, a village near Steventon. Their father was a wealthy landowner who sometimes used to add the name Wither to his surname to give it a double barrel. The five girls got on well and all of them looked forward to a few weeks together with a lot of chat and gossip round a winter evening's fire. However, their father was at home and it is possible that there was an agenda concerning their visit that Cassandra and Jane were unaware of.

The Bigg sisters had a brother who had returned from Worcester College in Oxford where he had been completing his education. His christian name was Harris and he had just turned twenty-one years old the previous May and although the Austen sisters knew him from years back, they knew him only as a shy stammering boy, uncomfortable in company. The young man that they saw now was rather different and was altogether more confident. He was tall, broad shouldered and his new found confidence was probably helped by the fact that he was heir to considerable estates. In the event, on the evening of the 2nd December, 1802, Harris Bigg-Wither proposed marriage to Jane, and she accepted. Given her views on marriage, and the woman's role within it, it seems an extraordinary decision to us today. However, the Austen family were not wealthy and when a wealthy young man made such an offer, there was enormous pressure on the woman to accept, as it would offer not only financial security for Jane, but more importantly for her, for the complete Austen family, especially of course, her parents. Harris was a perfectly respectable young man and there could be no objections to the match from any quarter, apart of course, from Jane herself. She had always maintained that she would marry for love only, and whilst everyone else around her rejoiced, Jane had a sleepless night comparing her feelings for Harris with those heady feelings that she had experienced with Tom Lefroy seven years previously. The feelings that she had for Harris simply did not compare, and the next day she explained to her fiancée of 24 hours that she had changed her mind. She would have done it gently and respectfully, but it caused consternation and she and Cassandra had to return to Bath immediately. Her mother with her aristocratic forebears was particularly furious as she saw a comfortable old age being taken away from her but Jane would not budge.

Harris Bigg-Wither did not mourn his loss for too long. He was married two years later to a woman who did seem to love him and bore him ten children. Jane would have been proud to have been the mother of his oldest son, who like Jane's own father became a clergyman but also a poet and a Whig, the forerunner of today's Liberal party. He translated the whole of Iliad, an epic poem describing the latter stages of the Trojan war, into English verse and later on he supported the Basingstoke Mechanic's Institute. The Mechanic's Institute was first formed in London in 1824 to provide cheap lectures for skilled workers, and then gradually, many other cities formed them as well. Bigg-Wither also helped to promote the case for agricultural labourers having allotment holdings so he must have been a man who had a great deal of humanity and thought for others.

Stepping back one year before Jane and Cassandra's visit to Manydown, Jane's family experienced a tragedy when in October 1801, Henry's wife Eliza's son Hastings died aged just fifteen. When he was two years old, Hastings could not speak or even stand and often had convulsive fits. Whilst so many babies with those types of afflictions were often sent away to be looked after by other families, including it has to be said, Jane's brother George, Eliza de Feullide as she then was, refused to do that, and insisted on keeping the child with her all his life. Eliza had a reputation for being frivolous and fun loving, but the decision to keep her son with her does her great credit. Eventually he learnt to speak, but he suffered from more physical afflictions than Jane's brother George had, and at fifteen, he died almost certainly worn out by the constant fits that had become more frequent as he got older. He was buried at Hampstead next to his grandmother, Philadelphia Hancock (nee Austen), the sister of George

Austen, Jane's father. Philadelphia had died in 1792, only nine years prior to her grandson. The inscription on the stone was interesting. It read 'Also in memory of her grandson Hastings, only child of Jean Capot Comt. De Feuillide and Elizabeth his wife born 25th June, 1786 died 9th October, 1801'. It is easy to read too much into it as the father is named as the Count, but the fact that Eliza chose not to use the title for her son could be a nod in the direction that Warren Hastings had been the father all along, or that as Henry was his stepfather, respect for him, or simply no more than a mother's love for her child who she saw as simply a vulnerable human being rather than someone titled.

There was another death three years later that affected Jane deeply. On 16th December 1804, Jane's twenty-ninth birthday, her long standing friend, Mrs. Lefroy died after falling from her horse. She had been riding to Overton to do some shopping when her horse, which had previously been quite docile, suddenly bolted. She had a servant with her but he was unable to catch the horse and she fell on to the road whilst trying to dismount. Dr. Lyford, the family's physician, could do nothing for her and she died within a few hours. She had been the wife of the Revd. George Lefroy and Jane had known them since she was a little girl when they had moved into Ashe, a village near Deane where the Revd. Lefroy and family had moved into the rectory. Along with her parents, Mrs. Lefroy encouraged the young Jane to read and had clearly been a huge influence on her life. She was also the aunt of Tom Lefroy, Jane's one true love, her husband George being the brother of Tom's father.

Even worse was just round the corner however. The following month, her father, the Revd. George Austen suddenly died. Jane must have been devastated but she kept her feelings under control, probably for her mother's sake. She took a pocket compass and a pair of scissors, both of which had belonged to her father, and sent them to her brother Francis. She wrote to him: "He had oppression in the head, with fever, violent tremulousness and the greatest degree of feebleness". It all happened very quickly, and "being insensible of his own state, he was spared all the pain of separation, and he went off almost in his sleep". She wrote more about seeing the body after he had died with the words "The serenity of the corpse being most delightful – it preserves the sweet benevolent smile which always distinguished him. The loss of such a parent must be felt or we should be brutes". The Revd. Austen died on 21st January, 1805 in a house in Green Park Buildings East to which they had recently moved. It had not been long since they had moved from Sydney Place and now they would have to move again. They found temporary accommodation at 25, Gay Street to give the Austen Brothers time to work out how best to look after Jane, Cassandra, and their mother.

The next four years left Jane, Cassandra and Mrs. Austen very unsettled. After spending some time staying in the rented accommodation in Bath, they stayed with Francis and his new wife Mary in Southampton. Edward eventually came to the rescue offering the three women a house in Chawton Village. They needed no encouragement to take it – it was in rural Hampshire where Jane had been brought up and Henry had a branch of his bank there, and so they moved in on 9th July, 1809. Added to that, James was but twelve miles away which would have pleased Mrs. Austen but even better was to come – after having to endure eight long years during which time her creativity had all but left her, a delighted Jane felt at peace and started writing again. At last she had escaped from Bath, the city she so hated with its noise, unhealthy air, and its meaningless round of parties and balls that she detested. At last, some peace and tranquillity had come back into her life and she was back in rural Hampshire that she loved so much. From Jane's point of view, the only possible thing in Bath's favour was that these endless parties that held no joy for her at least gave her some experience of how the marriage market worked, a knowledge which she used so effectively in her books.

She started a daily routine of writing and gradually refined the novels entitled *'Elinor and Marianne'* and *'First Impressions'* that as mentioned earlier became *'Sense and Sensibility'* and *'Pride and Prejudice'* respectively. At last Jane was happy with her life – she was away from the dreadful marriage market that was so prevalent in Bath and indeed, was happy with the thought that she would never marry. She saw no joy in having a child every eighteen months however rich any husband would have been and indeed, as far as she was concerned, her books were her creation, and therefore her children.

A bleak moment for Jane in this otherwise happy period was when three months before they moved to Chawton, she wrote a letter to Richard Crosby, the publisher who had purchased the copyright of *'Susan'* (later to become *'Northanger Abbey'*) over six years earlier at the beginning of 1803. He had promised her that the book would be published sooner rather than later, but after advertising it in a brochure called *'Flowers of Literature'*, he had seemingly lost interest in it. She requested the return of the original manuscript if he had no intention of publishing but Jane received little joy in this as Crosby wrote back saying that he had never given Jane a date for publishing, in fact had not agreed to publish it at all. He did however, offer her the manuscript back for the £10 that she had originally received for it. In some ways it was not an ungenerous offer as he had held the novel for some years and could have asked more for it, but in any event, it was too much money for Jane to raise and it had to be left with Crosby for a few more years until Henry purchased it soon after the publication of *'Emma'* in 1815.

When *'Sense and Sensibility'* was published in 1811, it was done anonymously, but when *'Pride and Prejudice'* came out to such acclaim in 1813, the Irish dramatist, Richard Brinsley Sheridan (1751-1816), said that that it was one of the best pieces of work that he had ever read. Sheridan had a great reputation as a speaker in Parliament, and this reputation rather ironically dated from when he had made some powerful speeches during the impeachment of Warren Hastings, the godfather to Eliza Austen's (nee de Feuillide) son, Hastings. The compliment paid to Jane for writing *'Pride and Prejudice'* from such an eminent source, plus a feeling in some quarters that 'the book was too good to have been written by a woman' was too much for Jane's brother Henry who then let it be known who the author was. Jane had tried what her hero Fanny Burney had attempted with *'Evelina'* before her, to keep the authorship quiet, but as with Fanny Burney, it was always going to come out one day so by the time the next novel would be published, Jane's secret was revealed.

When '*Mansfield Park*' was published in 1814, it was made known to Jane that the Prince Regent who was later to come to the throne in 1820 as George IV until his death in 1830, suggested that Jane make a dedication to him in her next novel entitled '*Emma*'. Jane's brother Henry, had been ill with what the doctors called a 'low fever'; in fact at one point, he was considered to be at the point of death. Happily however, he recovered, but it so happened that one of the doctors who attended Henry was a court physician who made a point of telling Jane that the Prince Regent had read and liked her books. The physician reported back that he had met Jane to the Carlton House librarian, Mr. James Stanier Clarke, and she was immediately invited to see the library at Carlton House which she duly did on 13th November, 1815. During the visit, Mr. Clarke, obviously being ordered by the Prince, suggested that Jane might like to dedicate her next novel to the Regent. Jane, like many of her fellow countrymen and women, was not too enamoured with the Prince. Since 1760, when George III came to the throne, the Royal Family had been very popular as he mixed openly with his subjects, was a good family man and devoted and faithful to his wife, Queen Charlotte. However, things changed when he had become ill and although he lived until 1820, he was too ill to carry out his duties and so his son, George had taken over his father's duties in 1811 as Regent, making him King in all but name. The Prince Regent, unlike his father who had always been very frugal, was extravagant in the extreme and gave a party at Carlton House costing £120,000 to celebrate the fact that he had been made Regent. This was an enormous sum by any standards but even more so when you realise that you would have to multiply that figure by something like fifty to calculate the amount in today's terms. This was at a time when the country had been at war with France for something like twenty years and was too broke to feed its own poor. He was at loggerheads with his wife, Princess Caroline and their daughter, Princess Charlotte was virtually out of control spending most of her time flirting with highly unsuitable young men, one of them being the son of Mrs. Jordan, the mistress of the Duke of Clarence, the Prince Regent's brother. The Duke of Clarence was no better than the Prince Regent. In 1811, the same year that the Prince of Wales became Regent, the Duke of Clarence dismissed the actress Mrs. Jordan as his mistress even though she had borne him ten children.

He had supported the slave trade during the period when William Wilberforce, Tom Clarkson, and William Pitt amongst others were trying to abolish it, and had become Admiral of the Fleet simply because his brother, the Prince Regent made him so rather than any particular talent that he may have had. Given all this, it would be hardly surprising to most people when Jane flatly turned down any idea of dedicating her work to the Prince Regent, but if it didn't surprise Jane's closest family and friends, it stunned James Stanier Clarke. Like her mentor, Fanny Burney before her, Jane soon found out that a royal suggestion was in fact a royal command and she therefore had no choice. She reluctantly suggested the words: "*Emma*, dedicated by Permission to H.R.H. The Prince Regent" until her publisher, John Murray told her what would be acceptable, and it certainly wasn't that. Murray was an experienced man in his field, being the founder of '*Quarterly Review*' as well as the publisher of Byron.

What eventually appeared, almost certainly written by Murray was the rather more sycophantic:

TO

HIS ROYAL HIGHNESS

THE PRINCE REGENT,

THIS WORK IS,

BY HIS ROYAL HIGHNESS'S PERMISSION,

MOST RESPECTFULLY

DEDICATED,

BY HIS ROYAL HIGHNESS'S

DUTIFUL

AND OBEDIENT

HUMBLE SERVANT,

THE AUTHOR

This was the dedication that Jane reluctantly agreed to when *'Emma'* was published in 1815.

The Prince wrote no thanks for the dedication, nor did he pass comment on whether he had read *'Emma'* or not. Instead, on 27th March, 1816, three months after receiving his specially bound copy, the Prince's librarian, James Stanier Clarke wrote:-

"I have to return you the Thanks of his Royal Highness the Prince Regent for the handsome Copy you sent him of your last excellent Novel..."

'Emma' in fact had proved a problem for Jane. She was pleased with it herself but she had a nagging fear that it would not receive the acclaim that *'Sense and Sensibility', 'Pride and Prejudice'* and *'Mansfield Park'* had received. This was not surprising given the attitude of her publisher, Thomas Egerton. He had published the first three novels but did not seem that interested in *'Emma'* at all. In fact, although *'Mansfield Park'* had sold out, Egerton

refused to print a second edition of it and that along with the fact that he did not make Jane a good enough offer for *'Emma'*, meant that she and Henry never worked with him again. Instead, the book was taken up by a new publisher, John Murray who was also offered the chance to buy the copyrights to *'Sense and Sensibility'* and *'Mansfield Park'*. Some critics today feel that *'Emma'* is Austen's best work, although *'Pride and Prejudice'* has always been seen as the favourite out of all her work. However, at the time, Jane had a reason for fearing the reaction towards *'Emma'* as none other than Walter Scott (1771-1832), the famous Scottish novelist and poet, gave it a fairly indifferent write-up when it came out. In fact he also wrote about *'Sense and Sensibility'* and *'Pride and Prejudice'* with a certain indifference whilst not mentioning *'Mansfield Park'* at all in his article which naturally upset Jane. Years later however, after Jane had died, he seemed to have had a change of heart and was fulsome with his praise for her work.

Jane was not impressed at receiving thanks from the librarian many weeks after receiving the book and nothing from the Prince Regent himself as to what he thought of her latest creation. The librarian however must have been impressed because he came up with the extraordinary idea of suggesting subjects for the next book that she would write, and these suggestions seemed to be based on events in his own life. Jane tactfully fended off these ideas at the time but a little later wrote a three page piece entitled *"Plan of a Novel, According to Hints from Various Quarters"* in which she *did* include some of his suggestions along with those of some of her friends.

Everything now seemed to be going well for Jane. She was happy living with Cassandra and their mother, and she had four major novels published. However, during this otherwise happy period, Eliza, Henry's wife died. Eliza had lost her son Hastings ten years before but in 1811 Eliza herself became unwell. It was known even then that breast cancer ran in families and after her mother's painful and protracted death from the disease in late February, 1792, Eliza knew exactly what was going to happen to her when she first noticed the symptoms. In those days there were none of the treatments that are available now, although the author Fanny Burney had undergone a horrendous mastectomy without anaesthetic at about this time, and after bearing the illness for two years, Eliza died on the 25th April, 1813. Henry remained alone for seven years until 1820 when he married Eleanour Jackson, a loyal wife to him for thirty years until his death in 1850. Although Eliza's death was a dreadful tragedy for the family, and Henry in particular, Jane's writing was blossoming and things seemed to be working out for her at last. However, in 1816 when Jane was just forty years old, she started to feel unwell. At first she ignored it, and carried on writing *'The Elliots'* which later was published as *'Persuasion'*, but in the middle of that year, people could see a visible change in her and a slow but obvious decline in her condition. Still she denied it, and at the end of January 1817, declared that she was "stronger than I was half a year ago".

She gave her illness several names depending on who she spoke to. She once described it as 'bile' and another time 'rheumatism' but still she got worse. Her niece Caroline, daughter of James, used to visit her and would often see Jane lying on a makeshift sofa which consisted of three chairs which she arranged herself with a pillow for added comfort. However, it didn't look remotely comfortable but as there was only one sofa in the room which Mrs. Austen used to lie on, Jane always used to use the chairs which she described as 'her sofa' and even if the actual sofa in the room was free, would never lie on it in case her mother came in the room and needed it. It was a lovely display of respect for her mother at such a time.

As a last desperate attempt to help her recover, Henry took Jane along with Cassandra to Winchester so that she could receive medical attention. They left on 24th May and it was not an easy journey for Jane as it rained all the way during the sixteen mile journey from Chawton to the lodgings at 8, College Street, Winchester. Henry rode alongside the carriage that carried Cassandra and Jane. It was a comfortable house with a small strip of garden. They had the first floor which gave them two sitting rooms, a bow window and two bedrooms at the back of the house. She wrote to her nephew, James-Edward, son of her brother James: "Mr. Lyford says he will cure me, and if he fails, I shall draw up a Memorial and lay it before the Dean & Chapter, & have no doubt of redress from that Pious, Learned & disinterested Body." This was to be her last letter to anyone.

Whilst she was at College Street, her friend Elizabeth Heathcote visited Jane every day. Elizabeth was one of the Bigg sisters and was the brother of Harris, who had proposed to Jane nearly fifteen years before and who had remained a good friend. Elizabeth had moved to Winchester with her sister Alethea four years previously when their father died. Cassandra allowed Jane to ride in a sedan chair and walk a little in the house whilst all the time Jane insisted that she was getting better, although Cassandra suspected differently. During the early evening of the 17th July the end came. The sun had been shining all day until the evening when rain set in. Jane had spent most of the day sleeping and didn't seem in a lot of pain, but at about 5.30pm she had a seizure of some kind. Mr. Lyford was sent for and he told Cassandra that Jane was close to death. He gave her some laudanum to settle her but by this time she knew that she was dying. Cassandra asked her if there was anything she wanted and Jane replied that she wanted nothing but death. Cassandra continued to stay with her but after sitting in the same position for six hours she had become uncomfortable, so at 1am, she allowed Mary, the second wife of James, who had also been looking after Jane, to take her place for two hours, but Cassandra returned to Jane's bedside at 3am. Jane died an hour later at 4am.

Cassandra later wrote "...I was able to close her eyes myself and it was a great gratification to me to render her these last services." The two sisters had been so close and Cassandra was devastated. She also wrote these very moving words: "She was the sun of my life, the gilder of every pleasure, the soother of every sorrow, I had not a thought concealed from her, and it is as if I had lost a part of myself."

Jane would probably have been happy to have been buried at either Steventon or Chawton but Henry asked the Bishop if she could be buried in the cathedral, and so that was where she was laid to rest. The funeral took place on 24th July although the cathedral register has the date incorrectly as the 16th July. Until the service Jane's body lay in an open coffin with a, "sweet serene air over her countenance". A few days later the *Salisbury and Winchester Journal* printed the following obituary:

"On Friday the 18th inst. died, in this city, Miss Jane Austen, youngest daughter of the late Rev. George Austen, Rector of Steventon, in the county, and authoress of *Emma*, *Mansfield Park*, *Pride and Prejudice*, and *Sense and Sensibility*. Her manners were gentle, her affections ardent, her candour was not to be surpassed, and she lived and died as became a humble Christian."

She was buried in the north aisle of the nave. Her brother Henry wrote the inscription that is on the fine black marble gravestone which reads as follows:

In Memory of
JANE AUSTEN
youngest daughter of the late
Revd GEORGE AUSTEN
formerly rector of Steventon in this County
she departed this life on the 18th July 1817,
aged 41, after a long illness supported with
the patience and the hopes of a Christian.

The benevolence of her heart,
the sweetness of her temper, and
the extraordinary endowments of her mind
obtained the regard of all who knew her and
the warmest love of her intimate connections.

Their grief is in proportion to their affection
they know their loss to be irreparable,
but in their deepest affliction they are consoled
by a firm though humble hope that her charity,
devotion, faith and purity have rendered
her soul acceptable in the sight of her

REDEEMER

The doctors of the day were not sure exactly what it was that Jane died of. Even today there does not seem to be agreement as to what the illness was. One school of thought is that it was Addison's disease, a tuberculosis of the adrenal glands that results in vomiting and dehydration as well as skin discolouration. Another idea put forward is that Jane suffered from Hodgkin's disease which is a form of cancer. Both of these illnesses are treatable today but sadly, were not in Jane's time.

She left us six of the greatest books in the English language – *'Sense and Sensibility'* (1811), *'Pride and Prejudice'* (1813), *'Mansfield Park'* (1814), and *'Emma'* (1815) all came out in Jane's lifetime whilst *'Persuasion'* (1817) and *'Northanger Abbey'* (1817) were published after her death. Sir Walter Scott, the great Scottish novelist and poet who was a contemporary of Jane and had written indifferently about her work twelve years previously, had obviously formed a different opinion of her literary talents over the previous decade because when reviewing her books nearly ten years after her death, wrote:

"That young lady has a talent for describing the involvements and feelings and characters of ordinary life, which is to me the most wonderful I have ever met with. The Big Bow-Wow strain I can do myself like any now going; but the exquisite touch which renders ordinary common-place things and characters interesting from the truth of the description and the sentiment is denied to me."

Had this been written straight after Jane's death, one would simply assume that he was being a little kind because of a recent loss of a fellow author, but this was ten years after Jane's death so we must assume that Scott's opinion of her had definitely changed and this tribute was written with complete sincerity. Her work was not immediately recognised when one remembers the publisher Thomas Cadell turning down the manuscript of *'First Impressions'* in 1797 that went on to become *'Pride and Prejudice'*, the best loved of all of Jane's work. The author and historian, Thomas Babington Macauley (1800-59) likened her to Shakespeare and felt that she was greater than Fanny Burney (1752-1840) and Maria Edgeworth (1767-1849), the Irish novelist who was very famous in her day.

However, Jane's nephew, James-Edward Austen-Leigh, the son of Jane's elder brother, James, points out in his *'A Memoir of Jane Austen'* that was published in 1870, if any of the Austen family had claimed that during her lifetime, his aunt was a greater writer than those two women, they would have accused them of being biased because she was part of the family.

It was very sad that Jane died so young as it was a personal tragedy for her friends and family, but for future generations who would never know her personally, we are all left to wonder as to how much more of this type of work she would have left us had modern treatments been available to her at the time. It is something that we can only guess at, but we can be grateful that she left us the brilliant work that she did, and despite her early passing, her descendants must be so proud of what she did leave.

The tribute in Winchester Cathedral says everything about her character but nothing about her writing. This was the family's wish but they could not possibly have known that in any event, any such mention would ultimately be unnecessary, and that these six great novels would make sure that Jane Austen would be remembered forever as one of the greatest writers this country has produced.

-oOOo-

9

John Harrison
(1693-1776)

Brilliant watchmaker who spent his entire adult life solving the age - old problem of sailors calculating longitude at sea.

Calculating longitude at sea was a problem that remained unsolved for centuries until John Harrison, this humble watchmaker from Yorkshire, finally solved it with the completion of his fourth timekeeper, now known as H4, in 1759. Harrison is described as a watchmaker, but he actually started his life as a carpenter, and all his early timekeepers were made out of wood. Although his fourth timekeeper was completed in 1759, Harrison's work was not officially recognised until 1773, in fact not until after personal intervention from King George III.

Harrison was born on 24th March, 1693 in Foulby, near Wakefield in Yorkshire and was to die on his 83rd birthday, 24th March, 1776. Despite his extraordinary contribution to modern science, little is known of Harrison's origins other than it is thought that he was the first of five children. His father was employed by the owner of Nostell Priory as a carpenter and custodian and there is a blue plaque on the house where John was born. At some stage in his early life, his father moved his family down to Barrow, a village in North Lincolnshire, which was also known as Barrow-on-Humber as it was situated on the south side of that river. John Harrison married a lady called Elizabeth Barrel on 30th August, 1718 and they had a son who they called John who was born a few months later. Elizabeth died in 1726 and Harrison married another Elizabeth shortly afterwards. His second wife was Elizabeth Scott and they married on 23rd November 1726. They had two children, William, who was later to become his father's long term assistant throughout his work with the Board of Longitude, was born in 1728 and Elizabeth arrived in 1732. In 1738, John Harrison's son, also called John, by his first wife died aged nineteen and John senior, second wife Elizabeth and the two remaining children moved to Holborn where he was to start work on his third timepiece.

John Harrison learned carpentry from his father and although we do not know who he acquired the knowledge from, he also learned music, playing the viola and eventually took over as choirmaster of the parish church in Barrow. Although generally unschooled, John had an inquisitive brain and loved learning. In 1712, a clergyman who was visiting the area lent him a textbook – it was a manuscript copy of a series of lectures on natural philosophy which had been delivered by a mathematician called Nicholas Saunderson at Cambridge University. By this time he had learned reading and writing, and made his own annotated copy of Saunderson's work, which he called *"Mr. Saunderson's*

Mechanicks". He studied this book over and over making his own notes, determined to understand the laws of motion.

Harrison made his first pendulum clock in 1713 at the age of just twenty. He was young, had no training in clockmaking at the time yet the extraordinary thing is that the clock still remains – it is housed in an exhibit case at The Worshipful Company of Clockmakers tiny museum at Guildhall in London. The other extraordinary fact concerning this clock is that it is made almost entirely of wood. Harrison built two more wooden clocks – one in 1715 which is housed in the Science Museum, and another two years later in 1717 making three in all. The third clock is at Nostell Priory in Yorkshire, and there is an inscription on the face saying 'John Harrison, Barrow'. There is a paper attached to the third clock which is Harrison's 'Equation of Time' table and this table allowed any user of the clock to differentiate between solar or 'true' time (ie-as shown on a sundial) compared to the artificial 'mean' time which is used more often and is measured by clocks striking noon every twenty-four hours. These days we rely wholly on 'mean' time but solar time was widely used in Harrison's day.

By 1720, John Harrison had achieved a good reputation locally as a clockmaker, and was asked to make a tower clock by Sir Charles Pelham at his stable at the manor house at Brocklesby Park. The clock still runs today and has done continuously since it was first built. There was a brief period in 1884 when it was stopped for refurbishing but that is the only time in which it has ceased to run.

John himself, had a younger brother James, and although eleven years younger than John, was considered a superb craftsman and when Harrison started to make more clocks, James helped John out and virtually became his right hand man, a role that John's son William was to fulfil many years later. During the period between 1725 and 1728, the two brothers built three long case clocks, or as they are known today, grandfather clocks. They kept perfect time because Harrison had solved the problem that was found in most pendulums. In the 18th century, most pendulums expanded with heat and slowed down when the weather was hot. Conversely, when the weather was cold, the pendulums would contract and the clocks would speed up. Harrison got round the problem by combining long and short strips of brass and steel and these metals being bound together counteracted each other's changes in length as the temperatures alternated between hot and cold, and so the pendulum did not vary in speed. The brothers carried out rigorous tests on these clocks and found them to be accurate within a 'second of a whole month' which was an amazing achievement as the finest clocks of the day by such master clockmakers as Thomas Tompian or George Graham differed by 'one minute per day'. It was about this time that Harrison decided on seeing if he could build a time-piece that would solve the problem of accurately calculating longitude at sea. Sadly, although his pendulum was responsible for the incredibly accurate timekeeping of the clocks that he had already made, he knew a clock with a pendulum at sea would never keep accurate time, so he had to go back to the drawing board to see if he could build a clock that would not need one. Harrison spent nearly four years trying to solve the problem, and when he felt that he was ready, went to London in 1730 in order to seek out the Board of Longitude. The Board of Longitude had been set up by Act of Parliament in 1714 but had not yet met – John Harrison was to change all that. Meanwhile, the Harrison brothers continued to work together for a few more years, but eventually, James went his own way and became a wealthy clock maker, bell-founder and industrialist. This then, is the very briefest of family histories on John Harrison and we must now look back at the problem of the calculation of longitude which had caused the navies of the world problems for generations. The calculation of latitude, that is, the angular distance on the meridian north or south from the equator, was relatively straightforward. The calculation of longitude was far more difficult however, and had caused sailors problems for centuries as seamen would never be able to calculate their exact position at any one time without knowing both their latitude and longitude readings.

In 1675, the Royal Observatory was founded by King Charles II with a view to solving the problem of the calculation of longitude. At that time, any such method was to be solved by the position of the stars. Assuming an accurate reading of the stars could be made if the position of the moon could be measured relative to the stars, then the moon's motion could be used as a natural clock to calculate the time at Greenwich. This method was known as the Lunar Distance Method. This method was unable to give an accurate reading twenty-four hours a day, seven days a week however, and whilst many distinguished scientists of the day thought that it was the only possible solution, another way of solving the problem had to be found. The problem of longitude manifested itself in two ways – it was not only where you were and where you were going, but how safe you were going to be due to the lack of knowledge as to your exact whereabouts and it was the tragedy in 1707 of losing over 2,000 men under the command of Admiral Sir Cloudesley Shovel (1650-1707) that brought matters to a head in England. Admiral Shovel had had a distinguished career in the navy and had taken part in the battle of Beachy Head on 10th July, 1690. This was an engagement in which the English and Dutch fleets fought against the French under Admiral Tourville during the so-called nine years war. The allied fleet led by Admiral Torrington was heavily defeated by the French and Torrington was court-martialled afterwards even though he had warned against engaging the superior numbers of the enemy. However, thankfully he was in fact acquitted. He was lucky however, as the navy seemed to take a dim view of cautious commanders as Admiral John Byng (1704-57) found out in 1757 when he was court-marshalled and executed when he had failed to relieve Menorca the previous year despite the fact that he was in command of a poorly equipped fleet.

Sir Cloudesley Shovel served under Admiral Sir George Rooke (1650-1709) when they captured Gibralter in 1704 and the following year took part in the capture of Barcelona. His fleet failed in the attack on Toulon in 1707 and it was from this action that he was returning when on 22nd October he mistook the position of his fleet as being near the coast of Brittany whereas in fact they were sailing right into the Scilly Islands off the coast of Cornwall. The first ship to strike land first was the *Association* and she sank within a very few minutes with all hands being drowned. Ships of this size could not alter course quickly enough to escape the danger and the *Eagle* and *Romney* were soon dashed on the rocks. Out of a total of five ships, four were lost and a total of two thousand lives perished. Most people assume that all the men drowned immediately but one version has it that two men initially survived, one of them being Sir Cloudesley Shovel himself. In this version he is said to have crawled ashore and if this is indeed the case, then he would have been horrified at what had happened given the fact that it was entirely his fault. It is said that a member of the *Association's* crew approached Sir Cloudesley on board ship in order to tell him that he, the seaman, had kept his own record of their location, and that the present course would lead to the fleet's destruction. The seaman was aware that it was against all regulations to question the Admiral's position, but he was so alarmed, he felt he had no choice. He was immediately hanged for mutiny and if Shovel did live for a short time afterwards, he would have bitterly regretted his decision as he would have been virtually the only survivor of this dreadful, and as it turned out, avoidable tragedy. The story goes on to say that a local woman saw the Admiral's emerald ring and murdered him for it. Whilst on her deathbed thirty years later, the woman is said to have made a full confession to her clergyman. Whether this story is accurate, or whether the Admiral simply drowned with the rest, his body was found and he was buried in Westminster Abbey. In the event, this appalling loss of life led to the setting up of a Board of Longitude in 1714 and the government offering £20,000 prize money for anyone who could solve the problem.

The Act was passed on 16th June, 1714 and was one of the last major pieces of legislation that Queen Anne, the last Stuart monarch prior to the Hanoverian dynasty starting with George I succeeding to the throne signed, prior to her death in August 1714. The Act stated:-

"...for providing a publick reward for such person or persons as shall discover the longitude... to a sum of ten thousand pounds, if it determines the said longitude to one degree of a great circle, or sixty geographical miles, to fifteen thousand pounds, if it determines the same to two thirds of the distance, and to twenty thousand pounds, if it determines the same to one half of the same distance..."

Trying to solve the longitude problem predated the act however. One extraordinary idea was the wounded dog theory put forward in 1687. This involved the use of the so-called 'Powder of Sympathy' which was apparently discovered in France by Sir Kenelm Digby (1603-65). Digby had been an English diplomat and writer. Grief stricken at his wife's death in 1633, he went into seclusion and in the civil war had his estates taken away from him, although he must have used his diplomatic skills to the full as he managed to establish a friendship with Oliver Cromwell. When the crown was restored in 1660 he retained his office as Chancellor to Queen Henrietta Maria (1609-1669), mother of King Charles II. In 1663, Digby was a founder member of the Royal Society and enjoyed his high status with the Royal family until his death in 1665 on 11th June, his sixty-second birthday. Digby claimed that the 'Powder of Sympathy' technique could heal from a distance and it was supposed to work by applying it to an article from the injured party. Thus if a dog was wounded with a knife a bit of bandage from the wound would be sprinkled with the powder which would hasten the healing even though neither the bandage nor the powder was near the dog. The idea was that the wounded dog would be taken on board ship whilst the bandage from the original wound along with the powder would stay on shore. Each day at noon, a person entrusted with the task would dip the dog's bandage into the sympathy powder which would help the wound heal. The treatment was not painless however, and it would cause the dog on board ship to yelp, thus telling the Captain and crew that it was noon in London. The captain would then compare that London time with local time on board ship and would therefore allow the longitude to be calculated. In order for this to work however, the powder had to have the power to work over thousands of sea miles in order for the dog to feel it, and there was also a suspicion that the dog would probably have to be continually wounded during a voyage for the wound to remain open. It says much for the high reputation that Digby's memory enjoyed that this bizarre solution was even remotely given consideration.

Another idea, only slightly less strange was put forward by William Whiston (1667-1752), an English clergyman and mathematician and his friend, Humphrey Ditton (1675-1715), also a mathematician. Whiston's mentor was Sir Isaac Newton (1642-1727), the celebrated scientist and mathematician, and for a while Whiston had succeeded him as Lucasian Professor of mathematics at Cambridge. Ditton had served as master of the mathematics school at Christ's Hospital in London so clearly neither men were fools but their idea still seemed far fetched and ultimately completely unworkable. They thought that longitude could be measured using sounds. Whiston had remembered that in 1690 he had been in Cambridge whilst the battle with the French had been fought off Beachy Head in Sussex. Although Whiston was in Cambridge during the battle, he heard the blasts of the great guns from the Sussex coast and thought that this could help measure longitude. Whiston and Ditton both thought that if there were enough ships placed in strategic positions at sea, sailors could calculate their distance from the gun ships by comparing the time known by the expected signal from these gun ships. It was hopelessly impracticable and would never work. Whiston and Ditton thought that they would need a fleet of ships anchored at intervals of 600 miles but that alone presented a problem. They thought that the Atlantic Ocean was no more than 300 fathoms at its deepest point, whereas in fact even the average depth was about 2,000 fathoms and deeper than that in places which would make it completely impossible for any ship to anchor. Another problem was how the ships were to be manned and when manned, how the crews were to be fed.

Although it seems ridiculous, Whiston and Ditton kept pushing their solution and in 1714, published their proposal in the form of a book entitled 'A New Method for Discovering Longitude both at Sea and Land'. The two men would not give up and managed to unite the shipping interests in London. In the same year that the book was published, they raised a petition signed by 'Captains of Her Majesty's Ships, Merchants of London, and Commanders of Merchant-Men'. Issac Newton then became involved, putting forward both the possibility of measuring longitude by time as eventually happened, and the lunar distance plan. And so it was that notwithstanding the fanciful ideas it produced, the Act of Parliament was eventually passed.

However, the longitude problem didn't start when Sir Cloudesley Shovel lost his fleet in 1707 – there were many people who attempted to find a reliable method of calculating longitude at sea long before this tragedy occurred. The first person who thought the longitude problem could be solved by a reliable clock was Regnier Gemma Frisius (1508-55), the Dutch Professor of medicine. He was interested in astronomy and astronomical instruments and he also constructed maps. He has the distinction that his celestial globe is the oldest one in the National Maritime Museum. However, although Frisius was a clever man and came up with the theoretical answer to the problem, he was no clockmaker and so there was no practical way that he could solve the problem. Another Dutchman, the brilliant Christian Huygens (1629-95) was a mathematician, astronomer, physicist and horologist. He invented the idea of a pendulum clock in 1657 but like Frisius, was not a clockmaker himself and instead got Salomon Coster (1620-59), the Dutch clockmaker, to build it for him. Huygens and Coster carried out a series of tests but they were unable to come up with a clock that was good enough to give an accurate longitude reading.

Another person who thought he may have the solution to the longitude problem was an English clockmaker by the name of Henry Sully (1680-1729), although despite the fact that he was English, spent many years living in France. In 1716, only two years after the Act of Parliament setting up the Board of Longitude was passed, he invented a very sophisticated marine clock which he hoped would determine longitude accurately. Sully was a skilled man and well respected. He was the first clockmaker in Paris to develop a chronometer and in 1718 he established a watch factory in Versailles. In 1726, he published *'Une Horloge inventee et executee par M. Sulli'* and also worked with Julien Le Roy, one of Louis XV's clockmakers. However, his efforts in trying to determine the method of measuring longitude accurately were doomed to failure because whilst his chronometers worked very well in calm weather, they were inaccurate in rough seas which of course meant that the problem of the accurate measurement of longitude remained unsolved.

Shortly after *'Une Horloge inventee et execute par M. Sulli'* was published, John Harrison felt that he could solve the problem of calculating longitude where Sully had failed, that is, with a timepiece. John Harrison had started his working life as a carpenter but after spending years with his brother James making incredibly accurate clocks, he felt ready to work on building a timepiece that would one day comply with the requirements laid down by the 1714 Act of Parliament. To work out the problem of longitude using a timepiece was very simple – actually solving the problem was very hard to achieve. The earth rotates at a rate of 360 degrees per day (24 hours). This means that for every hour it rotates at 15 degrees. Using Harrison's method to calculate longitude the Captain of the ship would need to keep a timepiece on board that would tell him the time in London. He would then calculate the local time of noon by seeing when the sun was directly overhead, and by comparing the local time with London time, would be able to measure the degrees of longitude and therefore the distance from London. By already calculating latitude, it would be a simple method of calculating an accurate position as to where they were. It seems simple, but there were to be two major obstacles in Harrison's path and they both took him years to conquer. Firstly, up until the time that he approached the Board of Longitude in 1730, it had been completely impossible to produce a timepiece that would keep accurate time on board ship – the movement of the ship had seen to that. Secondly, the Board of Longitude was full of members who preferred the lunar method which involved hours of complex calculations. Unfortunately, they were completely biased against Harrison's attempts at a solution, the chief of these being the Rev. Nevil Maskelyne (1732-1811), who was eventually to become the fifth Astronomer Royal in 1765 and was himself a candidate for the longitude prize. Being a member of the Board of Longitude hardly made him a disinterested party and he put obstacles in Harrison's path whenever he could. He was in favour of the Lunar Distance Method which entailed using new tables that had been drawn up by the famous German astronomer, Tobias Mayer.

However, all that was to happen later. John Harrison initially came down to London in 1730 before Maskelyne was even born with the express purpose of seeing the Astronomer Royal, Dr Edmond Halley who was a member of the Board of Longitude. Edmond Halley (1656-1742) was a distinguished astronomer and mathematician and had become Astronomer Royal in 1720 when the previous holder of the post, John Flamsteed (1646-1719) died. Halley had achieved much in his lifetime but it was in the field of cometary astronomy that he is best known. He correctly predicted that a comet that had been observed in 1683 would return in 1758, 1835 and 1910 and it is this comet that is named after him. Halley had spent many years calculating the moon's motion with a view to solving the longitude problem using the lunar method, but he kept an open mind and listened to what Harrison said about the use of time and eventually recommended that he showed his drawings to the famous watchmaker, George Graham. George Graham (1674-1751) was one of the most famous watchmakers of his day. He invented several improvements to the pendulum clock but his greatest invention was the deadbeat escapement in or around 1715. In 1722 he was appointed the Master of the Clockmakers Company and when he died in 1751, he was buried in the same tomb as his friend and mentor, Thomas Tompion (1638-1713). In the latter part of Tompion's life, Graham went into business with the man who is known as 'The Father of English Watch-making'. In 1675, Tompion made one of the first English watches equipped with a balance spring and this watch was subsequently given to Charles II. He had now gained a very good reputation and the following year was appointed Clockmaker for the newly opened Royal Observatory. The Observatory had been opened as a result of a suggestion by John Flamsteed (1646-1719) with a view to determining the problem of longitude. Flamsteed was an English astronomer and clergyman and began the observations that would lead to modern day astronomy. He was appointed the first Astronomer Royal in 1675 by King Charles II and in his warrant establishing the Observatory, the King charged Flamsteed to apply: "the most exact Care and Diligence to rectifying the Tables of the Motions of the Heavens, and the Places of the fixed Stars, so as to find out the so-much desired Longitude at Sea, for perfecting the art of Navigation". Thus it was that the Royal Observatory came into being and with it its philosophy that the answer to the longitude problem was in the field of astronomy. Directly with Edmond Halley and George Graham, and indirectly with Thomas Tompion, John Harrison, the completely self-taught clockmaker from a village in Lincolnshire, was already moving in illustrious circles.

After the recommendation by Edmond Halley, Harrison went to see George Graham. Although Halley was obviously favouring a lunar method, he was a fair man, and realised that George Graham would understand Harrison's methods better than he, Halley would be able to. When John Harrison and George Graham first met, they were suspicious of each other and they got off to a bad start, but by the end of one day's discussion, Graham became Harrison's patron. John Harrison described their first meeting thus:- "Mr. Graham began as I thought very roughly with me, and the which had like to have occasioned me to become rough too; but somehow we got the ice broke... and indeed he became as at last vastly surprised at the thoughts or methods I had taken."

After the meeting, John Harrison returned to Barrow with a generous loan from Mr. Graham which would enable him to spend five years building the first sea clock, later named H1, which was completed with the help of his brother James in 1735. It was a huge instrument weighing seventy-five pounds and was kept in a cabinet four feet in width, height and depth. The brothers tested it thoroughly on a barge on the River Humber before taking it to London where they demonstrated it to George Graham. Graham was very impressed and showed the sea clock to the Royal Society who were equally impressed. One of the members of the Royal Society who saw it was Dr. Edmond Halley. At this stage, the Board of Longitude had not yet seen the clock. Graham wrote this favourable report about H1 and its inventor, John Harrison:

"John Harrison, having with great labour and expense, contrived and executed a Machine for measuring time at sea, upon such Principle, as seem to us Promise a very great and sufficient degree of Exactness. We are of Opinion, it highly deserves Public Encouragement, In order to a thorough Trial and Improvement, of the several Contrivances, for preventing these Irregularities in time, that naturally arise from the different degrees of Heat and Cold, a moist and dry temperature of the Air, and the Various Agitations of the ship."

Although the first reaction to the clock was favourable, the Admiralty started what was to be many years of frustration for Harrison by delaying the trials for a year. Also, instead of sending the clock to the West Indies as the 1714 Act required, they ordered that the clock go to Lisbon and Harrison was ordered to take his clock to Spithead to board *HMS Centurion,* which was due to sail there. On 14th May, 1736, Sir Charles Wager, the First Lord of the Admiralty, sent a letter of introduction to the Captain of HMS Centurion, Captain Proctor:-

"Sir, The instrument which is put on Board your Ship has been approved by all the Mathematicians in Town that have seen it (and few have not) to be the Best that has been made for measuring Time; how it will succeed at Sea, you will be a Judge; I have writ to Sir John Norris, to desire him to send home the instrument and the Maker of it (who I think you have with you) by the first Ship that comes... The man is said by those who know him best, to be a very ingenious and sober Man, and capable of finding out something more than he has already, if he can find Encouragement; I desire therefore, that you will let the Man be used civilly, and that you will be as kind to him as you can."

Captain Procter replied immediately: "The Instrument is placed in my Cabin, for giving the Man all the Advantage that is possible for making his Observations, and I find him to be very sober, a very industrious, and withal a very modest Man, so that my good Wishes can't but attend him; but the Difficulty of measuring Time truly, where so many unequal Shocks and Motions, stand in Opposition to it, gives me concern for the honest Man, and makes me fear he has attempted Impossibilities; but Sir, I will do him all the Good, and give him all the Help, that is in my Power, and acquaint him with your Concern for his Success, and your Care that he shall be well treated...."

The *Centurion* sailed for Lisbon in 1736 and the journey took just one week, which was just as well as Harrison was not a good sailor and felt ill for almost the entire journey. Captain Proctor died very suddenly almost as soon as they reached port – he had not even had the time to write any kind of report up and only four days later, Roger Wills, who was the Master of *HMS Orford* was instructed to take Harrison and his clock back to England. This was an even worse journey for Harrison as it took a month to return due to the weather conditions but something happened on that journey that was to make it all worthwhile.

The ship was nearing home and when land was sighted, Wills, who claimed that he knew the waters well, had thought that it was the Start, which was a point on the south coast around Dartmouth. Although he had never been to sea before, Harrison contradicted Wills and told him that according to his calculations, the land sighted was the Lizard on the Penzance peninsula which was sixty miles west of where Wills thought they were. As it happened, Harrison was proved correct and Wills, being very impressed, generously admitted his mistake and gave Harrison a certificate of accuracy which was dated 24th June, 1737. This was to be a good week for Harrison as the Board of Longitude met for the first time ever on the 30th, twenty-three years after it was set up by the 1714 Act of Parliament.

Harrison took his H1 clock to the Board which at that point was well disposed towards him. Edmond Halley was there along with Sir Charles Wager. It was Wager who had written to Captain Proctor of the *Centurion* prior to the trip to Lisbon requesting that Harrison be treated with all due kindness. There were several others there, including the Speaker of The House of Commons, the Right Honourable Arthur Onslow. Most people in the room were well disposed towards Harrison and he would have been well within his rights to request a West Indies trial as specified in the 1714 act. If that had happened and it turned out to be successful, we can only guess as to whether he would have won the £20,000 prize at that point instead of waiting another thirty-six years and suffering all the trauma that went with it. There was only one person in the room who was prepared to criticise the H1 clock, and that was Harrison himself. On the trial run to and from Lisbon it had not lost or gained more than a few seconds, but Harrison, a perfectionist and a man who would never make life easy for himself, started to point out so-called flaws. He thought that H1 was too big and that he could make a smaller clock and one which could keep even better time. He asked for £500 and two years grace to make the new clock and an official trial to the West Indies, but he did not want the trial now. The Board promised to pay him £250 straight away and the balance of £250 when the clock was completed and handed over to the Royal Navy. The Board also required Harrison to hand over the second clock along with the first after the sea trial which Harrison surprisingly agreed to. Perhaps he felt that he had no choice, but he trusted the Board and felt that he had been commissioned by them, so at this stage of the proceedings he was fairly at ease with the situation.

Harrison then went off to build his second clock which he completed in 1739 although he was to spend a further two years testing it himself before presenting it to the Board in January 1741. By this time however, he was already unhappy with it and although by now he had been working on the two clocks for ten years, he basically asked the Board what he had asked them in 1737 – more time. This seems an extraordinary thing to have done at a time when they were so well disposed towards him. H2 was an improvement on the first timepiece and passed various tests with ease. The Royal Society brought out a report in 1741/2 saying that the tests subjected H2 to heating and cooling, and to being "agitated for many hours together, with greater violence than what it could receive from the motion of a ship in a storm". The Royal Society completely backed the H2 and went on to say "And the Result of these Experiments, is this; that (as far as can be determined without making a voyage to sea) the motion is sufficiently regular and exact, for finding the Longitude of a Ship within the nearest Limits proposed by Parliament and probably much nearer".

One is left to wonder why Harrison didn't press home his advantage and attempt to win the £20,000 with the two clocks that he had already built. After all, he would have been a rich man and nothing need have stopped him building the improved timepieces at a later date. John Harrison was now forty-eight years old and perhaps he thought he could retain the goodwill of the Board for ever, and that his pride would only allow him to accept the £20,000 if he presented them with as perfect a timepiece as was possible for him to make – he obviously thought he had not yet made it at this juncture. He told the Board that he would build a third clock and was awarded another £500 in order to do this but by the time that the third timepiece was built, almost another twenty years had gone by and the Board were made up of very different men.

Throughout these long years of building H3, the Royal Society had stood by Harrison, and awarded him the Copley Gold Medal on 30th November, 1749. This was a very prestigious award and some very eminent people, including Captain Cook and Albert Einstein were to receive it in later years. The Royal Society said that Harrison was – "…the author of the most important scientific discovery or contribution to science by experiment or otherwise…". The Royal Society then offered Harrison membership which would have allowed him to put the letters F.R.S. after his name but he refused, requesting that membership be awarded to his son William instead. William had spent most of his adult life acting as his father's assistant on the building of H3 but the Royal Society were adamant that this simply could not happen as people had to earn it in their own right. However, as it turned out, William was eventually elected himself in 1765. John Harrison was certainly a hard man to help. The Royal Society was set up in the previous century by brilliant scientists and early members included men such as Issac Newton (1642-1727), English scientist and mathematician, Robert Hooke (1635-1703), English chemist, physicist, and architect, Samuel Pepys (1633-1703), English diarist and Admiralty Official, and Sir Chrisopher Wren (1632-1723), architect and astronomer and the man who designed the new St. Paul's Cathedral after the Great Fire of London in 1666. One would think that for a man of so-called humble origins it would have been a dream come true to join such an august body, but clearly it wasn't for Harrison. He was simply intent on building the timepiece that would solve the problem of longitude and did not welcome distractions. Eventually H3 was complete – by now it was 1758 and Harrison had spent nearly thirty years building H1, H2, and H3. Despite Harrison's dissatisfaction with his own work, George Graham was housing H1 having it on loan from Harrison and put it on show for people who came from far and wide to view it. The English artist, William Hogarth was well known for having an obsession with time and timekeeping, and he wrote in his 'Analysis of Beauty', which was published in 1753, that H1 was, "One of the most exquisite movements ever made". But still John Harrison was not satisfied. However, at about the time he finished his H3 timepiece an extraordinary thing was about to happen that would lead to Harrison building H4 which would finally deliver him the money and the recognition that he deserved, although there was a very long way to go and many obstacles to overcome before he was successful.

Although Harrison was not completely satisfied with H3, he thought at the time that it was probably the best that he could do. He felt that the answer to the longitude problem was building a clock, and that as H3 was smaller than his first two, it might have to do, but something niggled at him. He felt that he would never solve the problem by building a watch as it would never achieve the same degree of accuracy as a clock. However, at about this time, Harrison had become friendly with a very clever watchmaker by the name of John Jefferys who was a Freeman of The Worshipful Company of Clockmakers. Harrison asked Jefferys if he would make him a pocket watch which Jefferys duly did. Jefferys fitted the watch with a very small bi-metallic strip and by so doing, he was using the same technique that John Harrison and his brother James had used over thirty years earlier before Harrison even started H1. This technique used on the pendulums of the earlier clocks had solved the problem of timepieces being exposed to extreme heat or extreme cold, and which allowed accurate time to be kept. John Jefferys had taken John Harrison's ideas of those early years and put them in a pocket watch. It also had the advantage of running normally when being wound as most watches either stopped or ran backwards. This remarkable watch is still in existence and is housed in the Clockmaker's Museum and it is the watch that gave John Harrison the idea for H4.

Harrison mentioned this watch to the Board of Longitude in June 1755 during one of their mutually frustrating sessions whilst he explained the latest reason for the delay in H3. He said that on the basis of a watch, "already executed according to his direction, that such small machines may be... of great service with respect to the longitude". After spending nearly twenty years building H3, Harrison wasn't even interested in sending it for trials which must have been hugely frustrating for his son William, who had grown up with H3.

Twelve years old when his father started it, William was now thirty years old and it must have seemed like a lifetime's work had gone to waste. However, John Harrison was nothing if not stubborn, and went ahead with concentrating on building a watch which he completed in 1759 – the watch that became known as H4. It was larger than a normal pocket watch, as it was five inches in diameter, but that size was nothing compared to H1, H2, and H3.

Harrison loved it and said: "I think I may make bold to say, that there is neither any other Mechanical or Mathematical thing in the World that is more beautiful or curious in texture than this my watch or Timekeeper for the Longitude... and I heartily thank Almighty God that I have lived so long, as in some measure to complete it". At last Harrison was satisfied, but it was to be a long time before he would satisfy the Board of Longitude who by virtue of the membership, tried every way that they could to thwart Harrison and to have the longitude problem solved by the Lunar Method.

As mentioned earlier, the person who was to embody the Lunar Method and to prove such a thorn in John Harrison's side was The Reverend Nevil Maskelyne. Maskelyne was born on 5th October, 1732 and the lunar method was entirely suited to his character, being obsessed as he was with observation and calculation of the most complex and intricate kind. He kept accurate records of virtually everything connected with his life. He recorded all his personal expenditure, astronomical positions and events of a personal nature that happened to him – a kind of diary-cum-ledger. In later life, he is often portrayed as the villain of the story of Harrison's clocks, both eventually becoming a candidate for the longitude prize as well as becoming a member of the Board. This put him in an impossible position of having a conflict of interest although it has to be said that he was not the only one. However, in his defence, in an age which was acutely class conscious, he who had been educated at Westminster school and then Cambridge University, probably thought that someone such as himself who had studied astronomy all his life could not possibly be bettered by a man of humble birth and little education such as John Harrison. He had also taken holy orders whilst at Trinity College which allowed him the title of Reverend. At some stage during the 1750's, whilst Maskelyne was still studying at Cambridge, he was introduced to James Bradley (1693-1762), the third Astronomer Royal who had succeeded Sir Edmond Halley in that post in 1742.

John Flamsteed (1646-1719) was the first Astronomer Royal from 1675 to 1719, Edmond Halley was the second from 1720 until 1742, Bradley the third, and on his death in 1762, the post was taken by Nathaniel Bliss who unlike his three predecessors, did not enjoy a long tenure, lasting only three years until his death in 1765. The fifth Astronomer Royal, appointed in January 1765, was none other than the Revd. Nevil Maskelyne. At the age of thirty-two, his appointment at the time did not bode well for John Harrison who by that time was seventy-two years old, whilst Maskelyne was nearly forty years younger. As it turned out, Maskelyne was to hold the post with some distinction for a period of forty-six years until his death on the 9th of February, 1811.

When he was at Cambridge, he befriended James Bradley although the latter was nearly forty years older, but Maskelyne took a great interest in the work that Bradley was undertaking. Bradley was close to codifying the lunar distance method with the help of tables that had been sent to him from Germany by an astronomer-mathematician-mapmaker by the name of Tobias Mayer (1723-62). Mayer was famous for much of his work but especially for his lunar tables along with new solar tables that he presented to the Konigliche Gesellschaft der Wissenschaften zu Gottingen (Royal Society of Sciences and Humanities at Gottingen) in 1752 and which were later published by that body. In 1755 he submitted an amended form to the British government and it was these tables that Bradley was using and comparing with the observations made at Greenwich. According to Maskelyne, Bradley had taken 1,200 observations at Greenwich between the years 1755 and 1760, which he followed with intricate calculations, the aim being to verify Mayer's predictions.

Whilst Maskelyne's interest in his work was entirely genuine, his friendship with Bradley who was the Astronomer Royal, certainly worked to his advantage as with the help of Bradley, he secured a place on the proposed trip to St. Helena, south of the Equator, with a view to studying the transit of Venus in 1761. After his trip to St. Helena in 1677, Sir Edmond Halley had urged the Royal Society to study the next transit of Venus from different parts of the globe, and by so doing, it would be possible to measure the distance between the Earth and the Sun.

Maskelyne set out for St. Helena in January 1761 at the same time as other voyages were setting out for places such as the Cape of Good Hope, Siberia, India, and South Africa to carry out the tracking of the transit. On the way there as well as the return journey, Maskelyne used an instrument called Hadley's quadrant in conjunction with Mayer's tables to calculate his longitude at sea and it has to be said that it worked well in Maskelyne's skilled hands. The quadrant was first demonstrated to the Royal Society thirty years earlier by a country squire called John Hadley, although an American by the name of Thomas Godfrey seemed to have hit on the idea at the same time. The Reverend Maskelyne also used lunar tables to work out the exact longitude of St. Helena which had never been calculated before. James Bradley, as Astronomer Royal and the man who for five years had worked so tirelessly on the method, was naturally delighted at the result of Maskelyne's work. Maskelyne was less happy with the results of the transit however as the weather was unsatisfactory, and he missed the end of the transit because of a cloud. Despite this set back, all in all he felt satisfied with the overall achievements made during the voyage and when he arrived home in May 1762, he felt very pleased with himself and quickly published *"The British Mariner's Guide"*, which was an English translation of Tobias Mayer's tables.

However, another important voyage was to take place – this time the testing of H4. H1 had only gone as far as Lisbon, whilst H2 had never gone to sea at all. H3 could have been tried, but the seven-year war (1757-63) was still being fought and there was fear that the secret of the clock would get into the wrong hands. Besides, despite spending nearly twenty years on building H3, Harrison was losing interest in it and was involved in and felt that he had found the answer with the completion of H4 which is the first of the four timepieces that he seemed to genuinely love and have confidence in.

By this time John Harrison was far too old and unwell to undertake a voyage, so William was to go instead. The Board of Longitude had decided to test both H3 and H4 together, and so in May 1761, William sailed from London to Portsmouth with H3 where he was to wait for a ship to take him to Jamaica. William waited for his orders at Portsmouth for five frustrating months and began to suspect that James Bradley deliberately engineered the delay to allow the Reverend Maskelyne to provide more proof concerning the viability of the lunar tables. Whilst some people might have thought that his mind was being over active on this matter, there is a note in William's diary recording how, during a chance encounter that he and his father had with Doctor Bradley in an instrument maker's shop, this view could be substantiated. The diary records that: "The Doctor seemed very much out of temper, and in the greatest passion told Mr. Harrison that if it had not been for him and his plaguey watch, Mr. Mayer and he should have shared the Ten thousand Pounds before now."

Whether this is true or not, William eventually embarked on *HMS Deptford* in November 1761 with just the H4 watch, his father having withdrawn H3. John Harrison had lost interest in the timepiece that he and William had worked on for nearly twenty years, all of William's adult life and more, and he was pinning all his hopes on H4 that in comparative terms, took him no time at all to build.

William received a boost on the first leg of the journey. It was very difficult to keep food and drink fresh on board ship in the 18th century and Captain Digges found that a large quantity of drink was completely unfit for consumption. The ship's master recorded: "….all the Beer was expended, the People obliged to drink water." The crew were none too pleased but William assured the Captain that they would reach Madeira in a day. Digges thought differently and was not happy at being contradicted, but as it happened, William and the watch were proved correct, allowing fresh barrels of wine to be brought on board the following day. Captain Digges graciously conceded and offered to buy the first watch that went on sale to the public. Captain Digges wrote to John Harrison from Madeira:-

"Dear Sir, I have just time to acquaint you… of the great perfection of your watch in making the island on the Meridian; According to our log we were 1 degree 27 minutes to the Eastward, this I made by a French map which lays down the longitude of Teneriffe, therefore I think your watch must be right. Adieu."

The ship arrived in Port Royal, Jamaica on the 19th January, 1762, the voyage across the Atlantic having taken a total of three months. The Board of Longitude's representative, John Robison, set up his astronomical instruments to establish local noon. Robison and Harrison then synchronised their watches to fix the longitude of Port Royal using the time difference between them. The result was a staggeringly accurate result for H4 – it had lost a mere five seconds after 81 days at sea. William was jubilant but it was not over yet. They were only in Jamaica for a week when William boarded the Merlin to journey home and it was a very rough crossing causing William to worry about the state of the watch which he wanted to keep dry. There was often two feet of water on the decks and a seasick, soaked and shivering William wrapped the watch in a blanket for protection and after the blanket got soaked, he slept in it hoping to dry the blanket with his body heat. Despite the anxiety and the horror of the journey home, by the time they reached England on 26th March, 1762, the watch was still working, and its total error amounted to no more than a little under two minutes. It was an incredible achievement, and by rights, John Harrison should have been awarded the prize without question at that time as the watch had done all that the 1714 Act required. However, when John and William Harrison attended the next meeting of the Board of Longitude to claim their prize, they were in for a very rude shock – it wasn't going to be so easy as yet more obstacles were to be placed in their way.

The first one was how Harrison's readings were to be evaluated. The Board seemed to think that the accuracy of the readings could have been by chance and wanted three mathematicians to check and check again the data concerning the times at Portsmouth and Jamaica. They also claimed that they did not know the exact longitude of Jamaica although that lack of information was known before the commencement of the trip. It all smacked of delaying tactics to John and William Harrison. The Board said in its report of August 1762: "the Experiments already made of the Watch have not been sufficient to determine the Longitude at Sea." It was decided that H4 must undergo a further trial in the West Indies. Harrison was not awarded the £20,000 but he did receive £1,500 because the Board recognised that: "tho' not yet found to be of such great use for discovering the Longitude… is nevertheless an invention of considerable utility to the Public." He was also promised a further £1,000 when H4 returned from the second trial.

Meanwhile, the Reverend Nevil Maskelyne arrived back in London in May 1762, only a few weeks after William had returned. He was pleased with his own efforts as he felt that his lunar method was accurate and reliable in determining longitude, added to which he had ascertained the exact longitude of St. Helena. He had been less successful with his reading of the transit of Venus but it has to be said that Maskelyne was a very talented man – it was just a pity that as a disciple of the lunar method, he was in direct conflict with John and William Harrison. He wasn't the only one. In July of that year, James Bradley (1693-1762), the Astronomer Royal died aged sixty-nine. Bradley, like Maskelyne, was a disciple of the lunar method and was a brilliant astronomer making discoveries that Jean Baptiste Joseph Delambre (1749-1822), who was a French astronomer said were: "the most brilliant and useful of the century". To receive praise such as that from a man like Delambre who was a historian of astronomy, would have made Bradley and Maskelyne proud indeed. Amongst other things, Delambre had received praise for his tables of the motion of Uranus. The discoveries that Bradley and Maskelyne had received praise for were the aberration of light (1725-28) and the nutation of the Earth's axis (1728-48). In fact it was Bradley who had spent so many years studying and verifying the tables of Tobias Mayer (1726-62), a brilliant astronomer and mathematician, and whose tables were brilliantly accurate, but who like Bradley died in 1762 although Mayer was aged just thirty-six at the time of his death. Whilst no doubt not wishing death on Bradley, the Harrisons must have hoped that the appointment of a new Astronomer Royal might have allowed them a more sympathetic hearing than Bradley had ever given them, but their hopes were soon dashed when it was announced that Nathaniel Bliss (1700-65), a firm believer in the lunar method, was to be appointed. During his career he had succeeded Edmund Halley as Professor of Geometry at Oxford University and now in 1762 he was to follow Halley once more as Astronomer Royal. Although John and William Harrison felt that after the trials in Jamaica, H4 had more than fulfilled the requirements of the 1714 Act, it was not surprising that obstacles were put in their way by so many people, all of whom believed the answer lay in the lunar method.

The matter of the second trial was still to be arranged however, and eventually in March 1764, William Harrison along with his friend, Thomas Wyatt, and the precious watch, set sail for Barbados on board HMS Tartar with Captain Sir John Lindsay. Sailing ahead of them on board HMS Princess Louisa, were, "two gentlemen well skilled in astronomy" who had been appointed by the Board to compare notes with William Harrison. One of these was Charles Green who in 1761 had been appointed as Assistant to James Bradley, the then Astronomer Royal. Green was born in 1735 in Yorkshire and was the son of a farmer. Being Assistant to the Astronomer Royal must have been a position that Green found boring as it was once described: "Nothing can exceed the tediousness of the life the Assistant leads, excluded from all society, forlorn, he spends months in long wearisome computations". Instead of accepting the Assistant's job he must have wished that he had gone with Maskelyne to St. Helena to observe the 1761 transit of Venus. However, he was to find his excitement by being chosen to be in charge of Harrison's watch on this 1764 trip to Barbados although he fell out with Maskelyne the following year when the latter was appointed Astronomer Royal. Green then became a purser in the navy before sailing with Captain Cook on the famous navigator's first voyage to study the transit of Venus from Tahiti in June 1769. Sadly, Green did not return from that trip with Cook because in 1771 he died of dysentery which was caught by most of Cook's crew at Batavia where Cook's ship the Endeavour had stayed for essential repairs.

However, returning to the 1764 trip to test Harrison's watch in Barbados, William Harrison was happy that Green was there as he felt that Green was a fair man but William was less than happy with the second gentleman chosen who was none other than the Reverend Nevil Maskelyne, although no doubt his presence was more than welcomed by Nathaniel Bliss, who in 1762 had succeeded Bradley as the Astronomer Royal. If the Harrisons thought that Nathaniel Bliss had a conflict of interest being as he was in favour of the lunar method, then Maskelyne, a skilled user of the lunar method and who had his own eyes on the prize money, was certainly in that position. Maskelyne almost felt that he himself was undergoing a second trial as he had thought his own findings during the trip to St. Helena had proved that he had provided the solution to the longitude problem. He also voiced out loud his certainty of winning the prize at the conclusion of this, the second trip.

It is hard to think of a more unsuitable person to help judge the Harrison watch, and William and Captain Lindsay said as much to Maskelyne. Maskelyne was outraged claiming that as a man of science he was impartial, but the accusation unsettled him and as a result he completely misread the astronomical observations, even though the weather conditions were favourable. It was very unsatisfactory for all concerned, but especially so for the Harrisons.

The 1764 trial was therefore a bad tempered period for everyone involved, but eventually they arrived back in England having completed their work. However, the Board of Longitude were silent for months afterwards, as the commissioners were waiting for the mathematicians to compare their findings with those of the astronomers concerning the longitude of Portsmouth and Barbados, all of which had to be taken into account. After receiving the final report, the commissioners said that they were: "unanimously of opinion that the said timekeeper has kept its time with sufficient correctness". Whatever the personal opinions of Board members were as to whether they preferred the watch or the lunar method, there was virtually no other statement that they could have released. The H4 watch told the longitude within ten miles which was three times more accurate than the 1714 Act required – the prize money was surely due now to be paid to John Harrison. He had waited over thirty years for this moment, but unbelievably, this moment was still yet to come – the Board wanted yet more from John and William Harrison.

In the autumn of 1764, the Board of Longitude offered to pay Harrison half the prize money, but there was a catch. Harrison would have to hand over all the sea clocks that he had made, H1, H2, H3, and H4. Added to that, he had to disclose all of the internal workings of H4. The Board added that if Mr. Harrison expected to win the entire £20,000, then he would have to supervise the manufacture of no less than two copies of H4 to ascertain whether the original could be successfully duplicated. By this time, John Harrison was seventy-one years old, exhausted and ill – it was a cruel blow but he had no option other than to comply. There was yet more to come however. In 1765, Nathaniel Bliss, the Astronomer Royal, died after only three years in post. Each of the three previous occupants of the post had been in office for a lengthy period of time. John Flamsteed had held office for forty-three years, Edmond Halley for twenty-two, and James Bradley for twenty.

Nathaniel Bliss was always a thorn in the side of John and William Harrison, but his successor was even harder to take because it was none other than the Reverend Nevil Maskelyne and barring accidents and illness, at thirty-two years of age, he could be expected to be in the post for a very long time. As it happened he was, staying in post for forty-six years which only his death in 1811 took him from. So in January, 1765 that was the position the Harrisons found themselves in. After two brilliant trials with H4, only half the money to be paid and then with conditions that would take years to fulfil, and their arch rival Nevil Maskelyne as Astronomer Royal with an ex-officio seat on the Board of Longitude. With Maskelyne himself a rival for the prize money, it was still going to be an uphill battle for the Harrisons.

Maskelyne didn't waste time in pressing his claim for the prize. His appointment became official on Friday, 8th February, 1765, and the following day he attended an already scheduled meeting of the Board when the matter of further payment for Harrison was to be discussed. Maskelyne read a memorandum to the board which extolled the virtues of the lunar method, and there to back his views were four captains from the East India Company. They confirmed to the Board that they had all used the method many times as outlined in *"The British Mariner's Guide"*, which Maskelyne had published in 1762 soon after returning from his trip to St. Helena and that they had managed to accurately gauge their longitude in no more than four hours. They backed Maskelyne's claim that the findings should be widely published for the benefit of other seamen. With these men behind him and the large number of men on the Board who were favourably disposed towards the lunar method, a groundswell of opinion was welling up against John Harrison's watch, because despite the fact that the watch provided a speedy answer, or even possibly because of it, they could not believe that something that calculated longitude so quickly could be reliable on a long term basis. Another thought was in the Board of Longitude's collective mentality in an age where religion played a greater part in people's lives than it does today. That is, that the Harrison clock was made by man whilst the heavens were made by God and had been there forever and would remain there forever.

There was more bad news to come however because yet another problem was to be put in the way of John Harrison. The spring of 1765 brought a new Act of Parliament concerning the calculation of longitude. It was called Act 5 George III and it was doubtless aimed at Harrison personally including as it did requirements that were never needed in the original act. Harrison was furious and at first refused to co-operate but in the end admitted defeat and had no choice but to try and meet the Board's requirements.

As required by the Board, on the 14th August, 1765, a group of experts gathered at John Harrison's house in Red Lion Square to examine H4 whilst Harrison took it apart, piece by piece, and explained the workings of it. John Harrison was dismissive of the whole exercise but knew that he had to go through with it. There were two Cambridge maths professors present which he was particularly annoyed about, but it has to be said that there were men there who were genuine experts. One of these was Larcum Kendall (1721-95) who was later to make an exact copy of H4 which Captain Cook was to use in his second South Pacific trip between 1772 and 1775. This was later to be known as K1. Another was the famous watchmaker, Thomas Mudge (1715-94). Kendall had previously been an apprentice to John Jefferys who had worked with Harrison for many years, whilst Thomas Mudge was a famous watchmaker who had once been apprenticed to George Graham who had financed John Harrison during his work on H1 in the early years. It should be said therefore, that both these men would be favourably disposed towards Harrison, as well as having an understanding of exactly what it was that Harrison was explaining. Harrison was unimpressed however, and to sour things for him completely, the figure of the Reverend Nevil Maskelyne was in the room with them.

During the next week, John Harrison took the watch apart piece by piece and explained each function to the assembled men and then signed a certificate for them saying that he had told them everything that he knew. The result of all this was that he now had to re-assemble the watch and surrender it to the Admiralty and then build two replicas without the aid of either the watch or the original drawings and descriptions. The Reverend Maskelyne had already taken possession of these and taken them to a print shop whereby they could be published and eventually sold to the general public.

To John and William Harrison, there seemed to be no end to the obstacles put in their path, and in April 1766, the Board demanded yet more from them. The Board wanted absolute assurance that there was no question of luck involved in the previous tests, and they demanded that H4 be transferred from the Admiralty to the Royal Observatory, where for a period of ten months it would undergo yet more strenuous tests carried out by Nevil Maskelyne in his capacity as Astronomer Royal. Meanwhile, the three clocks, H1, H2, and H3 were to be taken from Harrison's home and transferred to Greenwich where their performances could be compared to the regular clock at the Observatory. Since Harrison was only submitting the watch H4 as the answer to the longitude problem, it is not easy to understand why the Board should require the other three. John Harrison was deeply unhappy about this, especially as he was not convinced that they would be moved in a careful manner, but he simply had no choice. Yet another shock was in store for Harrison however as it was none other than Nevil Maskelyne who arrived at Red Lion Square with a warrant for the removal of the three clocks. The warrant read: "Mr. John Harrison, We the Commissioners appointed by the Acts of Parliament for the discovery of the Longitude at Sea, do hereby require you to deliver up to the Rev. Nevil Maskelyne, Astronomer Royal at Greenwich, the three several Machines or Timekeepers, now remaining in your hands, which are become the property of the public".

John Harrison, who had created and housed these machines for the best part of his working life, now had to surrender them to the person he considered his arch enemy, the Astronomer Royal. Concerned about how they were to be transported, Harrison asked Maskelyne to sign a written statement saying that the clocks were in perfect order when he took them, but Maskelyne refused, saying he was not in a position to make such a judgement. After words were exchanged between the two men, Maskelyne agreed that they were 'by all appearances' in perfect order and signed accordingly. It was the best that John Harrison was going to get. To his horror, he found that they were to be transferred to Greenwich on a cart with no suspension over roads that were badly maintained. John Harrison, unable to watch while the three clocks were removed, went upstairs, but heard the crash when the men carrying H1 dropped it. H4 was to fare somewhat better, travelling down the Thames to Greenwich by boat accompanied by Larcum Kendall, the great watchmaker who understood the delicacy of the property that was in his charge and who had been one of the experts that Harrison had explained the workings of the watch to. At least that timepiece was being looked after properly, or at any rate, it was being looked after properly when it was being transported to Greenwich but after that, Nevil Maskelyne was to assume responsibility for housing and testing H4.

H4 had sailed, both literally and metaphorically through two sea trials, and had praise heaped upon it by no less than three sea captains. Even the Board of Longitude had testified as to its accuracy so although Harrison was unhappy that Nevil Maskelyne was carrying out the ten-month trial which took place between May 1766 and March 1767, he was not unduly worried as it would be impossible for anything to go wrong. In this he was mistaken. The H4 Watch, so reliable at sea during its previous trials, suddenly started to go wrong. It was erratic and gained as many as twenty seconds a day and as a result, astonishingly failed its ten-month trial at the Royal Observatory. It is unclear why this happened. One theory is that it was damaged in some way when John Harrison had to dismantle it for examination. Others, less trusting of Maskelyne, blamed him saying either by accident or design, he did not carry out the tests properly. Maskelyne concluded: "That Mr. Harrison's watch cannot be depended upon to keep the Longitude within a degree in a West India voyage of six weeks". The major flaw in Maskelyne's findings was that John Harrison's watch had already kept the longitude to within *half* a degree on two actual voyages to and from the West Indies. Maskelyne did concede that it was impossible to use the lunar method all the time and the watch would therefore be of use as a back-up to that method, but it was easy to see where he was going with this report considering that he always had and always would favour the lunar method.

John Harrison was old and unwell, but was still full of grit and determination. He issued a booklet criticising the way in which Maskelyne had tested the H4 Watch and made several specific allegations as to why the test was unfairly carried out and therefore would produce a misleading result. Maskelyne did not bother to reply to any of the allegations however and the Harrisons and Maskelyne never spoke to each other again.

Harrison asked the Board for the return of H4 but was refused. He now had to make the two new watches that the Board required without the original for guidance, although he was given two copies of the book that Maskelyne had had printed, entitled *"The Principles of Mr. Harrison's Timekeeper with Plates of the Same"*. In addition to John Harrison making two further watches, the Board asked Larcum Kendall to make an exact copy if he could. The original Act stipulated that a 'Practicable and Useful' method of calculating Longitude must be found and Harrison thought that he had already complied with the terms of the Act. He did not realise that copies would be needed and told the Board that if given the money he would use it to build many such watches, but the Board were unmoved. Copies had to be produced first, the money would be forthcoming later. It has to be said however, that Larcum Kendall (1721-95) was a good choice of watchmaker to produce the copy. He had already acquired a good reputation and had been an apprentice to John Jefferys who had had such an influence on the creation of H4. Kendall had also been one of the experts who had had the workings explained to him in August 1765 so it was fair to assume that if anyone could, he would be able to produce a workable copy.

It took two and a half years for Kendall to complete his copy which is always referred to as K1. In January 1770, the experts who had examined H4 were reassembled to judge how accurate Larcum Kendall's copy was. Kendall, being the maker had to step down, and William Harrison took his place. As it happened, Kendall had done a brilliant job and William Harrison himself was lavish with his praise. It was KI rather than H4 which was chosen to be given to Captain Cook to take on his second great voyage between July 1772 and July 1775. The Board did not choose K1 over H4 because K1 was better, it was just that the Board felt that the two watches were, or should be identical, and they considered that H4 was their property. Cook was very like John Harrison in as much as they both came from humble beginnings and neither had the connections from an early age that in a class conscious period, helped people get on in life. Cook was born in Yorkshire in 1728 and was the son of a farm labourer. Despite the fact that he was a brilliant seaman, he didn't become a commissioned officer until 1768, when he was asked to take the *Endeavour* to Tahiti to study the June 1769 transit of Venus. The second orders that he received on that first trip were to explore the southern polar regions in order to ascertain whether the huge southern land mass that so many people thought existed did in fact exist or not. He returned in 1771 convinced that it did not but many scientists back home refused to accept it. Cook was asked to look again in July 1772, this time with two ships, whereby he captained the *Resolution* and Tobias Furneaux captained the sister ship, the *Adventure*. During the voyage the two ships were separated and the *Adventure* returned to England early, but Cook ploughed on and returned in July 1775 having mapped the entire Pacific Ocean and at the same time, putting to bed once and for all the idea that there was a great southern land mass. It was during this second trip that he took the Larcum Kendall copy K1.

Before that however, by 1770, the same year that Kendall had completed his copy of H4, Harrison had completed *his* first copy, now known as H5, but he could not see how he could possibly make another. He had spent three years making the first and another two years testing it until he was satisfied. By now he was seventy-nine years old, was unwell, had failing eyesight and was utterly exhausted. He felt that it would be utterly impossible for him to build another and live long enough to test it to the Board's satisfaction. Both John and William Harrison knew Lord Sandwich, who had previously taken an interest in the Harrison timepieces. Sandwich was a powerful man who had influence and the following year would become First Lord of the Admiralty. After hearing of the plight of John Harrison, he told the Harrisons that there was only one person who could put this matter right and bring some justice to the proceedings, and that person was King George III. King George was known as Farmer George, which was possibly partly derisory, but mostly it was meant in an affectionate way. He took a keen interest in the land and would often stop and talk to farmhands when he was out riding. However, he was also interested in science and had opened a Royal Observatory at Richmond in time for the 1769 transit of Venus which Captain Cook was to view from the newly discovered Pacific island of Tahiti. Captain Wallis in the *Dolphin* had discovered this island in 1767, although Wallis had originally named it King George's Island.

William wrote to the King in January 1772 and in the letter he detailed the whole story of his father's dealings with the Board of Longitude and the Royal Observatory. He asked if the Watch could be held at the King's Observatory and tested over a period of time to ascertain its accuracy. The King granted both John and William Harrison a lengthy audience in which the King is reported to have said to William: "By God Harrison, I will see you righted". In an account of this meeting, written much later in 1835 by William's son John, he claims that the King muttered under his breath that: "These people have been cruelly treated".

The King was very supportive and gave the H5 Watch to the Observatory Director, Dr. Demainbray for an indoor trial that was scheduled to last for six weeks. Dr. Stephen Charles Triboudet Demainbray (1710-82), the well known astronomer, had spent years lecturing in natural philosophy in Britain and Europe but in 1754 decided to live permanently in Britain and eventually tutored the Prince of Wales (the future King George III) in mathematics and science. It was much later that he was appointed to the post of Observatory Director at Kew, the Prince of Wales by now being King George III.

Dr. Demainbray and the King tested the watch for several weeks but it completely failed at first which shocked William who along with the King and Dr. Demainbray, monitored it each day. It wasn't a little way out, it was a long way out and William simply couldn't understand it. It was the King himself who solved the problem, remembering that he had left two magnets stored in a closet near the clock. Once these were removed, the problem was solved and the King started the tests again. The H5 Watch performed beautifully, and anticipating objections from the Board, the King extended the trial to ten weeks between May and July 1772. The H5 passed the trial admirably and proved accurate to within one third of one second a day.

This was an incredible result, but still the Board prevaricated about the balance of the prize money. In the end, the King advised John Harrison to appeal directly to the government, and in particular to Lord North, the Prime Minister. The government took on the Board who as a result, met on 24th April, 1773 to recapitulate on the whole sorry saga that had gone on for so many years. John Harrison appeared before ministers and simply appealed to their better nature, explaining that he was an old man who had devoted his whole life to solving the problem of longitude but was still being asked to produce the impossible. His arguments still cut no ice with the Board, but fortunately, they did with the government, who in June 1773 awarded John Harrison £8,750, the saga at last coming to an end. Its ending had been helped by a message getting through that Captain James Cook had written the following in his log: "I must here take note, that indeed our error (in longitude) can never be great, so long as we have so good a guide as the Watch". The log of the *Resolution* has several references to the Watch. Another reads: "It would not be doing justice to Mr. Harrison and Mr. Kendall, if I did not own that we have received very great assistance from this useful and valuable timepiece". To Harrison, it was only a partial ending however, as this was a payment made by Parliament to top up the previous £10,000 that he had received from the Board. After all those years, Harrison never did receive the actual prize money originally offered by the Board of Longitude as laid down by the Act in 1714 because nearly half of the original £20,000 had been paid by the government.

Whilst the Reverend Maskelyne was at the very least, unhelpful to John and William Harrison, his own contribution to the calculation of longitude must be acknowledged. Certainly he had a vested interest in the lunar method but it is not surprising given his educational background and the amount of work that he put into it. That he toiled on it for years shows that he was sincere in his belief in this method. He produced the first volume of the *"Nautical Almanac and Astronomical Ephemeris"* in 1766 and continued to have a hand in it right up to the day he died in 1811. In publishing this work, he had reduced the calculations a sea captain had to make from four hours to just thirty minutes. It came nowhere near Harrison's method which produced a reading virtually in seconds, but it was an extraordinary achievement nonetheless. Sailors continued to use the Almanac long after Maskelyne's death because his predictions contained in it went through to 1815.

Other astronomers continued his work and the Almanac is still valid today. Maskelyne cannot be written off and the Almanac is thought by many to be his long lasting contribution to the field of navigation. Included in it is the most extraordinary detail which has twelve pages of data for each month and the moon's position calculated every three hours with regard to the sun. The Almanac and its companion volume *"Requisite Tables"* enabled sailors to have a reliable method for them to calculate their positions when at sea.

After all the years of toil and arguments, John Harrison actually received more than the original £20,000 put up by the 1714 Act. Over the years, he received a total of £23,065 for his achievements. This was made up of £4,315 in various payments by the Board of Longitude to help him continue his work, £10,000 as an interim payment for H4 in 1765 and then the final payment of £8,750 from the government in June, 1773. After receiving the final payment from the government, John Harrison lived for less than three years and was probably too old and infirm to enjoy his money very much. However, at least that final payment meant that he could relax knowing that the job was done, that he had achieved recognition for helping to solve the longitude problem, and that he could live his final years out in peace. He left an incredible legacy and some highly talented watchmakers followed him and carried on his work. One was the famous Thomas Mudge (1715-1794) who in his younger days had been apprenticed to George Graham who in turn had helped John Harrison's early work. Mudge spent years making a series of timekeepers in order to come up with the perfect marine watch. The first of these was assessed in Greenwich by the Board in 1774 and is now in the British Museum.

Larcum Kendall of course was another and whilst Mudge and Kendall made three marine timekeepers each, another watchmaker called John Arnold (1736-1799) actually succeeded in making several hundred which were very high quality. He managed this by getting other craftsmen to carry out the routine work whilst he finished the timepiece off by adjusting the more difficult final areas of construction. During the period of Arnold becoming well known, the word 'Chronometer' came into general use and became the more popular way of describing the marine watch. The term caught on when it appeared in a pamphlet written by Alexander Dalrymple (1737-1808) of the East India Company, and it was entitled *'Some Notes Useful to Those Who Have Chronometers at Sea'*. Dalrymple was a clever man, an able navigator and astronomer, but he had too high an opinion of his own worth. He had spent years being a thorn in the side of Captain Cook, claiming for years that the great southern land mass existed and disbelieving Cook when the latter claimed that it didn't. However, that he had talent cannot be denied.

Another watchmaker who became a rival of John Arnold's was Thomas Earnshaw (1749-1829) who turned out brilliant chronometers on a scale not even managed by Arnold. Earnshaw actually managed to achieve what no other marine clockmaker achieved, his work finding approval from none other than the Reverend Nevil Maskelyne, although even then Maskelyne irritated Earnshaw by insisting on year long trials for the watches which eventually Earnshaw managed to get reduced to six months.

Arnold and Earnshaw sold their chronometers all over the world for use on ships. The first marine chronometer was built by John Harrison in 1737 and in that year there was but one. In 1815, thanks to the like of craftsmen such as Arnold and Earnshaw, the number grew to approximately five thousand and the problem of calculating longitude had been solved.

John Harrison's last home was in Red Lion Square, London, and there is a plaque to celebrate his life and achievements on the wall of Summit House which is situated in the south side of the square in which he lived. He died on 24th March, 1776, his eighty-third birthday and was buried in the grounds of St. John's Church, Hampstead alongside his second wife Elizabeth and William, their son who was such a support to his father over so many years. When we remember the constant battles that John Harrison had with the Board of Longitude who prevaricated over so many years before he received his just rewards, it seemed that in life, everything came late to him. Things did not change in death either, because it was not until the 24th March, 2006, the 313th anniversary of his birth and 230th anniversary of his death, that a memorial tablet to him was unveiled at Westminster Abbey. This tablet was well overdue but at last he was given the same recognition as George Graham and 'The Father of English Watchmaking', Thomas Tompion, both men actually being buried in the Abbey.

On the 22nd October, 1707, Admiral Sir Cloudsley Shovel lost two thousand men in one dreadful accident due to an inaccurate reading of longitude. With that thought in mind, it is impossible to estimate the thousands of lives that have been saved since John Harrison achieved final recognition from Parliament in June 1773. To imagine those numbers must be John Harrison's great and lasting legacy.

-oOOo-

10
Captain James Cook
(1728-1779)

*Brilliant naval officer who went on three exploratory trips round
the world between 1768-71, 1772-1775, and 1776 until his death
at Hawaii in February 1779.*

James Cook was born on 27th October, 1728 at Marton-in-Cleveland in
Yorkshire. Although born in humble circumstances in an age where status
reigned supreme, he rose to become one of the greatest naval officers of all time,
and a book on influential people of the 18th century cannot be complete without
a chapter on Cook.

His father was also called James, and he was a farm labourer. He was
Scottish, having been baptised on 4th March, 1694 in the kirk of Ednam, which
was a village near Kelso. Times were hard in Scotland and many people
emigrated to America to start a new life, others merely went south, and attracted
by the profitable mining area of north Yorkshire, James senior made his way to
Marton where he found work as a labourer. He met a girl named Grace Pace and
they married in 1725, Grace giving birth to her first child John in 1726. James
was born in 1728 and by the time that he was eight years old, he was already
helping his father working in the fields along with his brother John. James was
an intelligent boy, and his parents wanted a better future for him, so they
arranged for him to have an apprenticeship with a shopkeeper from the village
of Staithes, called William Sanderson. Sanderson's shop was both a grocery and
drapery, and the family consisting of Sanderson, his wife and two children, lived
above the shop.

Apprentices did not normally live with the family so James had to take his
meals downstairs and sleep under the counter of the shop – an extraordinary
scenario to us today, but one that was accepted by the young James. He carried
out his duties of sweeping the shop and closing and opening it as well as serving
in it, but he had met many of the fishermen in the evening and had become very
interested in the stories they told about their lives on the sea. James eventually
asked Mr. Sanderson if he could be released from his obligation and Sanderson,
agreed, arranging for James to have an apprenticeship with John Walker, a
shipowner and master mariner who was based in the port of Whitby, not far
from Staithes. The coal trade to London was the main source of profit for
Walker as London needed a million tons of coal a year in the 1740's and it
needed a thousand ships to keep up with this demand. The ship used was a
Whitby cat, later made famous by Cook himself as it was built with a shallow
draught which made it safer to sail closer to land. Cook's living conditions
improved somewhat when he joined John Walker, as he had his own room and

lived and ate with the family in the way we would consider normal today. When Cook was eighteen, a lady called Mary Prowd, who was employed by Walker as housekeeper, took him under her wing and encouraged him to study the subjects that would be useful to him in later life, such as learning about longitude and latitude, reading charts, and navigation. He also attended a school for apprentices that was situated in the town. In 1750, Cook had finished his apprenticeship and was no longer a boy. He was in fact, twenty-two years old, a fully fledged sailor and a man who was clearly loving what he was doing.

Cook was very confident of his own ability, and in 1752, at the age of twenty-four, had passed all his exams that would enable him to be Master's Mate. Three years later, Walker offered Cook a ship of his own, but to his surprise, James turned him down. He had sailed in the Baltic, the North Sea, the channel and the Irish Sea, but it wasn't enough and he wanted to further his horizons. He was a great reader, had studied previous exploration of the Pacific and now wanted to experience it himself.

It was to this end that he resigned from John Walker's employ and at the relatively advanced age of twenty-seven, volunteered for the Royal Navy. Cook was a talented sailor, and he joined up with the confidence that his abilities would be recognised and that he would soon reach officer rank but in this he was to be disappointed. It came eventually, but it took many years and this delay was almost certainly due to the fact that he was of humble birth and had no rich friends to sponsor him.

Cook signed on the *Eagle* on 17th June, 1755 which was being fitted out at Portsmouth. The Captain, Joseph Hamar, complained about the state of his crew and he wrote to the Admiralty – "I do not believe there is a worse manned ship in the navy". Cook, with his fine ability, stood out and although initially taken on as Able Seaman, was quickly promoted to Master's Mate, the rank he had held with Walker. The Admiralty was not best pleased with Hamar's command however, and he was eventually replaced by Captain Hugh Palliser (1723-96), a move that was to have beneficial results both in the long and short term for Cook. Palliser was an experienced officer having entered the navy at eleven years of age and received his first command in 1746 taking over the sloop *Weasel* and distinguished himself by capturing six French privateers in the English Channel. It was in recognition of this action that he was made Post Captain on 25th November, 1746. He took command of the *Eagle* in October 1755 which is when he first met Cook who had been serving on her for the previous four months. He was later to become an Admiral of the White as well as a Lord of the Admiralty and was a very positive support for James Cook throughout the latter's career.

It was in the *Eagle* that Cook first saw action. War with France was not formally declared until May, 1756, but there were sporadic bursts of action between the countries ships before then. On 15th November, the *Eagle* was part of the fleet headed by Admiral Lord Byng (1704-57) when they came across a French ship-of-the-line. It was being battered by the Atlantic storms and soon surrendered after a further battering by the British ships. That night, Cook entered in his log "Received on board from the *Esperance* 26 prisoners at 4 o'clock. *Esperance* on fire and there being no possibility of keeping her above water". The French ship sinking meant that Cook's first chance of prize money had disappeared with her to the bottom.

The *Eagle* spent a great deal of time after that being refitted in Plymouth, and she next saw action on 30th May, 1757. She had only left Plymouth two days before when along with the *Medway*, she sighted the 50 gun French ship, *Duc d'Aquitaine*. Palliser brought the *Eagle* alongside her and poured a broadside into the French ship. Fighting at sea in those days was absolutely deadly as ships simply came alongside each other and poured broadside after broadside into each other until one of them either struck her colours or simply could fight no longer. This method of fighting continued right to the end of the century and didn't alter until a few enlightened British Admirals changed tactics, notably Admiral Duncan at the battle of Copenhagen in 1797, Admiral Sir John Jervis at the Battle of Cape St. Vincent in the same year, and Admiral Nelson at Trafalgar in 1805. In these battles, the British Admirals employed two lines of ships to attack the enemy sailing at right angles towards them splitting the enemy fleet into three sections and virtually putting the van of the enemy fleet out of action until it had time to put about and re-join the battle. However, the traditional method of warfare was being used during the action that Cook was taking part in, and the battle between the *Eagle* and *Duc d'Aquitaine* was suitably bloody as the *Eagle's* log shows: "She returned fire. We engaged about three quarters of an hour at point blank range. She then struck. The *Medway* then came up astern. We were employed getting prisoners on board and securing our masts and rigging. We killed 50 men and wounded 30. Our casulties were 10 dead and 80 wounded." The *Eagle* did not get off lightly, sustaining great damage, and her "Sails rent almost to rags". Palliser reported that he was very pleased with the conduct of his crew during this action.

Cook was promoted to Master on 18th October, 1757, days before his twenty-ninth birthday and he took up his position in the *Pembroke*. She was a new ship having been built at Plymouth in that year and weighed 1,222 tons, carrying 60 guns. William Pitt the Elder (1708-78) was Secretary of State, and de facto Prime Minister. He conducted war against the French more aggressively than had been carried out by his predecessors, and his aim was to remove French occupation of North America. Sea power was essential, as in order to protect British interests, Britain had to have control of the St. Lawrence river which at the time was controlled by the French. The Pembroke was part of the fleet commanded by Admiral The Hon. Edward Boscawen (1711-61), a distinguished naval officer who had acquitted himself well in many battles over a lengthy naval career. His one possible black mark was the fact that he had been responsible for the court-martial of Admiral John Byng (1704-57), who with a poorly equipped fleet, had failed to take the island of Minorca from the French in 1756. He was arrested and brought back to England and although the court cleared him of cowardice, he was sentenced to be shot for neglect of duty. The court felt obliged to pass this sentence, but strongly recommended leniency which sadly was denied by the then reigning monarch, King George II. Byng faced the firing squad with courage and dignity when the sentence was carried out on board his ship, the ironically named *Monarch* and the decision to execute him remains controversial to this day.

Boscawen's fleet set sail from Plymouth on 22nd February, 1758 and crossing the Atlantic, Cook found himself busy with the day to day running of the ship. It was during this voyage that he first became aware of the effects of scurvy, prevalent on ships at that time but absolutely dreaded by sailors. The symptoms were so bad that death was often seen as a merciful release. Scurvy was caused by a lack of Vitamin C in the sailors' diet which was very limited due to the lack of fresh fruit and vegetables, and more men died from the disease than died in any wars that were fought, ferocious though these wars almost always were.

It was during this time that Cook became interested in surveying. He became friends with an army officer, Lieutenant Samuel Holland (1728-1801). Holland and Cook were born in the same year and took to each other straight away. The friendship between Holland and Cook developed in the relatively early stages of both their careers. Holland went on to play a very distinguished role in the army and was the first Surveyor General of British North America from 1764 until 1770. Holland had showed Cook how to reproduce outlines of coastlines in miniature and so can take credit for helping to start his friend's interest in the subject which would help Cook to achieve future greatness in his own career in years to come. This was a life changing time for James Cook – his interest in both surveying and the elimination of scurvy happened at almost the same time and would stand him in good stead for his future promotion to Lieutenant and command of his first ship, the *Endeavour* in 1768. However, he would still have to wait some years for that to happen and in the meantime, Quebec was eventually captured and the ever ambitious Cook served with distinction for several more years, firstly transferred in 1760 to *The Northumberland* under Captain Colville but there was less for the men to do at this time due to the end of hostilities after the capture of Quebec. The ship returned to England, docking at Spithead on 18th October, 1762 and Cook was discharged on 11th November. He made his way to London and found lodgings in Stepney. Whilst he was there he met a lady called Mrs. Mary Blackburn who had been married to a Samuel Batts before his death. Samuel and Mary Batts ran the Bell Alehouse at Execution Dock in Wapping and in 1742 had a daughter called Elizabeth. Elizabeth was baptised in Wapping on 31st January but sadly, Samuel died a short while later in the same year, although we cannot be sure of the exact date. This left Mary to run the alehouse and raise her daughter alone, but three years later, she met and married John Blackburn. Mary herself was originally Mary Smith, daughter of Charles Smith and his wife Elizabeth (nee Roper). Charles was a Bermondsey Currier, a currier being a person who treated and coloured leather and the trade was based in Bermondsey. On the Batts' side of the family, Elizabeth's grandfather (Samuel's father) was Richard Batts who had married Sarah. Unfortunately we know nothing more about Sarah, not even her maiden name. Richard Batts was a mariner based in Lambeth, South London.

Their son Samuel was baptised on 4th November, 1686 at St. Botolph near Aldgate. Samuel was apprenticed to Edward Hutchinson of the Poulters' Company on 15th October, 1702 and in December 1715, married a Sarah Thompson. They had a daughter, also called Sarah, who was born on 6th

September, 1716 and baptised a week later at St, Olave's in Bermondsey. This Sarah would become Elizabeth's half sister. Sarah Batts (Samuel's wife) died a few years later, and Samuel married Mary Smith on 21st December, 1726. This Mary Smith, now Mary Batts, was Elizabeth Batts' (later Cook) mother.

We do not know exactly how it came to be that James and Elizabeth met, but it is generally thought that it was when James was visiting Mary, Elizabeth's mother. James had just turned thirty-four whilst Elizabeth was an attractive intelligent young girl of twenty. James was a warrant officer in the navy and made it clear that he was looking for a wife, wanted to be married as soon as was possible, and was attracted to Elizabeth more or less straight away. They certainly married very quickly after meeting – 21st December, 1762 at St. Margaret's Church. James would have made it clear to Elizabeth that as a serving naval officer, he would be away much of the time, but this did not deter the feisty Elizabeth Batts and the marriage was a happy one, although as Cook warned, subject to the most painful partings, often for years during a period where there was little means of communication.

A very short time after their marriage, a week to be exact, Admiral Lord Colville sent the following letter to the Admiralty:

"Sir,

Mr. Cook, late Master of the *Northumberland*, acquaints me that he has laid before their Lordships all his draughts and observations relating to the River St. Lawrence, part of the coasts of Nova Scotia, and Newfoundland.

On this occasion, I beg to inform their Lordships that that from my experience of Mr. Cook's genius and capacity, I think him well qualified for the work he has performed and for greater undertakings of the same kind. These draughts being made under my own eye, I can venture to say they may be the means of directing many in the right way, but cannot mislead any-

I am sir, your most obedient and humble servant,
COLVILLE"

The *Grenville*, with the newly married Cook on board, sailed off to survey the southern coast of Newfoundland. Cook carried out his tasks with the usual distinction, and was sent home on the *Tweed* where she anchored at Spithead on 29th November, 1763. Cook returned home to find that he was the father of a seven week old boy, also named James, and he, Elizabeth and his new son moved into a new home - 7, Assembly Row in the Mile End Road. Cook had to commute to the Admiralty each day to work on the most recent charts that he had brought back from Newfoundland and Labrador, and whilst he had nothing against Thomas Graves, the Secretary to the Admiralty, he was delighted when Graves was replaced by Hugh Palliser who he already knew, and who was to have such a huge impact on Cook's later career. Although he felt that he was being held back for promotion to officer class by his humble birth, the tide started to turn very slowly in Cook's favour when he surveyed the Burgeo Islands on the south coast of Newfoundland on 5th August, 1766. There was to be an eclipse of the sun that day and Cook was prepared with his instruments for it. The observations that he took were brought to the attention of the Royal Society at a meeting on 30th April, 1767. Cook already knew Hugh Palliser; he was soon to know Joseph Banks, the great botanist and a member of the Royal Society. To get on in the navy, you had to have high ability, but that wasn't enough, you also had to have influential friends and whilst there was a long way to go, these were gradually getting to know James Cook.

In 1761, there had been a transit of Venus and the observing of this had had an international flavour. France, England, Sweden, Italy, Russia and Spain were all involved, but despite this co-operation the sighting hadn't been a success. There was to be another transit of Venus in June 1769 and then not another until 1874 and 1882, so it was imperative that the next sighting was more accurate. The Royal Society set up a committee with the following brief: "To consider and report on the places where it would be advisable to take observations, the methods to be pursued, and the persons best fitted to carry out the work." The committee first met on 12th November, 1767 – a little late given the fact that any expedition would have to leave England by the summer of the following year if it was to be sure of reaching one of the Pacific Islands by June 1769, which is where one of the exploration sites was to be. It was still undecided as to who was going to lead the expedition and a fierce argument started between Alexander Dalrymple and the Admiralty as to who it should be. Dalrymple (1737-1808) was a hot headed man who had a passion for travel, map making and exploration. There was no doubting that he had talent but probably not as much as he thought that he actually did possess. He was convinced that there was a great southern continent, Terra Australis Incognito, waiting to be discovered and he thought that the main purpose of the expedition was to seek and find it, claiming it for Britain. Many eminent scientists agreed with him feeling that it had to be there, if for no other reason than a southern land mass would balance the world. Dalrymple's talents were widely recognised, but when the Royal Society offered him the post of senior observer, he said that he would accept only on the condition "than that of having the management of the ship intended for the service". The reply from the Admiralty was swift and unambiguous – the answer was no. They said that the idea was "entirely repugnant to the regulations of the navy". It is believed that Sir Edward Hawke, Admiral of the Fleet and First Lord of the Admiralty was particularly furious with the suggestion and re-iterated that only a serving officer could command one of his Majesty's ships. Hawke (1705-81), later to become the 1st Baron Hawke, had had a brilliant career in the navy and as First Lord had immense power. Despite this, the egotistical Dalrymple wouldn't give up on the idea, but he hadn't a hope of succeeding as other powerful forces in the Admiralty were already taking notice of Cook, one of these being Philip Stephen, the Secretary to the Admiralty who knew Cook personally and was much impressed with his work. There was also Hugh Palliser, and with these two powerful men behind Cook, Dalrymple never had a hope. Cook's appointment was confirmed at a full meeting of the Royal Society on 5th May, 1768. He was also promoted to Lieutenant, the commissioned rank that he had hoped for for so long, and was given command of the *Endeavour*, a Whitby Bark that Cook loved so much, and this was to take effect from 25th May, 1768.

Up until now, it had still been undecided as to exactly which island in the Pacific that Cook was to observe the transit of Venus from, but five days prior to Cook's formal appointment, Captain Samuel Wallis (1728-95) of the *Dolphin* had arrived back in England. Wallis, along with Philip Carteret of the *Swallow*, had been sent to explore and find the great southern land, Terra Australis Incognito but the two ships had separated when they emerged from the Magellan Strait after encountering particularly rough weather. Carteret continued alone, and although his ship was inferior to the *Dolphin*, still made important discoveries, not least that of Pitcairn Island, which was to become famous years later as the home of some of the *Bounty* mutineers. Wallis however, had discovered an island in the Pacific which was far more significant, at least for the Admiralty's needs. He had come across Tahiti which he named King George's Island and moored at Matavai Bay on 19th June, 1767, taking possession of her in the name of the King. Lieutenant Tobias Furneaux, who was later to captain the *Adventure* in Cook's second voyage, was the officer who took charge of the landing and planted the flag. As this was the first time they had seen a European ship, there were inevitable misunderstandings between the *Dolphin's* crew and the local people, which led to tragic hostilities between the crew and the islanders. The local people, possibly believing that the *Dolphin* had come to invade their land and to take it from them, attacked the ship with stones which whilst hurled with great ferocity and accuracy, were no match for the power of the guns of the *Dolphin*. Naturally, Captain Wallis had to defend his ship but one has to question the necessity of the cruelty that happened next.

After ordering his guns to be fired at the canoes, the islanders were so frightened that they immediately dispersed and this had the effect of not only clearing the surrounding sea, but struck so much terror into the islanders, that they fled the beaches and went inland. The women and children, now so far away from the shore, thought that they were safe, but Wallis then ordered his guns to fire into the woods and so terrified were the islanders that they disappeared further inland. Wallis, seeing that the coast was clear then ordered his crew to be armed and go ashore and destroy every canoe that they could see, a task that they carried out with ruthless efficiency. Fifty canoes, many of them sixty feet long were smashed to pieces and the Tahitian people who had no tools that were made of iron must have been devastated as the construction of these boats would almost certainly have taken years to complete.

It says everything about the extraordinary forgiving nature of the Tahitian people, that once they were told that the European sailors wanted nothing more than to have friendly social intercourse with the natives and to be provided with fresh food and water, friendly terms between the two peoples were immediately achieved and peace broke out. A Tahitian woman of middle years came to the ship the next day. During the fight of the preceding day when the canoes had initially attacked the ship, her husband and three of her sons were killed and she was so grief stricken that she had to be helped on board the *Dolphin*. However, once she had partially recovered her composure, she requested that two hogs be delivered to the crew, and held out her hand to the gunner, the crew member put in charge of trading, as a gesture of friendliness, but once the hogs were handed over, she would accept nothing in return.

The ship only stayed six weeks before starting her journey home. The men of the *Dolphin* had never seen anything like this paradise island and George Robertson, the Master of the *Dolphin*, wrote "It is impossible to describe the beautiful prospects we beheld in this charming spot". It was a beautiful island with breadfruit, bananas, yam and other fruit growing in abundance – a perfect place for Cook's ship to settle and observe the transit of Venus.

One of the *Endeavour's* officers was an American born man by the name of John Gore. He had sailed in the *Dolphin* twice before, once with Wallis, and prior to that with Jack Byron, grandfather of the famous poet, so he had already circumnavigated the world twice by the time that he was appointed to the *Endeavour*. He was a Petty Officer on the *Dolphin*, but such were his outstanding abilities, that he virtually took over the running of the ship with Tobias Furneaux, the second Lieutenant, when Wallis and his first Lieutenant, William Clarke were unwell on the trip. He was barely home from this voyage when he was appointed to the *Endeavour*. He missed out on Cook's second trip but re-joined Cook on the latter's third trip, bringing the expedition home when Cook was killed at Hawaii. On Cook's first trip, Gore was to be Third Lieutenant on the voyage of the *Endeavour*. There were several others from the *Dolphin* who joined Cook on the trip but the man who Cook had most dealings with on the voyage was to be Zachary Hicks, a twenty-nine year old London born man who had just finished a voyage with the *Hornet*. Cook considered him very reliable and he was made second Lieutenant on the *Endeavour*. The ship's surgeon was William Monkhouse from Penrith and he was highly thought of by Cook, along with William Perry, the surgeon's mate, who was also held in high regard. Probably the most flamboyant person on the trip was Charles Clerke, the Master's Mate. Always cheerful, a great storyteller, womaniser, and was always good for a great story, which he usually told with the aid of the contents of a bottle.

Cook's orders were in two parts. They were signed on 30th July, 1768 and the first part was to observe the transit of Venus from the newly discovered island of Tahiti. The second part of the orders were to remain sealed until the first part were completed, but whilst officially secret, it was almost certainly known to Cook and his officers that they were to find and map Dalrymple's great southern continent. Cook didn't think it existed, but the received wisdom of the Royal Society, the Admiralty, and Joseph Banks was that it did.

Joseph Banks (1743-1820) and his nine-man entourage were to join the *Endeavour*. There is a separate chapter on Banks detailing his character and career, but at the time of the *Endeavour's* departure, he was a twenty-five-year-old wealthy largely self-taught botanist. Educated at Harrow and Eton, he was nevertheless totally disinterested in Latin and Greek and discovered a love of plant life that was to remain with him all his days during a life that was long and fulfilled. With him were the fellow botanist, Daniel Solander (1733-82), a clever man and a pupil of Carl Linnaeus (1707-78), the Swedish naturalist and physician whose method of plant classification is still in use today. Linnaeus was a brilliant man who studied both medicine and botany but settled for the latter as a career. His contribution to botany was huge and his writings are far too numerous to deal with here, but the Linnean Society which was founded in his honour in 1788 still holds his manuscripts and collections in London. His disciples, Solander and Banks, were to remain firm friends all their lives. With them were Astronomer Charles Green who had gone to Jamaica in 1761 to study the previous transit of Venus, the artist Sydney Parkinson, a rather gentle mannered Quaker who was loved by all the crew, the draughtsman, Alexander Buchan who was an epileptic and died after a fit soon after arriving at Tahiti, and Hermann Sporing, a watchmaker but who was on the trip as Solander's assistant and clerk. Banks also brought four servants and his two greyhounds with him.

The *Endeavour*, with Captain Cook, his officers and crew, along with Joseph Banks and the members of his entourage, set sail from Plymouth on 26th August, 1768 on the first leg of their voyage, to round the Horn, and once reaching the Pacific, to make their way north to Tahiti in order to observe the transit of Venus.

Their first port of call was on 12th September, when they reached Funchal, which was the capital of the Portugese island of Madeira. The weather was warm and they were greeted with great hospitality, Banks and Solander quickly taking advantage of this to travel round the island digging up as many different plants as they could. In the short time they had there, they managed to collect hundreds of different species. Given the warm weather and hospitality, it was especially sad that they were to lose one of the crew at Funchal. On the 14th, two days after arriving there, the stream anchor had slipped due to the carelessness of one of the crew who had made it fast, and a very experienced sailor, Alex Weir, the Masters Mate, launched a boat to find the anchor. Weir and the members of his crew found the anchor and were retrieving it when Weir got caught in the buoy rope and was pulled overboard by the weight of the anchor itself. Weir and the anchor were recovered, but not in time to save Weir who had long since drowned. It must have been a bitter blow for Cook who in addition to carrying out his orders, wanted to bring his crew back to England safely, and this incident happened very early in the voyage.

On the 16th September, two days after the drowning of Weir, another incident occurred. Two of the ship's crew, seaman Henry Stephens and marine Thomas Dunister were flogged with a dozen lashes each for refusing to eat fresh meat. To us today, it may sound harsh, but the disease of scurvy was so lethal on board ships, that Cook was determined to avoid it at all costs and felt that he had no option other than to set an example to the other members of the crew. Scurvy was an appalling disease and far more men died from it than died in battle. The symptoms included nausea, swollen and bleeding gums, teeth rotting and falling out, wounds that had been healed for years suddenly opening up again and the tongue swelling up until it was almost too big for the person's mouth. In fact, the disease was so dreadful that death was often considered a merciful release. The disease appeared when a person's diet was short of vitamin C, and Cook was determined that this would not happen to his crew although he knew that whilst the men would be perfectly happy to eat fresh vegetables, they would not be so keen on sauerkraut. Cook was adamant that they should and in order to achieve this, he ordered all the officers to eat sauerkraut as well as the fresh meat and lemon juice so that the crew had no option but to do the same. Prior to Cook taking the *Endeavour* out, scurvy was rampant throughout ships on long voyages and it was he who gained a great deal of credit for keeping his crews free of the disease, something that up until then, sea captains had singularly failed to do. In fact, Cook has sometimes been given the credit for actually discovering the cure for scurvy, but this simply is not true. What he did however, was to put into practise the ideas of James Lind (1716-94), the eminent Scottish physician who had worked on the problem years before Cook, and had written his famous *'Treatise of the Scurvy'* and published it in 1753. Today it is deemed a medical classic but it was inexplicably ignored for many years causing terrible suffering and unnecessary loss of life. Lind had started his naval career by serving as a surgeon's mate before qualifying in medicine at Edinburgh after which he became physician at the Gaslar naval hospital in Gosport. Sadly, very few sea captains followed Lind's ideas and Cook was one of the first to take them seriously and virtually removed scurvy from his crews by following Lind's ideas of taking fresh lemon juice along with the eating of fresh vegetables. For this he deserves great praise as it had never been applied strictly enough by officers before him, which meant that the disease carried on decimating crews for years longer than was necessary. Even after Lind and Cook's work on preventing scurvy, the Admiralty were slow to react, and it wasn't until 1795, the year after Lind's death, that the Admiralty issued the order that each ship should carry lemon juice. If the fact that the Admiralty were dragging its feet over such an important issue seems extraordinary, there was a naval pioneer who was sailing a century before Cook and who insisted on his crews being fed with oranges and lemons and where possible, fresh meat. His name was Sir John Narbrough (1640-88) and a quote from his journal circa 1670 reads:-

"I killed many ducks and geese and hars and ostorages here. There are good fowls in the winter, a great store of mullets in the summer and very good salt in the ponds".

Sir John was a man ahead of his time by a hundred years and some of his ideas resembled those of Cook. He cared about his crew and their health, and he was very accurate with his charting of new territories. Added to that his respect shown to the local people of wherever he visited shows him to have been a very knowledgeable as well as a humane man. Sadly, he was never given the credit that he was due during his lifetime and his journal was never published – indeed it has only recently been discovered at the Centre for Kentish Studies lying unread with the papers that belong to the Earls of Romney. However, none of this should detract from what Captain Cook achieved in terms of health at sea.

Before they set sail again, Cook had the crew load the *Endeavour* with stores to see them through the next stage of their trip. 270 pounds of fresh meat along with a live bullock for future slaughter, over 3,000 gallons of wine, 10 tons of water, along with sweetmeats and poultry were also added. They bade their generous hosts farewell and at midnight on the 18th September, slipped anchor and set sail for Rio de Janeiro.

On the 13th November they anchored off Rio and Banks was captivated by the beautiful scenery that beheld them. Miles of white sandy beaches flanked by forests and the surrounding mountains gave a very misleading scenario of peace and tranquillity. Cook sent Zachary Hicks and Charles Clerke ashore to make themselves known but Cook realised that some sort of trouble was brewing when after a period of time they failed to appear. The boat finally returned with a Brazilian army officer but without Hicks and Clerke who were to be detained until Cook himself came ashore. Two more boats full of soldiers then appeared, one boatload of soldiers coming on board the *Endeavour* along with several of the Viceroy's officers asking questions as to the nature of the English ships voyage.

Cook was informed that Hicks and Clerke would be returned once Cook himself came ashore. The problem the Viceroy had was believing that Cook, along with Banks and his fellow scientists could be remotely interested in the plant life and general natural history of this country. He also had problems believing that Cook wanted further provisions as it had only been eight weeks since they had left Madeira. Despite the British being given strict orders by the Viceroy not to venture ashore, the irrepressible Banks along with Solander and Parkinson took themselves off to explore and on 26th November, Banks went ashore on his own and even managed to ingratiate himself with some of the locals, visiting their houses and being warmly welcomed. Banks was not going to be held back by the "Illiterate impolite gentry" as he called the Viceroy and his officers. After nearly two weeks of negotiations conducted with a great deal of ill will, the *Endeavour* finally set sail and got clear of Rio de Janeiro on 7th December with a great deal of relief all round. Another tragedy was to happen however, as a seaman, Peter Flower, who Cook had known for over five years, slipped from the rigging and fell overboard, and like Alex Weir before him, drowned before anything could be done. They were now on their way to Tierra Del Feugo hoping for a more peaceful time. Christmas Day arrived and with it came calm weather and a great deal of alcohol was consumed. Banks noted in his journal: "All good Christians, that is to say, all hands get abominably drunk so that at night there was scarce a sober man in the ship, wind thank god very moderate or the Lord knows what would have become of us." On Wednesday, 11th January, 1769, the *Endeavour* sighted Teirra del Fuego and on Monday the 16th she anchored in the Bay of Good Success. They were greeted by thirty or forty local people who didn't seem at all nervous of Cook and his officers. Cook and his men tried to trade with the Feigians, but the only thing they seemed interested in were beads. Cook states in his journal for that day: "They are extremely fond of any red thing and seemed to set more value on beads made of small shells or bones about their necks. They did not taste any strong liquor, neither did they seem fond of our provisions." Meanwhile, Banks, Solander, Charles Green, Surgeon Monkhouse, Alexander Buchan and Banks' servants had gone in to the country to collect plants and any other specimens that they could find. Unfortunately, the weather became freezing and they had to stay out all night in the biting cold. Cook was very uneasy realising that they may not survive such extreme cold, and it was with great relief that he saw them return the next day, although it had been a close run thing. Solander had almost succumbed, Buchan had suffered an epileptic fit and two of the servants had perished. Cook could have been angry at the young Banks' recklessness, but it was more likely that he was merely relieved to see him return alive and seemingly fit. It would not have looked good for James Cook if he had lost the famous Joseph Banks on the voyage, let alone so early and before they had even carried out the first of their two tasks which Cook was hoping so desperately would make his name. It must have been with some relief when the *Endeavour* headed off from Tierra del Feugo on 21st January, 1769, rounded the Horn, and set a course for Tahiti.

Although the journey to Tahiti was fairly straightforward, there was a sad incident on the 25th March. A young marine, William Greenslade, who had been no trouble on the trip, had got involved in an argument with other marines over the sharing out of a piece of sealskin which was given to him to look after. It is thought that it was to be made into tobacco pouches but that no part of it was the property of Greenslade – he was merely looking after it. It is not clear why Greenslade had the sealskin in his possession, but he did, and although told he was not to have a share, he nonetheless cut himself a piece and although there was a lot of anger expressed on both sides, the other marines involved in the incident didn't feel it necessary to make a complaint. However, one man, Sergeant John Edgecombe did take exception, and wishing to report the matter to Captain Cook, pursued Greenslade who gave Edgecombe the slip and at 7pm went over the side and was drowned, apparently committing suicide presumably fearing the severity of the punishment that he was likely to receive. Captain Cook's entry into the log of the 26th showed that he knew nothing of the incident until Greenslade was reported missing – the end of Cook's entry reads:- "I was neither made acquainted with the theft or the circumstances attending it until the man was gone". Greenslade had been a quiet, withdrawn boy and had given no trouble prior to this incident, and it was particularly sad as for a first offence, his punishment may have been lenient.

The *Endeavour* continued to sail northwest and on 11th April they sighted Tahiti, or King George's Island as Captain Wallis of the *Dolphin* had named it nearly two years before when he discovered it. On Thursday, 13th April, 1769, the *Endeavour* anchored in Matavai Bay and were welcomed by the local people who came to greet the ship in their canoes. Many of the Tahitian people recognised some of the crew from the *Dolphin's* trip two years before, and the most notable of these was probably John Gore, a midshipman with Wallis, but a now a Lieutenant with Captain Cook. Although there had been initial problems between the sailors and the Tahitians on the *Dolphin's* trip, these had been settled well before the ship left the island, and so the welcome the *Endeavour* received was rapturous. Cook was aware that it was in the nature of Tahitians to be generous with gifts and with love, but he also knew that they had a propensity to steal anything that they saw, and was therefore determined that relations with the islanders would remain cordial and that there should be no misunderstandings or quarrels. He therefore laid down a set of five rules that the crew members had to abide by, the first of which was one of the most important:

"To endeavour by every fair means to cultivate a friendship with the natives and to treat them with all imaginable humanity."

This set the tone for the other four rules that dealt with the practical aspects of the trading between the two sets of people. William Bligh, who was to sail with Cook on his third trip which commenced in 1776, used a very similar set of rules when he was Captain of the *Bounty* which reached Tahiti in October 1788. He had obviously learned these rules from Cook, but sadly for Bligh, they were to work a little too well, as Bligh's crew grew very attached to the Tahitian people which almost certainly led to the famous mutiny.

Meanwhile, on the *Endeavour*, Cook and Surgeon Monkhouse had been extremely careful with regard to the health of the crew, and Cook was pleased that they had reached Tahiti without a single person becoming ill with scurvy. Some of the crew had shown signs of the disease but on 13th April, 1769, the day they reached Tahiti, Cook was to enter the following in his log:-

"...Wort was made of the Malt and at the discrition of the Surgeon given to every man that had the least symptoms of Scurvy upon him, by this Means and the care and Vigilance of Mr. Munkhous the Surgeon this disease was prevented from geting a footing in the Ship..."

The *Endeavour* had lost two men, Alex Weir and Peter Flower by accidental drowning, and marine William Greenslade by apparent suicide. They had not lost a single person through illness although sadly the draughtsman Alexander Buchan had an epileptic fit a few days later and died on the 16th April, three days after they had arrived in Tahiti.

Previously, on the 14th, they were entertained by two chiefs, Tubourai and Dootahah who brought them fish, breadfruit, and coconuts and relations between the crew of the *Endeavour* and the local people seemed very good. However, despite knowing about the Tahitians habit of stealing, Daniel Solander and Surgeon Monkhouse both had their pockets picked, one his spy glass and the other his snuff box. Cook told the chiefs that this was unacceptable and eventually he recovered the items, but it was a sign of things to come. Cook may have got the stolen items back but he couldn't change their nature. The crew began to build a small fort in order to have a private spot to study the transit of Venus, but trouble happened the next day when a musket was stolen from a sentry. The marines opened fire and shot the man dead which was the last thing that Cook wanted, but when he explained to the chiefs that the man was being punished for stealing the gun, they seemed to accept the explanation and surprisingly it did no harm to the long term relations between the crew and the Tahitians. The Tahitians it seemed, were very forgiving people as the crew of the *Dolphin* had realised two years earlier. The two chiefs, Tubourai and Dootahah came with presents of breadfruit and a pig which was welcomed by the crew who gave hatchets and linen in return, items which the Tahitians seemed to value and the people of the *Endeavour* settled down to life in their new temporary home.

Cook needed the fort in order to study the transit of Venus, and as many men as could be spared from the ship were brought ashore to build it. The local people seemed unconcerned and some even helped carry the wood that was being used to erect it. On the 28th April, two weeks after they arrived, several canoes full of people came to visit them, and in one of these was Queen Oberea. Cook had heard of her, but she had less power than he thought, the crew of the *Dolphin* crediting her with being Queen of the whole island. Perhaps she had been when Wallis was there two years before, but she was just one of a number of chiefs now. However, regardless of her status, Cook and his officers treated her with kindness and respect and they exchanged presents with the Queen.

The crew got on with building the fort and life was settling down to a normal pattern between the local people and the crew of the *Endeavour*, when on the 2nd of May, something occurred that was potentially a disaster. At 9 o'clock in the morning, Charles Green and Cook went to get the quadrant but it had gone missing. This was extraordinary, as it had only been brought ashore the day before and hadn't yet been removed from its case. Given that the instrument was heavy and that a marine was standing guard close to the door of the tent where it had been kept, Cook couldn't quite believe how they had managed it. He gave orders that the canoes were to be confiscated and Dootahah was to be detained until the quadrant was returned, but he thought better of holding the chief hostage as he didn't think that the theft had been instigated by him and was confident of getting it back. Banks heard that the quadrant had been taken to the eastern part of the island and along with Charles Green, Tubourai and a midshipman, set out to find it. After walking and half running for about five miles, they managed to locate the instrument and return it to the fort. No harm was done in the long run but after all the gifts that they had already made to the local people, Cook was at a loss to understand why they should have stolen it in the first place. However, Cook and his men had much to learn about the customs of the Tahitian people. On Sunday 14th May, Cook wrote in his journal:

"...this day closed with an odd scene at the gate of the fort where a young fellow above six feet high lay down with a little girl about 10 or 12 years of age publicly before several of our people and a number of the natives. What makes me mention this, is because it appeared to be done more from custom than lewdness, for there were several women present particularly Oberea and several others of the better sort and those were so far removed from showing the least disapprobation that they instructed the girl how she should act her part, who young as she was, did not seem to want it".

As Cook and the crew were finding out, the Tahitians had a completely different way of life from the Europeans. They had no work ethic as they sought no possessions but simply sat around with very little to do. They made a hut if they needed a home or they hunted and fished when they needed to eat. Other than that, it was a simple uncomplicated life style and with so much time on their hands, the art of love played a big part in their lives, and young people were initiated into that art at an early age. Many of the *Endeavour's* crew formed attachments to the local women, and some of the men would have loved to have spent the rest of their lives there enjoying this life style. Cook was aware of this and knew that the biggest danger he had to face could have been wholesale desertion when the *Endeavour* would eventually leave the island. That possibility was never far from his mind and hit William Bligh twenty years later on the *Bounty*.

On the 2nd of June, Cook arranged for the instruments to be set up for the observation of the transit of Venus, which took place on the following day. However, although the weather conditions were near perfect, the readings were wrong and Cook was bitterly disappointed. His readings were different from those of Dr. Solander and Charles Green. He wrote in his journal: "...we very distinctly saw an atmosphere or dusky shade round the body of the planet which very much disturbed the times of the contacts, particularly the two internal ones..." History has judged that his readings were more accurate than he thought at the time, but Cook was very downcast at the results.

Banks and his people continued to study the island and its plant life and he also acquainted himself with the customs and the language of the local people. One of the surprises was that Queen Oberea presented them with a meal that consisted of a dog that had been cooked, which after their initial reluctance, they found to be delicious. A month was spent in overseeing the island and getting the ship ready for departure, when on 9th July, it was found that marines Gibson and Webb had deserted with their womenfolk, hoping to stay on the island after the *Endeavour* had sailed. Cook was having none of it however, and fearing wholesale desertion later on if they were allowed to get away with it, determined to find them. He took Queen Oberea and some of the other chiefs hostage and whilst they met with some resistance from the local people who wanted to help the two marines, Gibson and Webb were eventually returned to the ship and the chiefs released. Much to Cook's surprise, the incident didn't seem to harm relations between the Tahitians and the crew however, and on the 13th July, 1769, when the *Endeavour* was ready to sail, the islanders were clearly sad at seeing the ship leave. Despite having been taken captive by Cook only two days before, Queen Oberea was as sad as the other islanders and the ship sailed leaving many of the islanders in tears. The *Endeavour* had been there exactly three months and fond attachments between the two sets of people had developed.

Once at sea, Cook opened his sealed orders from the Admiralty. He was to sail as far south as 40 degrees latitude and search for the southern continent that Dalrymple and other scientists were convinced was there, and take possession in the name of King George III. Cook doubted that it existed, although Joseph Banks disagreed, but in any event, that was the task laid down by the Admiralty and Cook was duty bound to carry out the task as thoroughly as he was able.

Cook sailed for Raiatea and took possession of it in the same manner as everything else he discovered. On 9th August, he set out for the south to search for the southern continent. They spent weeks searching and reached 40 degrees latitude as instructed by the Admiralty. However, at the beginning of September, convinced that there was no great land mass there, Cook decided to concentrate on what he knew to be there, namely New Zealand and then explore the east coast of New Holland (Australia), then to sail across the northern tip before stopping at Dutch Batavia before setting off for home. On 7th October 1769, Nicholas Young sighted New Zealand and Cook went on to explore and map this country. On 30th December, the *Endeavour* rounded Cape Marie Van Dieman situated at the northerly tip of New Zealand, and Cook began his exploration of the west coast.

On 15th January 1770, they sailed into Queen Charlotte Sound to carry out much needed repairs to the ship. After charting New Zealand, they then sailed off in a north westerly direction until on 28th April they entered what is now known as Botany Bay, so called because of the huge amounts of plant specimens that Joseph Banks and Dr. Solander found, although Cook didn't actually give it that name until 6th May, a week later. The discovery of this little bay was to have a huge significance on the future of Australia as in 1787, Joseph Banks was to suggest it to be a good place to send English convicts to ease the overcrowding in English prisons. For now though, such a future for the place was the farthest thing from their minds. Later on that day, they set sail to head north up the east coast of New Holland having first taken possession of the whole country in the name of King George III.

The next major event to happen was on 11th June when the *Endeavour* struck the Great Barrier Reef. She was stuck fast and in mortal danger because any attempt to heave her off could mean that her hull would be ripped open and the ship, alone in the Pacific would sink. They jettisoned all ballast including the ship's guns and waited for high tide. The water was rising rapidly in the bilges and the crew were taking it in turns to pump in order to keep the levels down. The jettisoning of the ballast did nothing as high tide came and went and the ship didn't move. Meanwhile their position worsened as the fourth pump didn't work and the water was gaining. At the next high tide, Cook decided to take a huge gamble and attempt to free her with one supreme effort. Cook wrote in his log for the 12th: "I resolved to risk all and heave her off... and accordingly turned as many spare hands to the capstan and windlass as could be spared from the pumps. About twenty minutes past ten o'clock in the evening the ship floated and we hove her off into deep water having at this time 3 feet 9 inches in the hold." They were not in any way out of danger however as there was a huge hole in the ship and the pumps were still being manned in fifteen minute shifts. Midshipman Johnathan Monkhouse, brother of the surgeon, knew of a way to temporarily plug the hole while still at sea – a method called fothering, which he had learned on a previous spell at sea. This was a technique whereby a sail, sewn with tufts of wool and oakum and spread with sheep's dung, was used to plug the gap. Monkhouse managed to carry this procedure out satisfactorily and in such a way that a single pump only was needed to keep the water at bay. Cook later said that: "Monkhouse executed the manoeuvre very much to my satisfaction". From Cook, who had a tendency to understate everything, this was high praise. What he was probably meaning to say, was that Monkhouse had done a truly excellent job. Brilliant though this was however, there was no way that this would get them all the way back to England, and Cook resolved to make for Dutch Batavia where he could make more permanent repairs before undertaking the final part of the journey home. Despite the perilous position that the ship and the crew had been in, there was complete calm and everyone had carried out their duties efficiently and quickly. Cook was never more proud of a ship's crew than he had been during this time. Now that they were seemingly safe, the crew were much more cheerful, but they had no idea that the place they were sailing into on 11th October 1770, Dutch Batavia, was rife with dysentery and disease, and whilst the local craftsmen made repairs to the ship, the stop proved a disaster for the health and welfare of the crew.

Cook had no choice other than to stop in Batavia, but the sanitary conditions were disgusting and the diseased city proved too much for what had been a fairly healthy crew. Dysentery and Malaria were rife in Batavia and many of the

Endeavour's crew succumbed to the diseases. Ironically, Surgeon Monkhouse was the first to die, Banks and Solander were both ill, but survived. Tupia, the Tahitian that Banks had brought with him died as did his servant, Tiata. Cook noted in his log that he felt that Tupia's death was not only the result of the diseases at Batavia, but also brought on by the lack of fresh vegetables that he enjoyed at home but were not available in enough quantities on the *Endeavour*. Hindsight is a wonderful thing, but it has to be said that it was a disastrous decision to take him away from his people, much as he had wanted to go. By the time they left Batavia on Boxing Day, 1770, Cook had recruited nineteen men to take the place of those crewmen that had died, but still further deaths were going to happen. Hermann Sporing and the gentle mannered Sydney Parkinson both died leaving hundreds of botanical drawings behind. Any death is to be mourned, but it seemed that the talented members of Joseph Banks' entourage were particularly vulnerable. Charles Green died and the aged John Ravenhill succumbed. They sailed on but still the deaths kept coming – Midshipman John Bootle, and Jonathan Monkhouse, the surgeon's brother whose temporary repairs had done so much to enable the *Endeavour* to stay afloat, also died. All in all, thirty-nine met their deaths as a result of them making repairs in Batavia. Apart from the overall tragedy of it all, it was a dreadful irony for Cook to return home having lost so many men after all his care in keeping the crew healthy.

The *Endeavour* sailed from Batavia and reached home on 12th July, 1771. The first voyage was finished and despite his own misgivings, Cook's achievements were immense. He had ascertained that New Zealand consisted of two islands; he had charted the eastern coast of Australia, and had explored and mapped more of the Pacific than any man before him. He had not quite disproved the existence of Dalrymple's land mass but had created doubts where there had previously been none, and reduced the area that was left to search in the event of future voyages.

Although viewed from a distance that the voyage could be considered a great success, at the time Cook was somewhat disappointed. Whilst Joseph Banks was welcomed home and feted for all the plant specimens that he had returned home with, Cook was left with negative feelings. He felt that he hadn't quite got the readings of the Transit of Venus right, although in retrospect, the readings were better than he thought. He hadn't disproved what he was convinced was the mythical southern continent, although again, he was proved correct in that, and he wanted to map even more of the Pacific Islands than he already had. As it happened, it wasn't going to be too long before the chance came.

Cook was promoted to Commander, a disappointment as he had hoped and expected to be promoted to Post Captain. For now though, that would have to wait. The Admiralty were soon planning a second trip for James Cook, and this time his orders would be to sail further south than before to prove or disprove once and for all the existence of the southern continent otherwise known as 'Terra Australis Incognito'. Joseph Banks was once again to sail with him but although Banks and Cook had become friends, there was soon to be a problem. At the age of twenty-eight, Banks was still young and had probably allowed the fame gained from the first trip to go to his head. On this second trip, there were to be two ships, not one, and whilst there was no problem with the idea of two ships which Cook agreed was necessary, Banks thought that he would be taking command of the expedition but this was never going to happen for the same reason that Dalrymple wasn't given command of the first trip. Given that Banks was well aware of the row that had happened between Dalrymple and the Admiralty before the first voyage, it was odd that he thought he would be allowed to take command. Banks also took issue with the type of vessel that Cook wanted which was of course, the Whitby Cat. Banks said that the Whitby Cats were far too small and he wanted frigates and for a while there was stalemate. In the end, it was agreed that two Whitby Cats, the *Resolution* and the *Adventure* would be used, but that Banks would supervise alterations to suit his needs. However, Banks was not a naval person, had no clue as to how a ship should be designed, and when finished, it was found that his alterations made the ship completely top heavy and totally unseaworthy. When told that his work would have to be reversed, Banks behaved in a petulant manner and in the end withdrew from the trip. Even without the unsuitable alterations, the trip as it stood was a complete non-starter anyway, given that the Admiralty would never have allowed Joseph Banks, a civilian, to command two ships, regardless of whether they were Whitby Cats or Frigates. By this time, Sir Edward Hawke had been replaced as First Lord of the Admiralty by Lord Sandwich, but the naval policy of who should take command remained unaltered much as they appreciated what Banks had achieved on the *Endeavour*. The new First Lord, John Montagu (1718-92), the 4th Earl Sandwich, had enjoyed a good career. He had been made First Lord of the Admiralty in 1748 at the age of thirty, staying there for three years until 1751. He was Postmaster General in 1768, Secretary of State in 1770 and back again as First Lord, holding the post for most of the time that Lord North (1732-92) was Prime Minister which was from 1770 until 1782. Sandwich held the post of First Lord from 1771 until March, 1782. He had a reputation for hard living and had been a member of the notorious Hellfire Club which was full of hell raisers like himself. He has also been given credit for inventing the sandwich which enabled him to keep gambling without leaving the table, or allowing him to carry on with working at his desk, whichever version people want to believe. Sandwich was a completely different man from Hawke, but where both men agreed was the fact that only a serving naval officer could be in overall command of the trip and this is possibly another reason why Banks misjudged the situation. Despite the difference in ages, Sandwich and Banks were close friends and it may have been this fact, along with the manner in which he, Banks, had been lauded after the first trip that made Banks think that he could lead the expedition. Banks has had a bad press over the years for his behaviour, and probably correctly so, but in fairness to him, he was putting up much of the money himself, and would argue that he merely wanted to be comfortable over what would be a three year voyage. In the end, he withdrew, and a replacement was found in Johann Reinhold Forster (1729-98) and his son George (1754-94). Forster senior was a German botanist-philosopher-church minister. He was rude, pedantic, self righteous, and managed to anger everybody he came into contact with. Fortunately, his son George was of a nicer disposition but there were many times that Cook and his crew yearned for Joseph Banks to be on board. Banks was many things and sometimes annoyed the officers, but he had charm in abundance, something that no-one accused Forster of having.

Tobias Furneaux was chosen to command the *Adventure*. A capable officer, he had sailed with Samuel Wallis in the *Dolphin* as second Lieutenant when they discovered Tahiti in 1767, and had taken a senior role in bringing her home safely when Wallis became ill. The *Resolution* and *Adventure* set sail on 13th July 1772, virtually a year to the day that Cook and the *Endeavour* had arrived home from the first trip. Cook also had a new chronometer made by the brilliant watchmaker, Larcum Kendal (1721-95) which would greatly assist Cook in the accurate calculation of longitude, a problem that had existed for years. The instrument that Larcum Kendall had made was a copy of the chronometer made by the extraordinarily clever self taught John Harrison (1693-1776), who had spent a lifetime perfecting his creation, responding to an offer by the Board of Longitude made in 1714 of a prize of £20,000 (Over a £1 million in today's money) for anyone who could solve the longitude problem. Eventually, Harrison did solve the problem but he only ever received half the money from the Board. It took many years before he finally received the full amount that was due to him, and only after an intervention by King George III was he awarded the balance of the money by Parliament in June 1773 – the Board never did pay Harrison in full due to the fact that it consisted mainly of men who had always favoured the use of lunar tables and saw their use as the solution.

As well as Johann Reinhold Forster and his son, Cook also had on board a brilliant painter by the name of William Hodges (1744-97). On the first voyage, in the *Endeavour*, Cook had taken Sidney Parkinson and Alexander Buchan with him, but both men had died on that trip. The artist on a voyage of this magnitude was a crucial appointment as it was the equivalent of being an official photographer today as they would be required to paint accurate pictures of any places that the ships would visit. Parkinson and Buchan on the first trip, and John Webber on the third trip were all very good artists, but it was now, on this second trip on the *Resolution*, that Cook struck gold with the appointment of William Hodges. Hodges painted the most beautiful pictures of Tahiti, New Zealand and other places that they visited on the second voyage, but he had a tragic end. When he returned, he found it difficult to earn a living as a painter, so he left London, gave up painting altogether and went into banking in Devon. It seems inconceivable today that he was unable to earn a good living as a painter as his pictures are quite beautiful, but the sad fact is that for whatever reason he couldn't and he died virtually bankrupt and in obscurity, his name almost entirely forgotten. It is only now that his extraordinary work seems to be gaining recognition. Over 200 years on, in 2004, the National Maritime Museum in Greenwich published a long overdue book of this man's great work giving him much deserved if very belated recognition. It's just a pity that he did not receive this recognition in his lifetime.

With his full complement of crew, Cook in command of the *Resolution* along with Furneaux in command of the *Adventure*, the two ships set sail and soon reached Cape Town with little difficulty. On the 17th January, 1773, they crossed the Antarctic Circle and he noted with some satisfaction that they were the only ship ever to have crossed it. At this point in time, he could see nothing but ice and certainly no hope of getting any further south. To this end, he headed northeast and commenced searching for the Kerguelen Island.

Both ships stayed together until the 8th February when amidst the swirling fog, they were separated. The *Resolution* spent two days firing her guns to try and locate Furneaux and the *Adventure* but to no avail. They decided to carry on alone to the south which they did for another six weeks before heading for Queen Charlotte Sound where they had a previous arrangement to rendezvous with Furneaux if they got lost. On 18th May, 1773, they arrived at Queen Charlotte Sound and met up with the *Adventure* who it appeared, had been there since 7th April having first landed at Van Diemans Land.

On 7th June, the two ships set sail dipping down south of the 45 degree parallel a little way below the southern tip of New Zealand. The weather was foul with very strong gales, but it was not deemed cold enough for the crew to need their fearnought jackets as there was no ice in the rigging or icebergs to be seen. They had been at sea for six weeks, when to Cook's fury he discovered that Furneaux had not been as disciplined as Cook himself had been with the diet, and no less than twenty men from the *Adventure* were struck down with the scurvy. Cook laid down the law to Furneaux about the importance of the officers to be seen eating the prescribed meals so that the men would follow. Although the *Adventure's* cook died, with the better use of the diet laid down by Cook, gradually the men started to recover. On 17th July, they tacked and headed towards a NE direction and on 18th August, 1773 they landed at Tahiti. It would be necessary to stay there as once again, scurvy had broken out on the *Adventure.*

The two ships eventually set sail from Tahiti on 18th September and came across and named the Hervey Islands and from there reached Tonga which he named the Friendly Islands. The ships left on 8th October but were separated again two weeks later during a howling gale. Cook anchored in Queen Charlotte Sound for three weeks, but again, with no sight of Furneaux, set sail again having left Furneaux a message in a bottle saying that he was heading for the Easter Islands and thereafter back to Tahiti. By Christmas 1773, he was again amongst the icebergs and by the end of January 1774, he was probably no more than 1,000 miles from the pole. Amazingly, his men wanted to continue although Cook had felt by this time that they had done enough, so they sailed to Easter Island which they reached on 12th March. Although initially disappointed with the island, he was amazed at the huge idols that he found there, and the locals could give no clue as to their origin. Cook again returned to Queen Charlotte Sound, reaching it on 19th October, but although there was no sign of Furneaux, the message that Cook had left in the bottle had gone so Cook assumed that the *Adventure* had returned there at some point.

Cook then sailed east in the vicinity of 55 degrees and in January 1775, he reached the point that he had reached during his first entry in to the Antartic Circle. He had exploded Dalrymple's mythical southern continent once and for all and reaching Table Bay on 21st March to find that he had missed Furneaux by only a few days, decided that it was time to return home. Cook eventually found out that Furneaux had decided to return home earlier from Queen Charlotte Sound after a landing party had been killed and to the horror of the crew, had been the victims of cannibalism by the local people. Cook arrived at Spithead on 30th July, 1775 after being away three years and eighteen days. The long suffering Elizabeth Cook must have counted each day as by now, he had been away for six out of the last seven years.

During this great voyage, Cook had crossed from New Zealand to South America in his third sweep across that ocean and had chartered the polar regions and all the islands in the southern hemisphere. He had crossed from the Cape of Good Hope to Cape Horn and through to the Cape of Good Hope again completing his second navigation of the world. He was indeed a hero and was welcomed home as such. On his return, he was elected a member of the Royal Society for his work on astronomy and seamanship generally, and in the summer of 1776, he was awarded the Copley Gold medal for his work in promoting health at sea. Whether he was being modest, or whether he genuinely felt that he was unworthy of the honour, on the 10th July, he wrote to Joseph Banks:- "Sir John Pringle writes me that the Council of the Royal Society have decreed me the Prize Medal this year. I am obliged to you and my other good friends for this unmerited honour".

It would be churlish to take anything away from Cook's achievements concerning his views on health at sea, but we have already seen that it was not true to say as many have claimed, that he eliminated scurvy because the man who deserves most credit for this was James Lind. Sadly for Lind, the credit he now receives is largely retrospective as his views were criminally ignored by the Admiralty at the time.

Today Lind is considered the 'father of naval hygeine' but it was not always the case. When Cook embarked on his voyages, he followed a more holistic approach than other naval officers had done and promoted the use of fresh vegetables, sauerkraut and malt, and by so doing, was not only using Lind's ideas, but the ideas of Dr. David McBride (1726-78), an Irish doctor who joined the navy in 1748 during the war of Austrian Succession. MacBride had the support of many influential people including amongst others, Sir John Pringle, the Surgeon-In-Chief of the army, who carried a great deal of influence at the time, Henry Tom, a Commissioner of the Sick and Hurt Board, and John Montagu, the 4th Earl Sandwich and First Lord of the Admiralty. Although MacBride had studied Lind's methods and agreed with many of them, he put more emphasis on the use of fresh vegetables generally as opposed to the very specific intake of lemon juice that Lind had advocated. Basically, Cook was throwing everything at the problem of scurvy rather than knowing whether it was any one thing that cured it. Still, it more or less worked although there were in fact, five cases of scurvy on board the *Endeavour* during Cook's first trip including Joseph Banks, although, thankfully, none proved fatal and all recovered. The extraordinary thing about Lind's ideas being ignored for so long, is the fact that Joseph Banks' journal entries for the 11th April, 1769, on board the *Endeavour*, clearly show that he used lemon juice to cure his own bout of scurvy. He was following the ideas of a Dr. Nathaniel Hulme (1732-1807), who in turn was following Lind's methods concerning the use of lemon juice as a curative. Unfortunately, a few years later, Hulme seemed to change his mind and recommended completely different methods to cure scurvy, and this fact, along with the different opinions being expressed by other doctors, resulted in the delay in implementing Lind's methods. Sadly for Lind as well as for the general health of naval personnel, David MacBride's ideas, rather than those of James Lind, found more favour with the likes of Lord Sandwich during the time of Cook, and scurvy continued to be a problem for the navy for many years after Cook's voyages. Nathaniel Hulme's change of heart merely added to the delay in the final elimination of this dreadful disease. However, Cook's first two voyages were brilliant achievements, and as well as receiving the Copley Gold Medal, he had been promoted to Post Captain, his commission being personally handed to him during an audience with King George III on 9th August, 1775.

Cook had been away for six out of the last seven years and was tired. He had been ill with severe colic pains on the second trip and it was considered reasonable to retire him. From a frustrating first few years in the Royal Navy where he felt his progress was impeded by his so called humble birth and lack of rich friends, he had come a long way and earned the affection and respect of everyone who worked with him, whether it be his crew members, or the people who held the reins of power and influence, such as Hugh Palliser, Joseph Banks and Lord Sandwich.

At the beginning of his first trip in 1768, Sandwich would hardly acknowledge him at all, now Sandwich was happy to describe Cook as the finest seaman in the navy. Not only that, but Cook had achieved the fame with the general populace that he had always wanted so badly. With retirement in mind, the Navy appointed Cook as Captain of the Greenwich Hospital, which had been set up in 1705 for injured and sick sailors. He was to receive £230 per year salary plus 1s 2d (6p) daily table money along with luxury quarters for himself and his family. He had also published his journals and would be keeping the profits from the sale of them. His wife Elizabeth was naturally delighted at the deal – after being alone for so many years, she could look forward to having a settled family life once more with no more long separations to endure. A settled future together at last seemed assured.

However, Elizabeth was sadly unaware of two things. The first was that the navy wanted an expedition to search for the elusive northwest passage which was believed to exist between Canada and the North Pole, linking the Atlantic and Pacific Oceans. Seamen of all nationalities had tried for centuries to find a way through without success and many lives had been lost in the process. If a passage could be found through it would shorten the journey considerably and negate the need to travel round the Cape of Good Hope and Cape Horn. The second thing that Elizabeth was unaware of, or possibly tried to pretend didn't exist, was the restlessness that Cook was feeling in the confines of Greenwich Hospital. It had after all, only been a few months since the Pacific Ocean was barely big enough to contain him, and he now felt completely underused where he was. The prize money of £20,000 for the person who found the passage was also an unsettling factor. In today's terms, that would amount to over a million pounds and the person who led the expedition would receive the lion's share of this. Cook was asked to attend meetings at the Admiralty where his advice was sought as to who could lead such an expedition. Names such as John Gore and Charles Clerke were put forward and whilst they were considered excellent officers, one man stood head and shoulders over all of them, and Cook knew it. Lord Sandwich knew it as well and on 9th January, 1776, he invited Cook for a meal at the Admiralty. The only people to be present were Hugh Palliser, Comptroller, Philip Stephen, Secretary, and Lord Sandwich himself as First Lord of the Admiralty. The meal was called so that a final choice could be made as to who was to lead the expedition, but Sandwich didn't want Cook's advice, he wanted Cook. The meal and conversation were agreeable and the wine flowed, and as time wore on and Sandwich's flattery grew more and more obvious, Cook finally succumbed and offered himself up – Sandwich had got his man. Everybody in the room was delighted, but when things seem too good to be true, they often are, and the man that Sandwich got was not to be the James Cook who took the first two voyages but a man who had been ill and was now very tired. In future months and years it would be seen that his judgement, once almost flawless, was to be fatally impaired.

Apart from the search for the North -West passage, the Admiralty had to return a Tahitian gentleman named Omai to his native Tahiti. Furneaux, for reasons best known to himself had brought this Tahitian to England in the *Adventure*. Although Omai had wanted to come, it was an extraordinary thing to do because there was no way that Furneaux, a serving naval officer could look after him. As it was, within ten days of Cook's return, Furneaux was given command of the *Syren* and was off to help quell the American revolt which had broken out the previous March. However, to give Furneaux the benefit of the doubt, it may be that he was given instructions by Joseph Banks to bring a Tahitian man back, given the fact that he, Banks, had attempted to do this on the first trip with Tupia, who had sadly died at Batavia. As it was, Banks and Lord Sandwich took it upon themselves to look after Omai who appeared to settle in to the European way of life with extraordinary ease. He was lauded by the aristocracy, and even had an audience with King George III. It is said by many historians, that being introduced to the King, Omai bowed low and said, "How do, King Tosh?" King George was apparently amused rather than annoyed at this form of greeting. Omai had survived because he knew a little English, whilst Banks was fairly competent in Tahitian. Omai also picked up the manners of the upper classes with ease and enjoyed the attention he was receiving, but like all fashions which Omai was, the novelty wore off. Although treated with kindness, he was seen as a novelty rather than an equal, and by the time Cook's third voyage was about to commence, it was considered that Omai should be returned to his people as he was beginning to feel isolated. Quite how he was to integrate back into his former way of life and with his people probably wasn't thought through when they took him from Tahiti and as it happened, the transition back was far from easy.

However, all that was considered trivial compared to the real reason for the third trip - the search for the North West passage. Crews had to be raised for the two ships that were to go, the *Resolution* and the *Discovery*. Although doubts were raised about Charles Clerke's ability to actually lead the expedition, he was a fine officer and Cook was in no doubt that he should command the *Discovery*. He also wanted and got John Gore who had been with him on the first voyage and who had been round the world on the *Dolphin* with both Captain John

Byron (1723-86) in the period 1764 to 1766 and Captain Samuel Wallis (1728-95) between the years 1766 and 1768, the latter being the voyage in which Wallis discovered Tahiti, both trips having been completed before Gore sailed in the *Endeavour* on Cook's first trip. Two extraordinarily fine officers was a good start to the huge trip that they were about to undertake. William Anderson who had been Surgeon's Mate on the second voyage and who again was considered first rate at his job, was taken on as Surgeon on the *Resolution* and again, Cook was very happy at this appointment.

Another appointment was that of 21-year-old William Bligh as Ship's Master. Bligh had streaks of brilliance – he was a good navigator, cartographer and surveyor. He had passed his Lieutenant's exams with distinction and a glittering naval career lay ahead of him which did in fact happen although it was a career that was dogged with controversy after the famous mutiny on the *Bounty* that was to happen thirteen years later in 1789. At this time however, he was a young man who had been recommended by no less a figure than Lord Sandwich and he was to turn out to be a good appointment for Cook. Another good man was second Lieutenant James King. King was a quiet, thoughtful, almost gentle man. He was very well educated and was considered so good at astronomy that it was felt that with him on board, there was no need for a professional astronomer. He turned out to be a valuable companion for Cook. A less obvious choice for the voyage was that of third Lieutenant John Williamson. Disliked by most people on board, he wasn't even respected as being that competent and it was a bit of a mystery as to why he was included in this voyage at all. Cook took a contingent of marines with him, one of them being Samuel Gibson. During the first trip on the *Endeavour*, Gibson had been troublesome, even to the point of attempting to desert, but by now he was a sergeant and a loyal supporter of Cook and a valued member of the expedition. He had been on all Cook's voyages and had taken trouble to learn the language of the Tahitian people and understand their customs. Less fortunate was the inclusion of Captain Molesworth Philips who had only just joined the marines and had no experience whatsoever of being to sea or any form of military action let alone being in charge of men. Eventually he was to marry the writer Fanny Burney's sister, Susan and became the brother in law of lieutenant James Burney, Fanny's brother. James was a lively man, good company and although not considered an outstanding officer, was still thought of as a good addition to the crew. He had sailed on the second voyage with Cook so already had a great deal of experience.

On the surface, everything looked good for the third voyage, but everything wasn't good. Cook, who before the previous trips, had been so careful in overseeing the work of the shipyards had neglected this task this time around, spending time with the King and was also having his portrait painted at Greenwich Hospital by Nathaniel Dance (1735-1811). Dance was one of the most famous portrait painters of his day and he came from a talented family. His father was George Dance the Elder (1700-68), a brilliant architect who had designed the Mansion House and many other London buildings and one of Nathaniel's brothers was George Dance (1741-1825), an architect like his father and a painter like his brother. Nathaniel had studied art under Francis Hayman

(1708-76) who in turn had influenced Thomas Gainsborough (1727-88) and had also studied in Italy. During his career Dance had been commissioned to paint many famous people, King George III and the actor David Garrick being just two along with Cook and many others. In 1768, Nathaniel Dance and Francis Hayman, along with others, co-founded the Royal Academy.

The portrait was completed in May, 1776, just one month before they were due to sail and a crucial time for Cook to inspect the condition of the *Resolution*. He was also finalising his journals which again was time consuming, and all the while, the shipyards were taking advantage and carrying out sloppy work that meant the ship was virtually unseaworthy from the first day. Another problem was that due to the absence of its Captain, Charles Clerke, the *Discovery* was unable to sail and the *Resolution* had to depart from Plymouth on 12th July, 1776 without its sister ship. Clerke was ordered to set sail in the *Discovery* just as soon as he was able. The reason for Clerke's initial absence was due to the fact that through no fault of his own, he was languishing in a debtor's prison in London. He had stood surety for his brother, Sir John Clerke, RN, who had sailed to the West Indies leaving debts unpaid. Clerke had been arrested and spent weeks in a foul smelling damp cell until he either bribed his way out or simply escaped, but either way he eventually managed to join his ship. The *Discovery* then set sail and eventually joined Cook at the Cape. However, it was not a good start, and if that wasn't enough, Clerke's joy at being free to take command of the *Discovery* and join his beloved mentor, Captain Cook, was tempered with the fact that he found out that he had contracted tuberculosis which would eventually kill him, almost certainly as a result of his prison experiences.

With both ships at the Cape, they realised that the work back at the shipyards had been very shoddy, and time was needed to carry out urgent repair work. The ships left on 1st December and reached Tasmania on 24th January, 1777 and on 12th February anchored at Queen Charlotte Sound. Canoes came out to meet them, and in one of the canoes was a Chief Kahourah, who had lead the attack on Furneaux's men when the *Adventure* anchored there on the second voyage. Furneaux's men had been killed and eaten by the natives but Karhourah, rightly as it turned out, showed no fear that any revenge attack would be carried out and actually was received on board the *Resolution* by Cook. This incident has often been used against Cook as ammunition to show that his behaviour was strange quite early on during the third trip, and given his aggressive behaviour with other south sea island people later on, it does seem a little strange that he had no desire to avenge Furneaux's crewmen. Cook stayed for two weeks before leaving for Tonga and this is where Cook's behaviour started to cause concern. They stayed at these islands for twelve weeks and on some occasions, Cook was his usual kind self to the island people, but at other times when he was exasperated at their constant thieving, would resort to dreadful brutality to try and make them change their ways.

Midshipman George Gilbert wrote:- "This (thieving), which is very prevalent here, Captain Cook punished in a manner rather unbecoming of a Europeann, viz by cutting off their ears, firing at them with small shot, or ball, as they were swimming or paddling to the shore; and suffering the people as he rowed after them to beat them with the oars, and stick the boat hook into them…" It wasn't only the crew who were puzzled at Cook's erratic and savage behaviour, but also the Tongan people who one day were being tied to a tree and lashed, and the next were treated with undue kindness.

The crew were also puzzled as to why they were staying so long at Tonga anyway. They had all the supplies they needed and there were the other Friendly Islands to explore, such as Fiji, but Cook seemed to have lost that burning curiosity that had been a hallmark of earlier trips. Eventually they left for Tahiti on 17th July, 1777, and arrived there and dropped anchor on 11th August. As usual, they were surrounded by canoes, and in one of these was Omai's sister, who had brought a boatful of provisions for her brother. As Omai had been away three years and had been part of the aristocracy in London, it was going to be a real test to settle him back in to the Tahitian way of life after all that had happened to him whilst he'd been living in England. Omai didn't pay much attention to King Otoo but socialised instead with the undesirable element of the island, and in so doing, he squandered many of the articles that he had brought back with him from England.

After a while, the ships made for an island called Eimeo, which even for seasoned travellers, was a paradise on earth. There was a great deal of fraternising with the local girls and the trading ensured that everybody was friendly. However, an incident occurred that seemed to make Cook go crazy. Two goats were stolen and whilst one of them was returned, Cook flew into a rage that none of his men had seen before and it was frightening to behold. He had his officers and men destroy canoes, whilst houses were burned as if Cook was at full scale war with the islanders. Williamson in particular, set about his task with relish and reported with some satisfaction that he had destroyed twenty houses and numerous canoes. It was disastrous for the local people and sickening to witness. On 9th October, Cook wrote in his log: "I desired Omai to tell them I was well assured that they had the goat, and therefore insisted on it being delivered up, if not, I would burn their houses and boats. But not withstanding all I, or Omai could say, they continued to deny any knowledge of it; the consequence was, my setting fire to six or eight houses, which were presently consumed, together with two or three war canoes that lay in some of them. This done, I marched off to join the boats, which lay about seven or eight miles from us, and in our way, burnt six more war canoes." Given that their houses and canoes were about the only possessions they had and how long it took to build them, this was an act of unspeakable cruelty, and totally unlike the Cook of the first two voyages – he seemed to have lost his mind completely. Eventually the goat was returned, but it was thought that it had been taken by Tahitians, making the islanders totally innocent, although it will never be known for sure.

Eventually, it was decided to settle Omai back to his people on a permanent basis, and on the 2nd November, 1777, the *Resolution* dropped him back on to the Tahitian island of Huahine. Omai was laden with gifts, but it has to be said that most of them, such as crockery, a jack in the box, and a suit of armour, were completely useless. The crew built Omai a wooden hut for him to live in but his homecoming was not a success. Omai left Tahiti a native, but because of the life that he had lived in England, when he returned, he was neither a native, but nor was he a stranger - he simply didn't fit in. The Tahitians were not impressed with his tales of court life and soon his hut was raided and his possessions stolen and he began to cut a sad lonely figure. It is almost certain that he died alone but we cannot be sure how. Captain Bligh, who had been on Cook's third trip and therefore knew Omai, went looking for him ten years later when in command of the *Bounty*, but was told that Omai had died approximately two years before.

Some say that he died of an unspecified illness, others say that he was killed by his enemies, but either way it was a sad end to a man who had had a grand life in England and had once had an audience with King George III. There is a school of thought that says his presence in England hastened the beginning of the campaign against the slave trade that was taken up so strongly by people such as William Wilberforce, Tom Clarkson and William Pitt the Younger, on the grounds that the people who mixed with Omai held the reins of power in England. That may be so, but there were other people who also held the reins of power and seemed to fight long and hard and for many years against the people who were trying so hard to bring about the abolishment.

After completing the task of taking Omai back to Tahiti, Cook returned to the main task in hand which was to seek out and find the North West passage. From the dropping off of Omai he sailed north and on the 24th December, 1777, he found an uninhabited island which he named Christmas Island. He left on 2nd January, 1778 and came across two more islands, Kauai and Nihau and to his amazement, found that they were populated with Polynesian people who he had not expected to find so far north. The language of these people was similar to that of the Tahitians and it is probably from this date that the idea of a common ancestry of the entire race of Polynesian people came into the minds of Europeans. The language of the people to Tahiti was similar, but the behaviour of these people was different, and puzzled Cook and his crew. They bowed down at his feet, almost treating him like a god, which as it turned out, they thought that he was. Cook saw another island, but at the time didn't explore it, but merely named the group the Sandwich Islands, the main one being Hawaii. Cook sailed north on 2nd February, 1778 and was soon off the coast of Alaska. During this time, an incident occurred that horrified the officers of the *Resolution*, Bligh in particular. On 26th June, Cook was sailing fast in thick fog which meant limited visibility and a sharp eared look out almost certainly saved them. He shouted the word 'Breakers' and Cook ordered 'Heave ho'. When the fog eventually cleared, they found themselves a few hundred yards away from the breakers which meant that they were no more than sixty seconds from a catastrophic incident. It was a terrible misjudgement on the part of Cook and a shock for Bligh, who had been brought up to believe that Cook was the greatest seaman alive, which he had been. It is hard to see your heroes with feet of clay and Bligh was upset at what he was witnessing on this, Captain Cook's third trip. Although the ship was leaking badly, Cook continued to explore the whole of the Alaskan Peninsula before entering the Bering Straits and reaching the mainland of Asia. He was a long way from finding a route through the North West passage however, and so in mid August, he decided to return south to the Sandwich Islands and effect repairs to the two ships. The ships had been separated but they were only apart for a short while and eventually made contact again on 7th January, 1779, and both captains were shocked at the others appearance. It was all too clear to Cook that Captain Clerke's consumption was getting far worse, although being Clerke, he continued to put a brave face on it, but Cook was also seen by Clerke as looking ill and his temper was becoming shorter all the time.

They anchored at Kealakekua Bay and the trading that had been going on for some time continued apace. The ships were invaded by islanders, the men wanting to trade and thieve, the women wanting to share their sexual favours. Some sort of order was reached on the *Resolution* when two chiefs, Kanina and Parea came on board. A holy priest also came on board and was introduced as High Priest Koa. It was then that Cook became not just a part of, but the subject of a religious ceremony, and it was quite clear that he was being regarded as a god, something that had not happened on the other Polynesian Islands.

It transpired that the Hawaian people thought that Cook was the great god Lono, who in their legend was due to arrive at the islands at almost exactly the time that the *Resolution* and the *Discovery* appeared. During their stay, the chiefs had asked their people if they would bring gifts to Cook or Lono as they thought he was. After a while, it became clear that the islanders were running short of food but Cook wanted to sail anyway to commence another search for the North West passage. The two ships set sail on 4th February, 1779 amidst the most friendly of farewells from the local people and everything was ready for another search. However, disaster was to strike, as four days later on the 8th February during a storm, the foremast split. Cook faced a dilemma as he needed a safe anchorage in which to carry out repairs and he could either search for one round the islands or return to Kealakekua Bay where it would be safe to assume that they wouldn't be so welcome back. The local people had virtually run out of food and in their eyes, the god Lono would not need to return to carry out repairs. In the end, despite grave misgivings from some of his officers, Cook decided to return to Kealakekua where he knew the facilities for repairing would be just right.

However, the crew's misgivings were justified. The local people were not glad to see them back and the friendliness was replaced by derision and aggression. The carpenters set about repairing the mast, and Cook thought that it would take two weeks. However, the local people went about the business of thieving from both ships with no fear, no respect and spent most of their time taunting the crews. Cook put up with this tense situation for a while and didn't seem to react when things were stolen, but in the end his temper snapped and he ordered the marines to load their muskets with ball instead of shot and gave orders that the Hawaiians were to be fired on if there was any more insolence or thieving. There was an affray on Saturday the 13th, and by now, Cook's temper was at boiling point. The following morning, James Burney, Lieutenant of the *Discovery*, was on watch between 4 and 8am and to his horror, saw that the large cutter was missing. To Cook, this was the final straw, the Hawaiians were finally throwing down the gauntlet. Cook ordered that Lieutenant Rickman was to be in charge of the launch whilst Burney was put in charge of the jolly boat.

Lieutenant Williamson was put in command of the *Resolution's* launch whilst Bligh was in charge of the cutter.

Cook decided that the best way of getting the cutter back was to take King Terreeoboo who he had previously been on good terms with, as hostage until the cutter was returned. He took Lieutenant Molesworth Philips plus Sergeant Gibson along with eight other marines as escort. In view of the mood of the people, both Lieutenant King and Gore were horrified at Cook's plan, but he was determined. He went ashore to Terreeoboo's hut, took him by the hand and invited him on board the *Resolution*. Terreeoboo came willingly at first, but he was surrounded by the natives who were in an ugly mood. However, it was all going to plan when suddenly one of the King's mistresses let out a loud shriek and begged the King to go no further. Whether it was out of surprise, or whether he simply slipped, we do not know, but the King was suddenly on the ground and Cook made the quick decision to leave him there as to do otherwise would involve killing a great number of local people. The natives began to throw stones at the marines, and at first, after the marines returned this by firing on them, they briefly fled. However, this did not last long, and they were soon back and a full-scale attack took place. Covering fire was given by the ship's launches, except from Lieutenant Williamson's, and Cook and the marines retreated back into the water as best as they could, surrounded by an angry mob. Molesworth Philips fought bravely, and although stabbed in the arm, managed to shoot his assailant dead with one shot. One marine, private Harrison, was literally hacked to pieces and all in all, four marines were killed.

Cook was the last to die. Perhaps they were too scared to kill Lono, but eventually in the struggle, a native came up from behind him and clubbed him before running away. Another, seeing Cook stumble, siezed his chance and stabbed Cook in the back of the neck with a dagger. Cook still struggled to keep his head above the water, but another native finished him off with a final terrible blow that sent Cook to the ground for the last time.

A silence then came over the bay as if the Hawaiians suddenly realised that they had killed Lono. The crews of the ships were in disarray, not knowing what to do as some of the men looked up to Cook almost as a father and were in deep shock at what happened. A discussion broke out between the officers as to what should be done. Bligh was all out for blood as were most of the men but John Gore was more cautious. Some of the men were still on shore and amazingly enough, were still on friendly terms with the islanders on the other side. When the ships started firing randomly at the island, Lieutenant King was seen being rowed back to the ships from the shore and gave the signal to stop firing. Clerke, despite his grave illness, was in command of the expedition now and gave the order to cease fire. Clerke's priority was to get the carpenters back on board safely which he managed to do despite repeated attacks from the natives. The date of this terrible carnage was 14th February, 1779.

Eventually, some sort of relations were built between the Hawaiians and the crew of the two ships, and some of Cook's remains were returned to the men who buried them at sea, his body having been chopped to pieces. The two ships with Clerke in overall command carried on, but Clerke was to outlive Cook by only four months, succumbing to tuberculosis on 22nd August, 1779. John Gore was now in command of the two ships, and after one last fruitless search for the passage, brought the ships home on 4th October, 1780.

Taking his three voyages in their entirety, Cook's achievements were staggering. He mapped the Pacific to such a degree that nothing else needed to be searched for, virtually to the present times. He sailed further south than anyone had previously done and in so doing, proved that the southern continent didn't exist. He also enabled Joseph Banks and his entourage to bring back over a thousand different species of plants and that first voyage in the *Endeavour* doubtless made Banks' name for him, setting his lifelong career up in a way that Banks's wealth alone would never have done. There is a certain irony in this, because it was Banks who was born into wealth whilst Cook came from humble beginnings in a period where rich people could virtually buy their commissions in the army, and wealth and influential friends certainly helped in the navy, although ability was important too.

Cook was a humane man who cared for his crew and was awarded the Copley Gold Medal in 1776 for his contribution to the elimination of the dreaded disease of scurvy. Revisionist historians often like to denigrate our heroes, and it has been said in some quarters that Cook did not deserve the Copley medal because the dietary ideas relating to scurvy had already been thought of by the Scottish physician, James Lind, who in 1747 set up the first practical medical research to find a cure. Cook, a non medical man, never tried to claim that he thought these ideas up, but he was the first captain to seriously look at the problem and whilst his methods may have lacked a specific medical knowledge, he put the combined ideas of Lind and David McBride, along with various other doctors, into practise over a three year voyage, and it was that extraordinary feat that Cook was being honoured for. Something else that Cook has been criticised for is the fact that he didn't try to change the so-called heathen morals of the Polynesian people, and that he actually colluded with them. This is a nonsensical argument and one that simply doesn't stand up. Apart from the fact that Cook wasn't there long enough to have made any impact on their way of life, he respected their beliefs and wanted to leave the people as quickly as he could to carry on with their way of life that had suited them over thousands of years. It was the Christian missionaries who went there twenty years later who wrecked their Polynesian traditions and even banned them from carrying out their traditional dances who are the people that should be criticised.

On Kealakekua Bay, a monument to Cook has been defaced by local people who blame him for the collapse of their history, but Cook was merely carrying out his orders in exploring the Polynesian islands – he certainly didn't want their traditions altered. Cook was a brilliant seaman and a humane man, but like a prizefighter who has one too many fights when he has passed his prime, so it was that Cook did not know when to give up and it is a sadness that he went on that third trip. He had been away from home for six out of the previous seven years, he had been ill on the second trip and was tired and unwell when he set off on the third and final voyage. After the second voyage, he was awarded semi-retirement in Greenwich by a grateful Admiralty where he could carry out light duties, stay with his family and write his journals – he was set up for life.

There was one major problem with this though, it simply wasn't enough. He was bored and restless and the lure of finding the North-West Passage was just too much for him and when it became clear that Lord Sandwich, the First Lord of The Admiralty, wanted Cook to lead that fateful search, Cook was all too willing to volunteer. However, the Cook who went on the third voyage was not the Cook who took the first two expeditions out. He was tired, his judgement gone, and some of the cruel punishments meted out to the Polynesian people for their customary thieving bore no resemblance to the man who all his crews had admired and loved. But we should not end this chapter on a negative note. From an early age Cook wanted fame and had he survived the third voyage, he would certainly have gained a knighthood and possibly even a Peerage and then in due course, maybe a burial at Westminster Abbey. That would have been an extraordinary achievement for the son of a farm labourer in the class conscious 18th century. As it is, Cook's achievements stand the test of time and he is still rightly regarded as quite simply one of the most remarkable seaman of all time.

-oOOo-

11
Admiral Cuthbert Collingwood
(1748-1810)

Nelson's second in command at Trafalgar who has virtually been
written out of history.

The famous battle of Trafalgar took place on 21st October, 1805 when the British naval fleet led by Admiral Lord Horatio Nelson took on and beat the combined forces of the French and Spanish ships. Nelson is rightly given credit for masterminding the tactics for that day, and he and his flagship, the *Victory*, remain in the public mind when thinking of the battle. However, there is another man who deserves praise for the victorious outcome of that day who never seems to get a mention, and that man is Admiral Cuthbert Collingwood, the forgotten hero of that action. Nelson's second in command, he became the senior British officer at the battle when Nelson was cut down by a French sniper's bullet during the action, although Collingwood was not given the terrible news of Nelson's death until the battle ended at 4.30pm.

Collingwood really is the forgotten hero of Trafalgar. Even when the country was celebrating the 200th anniversary of the victorious battle in 2005, Collingwood's name barely came up, and yet he played a very significant part in its successful outcome. The tactics that were drawn up before the battle were of course Nelson's. Naval warfare in the 18th century usually consisted of the enemy sailing in parallel lines firing broadsides at each other until one side caved in. Nelson's tactics were completely different, although contrary to popular belief, he was not the first to use them. He split his fleet into two lines of ships that would sail towards the enemy at right angles eventually splitting them into three sections. This had the effect of isolating the first third of the French and Spanish fleet who found themselves sailing away from the action and it would take them a long time to tack and return to the fray. The downside of this ingenious plan was that all the while the British ships sailed towards the enemy, they had to withstand ferocious firing without being able to return it until they could engage the enemy themselves. Nelson in the *Victory* headed one line whilst Collingwood in the *Royal Sovereign* led the other, and another fact that is not realised by the majority of people is that it was Collingwood who reached the enemy first.

Cuthbert Collingwood was born on 26th September, 1748 in Newcastle upon Tyne. His father was also named Cuthbert and he was a trader and for a long time earned an adequate living but eventually went bankrupt. We do not know when Cuthbert senior married, nor do we have any information about his wife other than her name was Milcah and that they had ten children, although four daughters did not survive into adulthood.

The three daughters who did survive were, Mary (1738-1815), Eleanor (1739-1835), and Dorothy (1741-1830) living very long lives, being 77, 96, and 89 years old respectively. The last three children were boys born in consecutive years, Cuthbert himself in 1748, Wilfred, baptised on 11th October, 1749, and John, who was baptised on 1st June, 1750.

Cuthbert was born in a house in Newcastle in a street called The Side. The street is still there but the house was demolished in the nineteenth century and these days an office stands on the site although a bust of Collingwood is placed above the doorway of the Victorian building that replaced his home. He went to the Royal Grammar School and was almost certainly there at the age of eleven. It is hard to calculate exactly how long he attended due to records being lost because of the school moving premises several times, but the records that do exist show that he may have only been there for six months. The curriculum concentrated on the classics with Latin being high on the agenda. When it came to deciding on a career, there was clearly no future in following his father into trade and in any event, Cuthbert wanted a life with more adventure and he was inspired by the Admirals Hawke and Boscawen as was his brother Wilfred who also joined up. The 1st Baron Hawke (1705-81), had entered the navy in 1720 at the age of fifteen, and by 1747 was a Rear-Admiral of the White. Amongst other achievements, in November 1759, he destroyed a French fleet in Quiberon Bay during the seven years war with that country that had been fought between 1756 and 1763. It was that action that foiled a French invasion of Britain. He was First Lord of the Admiralty between 1766 and 1771 and was Admiral of the Fleet in 1768. Edward Boscawen (1711-1761) was known as 'Old Dreadnought' and had many campaigns to his credit, amongst which was the capture of the French ship *Medee* in 1744 when he was in command of the *Dreadnought* in which he took 800 prisoners. In 1755, he intercepted the French fleet off Newfoundland and captured two 64-gun ships, taking 1,500 prisoners. Both men had other successful battles to their credit and it is not difficult to understand why both the young Cuthbert and Wilfred chose the navy for their careers rather than going into a possibly not very lucrative nor exciting business in Newcastle. Wilfred served with both Cuthbert and Horatio Nelson before dying on 20th April, 1787 at the age of thirty-eight in the West Indies on board *HMS Rattler* of which he was Commander. John, the youngest brother didn't follow his elder siblings into the navy, but joined the customs service instead, dying at the age of ninety-one in 1841.

When joining the navy, it helped to have connections in high places and Collingwood had none of these to speak of, but his maternal aunt had married a gentleman by the name of Richard Braithwaite who was a captain of a frigate. In 1761, the thirteen-year-old Cuthbert joined the frigate *Shannon* which Braithwaite commanded. This particular ship was a 600 ton vessel with 28 guns and was therefore considered small for a fighting ship. To give some idea of the small amount of power the *Shannon* had, would be to say that a ship of the line could discharge 1,500lb in a single broadside, whilst the total mass of shot that could be discharged from the *Shannon* could amount to only 126lb. Nevertheless, it was a ship and the young Collingwood was now in the navy. There was a crew of approximately two hundred, eighteen of which were officers, three of whom were commissioned. These were the Captain and two Lieutenants and then there were fifteen non-commissioned officers such as the Boatswain and Surgeon. There were also four Midshipmen who were neither commissioned nor non-commissioned, but who were normally young gentlemen who would eventually train to be officers.

However, Collingwood was not yet a Midshipman but a volunteer and as such he would now have to learn how to be a seaman as well as an officer. It is often thought that young gentlemen came into the navy, instantly became Midshipmen, and straight away gave orders to men much older and more experienced than they were. This is not quite true and the young men had to earn the right to become Midshipmen, as it was then that they would have to give orders to men who had been at sea for years, so it was important that they learnt quickly in order to gain the respect of the men. It actually took Collingwood five years before he reached this exalted rank.

Collingwood did not stay on the *Shannon* for more than a few months before Captain Braithwaite transferred to the *Gibraltar* and the young Collingwood was allowed to follow his uncle into the new vessel. In 1763, two years after Collingwood had entered the navy, Britain made peace with France after being at war with them for seven years. To make progress as an officer in the 18th century navy, a man had to have two things, the first being connections in high places and Collingwood did not possess these. It was true that his uncle commanded a frigate but this carried little influence at the time. The second thing that a man needed to do was excel at war, but there was little chance of this now that the country was at peace with France. Collingwood spent fourteen years learning how to be a seaman, but precious little time being involved in action against any kind of enemy. In the early years, Collingwood visited Menorca for the first time, where along with Gibraltar, Britain had held bases but had to give them up under the terms laid down in the Treaty of Paris, the treaty that had ended the seven years war. The lack of action against any enemy was probably part of the reason why it wasn't until 1766, five years after he joined the navy, that Collingwood was at last rated as a Midshipman. Soon after that, in 1767, he was transferred to another small frigate, the *Liverpool*, and this time his promotion was more rapid, as by 1770, he had been made a Master's Mate. The position of Sailing Master on a ship was a highly prestigious one as he was entirely responsible for the navigation of the vessel. Possibly the most famous Master was William Bligh, who in 1776, at the age of twenty-one, was appointed to that position on board Captain Cook's ship the *Resolution*, when along with the sister ship, the *Discovery*, set out on the ill fated expedition to find the North West Passage which linked the Pacific and Atlantic Oceans via the top of the Americas. The expedition virtually ended when Cook was killed in Hawaii on 14th February, 1779 in a needless fracas with the local people, although the ships did carry on with one more search until Bligh steered the ships safely home in October, 1780, the North West Passage still waiting to be discovered. To get on in the navy, you would needed to have excelled as Sailing Master which Bligh certainly did and he went on to captain the ill fated *Bounty* when in April, 1789, the crew mutinied, lured by the charms of the local women in Tahiti, where they had enjoyed the carefree lifestyle for five months whilst waiting for the breadfruit plants that they were to take as cheap food for the slaves to the West Indies, to be potted. Just as Collingwood has never had the recognition for Trafalgar that he deserves, most people only remember the name of Bligh in connection with the mutiny, having no idea at all that he went on to have a glittering career in the navy, fighting with distinction at the battle of Camperdown in 1797 and again at the battle of Copenhagen in 1801. Bligh in fact had a connection with Collingwood's friend Nelson when Nelson's ship, the *Elephant* was in trouble during the Battle of Copenhagen, and Bligh, commanding the *Glatton* gave covering fire and was personally thanked by Nelson for his efforts.

The position of Master's Mate was therefore an important one, as it enabled Collingwood to get himself on the first rung of the ladder to become a Master himself, followed by a Lieutenant and thence promotion through the ranks until hopefully attaining the position of an Admiral.

Whilst Collingwood was on board the *Liverpool*, the ship sailed to the Balearic Islands, and dropped anchor there on 10th December, 1770 by which time he was twenty-two years old. By now he was fairly experienced in every aspect of naval life, except warfare, a fact that he found deeply frustrating. Apart from him always feeling restless, it meant there were virtually no chances of promotion all the while this lack of action was taking place, and this state of affairs continued all the time he was on board the *Liverpool*.

Collingwood's Mediterranean posting finished without anything eventful happening, and in 1772 he was posted to the Portsmouth guard ship, the *Lennox* under Captain Roddam. Although the *Lennox* was a step up from the *Liverpool*, being a 74 - gun two decker, the posting wasn't, consisting as it did of supplying boats from one ship to another, and working on other ships that were anchored in the harbour. The upside of this was that Collingwood's brother Wilfred was with him on board, and being in port, there were no watches to be kept and he was allowed ashore. The work was tedious however, but the boredom was relieved in February 1773 when Collingwood along with eighteen seamen was transferred from the *Lennox* to the *Portland*, a 50 - gun two decker which was being fitted out in order to be ready to set sail to the West Indies. This was to be convoy work, and the ship anchored off the Downs in East Kent where it joined up with other men-of-war and merchantmen who would be sailing for the Indies, Baltic and the Americas. On the 2nd April, 1773, Collingwood was to write an entry into his log book which showed his style of being economical with words:-

"Mr. Gold, midshipman, fell from the gangway overboard, and every means to save him were abortive, thus died an amiable young man, respected and beloved most by those who best knew him. Fresh breezes and hazy weather".

On the 2nd April, they arrived in Jamaica where two Courts Martial were held. The first was when Harris, the Boatswain of the *Portland* was accused of embezzlement but was acquitted, an unusual outcome in such an instance. However, the second court martial made this outcome completely clear. At the end of May, whilst the ship was still at Port Royal, the defendant at the second trial was a one Thomas Bradley who had accused Harris, the boatswain who suffered the original charge of embezzlement, and this had led to Harris' trial. However, the charge against Bradley in the second court martial was false accusation, which is about as serious as it could get. Bradley was found guilty and sentenced to 300 lashes, which although dreadful, would have received no sympathy from his shipmates. If such a sentence had been carried out in one go, it would almost certainly have meant a slow painful death, but in such instances, the Captain who was in charge of the punishment would almost certainly have had it carried out in stages, thus making sure that the seaman could receive the punishment in full. It seems barbaric to us today, but it was how discipline on board a ship was kept and the men understood it.

On 26th May, 1773, Collingwood was transferred from the *Portland* and sent to the *Princess Amelia* commanded by Captain Berkeley with orders to sail to England. She left Port Royal on 15th June and arrived in England two months later. It was sometime in 1773 that Collingwood met Horatio Nelson who was to become a lifelong friend. We cannot be sure of the exact circumstances of their first meeting but despite some biographies of Nelson putting him anything between eight and ten years younger than Collingwood, the age difference is something we can be sure of. Nelson was born on 29th September, 1758 whilst Collingwood was born on 26th September, 1748 so that is ten years difference virtually to the day. Given that age difference and the fact that Collingwood had already had twelve years experience at sea compared to Nelson's three, it seemed an unlikely basis for a friendship. Perhaps Collingwood was simply taking the young boy under his wing and if that is the case, it speaks volumes for Collingwood's good nature that he remained on good terms with Nelson throughout the rest of their lives, despite the fact that it was Collingwood who seemed to follow Nelson, often replacing him on a ship if Nelson was moved on or promoted rather than the other way round. There is no question that Nelson possessed extraordinary talent and bravery to the point of extreme recklessness, but he also had friends in high places which must have been a partial reason for him being promoted to the rank of Post Captain at the very young age of twenty. Collingwood had no such connections but if he was envious of Nelson, he never showed it. Their friendship lasted until the day that Nelson died, which was on 21st October, 1805, when both men fought at Trafalgar together.

1773 started as if it was going to be a quiet year for Collingwood with his navigating the *Princess Amelia* from the West Indies back to England, but along with his meeting Horatio Nelson, it was to be a momentous year as it finished on 16th December with some young men calling themselves the Sons of Liberty throwing a consignment of tea imported from England into the harbour at Boston. This was the first act of the American War of Independence which was fought between the years 1775 and 1783 and the reasons are numerous and complex, but put very simply, the people who lived in the American colonies objected to their having no say in the governing of their country and yet were subject to certain taxes from the mother country. The cry that became commonly heard over the years was "No taxation without representation".

On 7th July, 1774, the Boston and Country Gazette and Journal, a republican newspaper, reported that Vice-Admiral Thomas Graves who was commanding a 50-gun British ship, the *Preston*, had arrived in Boston harbour. Collingwood was on board having been transferred from the *Princess Amelia* and unlike his friend Horatio Nelson, was still a Master's Mate even though he was twenty-seven. The next year saw the building up of tension all round as rebels conducted a guerrilla war against the redcoat soldiers, who the rebels came to see as an occupying army rather than troops that were there to defend them. This escalated however, when on the morning of the 16th June, 1775, Colonel William Prescott and the rebel forces under his command dug themselves into Breeds Hill and the next morning, the British soldiers tried to retake it but were forced back into a humiliating defeat. Three times the British tried to storm the hill, but they suffered dreadful casualties. The second wave was led by Major General Sir William Howe with Collingwood in command of the boats. The action probably lasted no more than two hours, but the fighting was fierce and the casualties were high. Collingwood spent all day sailing back and forth taking the wounded away from the action and returning with reinforcements. This was the first time that he had tasted action and he showed great coolness under the constant bombardment from the rebels. It was this action that showed his superiors his qualities and resulted in his promotion to Lieutenant. Whilst this episode helped Collingwood's career, it did nothing for the reputation of Britain's redcoat soldiers and for the first time, the rebels had shown their countrymen that the British soldiers were not invincible and that under the right conditions, could be beaten. In this instance, the British had grossly underestimated the strategic advantage that the Americans had at Breeds Hill and the British had suffered large casualties as a result. It was this action that signalled the beginning of the War of Independence.

Collingwood was only an Acting-Lieutenant at this stage and he had to return to England in order that his promotion could be confirmed by the Admiralty. The *Preston* had to stay in Boston and so Collingwood transferred to the *Somerset* which was under the command of Captain Edward Le Clas and set sail on 15th January, 1776 arriving in February after a severe battering due to the weather in the Atlantic Ocean. Collingwood's promotion was duly confirmed and he was anxious to see his family in the north again but was also tempted to stay in London as, although needing a rest, he was keen to stay close to the Admiralty in London so that he would not miss out on a posting, especially now that he was a Lieutenant. He did stay in London and in April was rewarded with a posting to the *Hornet*, a 14-gun sloop which was captained by Commander Robert Haswell and which was to sail to the West Indies. If Collingwood was disappointed with a posting to such a small ship, he would have been doubly disappointed if he knew in advance what he was to suffer in the hands of such an incompetent commander. As it was, he received a written order which survives to this day dated 1st April, 1776, in which he was ordered to form a press gang. The order read:-

"Whereas we intend that you shall be employed to raise Volunteer seamen and landsmen in and about London for the service of his Majesty's sloop *Hornet* at Woolwich, you are hereby required and directed to observe the following instructions...."

The instructions went on to detail exactly how Collingwood was to set about this unenviable task. It was not the best reward for what he had achieved in Boston. He was in a small sloop with a bad captain and an order to raise a press gang, an order which was not to his taste – he must have thought that the date of the order was highly appropriate.

The method of obtaining members of a ship's crew using Press Gangs was used by the Royal Navy from 1664 and through the 18th and 19th centuries. The gangs were hated and caused fear and alarm amongst able bodied men between the ages of eighteen and forty-five as these were the most likely to be taken. It was utterly cruel as it could take husbands away from wives and their children and the living conditions on board a Royal Navy ship were much more harsh than those that the sailors on merchant ships endured. Not only that, but the wages were about half those enjoyed by the crews of the Merchant Navy. The Royal Navy wages had been set in 1653 and did not alter until April 1797 after the Channel Fleet mutinied in order that their conditions be improved. Some historians have tried to defend the process by which the press gangs operated claiming that they were totally unlike the way in which it has been depicted in films over the years, and in many ways this is true. It is said that only experienced seamen were taken and this was certainly the first preference that the gangs operated under but then it would be logical for that to happen anyway. However, this very fact meant that injustices were still happening as it was perfectly possible for young men who had left the sea and had new families to look after and spend their lives with, to be taken after they thought that they had settled lives on shore to look forward to. One of the worst excesses however, was the way in which some Royal Naval vessels would wait just a mile or two out of harbour waiting for a merchant-man returning to port after possibly years at sea and taking some of the seamen from the returning ship. Collingwood hated the way this system worked and a few years later he wrote:-

"I have got a nurseryman here from Wrighton. It is a great pity that they should press such a man because when he was young he went to sea for a short time. They have broken up his good business at home, distressed his family, and sent him here, where he is of little or no service. I grieve for him poor man".

The *Hornet* sailed for the West Indies to try and help stop American privateers from operating, as British ships were supplying munitions to the army in support of the war effort but were being captured, an action that France was colluding in. It was a delicate situation as Britain had more than enough to worry about fighting the rebels and did not want to risk a war with France. However, for a situation that required sensitive handling, it was difficult to know quite how much use the *Hornet* would be given the fact that it was captained by Robert Haswell. Although called Captain as a courtesy title because he was in command of the vessel, he was in fact a Commander, and had been so for eighteen years. This seemed to make him hate everyone and completely ruined the way in which he ran his ship, which only compounded his problem because this attitude caused any promotion that the Admiralty would have made in the normal run of things to be put on virtual permanent hold. Despite his promotion to Lieutenant, Collingwood was deeply unhappy in the *Hornet* because of the way that Captain Haswell ran his ship. Collingwood had been on the ship for a year when he wrote to his brother:-

"My dear John, Every opportunity of writing to you is but too few. The 'Lively' brings this. Wou'd to god the 'Lively' brought me also for believe me I am heartily tired of my situation, and cou'd a letter contain half the causes of my dissatisfaction you wou'd not wonder at it. What a country is this at present to make a fortune in; all kinds of people wallowing in their wealth acquired by prizes and so extraordinary an exception are we that to be as unfortunate as the Hornet is become a proverbial saying, and the Black girls sing our poverty in their ludicrous songs".

The crew detested Haswell, and none more so than Lieutenant Cuthbert Collingwood. In the normal run of things, there were two ways in which an officer could obtain promotion; one would be the recommendation from his captain and the other was the capture of enemy ships and the prize money that would naturally follow. Neither of these avenues were open to Collingwood all the while he served in that ship under that captain and in the end he decided that he would endure the situation no more. He was later to write:

"I told him I was determined no longer to bear with his capricious humours, that I was not a mark to shoot his spleen at, and desired him did he disapprove of any part of my conduct to explain himself, nothing wou'd make me more happy than to correct what had given offence to him. Men who act without meaning, or who are ashamed to confess the passion that impels them, are always distressed when explanations are required of them. He had not a word to say and I had a respite from his malign broils, not that they ceased, but he kept out of my way".

As a result of this confrontation, Collingwood was court-martialled, which is probably what he wanted in order to bring the conduct of Haswell to a head. The Court-Martial took place at Port Royal, Jamaica, in September 1777 where he was charged with disobedience and neglect of orders. He was acquitted, but did not get off scot-free because the court made the extraordinary criticism of his 'want of cheerfulness' and told him to 'conduct himself for the future with that alacrity which is essentially necessary to His Majesty's Service'. Although Collingwood was acquitted, it is difficult to know quite what the court-martial achieved. It certainly didn't get Haswell thrown out of the service, and didn't result in Collingwood being posted to another ship or get him promotion because he had to stay on the *Hornet* for another agonising year knowing that if anything, Haswell would be even less likely to recommend him for promotion. Indeed, their relationship sunk to an all-time low and another long year went by before Collingwood went to another ship, the *Lowestoffe*, where his friend Horatio Nelson had been made second Lieutenant.

Nelson had gone to the *Lowestoffe* in the summer of 1777 and then in July 1778, he was transferred to the *Bristol* as third lieutenant. The nineteen year old's abilities were noticed by Admiral Sir Peter Parker and after a few months with the *Bristol*, on 8th of December, 1778, Nelson found himself promoted to Master and Commander of the *Badger*. Nelson now had an admirer at the Admiralty and this helped Cuthbert Collingwood, as Nelson used his influence with Admiral Parker to help Collingwood be transferred from the *Hornet* and her useless Commander, Richard Haswell, to the *Lowestoffe* under a captain who was far more amenable called William Locker. After what had seemed an eternity on the *Hornet*, Collingwood was transferred yet again, when on the 8th December, which was the day of Nelson's promotion, Collingwood himself was promoted to second Lieutenant and sent to the *Bristol*, in effect, replacing Nelson.

All this was going on in the West Indies, where the British were fighting the American privateers and the war with America generally was going quite badly. France was not at war with Britain, but was co-operating with the Americans, and as the British had assumed a peace-time policy of running her navy down, it had made the job of the British navy difficult. The Prime Minister at the time was Lord Frederick North (1732-92) who had taken office in 1770 when the Duke of Grafton resigned. North was a talented man, albeit overweight, but a clever speaker who could command the House of Commons and was also blessed with a great sense of humour. He was also prone to dozing off in the House of Commons if a speech bored him. His humour was never better expressed than on one occasion when George Grenville (1712-70), previously Prime Minister himself between 1763 and 1765 was making a long speech detailing the history of the government finances. Speeches in the House were very long at the best of times in the 18th century, but Lord North had no intention of listening to Grenville's all the way through. After requesting his neighbour to wake him when Grenville reached the present day, he then fell into a sound sleep. At what he assumed to be the relevant time, his neighbour duly nudged North in the ribs causing him to wake and listen for a few minutes before exclaiming: "Zounds, you have waked me a hundred years too soon".

Peers were allowed in the Commons if they held a courtesy title, and as he was heir to the Earldom of Guilford he was entitled to call himself Lord North but was able to attend the House of Commons. In fact, he did not succeed his father and become the 2nd Earl of Guilford until 1790, just two years before his own death. However, despite his command of the House of Commons and his great speaking ability, he did come in for a great deal of criticism over his handling of the war with the American colonies. Many politicians at the time condemned his aggressive response to what took place at Boston on 16th December, 1773, when a consignment of tea was thrown into the harbour, an incident that came to be known as the Boston Tea Party. The British Government were indeed very clumsy with their handling of the American colonies. They had given the East India Company a monopoly of imported tea to America and they were taken by surprise when the colonies decided that they would not pay tax on the imported tea if they had no representation in the British Parliament. This lead to them refusing to accept the consignment of tea that had arrived in Boston and this was the catalyst that would eventually lead to the American War of Independence (1775-83). North was blamed for both starting the war in the first place and also for eventually losing it. He did in fact offer his resignation to King George III several times but the King refused – he liked North, and in any event there was no obvious successor. It was North's stewardship that resulted in the 1st Earl of Chatham, otherwise known as William Pitt the Elder, although gravely ill, getting off his sick bed to make a dramatic speech in the House of Lords on 7th April, 1778, denouncing the government's handling of the war. The intervention by the Earl was dramatic enough but was made more so when he collapsed and had to be helped out of the chamber by his son, William Pitt the Younger, and his son-in-law, Charles

Viscount Mahon. The 1st Earl never recovered and died a month later in May. Eventually North's resignation was accepted, but only after the British surrendered at Yorktown in 1781, and so on 20th March, 1782, North stood up in the House of Commons and announced his resignation, leaving the House with a cheery wave, pleased to have cast off the heavy responsibilities of office.

Meanwhile, on 11th June, 1779, Nelson, who had been Master and Commander in the *Badger* was promoted to Post-Captain at the extraordinarily young age of just twenty and took over the *Hinchinbroke*. Collingwood's career was progressing well now, as Nelson needed to be replaced so at the age of thirty, on 20th June, 1779, Collingwood found himself promoted to the post that Nelson had just vacated, that of Master and Commander of the *Badger*. After a few months, Collingwood replaced Nelson yet again. In April 1780, Nelson was in command of the *Hinchinbroke* when it was in charge of escort ships in the San Juan River in Nicaragua and his friend Collingwood was in the *Badger*, one of the other escorts and was supporting Nelson. Although Nelson behaved with his usual recklessness, it was not his behaviour that nearly got him killed, but the dysentery he caught that had killed a large number of the sailors who made up the crews of the escorts. For all his incredible bravery, Nelson had a weak constitution, and he was so ill that he had to be sent home, many fearing that he would die before he arrived in England.

Because of Nelson's incapacity, Collingwood achieved another promotion, once again following in Nelson's footsteps and replacing him as Captain of the *Hinchinbroke*. Collingwood had followed Nelson in the last four ships, the *Lowestoffe, Bristol, Badger* and now the *Hinchinbroke*. Taking command of the *Hinchinbroke* was not to be the last time that Collingwood would replace Nelson, and the most famous occasion when he replaced his friend was of course when he took over command of the Battle of Trafalgar, but that was to be a quarter of a century away and the reasons for it gave Collingwood no happiness as it was due to his friend's death in Britain's moment of glory.

From the *Hinchinbroke*, Collingwood was transferred to the 24-gun frigate, the *Pelican* and was in command when he and the crew suffered a dreadful hurricane which appeared with no warning and not only wrecked the ship, but was of such force that it practically wrecked Jamaica as well. Collingwood managed to get his men off the ship onto makeshift rafts and made for land on an island where they remained for ten days with only a small amount of food to sustain them before being rescued. It hardly compared to a glorious victory such as would be had in war, but nevertheless, it was a remarkable achievement by Collingwood to keep his men in order, because it was usual in such circumstances for the crew to lose all discipline and panic in their fight for survival. What is not generally understood by people is that the majority of seamen, officers included, cannot swim, and will do anything to save themselves. The fact that Collingwood kept his nerve in such circumstances and brought his men through safely spoke volumes about him. Nevertheless, he had to attend a Court-Martial which was obligatory if a Captain lost his ship, but the result was a complete formality and no blame was attached to him.

Collingwood returned to England in the early part of 1782. It is always difficult to know his whereabouts when he was ashore at home, because although his natural instinct would be to return north to see his family, at this stage of his life, he was always on the lookout for a new command, and it was therefore quite likely that he stayed in London to be near the Admiralty. His new posting was not long in coming and he was given command of the 64-gun *Sampson*, but this was only for a short while before he was given command of the *Mediator*, a 44-gun, two decker frigate which was ready for sailing in September, 1783. It was to sail to the Leeward Islands station at Antigua and on board was some human cargo that was to prove to have a long standing effect on Collingwood. The dockyard at Antigua was to have a new Navy Commissioner called John Moutray and he along with his wife Mary were to take up residence. Initially, Collingwood did not take to the couple as he had to give his cabin up to them and they showed precious little gratitude once they arrived. They were also a financial burden to him as he had to spend a considerable amount of his own money to entertain them and so his new command was proving costly from a financial point of view along with the irritation the couple were causing him. However, Mary was considerably younger than her husband, and Collingwood found her attractive, so attractive in fact, that eventually his feelings of irritation were to give way to quite different emotions and he fell in love with her. Mary Moutray was another reason why Collingwood was connected to his friend Horatio Nelson as he too fell in love with her. In different circumstances, she could well have ended up marrying either man and both of them wrote to her for the rest of their lives. By the time he sailed to the West Indies, John Moutray was effectively retired from being a Post-Captain and his posting was in fact virtual semi-retirement that allowed him an easy life. He was twenty-eight years older than Mary and his health was not good, but she on the other hand was young, physically fit and no doubt attracted to Collingwood who was a younger man than her husband. Collingwood was tall, handsome, and like Mary, was physically fit himself, and the two were naturally drawn to each other given that the three of them spent so much time with each other, although nothing ever improper took place between Collingwood and Mary.

In 1783, Britain had no choice other than to recognise that America was now an independent nation, and in September of that year, she, Britain, also made peace with France and Spain. Two months later, on 19th December, William Pitt the Younger (1759-1806), the son of William Pitt the Elder (1708-1778) a.k.a. Lord Chatham, became Prime Minister at the age of twenty-four. When he first made his appearance in the House in this new role the opposition roared with laughter, none louder than the three main members of the previous administration, William Henry Cavendish-Bentick, the Duke of Portland, (1738-1809), the nominal Prime Minister, along with Charles James Fox (1749-1806) who had looked after foreign affairs and Lord North (1732-92) who had been Secretary of State for the Home Department. Fox and North were far more powerful men than the Duke of Portland and this government had always been known as the Fox/North coalition. As it happened, their laughter at what they assumed would be an extremely short reign by Pitt was rather ironic due to the fact that they had remained in office for only eight months, from April 1783 until December of the same year. By contrast, William Pitt lasted rather longer than anyone could have predicted, and certainly more than the Fox/North coalition as he was Prime Minister for twenty out of the next twenty-three years. He held the office from 1783 to 1801, and then again from 1804 to 1806 when he died exhausted at the age of just 46 years. He was a remarkable man and a great deal of his time and energy was spent in fighting the French, from 1793 until his death. He introduced income tax, which although unpopular at the time, is an essential part of our system of government today and he saw the country through the crisis of King George III's very severe illness. There will never be a Prime Minister who came to the job at such a young age again, and neither will there ever be one who stays in the post for anything like that period of time, although Robert Walpole (1676-1745), the first ever Prime Minister was in office from 1721 until 1742. Pitt the Younger had a small connection with Collingwood, as his brother, James Pitt, was a naval officer and died at the age of nineteen in Antigua in 1780 whilst Commander of the *Hornet* in which both Collingwood and Nelson had served. James Pitt was well liked, and the blow was huge to his brother William, but also felt by his brother officers. Despite their liking for James Pitt however, quite what Collingwood, an experienced naval officer aged thirty-five years and his fellow servicemen made of James Pitt's brother being Prime Minister at the age of twenty-four is unclear but William Pitt was to gain their admiration and respect in the coming years.

Horatio Nelson arrived at the station in July 1784 and he joined Collingwood and the Moutrays for evenings together. It was during this time that Nelson too became captivated by Mary's charms and now both Nelson and Collingwood were in love with her. The four spent a great deal of time socialising together until early in 1785 when John Moutray became very ill and the Moutrays were forced to return to England. Both Collingwood and Nelson were desolate at losing the company of Mary. Both men probably felt the loss equally but the different temperaments of Collingwood and Nelson are shown by the way in which they wrote of their loss. Collingwood, the more methodical, careful and thoughtful of the two, wrote in measured tones but nonetheless with feeling:- "I shall miss them grievously, she is quite a delight and makes many an hour cheerful, that without her would be a dead weight". Nelson, the more flamboyant of the two, wrote in a slightly more flowery manner:- "Her equal I never saw... I took leave of her with a heavy heart. What a treasure of a woman". John Moutray died soon after he and Mary arrived in England and both Nelson and Collingwood exchanged affectionate letters with Mary for the rest of their lives. If either man had met Mary before she married, it seems certain that one of them would have married her.

Collingwood may have been the more down to earth of the two men, but like Nelson, he was highly thought of by his crew and his man management skills were superb. He hated flogging, although he would do it when necessary, but preferred to use psychology instead, and this is what made him stand higher than officers like William Bligh, fine naval officer though Bligh was. Over the years since the *Bounty* mutiny in April, 1789, William Bligh has been portrayed as a tyrannical flogger but this is wholly unjust and wrong on both counts – he was neither a tyrant nor a flogger and in fact he flogged a great deal less than both Nelson and Captain Cook. It was just that Bligh did not have the man management skills that Collingwood had and would belittle the officers in front of the men which would cause unnecessary hurt which would then turn into resentment. As mentioned earlier, Bligh went on to have a great career in the navy before becoming Governor-General of New South Wales between 1806 and 1810. Collingwood was quite different, and two instances show how he put this into action. Midshipmen were the young gentlemen who were being trained to become officers and eventually be in charge of men much older and experienced than they were. Two of them clearly got above themselves, and one wrote later:- "Another midshipman and myself were put to mess with the common men, where we lived with them for three months... At first I was indignant at such treatment, but there was no help for it... and I am very glad I was so placed, as it gave me a great insight into the character of seamen... ". The last sentence says it all, and no doubt the midshipmen went on to become better officers as a result. The second occasion was when Collingwood felt that several midshipmen had fallen far short of the standards that he felt acceptable. As a result, he had them lined up, produced his penknife, and cut off their pigtails, giving them back to their owners saying that they could wear them again if their work came up to the required standard in future. No doubt the midshipmen were angry at the time, but the crew wouldn't have been, and again, the midshipmen no doubt learned valuable lessons for the future. Collingwood may not have wished to flog men if it could be avoided but neither was he a soft touch and his methods produced good results.

Collingwood was still in command of the *Mediator* when in early 1786, he set sail for England, arriving in July of that year. He had very mixed feelings about coming home, as he was to leave the two men that he probably loved most in the world. Nelson was one, but the other was his brother, Wilfred Collingwood, who since late 1784, had been working at the station arriving as he did in command of the *Rattler*, a 14-gun sloop. The three officers had worked well together but Cuthbert was destined never to see his brother again as Wilfred died in April, 1787, still in the West Indies and still in command of the *Rattler*. It was Nelson himself who wrote and told him of the news in a lengthy and fulsome letter and on 23rd June, 1787, it was reported in the *Newcastle Courant* with the following words:-

"On 20th April last, in the West Indies, Captain Wilfred Collingwood, Commander of His Majesty's Ship Rattler. By his death his friends have lost a most valuable and affectionate relative, and his country an active and zealous officer".

When Collingwood returned to England in 1786, naval officers were in a state of limbo. The war of American Independence had long since been fought and lost, whilst the war with France which would start in 1793 was yet to come. Whilst war wasn't wanted for the sake of it, the fact is that without it, many officers found themselves without a ship and on half pay as the government would inevitably run the service down during peacetime.

Collingwood spent a long time in London in order to keep reminding the Admiralty that he wanted a ship but he also spent time in Northumberland and whilst he was there, he planted a great many acorns so that there would be plenty of oak trees with which to make ships in years to come. It is highly likely that a 200-year-old oak tree in that area was planted by him.

In 1789 there was huge unrest in France which put Britain on alert. On the 14th July, a mob in Paris stormed and took over the Bastille and whilst France was completely bankrupt due to it helping the American colonies, it seemed to be entering a phase whereby it could become ungovernable, and therefore it was not beyond the realms of probability that she would cause problems with Britain. The French were finding the behaviour of King Louis XVI unacceptable as he seemed to think that he had some divine authority over the people of his country. It was this way of governing that Charles I exercised in England that brought about his own execution in 1649 and although leading to a bloody civil war that killed thousands and split families, it eventually led to the constitutional monarchy that came later. Louis XVI's failure to learn the lesson would lead to his own execution on 21st January, 1793, an event that shook the monarchs and governments of Europe, not least Britain.

Before this dreadful event took place however, Collingwood wanted a ship and quite understandably lobbied senior officers that he was acquainted with in order to find one. Two officers that he knew, Captain Conway and Admiral Bowyer lobbied the First Lord of the Admiralty, Lord Chatham on Collingwood's behalf. The 2nd Earl Chatham was John Pitt (1756-1835) and was the Prime Minister William Pitt's elder brother. Whilst never reaching the political heights that his more famous brother did, he nevertheless had a more than satisfactory political career serving in several governmental capacities before being made First Lord in 1788, a post he held for six years. His wife, the Hon. Mary Townshend who he married on 10th July, 1783, was the daughter of Lord (Thomas) Sydney, (1732-1800) who had a very distinguished political career and who, as Home Secretary, gave his name to the city of Sydney in Australia when the first penal colony was set up there in 1788.

Eventually, in June, 1790, Collingwood was offered command of a 32-gun frigate, the *Mermaid* that would be bound for the West Indies where Collingwood had already built up a wealth of experience. He had to raise a crew and because he was held in such high esteem by so many of the men who had served with him, the task was easier than it was for some other captains. A ship's crew that had spent a long time, sometimes years together forged a strong bond that only a good captain who was respected, and in some cases loved, could create. When raising a crew, Collingwood would select previous crew members that he liked, and ask them to join him and bring men that they knew along with them. The more men that he could recruit in this manner, meant fewer disgruntled men needing to be pressed at a later date in order to make up the numbers, the pressgang being a method Collingwood hated anyway. It was unfair to take men in this way, and disgruntled men would not help a ship run in a harmonious manner. One member of the ship's company that always stayed with him was his beloved dog Bounce. Collingwood wrote to his sister Mary:- "My dog is a good dog, delights in the ship and swims after me when I go in the boat".

The *Mermaid* was being fitted out right up to October 1790 from the previous June when Collingwood was first offered command. There were still tensions between Britain and Spain over Nootka Sound, a very small settlement on Vancouver Island. The East India Company had set up a fur-trading post there some time before not believing it was big enough for anyone else to worry about. However, Spain had other ideas and had decided to lay claim to it and sent a squadron there to seize the East India Company's assets. British ships were impounded and the crews taken prisoner which led to tensions between the two countries. So bad were relations, that Britain invested in the possibility of a full scale war but in the event, Spain eventually backed down. The incident did Britain a favour however, as it had helped her build a navy that would be prepared for the dreadful war with France that would commence in 1793, shortly after the execution of King Louis XVI.

Meanwhile, life was about to change for the bachelor naval officer. During all his naval career, he had always been keen to return to sea at the earliest opportunity, and instead of returning north, had often spent a great deal of each leave in London so that he could be near the Admiralty in the hope that he would be offered another command. This time was different however. Whilst still being a committed naval officer, he was not quite so keen to sail to the West Indies as he would normally have been. He had obviously spent part of this leave in Newcastle because during the course of it he became engaged to Sarah Blackett who was the daughter of John Erasmus Blackett, the Mayor of Newcastle. Sarah was a shy young woman whilst at the age of forty-two, Collingwood had sailed the world and fought wars. He had no choice other than to sail however and urged his sister Mary to be friends with Sarah in his absence. At the end of 1790, Collingwood and the *Mermaid* sailed to the West Indies, the squadron that they were part of being commanded by Admiral Cornish, but as Spain had retreated from her position over Nootka Sound, there was so little for them to do that they returned to Portsmouth in April 1791. Being able to return to England so soon after leaving was a piece of luck that Cuthbert Collingwood and his soon to be bride would never enjoy again, but they were not to know that when they got married on 18th June, 1791 at St. Nicholas' Cathedral in Newcastle, a stone's throw from where Collingwood was born.

Cuthbert and Sarah were together long enough to produce two daughters, Sarah, born in September, 1792, and a year later, Mary Patience. Mary was born in August, 1793, although by the time Mary, the second daughter was born, her father was at sea and he would not see her until she was some months old.

Meanwhile, events in France were proving chaotic and were causing European countries to be nervous. A Legislative Assembly had been formed and King Louis XVI had been imprisoned in Paris, whilst in Britain, Thomas Paine had published his book '*Rights of Man*' which was also causing nervousness in Britain. Paine (1737-1809) was a revolutionary writer who published a pamphlet called '*Common Sense*' in 1776, which detailed the history behind the events leading to the American War of Independence (1775-1783) and put forward the case for the American course of action. His '*Rights of Man*' published in 1792 supported the French revolution and went so far as to call for the abolition of the British monarchy. He was indicted for treason but fled to France where he was made a French citizen but fell foul of that country as well when he opposed the execution of the French King. The monarchy was formally abolished in September, 1792 and the General Convention came into being. More nervousness was spread amongst European countries who had a monarchy as the head of state when on 21st January, 1793, the French executed King Louis XVI and followed this up by declaring war on Britain ten days later on 1st February, 1793. They had already declared war on Austria and Prussia in April 1792 and Collingwood felt that a collective madness had taken over the country, although he put forward the rather forlorn hope that the new Convention would see sense and put a stop to it all, although he knew this was based more in hope than in reality.

As we now know, the Convention did not put a stop to it all, and once France had declared war, Collingwood knew that he would be required to leave his family (his second daughter Mary was not yet born) and on 17th February, 1793, he was in London waiting orders to take a ship. Dedicated to the navy, but now contented with a young family, it must have been the first time in his career that his hope of getting a command would be tinged with sorrow at leaving home.

It wasn't long before he was given the appointment of Flag Captain of the 98-gun second rate ship of the line named the *Prince*. Being given command of a flagship was always a bit of a double edged sword. Although an honour because a ship of the line was a big step up from a frigate, the 98 guns being spread over three decks, it was a mute point as to who was actually in command, the Captain, in this case Collingwood, or the Rear Admiral who was on board, in this case Sir George Bowyer. In any event, the matter was largely irrelevant in the *Prince* because both Bowyer and Collingwood were transferred to the *Barfleur* and took part in the battle that was to become known as the Glorious First of June.

The British fleet was taken out by Lord (Richard) Howe (1726-99) in the *Queen Charlotte* on 2nd May, 1794. Howe was a brilliant naval officer and like Nelson, had been appointed a Post-Captain at the age of just twenty. He distinguished himself in the seven years war with France between 1756-63 and in 1776 was commander of the British fleet during the American War of Independence. He was First Lord of the Admiralty in 1783 but returned to active service at sea in 1793 after France had declared war.

His aim was to destroy the French fleet and then pursue their unprotected convoy and subsequently destroy that. The convoy was essential for France as it would contain much needed food from the United States. His thinking was sound enough as many of the French captains had been executed in the revolution because they were seen as being part of the aristocracy, and so many lieutenants had been promoted above their capabilities to captain the ships. On top of this, the French fleet had been poorly fed and in August, 1793, left the French coast undefended whilst they took the ships into harbour in order to search for food. The National Convention then promptly executed even more officers, both commissioned and non commissioned, and this made the hierarchy in the French navy even weaker than before. The British were also far superior in their method of gunfire as they practised until they were so well drilled that they could outnumber the French by as many as five to one in the number of times they could fire. On top of this, the British had learned their lesson since the American War of Independence which they had not anticipated and the navy had been woefully unprepared for. This time, the ships had been built, the fleet was at full strength and the ships manned sufficiently. However, the one saving grace for the French was the presence of a Commander-in-Chief by the name of Louis-Thomas Villaret-Joyeuse who by his own wits, was saved from the guillotine. Although a talented officer, and an obvious asset to the French fleet, he was not given a free hand because the National Convention had sent out someone who had the power to overrule Villaret, and he was Jean-Bon Saint-Andre who frequently interfered with him and wrote back reports directly to the Convention. The aim of Villaret was not necessarily to beat the British fleet in a straight battle, but to save his convoy and he managed to do just that because Lord Howe did not go for the convoy first. Howe had pursued the French round the Atlantic until he found the fleet on 28th May, 1794 and attacked them. Viewed in terms of casualties suffered and prizes taken, then the battle was certainly technically won by the British but the convoy managed to escape as Villaret had taken his fleet to the west, thus putting Howe off the scent. There were huge casualties on both sides and although the British took several prizes, the main part of the French fleet escaped and without taking anything away from the enormous bravery shown by the British sailors, it is difficult in retrospect to see it as a great victory. Indeed, the French saw it as a victory themselves due to the fact that the convoy escaped which had been Villaret's aim all along.

Although the British were pleased with what they saw as their own victory, there was a sour aftermath suffered by Collingwood and some of his fellow officers. Admiral Bowyer had his leg blown off early in the battle and Collingwood effectively took over the running of the *Barfleur,* which at the time he would have seen as merely doing his job. However, he along with others was bitterly disappointed at not being mentioned afterwards in Lord Howe's dispatch which was written the following day. Several others were mentioned and all received medals, but not Collingwood and he was deeply hurt. He was not the only one – there were several other captains who were furious and the row over some of the omissions lasted years. Collingwood, deeply upset and affronted, refused all further awards for his service until he was finally presented with his 1st June medal. However, he was not to receive it for another three years, after the Battle of Cape St. Vincent that took place on 14th February, 1797. Then, and only then, did he feel that justice had been done.

When Collingwood returned to England he had been promised a new ship at some stage but in the meantime travelled north to see his wife and two young children. He had yet to see the younger daughter, Mary Patience, as he had been at sea when she was born. After a short time with his family and a couple of false starts concerning ships, he was offered the 74-gun two-decker *Excellent,* which would result in his not seeing his family again for four more years although fortunately he was not to know this at the time.

Collingwood had long since been worried about the conduct of the war. France had a new and young army commander called Napoleon Bonaparte who was successfully waging war on land and it seemed as if the war with France was going to be a long drawn out affair, especially as in August, 1796, Spain signed a treaty with France. It was not going to be too long after that treaty was signed before Collingwood could receive some sort of justice for not receiving a medal after the Glorious First of June battle as already mentioned. The battle that would help him achieve this was the battle of Cape St. Vincent which was fought on 14th February, 1797 between the British and Spanish fleets. The British fleet was led by Admiral John Jervis (1735-1823), an incredibly brave and possibly reckless officer in as much as he knew no fear and felt that he would win every battle he engaged in whatever the odds were that may have been stacked against him. With these characteristics he was virtually an older version of Nelson. He had entered the navy in 1749 at the age of fourteen and became a lieutenant in 1755. He had a very distinguished career and as an Admiral in 1795, he led the Mediterranean Fleet. He was created Earl St. Vincent in 1797 after the battle of the same name and was First Lord of the Admiralty from 1801 until 1804 during which time he improved the way that the Admiralty was run. He believed in training the men in gunnery and the men in the fleet were almost perfect in their ability to fire quickly and accurately. This impressed Collingwood greatly who had always believed in this type of preparation and the gunnery crew of the *Excellent* became incredibly efficient under his command. Also in the fleet was Collingwood's old friend Commodore Horatio Nelson who was in command of the *Captain.* The man who commanded the Spanish fleet was Admiral Don Jose de Cordova and one of the ships was the massive four-decker flagship *Santissima Trinidada* boasting 130 guns. Up against the British fleet of fifteen ships were set twenty-seven Spanish, and their guns outnumbered the British by two to one. This fact was not immediately clear to Jervis who wouldn't have cared anyway. He was on the flagship *Victory* with Captain Robert Calder. Calder was looking through his glass at the enemy fleet when the following conversation was supposed to have taken place:

Calder: "There are eight sail-of-the-line Sir John".

Jervis: "Very well Sir".

Calder: "There are twenty sail-of-the-line Sir John".

Jervis: "Very well Sir".

Calder: "There are twenty-five sail-of-the-line... twenty-seven Sir John".

Jervis: "Enough Sir, no more of that Sir. The die is cast and if there are fifty sail I will go through them. England badly needs a victory at present".

This conversation has been quoted as fact by historians and it certainly could have happened given the character of Sir John Jervis. Like Nelson, Jervis inspired his officers and made them feel invincible.

The two fleets met on 14th February, 1797. The normal way that naval battle took place was for both fleets to be in a parallel line with each other and then simply blast away until one either gave in or there were simply not enough ships in one of the fleets to carry on with any realistic chance of winning. Sometimes it simply wasn't clear cut as the battles were always ferocious and it was difficult to tell how many ships had struck their colours due to the smoke and general confusion. With the British so well drilled in gunfire, and with an Admiral like Jervis, had the number of ships been more equal, there would have been no question that the British would have won, but this particular battle was never going to be so straightforward as that. Many people think that it was Nelson at Trafalgar who was the man that broke with this tradition of ships simply blasting away at each other in parallel lines when he, Nelson, came at the combined Spanish and French fleets from the side, but Jervis did a similar manoeuvre at this battle, which was eight years before Trafalgar. At St. Vincent, the British were in a tight formation whilst the Spanish fleet were ill disciplined and their column had drifted into two. The Spanish were heading in an easterly direction and the British south. Jervis in the *Victory* signalled to the leading ship the *Culloden* under Captain Troubridge to attack. His plan was to cut the Spanish fleet in two which he did, the leading nine Spanish ships being separated from the rest of the fleet. The Spanish ships then turned northwards, the opposite direction to that of the British in order to escape the British fleet that was stronger than the Spanish originally thought. Although the *Culloden* tacked with a view to chasing the Spanish and attacking the rear, Captain Troubridge would not have reached the rear of the Spanish fleet in time before the van of the Spanish fleet could have carried out the exact same manoeuvre in reverse and tacked south in order to attack the rear of the British fleet. Commodore Horatio Nelson, in the *Captain*, saw exactly what was happening and being just two ships to the rear of the British fleet, broke away and went straight into attack against the van of the Spanish fleet in order to cut them off before they had a chance to attack the rear of the British fleet. The odds were so stacked against Nelson that it was virtually a suicidal mission as against his 74-gun two decker, was the enormous four decker Spanish flagship, *Santissima Trinidada* with it's 130 guns, and along with the flagship, two 112-gun three deckers and an 80-gun two decker. Sailing right behind Nelson, Collingwood in his ship, the *Excellent*, immediately followed Nelson and came to his friend's rescue before other ships of the British fleet, namely the *Culloden* and Captain Roderick of the *Blenheim* were able to join in the battle, which soon became a general melee which as it happened, was what Jervis had wanted all along.

Nelson's ship, the *Captain* was virtually wrecked by now as he was against huge odds, so he ordered her to run alongside the *San Nicolas,* which he proceeded to board with a group of seamen and marines, and after some hand to hand fighting, the Spanish officers surrendered their swords. Just as he had captured the *San Nicolas*, there was firing from the *San Jose* and Nelson and his boarding party took that ship as well. Whilst all this was going on, Collingwood and the *Excellent* were right in the middle of the melee and giving covering fire against the two Spanish ships and realising that both of them had struck her colours, carried on to fight the massive Spanish flagship, *Santissima Trinidada* which by the end of the battle was almost completely wrecked, although she survived to fight the British again at Trafalgar.

Nelson's cry when he led a boarding party was always "Westminster Abbey or Glorious Victory". Vainglorious, reckless, possibly having a death wish, perhaps just incredibly brave, perhaps all of these things, he was a great self publicist but would never have been able to achieve the glory that he had on this day without the bravery and support of Collingwood and other officers who without hesitation, brought their ships to support him with a great deal of bravery. After the battle, Nelson received and bathed in the glory, but Collingwood was content with the recognition of his peers, and the letter he received from his good friend, Horatio Nelson:-

"MY DEAREST FRIEND,

'A friend in need is a friend indeed' was never more truly verified than by your most noble and gallant conduct yesterday in sparing the *'Captain'* from further loss; and I beg, both as a public officer and a friend, you will accept my sincere thanks. I have not failed, by letter to the Admiral, to represent the eminent services of the *'Excellent'*... We shall meet at Lagos; but I could not come near you without assuring you how sensible I am of your assistance in nearly a critical situation".

It is sometimes difficult to get a true meaning when a word is taken so long after the event, but Nelson's inclusion of the word 'nearly' seems strange. It could be that he did not want to give his friend too much credit, or it could be that he was innocently understating the desperate situation that he was in because he simply knew no fear. Whatever the odds that were stacked against him, they would not have caused him any concern because like Jervis, he would have carried on regardless whatever support he may or may not have received from Collingwood and others. Either way, Collingwood was not bothered. He had received recognition from the friend that he loved, and was offered a medal for his part in this battle. As mentioned before, he initially refused it on the grounds that if he had deserved one for the Battle of St. Vincent, then he deserved one for the Glorious 1st June, 1794. Sir John Jervis, who was made Earl St. Vincent after the battle, agreed with him and so did the Admiralty. After a wait of three years and after suffering the hurt for that length of time, Collingwood received medals for both battles, and justice at last, was done and seen to be done.

1797 was not only notable for the Battle of Cape St. Vincent, but there were also two naval mutinies and the battle of Camperdown was to be fought. The first mutiny was at Spithead, which was an anchorage near Portsmouth, and this took place between the 16th April and the 15th May of that year. The channel fleet consisted of sixteen ships and were led by Admiral Lord Bridport, (1727-1814), otherwise known as Alexander Hood, and brother of Samuel, the 1st Viscount Hood (1724-1816). Lord Bridport had had a distinguished naval career and fought at the Glorious First of June battle. There was no criticism of Lord Bridport and in fact it may be a little harsh calling it a mutiny, as the men were actually on strike for grievances that many thought were reasonable; however, be that as it may, the fleet were ordered to sea on the 15th and they refused to sail so it was by naval rules a mutiny. The situation was badly handled initially as Bridport had recently taken over the command of the fleet from Lord Howe, and was not conversant with the sailors' grievances. The sailors liked and respected Lord Howe and had written several letters to him whilst he was taking the waters at Bath, but they somehow got lost because of poor administration by the Admiralty. There was a stand-off and five seamen were shot before Lord Howe was finally recalled to negotiate. The crews were protesting against the living conditions and the pay which had not been increased for over a hundred years. For the first sixty years or so after the rates were established in 1653, it did not seem to matter much as inflation had been low, but inflation suddenly

317

became a problem in the latter part of the 18th century and by 1797, the rates were hopelessly out of date. The mutineers elected delegates and apart from wanting better pay, they wanted the custom of the Purser keeping two ounces out of every pound of meat abolished. The mutineers also wanted a small number of officers whose behaviour the men felt was unduly harsh, to be removed and placed in different ships. Initially, it looked as if negotiations would break down, but once Lord Howe was brought in, matters settled down. The requests were put to the Prime Minister, William Pitt the Younger, and the First Lord of the Admiralty, Earl Spencer (1758-1834), who was the younger brother of Georgiana, Duchess of Devonshire. Spencer had first entered the House of Commons in 1780 but had to go to the Lords in 1783 when he inherited the Earldom after the death of his father, the First Earl Spencer. He was appointed First Lord in 1794 by Prime Minister Pitt and was in office when the British Navy won the battles of St. Vincent and Camperdown, both of them being fought in 1797.

He was also the Minister who appointed Horatio Nelson to lead the fleet that decimated the French fleet at the Battle of the Nile on 1st August, 1798.

However, so far as the dispute that the Channel Fleet had with The Admiralty was concerned, both Pitt and Spencer realised that the crews were making every attempt to be as reasonable as possible and also promising that they would take the ships out should it appear that the French fleet were heading towards British shores in order to attack. The men received a pay increase, the Purser's pound system was stopped, and some of the officers that had made themselves unpopular were transferred to other ships. Allowance was made for the way that the negotiations were handled by the men, and King George III agreed to pardon all the mutineers.

All seemed to be well and everything seemed to be settled to everyone's satisfaction, but unfortunately the crews of the ships at the Nore, instead of settling for what seemed to be a good deal that had already been negotiated, decided to push their luck a bit further. On 12th May, buoyed up by what they heard had happened at Spithead, the crews at the Nore followed suit with a mutiny but this was far more serious. The crew of the *Sandwich* seized control of the ship and the crews of other ships followed suit. The men elected delegates from each ship and Richard Parker was elected as 'President of the Delegates of the Fleet'. Parker was always going to be trouble as he was an agitator rather than a negotiator and he had sympathies with the French Republican cause. On the 20th May, a list of demands was presented to Admiral Buckner which included an increase in pay (these had already been won at Spithead anyway), and the modifications of the Articles of War. Had things been left there, then there probably would have been a settlement, but their demands then entered into the political arena which infuriated the Admiralty, including as they did that the King dissolve Parliament and negotiate an immediate peace with France. These ideas were extraordinary and were never going to be agreed to. It was one thing to ask for better pay and conditions, but quite another to attempt to dictate the policy of the government and the Admiralty in the politics of the war. They not only infuriated the Admiralty but frightened them too, because if the mutineers wanted an immediate peace with France, it would not be likely that they would fight the French in future battles with any meaning. Also, since the execution of Louis XVI in January, 1793, everybody feared that revolutionary ideas would spread to Britain. The government decided to get tough and Pitt ordered that gun batteries be set up in case events got out of hand. He also introduced two Emergency Bills which specified that harsh punishments would be meted out to anyone inciting the mutiny. Seeing that they had gone too far, one by one, ships drifted off leaving an isolated rump of ships and mutineers and by the middle of June the whole affair was over. Twenty-nine of the men deemed to be leaders of the dispute, including Richard Parker, were hanged and others were either flogged, put in prison or sent to the penal colony that had been set up in Australia in 1788. However, the majority of the crews suffered no punishment, but were left in no doubt as to what would happen to them should a similar incident happen again. The two mutinies combined took two months to settle and with Britain being at war with France, it had been a difficult time. Collingwood had not been impressed with the way that the Admiralty had handled the two situations. After the two strikes were over, he wrote to Alexander Carlyle, an uncle of his wife, Sarah:- "The state of the fleet in England has given me the most poignant grief. How unwise in the officers, or how impolitic in the administration, that did not attend to, and redress the first complaints of grievance, and not allow the seamen to throw off their obedience and to feel what power there is in so numerous a body".

Earl St. Vincent might well have chosen Collingwood to sort the matters out. He was reputed to have said:- "Send them (the troublesome men) to Collingwood, he will bring them to order". There was one man who *was* sent to Collingwood and he had been on the *Romulus* during the strike. He had loaded a gun, pointed it at the officers and threatened to shoot them. He was lucky not to have been hanged for that kind of behaviour but somehow he got away with it and was transferred to Collingwood's ship, the *Excellent*. In front of the whole crew, Collingwood addressed the man:-

"I know your character well, but beware how you to attempt to excite insubordination in this ship; for I have such confidence in my men, that I am certain I shall hear in an hour of every thing you are doing. If you behave well in future, I will treat you like the rest, nor notice here what happened in another ship, but if you endeavour to excite mutiny, mark me well, I will instantly head you up in a cask, and throw you into the sea".

It is often said that society is judged by how it treats the weaker members of that society. Similarly, officers were judged as to how they treated the common sailor, and Collingwood always treated his crew with respect and expected his officers to do the same. In turn, he was respected by his own crews and rarely had to resort to flogging which he hated even though it was accepted as part of 18th century naval life. He also hated any form of bullying in his officers which is why he was loved and respected by his crews, and on the occasions that he did have to punish men, it was usually accepted as being fair.

Collingwood was involved in both the battles of the Glorious 1st of June in 1794 and St. Vincent in February 1797 but missed out on the battle of Camperdown fought eight months later in October of that year. The British fleet led by Admiral Duncan fought the Dutch fleet after they had been blockaded by the British to stop them covering the planned invasion of Ireland by French troops. The Dutch had eventually come out of port and were engaged by the British fleet who attacked them using two columns rather as Nelson was to do at Trafalgar exactly eight years later in October 1805. Duncan led one column in the *Venerable* whilst Vice Admiral Richard Onslow led the other in the *Monarch*. Both fleets fought very bravely and there were heavy casualties on both sides. It was considered that there were no outright winners although the Dutch flagship, the *Vrijheid* received heavy casualties along with being dismasted and struck her colours. Captain William Bligh, who was in command of the *Director*, received Admiral de Winter's sword as he surrendered.

Instead of being where the action was, Collingwood was now taking part in the blockade of Cadiz which was essential because of the danger from the Spanish fleet. It was boring, monotonous work and it was hard to keep the crews occupied, especially when they wouldn't put in to any port for months on end. Not only that, but Collingwood's own thoughts would stray to Morpeth and he must have longed to be home to see his wife and daughters as by 1797 he had been away from them for four years. Apart from the obvious sadness at missing his young wife Sarah, he was also missing out on seeing his daughters grow up.

Collingwood was promoted to the rank of Commodore but whilst pleased at first, it meant little to him when he heard that he was not to be included when his friend Horatio Nelson was to lead a fleet to attack the French fleet which Napoleon Bonaparte had taken to Egypt in order to invade. After the disaster at Teneriffe in July 1797, when Nelson had lost an arm, he was back with his own fleet and raring to go into the battle which would finally make his reputation – the battle in which he destroyed the French fleet and was to be known as the battle of the Nile, fought on 1st August, 1798.

Prior to the Battle of the Nile, in July, 1797, Nelson had been ordered to take a fleet to the island of Tenerife and with a surprise attack, to capture the town of Santa Cruz which was not an easy prospect as although many of the troops were inexperienced, the towns defences in the form of the castle and forts were strong. It was essential that the attack would contain a large element of surprise and Nelson went ahead ignoring the caution expressed by the army commanders. Nelson dismissed their caution as cowardice and went ahead anyway but was proved wrong. There was no element of surprise due to the fact that the landing boats were easily spotted by the defending troops, and that, coupled with a rough sea and strong wind guaranteed high casualties and failure which is exactly what happened. The whole thing was a disaster and Nelson's right arm was shattered and he was rowed to the *Theseus* where the surgeon, Thomas Eshelby performed an operation to remove it. Although the operation was skilfully performed, for a long time afterwards, Nelson was ill at home and the stump would not heal. He was depressed not only because he was unwell and feeling pain from the stump, but the slowness of the wound to heal along with his failure to capture the town of Santa Cruz made him feel that his naval career was over. However, from this pit of depression, his comeback to naval duty was spectacular when he eventually recovered and came back in style to defeat the French fleet in the battle of the Nile, the battle that isolated Napoleon and his troops in Egypt, and the battle that Collingwood was so sorry to be excluded from.

Collingwood's anger spilled out in a letter that he wrote when he was back in England in December, 1798, four months after Nelson's triumph. It was not anger towards Nelson, far from it, it was due to the fact that Nelson was his friend and he wanted to be with him that made Collingwood so upset. His anger was directed at Earl St. Vincent and Collingwood was to write from Spithead:-

"The only great mortification I suffered was not going with Admiral Nelson. He (St. Vincent) knew our friendship; for many, many years we had served together, lived together, and all that ever happened to us strengthened the bond of our amity, but my going would have interfered with the aggrandisement of a favourite to whom I was senior, and so he sent me out of the way when the detachment was to be made".

If St. Vincent was favouring another officer who was junior to Collingwood, then Collingwood's anger and disappointment were quite justified and understandable, although apart from writing his feelings down, there was little he could do about it. The result of this was that whilst Nelson was making his name, and quite deservedly so, in destroying the French fleet at the Nile, Collingwood was forced to endure the boring work of blockading Cadiz until his return to England. Initially, he was not allowed to leave Portsmouth which was agonizing for him as he longed to return to Morpeth to be re-united with his wife Sarah, and their two little daughters, Sarah and Mary Patience. At last, in February, 1799, he was allowed home – he had not seen his family for six years, both his daughters being virtual babies when he had last left them. Being married to a naval officer was a very hard life as the men were often away for many years at a time, and coupled with this was the fact that there was practically no form of communication available to them to keep in any sort of contact. As well as Collingwood's absences, and the cruellest was yet to come for him, William Bligh was away from home for six out of seven years during the time of the *Bounty* episode, and again for five years when he was Governor-General of New South Wales, whilst Elizabeth Cook only saw her husband for two out of the last eleven years of her husband, Captain James Cook's life.

Collingwood enjoyed his time at home, but his mind was never far from his next command and what it would be. He and his wife Sarah enjoyed visiting friends and on a visit to London to discuss being offered a ship, Collingwood actually met Queen Charlotte, although he seems to be completely underwhelmed by the experience. Unlike his friend Nelson, who seemed to think that the Royal family of any country were practically deity, and was doing his best to ruin his newly found glorious reputation by staying in Naples with their King and Queen, Collingwood wrote of his audience with the British Queen:-

"It was an entertaining sight, to so new a courtier, to observe the pleasure that sprang into the countenances of all, when Her Majesty was graciously pleased to repeat to them a few words which were not intended to have any meaning; for the great art of the courtly manner seems to be to smile on all, to speak of all, and yet leave no trace of meaning in what is said".

Whilst he was waiting for his next command, Collingwood was promoted to Rear Admiral of the White and given the two decker, 74-gun the *Triumph* although neither the ship nor the Captain, gave him much satisfaction. The ship was probably the slowest in his fleet whilst he thought the Captain totally inadequate for the job. The quality of officers in the navy had deteriorated as there had been an expansion of the service in a short space of time that meant many officers were promoted above their abilities. Collingwood wrote of his own situation:-

"I have a captain here (Stephens), a very novice in the conduct of fleets or ships. When I joined her I found she had been twice ashore, and once on fire, in the three months he had commanded her, and they were then expecting that the ship's company should mutiny every day. I never saw men more orderly, or who seem better disposed, but I suppose they took liberties when they found they might, and I am afraid there are a great many ships where the reins of discipline are held very loosely, the effect of a long war and an overgrown navy".

The fleet was under the command of Admiral George Elphinstone, the 1st Viscount Keith (1746-1823), otherwise simply known as Lord Keith. Keith had had a distinguished career fighting in the American War of Independence (1775-83). He helped capture Toulon and commanded the expedition that captured Cape Town in 1795 and Ceylon the following year. In 1808, he married for the second time, his first wife being Jane Mercer, but she died in 1789 after just two years of marriage. His second marriage was to Hester Maria Thrale (1764-1857), the daughter of the celebrated Welsh writer, Hester Thrale, later Hester Piozzi (1741-1821) friend and confidant of the great Dr. Johnson (1709-84).

With his current command, Keith chased after the French fleet but failed to catch up with them before they entered Brest, and so the British fleet returned to Torbay and at Christmas, 1799, Collingwood found himself in Plymouth. By now, there was hope that there would at last be peace as Napoleon had written to King George III in a conciliatory fashion. Nothing came of it however, the King demanding the restoration of the Monarchy which the French would never agree to. Collingwood spent the next two years carrying out mundane blockades of various ports until on 25th March, 1802, the Treaty of Amiens was signed by Britain and France whereby Britain would recognise the French Republic. William Pitt the Younger had been Prime Minister since December 1783 but had resigned on 16th February, 1801. He was succeeded by Henry Addington (1757-1844) later 1st Viscount Sidmouth who was Speaker of the House when Pitt resigned and it was he who was Prime Minister when the Treaty was signed. For a while, it seemed that this signalled the peace that everybody craved but it was not to last. Britain felt that she had conceded too much to the French and this feeling simmered on and when Bonaparte refused to make further concessions, the Treaty broke down and war resumed on the 18th May, 1803. Another reason that the Treaty failed to last was that France accused Britain of illegally seizing six of her ships, although France never succeeded in naming either the ships or the captains. Addington was not a good Prime Minister during wartime, and he was unable to withstand the combined critical onslaught of Charles James Fox and William Pitt, who had joined the opposition after refusing a place in Addington's government. In May 1804, a year after the Treaty broke down,

Addington resigned and William Pitt took up the reins of power again on 10th May of that year. William Pitt, although not so effective a Prime Minister the second time around, was in office when Collingwood and Nelson were to have their finest hour, the 21st October, 1805, when the British fleet of twenty-seven ships of the line, defeated the combined Spanish and French fleets numbering thirty-three. Collingwood, by now a Vice-Admiral of the Red, was in command of the *Royal Sovereign* whilst the fleet was led by Admiral Lord Horatio Nelson in the flagship *Victory*, Collingwood being his second in command.

In 1805, France dominated the European continent with her army, whilst Britain had the better navy. The French had good ships, but their officers were nothing like the quality of those of the British navy due to the fact that most of their good ones had been executed, and the gunnery crews of the British were much better trained than their French counterparts. It is thought that the British could fire more accurately and at least three times the rate of the French, some historians even putting the number as five although this would be unlikely. The British fleet was led by Admiral Horatio Nelson in the *Victory* whilst the combined French and Spanish fleets were led by Admiral Pierre de Villeneuve in the *Bucentaure*. On 9th October, Nelson explained his battle plan to Collingwood before going through it with his officers. It would involve the British fleet coming at the French and Spanish at right angles with Nelson leading one column in the *Victory* and Collingwood leading the other in the *Royal Sovereign*. This would mean that the enemy would be split into three groups, having the effect of cutting off the van and removing them from the action until they had time to tack and return to the fight. The way Nelson explained it to his mistress, Emma Hamilton, shows the stark contrast between the characters of Nelson and Collingwood. Nelson, the more flamboyant of the two wrote to Emma Hamilton:-

"When I explained to them (his officers) the Nelson touch, it was like an electric shock; some shed tears, all approved, it was new, it was singular…"

In fact, it wasn't new at all – Admiral John Jervis had used similar tactics at the Battle of Cape St. Vincent in February, 1797, whilst Admiral Duncan had done the same at the Battle of Camperdown in October of the same year. Nelson certainly knew it, especially as he had fought at Cape St. Vincent, but he wasn't going to let a small detail like that get in the way of a good letter to Emma, although this should take nothing away from Nelson as a man and as an amazing naval officer. There is no doubt that Nelson had extraordinary charisma and inspired all around him with his exceptional courage and leadership qualities although Collingwood's style and temperament were completely different but nonetheless very effective. Cool, calm and always collected before a battle, he inspired his crews every bit as much as Nelson did, it's just that he did it in a different way.

Napoleon wanted to invade Britain, and in order for his invasion flotilla to land his troops, he needed the British navy to be beaten. Despite the numerical supremacy of the combined French and Spanish fleet, it was going to be a tall order, and although he was a brave officer, Villeneuve was nowhere near the calibre of Nelson. In fact, Napoleon wanted to replace him but Villeneuve wanted to fight Nelson, got wind of the fact that he was to be replaced, and this, more than anything else, meant that he changed tactics, and instead of allowing his fleet to be blockaded in Cadiz, determined to come out and fight. On the morning of 20th October, Villeneuve brought his combined French and Spanish fleet out of Cadiz in order to sail to the Strait of Gibraltar, but realising that he wouldn't make it, attempted to return to Cadiz, but was cut off by Nelson's fleet. At dawn the following day, the 21st, the two fleets met. Collingwood's servant Smith, on board the *Royal Sovereign*, entered the Admiral's cabin and was amazed at the calm way that he was shaving whilst discussing the oncoming battle to Smith in a measured, matter of fact way. It was this attitude that inspired men just as much as Nelson's flamboyant character trait.

The British fleet split into their two columns with Nelson leading one on board the *Victory* and Collingwood leading the other in the *Royal Sovereign*. Collingwood had recently changed from the *Dreadnought* and was unhappy about this for two reasons. The first being that the crew was new to him – he had built up a relationship with the crew of *Dreadnought* and had taught them the art of skilled gunnery. The second reason was that the *Royal Sovereign* was the slowest ship in the fleet, or so Collingwood thought, but unknown to him, the recent copper bottom that she had had fitted had transformed her into the fastest, which meant that once the battle commenced, she would reach the enemy fleet before Nelson and the *Victory* and this is precisely what happened. At 11.40am Nelson hoisted his famous signal "England expects that every man will do his duty". There are different stories as to how this signal was received. Most say that it had an inspired effect on all the crews and produced cheering round the fleet, but others say quite the opposite. It certainly produced a mild dose of irritation from Collingwood who said of his friend:- "I wish Nelson would stop signalling. We all know what we have to do". Collingwood's way was rather more low key but equally effective in raising the moral of his men. Just before the *Royal Sovereign* was to engage the enemy, he called his officers together and said:- "Now gentlemen, let us do something today which the world may talk of hereafter".

Everything was now ready for the battle – the cabins cleared for action stations and the deck wetted and sprinkled with sand to help mop up the inevitable blood that would soon flow. The two columns headed towards the enemy with the *Royal Sovereign* in the lead taking a heavy pounding from the enemy fleet with no hope of returning fire for twenty minutes. Collingwood, calm as ever, turned to his captain, Edward Rotheram and said:- "What would Nelson give to be here". At what was probably about the same time, Nelson was heard to cry:- "See how that noble fellow Collingwood takes his ship into action. How I envy him!" When at last the *Royal Sovereign* was able to turn her fire on the enemy fleet, the effect was devastating. The guns of the *Royal Sovereign* raked the huge three decker *Santa Anna*, the flagship of the Spanish Admiral Don Ignatius d'Alava and the first broadside alone killed or wounded over a hundred men and was so deadly, that it virtually finished the Spanish ship as a fighting machine because so many of her guns were destroyed. Nelson could only watch with envy as this was going on as he had yet to reach the enemy fleet. As the battle wore on, the *Royal Sovereign* was dismasted although at 2.30pm, the *Santa Anna* struck her colours and surrendered to Collingwood's ship. It was at this time that Collingwood was told the terrible news that Nelson had been shot by a sniper who was in the rigging of the *Redoutable*. The French used this method of warfare to great effect, putting Marines in the rigging with a view to shooting at the British officers, many of whom had not changed out of their conspicuous uniforms, thus making them an easy target. Nelson, with all his regalia, was a sitting duck and the one bullet entered his spine and was clearly going to be fatal. Collingwood didn't know this at the time but took an educated guess. Later on, he was to write to his and Nelson's friend, Mary Moutray:- "An officer came from the *'Victory'*, to tell me he was wounded. He sent his love to me, and desired me to conduct the fleet. I asked the officer if the wound was dangerous, and he by his look told what he could not speak, nor I reflect upon now, without suffering again the anguish of that moment".

Collingwood tells a different story to that of Nelson's captain and friend, Thomas Masterson Hardy, who says that Nelson would not relinquish command of the battle until the moment of his death. It is easy to understand that Nelson would have difficulty in handing over command, much as he loved and respected his friend Collingwood, but it is equally difficult to understand how Nelson, away from the action, mortally wounded and fighting for breath could play any meaningful part in the battle as he simply would not be able to see anything that was going on. He was dying a slow and painful death. However, it is also not easy to see that Collingwood would be able to play too much of a leadership role in the conduct of the fight, as the ships were in a melee, which is exactly as Nelson had intended with his right angled two pronged attack, and it would really be a case of each ship being on its own and doing the best that it could.

The battle continued in a ferocious way and prior to the *Santa Anna* striking her colours, Captain Lucas of the *Redoutable* had surrendered. He had 643 men wounded and just 99 fit men left. Nelson died at 4.30pm, his last words being:- "Thank God I have done my duty". The British won the battle which stopped any invasion plans that Napoleon had harboured. The victory at Trafalgar had justified the earlier comment made by the always supremely confident Earl St. Vincent when as First Lord of the Admiralty between 1801 and 1804, he had previously said:- "I do not say the French cannot come. I only say that they cannot come by water". Trafalgar was a great battle won, of that there is no doubt, but the price was heavy.

Although nineteen of the combined Spanish and French had surrendered without a single British ship striking her colours, the British fleet itself was all but destroyed, with many of the ships being dismasted and unable to function properly. The state of the fleet was not helped by the fact that there was a dreadful storm which commenced the next night and which damaged the ships even further and caused the British to lose some of their captured ships. In all, the British had a total of 449 officers and men killed and 1,241 wounded, whilst the French and Spanish fleet suffered many more than that. Estimates say that 2,600 officers and men were killed or wounded whilst 4,400 were captured – it had been an amazing victory and whilst it immortalised Nelson's name, the role of Admiral Cuthbert Collingwood has long been underestimated if not all but forgotten.

There were no great naval battles between France and Britain after Trafalgar, but it was nowhere near the end of the war with France – that would not happen for another ten years until August 1815 when the Duke of Wellington (1769-1852) beat the French army on the battlefields of Waterloo. Wellington was born Arthur Wellesley and after a distinguished military career became Prime Minister between 1828 and 1830. Meanwhile, Collingwood, despite ill health that had started before Trafalgar, had repeatedly asked to go home, but his requests were always denied on the grounds that he was too important to be allowed to retire. He was created Baron Collingwood of Caldburne and Hethpool, given a pension for life and was given the freedom of several cities and towns although whilst appreciated, none of these honours were of much use to a man who was kept at sea for the rest of his life. His dry humour never left him however, as in a letter to his wife Sarah after being made a Baron, he wrote of his dog Bounce:-

"I am all out of patience with Bounce. The consequential airs he gives himself since he became a Right Honourable Dog are insufferable. He considers it beneath his dignity to play with commoners' dogs, and truly thinks that does them grace when he condescends to lift up his leg against them. This, I think, is carrying the insolence of rank to the extreme, but he is a dog that does it".

Life was not good for Collingwood after Trafalgar. He had lost his great friend Horatio Nelson, was continually very ill and year in, year out, he was involved in the tedious blockade work in the Mediterranean where he had been made Commander in Chief of the fleet. It must have been a tremendous anti-climax after Trafalgar and he was always desperate for one last battle so that he could finish the French fleet off once and for all, but it was never to be. Despite being continually tired and ill, his repeated requests to be relieved of his command and return home to Morpeth were always denied him and he never saw his wife and daughters again. He was at Port Mahon on the island of Menorca when he finally wrote to Lord Mulgrave resigning his commission as Commander in Chief but it was far too late for him to get home and enjoy any time with Sarah and the girls in Morpeth. He was suffering from stomach cancer and was barely able to walk. On the 6th March, 1810, he was taken on board the *Ville de Paris* to commence his journey home, but the following day he died, unable to fight his illness any more.

His remains were brought home to Portsmouth and after being taken to the Nore, his body travelled by barge up to Greenwich where he laid in state from 26th April to 11th May. He was then laid to rest next to his great friend Horatio Nelson in St. Paul's Cathedral in a plain and simple tomb, which is probably what this modest man would have wished for. Many seamen of all ranks were at his funeral. Some of them had never even met Collingwood, but such was his reputation that they wanted to be there. Amongst the mourners was the extraordinary Admiral Sir John Jervis, Earl St. Vincent who lived until 1823, dying at the age of 88 years.

Admiral Collingwood came home in the end, and the nation was quite right to lay him to rest with Nelson, but this great hero deserved better than the way he was treated in the latter part of his life. Trafalgar should have been his crowning glory, and yet it seems typical of this modest man, that in a letter to his and Nelson's friend, Mary Moutray in the spring of 1807, less than eighteen months after the battle, he assumed that Trafalgar would have been all but forgotten. This was in a reply to a letter from her when she had asked him for a piece of wood from the *Royal Sovereign* as a souvenir. Trafalgar has never been forgotten, and probably never will be, but sadly, it does seem to many that the name of Admiral Cuthbert Collingwood has. The modest man from Morpeth probably felt that he was merely doing his job, but the victory over the combined French and Spanish fleet on that October day in 1805 was just as much his achievement as it was Nelson's. His courage, skill and a lifetime of dedication to his country must surely rank him alongside the great English heroes of his age - he surely deserves to be remembered as such.

-oOOo-

12

Georgiana, Duchess of Devonshire
(1757-1806)

*Society lady and fashion icon, an ancestor of Diana Spencer, and
supporter of the Whig Party.*

Georgiana was born on 7th June, 1757 at Althorp, the famous house just outside
Northampton, to John Spencer (1734-83) who was the 1st Earl Spencer, and
Margaret Georgiana (1737-1814) who was the daughter of the Rt. Hon. Stephen
Poyntz, the couple marrying in 1755. Margaret Georgiana Poyntz (usually
known as Georgiana) met young Georgiana's father, John Spencer in 1754 and
was immediately smitten – she was just seventeen but she knew her own mind
when she saw the handsome man who was just twenty years old. During this
period of his life, he would dress in the fashions of the French aristocracy, and
despite the fact that he seemed to value this somewhat shallow lifestyle, there
was obviously much more to him than that as he was equally attracted to the
clever Margaret Georgiana Poyntz. The future Lady Spencer was attractive to
look at but more importantly, was very clever, being able to read and write
French, Italian and Greek.

John Spencer was as deeply in love with her as she was with him and
courted Margaret Georgiana during the spring and summer of 1754. In late
spring of the following year, her family, the Poyntzes, and his family, the
Spencers, spent a week in Wimbledon together waiting for the shy John Spencer
to ask the question that they were all waiting for him to ask. Unable to cope with
a rejection, he seemed to not want to risk it, but at the last minute, just as the two
families were about to take their leave of each other, he produced a diamond and
ruby ring and the engagement became official.

John Spencer, Georgiana's father, did not inherit any titles on the death of
his father, the Hon. John Spencer (1708-1746). This John Spencer was
Georgiana's grandfather who married Georgiana Carteret (1716-80), the
daughter of the 2nd Earl Granville, in 1734. His elder brother (Georgiana's great
uncle) was Charles (1706-58) and was the Third Duke of Marlborough, so his
titles passed to his descendents. Charles had become the third Duke because his
mother, Anne (1683-1716) was the younger daughter of John Churchill (1650-
1722), the 1st Duke of Marlborough and the hero of the Battle of Blenheim.
John's eldest daughter Henrietta (1681-1733) had been created 2nd Duchess of
Marlborough on the death of her father, but to stop the line dying out, Charles
was given special dispensation and so he became the 3rd Duke of Marlborough.
Although Charles had inherited the title, he had no right to the Marlborough
fortune (although he inherited Blenheim Palace) until his grandmother, the 1st
Duke's widow, Sarah (1660-1744) died. However, Sarah had been greatly

angered when Charles opposed the government of the day against her express wishes and so she left her husband's (the 1st Duke of Marlborough) £1 million pound estate to Charles's brother John (Georgiana's grandfather) with the proviso that neither he nor his son (Georgiana's father) accept a post in any future government.

This arrangement allowed Georgiana's father to take a seat in Parliament but not to accept ministerial office which meant that not only was he to be immensely rich, he would never have to work in any meaningful way in his life. He did not have to wait long for his riches. John Spencer was only eleven years old when his father (Georgiana's grandfather) died in 1746 leaving a fortune of £750,000 which would be worth approximately £45 million in today's terms. Lord Spencer received an income of £700 a week (approx £42,000 in today's terms) along with several residences. This was an extraordinary amount of money by any standards, but to inherit it at such a young age almost certainly did him no favours in the long term as it would have robbed him of any ambition that he may have had. Some men could handle that kind of wealth accumulated at an early age such as the botanist Joseph Banks (1743-1820) whose life has been dealt with in another chapter. Banks went on to lead a useful and fulfilled life, but not so the young John Spencer. His life was spent in the pursuit of pleasure which would eventually lead to ill-health overtaking him.

Georgiana's father, John Spencer, was not very active politically, in fact the terms of his great grandmother, Sarah's will saw to that, but in any event, he was fairly indifferent to the frenetic world of politics generally. However, in 1765, Thomas Pelham Holles, the Duke of Newcastle, (1693-1768), who had been the Whig Prime Minister between 1754-56 and again in 1757-1762, but who was now Lord Privy Seal in the Rockingham government, awarded Spencer an Earldom for his consistent loyalty, but this did not change the now Lord Spencer's languid character. There was no universal suffrage in the 18th century and whilst there were some places, for instance universities, that had some sort of voting to create some idea of democracy, a great many boroughs were each owned by a wealthy family and these were known as pocket boroughs, and then later, rotten boroughs. The pocket boroughs came with the land that the particular landowner purchased. The electorate was miniscule and could easily be bribed to return a particular candidate that the landowner wanted, and the Spencers did this in the fashion of the day, which was for wealthy families to host what were known as Public Days, in which they invited the local people into their homes with a view to them voting for the candidate of the family's choice. The Spencers were no different from other wealthy families in taking part in this, but opening his house from time to time was the most that Lord Spencer did in the way of being involved in politics.

John and Margaret Georgiana Spencer had three children who lived into adulthood. Georgiana was the eldest, the other two being George John (1758-1834) who was to become the 2nd Earl Spencer on the death of his father in 1783, and Henrietta Frances (1761-1821). Georgiana's mother was to give birth twice more, to Charlotte in 1765 but she lived only one year, dying a short time after her first birthday, and Louisa who was born in 1769 but who only lived for a few weeks. Despite the fact that infant mortality was high in the 18th century, the two deaths shattered Lady Spencer. She had breastfed Charlotte herself instead of leaving her to a wet nurse and consequently had become closer to the child. When Charlotte died, both Lord and Lady Spencer were devastated but the other sadness was still to come. In 1769 she gave birth again, this time to Louisa, but sadly this little girl lived only for a few weeks. Distraught over this, the reactions of the Spencers affected the surviving children greatly. Lord and Lady Spencer started to travel abroad a great deal, hardly spending more than a few weeks out of the year in England, sometimes taking their children, sometimes not. They also worried about the children much more than they normally would and thirdly they became very religious. This affected Georgiana more than George and Harriet. Lady Spencer made Georgiana pray for hours on end confining her to her room in the process. Fortunately, when Georgiana ceased to be a child and started to become a young woman, Lady Spencer eased off but continued to worry about the children.

Despite being made to spend a great deal of her time in prayer, Georgiana had a happy childhood and her parents were affectionate and loving. Their marriage was essentially happy in the early years and as is usual in that situation, the children were happy, all that is, except, the youngest, Harriet. Georgiana excelled at writing and would delight her parents and their friends by composing little poems and stories that were often read aloud to everyone after an evening meal. George, the middle child was clever but being the only male offspring, saw it as his duty to be quiet and dependable and someone who could be relied upon. Harriet however, being the youngest received the least attention. She was sensitive and clever but was simply overlooked when compared to Georgiana who always received the bulk of the attention, whilst George continued in his role as the clever, mature and reliable child. Harriet tried to receive attention by default by being with Georgiana and almost acting as her assistant, hoping that some of the attention that Georgiana received would rub off; sadly however, most of the time it did not.

Overall though, it was a fairly happy household, but it was always Georgiana who was the favourite, and this never changed. The special love that existed between Georgiana and her mother continued right through until Georgiana reached adulthood. At seventeen, Georgiana wrote the following to her mother: "You are my best and dearest friend, you have my heart and may do what you will with it".

As a child, Georgiana was used to the good things in life, and like all wealthy families of their time, her parents had more than one house, in fact they had several. Their main residence was Althorp, but they also had a house in Grosvenor Street, London where the family stayed during the so-called 'season'. During the summer, they stayed at a Palladian villa at Wimbledon Park to get away from the stench of the London cesspools, and in the autumn they went to their hunting lodge in Pytchley near Kettering. During the winter, between November and March, they would return to Althorp, which even then had been the seat of the Spencer family for three hundred years.

The settled life that the children enjoyed however was to be interrupted in 1763, when Georgiana was six years old. Despite the fact that her father was not yet thirty, he suffered from ill-health due mainly to trouble with his lungs which caused him to be moody which in turn affected Lady Spencer who was having problems coping with the situation. John and Georgiana Spencer (he was not to become Lord Spencer until 1765) decided to travel to Spa (now in Belgium) with Georgiana leaving George and Harriet behind because it was considered that they were too young to undertake such a journey. It was not a success however, as by now, Georgiana's father had a propensity to see the negative side of everything and continued to complain. Georgiana's mother refused to give up however, and suggested that the couple go to Italy which they proceeded to do but made the strange decision to leave Georgiana behind. This was a double blow to the young Georgiana as she not only felt that she was being abandoned by her parents, but her siblings, George and Henrietta were back in England, so she did not have them for company. Georgiana had no idea why her parents had left her, and it made her feel very insecure as a result. She stayed behind in Antwerp, being looked after by her maternal grandmother, Mrs. Poyntz, and because she felt that her parents leaving her meant that she was being punished for something that she had done, did everything she could to please her grandmother. This went on for a year and when little Georgiana's parents returned, her joy at seeing them was overwhelming. Georgiana's mother immediately noticed the change in her daughter's behaviour and liked what she saw, although she did not realise that Georgiana's improved behaviour came at a cost to the child. Georgiana now lacked self confidence which meant that she relied on others and this lack of confidence, taken into adulthood, left her vulnerable to those who wished to manipulate her.

It was three years later that the family were to experience the double tragedy of losing Charlotte and Louise in 1766 and 1769 respectively. Lord and Lady Spencer not only turned to religion as mentioned earlier, but also paradoxically, to gambling. Lady Spencer certainly felt guilty about this, and although she talked often about the need to give it up, the will was weak and the gambling persisted. They had gaming tables set up at Althorp and Spencer House, and Georgiana used to creep down from her bedroom and saw quite clearly what was going on. Her parents even allowed Georgiana to take part when she was older which inevitably helped lead to her later addiction to gambling when she was away from home and married. The Spencer House that was now being used had been built over a period of seven years and that was the age that Georgiana was when the family moved in, becoming the house that the Spencer family used when in London, overlooking as it did Green Park. Besides taking seven years to build, it also cost an enormous £50,000 which in today's terms, would be about £3 million. Lord Spencer had acquired a large collection of antiquities and he wanted a house that would be worthy of that collection. When he first opened the house to the public, one of the first people to look round and admire it was Arthur Young (1741-1820), the writer and economist. Young had had many publications to his credit and was brother-in-law to the famous musician, Charles Burney (1726-1817), who in turn was father of the writer Fanny Burney (1743-1820). The two men had married sisters, Young marrying Martha Allen in 1765 and Burney marrying his second wife Elizabeth Allen, a wealthy widow from King's Lynn in 1767. Young wrote:- "I know not in England a more beautiful piece of architecture... superior to any house I have seen... The hangings, carpets, glasses, sofas, chairs, tables, slabs, everything, are not only astonishingly beautyful, but contain a vast variety". Everything connected with the house reflected Lord Spencer's taste, from the classical facade to the interior which was beautifully decorated with no expense spared. He also collected rare books and statues and would always bring something of that nature, along with a number of paintings back to the house when returning from one of his trips abroad.

In 1771, Georgiana turned fourteen years of age, and to Lady Spencer's dismay, was already becoming the object of speculation as to who she might marry. Lady Spencer told a friend that she did not want her daughter to marry before the age of eighteen which still seems very early today, but was quite normal in the 18th century. From an early age, girls were brought up to believe that their future role was that of a wife, which would entail producing children, preferably a male heir, and keeping house for their husbands. They were not expected to have political opinions or to undertake any, as they saw it, vulgar pastimes such as writing for a living, as Fanny Burney and Jane Austen were to do. Both Burney and Austen had published their early novels anonymously as women writers were frowned upon. Nothing much was expected of Georgiana other than to marry a member of the aristocracy and eventually produce a son and heir for the husband. Georgiana had so far obliged by acquiring a poise way beyond her years, which probably accounted for the early interest in her future.

In 1772, the family travelled again, this time taking all three children with them. When they were in Paris, Georgiana received a great reception at the French Court and impressed the courtiers there which confirmed Lady Spencer's worst fears, but after spending a few months travelling round France, the family moved to Spa during the summer of 1773 in time for Georgiana's sixteenth birthday. They were to catch up with many old friends there, but one man they met would change the family's life forever, and that was the twenty-four year old William Cavendish (1748-1811), the 5th Duke of Devonshire.

Spa was the place that William's father, the 4th Duke of Devonshire had died in in 1764 at the age of just forty-four years. He had been a Whig Prime Minister for a short while between 1756 and 1757, but he was clearly not suited to the job and was merely a stopgap. In fact he filled in for a few months between the two spells that Thomas Pelham Holles, (1693-1758), the Duke of Newcastle had held the post. Newcastle had been Prime Minister between 1754 and 1756 and again from 1757 to 1762 and it was he who had awarded Georgiana's father an Earldom in 1765 making him the 1st Earl Spencer. Sometimes people come to a job because of who they are not rather than who they are and this is what happened to the 4th Duke of Devonshire. The Duke was an amiable man who could not handle the rough and tumble and inevitable back stabbing that went on in 18th century politics in the same way as it does today. In 1754, Thomas Pelham Holles, the Duke of Newcastle, had succeeded his brother Henry Pelham (1695-1754) who had been Prime Minister since 1743 but who died suddenly in 1754. Thomas Pelham Holles had worked closely with his brother during all that time and was tired and therefore decided to retire in 1756. The obvious candidates for the succession were William Pitt (the elder, later the 1st Earl of Chatham) who lived between 1708 and 1778, and Henry Fox (later the 1st Lord Holland) who lived between 1705 and 1774, but these men would not support an administration with the other at its head. George II therefore found himself in the position of having to find an alternative man who would not upset either Fox or Pitt, hence the appointment to the post of Prime Minister of the 4th Duke of Devonshire which solved the King's problem in the short term but inevitably meant a brief tenure, as indeed was the case. The Duke of Newcastle returned to the job of being Prime Minister in 1757 but faced unexpected opposition in 1760 when George III ascended to the throne. The new king was determined to get rid of those who presently held power and in 1762, Newcastle and his Whig government were ousted and the king's former tutor, Lord Bute (1713-92) became Tory Prime Minister, making it the second time in six years for Newcastle that he had made way for a man who was totally unsuited for the top job. Bute did not last long, resigning the following year making way for the Whig George Grenville (1712-70) who held the post for two years from 1763 until 1765, before he made way for Lord Rockingham (1730-82). Meanwhile, in the abrupt and unexpected 1762 change of government that was brought about by King George III, the 4th Duke of Devonshire suffered, because although no longer Prime Minister, he had held the post of Lord Chamberlain in the second Newcastle administration and was removed from the post and removed also from the Privy Council. He never forgot what he considered to be a cruel insult, and when he died a few years later in 1764, his sixteen-year-old son William, who had become the 5th Duke of Devonshire, carried forward the family's dislike of the king.

The 5th Duke was a very reserved man and that has to be because of his upbringing. Born in 1748, he virtually had no relationship with his mother, Lady Charlotte Boyle (1731-54), who died at the age of just 23 years when young William was just six, and the future 5th Duke, along with his brothers Richard and George, and sister Dorothy, were brought up by aunts and uncles but without the parental love that one would normally hope for.

William Cavendish, the 5th Duke of Devonshire and the man who was eventually to become the husband of Georgiana, came into a fortune when he was just sixteen, his father dying in 1764. His inheritance was so large it was greater even than that which Georgiana's father, the 1st Earl Spencer had received. Apart from the properties that he inherited, Spencer had received an income of £36,500 per annum (over £2 million in today's terms). However, one estimate put the Duke of Devonshire's income at £60,000 a year (or £3,600,000 in today's valuation). He also inherited some enviable properties. The obvious one to mention first was the incredible Chatsworth House in Derbyshire that visitors marvel at to this day. He also had three properties in London; Chiswick House, Burlington House, and Devonshire House. Finally, there was Lismore Castle in Ireland, and in Yorkshire, Hardwick House and Bolton Abbey, making a total of seven properties in all.

The Duke was quiet and reserved, not unlike Georgiana's father, so she was not put off by that when she met him. Brought up by aunts and uncles, he was a lonely child and this made him the shy reserved adult that he became. Intellectually, he was a clever man and was considered an expert on Shakespeare and the classics. If an argument broke out concerning anything to do with the classics when the Duke visited Brook's Club, the members would look to the Duke for the definitive answer. Sir Nathanael William Wraxall (1751-1831), the English writer of memoirs wrote:- "On all disputes that occasionally arose among the members of the club relative to passages of the Roman poets or historianians, I know that appeal was commonly made to the Duke, and his decision or opinion was regarded as final". Georgiana spent a great deal of time during the summer of 1773 attending dinners where the Duke was also present, and had danced with him on several occasions. By the end of that summer, she had decided that she definitely wanted to be married, but it appeared that Georgiana seemed to be in love with the idea of marriage as opposed to necessarily falling in love with the Duke that worried her mother, Lady Spencer. Georgiana was still only sixteen, hardly worldly wise, and she took the simplistic view that because both the Duke and her own father were reserved men, then they were both of the same mould. This was not necessarily so, because after her marriage, Georgiana received a very touching letter from her father saying how much he loved and missed her. The 5th Duke had his good points, but it is difficult to imagine him ever expressing such tenderness towards her in the form of the written word. When he left Spa in the autumn of 1773, Georgiana was worried that he would choose someone else, although her mother was somewhat relieved, not because of any dislike towards the Duke, but simply because she felt that Georgiana was too young for marriage. Unbeknown to Georgiana and her mother however, the Duke had already come to the conclusion that Georgiana would one day be his bride; indeed, it would be strange if he thought otherwise. Her mother once said to a friend that:- "Georgiana is indeed a lovely young woman, very pleasing in her figure, but infinitely more so from her character and disposition". If this wasn't enough for him, there was the added attraction (as they saw it in the 18th century) that she would bring a large dowry to the marriage, and also that the Cavendishes and the Spencers were on an equal footing from the viewpoint of their social standing. Eventually, the Duke made his intentions known and the matter was discussed between the two families and finalised in the autumn of 1774. Georgiana was happy but not necessarily because she was madly in love, after all, she hardly knew the Duke and because of her age, had hardly had the chance to meet someone else. In fact Georgiana's happiness had more to do with the fact that she wanted to please her parents so much, that she allowed herself to believe that she was in love, and her joy convinced the Spencer family that it was a genuine love match. However, Lady Spencer was not entirely happy with the proposed union, still believing that Georgiana was being married at too young an age. Despite Lady Spencer's misgivings, the wedding date was fixed although Lady Spencer's reservations continued for the same reason - she simply felt that Georgiana was too young and inexperienced to understand the responsibilities that being the Duchess of Devonshire would bring. When they were apart, she would write to Georgiana criticising her behaviour and pointing out a lengthy set of rules that she should abide by. Lady Spencer would also confide in her friends that she thought Georgiana too young saying that she was 'amiable, innocent and benevolent, but she is giddy, idle, and fond of dissipation'. Despite this, there is no doubt that Lady Spencer loved Georgiana a great deal and would have been even more worried about the forthcoming marriage because of something that some of her friends had noticed, but Lady Spencer clearly hadn't, and that was the Duke's demeanour.

One of Lady Spencer's friends was Mary Hamilton (1756-1816) the famous diarist. In fact she was so famous that she was once called the 'the female Pepys' for her illuminating insight into the life at the Royal Court at the end of the eighteenth century. She was a niece of the famous Lady Hamilton, the mistress of Lord Nelson, and she was a member of the famous 'Blue Stocking Club' which consisted of a group of famous women who would meet on a regular basis for intellectual conversation. Mary Hamilton's striking good looks made her the object of the Prince Regent's (1762-1830) affections. He became Prince Regent in 1811 and reigned as George 1V between 1820 and 1830. In 1779, when he was sixteen, he sent her 78 love letters but as a callow youth six years her junior, his overtures towards her were unsuccessful.

With regard to Lady Georgiana and the Duke of Devonshire, Mary Hamilton recorded that:- 'We drank tea in the Spring Gardens; Lady Spencer and daughter, Lady Georgiana, and the Duke of Devonshire joined us: he walked between Lady Georgiana and I, we were very Chatty, but not one word spoke the Duke to his betrothed nor did one smile grace his dull visage. — Notwithstanding his rank and fortune I would not marry him — they say he is sensible and has good qualities — it is a pity he is not more ostensibly agreeable, dear charming Lady Georgiana will not be well matched.'

Like Mary Hamilton, Mary Delany (1700-88), the writer and diarist and also a member of the Blue Stocking Club, was equally unconvinced about the suitability of the marriage. She was at a ball which Georgiana also attended in May of 1774. Georgiana had danced so much that the combination of that, along with the constricting nature of the dress that she was wearing, caused her to faint. The Duke, who was on the other side of the room showed no emotion when told what had occurred and did not bother to go and see how Georgiana was. It was not the actions of a man in love with his future bride but such was the excitement at the prospect of these two famous families uniting, most people ignored this fact and the press were soon dubbing it as the wedding of the year. As it turned out, it was a very quiet affair, the wedding as it was taking place on the 7th June, 1774, at the parish church at Wimbledon Park. It seems extraordinary considering the expected nature of the wedding, but there were only five people present. These were Lord Richard Cavendish, the Duke's brother, their sister Dorothy, who was now the Duchess of Portland, and Georgiana's parents, Lord and Lady Spencer, along with her grandmother, Lady Cowper. Neither Georgiana's brother, George, the future 2nd Earl Spencer, nor her sister, Henrietta, attended. The expected date of the wedding was to be two days later than the actual wedding itself, but it was brought forward in great secrecy as it was felt that it would attract too many onlookers. The idea of a quiet, secret wedding appealed to the romantic side of Georgiana, and she was a happy bride that day, but the Duke of Devonshire looked anything but happy, his thoughts being far away. Not a great distance from the wedding venue, a lady called Charlotte Spencer was nursing a newly born girl, also called Charlotte. Charlotte Spencer was no relation to the Duke's new wife but the unfortunate connection was due to the new baby Charlotte being the Duke's child. The Duke of Devonshire was the father of a baby that was a few weeks old when he married a woman other than the baby's mother – it was not a good start to the marriage.

The newly married Duchess was expected to call on all the people that society deemed to be important, and for the next three weeks she did just that, spending a quarter of an hour making fairly meaningless but nonetheless polite conversation whilst she was being judged by the various families. A visit from the Duchess was deemed an honour by these families but the fact that she was able to visit as many as 500 in that short space of time would imply that any judgements that were made were fairly superficial.

In early July, after just a few weeks of marriage, the Duke and his new bride travelled to Chatsworth where they planned to stay for the summer. The journey from London to Derbyshire took three days by coach and was difficult for both the Duke and the Duchess, especially the Duchess as the taciturn Duke had barely said two words to Georgiana whilst she, nervous at his lack of conversation talked incessantly and almost certainly irritated him as a result. In fact, he had hardly spoken to her at all since the wedding but her role in the marriage, which was simply to produce a male heir, had not yet dawned on her.

Georgiana was taking a step into the unknown by going to Chatsworth. Althorp was big, but Chatsworth was far more daunting than anything that she had so far seen. As in so many aristocratic houses of the time, it was built to be more than a family home. The rooms were huge and decorated in such a way as to create an atmosphere in which the general public, or the lower orders as the aristocracy called them, would be awestruck when entering on Public Days, and awestruck they certainly were. However, although the public were impressed, the nature of a house like Chatsworth meant that it was hardly a home as such, it was there to show off the wealth of the family, but despite its grandeur, not everyone was impressed. The rooms were criticised for being too dark and one diarist criticised the grounds for 'lacking in taste'. The grounds were produced by the famous Lancelot 'Capability' Brown (1716-83) and although loved by many, some people thought he was lacking in ideas and his designs were much the same wherever he worked. He was however, highly regarded by the majority and worked at Blenheim Palace, Kew, and Warwick Castle amongst other places.

To the relief of the Duchess, she was not alone with the Duke for long, as her parents and sister Harriet came for a lengthy stay. Georgiana was more than happy with this situation as they provided support for her as some of the Duke's family had already started to arrive with the sole aim of inspecting Georgiana and her suitability of being the Duchess of Devonshire. She was always on show and she had little privacy. There were always servants around as well as neighbours and the general public, and being the wife of one of the most powerful men in the country meant that she was starting to be written about in the newspapers. She also had to make friends with the Duke's tenants which she did whilst the men went out shooting in the morning. Meanwhile, more and more of the Duke's friends were arriving at Chatsworth to cast their judgemental eye over the Duke's new bride and Georgiana derived great support from the fact that her mother stayed with her during this time. After her morning duties, Georgiana would normally rest at midday and get ready for dinner which usually started at 3.00pm. After dinner, she would play cards with the guests and often listened to music played by the Italian violinist Felice Giardini (1716-96), the director of the Opera and a friend of the Spencer family. Giardini was born in Turin and it was noticed early on in his childhood that he was a prodigy. He studied singing, harpsichord, and violin in Milan and mastered all three skills well, but it was on the violin that he really excelled. He was also a prolific composer and whilst he wrote in all styles, it was opera and chamber music that he favoured.

Georgiana enjoyed the music and all the while that she had her mother for support, she found her life relatively enjoyable even if slightly boring. Unfortunately however, the support that Georgiana had received from the presence of her mother was abruptly brought to an end, as Lady Spencer had suffered a miscarriage and wanted to return to Althorp as soon as possible which she did leaving Georgiana alone just as the Public Days were starting. She left so abruptly that she did not even say goodbye to Georgiana, setting off very early one morning merely leaving her a note. They continued to write to each other however, and their relationship was not seriously damaged by this, but it did leave Georgiana alone with the Duke at Chatsworth.

In September, 1774, three months after their wedding, the penny started to drop with Georgiana that her husband was not in love with her. She began to realise that although not overtly unkind, her husband was distant, continued to pursue his own particular interests as if he were still unmarried, and her role was merely to carry out the normal duties of looking after the Cavendish tenants, as well as to produce a son and heir. She would write to express her feelings to her mother, but Lady Spencer merely reinforced the fact that Georgiana's prime duty was to make her husband happy, and that in itself should make Georgiana happy. Even if the Duke did love Georgiana, he had received no love as a child and therefore did not know how to give love as an adult, and Georgiana's mother simply repeated the fact that the Duke loved her. Without the understanding of her mother, Georgiana became even more isolated, but nevertheless made a determined effort to please the Duke by extending her knowledge of books. She read Lord Chesterfield's *'Letters to His Son'* as well as undertaking the reading of ancient Greece and the life of Louis X1V. Lady Spencer again tried to re-assure Georgiana that her husband was still in love with her but it was to no avail, Georgiana knew differently.

In January 1775, the Duke and Duchess left Chatsworth and went to Devonshire House in London. This was good news for Georgiana who could look forward to seeing her family and friends in London and not only that, having come to terms with the lack of a fulfilling relationship with her husband, would have more chance to carve out some sort of separate life for herself, and this she did with style.

The aristocrats' lifestyle included what they saw as 'the season' which was basically an upper class cattle market whereby the young daughters would be shown off to potential suitors with a view to finding, or being found future husbands. The season ran from late October to the following June and it was no accident that those dates were the same as when parliament sat as it was also intended to provide amusement for the ruling classes. There were plenty of other activities for them to enjoy in the form of coffee houses and there were also the clubs such as Whites, which was the first to open and Boodles, Brooks, and Almacks. For evening entertainment, there was the chance to hear the great composer George Friederic Handel (1685-1759) at the Italian Opera House in Haymarket or to see David Garrick (1717-79) at the Drury Lane Theatre. Handel was a brilliant German-English composer who was the organist at Halle Cathedral at the age of just seventeen and had composed *'The Water Music'* to celebrate the accession to the throne of King George I in 1714, whilst Garrick was a huge name, being an actor, theatre manager and dramatist who as a young man studied Latin and Greek under the great Samuel Johnson (1709-84), writer, critic, racantour, and the man who wrote the great dictionary which was published in 1755 after nine years work. Although coming to London to study for the bar, Garrick turned his hand to acting in 1740 with great success. The people who attended the opera and the theatre and took part in the season were called the 'ton' and such was the deference shown to the aristocracy, these people were allowed to dictate fashion and on occasions, even have huge influence as to whether a play was going to be successful or not. Georgiana was seemingly head of the ton and what she wore one day, people copied the next. Lady Spencer could see what was going on and was critical, but Georgiana took no notice and turned frivolity into an art form. Already the fashion amongst the women of the aristocracy was to have their hair piled high but one day Georgiana turned out for an evening with a 3-foot hair tower. Occasionally she would have a ship in full sail at the top, or an arrangement of stuffed birds and waxed fruit, and despite the fact that it was clearly ridiculous, many tried to imitate her, even though it would take hours to create. Not everybody was impressed with this way of life however, and the writer and diarist Fanny Burney (1752-1840) poured scorn on them in her play *'Cecilia'* which was published in 1782. In *'Cecilia'*, Miss Larolles says of Mr. Matthews:- "Why, he's the very head of the ton. There's nothing in the world so fashionable as taking no notice of things, and never seeing people, and saying nothing at all, and never hearing a word, and not knowing one's own acquaintance, and always finding fault, all the ton do so". Ironically, Fanny Burney was to know first hand exactly what she was writing about when in July 1786, she became Second Keeper of the Queen's Robes, a post that she accepted with great reluctance and was done only to please her father, the renown musician, Charles Burney (1726-1814). She spent years of misery there before finally leaving exactly five years later in July, 1791. If she had written *'Cecilia'* after she had held the position rather than before, her scorn would possibly have been even more withering, although it has to be said that she was fond of the King and Queen.

If not particularly encouraged by Lady Spencer, although encouraged by the people who made up the ton, it was certainly accepted by the Duke that he and Georgiana led separate lives. He was not really interested in all the frivolity involved in the world of fashion although he did attend the opera with her. However, once there he would soon leave and visit his club, usually Brooks, in order to continue with his habit of playing cards until about 5am. The Duke was a quiet withdrawn man and was more interested in staying at home with his dogs and shooting with his male friends than attending what he saw as meaningless balls and rubbing shoulders with so-called fashion icons. Meanwhile, Georgiana was everywhere, accepting every engagement offered rather than sit at home on her own, but inevitably, her health broke down, and on the concerned advice of Lady Spencer, she left England in July 1775 to holiday in Spa. The Spencers and the Devonshires all went together, and on their return, stopped at Versailles to pay court to Louis XVI. Georgiana already knew Marie Antoinette and they became close friends which lasted until the Queen was executed in 1793 as part of the horrifying revolution that was taking part in France at that time. The two women found that they had a great deal in common, not least of which was the fact that they both married rather reserved men for purposes of position rather than love, they both had mothers who loved but suffocated them, and were both addicted to frivolous entertainment, both women turning into heavy gamblers which was to turn into a disaster for Georgiana. When they returned from Spa, Georgiana tried once more to please her husband and for a short while, all seemed well between them, but it was not long before they both realised that they had little in common and as the Duke was still conducting an affair with Charlotte Spencer who had given birth to his daughter Charlotte in the year that the Duke and Duchess married, he saw no reason to respond to Georgiana's emotional needs. By Christmas 1775, all pretence at a loving marriage was quashed and Georgiana once more threw herself into the social world to attempt to fill her emotional void. The Duchess was pregnant and this hectic pace of life inevitably led to her physical breakdown and no-one was surprised when she suffered a miscarriage in April 1776. By this time, the Duke was aware of the gambling debts that she had accumulated and she was banking on the fact that he would forgive her if she delivered him a son, but when this plan went wrong, she found that the resulting stress caused her physical health to break down once again. Frightened because the people to whom she owed money threatened to tell the Duke, Georgiana confessed everything to her parents who paid her debts on the understanding that she confessed to the Duke. He barely said a word when a tearful Georgiana told him. He paid Lord and Lady Spencer and never mentioned the subject again. There was hardly a word spoken by him, no emotion showed, and the matter was not brought up again. Georgiana would rather have seen anger from him, but his aloofness over the matter was proof, if proof be needed, that the marriage was virtually dead. They had been married just two years and there was no sign of a son and heir that the Duke wanted – the situation did not bode well for Georgiana.

Georgiana threw herself into a life of frivolity based around fashion and parties and being at the forefront of the so-called Devonshire House Circle. Many of the Whig party attended and the Circle itself seemed to consist of people who were wealthy, loved the theatre, politics, and in the case of most of the women, fashion. One woman in particular was to become important in Georgiana's life – Lady Melbourne. Lady Melbourne was older than Georgiana, but still beautiful and was very manipulative. Far from seeing Georgiana as any kind of rival, she took the younger woman under her wing much to the annoyance of Lady Spencer who tried to get Georgiana to drop the friendship, but without success. Lady Spencer knew that Lady Melbourne was a bad influence on her daughter but there was nothing she could do about it. Lady Melbourne was the wife of the 1st Lord Melbourne, and after first giving birth to a daughter, she gave birth to a son and heir, and then felt free to indulge in a series of affairs, producing three more children, probably none being fathered by her husband. The son and heir that she produced was William Lamb (1779-1848), the 2nd Earl Melbourne and the husband of Caroline (1785-1828) who as Lady Caroline Lamb, wrote novels but was more famous for her nine month affair with the poet, Lord Byron. Georgiana was living a life of extremes – partying, gambling, indulging in eating binges, and dancing so much that she would become too tired to leave her bed. Then there would be a period whereby she was the dutiful wife, would starve herself, say her prayers and involve herself in charity work. However, Georgiana could not hide what was really going on – her health was suffering, her weight was continually fluctuating and her name was always in the newspapers. She simply could not escape all the bad influences that were around her and another person who was to have a bad influence on her was Lady Jersey (1753-1821) whose main pleasure in life seemed to be to have affairs with her friend's husbands and then flaunt them afterwards. As seventeen-year-old Frances Twysden, she had married George Villiers, the 4th Earl of Jersey, who was nearly twice her age. He was Master of Horse to the Prince of Wales and a Lord of the Bedchamber. It is easy to see why this ambitious young girl would marry such a man, but it is less clear as to why *he* married *her*. She was young and beautiful certainly, but that fact made it all the more likely that she would not be faithful to him, although his later behaviour almost certainly meant that he was burying his head in the sand over her relationships with other men.

The American War of Independence was being fought and as France had entered the war on the side of America in February 1778, the Duke of Devonshire headed a voluntary militia in Coxheath, Kent where both Georgiana and Lady Jersey attended to add their support. It was here that Lady Jersey's cruel way of treating her friends extended to Georgiana when the Duke of Devonshire and Lady Jersey went in to each other's tents and afterwards made no attempt to hide the matter. Surprisingly, Georgiana did not know how to handle the situation and made no fuss, although a furious Lady Spencer did on her behalf and made it clear that the affair was to cease which it did, although the hurt to Georgiana was very deep. The whole way of life that was being carried on by the Devonshire House Circle was a mess, and the playwright, Richard Brinsley Sheridan (1751-1816), the Irish dramatist who later became a politician, becoming a member of parliament in 1780, satirised them with a play called *The School For Scandal*. The play was performed at the Drury Lane Theatre in May 1777. Some of Georgiana's set went to see it and were amused at the way in which they were portrayed, but Georgiana was beginning to question her own lifestyle which now included heavy drinking and gambling. The Duke of Devonshire, along with other members of the Cavendish family, began to blame Georgiana's erratic life style for the fact that she suffered a series of miscarriages – she was even accused of deliberately stopping her chances of producing a son and heir for the Duke. However, to the Devonshire

House Circle and the newspapers, she was still the first lady of fashion and it was Lady Sarah Lennox (1745-1826), one of the famous Lennox sisters, who was the only person with the courage to criticise Georgiana. Sarah was the daughter of Charles, the 2nd Duke of Richmond (1701-1750), and his wife, Lady Sarah Cadogan (c1704-51), and sister-in-law to Henry Fox, the 1st Lord Holland (1705-1774) who had married Sarah's sister, Caroline Lennox (1723-74). Sarah Lennox was the most troublesome of the Lennox sisters and had caused a scandal herself, so she knew what she was talking about. Her father died suddenly in 1750 and soon afterwards her mother died leaving Sarah an orphan at the age of five years. She was brought up in Ireland by her sister Emily (1731-1814) but returned to London in 1758 at the age of thirteen to live with her sister Caroline, and Caroline's husband, Henry Fox, the 1st Lord Holland. She was presented at Court in 1760 at the age of 15 and immediately caught the attention of the young George III, who had ascended to the throne that year. The family pushed hard for the marriage to take place, but this was stopped by the new King's advisor, Lord Bute, who feared that his influence over the King would be diminished by Henry Fox, Sarah's brother-in-law. Lord Bute held great power over the young King as George had lost his father Frederick nine years previously in 1751, before his grandfather, George II died in 1760, so he looked to Lord Bute for paternal guidance. Sarah was not too upset at losing the young King's favour and was in fact a bridesmaid when he married Charlotte of Mecklenburg-Strelitz in 1761. Sarah went on to marry Charles Bunbury on 2nd June, 1762 but the marriage was unhappy and she left him in February, 1769 when her baby Louisa was born. The father was her cousin, Lord William Gordon with whom she eloped. Charles Bunbury divorced Sarah in 1776 and as a result, she found herself left out in the cold as far as polite society was concerned. She did eventually find happiness with George Napier, an army officer and they married on 27th August, 1781 and had eight children. At the time she made the comments about Georgiana however, she was still out of favour with people like the Devonshire House Circle, so she was well aware of what she was talking about and was in fear of Georgiana's future. Sarah, whilst criticising the way in which Georgiana was leading her life, said what no-one else had the courage or foresight to say, and that was to question whether the Duke's behaviour had driven Georgiana to it for neglecting her so soon after their marriage when she was young and needing affection. Just as she was in despair with her situation however, Georgiana was about to meet two people who would have a profound and long lasting effect on her life, Mary Graham and Charles James Fox.

It was towards the end of 1777 and Georgiana was in Brighton where she was hoping to find a cure for the fact that she had had several miscarriages. The doctors had decided that the problem was a weak placenta and that Georgiana must undertake the water cures. The doctors would resort to water cures for a variety of medical problems and so the Duke and Duchess went to the south coast town where she would either bathe in the sea or drink warm spa water. As long as the male partner did not suffer from impotence, the problem of infertility in the 18th century was always considered the problem of the female. It was in the October of that year that Georgiana was introduced to Mrs. Mary Graham

(1757-1792) and her husband Thomas Graham, the 1st Baron Lynedoch (1748-1843). Mary was recovering from pneumonia and the two women liked each other straight away. Mary was different from many of the other women that Georgiana had associated with and many considered her a good influence. She was in fact the Hon. Mary Cathcart when she married, being the daughter of Lord and Lady Cathcart, and unlike most of the people that Georgiana knew, was kind and gentle and had led a quiet, sheltered life. Her husband seemed to be quite a different man from those that the aristocratic women would normally marry. He was a very brave soldier, Scottish, and was the son of the Laird of Balgowan in Perthshire. After a lifetime of brave service in the field of battle, he was created Baron Lynedoch of Balgowan in 1814. In addition to these qualities, he was also a loving husband and there is a story that when Mary discovered that she had left her jewellery box at Balgowan on the morning of an Edinburgh ball, Thomas rode the ninety miles to and from Balgowan so that she would have her jewellery in time for the dancing that would take place that evening. Georgiana must have been green with envy to find that such a husband existed but at the same time was very pleased for her new loving friend. Mary was very beautiful and had been painted several times by Thomas Gainsborough (1727-88), the great landscape and portrait painter, who never quite felt that he had captured her features correctly. Mary was born in the same year as Georgiana and both women married at the same time. Mary had lost her mother at the age of fourteen and therefore become a surrogate mother to her little sister, Charlotte. Although naturally gentle and quiet, the fact that she had to look after her baby sister from such a young age kept her from the sort of wild life style that Georgiana had embarked on and from the sort of people that she had mixed with.

After Georgiana had left Brighton to return to Althorp, the two women would write each other affectionate letters and by the spring of 1778, were writing to each other so often that Georgiana found little time to write to Lady Spencer. There was great tenderness between the two women and the physical warmth between the two contrasted sharply from the coldness that she experienced from the Duke. Georgiana was back with her gambling friends but now found the lifestyle empty and meaningless where once she had found it exciting. She could communicate this to Mary by letter but could find no-one in her circle who would listen and understand because they were part of the set that she was beginning to dislike.

Georgiana started to read seriously, and one of the books was the French author, Jean Jacques Rousseau's (1712-78) *'Julie ou La nouvelle Heloise'*. Rousseau was a brilliant man who produced both written and musical work, but his life was to end tragically when he went insane. The book is written in the form of letters about a man of low rank falling in love with someone of a higher social standing called Julie. The book changed the way that Georgiana related to the people that she loved, and she wrote intense letters to her women friends declaring deep love for them, sometimes causing them great concern as they had not come across this depth of emotion before. In particular, she would write to Mary in this manner and there is no doubt that she loved Mary deeply. Sadly for Georgiana however, Mary was ill and in 1781, the doctors ordered her husband to take her to a warmer climate because her lungs were not working properly and they felt that she would develop consumption if she stayed in England. Georgiana had lost her best friend and the woman she loved more than any other – she was devastated.

In late 1777, the same time as Georgiana had met Mary Graham, she also met the Whig politician, Charles James Fox (1749-1806). Fox was a brilliant man but a flawed character which, like so many politicians before and since, would ultimately stop him from reaching the highest position in the land, that of Prime Minister. Georgiana was captivated by him although it certainly wasn't for his looks, but rather for his intellect. Fox had huge eyebrows, was short and fat, and looked as if he always needed a shave. Fox was the third son of Henry Fox, the 1st Baron Holland and Lady Caroline, elder sister of Sarah Lennox. Henry certainly loved his children, probably too much as he let them do exactly what they liked and never chided them – throughout their lives they were thoroughly spoilt. There are stories of Fox junior smashing his father's gold watch simply because he wanted to know what it looked like when broken into pieces and another time destroying his father's speeches that he had spent so long in preparing. On neither occasion was Charles James reprimanded and there must have been many other examples of this extraordinary behaviour. When he was in his teens, Charles James was a compulsive gambler, in fact it was completely out of control and he would win and lose thousands of pounds in an evening without batting an eyelid, simply because he knew that his indulgent father would bail him out. With regard to gambling, he never learnt his lesson and never had any sense of responsibility; nor did he grow up which was not surprising given the behaviour of his father, who could always be guaranteed to pay his son's debts, however enormous they may be. When his father, Lord Holland died in 1774, Charles James had reached the age of twenty-five but was still gambling everything away at various clubs between attending debates in the house. Lord Holland's final payment on behalf of his son was the extraordinary amount of £140,000, which in today's terms would be approaching £8.5 million – a sum that is barely credible, both in terms of the amount gambled, but in the way an indulgent father could rescue his undeserving son. Although he was incredibly spoilt as a child, Fox turned out to be a likeable adult which is a surprise, but oozed confidence, which is not. He was clever, confident, opinionated, and was not afraid to express that opinion even if it was not the perceived political wisdom of the day and might cost him his job, which in 1783 it did. Charles James was a politician at nineteen and a junior minister two years later. He held several posts in Lord North's government but was dismissed by King George III because of his seemingly open support for America during the war of independence. Lord North was a weak Prime Minister, although he had held power for twelve years but eventually he fell in 1782 and Fox was appointed Foreign Secretary in Rockingham's short lived administration, Rockingham dying on 1st July, 1782 after only three months in office. When the Earl of Shelburne became Prime Minister Fox refused to serve with him and after joining forces with Lord North, succeeded in bringing down Shelburne's government in February 1783. After first sending for William Pitt (1759-1806) to offer him the job of Prime Minister and being turned down, the King then appointed William Cavendish Bentick, the 3rd Duke of Portland as Prime Minister on 2nd April, 1783. North and Fox became secretaries of state in a coalition but they were asked to resign when King George III effectively killed off the East India Bill that Fox was attempting to get on the statute book. He did not hold office again for another twenty years.

Fox never patronised Georgiana, and he spoke to her on equal terms, which when it is remembered that women were nowhere near getting the vote, resulted in a huge boost to her confidence. The Duke of Devonshire did not pay her the slightest attention but Charles James Fox, this huge name in politics, gave Georgiana an interest in the subject, which in turn gave her a focus and a meaning to her life. She made a point of attending debates in the house so that she could inform herself as much as possible about any subject that Fox would discuss. Politics was conducted in a very different way in the 18th century than it is in the 21st century. There were the labels Whig and Tory but there was no slavish adherence to a party manifesto that you get today. Instead, politicians tended to follow certain people, so you would get a certain number following Lord Rockingham, and these would be known as the Rockinghamites, Lord North, the Northites, and followers of Fox would be known as the Foxites, and so on. There was also another big difference. The media of today has television which informs people of what is happening in the world almost instantaneously, whereas the 18th century media consisted of newspapers and the newspapers could only report on what was said in Parliament. Therefore, the speeches were much longer and politicians actually made up their minds through listening to those speeches, as they were often getting their information on a subject for the first time during the parliamentary debate. Georgiana's knowledge and interest became so intense that Devonshire House became the centre of Whig politics and she was the first woman to actively campaign for a named politician when she assisted Charles James Fox in the 1784 election. William Pitt the Younger had been Prime Minister since December 1783 but did not enjoy a majority in the House. He was trying to get a new India Bill through parliament and felt that the only way to achieve this was to call a general election which he did in March 1784, and it was this election that introduced Georgiana to the rough and tumble of electioneering. It was not easy for her – she was manhandled physically by voters and abused by the press and her sister Harriet was continually asking her to give up which eventually she did on 12th April when she informed the Duke that she would be leaving London in order to stay with her mother in St. Albans. Lady Spencer had not objected to Georgiana canvassing as such, it was the way that she was going about it that upset her mother who felt that it shamed the family. The number of newspapers had expanded rapidly in the years leading up to the election and the people writing in them had more and more confidence when it came to lampooning people like Georgiana, which they did, mercilessly. They were successful this time but she would never lose her interest in politics that stayed with her until the day that she died. The 1784 election was a triumph for William Pitt who achieved the majority that he wanted but it was a disaster for the Whigs and Charles James Fox. However, it established Georgiana on the political scene and Devonshire House continued to be the centre for the Whig politicians and supporters to meet in large numbers.

Georgiana was certainly well informed about politics, but she still had a terrible problem with gambling, which she took to excess. She was not helped by the company she had always kept, except for the friendship that she had enjoyed with the gentle Mrs. Mary Graham but who had left to live abroad in 1781 for health reasons. Georgiana missed Mary terribly, and it is just possible that her gambling problems would not have been so great had Mary been able to stay in England as her friend, as she was one of the few people that Georgiana knew who had a good influence on her.

Instead, Georgiana met Lady Elizabeth Foster who was to have a profound effect on the rest of Georgiana's life, although not necessarily a good one. Both the Duke and Georgiana were in Bath in the summer of 1782, the Duke for his gout and Georgiana because she had failed to conceive, and the waters of Bath would appear to have contained cures for all ailments in the 18th century. Lady Elizabeth was born in 1759, two years after Georgiana. She was part of the Hervey family and her father became the 4th Earl of Bristol as his two elder brothers had died without either of them producing a legitimate heir. George, the 3rd Earl of Bristol, was the eldest son and died unmarried, whilst the second son, Augustus married Elizabeth Chudleigh, a lady-in-waiting at court, but the union was short-lived and they separated soon afterwards, pretending in fact, never to have been married. Bess's father became the 4th Earl of Bristol in 1779. Bess, however, had married John Thomas Hervey three years earlier in 1776. Bess later claimed that she married reluctantly but the parents both wanted the union so it took place. In 1780, the marriage was all but over; Bess was pregnant for the second time and whilst it is possible but not definite that she was having an affair, her husband certainly had seduced Bess's maid. Foster then demanded a separation and ordered that Lady Elizabeth, as she was now known, give up the second child as soon as the baby was weaned. In the 18th century, the father always had custody of the children so this was quite normal, even if somewhat callous when actually carried out.

When Georgiana and the Duke met Bess in Bath in the summer of 1782, Bess was in a desperate situation. She was without money as her husband was refusing to support her, and she could not find work because of her newly acquired title. Both women were lonely and desperate to befriend the other, whilst the Duke of Devonshire found that he liked Bess as well. The scene was set for a long-standing, complicated ménage a trois that was to last for over twenty years. Bess lived with the Duke and Duchess and both of them confided in her about the so-called shortcomings of the other. Georgiana's friends could see what was happening and so could Lady Spencer, but Georgiana couldn't, or possibly wouldn't. Meanwhile however, by December of 1782, Georgiana realised that she was pregnant and so was her sister, Harriet. Georgiana's physical state was good but her mental state was fragile and Lady Spencer feared the possibility of a miscarriage. Georgiana's fragile state of mind was caused for two reasons:- firstly, she had worried about her seeming infertility, and secondly, her debts that were mounting due to her continued gambling. However, despite her anxieties over Georgiana, it was some relief to Lady Spencer that Bess was going abroad at the end of the month to take in the warmer climate which would help the very bad cough that she had developed and she left with Charlotte, the illegitimate baby that the Duke Of Devonshire had fathered in 1774, the year of his marriage to Georgiana. So far as the outside world was concerned, Bess was taking Charlotte abroad with her to act as her governess.

With Bess out of the way, Lady Spencer felt that her family would be able to get on with their lives unhindered and the sisters' pregnancies continued without too many complications. Georgiana and Harriet both had their babies within a week of each other. Harriet had her baby first on the 6th July and she named him Frederick. It was her second boy, the first, the Hon. John William Ponsonby being born on 31st August 1781. She had married the two boys' father, Frederick, the 3rd Earl of Bessborough the year before. Georgiana's baby came six days after young Frederick, on 12th July and was a girl who she named Georgiana Dorothy. As was the custom of the times, she lay in bed for a month, but unusually for the aristocracy, she breastfed the baby herself and insisted on the windows of the room being left open to let the summer breeze in, again, unusual as it was always the custom to keep the windows closed. Georgiana was happy to have a girl, but the Duke was not, especially as his sister-in-law, Harriet, had managed to produce two boys.

Despite the birth of little Georgiana, it would appear that 1783 was not a good year for Georgiana. Bess was writing her pleading letters from abroad denying rumours that she was having affairs, Georgiana herself was accused of having an affair with Charles James Fox, a fact that she always denied, her gambling debts were being discovered by John Heaton, the Duke's agent, who actually accused Georgiana of swindling local tradesmen, and not only that, he told the Duke that she was having an affair with the Prince of Wales. If that wasn't enough, on 31st October, she was told that John Spencer, her father, and the 1st Earl Spencer, was dead at the age of forty-nine. Georgiana was devastated and even Bess went into mourning although she was in Rome at the time. Georgiana wrote to Bess on 3rd January, 1784:- "I feel more capable of talking to you about my sorrow, and receiving consolation from such discourse than anything else. Pray heaven I do not infect you with my grief". Georgiana was desperate for Bess to return, but Bess had other reasons that meant that she was in no hurry to come back to England as on a visit to Rome she had met Cardinal Bernis who she started a relationship with. After that fizzled out, she met a Swedish diplomat named Count Fersen who it was alleged, had possibly had an attraction to the French Queen, Marie Antoinette, and promptly fell in love with him, although it did not materialise into a full blown affair. Eventually, after another two years, in the summer of 1784, Bess and Charlotte did return.

Lady Spencer delivered a shock to Georgiana on her twenty-fifth birthday which was on the 7th June 1784 after Bess had been away from them for two years. She upset Georgiana by writing her a ferocious letter denouncing Bess and the situation that Georgiana found herself in, but rather than take heed of the contents of the letter, Georgiana chose to turn to Bess for comfort and advice, in other words, turning to the very person who was causing the problem that Lady Spencer was warning of. Over the years Lady Spencer tried to think up ways of getting Bess out of the way. She would exclude her from invitations, but to no avail, Georgiana simply found ways round the situation and so it went on. Although Georgiana would normally obey her mother in all things, it seemed that the presence of Bess in her life was non-negotiable, but the inclusion of Bess in the life of the Duke and Duchess would result in complications that just about everybody except Georgiana had seen coming for a long time.

Eventually Bess returned but was beginning to look ill and it was decided that she should go abroad again. She went to France with letters of introduction to the friends of the Duke and Duchess who lived in Paris, and it seemed that after a short while, she was enjoying a good social life and feeling better. Georgiana however, sent her a letter early in 1785 saying that she had become pregnant again and would be expecting a baby in August or September. This was very good news for Georgiana who was hoping that she could deliver a son and heir to her husband, but although Bess had similar news, she was rather less than happy about it as she too was pregnant with the Duke's child, and when she read Georgiana's letter, realised that the two babies could have been conceived within days of each other. Deeply troubled, she started an affair with the John Frederick Sackville, the 3rd Duke of Dorset (1745-1799) and carried on with the relationship for several months whilst remaining in Paris. The Duke of Dorset is remembered for very little other than his love of cricket and also his womanising, both of which he seemed quite good at. He was also a heavy gambler, although that was usual amongst the aristocracy anyway. He played for Hambledon Cricket Club which was the leading club of the day and in 1773, he presented the Vine Cricket Ground to Sevenoaks, Kent, which was the town that the ground was situated in. In 1784, The Duke of Dorset was appointed Ambassador to France but despite the seriousness of his post, he continued to encourage cricket both to the local people but also to the British people who were residents there. In 1790, back in England, he married Arabella Diana Cope and they had one son, George John Frederick. George was born on 15th November, 1793 and went on to become the 4th Duke of Dorset on the death of his father in 1799.

After some time, when Bess's pregnancy became obvious, the affair finished but whilst Georgiana was able to go into labour in the luxury of Devonshire House, giving birth to a baby girl on 1st September 1785, Bess had to keep her pregnancy secret and therefore had to resort to staying in a hostel in a small town called Vietri on the Gulf of Salerno where she gave birth to a baby girl on 16th August. Georgiana called her baby Harriet, and whilst the Duke was again disappointed that the baby was a girl, Georgiana wasn't and was able to get over the birth in opulent surroundings and enjoy the fact that she had a second child. Bess, however, was separated from her child who she called Caroline Rosalie although she could see her once a day.

Bess stayed away for a few months before returning to England in the summer of 1786 and on arriving at Chatsworth, spent little time before indulging in flirtatious behaviour with the Duke of Devonshire. This behaviour became even more marked when Georgiana became ill with strange spasms that kept her in her room almost the entire day each time it happened, although so besotted with Bess was Georgiana, that she refused to believe Lady Spencer when her mother brought her daughter's attention to the situation. Although there was probably no one occasion that caused the Duchess to reluctantly accept what was happening, it must have been a gradual acceptance of the affair, and one that she put up with for many years simply because Bess was her best friend and confidant, and she needed her as did the Duke. It was an extraordinary ménage a trois that lasted years. It probably explains why, along with Bess, that Georgiana started an affair with the Duke of Dorset who turned up at Chatsworth in September 1786, not long after his affair with Bess had fizzled out. Dorset saw what was happening between Bess and the Duke of Devonshire and promptly started courting Georgiana before having an affair with her much to Lady Spencer's distress as she could see what was happening between the two couples.

Meanwhile, over the years, Georgiana's gambling went on and on and was completely out of control. She had somehow run up a debt of £100,000 (approximately £6 million today) to a man called Martindale who threatened to tell the Duke, so there was nothing that Georgiana could do but tell all to her husband. The problem was however, that she didn't tell all, she only confessed to losing part of the amount that had actually gone but it was enough to lead the Duke into saying that he wanted a separation. Bess was delighted as she had visions of having the Duke to herself at last, although it was not long before she realised that if there was a formal separation, she would have to leave Devonshire House as society would not accept her openly living there as his mistress. All the while the three of them were there, everyone could pretend that there was nothing going on between the Duke and Bess but that would not be the case if Georgiana left. Discussions went on for months with neither side being able to agree to the other's suggestions about where Georgiana was going to live and by the end of 1786, the whole idea of a separation seemed to fizzle out and the Duke eventually stopped pursuing the matter. It was never formalised and life drifted on the way it had done for years with the Duke, Duchess and Bess carrying on living together in this strange and uneasy threesome. Meanwhile, Georgiana had met Martindale and managed to persuade him to settle for a much reduced figure but it was still too much for her – she asked Mary Graham for financial help who initially gave what she could until her husband discovered what she was doing and put a stop to it. Most of her friends knew that they wouldn't get their money back and so Georgiana turned to people who she hardly knew who had no idea that they would not have their loans repaid but merely thought it was a good idea to lend their money to such a high profile person. Their snobbishness would turn out to be costly to them and one of these people was Sir Richard Arkwright (1732-92). Arkwright had invented the water powered spinning frame and there was a great deal of public dislike of him on the grounds that his inventions cost a great many jobs, and in 1779, matters had come to a head when a large mill near Chorley that he owned was destroyed by an angry mob. However, Arkwright was more interested in society people than he was the loss of work his invention would cause amongst the working classes and he duly lent Georgiana several thousand pounds. Whether he was quite so enamoured with Georgiana later on must have been put to the test when she not only neglected to settle the debt but also asked for a further loan. Perhaps she was incredibly naive about her ability to pay it back, had no scruples about letting people down, was simply desperate, or a combination of all three. It is difficult to know, but virtually no-one had any of their money returned.

In January, 1788, Arkwright was to write to Georgiana:- "I flattered myself with the hope that everything had turned out as you wished. I am sincerely sorry to find I was mistaken..." Georgiana had been crafty because her story always included that each loan had to be kept a secret to save her from ruin, so that many of her creditors did not know of the existence of the others.

Bess had spent the summer of 1787 in London whilst the Duke and Georgiana were in Chatsworth, but in October she joined them but seemed decidedly subdued. This was because Bess had some bad news for the Duke of Devonshire, although it had nothing to do with Georgiana's gambling. Bess was pregnant, and although she had had an affair with the Duke of Richmond, she swore to the Duke of Devonshire that the baby was his, Devonshire's. They decided to tell Georgiana straight away and the reaction they received was extraordinary, although by this time not unexpected. She knew that Bess would have to have the baby abroad, just as Bess had had to do when giving birth to Caroline in 1785, but this time, Georgiana insisted on travelling with her in order to look after her. The fact that the Duke of Dorset was in France was an added attraction, but it was clear that Georgiana loved Bess dearly and genuinely wanted to care for her. However, Lady Spencer, interfering ever more in her daughter's affairs, insisted that Georgiana remain in England, fearing that she would take up with the Duke of Dorset again. Bess travelled through France and settling in Rouen in the middle of May, finally giving birth to a boy two weeks later on the 26th May, 1788. Bess called the boy Augustus although he was usually called Clifford, which was the surname that he was given as she already had an eight-year-old boy called Augustus by her husband John Foster. Like her daughter Caroline, born three years earlier by the Duke of Devonshire, Clifford was left in France when Bess eventually returned to England.

Georgiana and the Duke of Devonshire had got on well together in Bess's absence although they planned to travel to France in the summer to see her but postponed the trip much to the irritation of the Duke of Dorset, who had made several arrangements to make sure that they would be comfortable once they were there. However, although he did not immediately realise it, Dorset was being pushed out of Georgiana's life and this was because she had met the up and coming politician, Charles Grey (1764-1845) and found herself attracted to him. Grey was born in Fallodon, Northumberland and had been educated at Eton and King's College, Cambridge. He delivered his maiden speech as a Whig member of parliament on 22nd February, 1787 and became the 2nd Earl Grey in 1807 on the death of his father. He was Prime Minister when the Reform Bill of 1832 extending the franchise was passed. When he met Georgiana however, he was a rising young politician, very handsome and Georgiana found herself smitten. It was not long before they started an affair which went on for many years.

In May, 1789 the Duke and Duchess decided to travel to Spa (Belgium). Bess was to be included in the trip and she was delighted to go with them not least because along with her ongoing fight to gain custody of her two sons

Frederick and Augustus by her husband, John Foster, she also wanted to see her two children by the Duke, Caroline and Clifford, who she had been forced to leave in France. They left for Calais on 20th June 1789 and amongst the party was Charlotte Williams, who was the Duke's daughter by another woman, Charlotte Spencer, who was no relation to Georgiana, and who had been born in the same year that the Duke and Georgiana had got married. The Devonshires picked a strange time to visit France as the National Assembly had just been formed and the family had not understood the tension that was rising in France prior to a full scale revolution taking place. They visited the King and Queen and held huge dinners for their many friends out there before eventually realising how serious the situation was. When they were in Brussels, they eventually heard of the storming of the Bastille which had taken place on the 14th July, 1789, and the Duke immediately wanted to go back to the safety of England. However, Georgiana felt differently because she had found out that Coutts the bankers realised that she had been economical with the truth concerning her financial affairs, and wanted to stay in France to escape her obligations. It says much about the size of Georgiana's debts that she would rather risk the dangerous situation that was developing in France than face the man who was looking after her financial affairs back home. There was some good news for Georgiana however, because at the end of September, 1789, she discovered that she was pregnant. Desperate to produce a son and heir for the Duke, she was ecstatic, and after a few months, finding that Paris had quietened down, they returned to the city and on the 21st May, 1790, she gave birth to the son that the Duke craved for. He was to be called William (Hartington) Spencer George Cavendish and was to eventually become the 6th Duke of Devonshire when the Duke died in 1811. Although there was great joy at the birth of the Cavendish son, there was also great concern for the health of Georgiana to the extent that her life was thought to be in danger, but she recovered, and true to form, within two weeks was ready to organise a number of parties to celebrate. By the end of August it was decided that it would be unsafe to stay in France, especially as they had children with them and so they returned to England, Bess having her daughter Caroline with her, but her son Clifford, the second child she had with the Duke, being caught up in France and left behind. Georgiana had her baby boy but still the Duke was unaware of the horrific nature of Georgiana's debts. She had had so many opportunities to tell the Duke but had simply never had the courage, fearing a separation would result despite the fact that she had delivered to him what he wanted most in the world, a son and heir.

There was an understanding in 18th century aristocratic circles, that once the wife had supplied the husband with a son and heir, she could have affairs so long as she was discreet and Georgiana wasted little time in turning to the man who she was really attracted to, Charles Grey, the Whig politician. However, the attraction was so great between them that they made little effort in being discreet to such an extent that her close friends became concerned about the situation. Sheridan tried to reason with her and make her see sense but she refused to listen and eventually the inevitable happened and Georgiana became pregnant. Lady Spencer was furious and she made Georgiana send Grey back to London without so much as a heartbroken Georgiana being able to say goodbye. The

Duke had been away and on his return was furious – after a heated argument he demanded that Georgiana go abroad or there would be a separation. Not only that, he told Georgiana that she would have to give Grey up which she agreed to but with a great deal of sadness on both sides – it seemed that she and Grey were truly in love with each other.

Georgiana felt very ill as she lay in her bed in a room in Montpelier, and she made her last will and testament dated 27th January, 1792. Although only thirty-four years old, she felt that her life had probably reached the end. Certainly at that time, in her own mind it had. She had spent her entire adult life in a loveless marriage, she had done what was asked of her, that is, produced a son and heir and probably felt surplus to future requirements, was thousands of pounds in debt which her husband knew little about and which she would never be able to repay, and had to give up the man she loved and who she was about to have a child by. Added to all that, she would never be able to keep the child – she must have wondered whether life could get much worse. On 20th February, 1792, Georgiana gave birth to a baby girl who she called Eliza and to avoid there being any hint of who the father was, was given the surname Courtney. Almost as soon as she was born, the baby was taken away from Georgiana and after spending an initial time with a foster mother, was taken to Falloden, England to live with Charles Grey's parents. Whilst the child's parentage was never openly acknowledged, events such as this could never remain a secret forever, and eventually it became common knowledge amongst the aristocracy. Georgiana was not allowed to visit Falloden to see Eliza or even write to her, but on the few occasions when Grey's parents visited London, Georgiana was allowed limited access. Whatever Georgiana's faults, and she had many, she was a loving mother and it caused her deep distress whenever she saw Eliza, as it was clear that the child was not receiving the same amount of maternal love that Georgiana gave to her other children. Eliza was always made to feel an outsider within the family group and never received presents unless they were from Georgiana. For many years, Eliza thought that Mrs. Grey, Charles' mother, was her own mother and that Charles was her elder brother whilst Georgiana was nothing other than a very kind friend. Georgiana would loved to have openly acknowledged Eliza because apart from anything else, she was still in love with Grey, and later on, the couple did in fact try to resume their relationship. However, their love wasn't enough as Georgiana kept her distance, not wishing to provoke the Duke into further anger, terrified that he would demand a separation as he had done once before. Georgiana's misery at seeing the lack of love that Eliza was receiving over the years never left her but there was a happy ending for Eliza although sadly, Georgiana did not live long enough to see it. In 1814, Eliza was rescued from her misery by meeting and marrying Colonel Robert Ellice. Ellice was a nice man and was a husband who gave Eliza the love that she had missed out on thoughout her childhood. It is not clear when and if Eliza found out who her true parents were but it is probable that she found out in later life.

Georgiana suffered from migraines, and sometime in the 1790's, she started to experience an ache in her eyes not only when going through the migraine, but after it had subsided. One day in July, 1796, she retired to bed with one of her headaches, but there was no let-up with the pain and a swelling started to develop around her right eye which after a few days, became huge. The family's physician, Dr. Warren examined Georgiana and he in turn called out three of the top eye surgeons in the country, one of which was John Gunning, Senior Surgeon-Extraordinary to King George III. Given the nature of the treatment meted out to Georgiana, the word 'extraordinary' seems highly appropriate in this context. Medicine in the 18th century was often a hit or miss affair – doctors were very knowledgeable about some illnesses and completely clueless when it came to treating others. Sadly, it seems that in the case of Georgiana's illness, the latter was the case. They were years away from any anaesthetics to kill the pain and had no clue whatsoever about hygiene or how infections came about. Surgeons carrying out amputations would often go from patient to patient without cleaning their knives at all. In Georgiana's case, one of the surgeons practically throttled her because of the mistaken belief that the eye had to be flushed out with her own blood. Her sister Harriet and their mother Lady Spencer were present and would always remember Georgiana's screams. Lady Spencer wrote to a friend:- "The inflammation has been so great that the eye, the eyelids and the adjacent parts were swelled to the size of your hand doubled, and projecting forward from the face. Every attempt was made to lower this inflammation so as to prevent any ulceration, but this has been in vain. A small ulcer has formed on the top of the cornea and has burst, and as far as that reaches the injury is not to be recovered. If the inflammation should increase, the ulcer form again, and again burst, it would destroy the whole substance of the eye, which would then sink... The eyelids are still much swelled and scarred with leeches, and the little opening between them is always filled with a thick white matter. The eye itself, to those who see it (for I cannot) is still more horrible".

News of Georgiana's misfortune spread very quickly. The newspapers got hold of it and printed the story which resulted in a great deal of sympathy for her which probably would not have happened in the past, and there was also concern for Georgiana's sister Harriet, whose own health was not good, and how she would react to Georgiana's illness. Georgiana started to circulate again, but it was a different Georgiana that people saw. Her classic beauty had gone because her right eye drooped which was not surprising after what she had been through, her sparkle had gone and she became subdued. She was still only thirty-nine years old and that beauty that she had always had, she knew was lost forever, and as a result, this one time party going person became introverted and made excuses not to visit people. Life had changed for Georgiana, and not for the better, not yet anyway.

However, with Bess, things suddenly did change for the better. She had been conducting an affair with the Duke of Richmond that had been going on and off for something like eight years, and suddenly, in November, 1796, her husband, John Foster died, and this allowed her two sons, Frederick, now nineteen years old, and Augustus, sixteen, to travel from Ireland to see her. Soon after that, the Duchess of Richmond who had long since suffered ill health, also died prompting one or two caustic comments about the convenience of it all for the Duke of Richmond and Bess. However, they soon decided that they would not marry in haste, preferring to spend at least a year as a period of mourning, either as a mark of respect to their respective spouses, or possibly, and this seems more likely, simply so as not to appear that they were acting hastily.

One would think that Georgiana would be pleased with the possibility that Bess, her arch rival for the affections of her husband, would possibly leave Chatsworth House and start a life with the Duke of Richmond, but this was not the case. She loved Bess dearly, and relied upon her all the time for advice and support, and also for many years past, had been reconciled to the fact that she and the Duke effectively led separate lives. There was a surprise in store for her however, but not before she had to endure yet another excruciateingly painful operation which took place in December 1796. Once again, she had to endure the most dreadful torture for hours on end, but seemingly made a good recovery, despite it being an extremely cold winter. Two weeks after this operation had taken place, the Duke of Devonshire's uncle John died. John had been a surrogate father to the Duke since the Duke's own father had died when he, the Duke, was just sixteen and he looked up to his uncle. After the funeral, he returned home, took Georgiana into a private room and cried his eyes out. The immediate reason was obvious because he was mourning his uncle, but there was something else. Georgiana had been quite ill and there was the possibility of him not only losing his wife, but also his mistress if Bess left the Devonshire home for the Duke of Richmond. On top of losing his uncle, the thought was just too much, and he told Georgiana that he would like them to live together again properly as man and wife. Georgiana was only too pleased, because although she may have lost her looks, she had got her husband back after twenty years.

Because of this reconciliation between the Duke and Georgiana, life settled into some sort of normality. Georgiana began to feel more comfortable about her looks and her interest and involvement in Whig politics continued. However, there were two issues that remained unresolved; one was Georgiana's gambling debts and the other was the problem of Bess. Even after all these years, Georgiana had still not confessed to the Duke the full amount of that which she owed, whilst Bess had spent years waiting for a firm proposal of marriage from the Duke of Richmond. She never received it; instead the Duke finally admitted in October 1801 that he would never marry her. Bess was no fool – because of the length of time it had been since their respective spouses had died, she had guessed as much, but she still felt disappointed, humiliated and angry. Georgiana took a very magnanimous view of the matter towards Bess – there was no gloating because she, Georgiana, was happy with the husband who her friend had spent so many years trying to steal. Instead, Georgiana had genuine sympathy towards Bess and included her in many of the outings and parties that she and the Duke attended. Georgiana's debts were quite another matter and at the beginning of 1805, she had a meeting with the Duke which Bess attended where she would finally confess the entire amounts that she owed to her creditors, always assuming that she could remember all of them. The Duke was expecting approximately £5,000 (£300,000 today), but it was in fact, ten times that amount, being much nearer £50,000 (£3 million in today's terms). The Duke's response astonished both Bess and Georgiana. He neither shouted nor did he get angry, but took the news quietly and did not do what Georgiana expected and probably what Bess secretly hoped for, and demand a separation. Instead, he thought long, hard and logically as to how to deal with the situation, and when he had made up his mind, he was more than generous to Georgiana in terms of future money that he allowed her and the manner in which the solution was found.

Georgiana continued her interest in Whig politics but was sad when the Tory Prime Minister, William Pitt the Younger died on 23rd January, 1806, exactly twenty five years since he first became a member of Parliament. Pitt had been first Minister from 1783 to 1801 and then from 1804 until his death. Although only forty six years old, he had been Prime Minister for nearly twenty out of the last twenty three years and was ill certainly with exhaustion and possibly stomach cancer. Unable to find an alternative, King George III reluctantly sent for William Wyndham Grenville (1759-1834), the 1st Baron Grenville and Pitt's cousin but nonetheless a Whig. Serving with Grenville were Charles James Fox as Foreign Secretary, George, 2nd Earl Spencer as Home Secretary, Charles Grey as First Lord of the Admiralty, and Richard Brinsley Sheridan as Treasurer to the Navy. Fox and Sheridan were friends of Georgiana whilst George Spencer was her brother. Charles Grey was a man that she had once loved deeply and who was the father of one of her children so one would have thought that she would be ecstatic about the new government, and for a short time she was, organising parties to celebrate their power and said to Harriet, her daughter:- "We are all statesmen and stateswomen and grown very dull and important". Georgiana's happiness was not to last for long however. On or about the 12th March, 1806 she fell ill and doctors suspected jaundice and then changed their minds and thought it was a kidney stone which she had suffered from twice in recent years. She seemed to rally for a short while but on the 22nd March suddenly took a turn for the worse. Although the doctors could not know it, she had an abscess on her liver and there was absolutely nothing they could do for her, other than make her last hours comfortable. This they signally failed to do and instead, shaved her head and put blister plasters on her skin thus ensuring that her last hours were anything but easy. She died at 3.30 on the morning of 30th March 1806, a mere month after Prime Minister William Pitt and less than six months before her friend and political ally, Charles James Fox who died on 13th September of the same year.

The grief over Georgiana's death was shared by family and public together. The Duke was beside himself as were the children, Georgiana (Little G.), Harriet (Harry-O.), and William (Hart) as was Bess, although her grief was no doubt a little tempered by the thought that one day she may get her long standing wish and marry the Duke. Georgiana was loved by the public and thousands took to the streets in Piccadilly where Devonshire House, the place that she died, was situated. Her friends, including Charles James Fox and the Prince of Wales amongst many others, were grief stricken – their grief being compounded by the fact that Georgiana's illness was so short in duration, and her death therefore, so sudden.

Bess did in fact get her wish to marry the Duke which she did in October 1809 but it brought her little happiness. She was never accepted by the

Cavendish family, the Duke dying less than two years later, on 29th July 1811. The Duke's death caused subsequent rows between Bess and Hart and there were violent disagreements between them over money and possessions. She even made it publicly known that the Duke was the father of her two children, Caroline and Augustus Clifford and fully expected that Clifford be allowed to use the Cavendish arms, only giving up the claims after Hart had made a generous financial settlement. Bess herself died in Rome on 30th March, 1824, eighteen years to the day after Georgiana's own death. Over the years, there seems to have been some softening in Hart's attitude to her, as he was at her side during her last moments. He also arranged for Bess's remains to be brought to England and buried alongside the remains of the Duke, Georgiana, and his aunt Harriet who had died in 1821.

Like many women of her times, Georgiana has been underrated over the years and only seen as a spoilt rich girl who had it all but gambled it away, expecting others to pick up the debts. It is certainly true that her gambling habits were appalling, and even she realised that, as it caused her to lie to just about everybody about them, especially Coutts the bankers, but worse than that, she lied to the Duke himself. The Duke has always suffered a bad press because of the cold manner that he showed towards Georgiana over many years, but he deserves praise for the calm way that he handled the matter when finally confronted with the truth about the total amount of her debts. However, probably Georgiana's worse crime was to lie to people she knew in order to borrow more money in order to pay her creditors off as many of them would not have given her anything if they had known the truth and the fact that they would have no hope of ever being paid back.

One biographer actually went so far as to say that she stole off these people which would not be far from the truth given the facts. In her early years she was seen as a fashion icon, and she would arrive at the opera or at balls with the most extraordinarily outrageous hair styles, only to see them copied by those that could afford to the next day. But there was more to Georgiana than that. In late 1777, at the age of just twenty years, her life would change when she met the brilliant but erratic Charles James Fox, the famous Whig politician who would spend virtually his entire political career opposing the Prime Minister, William Pitt the Younger, along with the reigning monarch, King George III. Georgiana and Fox became firm friends and there were many who thought that they had actually been lovers, but she always denied it. Thanks to Fox, Georgiana became heavily involved in politics and Devonshire House became a favourite meeting place for Whig politicians and sympathisers over the years. Because women were more than a century from obtaining the vote, many people thought that their role in politics was minimal, but Georgiana was listened to by Fox when her advice was offered, and when the Prime Minister, William Pitt dissolved Parliament on 24th March, 1784, Georgiana canvassed for Fox as he attempted to secure the seat at Westminster during the resulting general election campaign. Despite winning a huge majority in parliament, Pitt spent a great deal of time and money challenging Fox's result at Westminster, but in the end, Fox was allowed to take his seat, sitting for the borough of Orkney in the interim.

Despite the totally irresponsible way that she behaved over her gambling habits and the resulting debts that she incurred, it should be said that Georgiana showed a great deal more responsibility in her role as a mother, as she was both loving and caring. Georgiana, nicknamed Little G (b1783), Harriet, also known as Harry-O, (b1785), and William Spencer George, otherwise known as Hart (b1790), and the future 6th Duke of Devonshire, all loved her, and these were the children she had by the Duke. Georgiana also had a daughter, Eliza Courtney (b1792) by Charles, 2nd Earl Grey and although it is probable that she eventually discovered that Georgiana was her birth mother, it is not certain. What is certain however, is that Eliza loved her as a friend by Georgiana's actions alone.

Georgiana was a product of her time and her class, and must be judged as such. Her initial youthful energy was spent in the rather frivolous world of fashion leader, but she rose above it, reading extensively in order to please her husband, and later on in an attempt to lead a fulfilling life. She fully embraced Whig politics for which she deserves praise, and was respected and admired by one of the most brilliant politicians of the day, Charles James Fox. She deserves praise too, for the courageous way she handled the severe eye infection that she suffered from, and the tortuous procedures the doctors inflicted upon her. During the latter part of her marriage, she won the love and respect that she deserved from her husband, and after the partial loss of her physical beauty, finally understood what she felt were the important aspects of life, and subsequently found an inner peace.

-oOOo-

13
Lord Frederick North
(1732-1792)

Prime Minister between 1770-1782, and who has been blamed
for Britain losing the American War of Independence.

Lord North, a little unkindly known as the Prime Minister who lost America, was born as the Honourable Frederick North on 13th April, 1732. His father was Francis North and his mother, Lady Lucy Montagu.

Francis North was born on the 13th April, 1704 and died on 4th August, 1790. He became the 7th Baron North in 1734 on the death of his cousin and became the 1st Earl of Guilford in 1752 which is why his son Frederick had the courtesy title of Lord North virtually all his life and was able to sit in the House of Commons. He did not become the 2nd Earl of Guilford until his father died in 1790, just two years before his own death on 5th August, 1792.

Francis North married three times. His first wife was Lady Lucy Montagu who he married in 1728 and who was the daughter of George Montagu, the 1st Earl of Halifax. She died in May, 1734 from smallpox aged just twenty-four years. She gave birth to Frederick on 13th April, 1732 who was later to be known as Lord North. There is also a suggestion that a daughter, Lucy was born in 1734, shortly before Lady Lucy's death that same year, but the existence of the daughter has not been verified.

Francis North was married again, this time in January, 1736 to Elizabeth Legge, Viscountess of Lewisham, the widow of the 1st Earl of Dartmouth's son George Legge, Viscount Lewisham. Elizabeth brought three children to this marriage, one son and two daughters. The son was William (Legge) Lewisham who was five years old when his mother married making him much the same age as his step-brother, Frederick North. He became a life long friend of Frederick's, and they later took up extensive travelling together and both served in government at the same time. William Lewisham succeeded his grandfather as the 2nd Earl of Dartmouth when the former died in 1750. Francis and Elizabeth (Viscountess of Lewisham) North had four more children together, one son and three daughters, and their marriage was a happy one, although the happiness ended after nine years when Elizabeth died in 1745. There was further sadness too, as one of the daughters had died just before Elizabeth, and then another daughter died soon after their mother. Francis was now left on his own with three of his own children, plus three stepchildren to look after.

Francis North married for the third and final time at St. Anne's Church, Soho, on 17th June, 1751. His bride was Katherine, Countess Dowager of Rockingham who was the widow of Lewis, the 2nd Earl Rockingham. Lewis was born Lewis Watson in 1709 and was the son of Edward Watson (Viscount

Sondes) who lived between 1687 and 1722, and Lady Katherine Tufton. The 2nd Earl Rockingham married Katherine Furnese (1715-1766) in 1736 and she was the daughter of Robert Furnese who in turn was the son of Sir Henry Furnese, a successful city merchant. Although Katherine was the second daughter of Robert Furnese, she inherited much of her grandfather Henry's wealth through her brother, who had died childless. The second Earl Rockingham died in December, 1745 and it was his widow Katherine, who married Francis North in 1751.

There has been some doubt cast as to the paternity of Frederick North. Frederick, the Prince of Wales, (1707-51) and father of the future George III was rumoured to have had an affair with Frederick North's mother, Lady Lucy Montagu. This was barely mentioned at the time, but the possibility was first aired by Sir Nathanael Wraxall (1751-1831), who was famous for writing memoirs. He also became an MP in 1780, initially as a follower of Frederick (by now Lord) North, who was then in his tenth year as Prime Minister, but Wraxall eventually switched sides and supported William Pitt the Younger (1759-1806). Francis North, Frederick North's father, had become a member of Prince Frederick's Household when he was appointed Gentleman of the Bedchamber in 1730, two years after he had married Lady Lucy and two years before Frederick North was born, so the timing does fit the conjecture. Lady Lucy was said to be a flirtatious young woman (she was just eighteen years old when she married) and it is certainly possible but by no means certain that she had an affair with Frederick, the Prince of Wales. If the Prince of Wales was Frederick North's father, it would make North and George III half brothers as they would have had the same father. There is a remarkable similarity in the looks of the two men, especially when they had reached middle age, and when one looks at the picture of Frederick (Lord) North painted by the celebrated Nathaniel Dance, it shows very clearly the extraordinary physical resemblance he shares with George III. Another argument put forward to support their shared paternity is the fact that both men went blind at the latter stages of their lives. Not only this, but their characters showed similarities and both men set a good example with the way they conducted their private lives. They were also both devoted to their wives in an age when it was almost expected that gentlemen of the aristocracy took mistresses but in fact both had a conservative and cautious outlook on life. Set against all this however, was the fact that the so-called affair was barely mentioned at the time, and on the few occasions that it was, nobody seemed to believe it. Both the monarchy and MPs were considered fair game by the cartoonists of the day, and if people had taken the rumour seriously, then the satirists would have been out in force. As it was, out of the 550 cartoons that could be traced whereby North is portrayed as the main subject, only two mention shared paternity, so it remains an idea that is unlikely to be proved either way.

As a boy and young man, Frederick North had a likeable, easy going character and never rebelled. He was part of a happy family unit which consisted of his father, his stepmother Elizabeth, and their children, but he was sent to Eton at the age of twelve which was just before Elizabeth, his stepmother died, along with two sisters. Frederick North had an obvious natural talent as he did well academically, but did very little work to achieve it. It was probably this that led to him coming across as being indolent in his middle years when he was Prime Minister. Unusually, for one doing well at his school, he was popular with his fellow pupils and one of his teachers wrote to his father:- "He deserves the Commendation and Love not only of his Relations, but of everyone about him". This popularity followed him through his life and even when he was Prime Minister, his opponents found it difficult to dislike him.

In 1749, at the age of seventeen, North attended Trinity College, Oxford where his stepbrother and friend, William Lewisham also studied, and who had matriculated a year before. North's father wrote to him asking him to be as good a student at Oxford as he was a pupil at Eton, but in the event, he needn't have worried, as Frederick was the model student at Oxford as well. He was always conscientious in attending lectures and turning in the required work, and he seems to have pleased his tutor with regard to his religious beliefs. In a letter to Frederick, the Revd. James Merrick enclosed the following sentence:- "It is an unspeakable satisfaction to me that you have by God's blessing been made sensible of the importance of religion before your entrance to public life." William was also considered an excellent student and so highly were both young men thought of that Frederick's father also received a letter from North's tutor, who alluded to:- "...the great honour they have done us by their publick example". He was referring of course to Frederick and his stepbrother William. Frederick had also been thought of as a good classical scholar excelling in Latin along with speaking French fluently.

Frederick North was travelling in Europe with William when he heard the news that his father, Francis, the 7st Baron North had been created the 1st Earl Guilford in April 1752, and from then on, Frederick became known as Lord North, a title by which he was always commonly known. His step-brother and friend William Lewisham had already succeeded to the title of 2nd Earl of Dartmouth two years previously on the death of his grandfather, the 1st Earl.

There were changes during this period – there are always changes in society but both these, the new calendar and the Marriage Act, were to have a lasting effect on life in Britain. The Prime Minister at that time was Henry Pelham (1695-1754) who held the office from 1743 until his death in 1754. A Whig, he was in office during the Jacobite Rising of 1745 and also the reform of the calendar. The Julian Calendar was adjusted by eleven days to become the Gregorian Calendar whereby the 2nd September 1752 was followed by the 14th September which brought Britain into line with most other European countries who had already adopted the new system. There were riots against this change, some thinking that they would lose eleven days pay whilst some people actually believed that they were going to lose eleven days off their life. Pelham also introduced the Marriage Act of 1753, sometimes known as the Hardwicke Act. Philip Yorke (1690-1764) was the 1st Earl of Hardwicke and was Lord Chancellor from 1737 until 1756. The Marriage Act of 1753 abolished common law marriages and decreed that unless both parties were aged 21 or over, consent had to be obtained from the parents or guardians. The Act also set the minimum age for a male as being 14, and 12 for a girl. Those ages seem very young to us in the 21st century, but prior to the 1753 act, children as young as seven years old were undergoing some sort of marriage. On his death in 1754, Pelham was succeeded as Prime Minister by his brother, Thomas-Pelham Holles (1693-1768) who retired in 1756 exhausted as he had already spent many years working with his brother, although he was persuaded to return in 1757, succeeding the Duke of Devonshire.

Frederick and William returned from their travels in 1754 and it was to be a fairly short space of time before both had become settled with both a wife and the beginning of a political career. Although Frederick had the courtesy title of Lord North, he was able to sit in the Commons, but William, being the 2nd Earl of Dartmouth, had to go to the Lords. On 15th April, 1754, soon after he returned from his travels with William, Frederick was returned as a Member of Parliament for the family seat of Banbury. Banbury was hardly a constituency, but was known as a Pocket Borough in the 18th century. Hardly a borough at all, it had an electorate of just eighteen and as there were so few in number, it was fairly easy to bribe them if need be which is why it was called a pocket borough, chiefly because of it's small size. As it turned out, North was the only person standing and so was elected unopposed. Getting elected unopposed with an electorate as small as eighteen was about as easy as it gets when entering parliament, but once there, he did make a good impression.

As mentioned earlier, the Prime Minister at the time that North was elected was the second of the Pelham brothers to hold the post, Thomas, the Duke of Newcastle. However, exhausted after many years holding high office, he resigned in 1756 and the 4th Duke of Devonshire nominally became Prime Minister before resigning the following year, only for the Duke of Newcastle to take over again. 1756 was the year that the seven years war with France started but it was also the year that Lord North was married.

The bride was Ann Speke and she was very young, being not quite sixteen years old. They were married on 20th May, 1756 at St. James's Church, Westminster. In aristocratic terms, Anne did not bring a great fortune to the marriage, but given that they had thirty-six happy years together, it does not seem to have been a problem for Lord North, although more surprisingly, it does not seem to have been a problem for North's father, Lord Guilford either who had married three aristocratic ladies. The relationship between Guilford and his daughter-in-law seems to have been warm and affectionate so it would seem that he was fond of Ann. Ann was the daughter of a squire in Somersetshire and on his death in 1753, she had inherited the family estate of Dillington which is near Taunton. No one can be sure of exactly how much she brought to the marriage three years later, but people were always apt to speculate and a figure of £4,000 per annum was mentioned more than once.

Historians have sometimes discounted that as being too large on the grounds that North suffered from financial worries all his life. However, that argument hardly bears scrutiny in the case of 18th century politicians as it was quite common for a senior politician of the time to be brilliant with the nation's finances, but quite hopeless with his own. A classic example of this was William Pitt the Younger (1759-1806) who was the Prime Minister who virtually invented income tax but was useless at managing his own affairs, with the result that he died owing a massive amount of money. Pitt should have been perfectly comfortably off given his income but he shared something with Lord North – both men entered parliament in their early twenties and stayed there virtually all their lives, which resulted in a complete inability at managing the minutiae of what they would have thought of as trivial amounts. However, if their personal creditors were in business, the amount owing was often the difference between them being able to continue trading or closing down depending on whether they were actually paid or not. Whatever Pitt and North owed to members of the aristocracy probably didn't matter so much as they too probably had money that they owed somebody else. Having said all that however, both William Pitt and Lord North were good at managing the nation's finances resulting then, as today, in the charge that politicians were divorced from reality.

Just over a year prior to Frederick's marriage, his friend and step-brother, William, 2nd Earl of Dartmouth, also married. The bride was Frances Catherine Nicoll, daughter of Sir Charles Nicoll and Elizabeth Blundell, the ceremony taking place on 11th January, 1755.

As mentioned earlier, the step-brothers were close in age as well as in the timing of their marriages, William having been born on 20th June, 1731, the year before Frederick. William outlived Frederick by ten years however, dying on 15th July, 1801 aged 70 years. William and Frances had six children:- Lady Charlotte Legge (d1848), Admiral Hon. Sir Arthur Kaye Legge (d1835), Right Revd. Hon. Edward Legge (d.1827), Sir George Legge, 3rd Earl of Dartmouth (1755-1810), Hon. Henry Legge (1765-1844), and the Rev. Hon. Augustus George Legge (1773-1828).

Frederick and Ann North's first child, George Augustus, arrived on 11th September, 1756 and as a result, North started having financial problems at an early time of his life. He had run up a debt as soon as he had married because he had had to raise a loan for a settlement on his wife. Even though he was given the family house in Grosvenor Square by his father in 1757, a year after he had married, debts continued to plague him throughout his life and he was always asking his father for help with loans, requests that did not stop even after three years working at the Treasury. His father, although wealthy, was not prepared to continually put his hand in his pocket to bale his son out, and subsequently Guilford has been criticised by historians for not helping his son with his finances. This earned Guilford the reputation for being mean with money, although he probably thought that the best way his son would learn was to leave him to sort out his own problems. North had, after all, a country house in Ashstead, Herts, which he could have parted with, but he simply kept putting the matter off. Local tradesmen didn't help either themselves or North, as they seemed to be willing to allow enormous sums of credit to build up so that North simply had no idea of what he owed, and the tradesmen probably never got paid everything that they were due. The best one can say of North with regard to this aspect of his life was that at least his debts were not due to excessive gambling as was the case of so many aristocrats.

In the 18th century, it always helped your political career to have somebody with influence to lobby on your behalf, and in the case of Lord North, it was his father, the 1st Earl Guilford who wrote to the then Prime Minister, the Duke of

Newcastle asking him if he could bear his son in mind when handing out offices of state. He actually wrote on his own behalf as well but in June, 1759, it was Lord North who was offered the job of junior Lord of the Treasury. There were three such posts of equal rank and two that were more senior, in other words, five altogether. The most senior was taken by the Prime Minister of the day, whilst the second by the Chancellor of the Exchequer. The remaining three were taken by backbench MPs although their jobs were important and held a high level of responsibility. MPs had no salary in the 18th century, but ministers did, and Lord North's ministerial income along with the amount that he received from his estates meant that he and Ann had an income of £3,000 per year on which to live. The rough guide that people use in translating 18th century amounts to the present day is to multiply by a factor of sixty, which meant that the couple had an annual income of about £180,000 in present day terms. Even an income such as this did not seem to help him manage his personal financial affairs properly, although his time at the Treasury earned him a good reputation for managing the nation's affairs.

On 25th October, 1760, sixteen months after North had gone to the Treasury, King George II died, and as his son Frederick, the Prince of Wales, had pre-deceased his father in 1751, Frederick's son, and George II's grandson, succeeded to the throne as George III aged just twenty-two. The new King was young and in some eyes, seen as poorly educated, but be that as it may, two years after his accession to the throne saw a change of premiership from the Duke of Newcastle to John Stuart, 3rd Earl of Bute (1713-1792) and who on becoming Prime Minister in 1762 broke a period of rule by the Whigs that had gone back forty years when Robert Walpole had become the King's first minister in 1721. When Frederick, the Prince of Wales died in 1751, the Earl of Bute became Groom of the Stole to Frederick's son George, the future George III. It was a recurring theme amongst the Hanoverian Kings that one generation did not get on with the previous one, and so it was that the new King had had precious little parental guidance from his father Frederick. When the shy young twenty-two year old was suddenly thrust into the role of King, he needed a father figure to help him. Bute was very friendly with the new King's mother, Augusta, the Princess of Saxe-Gotha, to the extent that some accused them of being lovers, but there is no direct evidence with which to back this up.

The new King made it crystal clear that he did not want either the Duke of Newcastle to remain in office at the Treasury (aka Prime Minister) or William Pitt the Elder as the other Principal Secretary. Pitt was persuaded to resign in October 1761, and Newcastle followed on 26th May, 1762, leaving the way clear for George III to appoint Bute who he, George, trusted and would work amicably with. Not only that, Bute would be able to give the young monarch the guidance that he so badly needed from an older man. A few days after Newcastle's resignation, Bute was appointed Prime Minister, but it was not a post he was happy with, and he resigned less than a year later and gave way to George Grenville (1712-70), brother of William Pitt the Elder's wife, Hester, and uncle of the future Prime Minister, William Pitt the Younger. Grenville took up office on 10th April, 1763. This was an unwelcome appointment so far as the King was concerned as Grenville had taken over from his friend and mentor, and he was once heard to say of the new Prime Minister:- "When he has wearied me for two hours he looks at his watch to see if he may not tire me for an hour more". In the meantime, Frederick and Anne North had been busy adding to their family. By 1763, when Grenville took over as Prime Minister to an unwilling King George III, the Norths had had two, possibly three more children to add to their first born, George Augustus who had arrived in 1956. In 1760, Catherine Anne (Kitty) was born followed by Francis in 1761. A fourth child called Charlotte was born, but we cannot be sure of the year, so it is not possible to say whether it was before or after 1763.

Despite the King's reservations about Grenville, Lord North respected him but was not keen to take up the request to lead for the government in the case that they intended to bring against John Wilkes. Wilkes was born in 1727 and was the son of a distiller. He lived life in the fast lane and was a prominent member of the Hell-fire Club along with people such as John Montagu, the 4th Earl of Sandwich. He entered Parliament at the age of thirty and was fiercely critical of Lord Bute, Grenville's predecessor and published a weekly newspaper called *The New Briton* that enabled him to express his criticisms. When Bute left office, Wilkes turned his attentions towards George Grenville and in the famous issue number 45 dated 23rd April, 1763, he wrote that King George III had merely read out lies which were contained in the King's Speech during the opening of Parliament that the Prime Minister had written for him. Wilkes wrote the following:-

"The King's Speech has always been considered by the legislature, and by the public at large, as the speech of the minister... I am in doubt whether the imposture is greater on the sovereign or the nation. Every friend of his country must lament that a prince of so many great and amiable qualities, whom England truly reveres, can be thought to give the sanction of his sacred name to the most odious measures, and to the most unjustifiable public declarations, from a throne ever renowned for truth, honour, and unsullied virtue".

The King had only been on the throne for three years and at the age of twenty-five, was still very young to take on the responsible role of being the monarch of the nation. He was anxious to establish himself in his own right rather than be a puppet of the government, and he was furious with Wilkes at implying that he, the King, was just that very thing, a weak man who could not stand up to his ministers. Because Wilkes had not actually put his name to the piece, it was doubtful whether it was in fact legal to take action against him, but in the event, the government had Wilkes incarcerated in the Tower. His case was heard at Westminster Hall, but he was discharged on the grounds of Parliamentary privilege, the Lord Chief Justice saying at the time, that he could only be charged for treason, felon, or breach of the peace. The House of Commons was not finished however, and stung by the judgement of the Lord Chief Justice, decided to bring three resolutions before the House. North led for the government on all three. The first was to charge Wilkes with seditious libel; the second proposing that Wilkes could not be protected by Parliamentary privilege; and the third to expel John Wilkes from the House of Commons. The first charge came before the House on the 15th November, 1763, and North won

the debate by 273 votes to 111. On the 24th November, North proposed that:-
"The Privilege of Parliament does not extend to the writing and publishing of
seditious libels". Once again, North won comfortably, and on the third motion
put forward on the 19th January 1764, it was decided that Wilkes should be
expelled from the House. There was no division on this issue which was held in
the absence of Wilkes, who by now had left the country and was residing in
France. North mistakenly thought that he had seen the last of Wilkes, but he
returned to England five years later when he was imprisoned in the Tower for
nearly two years and not allowed to resume his seat. He eventually came back
into Parliament, but despite the fact that Wilkes had seemed to outwit the
government, the debates had cemented North's reputation as a very good
Parliamentary performer. He had a good memory which allowed him to
remember points made by opponents and counter them some time later without
the aid of notes. Nathanael Wraxall (1751-1831), a writer of political memoirs,
touching on Lord North's humour, later wrote when North was Prime Minister;-

"Lord North was powerful, able and fluent in debate, sometimes repelling
the charges made against him with solid argument, but still more frequently
eluding or blunting the weapons of his antagonists by the force of wit and
humour. Fox, conscious of the First Minister's superiority in exciting a laugh,
and irritated at being the object of his talent for ridicule, more than once tried to
silence him by severity of animadversion."

Indeed, North was renowned for both his sense of humour, as well as his
habit of falling asleep during debates if they held no particular interest for him.
On one notable occasion, both characteristics were shown in the House when
George Grenville was making a very long speech which was virtually a history
lesson concerning government revenues. Lord North had no intention of
listening to it all and asked his neighbour John Robinson, the Member for
Westmorland, who was also North's political manager to wake him when
Grenville reached the present day. Grenville went droning on and on until
Robinson felt that the time was right and he gave North a dig in the ribs
whereupon the House heard Grenville saying:- "... I shall now draw the
attention of the House to the revenues and expenditure of the country in 1689".
North listened for a minute before exclaiming to his neighbour:- "Zounds! You
have wakened me near one hundred years too soon". Once, during a different
debate, an opposition member was attacking him in a lengthy and tedious speech
and said:- "Even now the Noble Lord is slumbering over the ruin of his country"
only to see North slowly open his eyes before muttering:- "I wish to heaven that
I was" before closing his eyes and nodding off again.

North was still at the Treasury when in April, 1765, King George III
suffered his first bout of illness which may have been the first showing of his so-
called insanity, but which did not really occur until much later in 1788. At the
time it was considered the King had gone mad but it was in all probability
porphyria, a disease which brings on the symptoms of insanity. The illness in
1765 was much more mild than that which the King was to suffer from years
later but was deemed serious enough for the King himself to wish for a Regency
Bill to be passed in the event of his being incapable of carrying out the duties
expected of the reigning monarch. The King wanted to nominate a list of names

as to who could be Regent and these names he wished to be part of the legislation. One of the people he wanted to nominate was his mother, Augusta, the Dowager Princess of Wales. For whatever reason, the cabinet would not include her name on the list, and the King, furious at such a rebuff, was determined to remove Grenville from office at the earliest opportunity. He succeeded in dismissing Grenville in July, 1765 and he was replaced by Charles Watson Wentworth (1730-82), the Marquis of Rockingham and leader of the Whig opposition. North would not serve under Rockingham, and for the first time in six years, found himself returned to the back benches.

When North next held office, William Pitt the Elder (1708-78), who since 1766 had been 1st Earl of Chatham, was Prime Minister, taking office in July of the same year. He appointed Augustus Henry Fitzroy (1735-1811), the 3rd Duke of Grafton, as First Lord of the Treasury and the Chancellor of the Exchequer was Charles Townshend (1725-67). Because of Chatham's poor health, Townshend was able to have more power than he would normally expect with the result that he imposed heavy taxes on goods, especially tea, that were bound for America and it was these taxes that began the first stages of unrest in the colonies that would ultimately lead to the War of Independence which would last from 1775 to 1783.

By March 1767, Chatham wanted to get rid of Townshend and wrote to Grafton suggesting that Lord North become Chancellor in Townshend's place. North initially refused and with Chatham's health deteriorating, plans to find an alternative man to replace Townshend were abandoned. However, on the 4th September of that year, Townshend suddenly died, and subsequently, Lord North was once again offered the post of Chancellor, and once again he refused due to the fact that his father, Lord Guilford was ill and quite possibly, would not recover. In the meantime, with Townshend dead, Grafton had had to make alternative arrangements should North turn the job down a second time, but then had to quickly alter them due to the fact that Guilford made an astonishingly rapid recovery allowing North to change his mind and accept the post.

Although he accepted this very important post, North was full of self doubt. A lack of confidence is an unusual and rather endearing quality in a politician and just over a month after accepting the post, he wrote to his father:- "I am afraid it will soon be found how unequal my abilities are to the task in which I am engaged, but if His Majesty and his ministers have made an insufficient Chancellor of the Exchequer they may thank themselves for it, for I can truly say I never obtruded myself upon them, and do not desire to continue in my place an hour after it shall be found prejudicial to the public".

North and his family moved into Downing Street, a quite common event in those days as the Prime Minister of the day often had a huge house in town that he was reluctant to leave. Meanwhile, because of the continual struggle with his finances, North was only too grateful for the use of the official residence which allowed him to rent his own house out which was situated off Grosvenor Square. Previous Chancellors of the Exchequer had attended Cabinet meetings but the first man to do this by virtue of the office as opposed to the person was North's predecessor, Charles Townshend. Now North was required to attend for the same reason and this pleased him as he felt that it was the only way that he could speak for the government with any meaning. In January of the following year, 1768, North was confirmed as Leader of the House, and these two posts, along with the illness of the Earl of Chatham meant that he was now the main spokesman for the administration.

In the political world of the 18th century, there operated a two party system, Whigs and Tories and on the surface, it was run in the same way as it is in the 21st century. However, there was a great deal less party discipline and there were no manifestos that were rigidly adhered to in the manner in which they are today. There being no television and radio, the media consisted entirely of newspapers and so members often listened with more interest to speeches in the House because in many cases, that would be the place where they came by their information. Speeches were often longer, and members often made their minds up about the direction their vote would take by what they heard in the House, so that the party label was therefore less important than it is today. However, what often did happen was that a person would have a following as opposed to a party, so there could be a contingent of Chathamites, Rockinghamites, etc., who tended to follow their man. North did not engage in this habit with the result that he did not make enemies and his easy going manner won him many friends. He was also seen as good at his job and seemed to have a good grasp of financial matters despite his early reluctance to accept the post of Chancellor due to a seeming lack of confidence. He did have a habit of falling asleep during some debates as seen earlier when he made no pretence of being interested in George Grenville's speech concerning the history of government finances, but this habit, far from making him disliked, was seen as an eccentricity that endeared him to other members. There was one occasion when Edmund Burke was castigating North whilst the latter appeared to be asleep with a hankerchief draped over his face. To add force to his argument, or merely to appear clever, Burke used a Latin quotation to emphasise a point that he was trying to make, whilst an unperturbed North woke from his apparent sleep long enough to correct Burke's pronunciation before covering his face again and returning happily to his dozing. In such circumstances, members found that it was difficult to get angry with North although doubtless they would have done if he had not been up to the job.

During the time that North took the job of Chancellor, there was a great deal of social unrest in the country. Britain was a rich nation and this could be seen by the extraordinary amounts of money that the aristocracy won and lost during their frequent bouts of gambling, but their riches were gained largely on the back of the working classes of the country. Unfair though the distribution of wealth was, the system worked reasonably well all the while there was work for people so that they could eat, but Britain was entering an age which was producing massive change resulting in a social cost. There was a poor harvest resulting in food prices rising, but at the same time, people were being put out of work due to the invention and introduction of new labour saving machinery. The century produced the industrial revolution, and Richard Arkwright who by co-incidence lived exactly the same time as Lord North (1732-92), invented the water powered spinning frame which produced cotton-thread that was strong enough to be used as warp. A few years previously in 1764, James Hargreaves (1720-1778) invented a machine known as the Spinning Jenny, but in 1768, fellow spinners broke into his house and destroyed his frame. These were but two inventions out of many, and the industrial revolution did not happen overnight, but the seeds were sown during this period of time.

Given the difficulties these social changes were producing, probably the last person that Lord North would want to be involved with was the political agitator, John Wilkes who returned to this country from France in February 1768 having fled Britain four years earlier. Wilkes decided that he wanted to return to Parliament and when it was dissolved on 11th March, he stood for the City of London in the subsequent general election. He was soundly beaten but undeterred, he stood for Middlesex and won with a large majority. However, having given himself up, he was sentenced to twenty-two months in prison and fined £1,000. After that there was confusion in government circles as to how to treat Wilkes. Many in the cabinet, including North, seemed to underestimate Wilkes and the damage that he was capable of doing, but George III was having none of it and wanted a tougher approach. North, being Leader of the House, had convened a meeting of the cabinet for 25th April, 1768, and just in case they harboured any thoughts of dealing lightly with Wilkes or even letting him off further, the King wrote to North:-

"Tho entirely confiding in Your Attachment to my Person, as well as in Your hatred of every Lawless Proceeding yet I think it highly proper to apprize You that the Expulsion of Mr Wilkes appears to be very essential and must be effected; & that I make no doubt when you lay this affair with Your usual precision before the meeting of the Gentlemen of the House of Commons this Evening, it will meet with the required Unanimity & vigour".

In writing this letter, the King was adopting his usual tactic of getting what he wanted by flattery, and it usually worked as no career minded politician wanted to upset the Monarch. However, despite the King's intervention and the fact that both meetings were chaired by North, no firm decision as to what to do about Wilkes was reached at the 25th April meeting, nor even the subsequent one held on 11th May. If Wilkes had been happy to keep a low profile after he had completed his prison sentence, it seems likely that he would have been able to resume his Parliamentary seat but unfortunately he did anything but. He presented Parliament with a list of the different ways in which he felt that he had been mistreated and demanded some sort of compensation, or at least an acknowledgement of how unfairly he had been treated. If Wilkes had set out deliberately to upset the Monarch and the government, he couldn't have made a better job of it, and was never going to get anywhere by adopting this approach. Wilkes had pushed his luck too far this time, and despite the fact that the Duke of Grafton offered an olive branch by promising that Parliament would drop their proceedings against him if he would drop his list of grievances, Wilkes refused and not unnaturally, the cabinet's patience finally ran out. North, showing a new determination, wrote to his father:-

"The Administration were well inclined to do nothing upon the subject of Mr. Wilkes, but he has resolved to force his cause upon them & upon the House by presenting a petition.... We shall probably have much tumult, noise & clamour in the course of this business but I do not see how it can end without his expulsion. He has brought it on himself & must answer for the consequences".

This was a different and altogether more confident Lord North from the man who reluctantly accepted the job of Chancellor less than a year previously after twice refusing it in the belief that he was not good enough. Not only that, he was now Leader of the House and responsible for the management of much of the government's difficult business, which included how to sort the problem of Wilkes out.

Wilkes's petition was presented to the House for debate on 27th January, 1769. The Earl of Chatham had by now resigned as Prime Minister in October 1768 due to ill health and his place as First Lord was taken by Augustus Henry Fitzroy (1735-1811), the 3rd Duke of Grafton. It was still Lord North who presented the government's case and Wilkes's petition was dismissed by a majority of 278 votes to 131 resulting in North being congratulated by the King who was getting what he wanted at last. It was then decided that something should be done concerning the possible expulsion of Wilkes and presenting the motion, North carried it successfully through on 3rd February, again with a large majority of 219 votes to 137. North and the cabinet, flushed with success, probably then went too far because North said during a third debate on the subject:-

"If ever this question should again come before us, I shall deem that man the true member for the county of Middlesex, who shall have a majority of legal votes".

The meaning behind this of course, was that any vote in any future election that was cast in favour of Wilkes would be deemed illegal and be null and void. Two months later, in April, this is exactly what happened in Middlesex during a contest between Colonel Henry Luttrell and Wilkes. They contested a seat in Middlesex which Wilkes won with a huge majority of 1,143 votes against 296, but Parliament refused to accept the vote and Luttrell took his seat in Parliament. It was doubtful that this was legal but as far as King George III was concerned, he had achieved the result that he wanted, and North went even higher in his estimation as it was North who had taken the leading role with the management of this unfortunate affair.

In April 1769, Lord North presented his second budget which received a mixed reception. He was careful with the nation's finances and was keen to repay government debt at regular intervals and as resources would allow. He had an interesting take on the use of the lottery as a tax raising method calling it a tax on the willing although some thought that it encouraged gambling. Others thought that he spent too little on the armed forces, thereby neglecting national security. However, his prudence won him friends in many quarters and one MP called Richard Rigby wrote:-

"Yesterday Lord North opened his budget in the Committee of Ways and Means; and in the four and twenty years that I have sat in Parliament, in very few of which I have missed that famous day of the Sessions, I verily think I have never known any of his predecessors acquit themselves so much to the satisfaction of the house".

There were further problems with John Wilkes that needed dealing with but it was the American colonies that would really present difficulties that would trouble the British government, and in particular, Lord North for many years to come. Both the government and the British people completely misread the resentment that was growing in the colonies over the attitude of the mother country and the taxes that were being imposed on the Americans, especially those on tea. The British had a patronising attitude towards the people in the colonies and treated them like naughty, ungrateful children who did not know what was best for them. In April 1769, the same time as he presented his second budget, Lord North said:-

"Let America look to Great Britain as a kind of parent and friend". A year later, William Pitt the Elder, the 1st Earl of Chatham, went even further and said:- "They (the Americans) must be subordinate. In all laws relating to trade and navigation especially, this is the mother country, they are the children; they must obey, and we prescribe".

Although he was no longer Prime Minister having given way to Lord Grafton in October, 1768, Chatham had returned to active politics early in 1769 having made a partial recovery and was still listened to. His attitude carried weight amongst many MPs but was a recipe for certain disaster in the future. During a cabinet meeting on 1st May, 1769, Grafton, the Prime Minister, asked his cabinet to repeal all the taxes on the colonies that the previous Chancellor, Charles Townshend, had introduced in January, 1767. Grafton lost by the narrowest of margins, with four members voting for him with five against. North voted against although the only tax that he was adamant about was that which was levied on tea. It seems barely possible that the American War of Independence could have been started by not only just one person's vote, but that vote concerned a tax on one item only. It seems that Parliament had not learned the lesson that laws should never be made if they cannot be enforced, and whilst it had become clear to many Members of Parliament during the previous year that these laws were just that, unenforceable, not enough members realised it until it was too late. The inevitable result of this muddled thinking and the vote that was taken on 1st May, 1769, was a war that could never be won by the so-called mother country although the actual war itself was not to start until 1775. North however, would not be criticised at the time for his attitude to the colonies, merely, that he was unsuccessful in bringing them to heel.

At the time of this vote, Lord Grafton looked vulnerable. His cabinet was split down the middle over what to do about the colonies and this state of affairs continued throughout the year. On the afternoon of 20th December 1769, North received the following note from the King:-

"Lord North – I wish to see you about eight this Evening".

It has been assumed by past historians that this note was the opening move of the King to make Lord North Prime Minister. Whilst there is no written evidence with which to back this assumption up, given the brief and very direct nature of the note and in the absence of any other crisis at the time, it seems a reasonable enough guess, especially in view of subsequent events. If the King was sounding North out about the prospect of he, North, agreeing to become the King's First Minister, it is also reasonable to assume, that given his reaction to being offered the post of Chancellor of the Exchequer, his reaction to this latest proposal would be to refuse it. If this was the case, then any caution on North's part would not have caused the King any undue concern, assuming of course that Grafton was not thinking of resigning in the immediate future. The only other reason that he should ask to see North was that the problem of John Wilkes had reared up again, although if the King wished to discuss this, it would be more likely that he would send for Grafton.

The beginning of the year saw a great many petitions calling for political reform, and many of these petitions complained about the fact that John Wilkes had been denied the right to take his seat in Parliament that he had won so handsomely in April, 1769. North however was very dismissive of these petitions and the people that had signed them. He considered that they were signed by a mass of people who knew little of that which they signed. In January, 1770, after a debate on the Address after the opening of Parliament, he said the following:-

"It is well known that by such activity men have been induced to set their hands to petitions which they have never read, and give countenance to complaints which they have never heard".

If this was dismissive, a determined North decided to finish the matter of the petitions off, and went on to say,

"I have as high a sense of the rights of Englishmen, as any gentleman of this house, yet I can never acquiesce in the absurd opinion that all men are equal, nor ever pretend to level all distinction, and reduce the various classes into which the polity of civil life has divided the individuals of this Kingdom, to a state of nature, for the sake of flattering my own vanity by a little popular applause".

The government won the debate quite easily by 254 votes to 158, but although the margin was high, the opposition had been fierce, and Grafton looked vulnerable as several important people resigned as a result. On 21st January 1770, he offered the King his resignation which was accepted in Grafton's subsequent version, "with a great deal of regret".

On 22nd January, the day after Grafton's resignation, the King sent Lord North another brief note requesting his attendance and this time there was no doubt as to what the meeting was about – that of the King offering North the Premiership. The King was determined to get his man, and directly after the interview between the two men, the King wrote North a letter leaving no doubt as to his, the King's, intention to persuade North to accept the job:-

"... You must easily see that if You do not accept I have no Peer at present in my Service that I could consent to place in the Duke of Grafton's employment, whatever You may think do not take any decision unless it is the one of instantly accepting without a further conversation with Me. And as to the other arrangements You may hear what others think but keep Your opinion till I have seen You".

North had still not given an answer three days later when the Opposition had tabled a motion of censure on the government concerning the Middlesex election involving Wilkes. It seemed that this matter would simply go on and on but in the debate that followed, the government won by the margin of forty-four votes – not huge, but certainly enough to give North the confidence to accept the King's offer although it was agreed to keep the decision a secret to allow North to rally supporters. This might be easier said than done as although North's fairly easy going manner had made him no enemies, it also meant that he had no particular following either which other leaders had had in the past. On the 31st January, 1770, North was officially appointed Prime Minister although acceptance of the post was never going to be easy as once again, he faced a censure motion on the subject of John Wilkes, his first as Prime Minister. Although the motion was on the subject of Wilkes, it was clearly held to try and throw North off balance before he could get settled into the job, but as it turned out, he put in a confident performance and the government won by a margin of forty votes. The King also recognised the motion for what it was and sent North a congratulatory letter the following day – North was now well and truly the King's First Minister although most people thought that he would not last long. It is easy to understand why. North had an amiable easy going personality which was not associated with someone who wanted to be at the top, and also, some of his predecessors had had a remarkably short tenure in the post. Prior to North becoming Prime Minister, there had been no less than six holders of the post in the previous eight years, The Duke of Newcastle, The Earl of Bute, George Grenville, Marquess of Rockingham, The Earl of Chatham, otherwise known as William Pitt the Elder, and the Duke of Grafton. As it was, North stayed in the job longer than the previous holders of the post put together, and lasted twelve years.

North had been Chancellor of the Exchequer since September 1767, and Leader of the House since January 1768 and it was decided that he should carry on with both of these posts after he became Prime Minister. At one level it seemed to be a sensible decision as he was an expert on Fiscal matters and had shown himself to be a good manager of the affairs of the House. On the negative side however, it meant that he was continuously overworked which was not good for someone expected to be able to take an overview of government business. Given his temperament however, it is difficult to see how North could have worked in any other manner, as he was amiable and modest, and never saw himself as the King's First Minister as such, telling his daughter that there was no such position in the British constitution. He saw his role as taking the chair in cabinet and being the link between them and the King, and this was partly due to the character of George III, who saw his role as very much hands on with his government. Sometimes, it must have felt that it was the King who was the First Minister – a somewhat dangerous idea given that the balance between Parliament and the Crown had been altered since 1689 when William and Mary took the throne.

When North became Prime Minister and First Lord of the Treasury, there was little or no reshuffle from the cabinet that he inherited from the Duke of Grafton due to the fact that he had little or no room to manoeuvre as all of the members who served were in the Lords. The most famous of these was John Montague (1718-92), the 4th Earl of Sandwich who became the First Lord of the Admiralty in 1771, the year following North taking over the role of Prime Minister. The person that Sandwich replaced was Admiral Sir Edward Hawke (1705-81), later the 1st Baron Hawke who held the post of First Sea Lord when Captain Cook set out in 1768 in the first of his three epic voyages. Admiral Hawke was a naval hero who had fought against the French in the seven years war between 1756 and 1763 and who destroyed the French fleet in Quiberon Bay in 1759, which almost certainly stopped a French invasion of Britain that year. However, Sandwich was an ambitious man and wanted the post back that he had already held twice before, firstly between 1748 and 1751 and then for a brief period in 1763. A gambler and a man who lived life to the full, it was he who was supposed to have invented the sandwich in order that he could stay at the gaming tables for hours on end although modern historians have treated Montagu more kindly. It is now felt that it was far more likely he invented the sandwich so that he may stay at his desk in order to keep working longer hours. It is also said that his third term as First Sea Lord showed him to be inept and helped to bring about Britain's defeat by America in the War of Independence. However, in making this claim, early historians have always been vague as to how his so-called ineptness manifested itself and have never given specific examples. In fact, he inherited a navy that was in chaos because the shipyards were badly run and there was not enough wood to make the required ships. Some of the existing ships also suffered from dry rot. Sandwich cleaned up the dockyards and was to oversee the improvement in the way that new ships were built which made them faster and which were to improve the British fleet so that France was unable to invade Britain in later years. He also improved the administration of the navy. Sandwich was a great friend of Sir Joseph Banks (1743-1820), the botanist who accompanied Captain Cook on his first voyage between 1768 and 1771 and who went on to become President of the Royal Society for forty-one years.

Sandwich was First Lord of the Admiralty throughout Lord North's Premiership, both men leaving their posts in 1782, and it adds credence to the more modern view of Sandwich that it was Lord North, not Sandwich, who history has cast as the man who was most to blame for the British defeat. Even this has seemed unfair as although Prime Minister, Lord North was nominally in charge of the way the war was fought, but the attitude of King George III was very influential in Britain's early reactions to the American people wanting to break away from the mother country.

The years between 1770 and 1775 were good years for Lord North. They were not always easy as there were the perennial problems of Ireland and the East India Company to be faced. However, his handling of the nation's finances were good and his reputation was high, but sadly for him, the problem of the American colonies were to start and which would overshadow his tenure at Downing Street eventually giving him the reputation as the Prime Minister who lost America.

When he was Chancellor of the Exchequer before his death in 1767, Charles Townshend had imposed heavy taxes on goods that were imported to America, and this had long caused resentment amongst the thirteen colonies that made the Americas. The British were guilty of both arrogance towards the people of the colonies and also complacency as to the power that they would have to organise any co-ordinated resistance. The colonies were made up of people with different roots and were run independently, but having said that, it is probable that even the people in the colonies recognised the odds that they were up against as John Adams (1735-1826) who was to become the second President of the United

States as they were later known, would recognise when he was to say after the war was finally over:-

"Thirteen clocks were made to strike together – a perfection of mechanism, which no artist had ever before effected".

The people in the colonies were angry with the taxes being imposed upon them and there was complete disagreement between the British and the Americans as to why the redcoat soldiers were there. The British saw them as a force which would protect law and order and keep the peace which is why the mother country felt perfectly justified at charging the taxes that would help pay towards the maintenance of them. However, with taxation being imposed upon them and no say as to how it should be spent, the colonials saw the soldiers as an occupying army. Angry at the Townshend taxes, the colonists organised a ban on British goods and with tensions mounting, there was a stand off between the redcoats and a large gathering of people that had crowded round the soldiers. On 5th March, 1770, only about five weeks after North had become Prime Minister, the crowd were pelting the soldiers with snowballs, rocks, and just about anything else that they could lay their hands on. A soldier was clubbed and fell and the soldiers fired into the crowd killing three instantly with a further two dying later on. In all, eleven people were hit by the soldiers' bullets. The soldiers were tried but to the anger of the local Bostonians, were acquitted, the person defending them being none other than John Adams, the lawyer who as mentioned earlier, became the second person to hold the position of President of the United States.

Because of the furious reaction of the colonies to the taxes that were levied by the British government that had been started by Charles Townshend in 1767, the government had reversed their taxation policy on everything bar tea, but this still caused unrest which came to a head on 16th December, 1773 in Boston Harbour. Three ships that had docked with a consignment of tea caused a furious reaction with the crowds that had gathered in the harbour. Thousands milled round the docks and after a mass meeting it was decided that the ships should leave without any payment of tax. The Collector of Customs refused to let the ships leave without the tax being paid and the resulting stalemate led to approximately two hundred men marching to the wharf and throwing the cargo of tea into the harbour waters.

The British government were furious and in March 1774 passed the Intolerable Acts, which amongst other things, closed Boston Harbour. The government had set something in motion that would be bound to lead to trouble, but despite all the unrest, the British government led by Lord North were not worried. There were several reasons for this. Firstly, the thirteen colonies were run independently and had no one voice with which to co-ordinate any action against the mother country. Secondly, as a result of this there was no single army, each colony using a largely untrained militia, who whilst quite effective at guerrilla attacks, had no central command. Thirdly, not all the people who populated the colonies wanted a fight with Britain. Those that did were known variously as Patriots, Whigs, Congressmen or Americans. It was these who wanted a break with Britain and to be able to forge their own destiny. However, there was a sizeable number, possibly as many as 15-20%, who wanted to stay loyal to the Crown, and these were known as Loyalists, Tories, or King's Men. Just as the English Civil War had divided families, so it was that the same thing happened in the American War of Independence. One famous example was Benjamin Franklin and his son William. Benjamin Franklin (1706-90) was a remarkable man who took a leading role in the events leading to America's final independence from Britain and it must have been painful for both father and son that William stayed loyal to the British Crown with the result that they never spoke to each other again.

In 1774, there was a unified Congress and at first it tried to stay loyal to the British Parliament but felt that the government was oblivious to their views and the King's subsequent heavy-handed response led to their attitude hardening. In 1775, the revolutionaries gained control of each of the thirteen colonies and formed the Second Continental Congress and once that had been achieved, they formed a Continental Army, formed in July of that year. The army was 17,000 strong and the Commander-in-Chief of this army was General George Washington (1732-99). During the quarrel between the states and Britain between 1765-70, he had always hoped for a peaceful solution, but once the problems re-surfaced later on, he became convinced that only a military solution would be possible. He was a dignified man and a natural leader and was the obvious choice to lead the new army.

Prior to this, the first fighting had started on 19th April, 1775 when 1,000 British troops clashed with local militia in Concord, a confrontation which was called the Battle of Lexington and Concord. This caused the thirteen colonies to assemble their militia and besiege Boston and two months later, on 17th June, 1775, the Battle of Bunker Hill followed. The British were led by General Sir William Howe (1729-1814) and whilst the battle was seen as a British victory, there were far more losses suffered by the British, losing as they did 1,000 men out of a total of 2,000, whilst the American losses were only 500 out of a much larger force. The British troops charged at the American forces twice but both times were forced back by a vicious volley of rifle fire. Victory was sustained only at the third attempt because by this time, the Americans had run out of ammunition and were left with only bayonets and stones with which to defend themselves. It was a victory for the British, but it was hardly a convincing one.

Despite now having an army, the Congress still hoped for a peaceful solution and on 5th July, 1775, they adopted the Olive Branch Petition which expressed hope for a reconciliation with King George III but in August, the King refused to even look at the petition and issued the Proclamation of Rebellion on 26th November, 1775 which was supposed to bully the Americans into line. It had quite the opposite effect however, and it merely hardened the attitudes of Congress and made war inevitable.

Soon after this, in January 1776, the Americans were given more encouragement when the English born American revolutionary writer and philosopher, Thomas Paine (1737-1809) published a 50-page pamphlet entitled 'Common Sense' in which he gave a brief summary of the causes of the war, and encouraged the colonies to immediately declare their independence. The pamphlet also criticised the whole idea of the Monarchy. Paine was to go on and fight in the Continental army before publishing a further series of pamphlets and later became secretary to the Congress Committee on foreign affairs between 1777 and 1779.

On 11th June, 1776, it was decided to set up a small committee to draw up a draft Declaration of Independence and on 28th of the same month, Thomas Jefferson, John Adams and Benjamin Franklin brought the document before the Second Congress. On 2nd July, 1776, the Congress voted for the independence of the United States whilst two days after that, on 4th July, 1776, the thirteen original colonies voted for a Declaration of Independence which effectively put them on a direct collision course with the British Government as well as the Monarchy. The Declaration established the United States as a separate country and was mainly the work of Thomas Jefferson (1743-1826) who was a lawyer and was also a member of the original Congress. Eventually he was to follow George Washington and John Adams to become the third President of the United States between 1801 and 1809.

In October 1777, Britain suffered a major setback in their conduct of the war when the two armies that they had in North America failed to co-ordinate their strategies properly. One army was led by Guy Carleton (1724-1808), who had served under James Wolfe (1727-59) in Canada many years before. Carleton had been Governor of Quebec from 1775 to 1777 and in 1782 would go on to become the Commander-in-Chief of the British Army in America. In 1777 however, he was in charge of an army that was in Quebec. The other army that the British had was led by General William Howe (1729-1814), 5th Viscount Howe and brother of the famous naval admiral, Richard Howe (1726-99), 1st Earl, and this army was in New York. General Howe successfully captured Philadelphia but the army of Guy Carleton that was in Quebec had sent an expedition led by General John Burgoyne (1722-92), to seize the Lake Champlain and Hudson River corridor so that New England would be isolated from the rest of the colonies. Burgoyne was a clever man, not only being a distinguished soldier but also a dramatist and had at one time sat as a member of the British Parliament. However, Burgoyne's detachment lost the battle of Bennington and in the process lost 1,000 men. Not wishing to be beaten, Burgoyne continued and with an army of 9,000 men attacked an American army of 8,000 led by General Horatio Gates (1728-1806), who, although born in England, from 1763 lived in America and considered himself an American citizen joining their army in 1775, instantly being made adjutant-general as he had previously served with the British army prior to 1763. However, two events sealed Burgoyne's defeat. The first was that the expected help from General Howe was not forthcoming as he had gone on to Philadelphia, whilst the American army were reinforced by a further 3,000 militiamen and after the ensuring battle, Burgoyne surrendered at Saratoga on 17th October, 1777. This was seen as a turning point in the War of Independence as America's victory encouraged France to enter the war on the side of the colonies, a massive boost to America which was negotiated by Benjamin Franklin early in 1778.

On 7th April, 1778, soon after France entered the war, William Pitt the Elder, the Earl of Chatham, by now very unwell, came off his sick bed to go to the House of Lords to make his dramatic speech denouncing Lord North and his conduct of the war. The fact that Chatham was there at all, as well as the contents of his speech, were enough to make the occasion memorable, but it was to prove to be the last speech that he ever made. He collapsed whilst delivering it and had to be helped out of the Lords and back to his sick bed where he died a month later.

France had entered the war alongside the Americans, but so far as Britain was concerned, worse was to come. The following year, 1779, saw Spain and then in 1780, the Dutch become allies of the French. Britain was now facing a totally different situation to the one that she faced just three years earlier. Then she faced a country that consisted of thirteen uncoordinated colonies with no major army; now Britain faced a global war which was going to be much more difficult to win.

It was a war they could not and did not win. The British were eventually beaten at Yorktown on 17th October, 1781 by a combined force of French and Continental armies, although General Charles Cornwallis (1738-1805), finally surrendered two days later. The British army had entered Yorktown, Virginia expecting to be picked up by a British fleet which would take them back to New York. However, with the French allied to the states since 1778, the numbers and skill factor on both sides had become much more equal and the British fleet were beaten by a French fleet. Cornwallis was an able commander but even he was unable fight his way out of the position he found himself in as the defeat of the British fleet had left him and his men marooned. The defeat at Yorktown effectively ended the war and brought about the recognition of the United States of America as a sovereign country, although it was a bitter pill for King George III to swallow. The news of the surrender at Yorktown reached London a month later, on 25th November, 1781. Nathanael Wraxall described North's reaction when told the news in Downing Street:-

"...I asked Lord George (Germain) afterwards how he took the communication when made to him. 'As he would have taken a ball in his breast' replied Lord George. For he opened his arms, exclaiming wildly, as he paced up and down the apartment during a few minutes, 'Oh God! It is all over!' Words which he repeated many times under emotions of the deepest consternation and distress".

The opening of Parliament was to take place two days later and the speech, already written, was barely altered, the King probably being in some sort of shock and denial. Part of the speech expressed a rather forlorn hope that:- "The King's deluded subjects in America would return to that happy and prosperous condition which they had formerly derived from a due obedience to the laws." The speech ended with the extraordinary call for the:- "prosecution of this great and important contest".

It was as if the King simply could not accept what he had always considered the unthinkable. He even wanted to fight on telling North the day after the King's speech:- "As soon as the men are a little recovered of the shock felt by the bad news... they will then find the necessity of carrying on the war, though the mode of it may require alterations".

Lord North had long since ceased to want to be the King's first minister. Although he was an able administrator he had never really had any appetite for the job and had asked the King if he could resign virtually every year since being appointed in 1770, but now his going was virtually inevitable. Early in 1782, Lord Rockingham and his followers sensed that they had victory in their grasp and just about everybody including Lord North, recognised it, everybody that was except the King. Various motions of Censure were tabled against the government with a formal motion brought by Lord John Cavendish on 8th March, 1782, and although it was actually defeated by ten votes, Lord North saw that he had little option other than to tender his resignation. Still the King would not let North go and there was another motion on 15th March which the government won by a margin of nine. Lord North could see the writing was on the wall but the King could not think straight and hinted to North that he would abdicate. North was very calm and after an audience with the King, wrote to him saying that:- "...the fate of the present Ministry is absolutely and irrevocably decided". It was a lengthy letter and quite brilliant and left the King in no doubt as to the fact that he, North, had to go, and that this time there was no room for negotiation about the matter. The King had no choice other than to accept North's resignation but was very ungracious about it. He wrote North a letter saying that he would have difficulty accepting the Opposition members forming a government, although this was hardly North's concern, and ended it with the words:- "If you resign before I have decided what I will do, you will certainly for ever forfeit my regard". These were a quite disgraceful set of words to a man who had served him so loyally during one of the country's most turbulent times in history.

North's resignation was carried out in brilliant fashion with cunning in the House and with style at the end. After entering the Commons in a full dressed suit he found that he was facing a motion to remove him and his government but North was determined to resign rather than be pushed out. The Earl of Surrey attempted the first motion but North got to his feet and the Speaker allowed him the floor to move an adjournment. However, the noise in the chamber was so loud that he could not be heard as it was clear to the members of the opposition what he was up to and they wanted to move the vote of censure. It was cat and mouse for about an hour as both sides fought to be heard, but in the end North won. Charles James Fox had got to his feet to propose that Surrey be allowed to put his motion but all this did was to allow North to say that the motion was unnecessary as the ministry had finished because the King wished the present Opposition to form a government. This was completely untrue of course, but it was a brilliant piece of thinking by North and Charles James Fox quickly realised that his proposal had produced the complete opposite effect than the one that he desired. North had got his way and had resigned before the opposition could push him out. His action had enabled him to achieve exactly what he wanted which was the desired effect of the House being adjourned to allow the King to form a new ministry. Even in defeat, North had outwitted his opponents as fully expecting a longer sitting, they had not ordered their carriages. North however had, and whilst the members were shivering outside in the snow and bitterly cold wind, Lord North calmly stepped into his own carriage which was already waiting for him, and with great good humour, said:- "I have my carriage. You see gentlemen, the advantage of being in the secret. Good night". With that, he stepped into his carriage and went off into the night to enjoy a dinner party with family and friends.

Lord North had enjoyed a good working and personal relationship with the King. Both men were patriotic, and both had a sense of decency about them. North even had a great deal of modesty in his character, something not normally associated with politicians, especially those who had reached the pinnacle of their profession, that of being Prime Minister. North had accepted the post of Prime Minister reluctantly and even after holding the position, had attempted to resign many times which was refused by the King again and again, only being accepted after the defeat by the United States had made his resignation inevitable. Although the King had little choice other than to accept the fact that North would have to go after Yorktown, it is not easy to blame Lord North entirely for the events of the war. The King, just as much as his Prime Minister, felt that the rebels in the United States should be brought to heel, and whilst the Prime Minister of the day makes the military appointments, with communications then being far more difficult than they are today, he is then dependent on the Generals and Admirals for carrying the military actions to a successful conclusion, and far more autonomy was given to the men on the field than they would later have in the 21st Century. Indeed, it is arguable that the King himself, whilst notionally under the control of Parliament, did more to start the war with the colonies than did North with his inflammatory Proclamation of Rebellion in November 1775 which had been very much the brainchild of the King himself as opposed to Lord North or any of his ministers.

The resignation of North could and possibly should, have signalled the end of his political career. The phrase 'Never go back' is one used time and time again and with good reason. Even the brilliant William Pitt the Younger failed to heed the warning nearly thirty years later but certainly if the phrase was in use at the time, North was not going to take any notice of it.

Before that, and in the wake of North's resignation however, the King was faced with the dilemma which he certainly did not want, and that was to form a ministry with the Whigs, and the only two candidates were Charles Watson–Wentworth (1730-82), the Marquess of Rockingham and William Petty-Fitzmaurice (1737-1805), the Earl of Shelburne. Neither particularly appealed to the King, but although Shelburne was the lesser of the two evils, he refused to form a ministry and so the King was forced to have Rockingham, although as it happened, not for very long because Rockingham died four months later, on 1st July, 1782. Those four months probably seemed like an eternity to the King however, as his two Secretaries of State were Shelburne, and serving alongside him, Charles James Fox, utterly despised by the King, although the feeling was entirely mutual.

Shelburne took over as Prime Minister on the death of Rockingham, and the blessing for the King must have been that this caused the immediate resignation of Charles James Fox, who was replaced as Chancellor of the Exchequer by the extremely young, but extremely brilliant William Pitt the Younger. However, Shelburne could not muster the support needed for an effective government and it was always going to be a short-lived administration. Shelburne certainly had more support than other MPs for the post of Prime Minister, but it was not enough to sustain him in office for any length of time. Lord North and Charles James Fox also had substantial support, but again, not enough to head an administration. The only course of action would be a combination of the two but there were complications. William Pitt the Younger, Shelburne's brilliant Chancellor, refused to serve with North which meant that so far as Shelburne was concerned, he could not form an alliance with North. Fox would not serve with Shelburne and it was unthinkable that the King would entertain the idea of Fox even if he could muster the required support, which was very unlikely. Indeed, the King's animosity towards Fox was so fierce that he probably wouldn't have allowed Fox to serve in any capacity, not at this stage at any rate.

Just as Shelburne's administration seem to be collapsing in the early part of February 1783, Lord North's son met Fox to see if he could broker some sort of agreement between his father and Fox. After several hours of discussion there seemed to be enough common ground for an alliance to be formed but by any stretch of the imagination, it was a strange partnership. It was not kept secret and the motives for it were called into question by many MPs. On 17th February 1783, there was a motion in the House attacking Shelburne's administration on the draft peace treaty with America which the government lost by sixteen votes. This was quickly followed by a motion of censure on 21st February which the government also narrowly lost and by the 24th February, Shelburne resigned. Initially, the King asked William Pitt to form an administration, but Pitt declined. He then asked North to return but he too declined the actual top job, although happy enough to return to a senior position in government. There was no question in the King's mind about Fox – he had no wish to offer Fox the top job and so an alternative arrangement had to be found and this was brought about by making William Henry Cavendish-Bentinck (1738-1809), Duke of Portland the Prime Minister whilst Fox and North were the two Secretaries of State, Fox being in control of foreign affairs whilst North looked after home affairs. This administration took office at the beginning of April, 1783, meaning that there had been no effective government for over a month. Although Portland was nominally the Prime Minister, this government has almost always been referred to as the Fox/North coalition, and almost from the beginning, it has seemed to everybody as a strange partnership and questions have always been raised as to why it ever happened. The King certainly hated it as it included Charles James Fox, but he had little option at that time other than to accept the situation.

It may have seemed a strange partnership, but it did allow for a permanent peace to be settled with the United States of America as the country was now called although the King loathed it and the loss of the Americas always rankled with him. The Peace Treaty, known as the Treaty of Paris, was eventually signed on 3rd September, 1783 and this finally ended the war. It was signed by John Jay, Benjamin Franklin and John Adams on behalf of the United States, and David Hartley on behalf of King George III of Great Britain. There were separate treaties with France, Spain and the Dutch Republics. They were called the Treaties of Versailles, one being signed with King Louis XVI of France and the other with King Charles III of Spain. The previous day, a treaty was signed with the States General of the Dutch Republic although the final treaty with the Dutch was not signed until 20th May, 1784.

The Fox/North coalition with the Duke of Portland as Prime Minister did not survive long, lasting less than a year. Prior to Lord North bringing stability to the post of Prime Minister in 1770, there had been six Prime Ministers in eight years and since North's resignation, the period of instability had returned and there had been three administrations in just over a year. The Fox/North coalition was eventually brought down by the King who had twice asked William Pitt to be Prime Minister and who was determined to get him and remove Fox from having any power. Although the King's methods were dubious, they were spectacularly successful and came about in December, 1783, when he finally persuaded Pitt to take office, the reason being, or rather the means used, because of the need to reform the manner in which the East India Company was run.

In 1781, a Select Committee had been set up to examine this and on 18th November 1783, Fox presented a bill to the Commons which would limit the influence of the monarchy as to how the company was managed, and despite opposition from Pitt, Fox was successful and was very confident when the Bill was presented to the House of Lords one month later on 15th December. However, the East India Company, attempting to look after its own interest, wrote to Parliament saying that Fox had not painted an accurate picture of the company's finances, and at the same time gained support from some of the newspapers. The final blow for the Bill however was delivered by the King himself. Before the Bill was due to go to the Lords, he did an extraordinary thing – he presented George Grenville (Earl Temple) with a card that read as follows:-

"His Majesty allowed Earl Temple to say, that whoever voted for the India Bill was not only not his friend, but would be considered by him as an enemy; and if these words were not strong enough, Earl Temple might use whatever words he might deem stronger and more to the purpose".

Fox was completely oblivious to all this and was astonished that during the final debate held on 17th December, twenty-seven peers had buckled under the royal pressure and switched their votes with the result that the Bill was defeated by nineteen votes. The next day, 18th December, 1783, William Pitt the Younger had an audience with the King and became Prime Minister which would result in an even longer period of stability than the King had enjoyed under Lord North. Later that day, a furious Portland, Fox and North were asked to surrender their seals of office but there was absolutely nothing they could do about it, and their short tenure of office came to an abrupt and undignified end.

Lord North carried on attending the House and making speeches, but his eyesight suddenly deteriorated badly in 1787. It had never been good at the best of times which is partly why he sometimes put a handkerchief over his face in the House. People assumed that he did this as it enabled him to carry on with his rather eccentric habit of going to sleep during debates which whilst partly true, hid the fact that he had a genuine need to keep the light away from his eyes. On 27th March of that year he was attending a debate and had to be led into the House by his son and a few weeks later North's wife Ann, wrote to her father-in-law, Guilford, that she and her husband would return to London from Bushy as he was hardly able to see. Not unnaturally, this caused Lord North to sink into a depression and although he travelled to both Bath and Tunbridge Wells in an effort to effect a cure, neither place could help at all and North's active political career was nearly over. However, there was still life left in him and when his father died on 4th August, 1790, it was only then, at the age of fifty-eight, that he inherited his father's title and went to the House of Lords where he made his maiden speech on 1st April 1791. The debate was on the subject of supporting Turkey during her war with Russia and North was still able to provide some of his old spark, but some ten months later, on 20th February, 1792, he spoke on the same subject for the last time, and after that his health then deteriorated quickly and it was obvious that his life was drawing to a close.

Questions have always been asked as to why Lord North returned to government after presiding over such a difficult period of Britain's history for so long and having asked the King for permission to resign virtually every year when he was in office. These questions have not only been asked retrospectively, they were also asked at the time. One possibility is that although he did not seem to enjoy power when he had it, he found that he missed it much more than he thought he would – he had after all, been Prime Minister for twelve years and been at the centre of power during a turbulent period. If he came back to power now, he could possibly take a back seat knowing that government affairs were more stable and he could enjoy the position more. Another reason could be that he simply felt that it was his duty to step in and help. Since he had left office, Rockingham had died suddenly after a brief tenure of office and Shelburne's ministry had always seemed weak and unstable added to which he probably thought that William Pitt was far too young to take over the top job. If it was the latter reason, he had miscalculated the ambition and talent of the young pretender and the King's determination to get Fox out and William Pitt in. He wrote a letter to his father which strongly hinted the reason was purely honourable:-

"I do not think I have much avarice. I have less ambition, &, if I do not flatter myself, still less malice. To see Peace Established in the Country by a firm Coalition, to see my friends satisfied, to see my honour safe, & a good government procured to this country by the sacrifice of my situation would be the most honourable, & the most eligible conclusion of my political warfare that I could possibly desire".

Of course, this does not necessarily prove anything, it may simply be a letter trying to hide what he has always been criticised for, that is, a thirst for the power that he once had and now missed, but perhaps, given the obvious decency of the man, it should be taken at face value. Certainly the story goes that he greatly regretted returning to government later on as he was supposed to have said to his wife who had always been against him working with Fox:-

"Oh Nance, it would be happy for me if I had taken your advice. There is no action in my life that I have such cause to regret".

He had some reason to express these sentiments. Although Lord North was always blamed for the loss of the American colonies, people always considered him a decent man, but his sharing power with Charles James Fox ultimately did the greater damage to his reputation, both in the short and long term because sadly, it brought that very decency into question.

North was not only a decent man, he was brave, especially when he was meeting his own death. During the first few months of 1792, his health took a turn for the worse with his legs becoming swollen and the doctors thought that it could be dropsy, a disease that causes watery fluid to collect in the body. By now bed-ridden, he asked the doctors just how ill he was and requested that they tell him the truth, which they did, telling him that he would not live for very much longer. The news did not frighten him, indeed, if anything, he seemed to discover a great peace of mind and no return of the depression that he had sometimes suffered from. He called the members of his family round to his bedside and thanked each of them, one by one, for their kindness to him, especially since the loss of his eyesight which had made him more dependent on them, and he died peacefully on 5th August, 1792. When describing his death, a friend was quoted as saying:- "No man ever met death with greater fortitude", and the same person went on to say:- "He expired without a struggle or groan".

North *was* a decent man, of that there should be no question and was also a beloved husband of his wife Elizabeth, and father to their children – George Augustus, 1756-1802, who became 3rd Earl of Guilford, Catherine Anne, 1760-1817, Francis, 1761-1817, who became 4th Earl of Guilford, Charlotte?-1849, Frederick, 1766-1827, who became 5th Earl of Guilford, and Anne?-1832. He was also blessed with a sense of humour as noted earlier and he was often underestimated as his tendency to seemingly go to sleep during lengthy debates gave the impression that he was not keeping up with what was being said, but this was totally untrue. In one such debate, he was being castigated by a member of the opposition who was asking: "Who is the chief architect of our misfortune as a country – it is the Noble Lord in the blue riband who is fast asleep on the treasury bench". Lord North simply opened one eye and said "I wish to God I were" before returning to what was seemingly a happy slumber. Had he been blessed with more luck concerning timing, history would almost certainly have judged North more kindly. Before the war with the Americas, things were going well and he was considered an acknowledged expert on financial matters as well as a very good manager of the House of Commons. He had managed to get the Quebec Act through Parliament in 1774 with little trouble. It was this act that gave Canada more independence, creating as it did a permanent administration there and giving the French Canadians religious freedom. This meant that the Canadians were less likely to support any form of war that the thirteen colonies of America were likely to engage in. He enjoyed a mastery of the House of Commons and was well liked and had he been Prime Minister in less troubled times, his reputation would have shown him to have been a good, possibly even a great Prime Minister.

Looking at the power of the United States of America today, one might come to the conclusion that Lord North was simply very unlucky, being in the wrong place at the wrong time, as one cannot help but feel that whosoever was Prime Minister, sooner or later, it would be inevitable that America would have become an independent country one day. It also has to be borne in mind that communications in the 18th century were totally different to the communications enjoyed in the 21st century. In North's time, it would take weeks for dispatches to reach another country whereas today, with modern technology, news can be dispatched from one continent to another in an instant. This meant that army generals in the 18th century were given much more autonomy and had to make decisions themselves, decisions that could make or break a battle and with that, heavily influence the outcome of the whole war.

North was exceedingly well liked by both sides of the House, not least because of his genial wit and sense of humour. He had been an able administrator, and had brought stability to the post of Prime Minister that had been lacking since the days of the Duke of Newcastle, and he, Newcastle, had only been Prime Minister a total of seven years over two periods of office, 1754-56, and also 1757-62. Lord North was a loving husband and father, and a very courageous man as the manner in which he met his dignified end showed. Modest as well as courageous, not for him a burial place in Westminster Abbey, but the family vault with his wife in the parish church at Wroxton.

-oOOo-

14
Mary Wollstonecraft
(1759-1797)

Early feminist writer with views years ahead of her time.

Mary Wollstonecraft was a feminist before the term had been coined. Author of the book called *'A Vindication of the Rights of Women'*, she lived in France during the time of the revolution, had two children, one being born out of wedlock, and Mary was thought to hold extremist views for her time. Her second child born shortly after she married William Godwin in 1797, was a daughter called Mary who would eventually become Mary Shelley, (1797-1851), author of *'Frankenstein'* and wife of Percy Bysshe Shelley (1792-1822), the great if short-lived poet.

Mary's roots seem to start at Spitalfields in London. Her grandfather, Edward Wollstonecraft (1688-1765), lived there when it was a centre for the silk weaving trade that was practised there at the time. Edward himself prospered because he was one of those men who altered the direct relationship that had previously worked between the weaver and his client. Instead, people like Edward became a middleman who arranged for weavers to be in effect piece-workers, whilst he and people like him arranged with the clients the delivery of the orders which were often large, making Edward and his like very wealthy. He married Jane, a woman four years older than himself, but as was usual in those times, she became pregnant on a regular basis and eventually died after giving birth to at least nine children. After a while, he then married a woman called Elizabeth (1716-46) who he also outlived. It was Elizabeth, Edward's second wife, who was to give birth to Edward John (1737-1803), who would later become Mary Wollstonecraft's father. The young Edward became a handkerchief weaver having been his father's apprentice, but in an effort to escape his father's domineering ways, Edward Junior stayed in a cottage in Primrose Street whilst his father had moved to a more salubrious house in Bishopsgate.

Edward junior married a young Irish lady by the name of Elizabeth Dixon in 1756. We do not know her date of birth, but we do know that she died in 1782, over twenty years before her husband, who died in 1803. They had a son, Edward Bland sometime in 1757, and then on 27th April, 1759, a daughter was born. They christened her Mary and she was the daughter that although living a short life, would become famous as Mary Wollstonecraft. With both Mary's paternal grandparents as well as her parents being called Edward and Elizabeth, it can be a little confusing when describing her background. However, her father Edward, born in 1737, lost his mother Elizabeth (Mary's grandmother) when he was only nine years old, dying as she did in 1746 at the age of thirty. Whether this affected Edward, Mary's father, it is impossible to say, but Mary certainly didn't have the best of upbringings. Her father would occasionally be affectionate but was also sometimes violent and was unreliable. Both he and Mary's mother made it plain that Edward, Mary's older brother was the family favourite and her feeling of being unloved was compounded when other children appeared and they were given more attention than she. Her feelings of being unloved were yet further reinforced by the will that her grandfather made in 1764, the year before he died. Even allowing for the times in which it was made, it was an extraordinary will. Basically, it was split three ways after allowing for payments to local paupers and the inmates of three debtors' prisons. After funeral expenses, one third was left to Elizabeth Ann Rutson, his forty-seven year old married daughter by his first wife Jane, and who had three children who were virtually grown up, one third to his son Edward John (Mary's father), and the final third to his grandson Edward (Ned), Mary's elder brother who when his grandfather died in February, 1765, was only eight years old. There was absolutely nothing left to Mary and her sisters Elizabeth (b.1763) or Everina (born the same year that her grandfather died, 1765). The two brothers, James (b1768) and Charles (b1770), were yet to be born. Daughters were treated very differently from sons in the 18th century, and it was a fact of life that was usually accepted by daughters in any family situation, but even at a young age Mary questioned this thinking and found it difficult to accept even when she was very young. It was to shape her future philosophy and actions for the rest of her life.

After Edward's father died, Edward, Mary's father, moved the family to Barking where he intended to continue to earn his living at farming, which he had tried to do for the previous two years when he had purchased a farm in Epping, but with little success. However, with the money received from his father along with the amount also left to his son Ned, he no doubt anticipated earning enough to enable his daughters to marry well into the local gentry, but even at the age of six years, Mary looked to be an unlikely candidate for such a plan. She seemed to have harboured resentment at both the lack of affection she received from her parents, and also the exclusion from her grandfather's will. It showed in both her appearance and her demeanour. Her younger sister, Elizabeth (Bess) was polite and her features were pleasant, whereas Mary was unsmiling and had a bad tempered look about her. She felt that she was given little or no affection compared to her elder brother, Ned, merely on the grounds that he was a boy, but also felt that her younger sister Bess received more kindly attention.

In 1768, the family moved to Beverley in Yorkshire. Mary's father always moved on if he did not achieve the success that he wanted, and moving to Yorkshire was certainly a drastic change from London. Although it must have seemed like the other side of the world to a nine-year-old girl in the 18th century, Mary liked it and the family settled there for several years. Mary found Beverley an arty type of place, and once settled in, grew to be fond of it quite quickly. The town has a large church called Beverley Minster, although it could be mistaken for a cathedral, and it has an organ with pipes by John Snetzler which had been installed in 1769, the year after the family had arrived in the town. Snetzler was born in 1710 and was considered to be one of the greatest craftsmen of his day, building organs for a great number of churches, including John Wesley's Chapel in Bristol in 1761, and Peterhouse College Chapel, Cambridge in 1765 as well as Beverley's church. To mark the installation of the organ at Beverley, a festival of George Frederic Handel's (1685-1759), George III's favourite composer, music was performed.

Local people also performed poetry in the nearby town of Driffield, and Mary often quoted the poets when writing to a new friend, Jane Arden. Mary was envious of her new friend because Jane's father was a far more sober and respectable gentleman than Mary's father was. Jane's father described himself as a philosopher and his behaviour and whole demeanour was in marked contrast to that of the violent drunken Mr. Wollstonecraft who would sometimes beat Mary's mother. Mary's letters to Jane tended to concentrate on poetry however until they suddenly changed into an emotionally charged series of what we can only call love letters. Mary had become obsessively jealous about Jane's friendship with another girl, and when Mary discovered that Jane's parents favoured the other friend, Mary became even more frantic. Her letter reads like that of a jealous lover and written by an older person:-

"If I did not love you I should not write so; - I have a heart that scorns disguise, and a countenance which will not dissemble: I have formed romantic notions of friendship, - I have been once disappointed:- I think if I am a second time I shall only want some infidelity in a love affair, to qualify me for an old maid, as then I shall have no idea of either of them. I am a little singular in my thoughts of love and friendship; I must have the first place or none. – I own your behaviour is more according to the opinion of the world, but I would break such narrow bounds."

Mary was very passionate – her words:- "I have a heart that scorns disguise" is one of many lines in various letters that basically say she wears her heart on her sleeve with little or no attempt to hide her feelings. This was completely different behaviour to that displayed by other young girls and women in the 18th century who tended to keep their feelings to themselves. The part in her letter that says she has already suffered disappointment possibly relates to her parents where she always felt that she was playing second fiddle to her older brother Ned and to a degree, her younger sister Elizabeth (Bess).

Mary's education in Beverley consisted of little more than reading and writing and she seemed to have little interest in clothes, certainly at this time of her life at any rate. At an early age, Mary seemed to develop a social conscience as she became aware of how the poor lived, be they servants or people that she knew to be in the workhouse. Her thought processes were very independent and she quickly made up her mind that she would marry for love and not money and social status – she seemed to be drifting away from her family at an early age.

Meanwhile, Mary's father Edward had not made a success at farming and in 1774, when Mary was fifteen years old, her father moved the family back to a place called Hoxton which was a little way to the north of the old family home in Primrose Street. However, Mary and her sisters were so young when they were previously there that they couldn't remember anything at all about it. Edward (Mary's elder brother) was the only person who seemed to benefit, being articled as a lawyer and forever bossing his younger sister about. Mary was very unhappy at this point, and would later write that Ned was:- "forever taking pleasure in tormenting and humbling me". Unable to find any love, friendship or role within the family, Mary looked elsewhere for company and love and found it with a nearby family called Clare. Mr. & Mrs. Clare had no children of their own and were very friendly and welcoming to Mary and took her under their wing. They encouraged Mary to read – this was probably Mary's introduction to writers such as William Shakespeare (1564-1616), the English playwright, poet, actor and joint manager of a London acting company, and John Milton (1608-74), the English poet who wrote the brilliant 'Nativity Ode', the wonderful epitaph on Shakespeare.

The Clare's had taken Mary into their household and made her feel one of the family, but there was another girl who they had also looked after called Fanny Blood. They had taught Fanny the sorts of skills that most people thought that young girls should have, and these were the usual subjects such as sewing, poetry, drawing, music, and letter writing. The Clare's wanted Mary to meet Fanny, but Fanny had already left the Clare home to return to the home of her parents who lived in south London so Mrs. Clare offered to take Mary there. Unlike Jane Arden who was the same age as Mary, Fanny was two years older, so by the time they met, Fanny was eighteen whilst Mary was sixteen. Mary was taken to the home of the Blood family, and almost the first person she saw was Fanny herself, looking after children that were obviously her brothers and sisters, and it seems that it was at this point, that Mary decided that she and Fanny would be lifelong friends. It seemed to Mary that she was with a kindred spirit, somebody that she could instantly relate to and even fall in love with. She felt that Fanny was in a similar situation to herself in as much as Mary felt superior to her parents, her father being a drunkard but also her mother, because although she was quite different from her husband inasmuch as she was both gentle and charming, she was quite unable to cope with her husband's violent and drunken ways. If Mary felt superior to her mother for those reasons, it seems a harsh judgement from a daughter.

Although identifying with Fanny due to their shared experiences, Mary felt that Fanny was superior to her in looks and character but hoped that Fanny would teach her to be as good as her new found friend was. As with Jane Arden, Mary decided that she would devote herself to a lifelong commitment to Fanny, but also as with Jane, Fanny did not seem to feel quite the same and certainly did not view a friendship with Mary to mean the exclusion of others. Indeed, it seemed that Mary's sisters, Elizabeth and Everina, meant just as much to Fanny as Mary did.

One can only assume that if Mary wanted a lifelong commitment to another girl, then she, Mary, had no intention of entering the marriage stakes, but unfortunately for her, Fanny did not feel the same and realised that marriage was the only way in which she would be able to escape her family who she was ashamed of. They were even poorer than Mary's family as Mr. Blood was often out of work and on the few occasions he found a job, was unable or unwilling to hang on to it. Because of this, the Blood family's finances were in desperate straits. With that in mind, Fanny became attached to a businessman named Hugh

Skeys who she had met at the Clare family home, but it seemed that, worried about what his own family would think of Fanny's parents, he had a very speedy change of heart.

The Wollstonecraft family were once more facing financial difficulties, and true to form, Mr. Wollstonecraft moved the family on again, away from Hoxton to Laugharne in Wales and Mary had to worship Fanny from afar, writing to her instead of seeing her. The move did little for her father's finances however, and so he moved the family back to Walworth, a place favoured by Mary as it brought her back near Fanny's family. She found a job as a companion to a widowed lady called Mrs. Dawson and still dreamt of a future life with Fanny despite the fact that Hugh Skeys was still involved with Fanny although making it somewhat clear that he was trying to get himself out of the situation that he found himself in. She would write to Jane Arden about her feelings for Fanny, possibly trying to make her jealous as some sort of petty revenge for Jane's rejection of her as she saw it. In any event, despite her dreams of setting up home with Fanny, she seemed to form a relationship with a man called Joshua Waterhouse. He was handsome, and although quite young, was a Cambridge don. Clearly clever, he was also vain and snobbish, although each seemed to enjoy the other's company. After a while he moved away and although she sent him love letters, the relationship petered out. He was murdered in 1827 and a nephew discovered a sackful of letters, some of them, although by no means all, from Mary.

When Waterhouse drifted away and Mary realised that he was not going to be part of her life, she began to wonder in which direction it would go. Jane had become a governess but had more qualifications than Mary and although she, Mary, did not want to commit herself to be in the employ of Mrs. Dawson in the foreseeable future, she had no other concrete future plans in mind.

In the early part of 1782, Ned, Mary's elder brother and the favourite of the family, had been married some time and he and his wife had a baby girl that they named Elizabeth after his mother, but just prior to that, Mary and Ned's mother had been ill and died in the spring of 1782. She was not old, being only in her fifties, but was probably worn out by her husband's drunken bullying ways and his inability to look after the family financially. She had also given birth to seven children in thirteen years and like many wives at that time, was probably exhausted at the continual pregnancies. However, given that she lived for her children, it was at least some comfort to Mary that her mother lived long enough to see a granddaughter born, and a girl who was named after her.

Mary had always felt ashamed of her family and resentful of the attention that her elder brother Ned received, but in the natural way of things, was upset at her mother's death. However, in the fullness of time when the grief had subsided, an objectivity set in that enabled her to write a fictional account of a mother apologising to a daughter on her deathbed at the treatment she had meted out to that daughter.

On the death of the mother, the family split up and went their separate ways, Elizabeth and Everina going to Ned and his wife. By this time they were nineteen and seventeen years old respectively, and it was made clear to them that apart from helping round the house, they would be expected to find husbands in the near future. Mr. Wollstonecraft took the twelve-year-old Charles and returned to Laugharne, married a lady called Lydia and spent the rest of his life there before dying in 1803. James eventually joined the navy and that left Mary who did not return to Mrs. Dawson but went back to live with the Bloods, the intention of which was to make a life with Fanny. It did not quite work out the way she wanted however, as far from it being just the two of them as in her dreams it would be, instead she found herself in a crowded house with no private time, either for herself or with Fanny. Mrs. Blood, Fanny and Mary all worked very hard at sewing jobs, often through the night until they were exhausted and Mary could not help noticing that Fanny looked ill. After reading some medical books, Mary worked out that Fanny was almost certainly suffering from consumption, which in the 18th century only resulted in one outcome. Mary still harboured the fantasy of going abroad to live with Fanny despite the fact that Hugh Skeys was still in Fanny's life, although he was still not committing himself fully to her.

Six months after Mary's mother had died, an altogether more happy event in the family took place. In October, 1782, Mary's sister Elizabeth was married to a young boat builder called Meredith Bishop and despite Mary's negative feelings towards marriage, she seemed to approve of her sister's new husband. Mary and Eliza's brother Ned also obviously approved as he was a witness to the marriage that took place in St. Katharine's on 20th October. Just one month later, Eliza was pregnant and nine months later on 10th August, 1783, she gave birth to a daughter who was named Elizabeth Mary Frances, thus both of Mrs. Wollstonecraft's grandchildren were named after her, although Mary always said that the child was known as Mary, possibly to escape confusion with her cousin.

However, the birth of the baby did not bring happiness to Meredith and Eliza, who Mary felt were unhappy in their relationship. Eliza seemed to go into a deep depression, possibly a breakdown after the birth, and by November it was clear that Meredith could not cope and asked his sister-in-law for help, a decision that he would come to regret. When Mary arrived at the Bishop's house, she found that Eliza was in a disturbed state, giving Mary the impression that she had not been treated well by her husband. Eliza made it clear that she did not want to remain with her husband – a fairly drastic situation given that divorce or separation was very rare in the 18th century as women tended to stick with their husbands come what may. Whether Eliza really meant it is open to question, but there was certainly no doubt in Mary's mind as she organised an escape plan for Eliza during a day in January 1784 when Meredith was away on business. Mary and Eliza left the family house but left the baby with its nurse and took a coach to Hackney, which was then a village, and settled in lodgings.

How much this action was carried out to help Eliza or some sort of statement against men in general is hard to say. Mary's experiences with men had not been happy and almost certainly coloured her attitude towards them for the rest of her life. She had had to put up with her bullying father, the equally bullying Mr. Blood, and those two men alone would have given her the idea that marriage did not give women much happiness in their lives. She did not get on with her elder brother Ned, there was Hugh Skeys, who although not violent, was always a threat to her relationship with Fanny Blood, and of course, there were the actions of Meredith Bishop himself. As if to cement her anti-male feelings, Mary organised a female only community, albeit a small one, which consisted of herself, Eliza, and Fanny Blood, the only problem being that it would be impossible for them to survive financially. An offer of a rescue of sorts came from an unlikely source. Mr. Blood, who Mary despised, offered Mary and Eliza, along with Eliza's baby refuge in his family home, probably so that he could at least make sure that his daughter Fanny was being looked after, but Mary could not see this situation in a crowded house working out. Although it was a way out, it was a far cry from Mary's dream of an all-female community.

The community never really came to fruition on a long term basis. They stayed in their cold damp lodgings until February 1784 and then Mary decided that she and Fanny and Eliza were going to run a school together. They initially moved to Islington but finding no pupils there, moved to Newington Green where they were joined by Everina and were more successful with Fanny teaching drawing and sewing and the others offering the basics of reading, writing and nature study. Mary, assuming charge as always, organised the necessities such as the timetables, and the day to day running of the finances. By the winter of 1784, Fanny's health had grown worse as her consumption took hold but Hugh Skeys was still in Lisbon and fortunately asked her to make the journey there in order for them to get married. Although she was pleased for Fanny, it meant the end of her dream of a life with her. Fanny left in January, 1785 and Mary, feeling bereft without the love of her life wrote:-

"I could as soon fly as open my heart to Eliza or Everina… without someone to love this world is a desert".

In her sadness, Mary took to the treatment that was used for most illnesses at the time, which was bleeding a patient by drawing blood from a vein in the arm, and then applying hot cups to the skin. This treatment was used for most illnesses during this period and it was almost certainly useless, hardly ever doing good and usually doing harm. If a patient recovered from any illness after being treated by this method, it was usually despite the treatment rather than because of it.

Fanny wrote to Mary from Lisbon often, and her description of married life was not exactly flattering which was hardly surprising. Soon after being married, she was pregnant which was the norm for young married women in the 18th century. Birth control was non-existent and sex usually consisted of gratification for the men and little pleasure for the women. Added to this was the fact that Fanny was very ill with consumption and so Mary made the decision to leave the school and visit Fanny, setting off in November and suffering a rough trip of thirteen days. When she arrived, she found that Fanny was already in labour but sadly, although not surprisingly, dying at the same time. Both Fanny and the baby died within a few days and Eliza and Everina, back home in the school without Mary, found themselves quite unable to cope. Eliza was also mourning the loss of her baby and the whole school project seemed to be falling apart. Mary returned home in February 1786 and almost immediately produced a hurriedly put together book entitled *'Thoughts on the Education of Daughters'*, which was published by a Mr. Joseph Johnson.

In the book, she eschewed the female habits of cosmetics, hair powder, the theatre and card playing, advised women not to marry young, and advised against teaching by rote which in some ways put her many years ahead of her time. Inevitably, the school collapsed, Everina returned to their older brother Ned whilst Eliza found a job in Leicestershire, courtesy of a Mrs. Burgh, a friend of Mary. Mary had previously befriended a Dr. Richard Price (1723-91), a Welsh moral philosopher and minister at Newington Green, but a radical intellectual who had supported the American cause in their war with Britain and who had several influential friends such as the famous Benjamin Franklin (1706-90), the American statesman and scientist and Thomas Jefferson (1743-1826). Both men were heavily involved in the American War of Independence. In 1746, Franklin started his famous research into electricity which resulted in him being made a Fellow of the Royal Society. He showed the distinction between positive and negative electricity and he also proved that lightning and electricity are identical. He also took part in the prolonged discussions that produced the Declaration of Independence on 4th July, 1776. Jefferson had no less an important career in terms of American independence, taking an active part in the foundation of the first Continental Congress in 1774, and it was he who drafted the famous Declaration of Independence which was signed on 4th July, 1776. He became the third President of the United States of America and like John Adams, who was the second President, died on 4th July, 1826, fifty years to the day when the Declaration was signed.

Richard Price attended a Dissenting Academy and had become a preacher at Newington Green when Mary was there and being very well known, it was a feather in Mary's cap to meet him and have him as a friend. His talents were remarkable, and he was admitted to the Royal Society in 1765 for his work on probability. His work entitled *'Observations on Reversionary Payments'* published in 1771 helped to bring about a scientific system for life insurance and pensions and he also wrote *'An Appeal to the Public on the subject of the National Debt'* which came out the following year, 1772, and which was to influence William Pitt the Younger when the latter became Chancellor of the Exchequer and then Prime Minister some ten years after the book came out. Price also wrote books on the American Revolution and the French Revolution, the latter entitled *'A Discourse on the law of our Country'* which was published in 1789 and which brought him to prominence.

When Mary met Price, he was mourning the death of his friend James Burgh, a writer and schoolmaster who like Price, worked for reform, and it was Burgh's widow, Mrs. Burgh, who had found Eliza her job. Mary herself went to Ireland to be the governess to Lord and Lady Kingsborough and their daughters. In the meantime, she remained friendly with Dr. Price who introduced her to the ideas of the Dissenters and it was from here that her views on equal rights for women began to form. The Dissenters had been barred from universities, but undeterred, set up their own and successfully taught subjects such as history, science and economics. They taught people, including Mary, to think for themselves rather than accept ideas that were merely handed down and also argued for the right of every taxpayer to vote. In his last book *'Political Disquisitions'*, James Burgh had put the idea to John Wilkes (1727-97) to introduce the notion of universal male suffrage and Price, in a further book, *'Observations on Civil Liberty'* published in 1776, had put forward the idea that the House of Lords be abolished, an idea that was way ahead of its time, as the idea was still being discussed with no agreement at the beginning of the 21st century. Wilkes was a politician who was very critical of King George III, and who was charged with treason for expressing his views in a weekly newspaper called *'The New Briton'* which he had set up as a vehicle for his views.

Given her new found ideas that had been fermenting for years, and now with the addition of Richard Price in her life, Mary was uncomfortable at going to Ireland to work for Lord and Lady Kingsborough, but a chance meeting on the boat with a young clergyman named Henry Gabell cheered her up considerably. Gabell and Mary got on very well in the short time that they travelled together and Mary was very cheered when Gabell told her that he too was travelling to work for an aristocratic family. Henry Gabell was a clever young man and went on to be the headmaster of Winchester School teaching Thomas Arnold (1797-1842). Arnold ended up as an English educationist and scholar, became headmaster of Rugby and had been a brilliant classical scholar whilst at Gabell's school in Winchester and later Corpus Christi College at Oxford. He was the father of two brilliant children, Matthew Arnold (1822-88), an English poet and critic, and Thomas Arnold (1823-1900), a literary scholar.

Mary arrived in Dublin and Lord and Lady Kingsborough had thoughtfully sent their butler to greet her as there was still 120 miles to travel. She parted from her new friend Henry Gabell and they both promised to write to each other as new friends tend to do. Mary arrived at Mitchelstown Castle after a fairly arduous coach journey. She had mixed feelings on arrival. On the one hand she had longed to visit Ireland for many years, but on the other, not in the circumstances in which she found herself. The position of a governess was a strange one in any situation, as she was not a servant, but neither was she part of the family, and therefore could often find herself feeling lonely. The one comfort is that the children of the family concerned could often build up a loving relationship with the governess, as by definition, the mother was often too busy to bond that closely with her offspring. However, the downside of this situation usually meant that the governess was starved of adult company once the children had retired to bed.

Lord and Lady Kingsborough had what was virtually an arranged marriage which was not uncommon amongst the aristocracy in the 18th century. Robert King, heir to the title of Lord Kingsborough was only sixteen when he married his fifteen-year-old cousin Caroline Fitzgerald in December, 1769. By the time Mary arrived in 1786, they had produced a large family, the oldest being a boy of fifteen followed by a girl of fourteen, despite the fact that they themselves were still only in their early thirties, not much older than Mary herself who was in her late twenties. They travelled a great deal, not counting the financial cost and when in Paris, even visited the Court of Louis XVI and Marie Antoinette at Versailles, the incredible palace built between the years 1676 and 1708 by his great great grandfather, Louis X1V. Caroline carried on with the role of an aristocratic wife which was essentially to give birth to as many children as possible, and this she did, producing no less than twelve children in all, although the habit of using wet nurses and governesses meant that there was little or no bonding with her children. Mary was to look after the three eldest girls, Margaret, Caroline and Mary and after her initial interview, was shown to her comfortable room and allowed to have the first evening alone in peace. The next day however, saw her busy with her charges and they soon took a liking to her, so much so in fact, that for the first time in her life, she began to show feelings of maternal love. That these feelings were reciprocated was shown clearly in what she later wrote about her time with the girls:-

"The children cluster about me. One catches a kiss, another lisps my long name – while a sweet little boy, who is conscious that he is a favourite, calls himself my son. At the sight of their mother they tremble and run to me for protection. This renders them dear to me – and I discover the kind of happiness I was formed to enjoy".

Mary seemed to get on well with her new employers and Lady Kingsborough even went so far as to say that she would help find good schools for Eliza and Everina should they come to Ireland. One of the reasons why Mary seemed to get on well with Robert and Caroline Kingsborough was the illness that beset Margaret, the eldest daughter. Mary nursed Margaret well, and despite the family at one stage fearing for Margaret's life, Mary nursed her back to a full recovery which produced further devotion from Margaret to her governess.

There was another pleasant distraction in Mary's life. Lord and Lady Kingsborough tended to have visitors, and one of these was a gentleman by the name of George Ogle, like Robert, an MP and a privy councillor and who arrived at Mitchelstown with his wife and sister. He was in his forties, polite and intelligent and also a talented poet. Mary found these qualities attractive – unfortunately so did her employer, Lady Caroline Kingsborough but despite the rivalry between them for George Ogle's attentions, they still managed to get on well for a while, although in time, the mutual affection between Mary and Caroline cooled, and Mary wished to be away from the family and back in England.

Caroline was almost certainly jealous of Mary's relationship with the children and again was envious of George Ogle's attentions to Mary. Mary for her part annoyed her employer who thought that Mary was getting above herself and forgetting that she was merely the governess of the house and not part of the family. There was tension between the two women that was soothed in part by Caroline's widowed stepmother, Mrs. Fitzgerald who also lived with the family. Relations were not helped when Mrs. Fitzgerald went away for a short period, a period in which Caroline and Mary had a huge row that only calmed down on Mrs. Fitzgerald's return. Mary stayed out of the way, working on a novel in her room whenever she could and in March 1787, she wrote to her sister complaining of various ailments such as trembling fits and faintness amongst many others. However all this passed and during another visit from George Ogle, she was made to feel uncomfortable again when Robert Kingsborough entered the room. Lord Kingsborough had previously been accused of having an affair with a governess and Mary knew this and it is possible that he made some sort of pass at Mary as she was later accused of wanting to have an affair with him herself.

Tensions built up and in August, when Mary and the family were in Bristol taking the medicinal waters, she was dismissed although the final reasons are unclear. It could have been Mary's good relationship with the children or Caroline's jealousy over George Ogle. It could have been the suspicion that Mary had had an affair with Lord Kingsborough, but in the event, she left the family under a cloud with the completed novel of *'Mary'* with her, the novel that she'd been writing in her room after the first row with Caroline. Based loosely on her own life, she includes the Kingsborough family under a different name although the character of Caroline in the book becomes Mary's mother and is a character clearly disliked by both the real and fictional Mary.

After Mary's departure, the Kingsborough's separated which was done at Caroline's behest. Margaret, the eldest daughter, had always been fond of Mary and continued to write to her, marrying her neighbour, the Earl of Mountcashel at the age of nineteen. She gave birth to many children and like her mother took little interest in them, preferring instead to involve herself with Irish republican politics much to the annoyance of her husband. Not that she let that fact worry her too much, as she'd never really loved him in the first place, marrying merely to get away from home. However, she seems to have had a dual personality when it came to the treatment of children because she left her husband and went to live in Italy with a gentleman by the name of George Tighe. She called herself Mrs. Mason and lived a fairly simple life, and was a loving mother to her daughters born to Tighe and all in all, led a completely different life to the one she had shared with Lord Mountcashel and their children. Despite the different way she interacted with the children of George Tighe, the Mountcashel children never altered their opinion of her, thinking of her as unloving and distant in the same way that she had thought of her own mother.

Mary meanwhile parted in disgrace so far as Caroline was concerned, but unlike other governesses, she did not go quietly and stuck to her fairly negative views of the women of the aristocracy who she thought of as frivolous and stupid, no doubt with some cause. She returned to the world of the London intelligentsia, a world that she felt more at home in.

When Mary left Ireland to return to England, she had no job, no home and no money. Despite her desperate situation, she was unwilling to teach in a girls' school even though she had the chance and it would have alleviated all the problems mentioned above. She had one card up her sleeve however, and that was in the form of her book publisher friend, Mr. Joseph Johnson. As soon as she arrived in London, she went to visit his shop and the move paid off beautifully as not only did he invite Mary to stay with him but went further than that as Johnson actually suggested setting up home together. This arrangement was not as man and wife, but as friends, and her payment would not be money, but in various tasks that she could undertake to carry out for him. There was nothing sexual in the arrangement – Johnson had never married and was considerably older than Mary – it was more like a father/daughter arrangement than anything else. He also had a genuine interest in the advancement of women and by giving a destitute Mary a home and an encouragement to write, he had enabled himself to have a way of giving some sort of practical expression to his beliefs.

Johnson (1738-1809), was a publisher and bookseller and held much influence in the eighteenth century. He had published works by people such as William Godwin (1756-1836), an English political writer and novelist who actually went on to marry Mary. Godwin took up writing at the time of the French Revolution and his *'Enquiry Concerning Political Justice'* which he brought out in 1793 brought him a great deal of fame and money. Other people that Johnson published were Joseph Priestly (1733-1804), the English Presbyterian minister and chemist, Gilbert Wakefield (1756-1801), English scholar and a controversial figure during this period, being opposed to the slave trade, war and public worship, and who fell out with the government of William Pitt, and there was also Anna Laetitia Barbauld (1743-1825), the feminist writer and poet who was successful until 1812 when she published her poem *'Eighteen Hundred and Eleven'* which criticised Britain's involvement in the Napoleonic wars. Stung by the heavy criticism that this work drew, she ceased to publish poems again although she carried on as a children's author.

Johnson had suffered from very bad asthma virtually all his life but early on in his publishing, paradoxically had earned his living specialising in medical books – perhaps it was in his efforts to know more about asthma and any possible cure that drew him to this area of publishing. Johnson soon branched out into selling books generally, regardless of subject matter, and this included religious literature. He distributed the literature of the Unitarian movement, whose belief in the one God contrasted sharply with other religions that split God into Father, Son and Holy Ghost. Quite soon his shop became the centre for people with radical and reforming ideas, including those mentioned above, and this excited Mary in the way in which being a governess in Ireland to an upper class family could never have achieved.

Another man who Johnson befriended in the 1760's was a Swiss born painter and writer named Johann Heinrich Fuessli, although he changed his name to Henry Fuseli as he came to see England as his adopted country, arriving here as he did in 1765. Fuseli (1741-1825), produced over 200 paintings, but he also drew 800 sketches which some felt were better than his paintings, good though his paintings were. Johnson asked Fuseli if he would live with him and while it is pretty certain that Fuseli was bisexual in his younger days, the same cannot be said of Johnson with any certainty. Fuseli had left letters after his death making his sexual preferences known very clearly, but with Johnson, the position was not straightforward at all. Johnson left nothing in writing that would have given any suggestions of homosexual feelings towards other men. Maybe this was because he *was* homosexual and wanted to protect his reputation or that he was simply asexual, had no sexual feelings towards either men or women and therefore it simply wasn't an issue. Fuseli had many interests, and besides the theatre, ancient and modern poetry, he had read Jean Jacques Rousseau (1712-78), the French philosopher. Rousseau had a great many books to his credit but it is in 1762 that he produced what was probably his masterpiece, *'Du Contrat Social'* or *'The Social Contract'* and which begins with the paradoxical line:-

"Man is born free; and everywhere he is in chains". The book became the bible of the French Revolution and included the famous line:- "Liberty, Equality, Fraternity".

Another person that Fuseli was attracted to was Johann Joachim Winckelmann (1717-68), the German archaeologist, and he translated Winckelmann's *'Reflections on the Paintings and Sculpture of the Greeks'* in 1765 which Johnson published along with Fuseli's own *'Remarks on Rousseau'* in 1767.

The friendship that Johnson and Fuseli had seemed to have ended when fire swept through the house that they both lived in in Paternoster Row in 1770 destroying everything that they owned. After encouragement by the great Sir Joshua Reynolds (1723-92), the great English portrait painter, Fuseli went off to Rome to study painting whilst Johnson set himself up again in St. Paul's Churchyard with the help of some friends and published a great deal of work written by the likes of Joseph Priestley (1733-1808), the Presbyterian minister and chemist and through him, made contacts with Priestley's colleagues in the Lunar Society. One of his biggest successes however, was translating the work of William Cowper (1731-1800) before Cowper was known and Johnson helped him become the famous poet that he eventually was to be.

Besides the above, there were a great many other well-known names in radical circles that Johnson mixed with, and each seemed to have their own agenda, so that there were very few oppressed groups who weren't supported by him and the people he published. These would naturally include the poor and hungry, but also slaves, Jews, women, press gangs and young children being used as chimney sweeps amongst others. Johnson's shop was used as a meeting place for all these radical people, and for Mary it was bliss, and a far cry from being a governess to titled people in Ireland.

When Mary walked around the streets in London, she was horrified by the grinding poverty that she saw and railed against it. In 1788, she published what she called a children's book entitled *'Original Stories'*, but it did not stop her writing about the dreadful landlords that caused this situation. She also wrote against the lack of proper medical facilities for the poor, the fate of the children who had no parents to look after them, bad housing and just about everything else that she saw as being wrong with society. Johnson published a second edition of the book and engaged a then unknown artist and engraver to illustrate it. The unknown artist was William Blake (1757-1827) who was born in London, the son of an Irish hosier and who went on to become famous for his poems, paintings, and engravings. As well as that, he was also a mystic and to the day he died, felt that he had regular visitations from the spirit world. To her delight, Mary found that Blake was a radical thinker as well, and that he shared her disgust at the unfairness of British society. Another friend that was to play a big part in Mary's life was Thomas Christie. She had met him at Johnson's when the two men set up a monthly magazine entitled *'Analytical Review'*. Christie was a very clever Scotsman whose father had been a banker and was also Provost of Montrose and had brought Thomas and his sister Jane up to worship in what was almost certainly the first Unitarian church that had ever been set up in Scotland.

Christie refused to follow his father's footsteps into banking and studied medicine instead, but got bored with that as well and in the end turned to journalism. He took to studying foreign languages and after corresponding with both French and German writers, he was able to persuade Johnson to co-produce the *'Analytical Review'* which sought to bring to Britain the ideas of continental countries. By now, he was disinterested in religion and was both a radical in his thinking, and eager to make as much money as possibly in business – he saw no conflict of interest in that.

Christie, along with Johnson and Feusli, wanted to bring foreign works to the British public and because of that, Mary spent the next few years working hard for Johnson, mainly concerning herself with translation, but she never felt that she was actually achieving anything. By 1790 she was just thirty-one years old but felt herself unattractive and a sexual failure. The man who awakened her sexual passions was Henry Fuseli, back from Rome where he had been studying painting. He visited St. Paul's Churchyard a great deal, had a high opinion of himself, and wherever he went, expected the other people in the room to share his opinion and what's more, show it openly to Fuseli himself. He produced many drawings, some of which were pornographic and many more just erotic. His most famous picture was entitled *'The Nightm*are' and depicted a woman asleep, with her head and shoulders dropping back over the end of the couch being visited by demons. There were several versions, one a grinning goblin crouched on her chest, and another a ghostly head of a horse. Fuseli first showed the picture in England in 1782, and it was well received and in fact made him famous. On the strength of it he was elected an associate member of the Royal Academy in 1788, a position to which he felt fully entitled, his self-esteem as high as ever.

Mary had never met anybody quite like Henry Fuseli, the Swiss born bisexual painter and writer. He spoke, or certainly had a knowledge of eight languages and his art reflected that knowledge, being drawn from classical mythology. A strange man, some of his pictures, especially those of women were uncomplicated and quite beautiful, whilst others seemed grotesque. He was not tall, being a few inches above five feet and he would often dress in a dandified manner. A Scottish writer called Allan Cunningham claimed that Mary fell in love with Fuseli the first time that she laid eyes on him. Cunningham wrote:-

"...and he, instead of repelling, as they deserved, those ridiculous advances, forthwith, it seems, imagined himself possest with the pure spirit of Platonic love – assumed artificial raptures and revived in imagination the fading fires of his youth".

Fuseli was older than Mary – when they met in 1788, Fuseli was forty-seven years old whilst Mary was twenty-nine, but it was not the age difference that had to stop any relationship between them getting too deep. Fuseli was about to be married to a lady called Sophia Rawlins, a lady who had not had the advantage of the kind of education that Mary had had and did not possess Mary's intelligence. In fact, Mary and Sophia were different in every way imaginable. Sophia had worked as an artist's model and was almost certainly very pretty but it is almost equally certain that Fuseli was not in love with her. It may have been that he was merely sexually attracted to her or that he wanted someone to keep house for him because she was certainly not included in many of his social outings. It would be unimaginable that Mary would put up with such treatment herself. It is very doubtful that Fuseli and Mary had a sexual relationship – rather, it was a meeting of minds. Fuseli could talk to Mary in a way he could never talk with Sophia.

Indeed, it is possible that Fuseli and Sophia's marriage was never consummated as she bore him no children. Despite the fact that Fuseli and Mary almost certainly had no sexual relationship, for a while they were certainly in love, and there is no doubting that Mary would have liked their mutual passion to have taken it's natural course but it was not to be. If her time spent with Lord and Lady Kingsborough had awakened Mary's passions, then the situation she found herself in with Fuseli ignited them to a dangerous level. She now became more demanding of the relationship, and Fuseli, unable to handle the situation, made a deliberate effort to cool things down and behave more like the married man that he was.

In 1789 the French revolution started which made the countries who had a monarch as head of state very nervous especially in Britain where King George III had begun to be ill with what was assumed at the time to be madness. The Prime Minister, William Pitt the Younger, was especially worried that the revolution in France along with the King's illness, would spark off something similar in Britain. Edmund Burke (1729-97), the Whig politician, found himself at odds with his party, many of whom supported what was happening in France. Burke was also at odds with a speech made by Dr. Richard Price, the radical clergyman, in which he supported the events in France and Price had added fuel to the fire by delivering his sermon on 4th November which was the anniversary of the 1688 bloodless Revolution in England. As if that wasn't enough, Price then went on to suggest a congratulatory message be sent to the National Assembly in Paris. This was all too much for a furious Burke who quickly published his 'Reflections on the Revolution in France' in November, 1790. In his piece, he urged all European countries to resist the revolution but this was completely against the thinking of the Whig intelligentsia and the Dissenters and as a result, Mary anonymously published her 'Vindication of the Rights of Men' as a direct answer to the points made in Burke's piece. 'Vindication' was not particularly well written – it was full of ideas, all of which had good intentions, but it was hastily put together. She talked of curing urban poverty by saying that large estates should be divided into smaller areas of land and distributed accordingly. She wanted slavery abolished, a cause that William Wilberforce was working on from Parliament. She wrote of more rights for women, the abolition of the press gangs, and more help for the poor. Both Joseph Priestley and Henry Fuseli didn't bother themselves to read the book, but many others did and Johnson published a second edition in January 1791, this time naming her as the author. Priestley and Fuseli may not have been impressed with the book, but Fuseli's friend William Roscoe was and as a result, found himself full of admiration for Mary. So much so in fact, that he commissioned a picture of Mary and she went so far as to try and improve her appearance by curling and powdering her hair for the sitting.

Roscoe (1753-1831) was an English historian and a poet and spent a great deal of his life supporting the arts. In 1787 he published a poem *'The Wrongs of Africa'* which was against the slave trade but it was his famous *'Life of Lorenzo de Medici'* (1796) that finally established him in the literary world. It was translated into German, French and Italian as was his follow-up book *'Life of Leo X'* which was published in 1805. He was so taken by Mary that he published a poem entitled *'The Life, Death, and Wonderful Atchievements (sic) of Edmund Burke'* in which Mary was named. Roscoe and Mary remained friends and continued to write to each other, Mary often talking to him about her feelings for Fuseli.

In April of that year, 1791, three months after her book had been published for the second time, Mary's friend, Dr. Richard Price died. It was Price who had introduced Mary to the Dissenters and given her life a new meaning and equally she was quick to defend Price when he was attacked for his November 1789 speech in which he spoke in favour of events in France. It was Price's speech that had caused Burke to write his *'Reflections on the Revolution in France'* and that in turn caused Mary to write her *'Vindication of the Rights of Men'* in which she came to a spirited defence of Price.

September 1791 saw Mary move to a bigger house in Store Street which was not far from the Tottenham Court Road. Mary found that a mixed bag of bohemian intellectuals along with writers and artists hung around this area and she felt at home there. About two months after moving into the area, she attended a small dinner party given by her publisher friend, Johnson and one of the guests was William Godwin, the English political writer and novelist who is mentioned earlier. Mary had never met him before but she knew of him by his considerable reputation. Their first meeting was not a success – Thomas Paine was also there and Godwin was far more interested in what Paine had to say than anything Mary had to offer, and he became irritable at the way in which Mary would interrupt when Paine was talking. Both Paine and Godwin had a great deal to talk about as Paine was busy writing the second part of his brilliant *'Rights of Man'* whilst Godwin had just commenced his *'Political Justice'* and consequently, neither man seemed that interested in Mary's unwelcome interventions. Paine (1737-1809) had already had an extraordinary life and had published books extolling the virtues of the American point of view during the War of Independence (1775-83) and was now turning his attention to the French Revolution, and his own *'Rights of Man'* was also an answer to Burke's *'Reflections on the Revolution in France'* as Mary's had been. None the less, it was William Godwin who Mary took to even if that particular evening was not successful. It was during this time at Store Street, September, 1791, that Mary started to write her *'Vindication of the Rights of Woman'* – a book that took a mere six weeks for her to write.

Although written in a hurry, the book seemed to strike a chord during a time when not all men had the vote, much less the women. The contents which must have seemed strange to many people at the time, make interesting reading today being a mixture of what we would think of as commonsense although with some rather idealistic thought patterns. Mary pointed out that by denying women a role in society whereby they could work in the way that men did, the world was being denied half of its talent. Mary was adamant on the subject of social equality and thought that society should get rid of monarchies, armies and navies and any form of church hierarchy. She described marriage as 'legal prostitution' and she also talked about prostitution in the way we know it today. She stated that prostitutes were not wicked, but that they were in fact victims in a society that did nothing for its poor. She wanted people's attitude to prostitutes to change and not to punish them and she even turned her fire on to the reformers, who whilst being well intentioned, she saw as being well wide of the mark when it came to solutions. She wanted justice, not charity for all people and wanted women to forgo passionate love even within marriage. She felt that sex was joyless for most women and once the initial courting had been completed, that sex was not much more than an assault on women by men. Although there was truth in what she said at the time she wrote this, Mary was very inexperienced sexually, and came to change her views after she had had a deep relationship which produced a baby followed by a marriage and another child.

With regard to education and family, she wanted co-educational schools which would mean that girls would have the same education as boys and be treated on an equal footing. She wanted children to stay at home and be nurtured by the family, and not sent away at a young age for years at a time. She thought that fathers should be friends to their children as opposed to someone that the children feared and she also felt that the emotional aspect of adults were affected by how they were treated when young. This was an extraordinary idea at the time but is common wisdom in the 21st century, well over two hundred years after Mary's book was written. She was also way ahead in her idea that parents should talk to their children in a sensible manner about sexual matters. She may have written the book in six weeks and the style may have suffered as a result, but there was certainly a great deal of ground covered in it.

The beginning of the following year, 1792, saw Mary at the height of her literary powers. Her book was an immediate best seller. However, it was not all plain sailing for Mary as there were certain people she thought would have approved but who in fact did not. Hannah More (1745-1833), the English playwright and religious writer wouldn't even read it and Horace Walpole (1717-97), the English man of letters, did not like it at all, although it seems that it was because he did not share her political views rather than objecting to her brand of feminism. However, be that as it may, she was now an established writer with a best seller to her credit.

Mary seems to have had three male loves in her life, Henry Fuseli, Gilbert Imlay and William Godwin. Henry Fuseli was the first and the relationship has already been dealt with – a sexual relationship between them was unlikely and certainly marriage was a complete non-starter due to Fuseli already being married to Sophia. However, there was certainly a meeting of minds and they could talk to each other in a way that he and Sophia could not and her feelings for him were certainly strong. So strong in fact, that she sprung an idea on Sophia by visiting her in August 1792, and asking that she, Mary, live with Henry and Sophia as a ménage a trois. She would not make sexual demands on her husband but be his partner in terms of their meetings of minds whilst Sophia continue with the usual wifely duties as seen in those times. Not surprisingly, Sophia reacted with fury, threw Mary out and told her never to show her face again. It was an extraordinary idea by Mary, showed incredible naivety for a thirty-three year old woman and was never going to be accepted by Sophia. The relationship between Mary and Fuseli effectively came to an end at that point.

In 1792, Mary had travelled to Paris to witness for herself the terror that was going on and in May the following year, 1793, she met Gilbert Imlay, an army captain who changed the direction of her life. It was a bad time for the French nation – it was all very well to strive for more equality but a great deal of blood had been shed in the process and it was never in Mary's mind that such events would take place. Gilbert Imlay was an army officer which did not impress Mary in the slightest, but what *did* impress her was the fact that Imlay had other strings to his bow, namely a wish to be a farmer once he had made enough money to buy some land. He had also written two books: *'Topographical Description of the Western Territory of North America'* which had been quite successful and a novel entitled *'The Emigrants'*, which was about to be published in London. What she did not know was that the thirty-nine year old Imlay had amassed debts over the years but he was an attractive man who was handsome and skilled at flattery. One of the things he told Mary was that he felt marriage to be a rather corrupt way of life and one in which he would not enter into. To justify this statement, he told Mary that he had been badly let down by a woman in the past and convinced Mary that he was a wronged man – a story that Mary, unfortunately was very keen to believe.

Mary soon fell in love with him and he had the skill of being able to say exactly what she wanted to say. He talked of many things, but one resonated with Mary when he spoke of getting a farmhouse in the backwoods and them having six children because this is exactly what Mary's mother had dreamed of but never achieved. He got on well with her friends and eventually they began to be seen as a couple. Despite the strength of her feelings towards Imlay, Mary stuck to her views about marriage – she was still firmly against it but she still expected fidelity and quite probably a lifelong commitment. Meanwhile, Mary was stuck in Paris which was very unsafe – Louis XVI had been guillotined on 21st January of that year, 1793, but Mary was offered a small house in Neuilly, a very small village, and well away from the troubles. Imlay came to visit her from June through to August, and by now they had been lovers for some time and by the latter part of the summer, she was pregnant.

The honeymoon period was now over and Mary returned to Paris and for a short while she and Imlay lived together, but it was not long before he said that he had to go to Le Havre on business and left Mary to face her pregnancy alone. Despite her sadness at losing Imlay for what she thought would be a short time, she carried on working on her latest book, *'A Historical and Moral View of the French Revolution'*. She also undertook prison visits and grew depressed at the news that filtered in about the execution of some of her friends. Fortunately Mary was safe as Imlay had registered her as his wife at the American Embassy which gave her protection by being an American citizen.

By Christmas she was still alone; Imlay had not returned from Le Havre and neither did Mary receive any encouragement from him that he wanted her to join him there. Because of his absences and the fact that Mary missed him, she decided to travel to Le Havre herself to see Imlay but soon after she arrived there he told her that he had to go to Paris for a short while. Mary used the time to finish her book *'Historical and Moral View of the French Revolution'*.

Imlay came back for the birth of the baby girl who was born on 14th May, 1794 and she and Imlay named her Fanny. In July, the terror that had taken over the country seemed to abate but if Mary thought she could now enjoy domestic bliss, she was mistaken, because a restless Imlay announced that he had to return to Paris and from there make his way to London.

In April 1795, Mary returned to London but she was only too aware that Imlay was cooling towards her and she took lodgings at Charlotte Street. It seems that Imlay had taken a mistress who was an actress and had set up home with her. Realising that her plans for a life with Imlay were in ruins, and thinking that she would face public humiliation, she made a suicide attempt with Laudanum. However, it was less a suicide attempt and more a cry for attention, and with the help of friends and a few reminders to think of Fanny, her little daughter, she rallied herself and tried to live normally again. However, she knew that Imlay was never going to set up home with her and the realisation of this caused her to go into a deep depression, and she made a second suicide attempt by jumping off Putney Bridge in October. This time she was more determined to succeed and she left Fanny with her maid, Marguerite, and made her way to the bridge. It was pouring with rain and her clothes were wet through which made her even more confident that she would sink quickly and drown when she jumped off. She did jump, but her plan went completely wrong. Instead of sinking she floated, whilst at the same time she was gasping for breath and in pain. Eventually, she did become unconscious but still floating, she was seen by two watermen and pulled out of the cold and filthy Thames water. She was less than grateful however and after recovering at a public house called The Duke's Head, she was taken to Finsbury Square at Imlay's behest and looked after there. She still harboured hopes that Imlay would return to her but there was no chance of that, and the affair was now effectively over.

After that, things seemed to improve for Mary. In January 1796, Johnson published her *'Letters Written during a Short Residence in Denmark, Norway and Sweden'* which consisted entirely of her letters written to Imlay when she was in Scandinavia. The book was well received by the public as well as professional writers and showed people that Mary was an observant traveller, picking up on how local people lived as well as making telling notes on the countryside.

She saw him again by accident in March 1796 when he approached her on horseback. He dismounted and they walked a little way together and she felt calm, but they never saw each other again. Mary settled in London in Cumming Street which was off the Pentonville Road with Fanny and her maid Marguerite. She was determined to put her affair with Imlay behind her, and with this in mind, she accepted an invitation from a long standing friend called Mary Hays to attend a small dinner party on 14th April, 1796, and this enabled her to renew her acquaintance with William Godwin who she had met three and a half years before, although neither person made a very good impression on the other at the time. Godwin (1756-1836) was a political writer and novelist and they had first met at a dinner party in November 1792. From Mary's point of view, the meeting had not been a success. Thomas Paine was there and he was in the middle of writing the second part of *'The Rights of Man'* whilst Godwin was working on his *'Enquiry Concerning Political Justice'* and this was the dinner during which Paine and Godwin had frozen Mary out of the conversation.

After a bad start all those years previously, the relationship between Mary and Godwin started slowly, but gradually they fell deeply in love with each other. Godwin was at the height of his fame at this point. The book that he was writing when Mary had met him earlier, *'Enquiry Concerning Political Justice'* had come out in 1793 and earned him a lot of money. It had gone down very well and had impressed people such as Robert Southey, Samuel Coleridge, William Wordsworth, and Percy Bysshe Shelley, (1792-1822), all of them famous poets.

Mary found herself in the midst of a group of women friends who were writers and who thought the same as her and who she could relate to. However, she was also popular with men as well and this was before she started a relationship with Godwin. John Opie, (1761-1807) the portrait and historical painter would often visit her, so often in fact that people were guessing as to what his intentions were, especially as he had recently become divorced. In his life he became famous for painting not only contemporary figures, but also historical pictures such as the *'Murder of Rizzio'*, *'Jephtha's Vow'* and *'Juliet in the Garden'*. He also published his *'Lectures on Painting'* (1809) at the Royal Institution. Robert Southey apparently told a friend that Mary was the person he liked best in the literary world. If she could impress someone like Southey, then Mary was certainly doing well. Southey (1774-1843), was a prolific writer and poet and was a good friend of Samuel Coleridge. In 1795, Southey married Edith Fricker whose elder sister Sara married Coleridge so the two men were related by marriage. In 1794, they had written a topical drama together called *'The Fall of Robespierre'* and in 1795 Southey had published an early volume of *'Poems'* and the same year produced an epic poem *'Joan of Arc'*. Later his views mellowed somewhat and he became Poet Laureate in 1813 and in the same year brought out one of the first biographies of Lord Nelson, amongst many other works. Samuel Coleridge's (1772-1834), career was no less impressive. Apart from his writings with Southey, he enjoyed success with William Wordsworth (1770-1850) and his wife Dorothy after meeting them in 1797. The meeting had a huge effect on English poetry and resulted in a move away from the neo-classic artificiality and the resulting 'Lyrical Ballads' started with Coleridge's famous *'Ancient Mariner'* and ended with Wordsworth's *'Tintern Abbey'*. Later the relationship between Coleridge and the Wordsworths cooled and Coleridge went on to huge success in his own right.

Coleridge enjoyed Mary's conversation although he was not quite so impressed as others were about the way her books were constructed. She began to get closer to Godwin during this period, although there was still no romance between them. Godwin in fact, proposed to another lady, a one Amelia Alderson (1769-1853) who was the daughter of James Alderson, a physician in Norwich. This was strange, as Godwin had always said that independence was necessary for a good life, but as it happened, Amelia turned him down and in May, 1798, she went on to marry John Opie, the painter who two years before had been so friendly with Mary. Godwin was at the height of his powers as not only had his *'Enquiry Concerning Political Justice'* become a good seller, but his latest book, a novel, entitled *'Caleb Williams'* was admired by just about everyone, regardless of whether they agreed with his political opinions.

Amelia Alderson's mother had died young and Amelia's father had spoiled her over the years although she ran his house for him in between writing little plays. Eventually she brought out a novel that was published anonymously entitled *'The Dangers of Coquetry'* and she always relied on Godwin for advice on her writings when she was in town. Godwin had a friend, a Thomas Holcroft, (1745-1809), who was a playwright and novelist. His first major work was *'Alwyn, or the Gentleman Comedian'* which came out in 1780 and was the first of four novels. He also wrote nearly thirty plays, the two best being *'The Follies of a Day'* (1784) and *'The Road to Ruin'* which was published in 1792. His life was touched by tragedy however when his eldest son William (1773-89) robbed him of £40 (Approx £2,400 in today's money) and when Thomas found him on a ship bound for America, his son shot himself. In 1796 Thomas was fifty-one and had been married three times, his most recent wife dying six years previously, but Godwin had never married. It is probably true to say that Holcroft was looking for a wife whilst Godwin was after love, but not marriage. As it was, both Holcroft and as previously mentioned, Godwin proposed to Amelia Alderson but she turned them both down. Amelia was obviously not short of admirers, because it was soon after Holcroft's and then Godwin's proposals to her that she eventually married Opie.

Meanwhile, Mary was writing a new book in the form of a novel, *'Maria, or the Wrongs of Woman'* which although supposedly fiction, contained several factual case histories of events that proved the fact that women enjoyed far fewer legal rights than did men, and very little sexual freedom either. In fact although it was a novel, she brought several people that she knew in to the story and used their experiences to make her various points, one of which was the fact that a woman's role was seen as having little purpose other than to please men sexually but not the other way round. Whatever the merits or not of the book however, Mary was enjoying herself socially at this point in time and was surrounded by a group of friends that she could relate to.

Amelia Alderson notwithstanding, Godwin and Mary starting courting each other soon after Godwin's unsuccessful proposal to Amelia. There was a definite love between them, but it has to be said that both of them were in the right place at the right time for each other. Mary, because of the breakdown of her relationship with Imlay, and Godwin, because he had been rejected by Amelia Alderson. However, the relationship got off to a shaky start which is not surprising. Mary was sexually experienced after her relationship with Imlay, whilst Godwin had reached the age of forty almost certainly never having had any sort of intimacy with a woman.

The relationship was sometimes strained through arguments and misunderstandings. If Mary was uneasy about Amelia Alderson, there was another woman she had strong misgivings about, and this was Elizabeth

Inchbald, an actress, playwright and novelist. She was a widow in her early forties and both Holcroft and Godwin enjoyed her company on numerous occasions. Elizabeth Inchbald (nee Simpson 1753-1821) hailed from Bury St. Edmunds and was the daughter of a farmer who she ran away from to pursue a career on the stage. In 1772, she married a fellow actor called John Inchbald but he died only seven years later in 1779. After her husband's death, she appeared at Covent Garden and as well as acting, she wrote many plays including 'The Wedding Day' (1794) and 'Lover's Vows' (1798). She also wrote novels and was editor of the 24-volume 'The British Theatre' (1806-1809).

Elizabeth Inchbald was a formidable rival to Mary if Godwin had designs on her, and there was certainly one occasion after some rows had been patched up between Mary and Godwin when she saw Godwin with Elizabeth at the theatre clearly enjoying each other's company. She attacked Godwin viciously which was partly brought on by the fear that she was pregnant. At this stage, Godwin had made no mention of wanting to marry Mary and she was terrified at the thought of another illegitimate baby by a different father from her first baby, the two-year-old Fanny Imlay. Godwin had always guarded his independence, and she could see no way that he would marry her, whether she was pregnant or not.

On 3rd February, Mary called upon a friend of hers, Dr. James Fordyce, and it was almost certainly he who confirmed that she was pregnant. She was feeling very low at this point as she was physically unwell, but as it happened Godwin did in fact agree to marry her, and the ceremony took place at St. Pancras on 29th March, 1797. It was a very low key affair with hardly anyone present. Thomas Holcroft was very disappointed that he only found out about the marriage after it had taken place, and in fact did not even know the identity of the bride earlier on. When he did find out however, he was very pleased for both of them saying:- "From my heart and soul I give you joy. I think you the most extraordinary married pair in existence. May your happiness be as pure as I firmly persuade myself it must be." However, they had been nervous at the reception they would receive from some quarters, and as it turned out, they were right to be concerned. Just over a week after Holcroft had sent his nice letter, Mary and Godwin went to the theatre in a party that included Elizabeth Inchbald and Amelia Alderson. Apparently when Mrs. Inchbald was told the news, far from showing pleasure, she simply insulted the couple and instead of pulling together in that situation, the couple had a huge row.

Despite this, the couple moved to a new house and Mary started to thrive in the new situation that she found herself in. She liked the domestic life, was happy to be a mother to Fanny, her daughter by Gilbert Imlay, and started to look forward to the new baby that she was expecting. Although happy at being married, after all that she and her husband had said about the marriage state so many times before they themselves married, Mary felt time and again that she had to justify her decision to wed. One of the first people she wrote to was Amelia Alderson, who had been in the theatre party. She wrote that she could have married before to men who were financially better off than Godwin but had chosen not to. She could write what she liked however, but in that situation, people on the receiving end of the justification are never convinced and at the end of the day, Mary wanted a father to not only her as yet unborn child, but Fanny, the child that she had had with Gilbert Imlay.

Some time before the baby was due, Godwin was invited to spend some time in the country by Basil Montagu, a friend of both Godwin's and Mary, and with a singular lack of tact, accepted. This left Mary alone in London, feeling alone and vulnerable, and not a little disgruntled as she had had a prior invitation from Montagu to do the same thing, but had declined due to a prior engagement with Godwin's sister, Hannah. Once away, Godwin seemed in no hurry to return home which caused Mary considerable anxiety, and although he wrote her affectionate letters, his reasons, or excuses, for not returning more quickly cut little ice with Mary. Eventually however, he did return home but then they started arguing over her religious beliefs which he tried to make her drop, but she refused, saying:- "How can you blame me for taking refuge in the idea of God, when I despair of finding sincerity on earth?" The couple argued a great deal in the months before the baby was due, but about a month before the birth, they seemed to grow more affectionate towards each other, and when Mary thought the birth was imminent, she kept Godwin informed of her progress by writing him notes describing what Mrs. Blenkinsop, the midwife, was saying as to when the birth was likely to be.

At 5am on Wednesday, 30th August, Mary felt that the labour pains were starting. She was feeling well, and was expecting to present the baby to Godwin straight after it had been delivered, and then get up and have dinner with him the next day. This is the sort of timetable that is considered quite normal in the 21st century, but in the 18th century, women tended to stay in bed a full month, an idea that Mary poured scorn on. When the midwife thought the birth imminent, she would apply butter to ease the delivery. Sometimes there would be a log of wood at the bottom of the bed for the mother to press her feet against. Other precautions were thought of, such as hot drinks to ease the mother's throat after the inevitable shouting during the birth, all the precautions in fact, apart from the most important, cleanliness, and it was the lack of cleanliness that was to have devastating results, not just for Mary on this occasion, but for countless other mothers in the 18th century.

At 11.20pm, Godwin heard the baby cry but Mrs. Blenkinsop sent a message to Godwin not to come up – the baby had been born but the placenta had not come away and he went to fetch Dr. Poignand, an eminent doctor in his day. If the placenta does not come away there is a risk of infection and the womb will keep bleeding. In modern times, the placenta is taken away quickly under anaesthetic but in the 18th century it had to be removed quickly and without anaesthetic which Dr. Poignand endeavoured to do with his hands and at 8am he informed Godwin that he had managed to take it all away. Tragically however, he had caused infection to break out although no-one knew that at the time. Mary thought her ordeal was over and after some sleep, seemed to her husband to appear very well and rested after the ordeal of the birth and the treatment afterwards. Dr. Poignand said that he felt he was no longer needed and another doctor, James Fordyce, who was a friend of William and Mary's, looked in and said that everything was fine – there were no problems. The baby was a girl and was named Mary after her mother and had been born on the Thursday.

Two days later, on the Saturday, Mary was still feeling well, but it was on that day that she started to feel unwell and asked for William to come to her bedside, but he had gone for a long walk. By the time he got home Mary was shivering uncontrollably and no-one knew what to do to ease her symptoms. They didn't even know what was causing them but with modern medical knowledge we now know that it was clearly septicaemia (blood poisoning) coming on, although this was not known of at the time. Dr. Poignand came back on Sunday but never returned – he handed over to Fordyce, probably because he knew that Mary was beyond help. It was now clear that Mary was dying and Godwin brought in his close friend Anthony Carlisle who was also a doctor, and whilst he provided moral support to his friend William Godwin, could do nothing medically. On the Thursday, a week after the birth, Carlisle warned Godwin to expect Mary's death at any time but still she hung on through Friday and Saturday, finally succumbing to the inevitable on Sunday, 10th September at 7.40 a.m.

In the short term, the new baby Mary was taken care of by a variety of women friends, and the funeral was held the following Friday, 15th September at St. Pancras where the couple were married a mere five and a half months earlier. William Godwin was too upset to attend the funeral. She was buried in the churchyard there and the memorial was a large slab of grey stone and it read:-

MARY WOLLSTONECRAFT
GODWIN
Author of
A Vindication
of the rights of Women

Born 27th April 1759
Died 10th September, 1797

Mary was an ardent feminist before the term was used. She wanted equal rights for women not only in education, but in terms of work and career paths such as being doctors or lawyers, but stopped short in advocating universal suffrage, although it must be remembered that not even all men had the vote during the period in which she lived. She was responsible for a great deal of feminist writing including *'Thoughts on the Education of Daughters'* which was published in 1786, and *'A Vindication of the Rights of Man'* published anonymously in 1790 which was a reply to Burke's *'Reflections on the Revolution in France'* written in the same year. A second edition of Mary's *'Vindication'*, this time under her own name was published the following year and in that year, 1791, she started work on her *'Vindication of the Rights of Woman'* which was completed and published the following year, 1792. In 1794, she published the *'Historical and Moral View of the Origin and Progress of the French Revolution'* and in 1796 she brought out the *'Letters Written during a Short Residence in Sweden, Norway and Denmark'*.

Whilst Mary's views could be seen as ahead of their time, she could also be naive, although no more than some of the men that she surrounded herself with.

She was completely supportive of the French Revolution and made excuses for the bloodshed and excesses that occurred in that country. She was ambivalent about marriage, seemingly in love with Fanny Blood and wanting nothing more than to spend her life with Fanny, yet formed a relationship with Gilbert Imlay and had a daughter, Fanny (1794-1816) by him, but Fanny tragically committed suicide. Fanny's birth was followed three years later by Mary marrying William Godwin, and then giving birth to another daughter, this time by her husband, the daughter being called Mary and who was to become Mary Shelley (1797-1851), this Mary marrying the famous poet, Percy Bysshe Shelley (1792-1822) in 1816, the year her half-sister Fanny killed herself.

With amazing speed, Godwin wrote a biography on Mary straight after her death entitled *'Memoirs of the Author of A Vindication of the Rights of Woman'* and it was published by Johnson in January 1798. Godwin had started writing the book only two weeks after Mary's death and as a result there are mistakes both in fact and in his judgement. He intended it to be a tribute written with great love and affection but his decision to include details of her love affairs and her illegitimate daughter Fanny by Gilbert Imlay caused Mary's reputation to be badly tarnished, and her contribution to women's rights was largely ignored for a hundred years until feminists took her ideas up at the latter part of the nineteenth century. Even some of her friends had seemed to turn against her memory, one of the worst examples being Amelia Opie (nee Alderson) who wrote two novels after Mary's death, the second, entitled *'Adeline Mowbray'* was supposedly based on Godwin and Mary's marriage but it was unkind and untrue in it's depiction. Godwin felt badly let down by her.

Mary was very controversial in her day and very courageous – the two went together. She had to be courageous in order to print her views that were certainly controversial and looked at in the 21st century, could have been written by a feminist two hundred years later. For all her forthright views however, she seemed to be on a constant lookout for love, whether it was from another female such as Jane Arden or Fanny Blood, or in later years, from men such as Henry Fuseli, Gilbert Imlay and finally, her husband William Godwin. In the end, she opted for a more conventional relationship, that is, a husband and two children, but that does not detract in any way whatsoever from her lifelong commitment to women's issues.

-oOOo-

15

Dr. Samuel Johnson
(1709-1784)

*Raconteur and wit and producer of the first proper dictionary in
1755.*

Samuel Johnson, writer, critic, lexicographer, essayist, raconteur and biographer,
was born in Lichfield, Staffordshire on Wednesday, the 18th September, 1709 to
Michael Johnson (c1657-1731), who earned his living as a bookseller, and his
wife Sarah. Samuel's father Michael, had gained a reputation as the first eminent
bookseller at Lichfield. He also produced his own books being the owner of a
parchment factory. Michael's father was William Johnson who was described on
different occasions as a 'yoeman' and a 'gentleman'. He was the first Johnson to
move to Lichfield which he did with his wife Catherine and their four children
in the 1660's from the agricultural village of Cubley, Derbyshire, and was also
the first Johnson to attempt to earn his living selling books. His eldest son
(Samuel's father) was called Michael and was born in 1657. It is not certain
where he went to school but it is assumed that it was the grammar school in
Lichfield as he possessed a good grasp of Latin. In 1672 when Michael, the
eldest, was fifteen, his father William died and the family had to rely on charity
to get them through. Michael then had some luck as one of these local charities
enabled him to be apprenticed to a London stationer by the name of Richard
Simpson. This apprenticeship lasted for eight years and at the age of twenty-
four, Michael returned to Lichfield with the aim of following his father's
footsteps and going into the book trade.

Michael did eventually marry, but relatively late in life although he had had
an earlier relationship. In 1686, when he was 29, Michael had become engaged
to a Lichfield woman called Mary Neild, but at some stage she ended the
arrangement and another twenty years went by before he married Sarah Ford
(c1669-1759) on 19th June, 1706. By this time Michael was approaching 50,
although his bride was twelve years younger. Sarah was the daughter of
Cornelius Ford, the grandfather of the Cornelius Ford who would later become a
good friend and mentor to Samuel. The Fords were a middle class family who
were involved in both milling and farming so when Michael and Sarah were
married, it seemed that they would be financially secure for life although it was
not to be. It was difficult to see how, with the combined wealth of both families,
that they would have financial problems, but by the time that Samuel was born
three years later in 1709, Michael found himself in a great deal of debt from
which he never recovered. The financial arrangements between the families
were certainly complicated and it was unclear as to why Michael Johnson had
purchased such a large house, certainly one that was bigger than the Johnson
family ever needed. Perhaps it was to impress his future in-laws who were

certainly comfortably off. Sarah's father, Cornelius Ford was a person who owned property and had been connected by marriage to a wealthy family. Cornelius had a son called Joseph, who had studied at Cambridge and then went on to run a medical practice as a physician in Stourbridge. It was Joseph who was the brother of Sarah and therefore Samuel's uncle and it was this same Joseph who was the father of Samuel's cousin, the young Cornelius Ford who would later become a good friend of Johnson.

Samuel was born in the bedroom of the house above Michael Johnson's shop, and the shop is still there overlooking the Market Square. Sarah was approaching forty years of age when she gave birth to Samuel, and at the time this was considered quite late in life and so as a precaution, a gentleman by the name of George Hector was brought in to assist with the birth. The usual name for a man in his profession at that time was a 'Man-midwife' and Hector was held in very high regard. He delivered Samuel but the little child did not cry and as it was thought that he might not live, they had him quickly baptised by the Vicar of St. Mary's. When it came to choosing a name for the infant, the baby's parents could not initially agree and Sarah wanted the boy to be called Samuel after her elder brother. She would later express the wish that her second son be called Nathaniel, and as it happened, her wish was granted on both counts. The two godfathers were Richard Wakefield, and Dr. Samuel Swynfen. Richard Wakefield was a Coroner and for nine years was the Lichfield Town Clerk as well as being a lawyer. He was a man who was comfortably off and although he had no children was a widower and very fond of books. He was also a frequent visitor to the Johnson bookshop. The other godfather, Dr. Samuel Swynfen, was a physician and a graduate of Pembroke College Oxford. Swynfen lived in an ancestral estate just outside of Lichfield, but would often stay at Michael and Sarah Johnson's house in order to be nearer his medical practice.

Samuel's father, Michael, had been elected Sheriff of Lichfield the previous July. It was a long held tradition that the Sheriff would conduct the annual 'Riding' which consisted of the Sheriff plus a great many of the townsfolk riding round the circumference of the city, the reason being that the various points of the city boundaries could be checked. The other custom that was popular in Lichfield is that the Sheriff provides refreshments during the ride and then a light meal at the Guildhall. This custom was always carried out on the 19th September each year, which as it happened, was the day following Samuel's birth and so it was a specially happy Sheriff who "feasted the citizens with uncommon magnificence..." in that particular year.

However, to return to Samuel's birth, after the initial scare when he was born, his health began to improve but he contracted scrofula, almost certainly as a result of being given to a wet nurse called Joan Marklew. Joan Marklew wasn't just anybody – she was chosen with great care which is what makes the tragedy that followed even more poignant because Samuel's parents had put a lot of thought into who they would leave Samuel with. Joan Marklew was the wife of John Marklew, a bricklayer and she had previously been employed as a servant to William Robinson, a neighbour who was known to the Johnson family. In her early thirties, Mrs. Marklew was reasonably young, seemed very fit and had been nursing her own child for eighteen months, so Michael and Sarah had no qualms about asking her to be Samuel's wet nurse.

Although confident that young Samuel was with the right people, Sarah, Samuel's mother, made excuses to visit the Marklew family as often as she could in order to see her son, and it was not long before she felt that Samuel didn't look right. His eyes looked as if they were infected and it was not long before Michael and Sarah Johnson discovered that their baby had scrofula which had spread to the eyes to such a degree that baby Samuel was almost blind in the left eye and had impaired vision in the right. Another reason that Michael and Sarah were almost certain that the disease was caught from Joan Marklew is the fact that Joan's son had also caught the disease and so after ten weeks, the young Samuel was taken home and he was later to write:- "I was taken home, a poor diseased infant, almost blind".

The disease of scrofula is a form of tuberculosis and it affects the lymph nodes of the neck. In Johnson's time it was often referred to as 'The King's Evil' as from the Middle Ages it was thought that sufferers could be cured by a mere touch from royalty. It was thought that the power for Monarchs to cure this disease was due to their descent from Edward the Confessor (c1003-66) who ruled England from 1042 and who was the last Anglo-Saxon King. He was the eldest son of Ethelred the Unready and his wife Emma. He was buried in Westminster Abbey and became a cult figure and was canonized in 1611. In turn, he was said to have received his healing powers from St. Remigius (c438-533), a Frankish Prelate and Bishop of Reims. He was known as the Apostle of the Franks who were said to have originated in the third century and were of West Germanic descent.

Sir John Floyer (1649-1734) the famous Lichfield physician, recommended that Johnson should receive the touch from Queen Anne and although this practice carried on right through to Johnson's time, it was stopped by King George I, who had succeeded Queen Anne to the throne in 1714. The Queen's Touch was not successful in Johnson's case because no cure resulted when he received the royal touch from Queen Anne on 30th March, 1712. It was surprising that Floyer should have recommended this as he was a highly respected physician who had a great deal of knowledge concerning medicine. This knowledge enabled him to be one of the first physicians to recognise the importance of counting pulse beats whereas a touch from the reigning monarch would seem to be based on nothing more than superstition. Floyer brought out several highly respected medical papers which included *'A Treatise of the Asthma (1st ed. 1698)'*, *'The Physician's Pulse-watch (1707-1710)'*, *'An Essay to restore the Dipping of Infants in their Baptism (1722)'*, and *'Medicina Gerocomica, or the Galenic Art of Preserving old Men's Healths' (1st ed. 1724)'*. That he was an able physician was not disputed, but the claim by his family that he had been the Physician to Charles II was doubted by many.

Be that as it may, Samuel was not cured by the Royal Touch and therefore had to undergo surgery, which in the early 18th century would probably have been a rather crude affair, and certainly very painful as there were no anaesthetics then, added to which the young boy was left with a disfigured face. Samuel's parents would have had to have paid for this operation and to add to

411

the family's financial troubles, they began to go further into debt when Samuel's brother Nathaniel was born a few months later, and Michael and Sarah were then unable to enjoy the lifestyle that they were once used to. From a very early age, young Samuel showed that he had a high level of intelligence and his parents liked him to demonstrate this in one form or another to their friends, something which Johnson was disgusted with when he recalled it when older. At the age of three, his mother, a devout Christian, made Samuel read and then memorise passages from the *Book of Common Prayer* and it was then that she realised what a phenomenal memory Samuel had. James Boswell, 9th Laird of Auchinleck (1740-1795) was a lawyer and a diarist who befriended Johnson later in Samuel's life and wrote the famous biography, *'Life of Samuel Johnson'*. In his biography of Johnson, Boswell wrote of the incident between Johnson and his mother:-

' "Sam" (his mother said after giving him the book), "you must get this by heart". She went up stairs, leaving him to study it: But by the time she had reached the second floor, she heard him following her. "What's the matter"? said she. "I can say it", he replied; and repeated it distinctly, though he could not have read it over more than twice.'

The following year when he was four, Samuel was sent to a school of sorts which was run by a woman named Dame Anne Oliver. She ran it from her cottage and taught the basics to a group of young children, and although not properly qualified to teach, she nevertheless ran it in such a way that the children were happy, and Johnson always had fond memories of his time there. He was with Dame Oliver for two years before being sent to a retired shoemaker for one year to further his education before being sent to Lichfield Grammar School. A gentleman by the name of Humphrey Hawkins taught young Samuel Latin and even at a young age, he demonstrated that he excelled at the language.

It was during this period that the young Johnson began to display the tics and gesticulations that plagued him for years to come and caused people to view him in an unfavourable light – certainly people were probably more unkind in Johnson's time than they are now especially as they did not understand what was causing the tics. However, even allowing for that, it did not make him physically attractive and it has had to be a posthumous diagnosis that has drawn medical experts to the conclusion that Johnson was suffering from Tourette's Syndrome which may have been partly caused by the scrofula he suffered from when he was a child. Tourette's Syndrome is often inherited, although there is no knowledge of anyone else in Johnson's family suffering from it, and is a neuro-psychiatric illness which lends further credence to the idea that it may have been brought on by the scrofula. Healthwise, Johnson was to suffer all his life, having to fight amongst other things, depression, insomnia and a morbid fear of death and dying. He also suffered severely from hypochondria.

Despite his problems however, Johnson impressed his teachers at Lichfield Grammar and he was placed in the upper school when he was only nine years of age where his tutor was Edward Holbrooke. However, the school was run by a man known as the Reverend John Hunter who was known equally for his brutality along with his desire to obtain good results for his pupils, and as a result, Johnson was unhappy with the way that he was being educated. He had once been quoted as saying that: "Hunter never taught a boy in his life – he whipped and they learned". He also knew Anna Seward, Hunter's granddaughter who looked so much like her grandfather that "he could tremble" at the sight of her.

Many years later however, it seemed that Johnson's attitude to Hunter had changed, probably softened because of the passage of time. Johnson later said that he would not have learned Latin as well as he did without the whipping he received from Hunter. A curiously fond memory for someone who it would appear did not deserve it. However, he did meet and befriend John Taylor and Edmund Hector, the latter being the nephew of George Hector, the 'Man Midwife' who delivered him at his birth. Both of these men remained friends with Johnson throughout his entire life. Another man who became very friendly with Samuel was Cornelius Ford (1694-1731). Cornelius was the son of Dr. Joseph Ford, who was Sarah's brother as mentioned earlier, thus making Cornelius Samuel's cousin. Dr. Ford died in 1721 and a year later, his widow passed on. There had been a complicated financial agreement when Michael Johnson had married Sarah Ford and so Cornelius (the elder Cornelius' grandson) travelled to the Johnson's house to sort the financial affairs out and it was when he was there on 16th September, 1725 that the thirty-one-year-old Cornelius met his sixteen-year-old cousin Samuel for the first time.

Cornelius had spent twelve years at Cambridge, first as a student, then as a Fellow at Peterhouse but found that he was bored with the tranquillity of the place. Like his father, and like his young cousin would do after him, he married a lady who was older than himself, her name being Judith Crowley. Cornelius was twelve years younger than his bride but he found her attractive and she was financially comfortably off. The fact that Judith married later than was usual for a woman in the eighteenth century had nothing to do with her looks. Judith had received offers of marriage before but had turned them down. However, Cornelius was very determined despite opposition from her family, not just because of the age difference, but because they were Quakers, and they wanted their daughter to marry one. Certainly the Ford family had no objections, as Cornelius' father Joseph had done the same thing, that is, he married a lady older than himself. She was the widow of Gregory Hickman whose family were based in Stourbridge. Joseph's son Cornelius persisted over a five year period however, and his patience finally paid off as he and Judith were married in 1724. The Johnsons were impressed with the thirty-one-year-old Cornelius, and allowed the sixteen-year-old Samuel to stay with Cornelius at his home in Pedmore, Worcestershire. During this stay, Samuel became very friendly with Cornelius and they remained close until Ford's death from alcoholism six years after Johnson had stayed there. Although dying tragically young, Ford was a clever academic and whilst Johnson stayed with the family, Ford spent considerable time with Samuel teaching him the classics. Ford's death affected Johnson deeply as he had become a valued mentor to Samuel. However, despite the fact that Ford was an alcoholic, all the while Johnson stayed with him and the rest of the Ford family, Cornelius remained a good influence on Samuel, at least from an academic point of view. Johnson spent six months with his cousins and clearly showed no great inclination to return to the school in Lichfield and the Reverend John Hunter and his brutality. Return he had to however, but luckily for the young Samuel, Hunter was aggrieved that Johnson had been away for so long and refused to have him back, no doubt to the delight of young Samuel.

Johnson was enrolled at the King Edward V1 Grammar School in Stourbridge which again pleased Samuel as the school was quite close to his cousins in Pedmore which again enabled him to spend more time with them. The headmaster was John Wentworth who took great pains to work with Samuel on his translations. It was during this period that Johnson began to write poetry and undertake translations although once again he was allowed only six months there before returning to his parents in Lichfield. One reason put forward for Samuel having to leave after such a short time was suggested in later life by one of his best friends, Edmund Hector, who said that Johnson and Wentworth had had a disagreement over Latin grammar. Another reason was his father's debt which meant that Samuel had to return home in 1727 at the age of eighteen to help his father with stitching. He was clearly a clever young boy and it was a frustrating time for him, although his consolation was that he had remained friends with John Taylor and Edmund Hector so he had companionship. Companionship of a different order came to Samuel when he fell in love for the first time. He had met Ann Hector, Edmund's sister and had fallen for her, although the feelings were short-lived. Many years later he would tell Boswell, his friend and future biographer that:- "She was the first woman with whom I was in love. It dropped out of my head imperceptibly, but she and I shall always have a kindness for each other".

Johnson carried on working at his father's shop for two years and whilst he was there he met the lawyer Gilbert Walmesley (1680-1751), who was the Registrar of the Ecclesiastical Court and was often in Michael Johnson's bookshop. A strong friendship developed between Samuel and Walmesley which remained constant throughout Walmesley's life; in fact, it is probably safe to say that the two men who had the greatest influence on Johnson were Cornelius Ford and Gilbert Walmesley. Walmesley was a lot older than Samuel being forty seven to Johnson's eighteen when they met in 1727. There were differences between the characters of Ford and Walmesley that Johnson recognised, but thought was no bad thing. Being a lawyer, Walmesley was skilled in argument and debate. He was very interested in politics and strongly supported the Whig party, not being afraid to let people know. Johnson, being just eighteen had not formed his political views at this point and had been brought up in a different atmosphere, that of Michael Johnson's Toryism. Samuel kept to his father's views which were certainly different from Walmesley's, but meeting the man meant that he was able to debate with him and argue his corner which he had never had to do before now. Walmesley was a batchelor when he met Samuel but nine years later, in 1736 when he would have been fifty-six, he married Magdalen Aston who it so happened, had a sister called Mary who Johnson considered "the loveliest creature I ever saw". There is no doubt that Johnson loved her but quite why he did not court her is not clear.

Meanwhile, Johnson continued to work at his father's shop because the family had no money to send him to university. However, in February 1728, his mother's wealthy cousin Elizabeth Harriotts died and left Johnson's mother £40 (between £3,000 and £4,000 in 2010). Rather than keep it for themselves, Samuel's parents generously used the money to send their son back to school, and from there, to Oxford. On 31st October, 1728, just over a month after he had turned nineteen years of age, Samuel entered Pembroke College, Oxford as a fellow-commoner. The money that his mother had received from her cousin was not enough to cover all of his outgoings but a fellow student who was also a friend from school days, Andrew Corbet, offered to finance the difference for Samuel, which on the surface seemed a very generous act. However, Corbet made the offer in haste and was unable to fulfil his promise. Corbet's father had long since been dead, but his mother, the daughter of Sir Francis Edwardes, a wealthy baronet, had died at about the same time as Johnson's cousin, Elizabeth Harriots. This left Corbet with rather more money than he thought he would have and he suddenly left Pembroke seemingly without any thought of the promise that he had made Samuel who, financially speaking, was now back to square one without adequate funding. Not wishing his son to miss out on the chance of studying, Michael Johnson, Samuel's father, stepped in at that point and allowed Samuel to borrow as many books as he wished from his shop. Samuel took his father up on his generous offer and to his father's surprise, selected a hundred books. However, Michael had confidence in his son and was happy for the young man to have them but what he didn't bargain for was the fact that when he left Oxford, Samuel left the books there and had to write asking for them back some years later. This left the father with a depleted stock in his shop for some time afterwards although he was to recover them eventually. One of the people who said goodbye to Samuel before he went off to Oxford was Dame Oliver who had taught him at infants' school. She was no longer teaching but was now running a sweet shop and she brought Samuel a present of gingerbread, telling him that "he was the best scholar she ever had". Samuel never forgot this compliment and would often quote it to his friends in later life.

Michael Johnson was a doting father who had confidence in his son and he had taken Samuel to Oxford for his original interview, introducing him to William Jorden, who would become Samuel's future tutor. When Samuel arrived at Oxford, Jorden was Chaplain to the College and had recently become Vice Regent of Pembroke and was an important person to get to know. During the actual interview itself, Samuel was embarrassed by his father's well meaning but unwise behaviour, which consisted of him telling the interviewing panel how talented his son was. However, after a fairly lengthy time of keeping his own counsel, Samuel suddenly interrupted his father and quoted Macrobius, the 5th century Roman writer and neo-Platonist philosopher. This caused surprise amongst the people who were interviewing him – it was unusual for someone of Samuel's age to have that kind of knowledge, and consequently he was immediately granted a place. William Adams, at the age of 26 was one of the interviewers as well as being a cousin of William Jorden. Adams was also later to become the Master of Pembroke and he said of Johnson that he was "the best qualified for the university that he had ever known come here".

Johnson almost certainly enjoyed himself at Oxford; he certainly did little work and despite his lack of money, made no effort to economise. He stayed away from many of the lectures and often took no notice when the tutors asked for poems from the students. When he was young, Johnson was one of these brilliant people who were capable of producing great work for short bursts of time, and so it was that his tutor, William Jorden, who realised that Samuel had talent, asked him to produce a Latin translation of Alexander Pope's *'Messiah'*. Alexander Pope (1688-1744) was a famous 18th century English poet best known for his translation of Homer and satirical verse. Like Johnson, Pope suffered from various illnesses, one of these being Pott's disease, which was a type of tuberculosis that affects the bone and in Pope's case deformed his spine and left him a hunchback. However, he was a brilliant poet and it would not have been seen as slow if Samuel had finished the translation in a month or possibly even longer, but as it was, he finished it in a matter of hours. Johnson completed half of the work in one afternoon, and the balance the following morning. The poem was highly praised but it brought no money for Samuel although it was published in *'Miscellany of Poems'* in 1731 and was edited by John Husbands who was a Pembroke tutor. This was the earliest of Johnson's writings that have survived.

After Johnson had been at Oxford for just over a year, he found that he did not have enough money to pay his student fees and was forced to leave and return home to Lichfield. He set off on foot in December 1729 with his friend John Taylor, who he had met and stayed friends with since they were at Lichfield Grammar School. Taylor went as far as Banbury with him and then left him. Johnson, having first made a careful list of the books that he had borrowed from his father, left them in Taylor's charge because he did not have the necessary funds to send them home. This huge collection of books were left behind not only because of Samuel's finances but almost certainly as a gesture to both the college and his father that he wanted and expected to return there one day. It was always a bone of contention with Johnson that he was not able to stay at Oxford to finish his studies but he was to eventually receive a degree as Oxford University awarded him a Master of Arts in 1755, the year his famous dictionary was published. He was also awarded an honorary doctorate in 1765 by Trinity College, Dublin, and in 1775 by Oxford University.

However, in the meantime, Johnson had left Oxford without these qualifications, but despite that, he found that after Oxford, somehow selling books in his father's shop was beneath him. It was at this time, the autumn of 1731, that Michael Johnson fell very ill with what Johnson described as an 'inflammatory fever' and after a rapid decline, died in the first week of December, being buried at St. Michael's Church on 7th December. It was during the last few months of Michael's life that Samuel did an uncharacteristic thing, and disobeyed his father's request for help. His father ran a bookstall at Uttoxeter but on this occasion he was very ill and bed-ridden. He asked Samuel to take his place and run the bookstall but Johnson refused – a decision that he was later to feel remorse for as his father was soon to die after this incident.

Years later, he was to feel such guilt that he travelled to the very spot where his father would have traded, and stood quite still in that same spot for hours in the pouring rain by way of exorcising his guilt. Although distraught at the way he had treated his father, he was also in a deep depression and worried that he was heading towards insanity. Years later, he purchased a padlock and told someone who would one day become a close friend, Mrs. Thrale, that she was to use it to keep him imprisoned if his insanity was to surface. Sometime during this period immediately after leaving Oxford, his friend John Taylor told Francis Munday, another friend, that Johnson had at one point entertained the thought of committing suicide. This very deep depression went on for two years but in 1731, Johnson recovered enough to realise that he had to earn a living somehow and was keen on being an usher at Stourbridge Grammar school. However, he was still suffering from his depression and was worried about his lack of qualifications. In the event he was turned down for the position in September 1731 for that very reason – he had no qualifications. It was not a good time for Johnson as he was struggling to find work generally, still very depressed and had had to cope with the death of his father in December 1731.

Johnson was now twenty-two years old, and in March, 1732, he was taken on as an undermaster at a school in Market Bosworth which was run by Sir Wolstan Dixie, the 4th Baronet for an annual salary of £20. Johnson was also allowed the use of a house free of charge and fortunately for Samuel, Sir Wolstan was not too concerned that Johnson did not have a degree. Johnson could have stayed at home working with his mother who now owned the shop, and his brother Nathaniel who was now nineteen years old but he knew that he wasn't needed and felt that he should get away from the family home and spread his wings as severe depression was setting in. It was not a happy time for Samuel as Dixie had not appointed him to the job for any qualities he had, but was merely using Samuel as a means of proving a point. Dixie was the Chief Trustee at the school and was an unpleasant man and a bully. He had once boasted that he could ignore the rules and employ anyone he liked which is how Samuel got the job. Samuel found teaching boring and repetitive and found that he was also used as a servant by Dixie. There is a story that Dixie stopped the use of a public path that ran through his grounds and when a local Squire objected, Dixie beat him up very badly. Two years later, Dixie was presented to King George II and was introduced as "Sir Wolstan Dixie of Bosworth Park." The King responded to the introduction by saying "Bosworth – Bosworth, big battle at Bosworth wasn't it?" The King had of course, meant the Battle of Bosworth that had been fought in 1485 between the House of York and the House of Lancaster, the battle being won by the Lancastrians. "Yes Sire. But I thrashed him" the Baronet replied. Exactly what the King made of that answer is not recorded. Johnson's friend, John Taylor once described Dixie as "an abandoned brutal rascal". Although Dixie no doubt tried to bully Johnson, it was not the bullying that would have driven Johnson to leave this unhappy place of employment, but the depression that was always within him, and after an argument with Dixie, Johnson left the school at the end of July, 1732 and returned home.

It may be that at this time, 1732 onwards, Johnson had a delayed reaction to the terrible stress that he had had to endure as a child with the scrofula and the dreadful surgery that he had had to undergo as a result. He had been very depressed since he left Oxford in December, 1729, and in 1734, he wrote to one of his godfathers, Samuel Swynfen, and said that he, Johnson, felt that he was suffering from a disease that would make him insane. Swynfen's reply did not help Johnson at all, in fact it merely confirmed what he already thought. Swynfen wrote: "From the symptoms therein described, he could think nothing better of his disorder, than it had a tendency to insanity; and without great care might possibly terminate in the deprivation of his rational faculties". However, back in 1732, prior to his writing to Swynfen, Johnson had always tried to look for employment, hopefully at Lichfield but without much success although he did spend a lot of time with his friend Edmund Hector who by now had followed his uncle George Hector into medicine and was practicing as a surgeon. As it happened, Hector was sharing a house with a publisher called Thomas Warren who was starting his Birmingham Journal and found Johnson an all too willing helper in this project. *The Birmingham Journal* would print local stories but obtain the main news from the London papers which was the common method that most local papers used in those days. Johnson went to live with Hector and Warren in October or November, 1732 and Warren used Samuel for suggestions and advice along with a few essays for publication, although sadly, none survive to this day.

Johnson only stayed at Warren's house for six months but he had felt a little better and in June, 1733, moved to another house, this one being owned by a Mr. Jarvis. However, no sooner had he arrived he seemed to sink into a depression again and when the loyal Edmund Hector visited him, he never knew which mood he would find Johnson in. Sometimes, Johnson could be quite aggressive towards his friend, but it didn't put Hector off and the friendship continued until Johnson's dying day. Meanwhile, Johnson spoke to Warren about a book that with alterations, he thought Warren might be interested in publishing. In the seventeenth century, Father Jerome Lobo, a Portugese Jesuit, had written an account of his life in Abyssinia and the book had lain in a monastery in Lisbon, unpublished and unnoticed for years. Lobo had written an interesting book, containing as it did details of the customs and religion of the Absyssinians and he had also written about the Jesuit missionary effort between 1625 and 1634. There was a French version which Johnson discovered in 1728, the year he went to Oxford, and although the length of it made for tedious reading, Johnson thought that if it could be reduced, it may improve the book and therefore provoke interest. Johnson was in a depressive state and was not looking to undertake the work himself, but was persuaded to do so by both Hector and Warren. He found the task difficult because of his mental state, and would often write whilst in bed, although he eventually completed it with the help of Edmund Hector, who would write a clean copy once Johnson had delivered him the drafts which were full of alterations. Johnson returned to the family home in Lichfield in February 1734 and the book was published a year later in 1735.

Johnson had a good friend by the name of Harry Porter but Porter died in Birmingham on 3rd September, 1734 at the age of forty-three. Porter was a woollen draper and Edmund Hector had introduced them to each other a year or so before. Johnson had been a good friend to Porter, and had spent a great deal of time with him at his sick bed, trying to look after him. It was a side of Johnson that people do not seem to hear about, but his character always showed a caring side throughout his life. Porter had left a widow, Elizabeth Jervis Porter who at the age of forty-five, was two years older than her late husband. Porter had also left three children – a daughter of eighteen named Lucy, and two sixteen year old boys, Jervis Henry and Joseph. Mr. Porter had been in business but had not been successful and he lost money. However, his widow's father was a Warwickshire Squire who as well as being a squire himself, was descended from a long line of country squires. Her ancestry on her mother's side was also distinguished, going back as it did to members of the royal household. She would bring a handsome dowry to any marriage which remained hers if her husband died before she did which of course is what happened in this instance. Johnson, despite being over twenty years younger than Elizabeth, found himself attracted to his friend's widow and after a few months had lapsed began to court her. Elizabeth, or Tetty as she was sometimes known, encouraged Samuel and in fact, initial advances could possibly have come from her. Lucy Porter, Tetty's daughter told James Boswell, the future friend and biographer of Johnson's, that:-

"when he was first introduced to her mother, his appearance was very forbidding: he was then lean and lank, so that his immense structure of bones was hideously striking to the eye, and the scars of the scrophula (sic) were deeply visible. He also wore his hair (as distinct from a wig), which was straight and stiff, and separated behind; and he often had, seemingly, convulsive starts and odd gesticulations, which tended to excite at once surprise and ridicule".

Elizabeth was not bothered by these outward defects however, she was attracted to the inner man and told Lucy that: "This is the most sensible man that I ever saw in my life".

It would be ungracious as well as incorrect to say that Samuel was only interested in her money, but the fact remains that Elizabeth was wealthy and promised Samuel financial security which is a situation that he had never experienced before. The couple were self conscious about the difference in their ages and felt that rather than get married in Lichfield, they would wed elsewhere so they were married on 9th July, 1735 at St. Werburgh's Church in Derby but the couple inevitably attracted criticism regardless of where they were wed. Elizabeth also took a few years off her age when signing the marriage certificate and instead of writing her actual age of forty-six, she simply wrote her age as forty. The first problem came from Elizabeth's children who were split on the issue of this marriage. Lucy accepted the union from the start although Elizabeth was not so fortunate with the boys. Jervis was disgusted with it all and had no connections with his mother ever again but after initially receiving a negative reaction from Joseph, he gradually accepted the situation. It was probably not just the difference in ages that had caused the problem, but the speed of the marriage so soon after their father's death.

Whilst courting Elizabeth, Samuel had managed to get a job, albeit a temporary one lasting only two months in June 1735. This was to tutor the children of Thomas Whitby. The main job was to tutor the eldest son in preparation for his entrance to university although he taught the four other children as well. The Whitby family attended Colwich church every Sunday and during the time that he was with them, Johnson would accompany them and would entertain and amaze the family by repeating the sermon practically word for word after the service ended adding pieces if he thought that he was improving it. His confidence seemed to have improved because he also wrote to a friend in May asking for all his books to be returned from Oxford – they had been left there for over five years. It was also during this time that he applied for a job as Headmaster of Solihull School and his application was supported by Gilbert Walmesley. The headmaster at this school was a Mr. John Crompton who had left to go to Market Bosworth to work for Sir Wolstan Dixie. Crompton was a morose man and carried "a birchen sceptre, stained with infant gore", in other words, exactly the sort of man that Dixie would have liked working for him. However, despite the support of Gilbert Walmesley, Johnson was turned down to be Crompton's replacement at Solihull because the school's directors thought him "a very haughty, ill-natured gent, and that he has such a way of distorting his face, the gents think it may affect the lads."

This setback was a blow to Johnson because he needed to earn his living somehow, and so Walmesley encouraged him to set up his own school. After the job tutoring the Whitby family finished, Johnson did indeed set up his own school and called it Edial Hall School which was situated at Edial near Lichfield. The title of the school gives it a grandness which was not matched in reality as Johnson was initially only able to muster three pupils, Laurence Offley, twelve-year-old George Garrick, and George's brother, eighteen-year-old David Garrick (1717-79), who became a long standing friend of Johnson's as well as being one of the most famous actors of his day, although not before he had tried his hand at becoming a lawyer and then a wine merchant. He was a very successful actor over many years before settling at the Drury Lane Theatre where he became an actor manager in 1747. He became as famous as Johnson and when he died in 1779, he was buried in Westminster Abbey. However, to return to his youth, David Garrick had been educated at Lichfield Grammar School and then went on to Johnson's school to learn Latin and Greek in 1735. It is widely assumed that there were only ever three pupils, possibly because that is what Johnson's future friend and biographer, James Boswell thought. However, there were a few more pupils later on, although certainly not more than eight at any one time which was not enough for the school to be a financial success however well the subjects were taught. Johnson had two major things against him – first, there was the fact that he had no degree which did not impress parents of potential pupils, and also the tics and involuntary gesticulations that he suffered which sadly were a cause of laughter that would cause the pupils to lose concentration. Despite the grand name, Johnson's school was not a financial success and he had to use a large amount of his wife Tetty's fortune to keep it afloat. Despite advertising in the *Gentleman's Magazine* in June and July of 1736, Samuel and Tetty eventually had to admit defeat and close the school which they did in January, 1737. At this stage, it is worth taking a few sentences to describe the *Gentleman's Magazine* and Edward Cave, the person who founded it six years earlier in 1731. Edward Cave was an extremely clever man who was way ahead of his time in starting this publication. He was brought up in Rugby where his father was a cobbler and had been academically clever at the grammar school that he attended. However, he was accused by his schoolmaster of robbing his hen roost and had to leave. We do not know whether Cave was innocent or guilty of the charge, but this setback did not stop him in his career when he became first a printer, then reporter, then editor before coming up with the idea of this magazine. Unable to interest a publisher, he proceeded to put the small savings he had into the project, and started the magazine himself. Cave initiated several features and different ways of presenting news, including the previously unheard of practice of reporting debates in the Houses of Parliament. Years later, when Johnson was in London, Cave would go on to use Johnson as a contributor to the magazine which became very successful. In the meantime however, Johnson's own project, the Edial school, had failed and instead, he decided to concentrate on a career that would enable him to use his talents but would allow him to hide away – he started writing, and the first major piece of work that came out of this was the historical tragedy, 'Irene'.

By this time Johnson was feeling very guilty at having used up so much of Tetty's fortune and resolved to do something about it. On 2nd March, 1737, he set off for London with David Garrick, the intention being to find work and make some money as a writer. By a sad piece of timing, it was also the day that Johnson's brother, Nathaniel died. A few months earlier, sometime in 1736 when Nathaniel was twenty-three, he had gone into the book business like his father, opening a shop in Stourbridge but somehow, something had gone very wrong and it seems he acquired some debt. He wrote a letter to his mother in September, 1736 explaining his circumstances, and it appears that he made his way to Somerset and with the aid of his mother, worked as a book-binder and stationer in the town of Frome. He then died on 2nd March the following year when Samuel set off for London. There is little information as to what exactly happened between September, 1736 and March, 1737, but there were some murmurings that his death was suicide due to his financial situation. It was another forty years before Samuel made concerted efforts to find out what had happened to his brother but he discovered very little. No-one can rule suicide out completely but it is unlikely because Nathaniel was buried in consecrated ground on 5th March, 1737, and also in later years, Samuel referred to Nathaniel's "pious death". Samuel never did find out exactly what happened and often worried over the years whether he could have done more for his brother.

Meanwhile, David Garrick and Samuel were making their way to London. Garrick was actually making his way to Rochester but Johnson, who had never been further than Oxford, was glad of the company. Because of their financial situations, they travelled the distance of 120 miles by a curious but cheap way which was called "rode and tied". This consisted of them having just one horse between the two of them and riding it alternatively. The way it worked was that one would ride ahead for a certain distance and then stop and tie the horse up letting it rest. That person would then walk on ahead whilst the second person would eventually catch up with the tethered horse and ride it himself until he caught up with the first person. Eventually they found out that Samuel's brother had died on the day they started their journey and David's father, Peter Garrick had died without warning a week later. Once in London, they each borrowed a sum of money from a bookseller called Thomas Wilcox who worked in the Strand, and who they probably knew via Gilbert Walmesley. They asked for and received £5 each and both amounts were promptly repaid. They both took a room at the home of Richard Norris who had some connections with Garrick although he, Garrick, soon left the house and continued his journey to Rochester where he was to be tutored by the Revd. Mr. Colson.

Johnson still had no work and had little to live on. He sometimes dined at the home of Henry Hervey who was the fourth son of the Earl of Bristol. Once again, the connections that Gilbert Walmesley enjoyed had helped Johnson as it was through Walmesley that he had met Hervey. Hervey was an officer in the Dragoons, and Hervey and Walmesley had married the Aston sisters, Hervey marrying the heiress Catherine Aston whilst Walmesley had married her sister, Magdalen Aston. Johnson was a very loyal person, and he remained grateful to Hervey all his life.

Meanwhile, Johnson had a play to finish as he was still only halfway through 'Irene', so in order to escape the distractions of London, he went to live in Greenwich. However, a combination of missing Tetty and thinking he could finish the work just as easily in Lichfield, caused him to return there where he did indeed manage to finish the play. He then returned to London with Tetty in October 1737.

Johnson's first work was published in May 1738 and was a poem called 'London' which was about a character called Thales who escaped London to live in Wales, thinking that London was a place that neglected the poor and was full of crime. For some reason he published it anonymously but it was well received. The subject matter was strange too as preferring the country to London was so far removed from Johnson's own view of London. Alexander Pope felt that the author would soon be well known and although true, it took many years to happen. Johnson was hoping to receive payment for it as he had earned nothing from 'Irene' but desperately wanted to pay his own way in life and also pay Tetty back the money that she had lost in their school project. Robert Dodsley agreed to publish it and paid Johnson ten guineas (£10.50p) which he was more than happy with. The poem sold well, so well in fact that a second edition was printed in the space of a week, followed by a third and fourth edition.

During the eighteen months between December 1737 and May 1739, something rather sad happened. For whatever reason or reasons, Samuel and Tetty seem to have split up and lived apart. It could well be that money, or Johnson's lack of it may have been the cause. Always feeling guilty that he had lost a large portion of her fortune in the failed Edail school, he now became very depressed at his low income and inability to repay her. He wasn't completely broke however because he did some work for Cave over the period August, 1738 to April, 1739 that brought him £49./7/0d shillings (£49.35p), which Johnson certainly felt was enough to see him through that period. However, it is possible that in order to compensate Tetty for the loss of part of her fortune, he was stretching himself too much and repaying her more than he could afford leaving himself with barely enough to live on. Whether this caused tension between the two, we cannot be sure but during this period he met a man named Richard Savage (c1697-1743) who was an English poet. Savage was similar to Johnson in as much as he always seemed to be short of money and the two men would sometimes wander the streets of London together if they did not have enough for a room.

Richard Savage was quite a character and his origins are a mystery. He always claimed that he was the illegitimate son of The Countess of Macclesfield who had been divorced from Charles Gerard, the 2nd Earl of Macclesfield in 1698. The Countess married Colonel Henry Brett soon afterwards. However, the divorce happened because The Countess had given birth to two illegitimate children by Richard Savage, the 4th Earl Rivers, the second of whom was born on 16th January, 1697 and christened not as Richard Savage but as Richard Smith at St. Andrews, Holborn. A few months later he was taken to Ann Portlock who lived in Covent Garden although quite when he took the surname of Savage is unclear. He claimed that his mother had always been hostile towards him, and stopped Lord Rivers from leaving £6,000 to him and added that his mother attempted to have him removed from this country and taken to the West Indies. If this sounds fanciful then it's quite possibly totally untrue, although it seems that Savage was perfectly sincere in his belief that it *was* true. Whilst the Countess (Mrs. Brett) had always admitted that she had given birth to two illegitimate children, she always insisted that Richard Savage was not one of them and she never wavered from that view. Having admitted the births it would seem pointless to deny that Richard Savage was the second boy if he had been, and there were certainly some discrepancies in his story. He was wrong about who his godmother was and there was no evidence that Mrs. Brett was cruel as he had claimed – in fact there is plenty of evidence to show that she provided financially for them.

Savage had written poems and plays, and he was aptly named as he was best known as a satirist and he also loved gossip. His best known work was the poem called *'The Bastard'* which was published in 1728. Savage was expecting to be made Poet Laureate but this eluded him and although his income was minimal, he spent his life as a spendthrift and was always in debt. In 1732, King George II (1683-1760) had been on the throne for five years, and in that year his wife, Queen Caroline (1683-1737) awarded Savage a pension of £50 per year but on the Queen's death five years later, this was discontinued and Savage was reduced to complete poverty. He soon built up a string of creditors and his friends, who included Alexander Pope, were well aware of what was going to happen to Savage if action wasn't taken – they could see the debtor's prison looming. They came up with a scheme to give him an annual pension if he went to Wales to escape his creditors. However, Savage was one of these people who didn't make life easy for themselves and although he did go to Wales, he didn't stay there long before going to live in Bristol, continued the lifestyle that he had adopted for many years previously and he ended up in a debtors jail there and died on 1st August, 1743.

Meanwhile, Johnson was trying to work out how he could earn some money in order to pay Tetty back the part of her fortune that he had lost in the Edail

School project that had failed, and by so doing, feel able to live with her again. He was earning little money from his writing but he suddenly learned that the post of Headmaster was vacant at Appleby Grammar School which was a short distance from Lichfield. It was a job that he craved as carried with it was a salary of £60 plus accommodation, and if appointed, it would allow Tetty to live in the country which she loved, as opposed to London that she loathed. Unfortunately, Johnson was at a disadvantage as there was another candidate, Thomas Mould who was twenty five and had an M.A. from Oxford, whilst Johnson had no such qualification and he was also suffering from the tics and involuntary gesticulations that had always haunted him from his childhood. Johnson had friends who were supportive towards him however, and one of these was Lord Gower who had influence locally. Gower wrote to Oxford to see if an honorary degree could be awarded but was refused. Gower then wrote to a friend of Jonathan Swift (1667-1745), the Anglo-Irish poet, satirist and clergyman. Gower had asked the friend to ask Swift if he would use his connections to obtain a Masters Degree from the University of Dublin which would then give Johnson the possibility of obtaining a degree from Oxford. However, Swift refused to become involved in the scheme and declined Gower's request. Johnson was therefore unsuccessful in his application for this post but it did mean that he could stay with his mother Sarah who still lived in Lichfield and was being looked after by Tetty's daughter, Lucy Porter. Lucy Porter not only looked after her step-grandmother, but helped with the ailing bookshop which had very few customers. Lucy could easily have had a better life with people her own age, but seems to have willingly carried out her caring role with good grace.

Although Johnson loved his wife Tetty and wanted to achieve an arrangement whereby they could live together again, it is also true that he fell in love with someone else during this period, and although seemingly a passionate love, somehow it didn't interfere with his marriage or his desire to share his life with Tetty once more. However, whilst he was staying at Lichfield, he was seeing Gilbert Walmesley and had met Walmesley's sisters-in law. As mentioned earlier, Walmesley had married Magdalen Aston whilst Johnson's other friend who was involved with the Aston family was Henry Hervey, the son of the Earl of Bristol who had married Catherine Aston. There were however, eight sisters, all daughters of Sir Thomas Aston and it was the second daughter, Molly Aston, who had captured Johnson's heart. Johnson was thirty whilst Molly was thirty three and he loved her not only for her looks but for her intelligence. She was never nervous about meeting new people and engaging in conversation with them and she loved to talk economics or anything about literature. About twenty five years later Johnson was asked to describe the happiest time of his life and he replied that it was the year "in which he spent one whole evening" with Molly Aston. He even said that it didn't constitute mere happiness but described it as "rapture" and the thought of that one evening made that whole year special. He was also asked what his wife thought of the relationship and he replied:-

"She was jealous to be sure, and teized me sometimes when I would let her; and one day, as a fortune-telling gipsey passed us when we were walking out in company with two or three friends in the country, she made the wench look at my hand, but soon repented her curiosity; for (says the gypsey) Your heart is divided Sir, between a Betty and a Molly; Betty loves you best, but you take most delight in Molly's company; when I turned about to laugh, I saw my wife was crying Pretty charmer! She had no reason!"

Johnson spent some considerable time on a visit to Ashbourne to see his friend John Taylor, who he had known since they were both at Lichfield Grammar School together. Johnson eventually returned to Lichfield in January 1740 spending time with Gilbert Walmesley and his sister-in-law, Molly Aston. However, he was not there long before he received word from Tetty that she had injured her leg. The winter of 1740 was a particularly hard one and it's quite possible that she had slipped on the ice and either torn or sprained her tendons. Johnson was very concerned but did not return to London straight away, although he sent Tetty money towards the surgeon's costs. He wrote to her expressing his concern and guilt which was certainly genuine and ended the letter:

"...when I reflected that the most amiable woman in the world was exposed by my means to miseries which I could not relieve. I am My charming Love, Yours Sam: Johnson"

Johnson returned to London and Tetty in the early part of 1740. Her fortune was spent but they stayed together and economised as best as they could. Johnson scraped a living as best as he was able but never made the money that he hoped for. Meanwhile, the opposite was happening to a friend of theirs, David Garrick whose star rose quickly after his appearance as Richard III at Drury Lane. Johnson did not envy Garrick his success, but disliked the airs and graces that Garrick put on and a coolness descended upon their friendship. However, years later, when Johnson himself became famous, he would not allow any talk which was a criticism of Garrick to take place in his presence. Johnson's output of work was prolific and when his friend Richard Savage died in a debtor's jail in 1743, Johnson wrote *'Life of Savage'* in 1744 which to this day is considered a great piece of work, and other works he was known for were the play *'Irene'* and poems such as *'London'* and *'The Vanity of Human Wishes'* although the work that Johnson would always be best remembered for was yet to come.

A person who became a friend of Johnson's at about this time who should be mentioned was Sir John Hawkins (1719-89), the English musicologist and later an attorney. He was a good friend to Johnson until the end of Johnson's life when he became an executor and drafted Johnson's will for him. Hawkins was knighted in 1772 and he had a very valuable library of rare pieces of music. In 1776, he published a five volume book entitled *'General History of the Science and Practice of Music'*, which while considered good, was overshadowed by the more famous Dr. Charles Burney's four volume *'General History of Music'* (1776-89). Years later, Hawkins was to lose out again, publishing a biography of Johnson in 1787, only to be eclipsed by Boswell's *'The life of Samuel Johnson'* which came out in 1791 and which is certainly the most famous biography of Johnson ever written.

By this time, Johnson was mixing with many of the London publishers, and one of them, Robert Dodsley, suggested to Johnson the idea that he, Johnson, should write a dictionary. Johnson was not keen at first, but early in 1746, Dodsley and Johnson came to an understanding that Johnson would in fact take this enormous project on. Dodsley was not alone as there were about half a dozen other booksellers who wanted Johnson to undertake this work. Contrary to some beliefs, this was not going to be the first English dictionary as there had been dictionaries before, but Johnson's colleagues wanted him to write the definitive version. After some discussion, Johnson signed a contract with the publisher William Strahan on 18th June, 1746. Johnson said that he would finish the project in three years and when it was pointed out to him that the Academie Francaise had forty scholars working on the French dictionary and that it took them forty years, Johnson was unperturbed. He said, "This is the proportion. Let me see; forty times forty is sixteen hundred. As three to sixteen hundred, so is the proportion of an Englishman to a Frenchman". Johnson really believed that he could do it in three years and accordingly his contract stipulated 1,500 guineas to be paid over that period of time. This amount at last took Johnson out of poverty and allowed him to employ six amanuenses who were there to copy what Johnson required. It also enabled him to rent 17, Gough Square, a house just round the corner from Fleet Street.

Lord Chesterfield (1694-1773), an English Statesman was asked to be the patron of the dictionary. He had had a distinguished career in politics and was an excellent Lord-Lieutenant of Ireland in 1745 and the following year was one of the leading Secretaries of State. He came to the dictionary in 1746 and Johnson, having written his 'Plan' for the dictionary, wrote a dedication to Chesterfield in it. Chesterfield's involvement was arranged by Johnson's friend Robert Dodsley. Dodsley felt that if the dictionary had Chesterfield's name attached to it, the dictionary would resonate with the public that much more. The 'Plan' was printed and has been reprinted thousands of times but given Johnson's letter to him at the conclusion of the dictionary in 1755, it has put Chesterfield in a poor light as someone who had little involvement with the project.

There had been dictionaries before, notably in Italy and France as well as England, but Johnson wanted his to be the definitive version and he started off by collecting the existing English dictionaries and took the words from them with a view to elaborating their meanings. However, he found that this method didn't work for him and he changed the way he approached the project completely. By using brilliant writers such as William Shakespeare (1564-1616), John Milton (1608-74), and John Dryden (1631-1700), he took about 2,000 books and picked out words which he felt were appropriate. He didn't own anything like that number of books so had to borrow a great many from friends and it is highly unlikely that the owners were too pleased with what Johnson did to them. If he saw a word that he thought should be in his dictionary, he'd mark both the word and the page heavily, and over a period of years caused the books considerable damage. Johnson didn't just give a definition of each word – he put it in a quotation so that readers would be able to see how the word was used in a sentence and as each word had several meanings, Johnson wrote the number of sentences with each meaning shown. It was to be a massive project but as has already been shown, Johnson was very confident that he could manage it. At first Johnson thought the dictionary would provide a lasting definition of each word, and his dictionary would actually safeguard their meanings, but after a while he realised that this was impossible. The English language consistently evolves and all Johnson would be able to do is to record their meanings at the time the dictionary was written.

Things then started to go wrong for Johnson in two ways. The first was that after a while he became very dissatisfied with the way in which the dictionary was turning out and by 1750 had run out of money which meant that he had to lay his helpers off as he was unable to pay them. The second thing that distressed him was the illness of his wife Tetty. She was living at Gough Square but was using her illness as a reason for leaving London and visiting Hampstead which was then just a village. She was spending most of her time in bed and taking large amounts of laudanum and drinking copious amounts of gin. Eventually she rented a house in Hampstead and stayed there most of the time until her illness became worse, and then for the last year of her life she returned to Gough Square. As if her illness wasn't bad enough, something very sad happened to Tetty at this time. When she had married Johnson in July, 1735, her son Jervis cut himself off from his mother, vowing never to have anything to do with her again. Jervis Henry always stuck to this vow and at the time of her illness was now a Captain in the navy. One day during the course of her illness, he knocked on her door and asked the maid if her mistress was at home. The maid replied that she was but was ill and Jervis instructed the maid to tell Tetty that her son called to see how she was. The maid asked Jervis if he would come up to see his mother and ran up herself to tell the overjoyed Tetty that her son had come to see her.

Naturally Tetty was beside herself with happiness at this news and asked that the maid tell Jervis that she longed to embrace him. However, when the maid arrived at the bottom of the stairs, Jervis had gone and the experience of having her hopes raised and then dashed left the very sick Tetty bereft. It had been the only time he had made the effort to see his mother in the seventeen years since her marriage to Samuel and he had dashed her hopes in the cruelist way possible. Tetty died on 28th March, 1752 at the age of sixty-three and a distraught Johnson was quite incapable of organising the funeral so his friend John Hawkesworth took over the arrangements and she was buried at his parish church in Bromley, Kent.

Meanwhile, to go back a year or two, Samuel had two problems to worry about, and given the natural depressive nature of the man, it is a wonder that he survived them. Tetty's illness devastated him, but another problem was the dictionary itself. His financial position was critical as the dictionary money had run out and he could not work on it without funds to pay his helpers. He also needed money to pay for Tetty's medical care but for two years he did no work on the dictionary which enraged the printers who had paid for the work but had not received it. By 1750, he had written the first 120 sheets which represented the first three letters of the alphabet, but as already mentioned, he had run out of money and had laid his amanuenses off being unable to pay them. However, after difficult negotiations between Johnson and the publishers, they agreed to pay Johnson more money, and he managed to start work on it again. Despite his constant depression, Johnson somehow found the energy to continue and he completed volume one by April 1753. Having got their fingers burned at the beginning of the project by paying Johnson in advance, the publishers now paid him a guinea (£1.05) per sheet completed which meant that Johnson had very little money and could only re-employ two helpers. This was a smart move on the part of the publishers as Johnson's desperate need for money spurred him on and another fourteen months saw the second volume finished in July 1754. Johnson's spirits seem to improve greatly along with his energy levels, and not only did he work hard at the dictionary, he also socialised more in the evenings, meeting friends in the local taverns. This renewed enthusiasm lasted until the death of Tetty when he slipped back into the depression that had been there before, but this time there could be no way that the dictionary could be held up. He tried to get over his grief by filling his house with people, and one of these was the twelve year old Frances Barber, a rescued slave boy who Johnson more or less treated as a son. Originally from Jamaica, Frank Barber had been brought to England by Colonel Bathurst, who was the father of Johnson's friend, Richard. Colonel Bathurst hated slavery and because Frank was an orphan, Bathurst was doing him a great favour by bringing him to England where he would have his freedom. Eventually, the Colonel asked his son to take care of the boy but Richard couldn't cope with the responsibility and handed him over to Johnson who he knew as a kindly person who was also very lonely. Richard Bathurst had been at Peterhouse, Cambridge between 1738 and 1745 where he had studied medicine, and once qualified, had gone to London in an attempt to set up practice. He and Johnson became great friends and in 1749, Johnson founded a club based in Ivy Lane, which was to be a place where friends could meet for interesting conversation. Richard Bathurst, along with Johnson and about eight others met regularly and Johnson was mortified when Bathurst died in 1762. For years afterwards, Johnson could not speak of him without tears welling in his eyes and many years later he once wrote of Bathurst to his friend Mrs. Thrale:

"...you would have lov'd Bathurst as well as I did, if I would have suffer'd you ever to see him, but that I would never have done, I should have lost somewhat of each of you".

Johnson took Francis Barber into his home, and when he, Johnson, died, he left Barber, by then in his early forties, the sum of £700 plus Tetty's wedding ring. There was also a man living in Johnson's house by the name of Robert Levet, a man who pretended to be a doctor but had absolutely no qualifications whatsoever. What he did know about medicine he picked up by attending lectures with some French surgeons who seemed to take a liking to him when he worked in a cafe that they ate and drank in in Paris. Although unqualified, his heart seemed to have been in the right place because when he returned to London, he set up his own practice and treated poor people who would otherwise not be able to seek medical help through lack of money. Levett charged little, sometimes a small drink of spirits, sometimes nothing at all. He was a good friend to Johnson over the years and was another person who lived in Johnson's house. There was also a blind poet by the name of Anna Williams who over a period of years continually asked Johnson if he could arrange to have her work published. However, this put Johnson into a difficult position as he felt her poetry was simply not good enough for any publisher to be remotely interested and therefore kept trying to stall her. His kind and generous nature made it difficult for him to tell her the truth and she was too naive to realise that he was using delaying tactics which resulted in her often getting cross with him over his seeming lack of help. Also residing in Johnson's house was Elizabeth Swynfen, the daughter of Johnson's godfather, Dr. Swynfen but who was later known as Mrs. Elizabeth Desmoulins as she had married a French writing teacher with that surname. Mrs. Desmoulins had been Tetty's companion but during Tetty's final illness Elizabeth would go to Johnson's room at his behest and talk to him until he fell asleep. After Johnson's death, Boswell interviewed her and asked her if he had made any sexual advances. She appeared to give conflicting answers by first saying that he had, but then saying that "he never did anything that was beyond the limits of decency".

Johnson desperately wanted letters after his name and in fact said that he would not allow the dictionary to be published until he had achieved this. He had become friendly with Thomas Warton (1728-90) who at the time of the dictionary, had just started a long career as a Fellow of Trinity. An English critic, he was the brother of the equally well known Joseph Warton (1722-1800), who was also an English critic and like his brother, also went on to know Johnson as both brothers joined the Literary Club along with Samuel. Thomas had been educated at Winchester and Trinity College, Oxford, and it was in 1751 that he became a Fellow. Thomas Warton introduced Johnson to the Radcliffe librarian, Francis Wise, and between the two of them, they helped Johnson attain his much sought after degree from Oxford which was conferred on 20th February, 1755, allowing him to put the letters M.A. after his name at the beginning of the dictionary. The dictionary itself was published in April, 1755 and is considered to this day to be an amazing piece of work. The pages were nearly 18 inches tall and the book itself was 20 inches wide when it was open and contained 42,773 entries. Each dictionary sold for £4. 10 shillings, (£4.50p), roughly the equivalent of £300 in the currency value of 2010. It was known as Johnson's Dictionary and many of the quotations contained within it were used by the people who compiled the New English Dictionary and Webster's Dictionary but despite its brilliance, it was several years before the publishers made a profit from their investment. Johnson himself made no profit whatsoever because there were no such things as royalties in the 18th century. Writers sold their books to a publisher for a flat fee and Johnson had already received his payment in the form of the initial 1,500 guineas and the payments for each sheet that he had produced after that.

During the nine years he was involved with the dictionary, Johnson wrote various essays, sermons and poems. He wrote *The Vanity of Human Wishes'* in 1748 and received fifteen guineas from Robert Dodsley for the copyright. He also wrote a series of essays for a periodical he called the *'Rambler'*, and the work that he carried out on this happened twice a week between 20th March, 1750 and 14th March, 1752. The *'Rambler'* became very popular and was re-printed nine times during Johnson's life, although few people knew exactly who the author was. After that, Johnson spent a year producing articles for the *'Adventurer'* every two weeks from 3rd March, 1753 to 2nd March, 1754.

Johnson continued to write prolifically but his work didn't make him wealthy or happy and on 16th March, 1756 he was arrested for a debt of money that he owed which was £5.18s (£5.90). He was horrified at the thought of going into Marshalsea Prison where the conditions were absolutely barbaric. Either unable or unwilling to contact his publishing friends, he wrote to the publisher Samuel Richardson who had lent him money before. Richardson not only lent him the money, but rounded it up to six guineas which was more than enough to save him from the debtor's prison. Johnson's gratitude was immense and the two men became firm friends after that. On 2nd June, 1756, shortly after his problems with the arrest, Johnson signed a contract to prepare an eight volume edition of Shakespeare in eighteen months, an idea that had been simmering in his mind for the best part of ten years. Johnson had been fascinated by Shakespeare since he was a very young boy, but now that he was older he felt that he could improve their presentation. He felt that:

"…were transcribed for the players by those who may be supposed to have seldom understood them; they were transmitted by copiers equally unskilful, who still multiplied errors; they were perhaps sometimes mutilated by the actors, for the sake of shortening the speeches; and were at last printed without correction of the press".

Given the erratic way he wrote the dictionary, it was either foolish or an amazing act of faith by the publishers to give Johnson a contract because to finish it in eighteen months would mean a volume every two months with an additional two months at the end to finalise everything. That was not all, because added to that, he would need to write a preface. It was ill thought out by both parties, Johnson and the publishers, to think that he could finish it within that period of time, and given the nature of his method of writing, it was never going to be finished in the space of eighteen months. Johnson did complete the work but it was nine years before it was published on 10th October, 1765 under the title *'The Plays of William Shakespeare, in Eight Volumes… To which are added Notes by Sam. Johnson'*. One thousand copies were initially printed but they sold out so quickly that a second edition was printed very soon afterwards. Another edition was published in 1773 and a further revised edition five years later in 1778 making it a success story in every way.

Another important friend that Johnson met at this time was Joshua Reynolds (1723-92), later Sir Joshua Reynolds. He was in his thirties when he met Johnson, and he went on to become one of England's most famous painters. He was probably at the height of his fame in 1760 and in 1764 he founded the Literary Club of which Johnson was one of its famous members along with others like Edmund Burke, the English statesman, David Garrick, actor and theatre manager, and James Boswell, who would later become Johnson's closest friend and biographer, to name but three. Reynolds and Johnson became very close – Reynolds had read Johnson's *'Life of Savage'* and was impressed by both the book and Johnson the man. Reynolds was probably only second to Boswell in his knowledge of Johnson and when Boswell wrote his biography of Johnson, he dedicated it to Reynolds. It was not too long after their first meeting that Reynolds painted the first of several portraits of Johnson. It was also during this time that Johnson's financial pressures had eased. He had produced a large amount of work which gave him a living of sorts, but he was also granted a pension of £300 in July 1762 by a youthful King George III who had only come to the throne two years before. The King granted this to Johnson in recognition of the dictionary he had finished seven years earlier, and it certainly took the financial pressure off Johnson for the first time in his adult life. Johnson went on to meet the King five years later in 1767. Johnson would often walk up to Buckingham House to use the library there which was massive. The King's librarian was a man named Frederick Barnard who was always very helpful to Samuel, and on one occasion when Johnson was there, Mr. Barnard told the King who expressed a wish to meet him. They talked about the various libraries at Oxford and Cambridge and the King then asked Johnson if he was undertaking any writing at present. Johnson replied that he wasn't, saying that he felt he had said all he knew and had nothing more to say that would interest anyone. The King replied by paying a compliment about Johnson's writing and asked him whether he would undertake 'the literary biography of this country' which Johnson agreed in principle to write. His *'Lives of the Poets'* came closer than any of his fellow writers did to complete the King's request.

Johnson had many people who entered his life, and one of these was Charlotte Lennox (1730-1804), the British author and poet. She was born Charlotte Ramsey in Gibralter and her father was James Ramsey, either a Captain in the Royal Navy or an army officer, historians cannot seem to agree as to which. Her mother is thought to be half Scottish and half Irish, although again, information on her is unclear because we do not know her name. Charlotte's first printed poetry was entitled *'Poems on Several Occasions'* which was published in 1747 and she was hoping for some kind of position at Court but her life changed when she married Alexander Lennox. Lennox seemed to be a strange choice as he was rarely employed but undeterred she carried on with her writing and her most successful poem *'The Art of Coquetry'* was published in *'The Gentleman's Magasine'*. She also had a successful novel entitled *'The Female Quixote'* published in 1752 but it was not really recognised until after she died when it also came out in 1783, 1799, and 1810. Johnson took her under his wing and both he and Samuel Richardson encouraged her at a time when it was difficult for women writers to be accepted. She mixed with the likes of Johnson, Reynolds, and Samuel Richardson and enjoyed a lengthy career. Johnson was a loyal person and appreciated all his friends, but maybe one of the most important, if not *the* most important friend he had was James Boswell (1740-95), the diarist and lawyer as mentioned earlier, and they would become friends until Johnson's death in 1784.

Boswell's father was Alexander Boswell, 8th Laird of Auchinleck who was a judge on the Scottish bench and his mother was Euphemia Erskine. James was the eldest of eight children and would one day inherit his father's title. When he was five years old, he attended James Mundell's Academy where he was taught Latin, English, writing and arithmetic. The Academy was considered to be very advanced for its time but Boswell was unhappy whilst he was there and at the age of eight years, was eventually removed and educated at home by a succession of tutors. This carried on until 1753 when at the age of thirteen, he started studying arts at the University of Edinburgh and stayed there for five years until 1758. In the middle of that course, he became ill with depression and some sort of nervous illness, but fortunately he recovered and if anything, he became even more healthy than he had been before he had become unwell. He put on weight, was more outgoing and on many occasions, showed that he had a good sense of humour. The following year when he was nineteen, Boswell attended the University of Glasgow and he was taught by, amongst others, Adam Smith (1723-90), the great Scottish economist and philosopher. However, he was not there long because he decided to become a Catholic which would bar him practicing as a lawyer and becoming a Member of Parliament amongst other things. Upon hearing this his father ordered him home which resulted in him running away to London where he spent three months living a free and easy lifestyle, worlds away from the behaviour expected by his father. The 8th Laird retaliated by ordering Boswell's return to Scotland whereupon he went back to Edinburgh University and studied law with his allowance cut to £100 per annum. However, he seems to have knuckled down to some hard work because he did well with his law exams, and the result was that his father increased his allowance to £200 per year and let him return to London where he arrived in November, 1762. The scene was set for the famous meeting between himself and Johnson. Boswell has certainly been famous since his death in 1795, but this is largely due to the fact that he knew Johnson and wrote the famous *'Life of Johnson'* after his friend's death and which was published in 1791. However, there was more to Boswell than that and much of his other work has only been recognised in recent years. It is only in the 20th century that his journals, kept throughout his life, have been discovered, the contents of which have consisted of Boswell writing down the conversations that he had with famous people. The contents of a *'Life of Johnson (1791)'* and the *'Journal of a Tour to the Hebrides with Samuel Johnson (1785)'* were taken from the information recorded in Boswell's writings. Boswell was just twenty two years old when he met the fifty three year old Johnson and was certainly in awe of the older man in the initial years.

Boswell's father was about the same age as Johnson and given that Boswell was a totally different person than his father, he almost certainly saw Johnson as a father figure in the first few years because Boswell's own father had always been moralistic and dour, whilst James was sexually promiscuous, very idealistic and had a romantic nature and he had even managed to get a serving girl pregnant.

Boswell had still to meet Johnson and he finally managed this at a bookshop at 8, Russell Street, Covent Garden, that Johnson would frequent from time to time. The shop was run by an actor named Tom Davies who had invited Johnson to meet Boswell several times, but each time Johnson had refused. When they did meet on 16th May, 1763, it was purely by chance as Boswell and Davies were in the back of the shop drinking tea and it was on that day that Johnson just happened to enter the shop. Boswell was very nervous at first meeting Johnson as he had heard that the great man did not like Scottish people. Boswell asked Davies not to tell Johnson where he, Boswell, came from. Davies immediately cried out "From Scotland". Boswell then cut in and said, "Mr. Johnson, I do indeed come from Scotland, but I cannot help it". Johnson's reply, which has since become quite famous was, "That Sir, I find, is what a very great many of your countrymen cannot help" and it initially left Boswell stunned and speechless and nervous as to how to continue the conversation. He needn't have worried because it was Johnson who did most of the talking and after Davies had shown him out, he told Boswell that Johnson did in fact like him. The friendship had to be put on hold however as Boswell was due to leave England in August and settle in Holland for over two years to study law, although he did see Johnson several times before he left and the two men held long conversations. Johnson actually went to Harwich with Boswell on 6th August 1763, to see him onto the packetboat and the two men left each other with an affectionate embrace.

Boswell did not return to England for two and a half years because after he had studied law at Utrecht, he did not return home immediately, but travelled the continent and interviewed notables such as Jean Jacques Rousseau (1712-78), the French political philosopher, Francois Marie Arouet de Voltaire (1694-1778), the French author and the embodiment of the 18th century enlightenment, and Pasquale de Paoli (1725-1807), the Corsican patriot, who had returned to Corsica in 1755 to help lead the fight for Corsican independence. Many people think that once James Boswell had met Johnson, the two men spent almost every waking hour in each other's company but this is simply not the case at all. When Boswell arrived home in February, 1766, he didn't live in London initially but travelled back to Edinburgh to finish his law degree and then he stayed there for more than ten years practicing law, although he was to make several trips to London to meet Johnson before finally settling back so that the two men could resume their friendship. Another idea that has often followed Boswell around is the impression that he was simply a young man hero-worshipping an older man, and consequently an air of innocence has often been attached to him. This is far from the truth however. Boswell married his cousin, Margaret Montgomerie in November, 1769 and they had seven children, four sons and three daughters. Boswell was often unfaithful to his wife, not by having a serious relationship with someone else, but by frequent visits to prostitutes, and each time she forgave him, staying faithful to him until her death from tuberculosis in 1789.

Despite his obviously flawed character, Boswell was a clever man and had interviewed many great men as well as Johnson, and apart from Rousseau and Voltaire as already mentioned, he had also interviewed William Pitt the Elder, later Lord Chatham (1708-1778), one of the greatest politicians in our history. However, it was Johnson who stood out as the interviewee who was the most interesting and it was Johnson's qualities and intellect added to the close friendship that he shared with Boswell that gave him so much material with which to work from when he, Boswell, wrote his 'Life of Johnson', which was finally published in 1791, seven years after Johnson's death. During their friendship, Boswell had almost always carried a notebook with him to note down what his friend and surrogate father was saying. Their friendship culminated in their trip to the Hebrides which commenced on 18th August, 1773 and finishing on 2nd November when they arrived at the home of Boswell's father where they were to spend a fairly tense week. Johnson was to write his *'Journal of the Tour of the Hebrides'*, which was published in 1785, the year after his death. It was Johnson who had made the original suggestion to Boswell in July, 1763, that he, Johnson, would like to go to the Hebrides and whilst at first dismissing the idea, Boswell began to realise that Johnson wasn't getting any younger and if it were to be done, it would be better that it was done sooner rather than later. However, it was another ten years after the original idea was mooted that the two men started talking about it seriously and it was decided that August, 1773 would be the right time to commence. On 6th August, Johnson travelled to Edinburgh and arrived at Boyd's Inn on Saturday, 14th August whereupon he sent a note to the waiting Boswell, who immediately came to the inn to fetch him. Johnson stayed at Boswell's house and met his wife Margaret and his first impression of her was very positive. The same could not be said for Margaret's feelings for Johnson however, as she disliked the strange hours that he kept which got on her nerves, and she was also against the trip to the Hebrides anyway. She was supposed to have angrily said to her husband of the proposed trip: "I have seen many a bear led by a man; but I never before saw a man led by a bear". Fortunately, Johnson only stayed there for four days before the two men set off on the 18th August.

Boswell took his servant, Joseph Ritter, with them and they started the trip which was planned to take twelve weeks. They went due north along the east coast with the idea of reaching Aberdeen and then head west and go further north to Inverness, then south along Loch Ness and upon reaching Fort Augustus, they were to travel to Skye and the Hebrides and then return to Edinburgh, possibly stopping off at Auchinleck to see Boswell's father. The trip went pretty much to plan and although at times Johnson was unwell, he was in good spirits. Meanwhile, Boswell kept a record of all the things that Johnson spoke of and immediately after Johnson's death, published *'The Journal of a Tour to the Hebrides with Samuel Johnson L.L.D. (1786)'* which was brought out before his monumental biography, *'The life of Samuel Johnson'* which came later in 1791. Johnson was really enjoying himself as they travelled across Scotland and he decided that he too would write a book about his and Boswell's travels. He didn't write it until they had been home some time and it was published in January 1775 having the title *'Journey to the Western Islands of Scotland'*. Although it was written some time after their return it was couched in the present tense but Johnson was able to refresh his memory by using the letters he had written to Hester Thrale at the time. They finished travelling more or less to the timescale that was planned and arrived at Auchinleck on 2nd November where they spent almost a week with Boswell's father. Although Boswell warned Johnson in advance to keep off certain topics, it was almost inevitable that the two older men would clash once politics was discussed, but they did manage to reach an accord before Boswell and Johnson left for Edinburgh where they spent a few days before Johnson caught the coach to London which he did on 22nd November, arriving in London four days later.

Hester Thrales' name has been mentioned earlier in this chapter, and it is time to write about her in a little more detail. If Johnson's meeting with Boswell was to change Johnson's life, then his meeting with Hester and Henry Thrale changed it again when they met on 9th January, 1765, eight years prior to Boswell and Johnson touring the Hebrides but less than two years after the two men originally met. Hester and Samuel were introduced by Arthur Murphy, who had known Henry Thrale for many years before Henry married her. She was born Hester Salusbury in 1741 and lived to the age of eighty years, eventually dying in 1821. She was a welsh writer, born in Bodvel, Caernarvonshire, and had married Henry Thrale, a wealthy Southwark brewer on 11th October, 1763, at St. Anne's Chapel, Soho, London, just over a year before the couple met Johnson. They had twelve children before Henry's death on 4th April, 1781. Their house in Streatham was always full of the fashionable people of the day, such as David Garrick (1717-79), the dramatist and writer, Richard Brinsley Sheridan (1751-1816), the Irish dramatist, Joshua Reynolds (1723-92), the English portrait painter, Warren Hastings (1732-1818), best known for being the English administrator in India and of course Johnson himself. Later on can be added the name of Fanny Burney (1752-1840), the novelist who would one day inspire Jane Austen. At the early part of her career, Fanny had written a novel entitled 'Evelina' but it had been published anonymously on 29th January, 1778 and whilst practically all who were a part of Hester Thrales' set had read it, none could guess who the author was which was a source of amusement to Fanny who was often in the room whilst they were discussing it. Some thought that her father, Charles Burney (1726-1814), the well known musician had written it whilst others dismissed the possibility that it could have been written by a woman. However, the cause of the greatest pride for Fanny was that Johnson himself liked it. Hester wrote to Dr. Burney on 22nd July, 1779 and said that:

"Dr. Johnson returned home full of praise of the book I had lent him, and protesting that there were passages in it which might do honour to Richardson..." The Richardson that Johnson was referring to was Samuel Richardson (1689-1761), the famous English novelist, and to be compared to him by someone such as Johnson filled Fanny with pride. Eventually of course, Fanny was identified as the author and went on to become famous in her own right and a favourite of Johnson's.

However, to return to the Thrales household, although the Streatham house was always full of interesting people, and despite the fact that Henry Thrales was a wealthy man, the marriage was not always happy. Despite his wealth and enjoying the company of a clever wife, he seemed dissatisfied with his lot. At one stage he developed feelings or possibly just an infatuation for a young woman by the name of Sophia Streatfeild – a beautiful young girl much younger than Thrale and rather manipulative. She was not only beautiful but also clever having been taught the classics when she was younger. Hester, not unnaturally, did not find the position she was in comfortable, and it may have allowed her to fall in love with another man rather sooner after her husband's death than she might otherwise have done.

However, in the meantime, the Thrales took Johnson in and he was treated as one of the family, and he relied on the arrangement over many years. When he first arrived there, he would confine himself to his room and involve himself in complex mathematical calculations in an effort to focus his mind. Hester was very caring towards Johnson, and gradually managed to coax him out and take some fresh air. He couldn't have had a better home; there were always people around to provide stimulating conversation, he had privacy if he wanted it, and there were servants around should he need anything. On top of that, Hester would sometimes sit with him until 3 or 4am making him tea or simply talking and listening to him. It was not just Hester who Johnson was fond of, he was also fond of her husband, Henry, and when Henry became ill, Johnson was upset when he, Johnson, was excluded from a trip to Bath followed by another to Brighton. The reason that Hester gave him was that she and Henry had Fanny Burney with them and there was no room for Samuel. Johnson was deeply hurt at this as he had been friends with Hester and Henry for a far longer period of time than Fanny had been, and it was at this point that he knew the relationship he had with her, not to mention a change in his way of life, would result. Although the trip did not really have the effect of making Henry better, he decided that he would socialise more and when they returned, Henry took a house in Grosvenor Square and to his delight, Johnson returned to the Thrale family home and had his own room there. They moved there on 30th January, 1781, but soon afterwards, Henry became very tired and apathetic. Doctor Lucas Pepys was asked to attend and all knew that Thrale was dying. During that night, Johnson sat with his friend and was with him when he died at 5am on the 4th April 1781.

By the time that Henry died, Johnson had spent many years at the Thrale house in Streatham more or less becoming part of the family, but after Henry had died, he found that Hester would share her time with someone else, her own mother, Mrs. Salusbury, and Johnson and Mrs. Salusbury would therefore vie for Hester's attention and did not get along at all. At some stage however, Hester's mother became quite seriously ill and Johnson softened his attitude towards her with the result that they eventually became friends. However, a much bigger obstacle to his friendship with Hester came when she met and fell in love with the Italian music teacher, Gabriel Mario Piozzi and she married him on 25th July, 1784. Johnson felt very threatened because he knew that everything would now change and it is probably fair to say that his feelings were more of fright as to what the future held for him rather than any feelings of anger.

Hester had been a good friend over the best part of eighteen years and despite the fact that she was many years younger than Johnson, she was also possibly a sort of mother figure. She even looked like Samuel's mother, Sarah Johnson and when the subject of Hester marrying Piozzi came up, then Samuel let his views be known and it may well be that he genuinely thought that Piozzi was not the right man for Hester. However, it is far more likely that he hoped that the marriage wouldn't take place simply because he could see that his home life as he knew it was almost certainly at an end. In the event, this marriage and Johnson's reaction to it caused a rift between himself and Hester that was barely healed by the time of Johnson's own death in December of that year.

Johnson had been unwell for some time prior to August, 1782 but appeared to be getting better so it was at that time that Hester decided she had to tell Johnson about her plans for travelling and living abroad for a period of time. However, she felt that she had to tread carefully as on the 17th January previous,

Johnson's friend Robert Levett died of a heart attack when he was seventy seven years old. Levett was important to Johnson and this was a bitter blow to him as he suspected that his life at Streatham was drawing to a close, and wanted to keep close to those people who had been close to him before he went to Streatham in order that he may feel some continuity to his way of life. For some time Johnson had dreaded hearing what Hester had to say but when she did get round to telling him, she was surprised at his reaction. She thought that he would be completely against it as he had been when first told of its possibility, but because of the kindness shown to him by the Thrales over the best part of eighteen years, Johnson reacted by being supportive of Hester's future plans, even though they did not include him. However, his supportive manner had the opposite effect on Hester than that which he had hoped for. It was almost as if she wanted Johnson to be upset but when they talked about it, instead of being upset at her movements, his encouraging manner confused her. Instead of her realising that he was being gallant and brave, she took it that he simply didn't care that the Streatham home was coming to an end and they would see very little of each other in the future. Letters went back and forth between the two and an uneasy truce broke out. When Hester went to Brighton in the latter part of 1782, she asked Johnson to accompany her which at first he was reluctant to do because he knew that the situation there would not be as homely as Streatham had been. However, worse than that would be a return to his own home in Bolt Court which would mean him being virtually alone as Levett had already died and Miss Williams was very unwell. Not only that, but he too was unwell as Hester had found out on 4th January, 1783 whilst they were sitting together at dinner. He could hardly eat and kept saying: "You little know how ill I am".

On 20th March 1782, Boswell had returned to London – his first visit for nearly two years. When he saw Johnson the following day, he too realised how ill his friend was. Boswell stayed several weeks, but when he left Johnson on 29th May, he was very concerned about Johnson's health and wondered whether he would see him again. He was right to be worried as on 17th June, 1783, Johnson had a paralytic stroke. He managed to write a scribbled note to his neighbour to ask if he could write to Hester at Bath to tell her and ask for her support as he had virtually none at home. Mrs. Desmoulins had left the house and Miss Williams, blind and unwell herself could offer nothing. Hester offered none herself and not only did not go to London as Johnson clearly wished for, but failed to invite him to Bath once he had recovered, an oversight which hurt him deeply.

In the event, Johnson was never going to recover as there was little treatment for what he was suffering from. First of all, he had circulatory problems, the sign of which was probably the stroke that he had in June, 1783. Secondly, he had chronic bronchitis and quite possibly emphysema. Thirdly, he had heart failure for which there was little or no treatment, and although not as serious as above, the fourth condition he suffered from was arthritis, although Johnson always referred to it as gout. It wasn't life threatening as such, but added to the others, combined to make him ill and depressed. The arthritis also stopped him walking any distances which he used to do to help his depression. Johnson's friend, Sir John Hawkins, drafted a will for Samuel but left the blanks for Johnson to fill in but instead of doing that Johnson merely signed it as it was. When Hawkins pointed this out to him, he merely replied that Hawkins should have completed the blanks himself.

However, after another reproof from Hawkins, Johnson eventually completed a will but it was only just before he made it that he realised how much money he had which was £2,300, a sizeable sum in 1784. He left £200 to the representatives of Thomas Inneys, a bookseller who many years before had helped his father; £100 to a domestic, the sale of his Lichfield house to some distant relations and the balance was to go to Francis Barber in the form of an annual payment. Hawkins was furious that he had been left out completely and was also annoyed that Francis Barber should receive so much but there was nothing he could do about it. However, in order to make up for being omitted, Hawkins took Johnson's watch, a totally mean thing to do as Johnson had earmarked it for Barber. Thankfully, Hawkins did not get away with this mean spirited act, because the watch was recovered and given to its rightful new owner, Francis Barber.

Johnson was never going to get any better and he had to take to his bed for the final week in December 1784. He asked Dr. Brocklesby who was attending him whether he would get better and Brocklesby confirmed that he wouldn't. He then stopped taking medicine on the grounds that if he wasn't going to recover, there was no point. The pain in his legs was becoming unbearable and he asked for a lancet which along with scissors that he had hidden in his bed, enabled him to make deep incisions in his legs which had the effect of relieving the pain. At one point he refused food but by the 12th of December he was becoming delirious. There were several people in the house during his final hours, but Johnson's final words were to an Italian teacher called Francesco Sastres who had become a friend, and Johnson spoke his final words to him which were: "I am Moriturus" meaning: "I who am about to die". He died quietly at 7pm on 13th December, 1784 thankfully at peace and with no pain.

It is difficult to sum Johnson up – his character cannot be easily drawn in a few words. He had a brilliant brain, eccentric, he cared not for appearance as he was often seen as scruffy, a brilliant writer, a loving husband, a hypochondriac, a caring person who took the young Jamaican born Frank Barber in to his home, a man capable of creating brilliant literary works, a wit, a man who loved company so long as it was not his own, and a devout conservative Anglican who had great respect for people who held different views from his own. He was an opponent of slavery and in that he was years ahead of his time and would no doubt have supported William Wilberforce's campaign against the barbarity of the dreadful trafficking of fellow human beings. The campaign was started by three young politicians who had all been born in 1759, William Pitt the Younger, William Grenville, and William Wilberforce in that famous meeting between the three men on 12th May, 1787, under an oak tree on Pitt's estate.

In later life, Johnson loved to be holding forth on a subject surrounded by friends in a tavern in the centre of the place he loved more than anywhere else – London. He was always quoted as saying: "The man who is tired of London is tired of life". However, despite his many pieces of written work and the different facets of his character, the thing that he will always be remembered for is the creation of the amazing dictionary, and his burial in Westminster Abbey is justly deserved.

-oOOo-

16
Thomas Paine
(1737-1809)

Writer and political agitator.

As there is a chapter on Lord North, the British Prime Minister who fought against the Americans in the War of Independence from 1776 to 1783, it would seem fair to cover another person who would look at the conflict from a different light, that man being Thomas Paine, variously described as a radical, pamphleteer, revolutionary, writer, intellectual and inventor, amongst others.

Paine was born on 29th February, 1737 in Thetford, to Joseph and Frances Pain (nee Cocke). Young Thomas was brought up in a religious household. His father was a Quaker, a member of the Society of Friends which was formed nearly a hundred years before, in the 1650's. Slightly (some say very) puritanical, the Quakers did not believe in priests being paid or deferring to people of so-called superior standing. They also refused to pay any tithes and their stance was acceptable in the republican Britain of Oliver Cromwell, but with the restoration of the Monarchy in 1660 under Charles II, they suffered a great deal of persecution. However, Joseph was expelled from the Quakers when he married Frances because he had committed the sin of marrying someone with a different faith. Frances was an Anglican, a member of the established church and she made sure that if Thomas was exposed to the Quaker religion, he would also receive a grounding in the virtues of the more establishment faith. Thomas was baptized into the Church of England and was also persuaded to be confirmed, but in later life, he rid himself of any confusion or mixed loyalties towards his parents that he might have had by simply rejecting both faiths although he tried to abide by both their teachings.

Thomas's birthplace, Thetford, was an important market town as well as serving as a coach stage post in this rural area. It is not certain when he added an 'e' to the name, some sources saying it was when he went to America in 1774 although others say he was using the new name in 1769 whilst he was still in Lewes, Sussex. There was no compulsory education then, but in the event, he attended Thetford Grammar School between the years 1744 to 1749, going there as a seven-year-old and finishing when he was twelve. His father earned his living as a stay maker, which is someone who manufactures women's corsets and shortly after leaving Thetford Grammar, young Thomas was apprenticed to his father. The parents weren't wealthy, but Thomas's father earned £30 per annum which was considerably more than labourers would receive, but when he was older, Thomas realised that his parents hadn't been wealthy and had struggled to give him the education that he had received.

Thomas had no brothers and sisters which was unusual in the 18th century as at that time there was virtually no form of birth control and wives seemed to be pregnant every eighteen months. There was a sister called Elizabeth who was born in 1738, the year after Paine was born but she died shortly afterwards. The reason that there were no other children may well have had something to do with the fact that Thomas's mother Frances, was eleven years older than her husband Joseph, and went past childbearing age, or maybe she simply didn't like intimacy. It does seem that she was not a very likeable person and did not show affection, either to her husband or her son, and it is a sad indictment of her that many years later when Thomas was in America he met a woman he found thoroughly unpleasant, and remarked to a friend that she reminded him of his mother.

Paine's apprenticeship lasted six years and in that time he learned how to cut, shape and stitch corsets prior to him presumably following in his father's footsteps and becoming a master staymaker. However, the ending of his apprenticeship co-incided with a downturn in his father's fortunes – the fashions had changed and there simply was not the demand for the kind of garment that he was producing. This meant that Thomas saw no future for himself in that kind of profession and so in the summer of 1756, he left Thetford and travelled to London.

It is difficult to know quite why he went to London, unless it was simply to broaden his horizons, but it wasn't long before he was able to do just that. On the 28th of May 1756, Britain declared war on France and it did not end until 1763 and was known as the Seven Years War. Paine may have found work as a staymaker when he was first in London, but it was not long before he found the adventure he obviously craved. He answered an advertisement in the *Daily Advertiser* from a ubiquitously named Captain Death who was in command of a privateer named the *Terrible*. A privateer was a perfectly legal ship that as the name implies, was a privately owned vessel operating against any enemy of the country that owned it to reinforce that country's navy. They mainly operated from the 16th to the 19th century and nowadays would be deemed illegal but that was not the case in Paine's time. In any event, Paine answered the advertisement and was all set to sail in November 1756 but was stopped when his father found him and dissuaded him from going. Paine had completely rejected the Quaker teachings in order to sign on but his father, worried not just for his son's safety, but anxious that his son retain his religious beliefs did in fact manage to stop him sailing. He didn't know it at the time, but his actions saved Thomas's life, as the *Terrible* was involved in fierce fighting with the French in a battle that took place in the English Channel that involved 150 crewmen losing their lives. It was absolute carnage and at the most, only about twenty men survived, possibly less than that.

After a brief spell working in Covent Garden as a staymaker, Paine, completely fed up with the long hours and the monotony of the work, decided he wanted adventure, and this time, he wasn't going to allow parental pressure to stop him. On 17th January 1757, with Thomas Paine on board, the man-of-war, the *King of Prussia* left London to seek and fight the French. Despite the fact there were 250 on board, Paine calculated that probably only 20 were sailors who were properly trained in their jobs. Men learned how to crew while they went along, and it is extraordinary that given the inexperience of the vast majority of the crew, the ship nevertheless had enormous success, capturing nine ships in seven months. It says a lot for the skill of the *King of Prussia's* commander, Captain Mendez, that the ship had this sort of success. On 20th August, seven months after they had left London, the ship came back to Dartmouth and the men were paid off, Paine receiving £30 which was a great deal more than he would have earned as a staymaker.

Determined not to return to his old job, Paine used his money to educate himself in the scientific field. He did nothing by halves as he was taught the use of globes by none other than James Ferguson (1710-76), an eminent Scottish astronomer. Born on 25th April at the Core of Mayen, near Rothiemay in Banffshire, the son of a farm labourer, he worked tending sheep when he was merely ten years old. However, he had gained an interest in mechanics and astronomy at an early age and as a child he studied the stars at night. He seemed to be extraordinarily talented as whilst employed as a young man cleaning clocks amongst other things, he built a wooden clock which operated using wooden wheels and whalebone springs. He kept his interest in the stars and in the 1740's he published an astronomical table and two years later he made an orrery, a mechanical model of the solar system which could show the various planets and revolutions. Unschooled in these skills, and entirely self taught, he reminds one of John Harrison, who followed the same path as Ferguson, even dying in the same year, although Harrison was born seventeen years before in 1693. It is extraordinary the talent and skills that both these men possessed.

Ferguson was to become a great friend of Benjamin Franklin (1706-90) who was to play a leading role in the American War of Independence, and Ferguson would in turn one day eventually introduce Paine to Franklin.

Paine attended lectures on Newtonian science, one of the lecturers being Ferguson, and it was during these lectures that Thomas felt that he had realised what he wanted to do with his life. Issac Newton (1642-1727) was a scientist and mathematician and was made a fellow of Trinity College, Cambridge in 1667 as well as Lucasian Professor of Mathematics in 1669. His whole approach to science had been totally different from anybody before him and greatly appealed to the twenty-year-old Thomas Paine. Paine attended the lectures and met up with people of a like mind which merely confirmed his views that he was on the path that he wished to be on. The audiences at these lectures were an interesting set of people, ready to challenge the orthodox view of religion and also the social order which saw some people incredibly wealthy whilst others, trying to make a living where there was no social security safety net, were very poor. However, whilst Paine knew what he wanted to do, he found that there was no way that he would ever earn his living at it, so once again, with his money having run out, he found that he had to return to the boring job of being a staymaker. He travelled to Dover, worked there for a year and then moving to Sandwich, set himself up with his own business as a Master Staymaker in April 1759. This part of his life started happily enough, especially when six months after he had started his business, he married Mary Lambert, the service taking place on 27th September, 1759.

Although Paine was happy at this point, he obviously had little idea on how to run a successful business because he was soon in financial difficulties, and so he and his wife left Sandwich and moved to Margate, just ten miles away. If his debts were to cause him to be distressed, then worse was to come. Early in 1760, Mary became pregnant and went into early labour, and sadly both mother and child died. Although he was only twenty-three years old, he had to start looking at his life again.

Paine decided that he would work as an Excise Officer – there was more stability in terms of pay and it also took him away from the job of staymaker which he did not like, and in any event did not bring him the steady income that he needed. His job did not make him popular – no Excise Officer was but he thought that it would bring him in a steady salary.

His job, like other Excise Officers, was to check the stock of Shopkeepers along with publicans, see what they had in the way of beer, wine, spirits, soap, salt, and tobacco, and collect the customs duties that were owed. At the beginning of December 1762, Paine started work inspecting brewers' casks in Grantham, Lincolnshire, and in August of 1764 he found that he was stationed in Alford collecting the revenues due on tea and coffee as well as watching out for the smugglers who were attempting to bring in cargoes of gin from Holland. Paine seemed to be doing well until he fell into the trap that many customs officers fell into, which was to short circuit the system and sign for goods without actually inspecting them. For this he was sacked on 29th August, 1765 but after spending an unhappy few months in Lincolnshire working yet again as a staymaker, he returned to London and on 31st July, 1766, he applied to the Board of Excise to be re-instated and was told that he would have a post when one became available. Whilst waiting for a position, he returned yet again to working as a staymaker, moving to Norfolk in order to do this, and at the same time he also applied to become an ordained minister of the Church of England and some reports say that he preached in Moorfields although it's difficult to verify this. Sometime after this, he had a complete career change becoming a teacher of English. He had been working as a servant for a Mr. Noble who ran a boys' academy and persuaded Noble to allow him, Paine, to teach. This seemed to be a short-term arrangement and on 19th February 1768, Paine was on the move yet again, this time to take up a position working for the Excise once more, but this time in Lewes, Sussex. Paine lived in a fifteenth century house called Bull House, above the tobacco and grocery shop of Samuel and Esther Ollive. Lewes was an important town for Thomas, as it was in this town that he started to become the person that people recognise today as Thomas Paine, and the date that he arrived in Lewes has some significance as well, as it was virtually his 31st birthday that he took up residency there.

Lewes began its existence as a Saxon village in the 6th century. By the 10th century it was deemed to be important by virtue of the fact that it had two mints although at the time of the Norman Conquest, it probably had no more than 2,000 people living there. It was the Normans who founded the priory there although it was dissolved in 1537 by Henry VIII and later on some Caen stone from the building was used to build Southover Grange. It was a centre for the Republican cause during the English Civil War and in 1649 a local MP signed the death warrent of Charles 1. When Thomas Paine moved there in 1768, it was a busy port and probably the main town of the county of Sussex.

It seems as if Samuel Ollive probably fired Paine's enthusiasm for politics. Ollive had been a constable and was a member of the Society of Twelve, a group of people who were not elected, but recruited themselves to their number, and dealt with much of the day-to-day administration of the town – an early form of local government. It was not long before Samuel Ollive was so impressed with Paine that he, Paine, found himself co-opted on to it as a member and it was therefore during this time that Paine became involved in civic matters. He also became a member of the Vestry church group which was concerned about the welfare of the poor - their function being to collect taxes to re-distribute to those in need. At an early age, Paine had been faced with a spiritual dilemma due to the differing religions of his parents and this was only resolved in his own mind by him rejecting all forms of organised worship. However, Christian beliefs had been drummed into him from an early age and those, coupled with the radical ideas he was forming in his own mind, meant that being a member of the Vestry church group was completely logical to him.

Along with the Society of Twelve and the Vestry group, Paine also became a member of the Headstrong Club which met on a weekly basis at the White Hart Hotel to discuss political matters over large quantities of food and wine. It was at these meetings that Paine's debating skills became honed and he regularly won the prize that the club awarded at the end of each session for the best speaker. He also started writing and produced a poem about an extraordinary event whereby a dog was put on trial and executed because the owner had voted against a wealthy landowner in an election. He also wrote a lament describing the death of General James Wolfe (1727-59) who had been killed in the Seven Years War whilst he was capturing Quebec. Wolfe had had a brilliant career in his relatively short life, amongst other things, serving against the Scottish Jacobites at Falkirk and Culloden in 1745/46, and when William Pitt the Elder decided to expel the French from Canada, he entrusted Wolfe with the command to capture Quebec. Wolfe was killed just as his mission became victorious and he was buried at Greenwich Church. The paper that Paine wrote about this was actually published in 1775 in Pennsylvania.

Meanwhile, Samuel Ollive died leaving Esther a widow along with three daughters and a son. Paine felt that it would be improper for him to continue living at the Bull House and moved out, although he had become close to Elizabeth, one of the daughters of Esther and on 26th March, 1771, Thomas and Elizabeth were married at the Nonconformist Westgate Chapel, completing their vows as they were legally bound to do at the nearby Anglican church. Paine was thirty-four years old and was twelve years older than his new bride. He seemed to have got over his first marriage – in fact he doesn't seem to have recall of it because he described himself as a batchelor and made no mention of the fact that he was in fact, a widower. It wasn't long before Paine's marriage to Elizabeth was in trouble. He was supposed to be running his mother-in-law's shop but he seemed to neglect that as well as his wife, both the shop and his wife coming a poor second to his politics which seemed to take up more of his time.

It was at this time that Paine started to write in earnest. He was still employed as an Excise Officer despite the fact that he was supposed to be running the shop, and his fellow workers were agitating for better pay and improved working conditions. In the summer of 1772, he produced a twenty-one page pamphlet entitled *'The Case of the Officers of Excise'*, setting out the demands of his fellow workers and he spent the winter of that year helping to distribute 4,000 copies to Parliament. The pamphlet was also presented to the Commissioners of Excise along with a petition with 3,000 signatories. It took a huge amount of work to have arranged for all this to happen but the Commissioners of Excise immediately rejected their employees demands seemingly without considering the merits of their arguments at all, whilst Parliament more or less ignored it.

It was a bitter blow for Paine who in late December of that year had met Oliver Goldsmith (1730-74), the Anglo-Irish writer who almost certainly would have supported Paine's cause. Goldsmith was an unschooled man and unreliable with it, but he possessed talent, and had written such works as *'The Citizen of the World'* (1762), *'Life of Richard Nash of Bath, Esq.'*, *'The Traveller'* (1764), *'Deserted Village'* (1770), and *'She stoops to Conquer'* (1773), amongst other works. He was an acclaimed writer who had friends such as Samuel Johnson, Sir Joshua Reynolds, David Garrick and James Boswell amongst other luminaries. Paine received a great deal of encouragement from Goldsmith, but it was too late as his paper had already been rejected, and just over a year later, on 4th April, 1774, Goldsmith was dead, dying of a short, unspecified illness.

Four days later on the 8th April, Paine was sacked from his job by the Board of Excise for leaving his post and less than a week after that, on the 14th, he was declared bankrupt. He could have ended up entering a debtor's prison but he sold his possessions to clear his debts and to make sure he retained his freedom. On 4th June, he gained another freedom which he may or may not have wanted. It was on that date that he and his wife, Elizabeth, formally separated and whilst this period in his life would seem to be disastrous, it gave him the opportunity to be single minded about the growing passion in his life – politics.

Paine wanted to leave Lewes – after all, he had little reason to stay with his marriage at an end and being bankrupt, but he also wanted to go for positive reasons. He travelled to London and made contact with old friends again, one of whom he had been introduced to but still hardly knew, and that was Benjamin Franklin (1706-90). Franklin was an American statesman and scientist, having been born in Boston, Massachusetts and who was to have a leading role in America's fight for independence. From 1746, Franklin had also commenced his research into electricity, and as a result was made a Fellow of the Royal Society (FRS). In October, 1774, armed with a letter of introduction from Franklin addressed to Franklin's son William, at that time the Governor of New Jersey, Paine boarded a ship called the *London Packet* whose captain happened to be a friend of Paine's from Lewes, and sailed for America where a new life beckoned. However, up to this point in time, Paine's journey through life had been anything but smooth, and there was an outbreak of a form of typhus or typhoid fever aboard affecting the majority of the 120 on board ship. It was difficult to know quite what the disease was that they were suffering from as it was not until 1851 that the famous physician, Sir William Jenner (1815-98), discovered the difference between the two illnesses. However, whichever one it was, it was fierce and five people actually died, Paine himself being close to death at one point, but on 30th November, he was taken ashore in Philadelphia and cared for by a doctor who had been told of his links with Franklin. Paine recovered and eventually presented his letter of introduction to William Franklin. The year of 1774 was coming to an end, and Paine's life, along with most Americans who, whether they agreed with it or not, would soon be fighting the British to gain control of their own affairs, would never be the same again.

There had been unrest in the American colonies for years about the taxes that Britain had levied on them. In the year that Paine had emigrated to America, Britain's Prime Minister was Lord North (1732-92) who held that office from 1770 until 1782 and London held a very different view as to what the taxes were levied for, although the feud between Britain and the colonies started well before North's period of office. The main problem seemed to start after Britain's victory in the seven years war with France. Although victorious, Britain had a national debt that had nearly doubled, going from £72 million to nearly £130 million. John Stuart, 3rd Earl of Bute (1713-92), was Prime Minister at the end of the war, and he decided to keep large numbers of soldiers based in the Americas. The idea behind this was to keep 1,500 officers in work and was therefore politically expedient, but in order to do this, he had to raise the revenue from somewhere. However, in April, 1763, Bute was replaced by George Grenville (1712-70) and it was his administration that passed the American Revenue Act of 1764 (Sugar Act), Quartering Acts of 1765, and the Stamp Act also in 1765. By the time the Declaratory Act of 1766 was passed Grenville had resigned and Charles Watson-Wentworth, 2nd Marquis of Rockingham (1730-82) had become Prime Minister but resigned that year and when the Townshend Acts of 1767 were passed, William Pitt the Elder (1708-98) was Prime Minister, also becoming Lord Chatham in the process. Given the failing health of Pitt along with the fact that he was in the House of Lords, Charles Townshend (1725-67) became Chancellor of the Exchequer and was able to wield a great deal of power as he was operating from the House of Commons. Townshend was a very witty and clever speaker in the House and would almost certainly have become Prime Minister in 1767 but died that year.

None of these acts were at all popular – no act that proposes taxes ever are. However, up until the Sugar Act of 1764, America had been divided into thirteen colonies, and each had a Governor who was a link with the British Crown. By the imposition of taxes from the British Parliament that they were not represented in, the colonists were aggrieved and the popular cry after that was 'No taxation without representation'. When the Sugar Act was passed, a petition from the New England merchants was sent to the King that their trade with the Caribbean was being put in jeopardy. They were not wrong. The trade with Madeira, the Azores, Canary Islands, along with the French West Indies were all adversely affected. The Quartering Act of 1765 was passed by the Grenville administration in order that the troops still employed in the colonies could be billeted and again, this bill caused resentment amongst the colonists. It had gone much further than anything that Lieutenant Thomas General Gage, the

Commander in Chief of the British North American forces had requested. The local people were not unhappy to billet soldiers in time of war but were resentful of doing it in peacetime. Many questioned the legality of the bill as it seemed to clash with the 1689 Bill of Rights which forbade taxation without representation. No army had been billeted before the war so questions were asked as to why it was deemed necessary now. The Stamp Act of 1765 followed and again, this produced unrest among the colonists. Britain saw this act along with others as helping to meet the costs of maintaining 10,000 soldiers who would afford protection to the Western and Canadian frontiers. The Stamp Act of 1765 was a tax on legal documents, magazines, and newspapers as well as other form of papers used in the colonies. At this point in time, Parliament tried to reinforce its own position concerning its right to tax by passing the Declaratory Act in 1766, which said that Parliament had the right to make laws for the colonies "In all cases whatsoever". Meanwhile, the Stamp Act of 1765 was repealed after organised resistance from representatives of nine colonies, who called themselves the 'Sons of Liberty'. It had been passed by the Grenville administration but was repealed when Lord Rockingham took over as Prime Minister. Rockingham was better disposed towards the colonials and had not got on with Grenville so he was not sorry to see the Act go. The Stamp Act was repealed and the Declaratory Act passed on the same day, 18th March, 1766.

Although there was widespread anger towards all these taxes, opinion in the colonies was by no means unanimous as to what to do about it as many Americans still felt their allegiance was towards the King. However, they were affronted that although expected to pay these taxes, they held no representation in Parliament and these feelings were further aggravated when Charles, 2nd Viscount Townshend (1725-67) was Chancellor in 1766 during Pitt the Elder's ministry and had levied swingeing taxes on various goods, notably tea. These were named The Townshend Acts and they were primarily for raising money in order to pay the salaries of governors and judges and as other acts, establishing the right of the British Parliament to tax the colonies. This was met with resistance as they imposed duties on just about all imports. The resistance resulted in troops being stationed in Boston, Massachusetts and although that resistance tended to be mere scuffles to begin with, it turned into a disaster when on 5th March 1770, troops opened fire on civilians and killed five people, this tragic incident becoming known as The Boston Massacre. Eight British soldiers were accused of murder and put on trial and a very courageous lawyer called John Adams (1735-1826), who, not only putting his practice but also possibly his life at risk, successfully defended the soldiers and they were acquitted. Adams went on to play a leading role concerning the way the colonists reacted to the British Acts, and went on to become the second President of the United States of America as they would eventually be named between 1796 and 1800. In 1773, Parliament passed the Tea Act, which allowed the ailing East India Company a monopoly of imported tea. Events were getting worse now and on 16th December a group of protesters threw three shiploads of tea into the harbour, an incident that became known as 'The Boston Tea Party'. By this time Lord North (1732-92) was Prime Minister, having taken office in 1770, and he felt that the situation had to be controlled by force, feeling that it had gone too far for anything else. It was his government that passed the Coercive Acts which were a series of five laws passed in 1774 and were set up to limit the rights that the Massachusetts Assembly had in administering the local affairs.

The Boston Port Act was passed as a reaction to the Boston Tea Party and resulted in the port of Boston being closed until the East India Company had been recompensed for the destroyed tea.

The Massachusetts Government Act brought further outrage to the colonists when it was passed by the British government. Its purpose was to curtail the powers of the Massachusetts government and transfer its powers to that of the British Parliament, but it merely put the other colonists on guard as they thought that it would happen to them.

The Administration of Justice Act said that trials of accused royal officials could be transferred to other colonies and even Great Britain if it was felt that a fair trial would not result if tried in America. This would have been totally unworkable, as very few potential witnesses would be able to leave their place of work to attend trials on the other side of the Atlantic. Besides, after the 1770 Boston Massacre, it was felt that the soldiers involved did in fact receive a fair trial when they were defended by the lawyer John Adams who, as mentioned earlier, went on to become the second President of the United States.

The Quartering Act of 1774 was merely an update of the 1765 version extending the type of buildings that soldiers could be billeted at. Contrary to popular belief, it did not specify that troops could be housed in buildings that were occupied by local people, but only unoccupied buildings.

The final act in this series was the Quebec Act which enlarged the boundaries of the Province of Quebec and brought about reforms that were favourable to the French Catholics but at the same time denying them an elected legislative assembly. Many were suspicious of this law, feeling that it was designed to get the French Canadians on the side of the British.

If the situation in the American colonies was tense before the Coercive Acts, they were certainly worse afterwards because they simply inflamed the situation within all the colonies, and the First Continental Congress was brought about by twelve of the thirteen colonies and that Congress created a Continental Association whose role was to review the British legislation insofar as it affected the colonies and to enforce any boycott of goods from Britain and the Caribbean areas. By the time Thomas Paine arrived in Philadelphia in late November, 1774, the situation in the colonies was very tense.

In January 1775, Paine took lodgings in the centre of town and befriended a Scottish printer by the name of Robert Aitken who, recognising Paine's talents, made him editor of 'The Pennsylvania Magazine' at an annual salary of £50. Despite being criticised by John Witherspoon, the president of the College of New Jersey, the subscriptions to the magazine increased rapidly from its original 600 and by March had arrived at 1,500, making it bigger than any other similar publication in the colonies.

Thomas Paine embraced the political happenings in America very easily. In March, 1775, he started writing under the pseudonym of 'Atlanticus' in which he criticised Britain's rule over India and it was not hard to see this as an attack on Britain's rule in America. He also attacked slavery and certainly seemed to be taking on issues well before his time. As well as putting into words his vision of an America free of the mother country, he also wrote of a world where slavery did not exist along with an America that gave freedom for the American Indian which was the only logical extension of an independent America. Sadly, too many white Americans wanted their own freedom but were unwilling to give it to the American Indian for many years to come.

In time there were many people who referred to Paine as 'The Father of the American Revolution' which was as a result of the pamphlet he wrote called *'Common Sense'* which was published on 10th January, 1776 although it was published anonymously as *'Written by an Englishman'* in the early days. It was a huge success, selling 100,000 copies in three months, an extraordinary achievement when it is realised that there were only two million inhabitants. Paine was originally going to call it *'Plain Truth'*, but it was his friend, Benjamin Rush (1745-1813), who he had met after Rush had seen his article on slavery, who persuaded him to change the title. Rush was an American politician and physician and having studied medicine in Edinburgh and Paris, became President of Chemistry at Philadelphia and at Pennsylvania in 1791. He signed the Declaration of Independence in 1776 and in the following year was Surgeon-General of the Continental Army. In coming to America, Paine had met the right like minded people and seemed to have found his spiritual home along with a cause that he could relate to.

Although *'Common Sense'* sold well, there were no particular ideas that were considered new expressed within its pages, and it is uncertain as to whether it actually converted that many people to the cause of independence. However, what he did achieve was to take fairly complicated ideas and write about them in such a way that people with only average reading skills could understand. A book of this nature was bound to cause controversy and it duly came from Loyalist quarters, but another aspect of this book was the fact that some people disagreed with it who would normally have been thought of as supporters to his view. In particular, John Adams, a man who was in the vanguard of the independence movement, called Paine's book a "crapulous mass". He went so far as to publish his own pamphlet entitled *'Thoughts on Government'* in 1776, which argued for a more measured form of government for any new country that came out of these discussions. One of the things that Paine argued against in *'Common Sense'* was what he considered to be the myth of the British constitution which he felt did not deserve the self congratulatory praise heaped upon it by the mother country. He questioned the very existence of monarchy and wondered how it was that certain people were born and then treated as exalted from the cradle to the grave – he also challenged monarchists to find such people anywhere in the scriptures. He did concede that Britain did not suffer the tyrannical monarchies that some other countries had, but felt that this was due to the revolution in Britain in the 1640's and the subsequent beheading of Charles I in 1649. Paine ignored the fact that Britain could not make republicanism work and restored the monarchy in 1660 by placing Charles II on the throne, but instead tore into the origins of the British monarchy. He referred to the 1066 conquest of Britain by William of Normandy and described the event as: "A French bastard landing with an armed banditti, and establishing himself as King of England against the consent of the natives..." Paine went on: "... the King was paid £800,000 a year to do hardly more than make war and grant offices. Monarchy had entered the world through violence and it was on war that monarchy thrived". He finished off this section with the words: "Of more worth is one honest man to society, and in the sight of God, than all the crowned ruffians that ever lived".

Paine proposed not just a separation from Britain, but once separated, a new form of democracy – he was certainly unimpressed with the way the mother country was run and wanted nothing that resembled an American equivalent of the House of Lords. He did make specific proposals such as convening a Constitutional Convention to frame a Charter of the United Colonies and he also pressed strongly for a Declaration of Independence which may or may not have caused John Adams, who at this point in time did not know the identity of the author of 'Common Sense', to comment to his wife Abigail that whoever had written the pamphlet had a "better hand at pulling down than building". Be that as it may, a second edition went out and was translated into several languages, German and French among them but Paine's name was only credited when the third edition was printed in February 1776. Paine was convinced that the only way to solve the problems with Britain was for the American people to become completely independent and become a republic.

Even people who wanted to separate from Britain did not agree with everything that Paine wrote, and a notable critic was John Adams. He did not agree with Paine's idea that there should be one legislative chamber and in his 'Thoughts on Government', Adams made a personal attack on Paine saying he was a newcomer to America and didn't understand the country. Adams himself preferred a system whereby there were two chambers, one being controlled by the wealthy and considered to be the upper house, whilst the second would be run by ordinary citizens. Paine actually went to Adams' lodgings to argue his case for a single legislative chamber which was based on the fact that with no monarchy, there was no need for more than one. Paine felt in fact, that this was a heaven sent opportunity to go one further and get rid of any class system. The two men could not agree although it was clear that by the end of the evening, Adams held a great deal of respect for Paine.

Thomas Jefferson (1743-1826), who would eventually become the third President of the United States after George Washington and John Adams, drew up a draft of the famous Declaration of Independence. On 2nd July, Congress voted for the independence of the United States and two days later, on 4th July, 1776, Congress adopted the Declaration of Independence. Jefferson was a clever man and an astute politician. He had been heavily involved in the discussions concerning the future independence of America and was Governor of Virginia from 1779 to 1781. In 1783, when the battle for independence was won, it was he who secured the adoption of the decimal coinage which was a totally different system to the one that operated in Britain at the time. It would be nearly two hundred years before Britain changed over to a similar system in 1971 that America had used in its infancy. It was a remarkable document, written as it was when Jefferson was just thirty-three years old. Jefferson in fact had wanted friendly relations with Britain, but could not stomach the price that he and his countrymen were expected to pay. On 29th November, 1775, some six months before the Declaration of Independence had been passed, he said the following:-

"Believe me, dear Sir: there is not in the British Empire a man who more cordially loves a union with Great Britain than I do. But, by the God that made me, I will cease to exist before I yield to a connection on such terms as the British Parliament propose; and in this, I think I speak the sentiments of America."

In other words, the British had stretched the loyalty of the majority of the American people to breaking point, and left them with no choice other than to fight for their independence.

On 12th July, 1776, the Second Continental Congress decided to appoint a committee of thirteen to draw up a draft agreement on a constitution that related to the running of the union of the states. The first ever document which related to the governing of the states was called the *'Articles of Confederation'* or sometimes just the *'Articles'*. The Second Continental Congress approved the Articles on 15th November, 1777, but they were not formally passed until the representatives of Maryland added their signatures on 1st March, 1781. The Continental Congress was then dissolved and the next day, a brand new government of the United States in Congress Assembled replaced it, and Samuel Huntington (1731-96) was made President. He had signed both the Declaration of Independence and also the Articles of Confederation. Samuel had a very limited formal education but educated himself to such an extent that he was eventually admitted to the bar in 1754 and moving to Norwich, Connecticut, practiced law. Thereafter, he dedicated himself to American politics and in 1775 was elected to serve as a delegate to the Continental Congress where he represented Connecticut. When on 1st March, 1781 he was chosen as President of the United States in Congress Assembled, many felt that he should be recognised as the first President of the United States. However, his role differed from future Presidents in that it was largely ceremonial although he did have to carry out administrative duties.

On 9th July, the Declaration was publicly read to the people of Philadelphia at the same time as Paine was on his way to Perth Amboy, New Jersey. He had joined up as a volunteer in the 'Associators' which was a militia unit. Although Paine was part of General Greene's army which was retreating from 6,000 British and Hessian troops, his own part in the fighting that preceded it was possibly overblown, as another member of the militia wrote rather dismissively that Paine may be good at philosophising, but as a soldier was somewhat lacking as: "He always kept out of danger".

Eventually Paine returned to Philadelphia and if he didn't know before, he was soon to find out that there were a sizeable number of people living in the colonies who were still loyal to the crown. These were referred to as Loyalists or Tories, and it was estimated that these numbered about 500,000, and of these, 20,000 took an active role in fighting for the British crown. Some were not necessarily against independence, but felt anxious about the economic future of the new country if it were formed. Others thought that the size of the Americas was unwieldy and that if they beat the British, then chaos would result. Paine was desperate for the undecided to be brought round and during the war, produced sixteen papers under the collective heading of *'The American Crisis'*, the first one appearing in *'The Pennsylvania Journal'* on 19th December, 1776 and within a matter of days, eighteen thousand had been printed in the form of a pamphlet. Paine had received no payment from writing *'Common Sense'* as he had not wanted to profit from the war, and he again accepted no payment for his latest work. However, it meant that he was always living in poverty and his friends continually came to his rescue.

The war between America and Britain had started on 19th April 1775 and the first fight was known as the Battle of Lexington and Concord. After that but before the allied states had declared their independence as one body, some states had become independently sovereign and Virginia for one, had declared itself independent in May, 1776. The war was being fought and at different times since it started, both the American states and the British had sought a peaceful solution, but to no avail. Meanwhile, the Battle of Bunker Hill was fought on 17th June 1775, and whilst it was considered a British victory, they suffered far more casualties than the American forces. The Second Continental Congress had convened by this time and extended the Olive Branch Petition to the British as a way of reaching a peaceful solution, but King George would have nothing to do with it. He in turn issued the Proclamation of Rebellion on 23rd August, 1775 which required military action against the American people who he labelled as traitors. It was at this critical point that Paine's words came into their own. He tore into the Tories, denouncing them all as cowards and he lashed out at the British Monarch George III, describing him as a 'sottish, stupid, stubborn, worthless, brutish man'. Washington read Paine's words and was so impressed that he ordered his officers to read them aloud to the troops on Christmas Day. Later that day, they fought the Hessians at Trenton and soundly beat them, taking 1,000 prisoners. A few days later they marched on to Princeton and had further success. By March, 1776, George Washington, commander of the American forces, had forced the British out of Boston and by now, all thirteen colonies were prepared to declare independence, all the Royal officials having made their escape. On 13th January, 1777, Paine published the second of *'The American Crisis'* and it was in this issue that he first used the term, 'The United States of America'. He specifically aimed the contents at the British Admiral, Lord Howe (1726-99), brother of the army commander, William, 5th Viscount Howe (1729-1814). It was Admiral Howe who Paine aimed his message at more or less telling him that the British were in a war that they could not win, although both brothers were involved in the war as Admiral Howe was Commander of the British Fleet whilst his army officer brother, the 5th Viscount Howe had won the Battle of Bunker Hill.

Because Paine always refused payment for any of his writings, he was forever broke and so on 17th April, 1777, he accepted a post of Secretary to the Committee of Foreign Affairs for Congress. The work did not stretch him in any way because it was really just doing the routine work of servicing the Committee – he wasn't involved in the decision making that the Committee would be involved in but he seemed to enjoy it – he even told people on occasions that he was Foreign Affairs Minister. However, he had a salary of $70 dollars a month and this helped him stabilise his finances.

Two days after being given the job, he published a third edition of 'The American Crisis'. It was not his best effort by any means and was almost ludicrous in content. He over-simplified the issue of independence by asking who was for and who was against, and then suggesting property tax for those who were against independence and then went even further by suggesting that those who openly opposed independence should be put in jail.

This was never going to happen and it was not long before he started work on the fourth 'American Crisis' which he hoped would be better received. This he did on 12th September, 1777 during the time that the British were beating the Americans at Brandywine Creek and he had 4,000 copies printed which he paid for himself before leaving Philadelphia and seeing Washington and his very demoralised army at Valley Forge. However, on 7th October, the American troops led by General Horatio Gates (1728-1806) had a victory over the British forces led by General John Burgoyne (1722-92) at Saratoga which led to Burgoyne surrendering his army ten days later. Gates was actually English born but moved to America and lived in Virginia. When the War of Independence started he took the side of his adopted country and fought for the Americans, being made an Adjutant-General in 1775 and in 1777 was given command of the northern department which then forced Burgoyne's surrender. Burgoyne himself was no mean soldier, distinguishing himself in the seven years war and was sent to America in 1774. Earlier in his career he had sat in the British parliament and had also published several plays. In 1777 he led an expedition from Canada and took Ticonderoga, but was later forced to surrender to Gates.

On 13th February, whilst staying at the home of a friend called William Henry, Thomas Paine wrote the fifth edition of 'The American Crisis' – a 24 page pamphlet, it was published the following month and was basically in two parts. The first part was aimed once again at Lord Howe, the British Admiral who he attacked in the second edition. He again warned Lord Howe that he was engaged in a battle that he could not win and urged him to return home and tell his government exactly what was happening. The second part was written to raise the morale of the American troops.

On 6th February 1778, America signed The Treaty of Amity and a Treaty of Alliance with France, which was a blow to Britain and they could now see that their task of defeating America was going to be a great deal harder. On the American side, it was negotiated by Benjamin Franklin, Silas Deane and Arthur Lee and created a military alliance between America and France, neither of whom could now make a separate peace treaty with Britain. The Treaty also recognised American independence and no future peace could be negotiated with Britain unless that basic requirement was met. Silas Deane's brother, Simeon Deane, presented the Treaties to Congress on 2nd May, 1778 and these were then passed on 4th May, two days later. Paine again questioned the ability of the British to win the war in a sixth edition of 'The American Crisis' when he urged the Commissioners who had come from Britain to negotiate a return home with nothing less than a recognition of American Independence. In November, he was at it again with a seventh version of 'The American Crisis' telling the

British people to rise up against the King and government but in this he was never going to be successful – the British way of life had been more or less settled after the restoration of King Charles II in 1660 and the bloodless revolution of 1688 when William and Mary took the throne. Besides which, King George III was very popular and in 1778 was ten years away from being struck down by his illness which at the time, people thought was insanity.

Paine possibly didn't help himself when he also wrote that he wasn't thinking of just America but stating his philosophy generally, which wouldn't have helped him have his arguments accepted in Britain. His arguments were not particularly well received in America either because from December 1778 to January 1779 he attacked in print the Connecticut lawyer named Silas Deane who had been one of the negotiators in France. Paine more or less accused Deane of corruption concerning the expenses he was claiming, and to make matters worse, he also accused another, Robert Morris, a wealthy and respected merchant, of the same misdemeanour. Although possibly correct in his opinions of Deane, Paine's star fell and when he gave away details of secret negotiations between America and France, he was heavily criticised by the press and found himself out of favour with just about everybody bar the true radicals who continued to support him. As a result, he had to resign his position of Secretary to the Committee of Foreign Affairs although a friend, Owen Biddle, who was head of the Pennsylvania Board of War, offered him a temporary job which although poorly paid and mundane, enabled him to buy food and pay his rent. However, he found it a huge comedown from being at the centre of the American Revolution and knowing that his words were once listened to and read throughout the world.

Because he had been so heavily criticised by the press and public, Paine's health deteriorated under the strain, and he stayed in bed with a fever for several weeks before being employed by the Pennsylvania Assembly's Executive Committee in October, 1779 as the Clerk to the Pennsylvania Assembly. Like other jobs that he had taken, it was fairly mundane but it meant that he was on a salary and also still enjoyed support of the Assembly. Paine felt his energy and enthusiasm return and in February 1780, he produced the eighth version of 'The American crisis' which was supposed to have the twin effect of raising American moral and denting the British which given the involvement of France in the war, was fairly successful. Meanwhile, Paine had always hated slavery and he had written about this in the 'Pennsylvania Magazine' in 1775, but it wasn't until March, 1780 that the Assembly passed legislation that would free the children of slaves and only when they had reached the age of twenty-eight. To Paine, this was a massive disappointment as he felt it didn't go anywhere near far enough – just as he felt that American people should be set free from Britain, so he felt that all slaves should be free.

On 12th May, 1780, Charleston was taken by the British in what was to be the heaviest defeat of the war for the American cause and it was at this time that Paine issued his ninth 'American Crisis' in which he called on the wealthy few to donate to a fund to help the beleaguered American troops. Paine himself donated $500 which he couldn't possibly afford but which was returned to him when Congress set up the Bank of Pennsylvania.

Paine's standing in America was still low and he was now contemplating moving back to Britain which seemed an extraordinary idea. If he thought he was unpopular in America, his standing in Britain would have been low to say the least, and almost certainly would have cost him his life. Fortunately, he was talked out of this idea by General Greene, who Paine had once acted as an aide to a few years previously. Paine was still writing however, and nothing or no-one would ever stop him doing that. In October, 1780, he published a pamphlet called 'The Crisis Extraordinary' which had him expressing the view about extra taxes being raised to cover the war. He came up with all sorts of different scenarios as to what Congress needed to do to win the conflict, which he said would cost less if America won than if Britain continued to rule. In December 1780, Paine argued for the present constitution, which basically still had thirteen states running the country to be altered to allow a strong central government. He argued this in a pamphlet called 'Public Good' but by the time it was printed, he was preparing to sail to France. He had resigned his post as Clerk to the Pennsylvania Assembly which he had only taken the year previously, but before the lack of finances could begin to worry him, it was arranged that he would accompany Colonel John Laurens, who was the son of a friend of Paine's, Henry Laurens, and be one of the negotiators in France in an attempt to get a loan from the French government. Congress was against Paine going to France and the attitude of some of its members hurt him deeply. He volunteered to accompany Laurens as a private citizen after selling his possessions and clearing his debts. He set off from Boston on 11th February with Lauren and his secretary and they arrived in France one month later, on 9th March.

When he had arrived and settled in France, he met two people whose company he valued, the first being the Marquis de Chastellux. The Marquis later wrote that Paine was a typical writer in as much as his room was very untidy, but he also expressed the view that Paine was no politician as he was better at writing about events rather than being able to carry any of them off. Paine also met Gilbert du Montier, Marquis de Lafayette (1757-1834) who in 1777 had joined the American forces to support the country's struggle for independence, and served with distinction under George Washington who gave him a division. Lafayette fought to save Virginia, and also took part in the battle at Yorktown. On his return to France he showed the National Assembly a declaration of rights which was based a great deal on the American Declaration of Independence before being put in command of the National Guard, and whilst he supported the 1789 revolution, had to flee as it was felt that he had sympathetic feelings towards the monarchy. Anyone holding those views was always in danger although he returned to the political life of France and sat in the Chamber of Deputies from 1818 to 1824. From 1825 to 1830 he was a leader of the Opposition but not before he had returned to America for a visit in 1824 where a grateful Congress voted him $200,000.

Meanwhile Paine was very happy with the reception he received when he arrived in France although he would have been less happy to hear what Elkanah Watson, a man originally from Philadelphia thought of him. Watson had been persuaded to put Paine up for a while but was clearly pleased to see him go when the time came. He wrote about Paine:- (He was) "coarse and uncouth in his manners, loathsome in his appearance, and a disgusting egotist." Watson also said that Paine:- "Spoke incessantly, rejoicing most in talking of himself and reading the allusions of his mind". Watson also thought little of Paine's ideas on hygiene, stating that he had to persuade Paine to take a bath because of his 'brimstone odour' – a not unreasonable request considering Paine had been at sea for three weeks. It must have been somewhat of a relief to Watson when Paine left and travelled to Paris where he stayed with his friend Benjamin Franklin.

Paine must have had the results of negotiations with the French government fed back to him afterwards because although he and Franklin met the French representatives, Paine could not really involve himself in the discussions as he did not speak French. However, he seems to have been busy writing various memoranda outlining the military capabilities of the American forces. The French government was generous – they made a grant in the form of a loan and sent the American army 20,000 uniforms as well as providing supplies. Near the end of May, Lafayette left on a ship that took the much sought after supplies to America whilst on 1st June, 1781, John Laurens and Paine set sail from Brest with the cash that had been promised.

Whilst Laurens received $200 dollars for his part in everything, Paine was given nothing at all which is difficult to understand, especially as both the supplies and cash had a significant impact on the course of the war. On 17th October, 1781, the British army under General Cornwallis surrendered although the news did not reach Lord North at Downing Street for another month, on 25th November to be precise. When he heard the news, Lord George Germain Sackville (1716-85), the Colonial Secretary, was with the Prime Minister. According to Sackville, North clutched his hand to his chest as if shot, and said:- "Oh God, it is all over". The British could have fought on, but the defeat at Yorktown seemed to have made them lose the will to continue and whilst Lord North carried on as Prime Minister for a few more months, it hastened his departure and left his reputation in tatters. From that day forward, he was always known as 'The Prime Minister who lost us the American Colonies'.

Although Paine received no lump sum such as John Laurens had been awarded, he was given the job of propagandist for Congress which carried an annual salary of $800. Paine received an agreement that his salary would be drawn from a secret services fund so that it would not generally be known that he held that post. Paine wanted the freedom to write and always expressed the view that anyone who wrote for money was no better than a prostitute who sold her body. Whether Paine ever met the great Samuel Johnson (1709-84) is not generally known, but they certainly held different views on that particular subject, Johnson believing quite the reverse, saying once that no man ever wrote *except* for money. The implication in his statement meant that he felt anyone who wrote without receiving payment had generally taken leave of their senses.

One of Paine's friends was a man by the name of Robert Morris, who after a shaky start between the two men when they first met a few years earlier, became firm friends. Morris was one of the men who Paine had negotiated with to get his job, Morris's post at the time being Superintendent of Finances but he resigned early in 1783, and at that time, Paine's payments were stopped.

Despite the fact that the war had to all intents and purposes been won by the American states, no long-term system of government had been completely finalised. Some felt that each state should be autonomous whilst Paine, accepting the need for an enlarged system of local government, felt strongly that there should also be a strong central government to bring to fruition his vision of a 'United States of America'.

Now that Paine had no job, he was free to write again and so he published the tenth edition of *'The American Crisis'* in which he again defended taxation as being necessary for such things as looking after the very old and very young. That was in March 1782, and the following month he wrote an article in the *'Pennsylvania Journal'* taking up much the same theme. At this time, Paine seemed to be restored to the centre of events and as such, he was invited to France along with a great many others who were part of the elite – the reason being there was a banquet at the French Embassy to celebrate the birth of a son to Louis XVI. As it happened, although Paine was happy that he was back in favour, he was very uncomfortable amongst such company, refusing to dance and if that wasn't enough, refusing to speak.

A radical French theologian, Abbe Guillaume Raynal (1713-96) was also a fairly radical historian who had written about the Dutch Stadholderate as well as the English Parliament. His most famous book was the 8-volume *'Histoire philosophique et politique, des etablissements et du commerce des europeens dans les deux Indes'* (1770). By 1789 some thirty editions had been printed but many people found it objectionable because of its approach to religion and the way he advocated the right of governments to tax. It also took the barbarity of the slave trade head on and was publicly burned as a result. Raynal also wrote about the causes of the American Revolution and Paine immediately wrote a critique under the title of *'Letter to the Abbe Raynal, on the Affairs of North America'*. Paine disputed two points that had been made. Raynal had said that the revolution had happened because the Americans did not want to pay their taxes. This was not true. They did not want to pay them to Britain but they understood the necessity of them once America became independent. The other point that Paine took Raynal to task for was his assertion that America only rejected Britain's offer of peace in 1778 because France and America had joined forces, but this was not true either as France had not entered the war until after Britain's offer.

On 18th April, 1783, Washington said that the war between America and Britain was over and this co-incided with Paine producing edition number thirteen of *'The American Crisis'*. Paine was proud of his own contribution to the war and in his pamphlet he had written:- "The times that tried men's souls are over – and the greatest and completest revolution the world ever knew, gloriously and happy accomplished". He also wrote that he would:- "Always feel an honest pride at the part I have taken and acted..." Paine, although obviously relieved that the war and suffering were over was afraid that he would be forgotten. He was also broke and he became homeless having to leave his lodgings in Philadelphia and had to rely on friends to put him up. Having no money at all, he set about the humiliating business of asking Congress for help and it was George Washington who advised him to attend Congress so that he could make his arguments for financial help personally. Eventually after a personal intervention from George Washington himself, he was given a house and 270 acres of land. Paine did not wish to seem ungrateful but he told Washington that he would have preferred cash, but feeling unable to sell it, he let it out so that he would have a regular income. Still wishing to be at the centre of power, he published the last edition of *'The American Crisis'* and once again, argued strongly for a central government which he felt was essential for the good of the nation.

Paine was not to stay in America for much longer, but in February, 1786, he did produce another paper entitled *'Dissertations on Government; the Affairs of the Bank; and Paper Money'*. He published this because the Bank of North America had had its charter removed by the Pennsylvania Assembly in September 1785 because of its refusal to accept a new paper currency. Paine, who had always disliked paper money argued for the Bank to have its charter restored. It also threw up another idea that Paine had always argued for, the single chamber type of government, usually supported by radicals but now questioned by Paine who felt that the two chamber system would be better.

With all his campaigning for an independent America, Paine had put aside a great love of his which was science. As he now had no money worries, he felt that he could spend more time on two inventions that he was hoping to work on – the design of an iron bridge and also smokeless candles. On 1st January, 1786, he and Benjamin Franklin dined together and tried the candles out after their meal. However, interruption on any more work on both the bridge and the candle happened and meant that work on these two projects was put on hold as his involvement in the affairs of the Bank of North America took over, although it was only a few months before he was working on his inventions again. In November of 1786, Paine found out that the Pennsylvania Society wished to construct a bridge over the Schuylkill River, and so working with the help of others, he produced a bridge made of wrought iron and on 1st January, 1787, one year to the day that he and Franklin had talked it through, Paine presented his model in the Pennsylvania State House Courtyard but to no avail as first one committee then another failed to give him the endorsement he needed.

Paine had received a letter from his parents in September 1785, the first time in ten years that he had heard from them, and now knowing that they were both living, naturally wanted to see them. He decided to go to France in April 1787 to see if he could muster any interest in his bridge and from France he intended to return to England to see his parents. He left for France on 26th April, 1787 and it was only a month later that the Philadelphia Convention met to formulate a Constitution for the newly formed country, which they drafted in the middle of September. The commencement of the work on the Constitution coincided with his arrival at Le Havre which happened on 26th May and from there he went to Paris where he met Benjamin Franklin. Franklin supplied him with letters of introduction which in turn resulted in him receiving a great many invitations from radicals and intellectuals. He had met the Marquis de Lafayette again who had fought for the Americans from 1777 until the end of the war. Lafayette now brought Paine into his circle of influential friends and one of these was the Marquis de Condorcet (1743-94) who was a brilliant mathematician as well as being a radical, and as such, had a lot in common with Paine. Condorcet, or to give him his full name, Marie Jean Antoine Nicolas de Caritat, Marquis de Condorcet, was the son of a cavalry officer and excelled at the Jesuit school at Reims before going to the College of Navarre in Paris when he was thirteen years old to begin studying mathematics. In 1765, he won a seat in the Academy of Sciences and in 1781 he entered the French Academy.

Paine was in his element arriving in France at this particular moment in time when there was revolution in the air. He had felt that his work in America was complete as he was better at agitation for change rather than dealing with the day-to-day governing once that change had taken place. Now in 1787, he felt the same excitement being in France as he had felt when entering America at the tail end of 1774. Louis XVI's Finance Minister had proposed to the Assembly of Notables, the Assembly being made up of the so-called great and the good, that taxation should be increased. This was due to the fact that France's economy was in bad shape but although there was no doubting the bleak economic outlook, the suggested means of rectifying the situation did not achieve universal agreement in the Assembly, mainly because Condorcet was a member. He claimed that the main reason for the state of France's economy was the extravagance of the Royal Family which led to an angry King dismissing the Assembly and asking the regional parliaments to bail him out. This move did not work out for the King at all as the Paris Parliament decreed that taxation could only be levied by the Estates-General, and they had not met since 1614.

The Estates-General was a general assembly split into three:- the First Estate represented the Clergy, the Second Estate the nobility, whilst the Third Estate represented the commoners and whilst this was 97% of the population in theory, in practise it meant that the Third Estate was contributing an ever increasing proportion of tax revenues. Also, it wasn't until the Estates-General met in May, 1789, that the Third Estate was allowed to participate in the decision making process.

However, that was some time in the future. In June 1787, Thomas Jefferson returned to Paris from Italy and it was not long before he and Paine formed a close friendship due to their shared interest in the sciences and their radical politics. Jefferson introduced Paine to Jean-Baptiste Le Roy who was an eminent scientist and mathematician and he too, struck up a friendship with Paine. Paine had obviously discussed the design of his bridge with Le Roy because when he, Paine, took that design to the Academy on 21st July, he found that Le Roy was Chairman of the committee that was going to study the proposals that Paine was putting forward. Just over a month later at the end of August, Paine received some good news in the form of a favourable report on both the bridge and the design. Paine immediately set off for England and the Royal Society whom he hoped would give him similar feedback, but it was not to be. Armed with letters of support from Thomas Jefferson, Paine attempted to court the people who had power such as Edmund Burke (1729-97), a leading Whig politician amongst others, but events were happening in America and Paine was interested in their new constitution that had been adopted on 21st June, 1788 and which he broadly supported, although he was concerned that a great deal of power would be in the hands of just one man, in this instance, George Washington who was made the first President.

During this time, John Adams, who one day would become the 2nd President of the United States but at this point in time had been America's representative in London, returned to the United States and Paine became a sort of unofficial representative of America in London. It was a strange turn-around for Paine after his total commitment to the American struggle for independence that England should take such little notice of him. Paine was trying to curry favour with Whig politicians but in November, 1788 fell out of step with them when King George III became very ill and it was not at all clear that he would recover quickly if he recovered at all. If the King died, then his son the Prince of Wales would become King but if he was seriously ill but remained alive, the Prince of Wales would become Prince Regent. The British Prime Minister William Pitt was desperate for the King to recover and held off passing legislation that would allow the Prince of Wales to take over as Regent as long as he could. The Whigs, meanwhile, realised that Pitt was using delaying tactics, and were equally determined to put Pitt's political rival, Charles James Fox in number 10 as Prime Minister and they also wanted the Prince of Wales to become Regent. Paine wished for no such scenario. He wanted Britain to seize the opportunity of getting rid of the monarchy altogether, and to follow the American style of government. Britain wasn't ready for that however, and in the end Pitt won the day when the King recovered and was able to take over his duties although his son, the Prince of Wales did rule as Regent from 1811, when it became clear that George III was totally incapacitated, until 1820 when he finally died and the Prince Regent came to the throne as George IV.

Meanwhile, in the spring of 1789, Paine had achieved a certain success with his bridge when he found an ironworks in Yorkshire who agreed to construct a full-scale bridge to Paine's design, although true to form, despite the fact that he was broke, he received no payment for this.

Meanwhile, the French King had agreed to summon the Estates-General but when they met on 5th May 1789, they were unable to agree on the reforms that King Louis XVI had in mind and the Third Estate broke away from the others and became the National Assembly. In effect, the Assembly became the government and felt that their first job was to draft a new constitution. The King attempted to hold on to what power he had left but the Parisien people flexed their collective muscles and on 14th July, 1789 stormed the Bastille prison. It was almost impossible for the King to know who was on his side and who wasn't as the demonstrators who took the prison were helped by many of the soldiers. This action gave the new Assembly added weight as the government of France and on 4th August, the National Assembly proclaimed a 'Declaration of the Rights of Man and of the Citizen.' By now the powers of the First and Second Estates, in other words, the Nobility and the Clergy, had all but gone and a few months later, the National Assembly took away the lands that had previously belonged to the church. After his experiences in America, Paine could see where this was going and was ecstatic at being part of another revolution.

In November 1789, Paine travelled to France and joined his friends, Condorcet and Lafayette but he also befriended Thomas Christie whose ideas more closely resembled those of Paine. Christie had studied medicine and tiring of that, went into journalism and after studying various languages, co-published the *'Analytical Review'* with Joseph Johnson, a radical book publisher, the idea being to bring to Britain some of the ideas of continental countries. Christie was the nephew of the famous English Presbyterian Minister and scientist, Joseph Priestley (1733-1804). Priestley was a friend of Benjamin Franklin and it was Franklin who helped Priestley in the research that the latter studied in order for him to write his *'History of Electricity'* which was published in 1767. Priestley wrote a reply to Edmund Burke's *'Reflections on the French Revolution'* which had been published in 1790 and the following year this caused a mob in Birmingham to break into his house, destroying all the contents in the process.

At this time, the revolution that was happening in France was virtually bloodless and on 17th January 1790, Paine wrote to Edmund Burke enthusing about the situation there. Burke was unhappy however, and told Paine by letter that what was happening in France could spell danger, not only to France but to Britain as well. In March, Paine returned to London to look after any further developments with his iron bridge. Whilst in London, he tended to mix with friends who were sympathetic to the events that were happening in France. One of these was the possibly the most famous politician of the day and that was Charles James Fox (1749-1806), a leading radical who was a strong supporter of both the American revolution and now the French revolution. He had been a Lord of the Admiralty and also a commissioner of the Treasury but had been sacked by the then Prime Minister, Lord North (1732-92) who had been in office from 1770 until 1782 and had overseen the handling of the war against American independence. Edmund Burke meanwhile, wrote his *'Reflections on the Revolution in France'* which was published in November 1790. This put Burke at odds with many of his colleagues in the Whig party, especially Charles James Fox, although the mutual respect the two men had for each other remained intact. Burke once described Fox as 'the greatest debater the world ever saw.' Besides Fox, there was another prominent person who had sympathy with the French revolution and that was Mary Wollstonecraft (1759-97) who was a feminist before the term had been coined. She wrote *'A Vindication of the Rights of Women'* and was the mother of the future Mary Shelley (1797-1851), Shelly being the author of *'Frankenstein'* and the wife of the poet Percy Bysshe Shelley (1792-1822). Wollstonecraft was also close to Thomas Christie, who as already mentioned, was the nephew of Joseph Priestly. Paine befriended both Mary and William Godwin (1756-1836), a radical English political writer who in 1793 published his *'Enquiry Concerning Political Justice'* which brought him both fame and money. Godwin clearly had different views on accepting payment for his written work than Paine did who constantly refused remuneration, although it did not stop him complaining about his lack of material wealth compared to the effort that he had put in producing his work and requesting payments later on as compensation.

Once Burke's *'Reflections…'* came out in November 1790, Paine decided that he would respond immediately and started work on his response only a few days later. Burke was very worried about the seizure of the Bastille and had been annoyed by a sermon that Dr. Richard Price (1723-91) had delivered on the anniversary of the Glorious Revolution that had happened in 1689 when William and Mary came to take the English throne after being invited by the British government. Price was a radical clergyman who supported both the American and the French revolutions. He had attended a Dissenting Academy in London and had become a preacher in Newington Green and Hackney. He was made a member of the Royal Society in 1765, and his *'Observations on Reversionary Payments'* which was published in 1771 helped to establish a scientific system for life-insurance and pensions, which was something that Paine was very interested in. Price also published *'An Appeal to the Public on the subject of the National Debt'* in 1772 which heavily influenced William Pitt the Younger when he became Prime Minister in 1783, as it was Pitt who introduced income tax and a sinking fund, the latter being introduced to help pay off any such debts. Burke's paper upset a great many of the left wing radicals. Mary Wollstonecraft quickly brought out her *'Vindication of the Rights of Man'* whilst there were attacks too from Thomas Christie and his uncle, Joseph Priestly. However, the work that everybody was keen to read was Paine's offering and his *'Rights of Man: Being An Answer to Mr. Burke's Attack on the French Revolution'* took three months to write despite the fact that he had previously claimed that he could complete it in three days. Paine argued that there should be no hereditary right to rule based on what he considered to be the misguided belief of the day that the aristocracy should rule as they had the inherited wisdom to do so.

Paine also argued for a written constitution composed by a National Assembly in the way that the newly formed United States of America had. There were 40,000 words in Paine's piece in total but the first part was finished at the end of January, 1791 and he duly gave the draft manuscript to his publisher friend, Joseph Johnson who said that he would have it ready in a month's time. However, Johnson was leaned on by government agents not to publish, or at the very least, to wait awhile, so Paine found another publisher, J. S. Jordan and the *'Rights of Man'* duly appeared on 13th March. Paine set out to dismiss Burke's fears about the revolution and then to talk about the positive aspects to it. Unfortunately, Paine was overtaken by events concerning one of the points he made when he said that the French revolution had involved no violence. At the time of his writing this it was perfectly correct, but as time went on, this assertion proved to be disastrously wrong. Burke wanted the system of government to be formed in the traditional way that preceded the revolution, whilst Paine felt strongly that more equality should be built into the system. He pointed out the new equality that seemed to be working in France – universal suffrage that was unheard of in Britain, equal constituencies which compared favourably with the system of rotten boroughs that was used in Britain, and a fixed seven-year term in Parliament.

Paine's views concerning previous revolutions were that they had simply meant that the leaders had been deposed and someone equally autocratic had replaced them but the system of government had remained the same. Paine thought that such a way of thinking solved nothing, and he argued that a revolution needed to be when the old *style* of how governments work was changed, and a completely new system was brought in to replace it.

Where Paine did alter his views however, was his attitude to the French monarchy. Whereas in *'Common Sense'* he wanted their abolition but that was written when he was talking about the events in America. Now he was writing about France and he argued that you could have republican principles but retain a monarchy. His change of attitude may well be down to two things. Firstly, America was striving to be a new country and it would be easy to dismiss King George III as their Monarch given the King was so far away geographically, and secondly, Paine felt some sympathy towards Louis XVI and Marie Antoinette as he felt that they had been helpful to America during the War of Independence.

The *'Rights of Man'* was a great success and the first edition sold out within a few hours and the sixth edition was printed within two months, coming out as it did at the end of May 1791. By now, the British government was worried about Paine and his ideas but couldn't make up their mind whether to arrest him and prosecute on the grounds that his book was likely to inflame the populace. In the end, they decided against prosecution as they felt it was overkill, so decided instead to hire a man named George Chalmers (1742-1825) to write a biography about Paine entitled *'Life of Thomas Pain; the Author of the Rights of Men, with a defence of His Writings'*. Chalmers was a Scottish antiquarian and political writer as well as being a lawyer having completed his studies in Edinburgh before going to America in 1773 and starting a practice in Baltimore. He returned to Britain two years later to specialise in writing about Ireland, American affairs, and the British Monarchy and had a good reputation to maintain. The book that he wrote about Paine did exactly the opposite of what the title suggested, but exactly what the government had planned it to do, which was to undermine Paine's arguments by pointing out so called weaknesses in his character, including the untrue statement that he had treated his first wife badly. It was probably the dubious nature of the book that caused Chalmers to write it under the name of Francis Oldys because as George Chalmers, he was considered a serious writer. Although hurt by the criticism, especially the charge that he had treated his first wife badly, Paine kept quiet and eventually it all died down without the sales of *'Rights of Man'* being adversely affected. In fact Paine's book was published in Holland, Germany, and France amongst others along with an American edition which had a preface by Thomas Jefferson (1743-1826). Jefferson was a Secretary of State in President George Washington's administration and he would go on to be Vice President when Washington left office in 1797 with the present Vice President, John Adams (1735-1826) taking over as President, serving until 1801. Jefferson himself then took over as President becoming the third person to hold that office. Jefferson was the ideal man to write a preface in Paine's book as both men shared the same views on the importance of all men being equal, whilst Adams took the view that America should continue the British system of retaining a King, as well as a House of Lords and a House of Commons but in this he was voted down.

Up until this time, Paine had assumed that France could be a republic as well as having a monarchy, but on 22nd June, 1791, whilst staying at Lafayette's home in Versailles, his host told him that the King and Queen had fled Paris under heavy disguise and had made their way towards the border where they thought that they could be sheltered by the Austrian army. Paine felt let down and expressed the view that he hoped that no effort would be made to bring them back but in fact this is exactly what happened. Captured at Varennes they were brought back to Paris three days later whilst running the gauntlet of jeering crowds. It had been a disastrous move by Louis XVI and Marie Antoinette because the country having previously accepted the fact that they could rule as a puppet monarchy, were now not so sure that they wanted a monarchy at all.

The Marquis de Condorcet became a republican virtually straight away and with others formed the Republican Society and also a newspaper, *Le Republicain* although the journal did not last long. Despite this however, it held the distinction of being the first paper in France to support the idea of abolishing the monarchy completely. Although he could speak no French, Paine offered to write for the paper under the pen name of *'Common Sense'* and also helped to write the Society's manifesto. They argued that this would be a good time as Louis XVI had by definition abdicated when he and Marie Antoinette had fled Paris although the Society also took the view that no punishment should be meted out to the King and Queen. Members of the society could not agree with each other about the future of the monarchy whilst Paine himself had again changed his mind and decided that it was not possible after all to be a republic whilst retaining a monarchy. However, amongst all these arguments there were two people who were very much in agreement, Condorcet and Paine, and between them they wrote an essay *'Answer to Four Questions on the Legislative and Executive Powers'* which they brought out in 1792. In it they suggested the formation of a national convention to look at what they saw as a constitutional crisis. Meanwhile Paine was working on the second part of the *'Rights of Man'* and his influence from Condorcet was clear.

Paine travelled back to England and in August 1791 he stayed in London with a friend from his days in Lewes, 'Clio' Rickman who was now a wealthy bookseller. Whilst there Paine spent a great deal of time writing *'The Rights of Man – Part two'* taking up all of the summer and part of the autumn. Paine's views were still differing greatly from those of Edmund Burke who had a pamphlet out entitled *'Appeal from the New to the Old Whigs'* and who was by now clearly contemptuous of Paine, not mentioning him by name and saying that he would not dignify the second part of *'Rights of Man'* with any counter arguements. However, there were many who thought highly of Paine and put him on a pedestal causing the government to fear what he would write in the second part of *'Rights of Man'*. Paine was finding writing difficult but at long last it was finished and on 16th February 1792, it was published by J. S. Jordan, who had also published the first part. The second part had the title of *'Rights of Man Part the Second, combining Principle and Practice'* but only after Paine had promised to take full responsibility for any trouble that the production of it might cause. Just as they had done with George Chalmers and the first part of *'Rights of Man'* the previous year, in the following year, 1792, the government paid someone called John Bowles to publish a piece entitled *"A Protest against*

Tom Paine's Rights of Man' although it appeared to cause little detrimental effect on Paine's work.

Paine's latest work was an interesting mixture of the positive and negative. Any previous affection he had for the French monarchy was now gone, and his views were now fixed that any monarchy in any country would have to be abolished to have anything resembling fairness in society. He tore into the British royal family not just because of the fact that they were royal, but for having originated from Germany. He wrote:- "I compare it (the monarchy) to something kept behind a curtain, about which there is a great deal of bustle and fuss, and a wonderful air of seeming solemnity; but when, by any accident, the curtain happens to be open, and the company see what it is, they burst into laughter." To press home his hatred of inherited power, he also wrote:- "Kings succeed each other, not as rationals but as animals". He also talked about democratic government but it was when he reached his fifth chapter that he really excelled. He wrote about social security for everybody, which just as it is now, would be financed by a taxation system. He refused to accept the well used phrase that:- "The poor will always be with us" because he considered that poverty was man made and did not happen by chance. He wrote:- "When it shall be said in any country in the world, my poor are happy; neither ignorance nor distress is to be found among them; my jails are empty of prisoners, my streets of beggars, the aged are not in want, the taxes are not oppressive; the rational world is my friend, because I am the friend of its happiness: when these things can be said, then may that country boast its constitution and its government."

Paine assumed that large families meant poor families and felt that the elderly part of the country would be unable to work. He felt that education was vital and proposed a grant system for every single child below the age of fourteen feeling that if this system was used, the financial hardships on families would be relieved and that ignorance would be a thing of the past. On and on his ideas came bursting out of the pages. One of the most extraordinary was the provision he suggested for old age which we do not even have today. He suggested a system of gradual retirement with the final retirement age being 60, qualifying for a pension of £10 per year, whilst people who were younger but who were beginning to find work harder, would receive a pension of £6 per year between the ages of 50 and 60.

Paine saw nothing but good in this system. He costed it and felt it perfectly feasible and said that if used, would mean the end of the dreaded workhouse that so many people ended up in and poverty would be eliminated. Reading these ideas today, people could be forgiven for thinking that although the Labour party was a hundred years or so away from being formed, Paine had definite socialist ideals. He hadn't however, because if he'd been an MP, he almost certainly would have been a Whig, but that was quite a different matter. Paine was never going to try and impose any state monopolies but simply, and possibly naively, he felt that the taxes would be redistributive and would be paid willingly. He also seemed to think that government should rein back its responsibilities and be minimalist in its functions, writing that:- "The instant formal government is abolished, society begins to act." There is no doubt that Paine struck a chord with people as 200,000 copies of the *'Rights of Man, Part*

2' were circulating as opposed to the 30,000 copies of Edmund Burke's *'Reflections'* which had been sold over a period of two years. *'The Rights of Man's'* popularity was such that it worried the government to such an extent that Paine was arrested in April 1792 for an alleged debt although he was bailed by his publisher friend, Joseph Johnson. Johnson had withdrawn from publishing the first part of Paine's *'Rights of Man'* due to government pressure but was now probably feeling guilty as a result.

Meanwhile, on 14th of May, the man who did publish Paine's work, J. S. Jordan, was indicted for printing work that was considered to be challenging the work of the state. Despite Paine's encouragement to plead not guilty, Jordan accepted the charge and paid a small fine. A week or so later, Paine himself had to appear in court charged with seditious libel and on 8th June he appeared again only to find that his trial had been postponed until 18th December. Meanwhile, he did not make life easy for himself as two days previously, on 6th June, he had written an open letter to the Home Secretary, Henry Dundas (1742-1811) mocking both the government led by William Pitt the Younger (1759-1806) who had become Prime Minister in 1783 at the age of twenty-four years, and King George III who he referred to as 'his Madjesty'. Distinguished though Dundas and Pitt were, they were used to criticism, Dundas having held senior positions in government under several Prime Ministers, whilst Pitt was the brilliant son of a brilliant father, William Pitt the Elder (1708-1778), later 1st Earl of Chatham. Pitt the Younger had risen to power at an incredibly young age, but the reference to what at the time had been King George's perceived madness only four years before in 1788 was highly insensitive to say the least and was a high risk factor. Although it was not known at the time, it is now felt that the King was almost certainly not insane, but had suffered a dose of porphyria, a genetically inherited disease which produced the symptoms of temporary insanity. However, whatever people felt his illness to be at the time, the King was very popular with the British people and Paine was taking a big gamble in writing in this manner.

It is possible that the reason the government postponed Paine's trial from June until December was their hope that he would leave the country and return to either America or France. If that was the plan, it worked because after having several honours bestowed upon him by France in his absence, Paine, accompanied by two friends, left Britain on 13th September, 1792 to return there. He was trailed by government agents who wanted to make sure that he was going to board the ship which although he did, it was in marked contrast to the positive reaction to his *'Rights of Man'*, and he was given a stormy send off by crowds who booed him, shouted at him and called him a traitor. There were even some who called for him to be killed. Although by now he was abroad, Paine's trial commenced at Guildhall on 18th December and despite the fact that he was out of the country, or possibly even because of, Paine wrote a letter to the Attorney General, Archibald MacDonald which could not have been more rude and insulting if he'd tried. Paine insulted the King as well as the government who he said were an example of:- "a great, if not the greatest, perfection of fraud and corruption that ever took place since governments began". If Paine was expecting to return to Britain at some stage, then he was not going the best way round it as the King was very popular, and the Prime

Minister, William Pitt the Younger was generally accepted as being a brilliant man and stayed in office from 1783 until 1806 with a break of just three years from 1801 until 1804. The letter that Paine wrote never gave Thomas Erskine, his defence Counsel, a chance as Erskine hadn't even known that it had been written until MacDonald used it to good effect in his opening address to the jury. Not surprisingly, Paine was found guilty which meant that he could not return to Britain as he would almost certainly have been imprisoned or possibly even worse, he could have been facing the death penalty. Booksellers stocking Paine's books were prosecuted and five years later, all of Paine's books were banned. Paine was stunned when he heard the news but it is difficult to understand why – in a period when people could be sentenced to death or transported to New South Wales for sheep stealing, Paine's insults to the monarchy and government must have seemed far more serious.

Paine arrived in France in September 1792 and received a warm welcome which contrasted sharply with the way he left Britain. In France he was welcomed with an armed guard who fired a salute for him and on the 21st September, he became a deputy with the National Convention. However, if a revolution in America and a further one in France wasn't enough, he walked into a situation whereby France appeared to be suffering further problems, if not another revolution. The National Assembly suspended Louis XVI from being King and demanded that there be elections to a body called the National Convention. The National Convention was charged with writing a new constitution and if anyone was even suspected of having Royalist sympathies, they were arrested. The whole situation was a nightmare because from 2nd September, 2,000 such people were thrown into jail and killed, a process that took less than a week. Although not approving of these killings, Paine was granted French citizenship.

Paine was in attendance at the first meeting of the National Convention. There were several factions but Paine, although not a member of any of them, seemed to be closer to the Girondins who were the most moderate. They were a very loosely affiliated group of people who included the Marquis de Condorcet. They had six deputies who sat in both the Legislative Assembly as well as the National Convention. The Girondins had no formal leader as such but many of their views were voiced by Jacques Pierre de Warville Brissot (1754-93), a revolutionary politician who had been imprisoned in the Bastille for four months on the charge of having written a brochure against the Queen, although the charge was false. As the revolution gathered momentum, he was seen as the mouthpiece for the Girondins and was eventually guillotined in 1793. Another faction were the Jacobins who were far more radical. They were formed in 1789 by deputies from the National Assembly and their aims were to protect the gains of the Revolution in case there was a movement amongst the aristocracy to thwart the revolution's progress. They were instrumental in turning France into a republic and doing away with the monarchy and were determined to look after the interests of the so-called lower classes. They were led by Maximilien Marie Isidore de Robespierre (1758-94) and organised the reign of terror in 1793. For a while, his popularity was high, and in 1791 he was appointed public accuser, having great power during the upheaval that the country was going through, but it was not to last, and in July 1794 he was guillotined.

On 11th October, 1792, Paine was appointed to a committee consisting of eight men with the idea of drawing up a constitution. This was always going to be a long job and meanwhile, Paine could see that power was slipping from the Girondins to the Jacobins, which meant that the King's life would be in danger. After three weeks, Paine warned the Convention against executing Louis, saying that it was the office of monarch rather than Louis himself that was causing the constitutional problems. The tide was turning against Paine however, and October and November saw the Girondins fighting a rearguard battle against the Jacobins over the future of Louis XVI and on 15th November, the Convention decided to put the King on trial. The trial commenced on 11th December and whilst Paine made clear that he was anti-monarchy, he made a strong appeal for mercy to be shown to the King but to no avail. With a majority of just one vote, the King was sentenced to death on the 17th January which was carried out on 21st January, 1793. Paine did not want to stay in a country that would carry out such a barbarous sentence and probably had put his own life in danger at the stance he took in asking for mercy for the King. Given the fact that he felt he could not travel back to Britain because of almost certain imprisonment and possibly execution, the stance he took in France was a very courageous one. He retreated to St. Denis, a quiet place just outside Paris where he received visits from Mary Wollstonecraft and Joel Barlow (1754-1812), the American poet and politician and Barlow's wife.

Barlow was born in Redding, Connecticut. He had served as a chaplain in the American War of independence and then went abroad for sixteen years, spending the majority of that time in France where he involved himself in politics and writing.

Paine had played a major part in what was happening in France, but he had often found himself out of step with certain issues, the execution of Louis XV1 being a prime example. He was now unclear what to do or where to go because on 2nd June, 1793, the Jacobins ousted the Girondins and a great many people who had supported the revolution but not so much the violence it produced were considered traitors. The reign of Terror had begun and some of the Girondins' leaders were unsafe - some of them were being executed whilst Robespierre and Louis St. Just prepared a new constitution. Among those executed were Mary Antoinette who faced the guillotine on 16th October, 1793 and also the Marquis de Condorcet who was politically close to Paine which made him realise that his own life was far from safe. In fact he was arrested on 28th December, 1793 and detained in Luxembourg prison. Up until his arrest, he was writing his latest book, *'The Age of Reason, Being an Investigation of Truth and of Fabulous Theology'*. Paine wrote about his religious views but confused people into thinking he was an atheist but he wasn't, it's just that he did not believe in organised religion. He wrote:- "I do not believe in the creed professed by the Jewish church, by the Roman church, by the Greek church, by the Turkish church, by the Protestant church, nor by any church that I know of. My own mind is my own church." He was a believer, but in one God only. Paine believed the Old Testament to be cruel and dismissed its writings, but he believed in

Christ although he thought that the people who wrote the New Testament had completely distorted the truth, the end result being what he thought was mere nonsense.

In January 1794, Paine was in jail pondering his predicament and wondering how long he had to live. He was ready to meet his death as he was convinced that it was to come soon, although an extraordinary piece of luck saved him. Lying in his prison cell, he became ill with a high fever and suspected typhus. In May 1794, he was transferred to a larger cell with three other prisoners. One night in July, the guards were going round the cells chalking on the cell doors that housed the prisoners who were to meet their deaths the next day. Because he was so ill, Paine's cell mates asked the guard to open the cell door which opened to the outside. The guards then chalked who was to be guillotined on the door but because it was open fully and the outside of the door was against the wall, the guards had written the names on the inside part of the door, which when closed, had the names of those prisoners on the inside of the cell. Although his illness was severe, it was that, plus the ingenuity of his cell mates along with a huge slice of luck, that saved his life.

France had a new American Ambassador called James Monroe (1758-1831), who Paine thought would be better disposed towards him. Monroe was American, being born in Westmoreland County, Virginia and had fought in the American War of Independence. In 1783 he was elected to Congress and in 1785 was Chairman of the committee that helped set in motion the drawing up of the new constitution. He had a fine career before being elected the 5th President of the United States in 1816 and was re-elected in 1820. On 2nd November, 1794, being the American Ambassador in France, he sent a letter to the Committee of General Security requesting Paine's release arguing that Paine was an American citizen. Fortunately this worked, Paine being released two days later having spent just over ten months incarcerated. Paine went to stay with Monroe at the latter's invitation although after borrowing some money from Monroe, stayed with him for over a year prompting Monroe to say in a letter to a friend that Paine would still be there until he died or returned to America, but held no hope that either event was going to happen in the near future.

Paine was still unwell but it did not stop him from taking his seat in the Convention in December 1794 which he had been invited to resume although he did not attend and make his first speech until 7th July, 1795. This speech coincided with his publishing 'Dissertation on First Principles of Government' and although members of the Convention listened to him politely, they ignored him afterwards. The new constitution came into being on 23rd September 1795, and allowed for elections to two chambers but with the executive power being in the hands of a five-man group making up the Directory. Paine was bitterly disappointed – this was not what he wanted at all and soon he lost interest in French politics and began to take a less active part.

August 1795 saw Paine finishing off the second part of 'The Age of Reason' and having an increased hostility to both the New and the Old Testaments. The New Testament he thought was ridiculous whilst the Old he simply saw as cruel. During this time his illness grew worse along with his anger towards George

Washington for seeming to ignore the situation that he, Paine, was in. However, there was little he could do about it although he wrote a very bitter letter where he expressed that bitterness to James Madison (1751-1836) although he was persuaded not to send it by James Monroe. Madison was an American and had a distinguished career in the American Political arena and on 26th August 1792, he, along with other Americans including George Washington, was made an honorary citizen of France. In 1801 when Thomas Jefferson became the third President of the United States, Madison was made Secretary of State before becoming the country's fourth President himself in 1809.

In February 1796 a treaty was negotiated between America and Britain known as Jay's Treaty and this was meant to formalise relations between the two countries and to tie up any loose ends that were left over from the war. The treaty enraged Paine who thought it was pro-British and anti-French and felt this totally unfair considering the fact that France had been the main ally of America throughout the war. In 1796, Paine wrote a furious open 70 page *'Letter to George Washington'* which he finished at the end of July, but released it in two stages, the first in October of that year, the second in November. It was released as a single pamphlet in February 1797. After criticising the treaty generally, Paine then turned his anger towards Washington personally as page after page of bitterness was turned towards the President. Paine felt that he had defended Washington's abilities as a Commander during the War of Independence but felt that when he had needed Washington's help, he had been ignored and left to rot in the Luxembourg prison. Washington almost certainly read the letter but did not reply.

Paine's final major piece of work was *'Agrarian Justice'* which was brought about by the arrest of Francois Noel Babeuf (1760-97) in May, 1796. Babeuf was a French communist who had advocated a system of communism in France but was sent to the guillotine for along with others, plotting against the Directory and trying to bring a system whereby all property would be equally divided. Paine had disagreed with the extreme views that Babeuf had been putting forward but felt that both he and Babeuf had wanted the equality that had not been brought about. Paine's *'Agrarian Justice'* was published in France in 1796 and America the following year. If Paine had a problem with George Washington, then he had even bigger problems with his successor as President in John Adams who was elected to the post and took office on 4th March, 1797. Paine wanted an egalitarian society and wrote about it in the second part of *'Rights of Man'* but felt that Adams was too comfortable with large differences of wealth, and also suspected that Adams would have preferred a monarchy as head of state based on the British system.

Paine had been staying in Le Havre for a few weeks in the spring of 1797 and on his return he was invited by his friend, the radical journalist, Nicolas de Bonneville (1760-1828) to stay with him and his family for what was supposed to be just a week or so but ended up with Paine staying five years. Bonneville was an interesting man, being a student of English and German literature and translated Shakespeare as well as founding several newspapers and in 1792 had finished writing a history of modern Europe. At the turn of the century, Paine was developing an urge to return to America and there were two reasons for this.

Firstly, he had fallen out of love with France, being disillusioned with the way that the revolution had turned out. It had not brought the equality that he had hoped for and felt that the American War of Independence had produced a far more equal society. The second reason was that the man in America that he hated so much, John Adams, was no longer President, Thomas Jefferson taking over the post as third President on 4th March 1801.

Paine decided that he would now like to return to the United States as a year later, Britain and France had both signed the Treaty of Amiens so that he thought it a good time to sail across the Atlantic. Paine left Le Havre on 1st September, 1802 and arrived in Baltimore two months later on 30th October. Bonneville's wife and children were to follow him over, followed by Nicolas de Bonneville himself at a later date.

Paine did not receive the reception he was hoping for when he arrived in America. He had been away for fifteen years and there were many who felt he was linked too closely with the dreadful mass murders that had happened in France. The two revolutions were quite different because America had one common enemy that she was fighting – Britain. The situation in France was internal with the result that people were committing the most dreadful crimes against their own people. Paine was not given enough credit for the fact that he himself was totally against Louis XVI being executed and that he, Paine, had also been incarcerated and only just escaped the guillotine. A Boston Federalist newspaper wrote that Paine was:- "A lying, drunken, brutal infidel, who rejoices in the opportunity of basking and wallowing in the confusion, devastation, bloodshed, rapine and murder, in which his soul delights". There were many articles in different papers written about him, and it has to be said that some were very much in his favour, but there were many who weren't but it seemed that there was no-one who was neutral.

Since Paine had been away from America, they had developed a political party system for elections to President. The Federalist Party was formed by Washington's former Aide-de-camp, Alexander Hamilton, and the support they received was largely from merchants, bankers and businessmen. The party was formed in 1792 and lasted until 1816. The Federalists controlled the government until 1801, because Washington, who was President from 1789 until 1797, had Federalist sympathies and the second President, John Adams, who was President from 1797 until 1801, actually called himself a Federalist but when he left office, he was the first and last President to run on that ticket.

The other party was the Democratic-Republican Party that was founded by Thomas Jefferson and James Madison on or around 1792, the exact date being unknown. Sometimes called Democrats, other times they were called Republicans but mostly their enemies would refer to them as Democratic-Republicans. The party was formed to counter the views of the Federalists and was the dominant party from 1800, the year before John Adams, the Federalist President was beaten in the election, and lasted until 1824 when it split into different groups, and one of these groups became the Democratic Party that we know today. It favoured the rights of the yeoman farmer over the businessmen who were favoured by the Federalists. John Adams' son, John Quincy Adams (1767-1848), who was the sixth President from 1825 until 1829 represented the

National Republican Party, whose policies were closer to the old Federalist Party after the latter had broken up.

Having arrived in Baltimore on 30th October, 1802, Paine was to live the rest of his life out in the States. At first he involved himself in politics but at 65, this was limited to writing and at first he wrote a series of open letters *'To the Citizens of the United States'*. The first one was published on 15th November, 1802 and in this and subsequent letters he attacked the Federalists but saved his venom for John Adams. Paine certainly seemed to have a personal vendetta against Adams who he seemed to hate with a vengeance but quite why is not clear, as Adams had lost office eighteen months prior to this and mentally bruised after his election defeat, had more or less retired from politics and had returned to his home in Quincy.

Paine began to feel more isolated from the American people and felt that now Jefferson had replaced Adams as President, he, Paine, had very little more to say. The man who had coined the phrase 'The United States of America' now seemed irrelevant to the American people. Always a restless spirit, on 24th February, 1803, he moved to a friend, Colonel Joseph Kirkbride's house in Bordentown where he was joined by Madame de Bonneville and her children, but not her husband, who was still detained in France. In January 1804, he returned to his farm at New Rochelle but had to sell 60 acres of the land that was once given to him by the government to clear debts. He had no money and was ostracized by those who once had a high regard for him, much of these feelings of anger being a reaction to Paine's book *'The Age of Reason'*, which had been published in two parts in the mid-1790's. People had incorrectly felt that the book was the work of an atheist but this was not true. Paine believed in God, but one God only although he disbelieved in organised religion and even George Washington cooled towards him.

Possibly the worst humiliation happened to Paine when he went to vote in November, 1805. He had travelled to New Rochelle in order to vote in Congressional and state elections but was not allowed to as he was deemed not to be an American citizen. A naturally hurt and indignant Paine, fought this in the courts but despite lobbying influential people including James Monroe, the man who had secured Paine's release from the Luxembourg jail in November 1794, he lost the case and the man who had coined the phrase 'United States of America' was not allowed to vote.

Paine was largely forgotten apart from a few close friends and some hangers on who would listen to his stories in various taverns, but basically, he was heading towards a sad ending to a life that was now becoming meaningless. His health was poor and he lost the use of his legs so he propped himself up at a table, still with books and papers around him. On 18th January 1809, Paine wrote his last will, his one last hope being that he be buried in a Quaker cemetery but even that was denied him when he made the request on 19th March, 1809. The reason given for this decision was that if anyone wanted to erect a monument to him this would be against the Quaker rules. There was now no way that he could recover and he was moved to a house where Madame de Bonneville was to care for him in the short period of time that he had left.

Thomas Paine died on the 8th June, 1809 and he was taken to his farm in New Rochelle the following day where he was to be buried. There were very few people there – Madame de Bonneville and her children and about seven others. The papers were largely silent on the matter and no word came from any of the people he had associated with in the mid 1770's when the War of Independence started. There was one more indignity he had to endure though, even in death. In 1796, an English journalist by the name of William Cobbett (1763-1835) had attacked Paine in print but subsequently become an admirer. When he started his journalistic career he was a Tory but eventually became a champion of the poor leaving the Tories in 1804. In 1819, he and two friends dug Paine's bones up with the idea of giving him a proper burial in England, but it simply never happened and the bones disappeared or certainly the secret as to where the bones were, disappeared when Cobbett died in 1835. A sad end for a man such as Paine who took a leading role in two revolutions in two different countries and put his life on the line in two events that would dramatically change the way these countries were governed. He certainly made mistakes, but for every person who disliked him and what he stood for, there were just as many if not more, who loved him and who owe a debt of gratitude to a man who worked tirelessly for what he perceived to be a better world for virtually no monetary gain. His whole life seemed to be a labour of love. His ideas were certainly way ahead of their time. He was against slavery many years before it was abolished, he advocated taxation which he saw as a way of re-distributing wealth, hated poverty and refused to accept the often quoted saying 'That the poor will always be with us'. He suggested an ingenious way of not only retiring people with a pension, but carrying it out gradually which was a completely novel idea, and he suggested a sinking fund so that money would always be kept in cases of emergency, such as re-payment of debts. Paine was a committed republican although he was totally against the execution of Louis XVI even though his beliefs nearly cost him his life in France. He was against any kind of violence towards any Royal Family, it was simply that he never understood the idea of people inheriting vast wealth and receiving undue deference without having earned it.

History has been kinder to Paine and there are memorials in various places in the world. In Britain, there is a statue of Paine in King's Street, Thetford, Norfolk which was his birth place, and in America, there is a bust of him in the Hall of Fame of Great Americans at Bronx Community College. There are also statues in Morristown and Bordentown, New Jersey and in France there is a further statue in the Parc Montsouris in Paris. There are other various plaques and back in Britain, Lewes Town Council celebrate the life and work of Thomas Paine between the 4th and 14th July each year.

Abraham Lincoln (1809-65), possibly the most famous President of them all and Thomas Edison (1847-1931), the American inventor and physicist admired Paine's work, and whilst Lincoln was persuaded to burn the work that he, Lincoln had written about Paine to save his career, Edison, a non-politician, had no such constrictions. Perhaps the last words on Paine can be left to Edison who wrote:-

"I have always regarded Paine as one of the greatest of all Americans. Never have we had a sounder intelligence in this republic… It was my good fortune to encounter Thomas Paine's works in my boyhood… It was, indeed, a revelation to me to read that great thinker's views on political and theological subjects. Paine educated me, then, about many matters of which I had never before thought. I remember, very vividly, the flash of enlightenment that shone from Paine's writings, and I recall thinking at that time, 'What a pity these works are not today the schoolbooks for all children!' My interest in Paine was not satisfied by my first reading of his works. I went back to them time and again, just as I have done since my boyhood days."

High praise indeed from an eminent man – Paine would surely have been pleased with such a tribute although it will always remain shameful that he never heard anything like it in the last few years of his life, only after his death were these thoughts and feelings articulated.

-oOOo-

17
King George III
(1738-1820)

The reigning Monarch between 1760-1820, although his son George, Prince of Wales ruled as Regent from 1811 when his father was too ill to carry out his duties. The Prince of Wales continued to rule as Regent until 1820 when George III died whereupon he took the crown as George IV and ruled until his own death in 1830.

During the morning of 25th October 1760, George, the twenty-two-year-old Prince of Wales, accompanied by a collection of people who were mainly servants, was out riding along Gunnersbury Lane, then a country road, when a rider approached with the news that George II had had a bad accident and was likely to die. If this was the case, then the young Prince of Wales would inherit the throne and become King of Great Britain whenever that moment came. On hearing the news, the Prince immediately rode back to Kew to write a letter to his mentor, Lord Bute (1713-92), the Groom of the Stole to the Prince and inform him of the situation. The Prime Minister of the day was Thomas Pelham Holles (1693-1768) but it was in fact William Pitt the Elder (1708-78), later to become Lord Chatham, who was Secretary of State and was responsible for prosecuting the war with France, that the Prince saw first when he and his mentor Lord Bute summoned Pitt to Kensington on hearing that King George II was dead.

The new King George III was the third of the Hanoverian Kings of Britain. The Kingdom of Great Britain was formed on 1st May, 1707 when England and Scotland were merged in the Acts of Union of that year. Britain had been ruled by the Hanoverians from 1714 – prior to that the monarchy came from the House of Stuart. The last Stuart monarch to rule was Queen Anne who was born in 1665 and became Queen in 1702 until her death on 1st August 1714, and because she had no immediate heir that was acceptable, George I was chosen to become the first King from the House of Hanover. George I was born in 1660 and ruled from 1714 until his death in 1727 and was succeeded by his son George II (1683-1760) and who ruled from 1727 until his own death in 1760 when his grandson became George III.

George I, the first Hanoverian King, was only distantly related to the Royal Family but because there was no Protestant heir to succeed Queen Anne, was chosen to become King in 1714 as he was the closest that Britain had as the Act of Settlement which was passed in 1701 decreed that no Catholics could take the throne. George I was German in every way. He spoke no English but the upside of that situation was that he refrained from interfering in politics and trusted his ministers. It also meant there was a constitutional change of the first magnitude which remains with us to this day and for the foreseeable future. It was felt that one chosen minister would be helpful when it came to keeping the Monarch informed of events and thus Sir Robert Walpole (1676-1745) was the man who chaired regular meetings of his ministers, these being the forerunner of today's cabinet and in effect making Walpole the first ever Prime Minister. He held the position from 1721 until 1742 when a grateful King made him the Earl of Orford.

George II had married Caroline of Ansbach on 22nd August, 1705 and they had eight children, three sons and five daughters, although one of the sons, George William was born in 1717 and died the following year. The eldest son was Frederick, Prince of Wales who was born on 1st February, 1707 and lived until his death by accident on 31st March, 1751, nine years before his father, George II died, thus the monarchy from George II to George III skipped a generation. George II was not particularly liked as he was petty minded, self-important and a womaniser although he did have one redeeming feature – he had great courage. He was the last reigning Monarch of England to lead his troops into battle which he did on 27th June, 1743 at Dettingen. Despite the French having 70,000 troops and the combined Austrian, British and Hanoverian having only 50,000, King George II fronted his infantry on foot and defeated the French. George II was a lucky man when he married Caroline of Ansbach in 1705. She was attractive and sexy and used it to good effect when the need arose although she was never unfaithful unlike her husband. Along with her looks, she had a brilliant mind and an understanding of politics that few women, certainly amongst the aristocracy, could lay claim to. Queen Caroline died in 1737 and the King was heartbroken. Although he had taken mistresses during their marriage, none of them came close to the Queen in looks and intellect, and despite the Queen's deathbed wish that he should marry again, the thought never crossed his mind.

It was a feature of the Hanoverian dynasty that father and son did not get on, and so it was with George II and Frederick the Prince of Wales. In fact, not only did Prince Frederick not get on with his father, his mother and her five daughters didn't like him very much either. His mother, Queen Caroline said of him:- "My dear first born is the greatest ass, and the greatest liar, and the greatest canaille, and the greatest beast, in the whole world, and I most heartily wish he were out of it". She also called him 'a wretch and a villain' and made no secret that she preferred her younger son William Augustus, the Duke of Cumberland (1721-65), later known as 'The Butcher of Culloden' after the cruelty that the English troops inflicted on the highlanders after the Battle of Culloden in 1745. As if Frederick's mother's opinion of him was not enough, his sister, Princess Amelia (1711-86) said of Frederick that:- "He was the greatest liar that ever spoke and will put one arm round anybody's neck to kiss them, and then stab them with the other if he can". Possibly the most damning comment made about Frederick was again from his mother, Queen Caroline who on her deathbed on 1st December, 1737 said:- "At least I shall have one comfort in having my eyes eternally closed – I shall never see that monster again".

Thus it was that when Frederick died in 1751 at the age of forty-four, his father George II didn't even try and show sorrow. It is not entirely clear quite how Frederick died – some accounts say that he was hit on the head by a tennis ball, others say it was a cricket ball. The fact remains however, that his death was an accident and was very sudden. He was put to bed but the blow caused an abscess which burst causing him to cough violently and he died shortly afterwards. Prince Frederick had had a succession of mistresses before he was persuaded to marry Princess Augusta of Saxe-Gotha (1719-72), which he did in 1736.

Although the bride was chosen for Frederick by his father, it seems that most of the royal household felt very sorry for her from the beginning and even after the marriage ceremony had taken place at St. James' Palace, he displayed inappropriate behaviour at the reception afterwards when he was seen to be too familiar with the servants, laughing and winking at them instead of paying attention to his new bride. His poor behaviour towards his new wife continued even when she became pregnant. The King and Queen wanted the baby to be born at Hampton Court and also wanted to be present at the birth but Frederick felt differently. This was in part due to the annoyance that he felt because in his view his father had not granted him enough money to live on from the civil list. As a single man he received £24,000 p.a., plus a further £14,000 from the estates of the Duchy of Cornwall, but he thought that as a married man, he should receive much more. However, when he married, he was allowed a further £12,000 a year taking the total to £50,000 which he felt was totally inadequate. Bearing in mind that in 2010, that amount would probably translate into roughly £3 million per annum, it is difficult to understand what he would have deemed to be a reasonable amount. Frederick decided to bypass his parents and took the case to parliament where he thought that politicians, hoping for future glory when Frederick became King, would support him. Some did but not enough for him to effect any change in the amounts as the motion was defeated in both the Commons and Lords. The King and Queen were annoyed because although the motion was defeated, it attracted enough support to ruffle the royal feathers but there was more to come. Late at night on 31st July, 1737 and with his wife expecting a baby at any time, Frederick took the Princess to St. James's Palace although no notice of this fact was given to the staff and nothing had been done to make them comfortable. The beds were damp and the baby was born soon after the couple's arrival – a girl, she was named Augusta and although she lived a long life until 1813, it was not a good start for her.

Frederick's behaviour in causing his wife unnecessary discomfort when Augusta was born was the last straw for the King and Queen who ordered him away from the Royal Household as soon as his wife, Princess Augusta had recovered from the birth and he was effectively banished from the King's palaces. Lest Frederick be in any doubt about the depth of his parent's anger, copies of George II's letter to Frederick were sent to foreign embassies in London as well as abroad. It was also made clear that if any of these ambassadors were to visit the Prince, it would be frowned upon by the King and Queen.

The second child that Prince Frederick and Princess Augusta had was a boy named George after the baby's grandfather, King George II and great grandfather, the late King George I with the additional names of William Frederick. If this was a ploy by Frederick to try and curry favour with his father George II, it did not work. The future King George III was born on 4th June, 1738 but George II's wife, Queen Caroline had died the year before, and the child did not excite his grandfather one little bit and he showed little interest in the boy. Baby George was premature by two months and with infant mortality being so rife in the 18th century, it was felt that the child would not survive so he was baptised later that day. He did survive however and a great deal of credit for this was due to the care that he received from his wet-nurse, Mary Smith who was married to one of the gardeners. She was later rewarded by being made laundress at Windsor Castle and the position was later taken by her daughter. All told, Prince Frederick and Princess Augusta had nine children, five sons and four daughters. These were Augusta (1737-1813), George, later King George III (1738-1820), Edward Augustus, the Duke of York (1739-67), Elizabeth Caroline (1740-59), William Henry, Duke of Gloucester (1743-1805), Henry Frederick, Duke of Cumberland (1745-1796), Louisa Anne (1749-68), Frederick William (1750-65), and Caroline Matilda (1751-75).

Although Prince Frederick was disliked by a number of people, he was a good father and took a keen interest in his children's studies. Prince George and his brother Edward, born the following year after George, were tutored by the Rev. Francis Ayscough, (1700-63), a Fellow of Corpus Christi College, Oxford and who was also a Doctor of Divinity. Whilst he was at Oxford, Ayscough tutored George Lyttelton and later became his brother-in-law by virtue of the fact that he married Lyttelton's sister – Lyttelton later became Prince Frederick's Private Secretary. However, King George II was unhappy with Ayscough being employed to tutor his grandson and there were two reasons for this – the first being that Ayscough was a rather dull uninspiring teacher but the second reason was due to the fact that the King had resented the fact that Lyttelton had supported Prince Frederick's attempt to receive a larger allowance when he, Frederick had married. However, despite the fact that Ayscough was an uninspiring tutor, the two princes did rather well at their studies and George would later become fluent in German as well as in English and Frederick was always encouraging both boys in their studies. Frederick had many interests such as music, science, art, gardening and astronomy amongst others and always hoped that young George would do well in some if not all of these subjects. Frederick's love of science and the arts was genuine and he played the cello quite well and even tried his hand at writing, succeeding in co-writing a play that was performed at the Drury Lane theatre. He was also a patron of the landscape gardener William Kent (1684-1748) who amongst other things gave the Prince advice on the layout of the gardens at Carlton House. Kent's fame has been somewhat overshadowed by that of Lancelot 'Capability' Brown (1716-83), but whereas Brown was a landscape gardener only, Kent was also an architect who had designed many public buildings in London which included the Royal Mews in Trafalgar Square, and the Treasury Buildings as well as the

Horse Guards block in Whitehall. He also designed the Gothic screens in Westminster Hall and Gloucester Cathedral.

Despite Frederick's sons, George and Edward doing fairly well in their studies, it was decided to replace Francis Ayscough with George Lewis Scott, a barrister and mathematician who was highly thought of by many in Royal circles. Scott had been born in Hanover and his father had been a friend of Frederick's grandfather, the late King George I. However, despite his undoubted capabilities, some had reservations about Scott's appointment because he was suggested to Prince Frederick by Lord Bolingbroke (1678-1751), who was known to have had Jacobite sympathies and it was felt his views would influence Scott. Prince Frederick ignored such doubts however and kept Scott on. To help Scott educate the princes, Frederick appointed Lord Francis North (1704-90), as Governor. North became the 1st Earl of Guilford in 1752 and was the father of the future Prime Minister, Lord (Frederick) North (1732-92). Many years later, people were to comment on the close physical resemblance between Frederick North (1732-92), Francis North's son and future Prime Minister, and Prince George (1738-1820), son of Frederick, the Prince of Wales, (1707-1751), and certainly there is a marked likeness between the two sons. Francis North had joined the Royal Household in 1730 as Gentleman of the Bedchamber, many years before he tutored the young Prince George. In 1728, two years earlier, he had married Lady Lucy Montagu, daughter of the 2nd Earl Halifax and who had a reputation for being rather humourless and although she was considered attractive, she was not seen as an outstanding beauty. Their first child was Frederick (North) who was born in 1732, four years after the marriage. Although nothing was said at the time, in later years Nathaniel Wraxall (1751-1831), an English writer of memoirs, suggested that Prince Frederick had had an affair with Lady Lucy, and that Prince George and Frederick North were in fact halfbrothers both having the same father, Prince Frederick. Most people did not believe it although at one level it is hard to understand why. The likeness between Prince George, the child born of Prince Frederick and Princess Augusta, and Frederick North, son of Lucy Montagu and possibly Prince Frederick is certainly strong and Frederick certainly had many affairs. Having said that however, prior to these rumours being spread, there had never been any scandal spread concerning Lady Lucy.

As mentioned earlier, it was a feature of Hanoverian Kings that each generation of sons seemed to detest their father and whether it was a simple clash of personalities or the sons rebelling against their upbringing cannot be certain. Possibly it was a little of both, but certainly the Princes George (the future George III) and Edward (the Duke of York) had little time for fun when they were children. Scott and North set about organising a very heavy workload for them starting in their schoolroom at 8 am and often not finishing until 9 or 10pm that night. Amongst other subjects, they were taught reading, writing, arithmetic, geometry, as well as the obligatory Latin and Greek and this timetable continued without respite for six days a week. On Sundays, there was a little time for relaxation and games, but only after the Bishop of Norwich had visited the princes and read to them a book on the principles of the Christian religion.

However, on the death of Prince Frederick in 1751, the Royal Household was to change. Previous tutors had been chosen by Frederick, but King George II wanted to have more say now that the boys' father was dead. Lord North was replaced as Governor by Lord Harcourt whilst George Lewis Scott went and was replaced by Dr. Thomas Hayter. Harcourt had served in the army and had reached the rank of Lieutenant-General, serving with George II at Dettingen in June 1743 when the latter had been the last monarch to command his troops from the front in battle. It was probably the fact that he was at that battle with the King that enabled Harcourt to be appointed as the Prince's Governor because it was certainly felt by a number of the Royal Household that he was not the right man for the job. However, Hayter was also deemed to be unfit to teach his charges. He was pedantic and harsh with Prince George and his brother, Prince Edward. Hayter had come through the church due to the influence of the Archbishop of York who was rumoured to be his natural father. Hayter later became Sub-Dean of York although he came to that position before he was thirty years old and again powerful influences helped, although this time it was the Duke of Newcastle, Thomas Pelham Holles, (1693-1768), a Secretary of State in his brother Henry Pelham's (1695-1754) government who was to lend a helping hand.

However, despite being given their respective positions, Hayter and Harcourt were frustrated because they were deemed to be unsuitable for the Princes needs and consequently, had little involvement with their education. There were three men who it appeared had more influence and although Hayter and Harcourt were unhappy with the situation, there was precious little they could do about it. Scott was still in the Royal Household as Sub-Preceptor and Andrew Stone, a friend of the Duke of Newcastle's was brought in as Sub-Governor. He was a talented man who was thought to have great knowledge and a good memory but whether he had the talent to inspire the Princes was open to debate. The third man who had influence was James Cresset, the clever secretary of Princess Augusta. Eventually however, both Harcourt and Hayter left after falsely accusing the new men of harbouring Jacobite tendencies and passing these thoughts on to the young Princes. Eventually Harcourt was replaced by Lord Waldegrave as Prince George's Governor, not that he particularly wanted the position and although the Prince resumed his studies of Latin, French, German, and algebra, amongst many others, Princess Augusta never felt that Waldegrave was the right man for the job. Stories had been spread about a so-called affair between Princess Augusta and Lord Bute and she felt convinced that they came from Waldegrave. The story was almost certainly nonsense as Lord Bute was devoted to his wife whilst Princess Augusta, the Prince's mother, was a very pious woman and almost certainly incapable of conducting an illicit relationship.

However, it was Lord Bute who was the man who really influenced the young Prince George. John Stuart, the 3rd Earl of Bute (1713-92), was a Scottish statesman who succeeded to that title at the age of ten years when his father died in 1723. He was made one of the Lords of the Bedchamber in 1737 by Frederick, Prince of Wales and after Frederick died suddenly in 1751, there was a re-organisation of the Royal household by King George II, and in 1756,

Bute became Groom of the Stole to Frederick's son, Prince George, the future King George III. In May, 1762, he was to eventually, albeit reluctantly, become Prime Minister being the first ever Tory to hold the job, the position being in the grip of the Whigs since 1721 when Robert Walpole held the position first. Bute was never keen on taking the job however and lasted just less than a year before resigning in April, 1763.

However, it was after the death of the Prince's father Frederick in 1751 that Lord Bute had the most influence on Prince George. Bute became a surrogate father to George and advised him on many things both as to his future role as King but also on personal matters.

Bute was a serious man and his views held enormous sway with the shy young Prince and when George became King in 1760, Bute continued to hold enormous influence over his charge. In fact, it is probably true to say that the Prince not only greatly trusted Lord Bute, but that he *only* trusted Lord Bute, once saying to him that:- "You are the only man with whom one's reputation and honour can with safety be entrusted".When George became King George III in 1760, the Prime Minister was Thomas Pelham-Holles, the Duke of Newcastle, although the country was effectively being run by William Pitt the Elder (1708-1778) and Bute was forever running government ministers down to the new King as self serving scoundrels.

King George III as he now was had never really had any opportunities to meet women, and yet as King he would be expected to marry and produce a son and heir. The King's choice was limited because he couldn't marry a commoner nor under the terms of the 1701 Act of Settlement could he marry a catholic. For a while he was very attracted to and possibly in love with, Lady Sarah Lennox (1745-1826) who was part of the famous Lennox family who were direct descendants of Charles II. There were five sisters and two brothers whose parents were Charles, 2nd Duke of Richmond (1701-50) and Sarah Cadogan (c1704-51). Lady Sarah's older sister was Caroline (1723-74) who defied her parent's wishes by marrying Henry Fox, the 1st Baron Holland (1705-74) and was only just reconciled with her parents shortly before they both died. Henry Fox was a fairly dubious character who was keen for his sister-in-law Sarah to marry the new King, or even have her installed as a Royal mistress – he didn't really seem to care either way. Fox was after an earldom and was also hoping to supplant Lord Bute as the Kings advisor and seemed quite happy to use Sarah to achieve his ends. In the event, Sarah neither married the King nor became his mistress because when the King married, he didn't marry Sarah Lennox, but instead married Sophie Charlotte, Princess of Mecklenburg-Strelitz (1744-1818) to whom he remained completely faithful. Henry Fox didn't achieve his hope of supplanting Lord Bute either although as already mentioned, he did become the 1st Baron Holland.

When the subject of who the King should marry was discussed, six names were put forward but each one was rejected for various reasons. In the end it was Lord Bute who advised King George strongly that he should not marry Sarah Lennox but instead marry Princess Charlotte. However much in love with Sarah that the young King was or imagined himself to be, if Lord Bute was against the marriage taking place, then there would be no marriage. Bute gave no particular reason for his objection to Sarah Lennox, but it is almost certain that he feared Henry Fox would supplant him as the Kings advisor, a fear that was probably justified as not many people trusted Fox and Bute certainly didn't.

However, prior to that final decision being taken, the King certainly paid Sarah a lot of attention. She was certainly given the strong impression that the King wished to court her – he sought her company a great deal at Court and seemed upset when he heard that Lord Newbattle also seemed to want to marry Sarah. Lord Holland still thought that his sister-in-law and the King would end up together even if she was merely the King's mistress, but once Lord Bute ruled otherwise, then it was not to be. However, before that decision was made, Sarah had been staying with her friend, Lady Susan Fox-Strangeways and during the course of her stay, she fell off her horse and broke her leg. Lord Newbattle, who had previously asked his parents permission to marry Sarah but much to her hurt and surprise had been refused, seemed to adopt an unkind, uncaring attitude to Sarah, and was quoted as saying:- "It will do no great harm for her legs were ugly enough before". The King however was very concerned and was constantly asking after her, and during a birthday ball a few days later, spoke to hardly anybody other than Sarah, and his obvious fondness for her was being reciprocated. Many years later, Sarah was to tell her own children that the King had made a proposal of marriage but we cannot be sure of this. He would not go against Lord Bute in any way, and it's hard to believe that a marriage proposal if made, would have been refused by Sarah. Whatever the truth or not of Sarah's version of events, she did not seem to harbour any bitterness towards George because at his marriage to Sophie Charlotte, she was one of the bridesmaids.

After the original six names for a possible bride for King George were rejected, more names were put forward, one of them being Charlotte of Mecklenburg-Strelitz. Born in 1744, she was just seventeen years of age when she was finally chosen as the bride for the young King. She came from a good family, although they were not distinguished, and she was neither particularly intelligent nor pretty but so far as could be ascertained, she had led a blameless life. The Princess of Mecklenburg-Strelitz's mother, the Duchess of Mecklenburg-Strelitz was approached in June, 1761 and said that she would be pleased to receive a proposal from King George's mother, Augusta, the Princess Dowager which she duly received and accepted.

On the 8th July, 1761, the Privy Council met to discuss the arrangements that would have to take place concerning both the wedding and the Coronation and soon after, Lord Harcourt, once the King's Governor, was sent to Princess Charlotte's duchy with instructions to bring her back to London. The King wanted the arrangements to be carried out with all speed, but although the decision had been made, carrying it out was not going to be so easy. Princess Charlotte's mother died on 12th July, just four days after the meeting of the Privy Council, and then the King became ill with chickenpox. Nevertheless, the wedding date was set at 8th September and the Coronation just two weeks later, on the 22nd. Lord Harcourt left England at the end of July and arrived at Elbe off Stade on 7th August. Harcourt's friend, Colonel David Graeme was there before Harcourt and by the time Lord Harcourt had arrived, he, Graeme had got to know the Princess a little and liked her, thinking her a very suitable match for King George. She spoke no English and spoke only a little French as she had received only a very rudimentary education but she was willing to put this right with all speed. She was mild mannered and although short on academic subjects, she was a good musician, able to play the harpsichord and glockenspiel.

Everything was arranged for her to leave and come to England to face a future full of uncertainties. She had never left her home country and she had not even been on a ship before and she was also acutely aware that she might never see her homeland again, which indeed she didn't. She was on her way to marry a man she had never met and at seventeen, the whole adventure must have been daunting for her. However, if she was nervous or in any way unhappy she didn't show it and given the fact that it was a very rough crossing, her continual cheerfulness did her great credit although like many of the other passengers, she was very sea sick.

Meanwhile, the King awaited her arrival with growing anxiety but on the 6th of September was told of her safe arrival at Harwich, a mere two days before the wedding. From Harwich the Princess still faced a long and tiring journey before she would arrive at St. James's Palace where the King and his bride would meet for the first time. An obviously tired and nervous princess was supposed to have 'thrown herself at his Majesty's feet' but the young King was very chivalrous and helped her up before guiding her into the palace. The reports that the King had previously received concerning the appearance of Princess Charlotte were not exactly flattering but as it happened, he seemed perfectly content although how much of that was a gentlemanly act on his part is uncertain.

She was introduced to some members of the Royal family, and although nervous and tired, did very well and at the dinner party later on that day, she seemed in good spirits, although it must have been a nerve-wracking experience for someone in a strange country with a family she'd never met, and no grasp whatsoever of the English language. The other ordeal she was being made to go through was her marriage to the King later that day having had little time to rest after her journey and no time at all to familiarise herself with her new surroundings. The couple were married in the Chapel Royal by Thomas Secker, the Archbishop of Canterbury. John Thomas, the Bishop of Winchester was also in attendance.

There was a ball the following evening and the King seemed perfectly happy with his new bride, paid her much attention and in fact hardly left her side all evening. This was partly to help her get through the evening, but was also to be a pattern of the early years of their marriage. The King was very careful who he allowed her to meet, the reason being that he did not want the new Queen to be involved in any way with the inevitable political intrigues that follow a monarch around and it's quite possible that he was overprotective. However, there was someone in her life who was even more protective, and that was Mrs. Schwellenburg, her Keeper of the Wardrobe who denied her charge the company of anyone that she thought unsuitable. Even the King objected to how far Mrs. Schwellenburg took this and spoke to her sharply about it, threatening to send her home. It may have been better if he had, because this particular lady made Fanny Burney's life a misery when years later, in 1786, Fanny was appointed as Assistant Keeper of the Wardrobe. Fanny Burney (1752-1840) was an established author and the daughter of the famous musician, Charles Burney (1726-1814). Many people were astonished that she accepted the post thinking that her status as an author did not sit well with the tedious nature of the role that she had just taken on, but Fanny reluctantly agreed to it as a way of helping her father move into Royal circles. Life must have been tedious for the Queen as well, because from the moment she rose in the morning, until the evening when she retired to bed with her husband, she never had any time alone. Having said that, the King and Queen seemed happy together and she gradually began to learn English with her husband and a Canon of Westminster, Dr. John Majendie. She took singing lessons from none other than Johann Christian Bach (1735-82), eleventh son of the more famous composer, Johann Sebastian Bach (1685-1750).

Johann Christian did not gain the kind of fame that his father had but nonetheless was a clever musician and composer. He studied in both Berlin and Italy and after becoming a Catholic, he was appointed Organist in Milan in 1760 and composed both ecclesiastical music as well as operas. Mozart admired him greatly and he became musician to Queen Charlotte in 1762. He was twice painted by Thomas Gainsborough (1727-88), the famous portrait and landscape artist.

It was no surprise then that the King and Queen had many musical evenings together, which involved her singing and playing the harpsichord, whilst the King accompanied her, he too playing the harpsichord as well as the flute. When he was a child, the King had had little family life as it is traditionally thought of and he was determined to create a life that would be good for his wife and any future children that they would have together. As it turned out, they were to have fifteen children, nine sons and six daughters.

The Queen's life was changing rapidly. She married the King after meeting him on the same day that she arrived after a long journey and with no time to recover. The Coronation was arranged for the 22nd September, a mere two weeks after her arrival and her marriage to the King. The ceremony was a grand occasion and the couple were married at Westminster Abbey. Some people paid upwards of fifty guineas (approximately £3,000+ in today's money) for a box high up in the Abbey which provided them with a wonderful view of the proceedings, whilst others paid much more to rent rooms that were nearby and would also provide a good view. Some people even paid £1,000 (approx. £60,000 in today's value) for renting a nice house just for the day. The lengthy proceedings were exhausting for the King and Queen but especially so for the Queen. Still only seventeen and with little or no grasp of English as yet and married only two weeks previously, she was to be under public scrutiny for no less than twelve hours on that day.

After leaving the Abbey, the newly crowned King and Queen were taken to Westminster Hall for the Coronation Banquet where the Royal couple could at least relax a little and enjoy the feast that was put down before them. They were starving and apparently ate with great relish.

George III ruled in a very different manner than his immediate predecessors, his grandfather, George II and his great grandfather, George I. The Hanoverian dynasty had started in 1714 when Queen Anne died and George I took the throne, but speaking no English at all, he left much of the decision making process to his ministers, whilst George II carried on in a similar vein thus enabling Robert Walpole to be Prime Minister for so long. This was to change when George III took the throne in 1760. Although at twenty-two years of age he was very young to take the throne, he was the first Hanoverian Monarch to be born in England and to speak English as his first language. In fact he thought of himself as English in every way which meant that he wanted to be involved in politics more. The problems soon arose. When George III ascended the throne, the Prime Minister was Thomas Pelham-Holles, the Duke of Newcastle but the new King did not approve and wanted his mentor and the only man he felt he could trust, Lord Bute, to be First Lord of the Treasury. Bute had many fine qualities and since the King's father, Prince Frederick had died nine years earlier, Bute had been more or less a surrogate father to the young King. However, Bute did not have the parliamentary skills that Newcastle possessed although there was no doubting his skills in controlling the House of Lords, whilst William Pitt the Elder was equally adept at controlling the Commons. When George III took the throne Britain was in the middle of the seven years war with France (1756-63) and Pitt was a lone voice in the government as to the terms in which peace could be negotiated. Britain was practically broke because of the cost of the war but Pitt took a very hard line approach whilst many of his colleagues would have been happy to negotiate peace on far less agreeable terms than Pitt. Pitt also wanted to declare war on Spain who had entered into a pact with France. Although the public were on Pitt's side, his colleagues weren't, and he resigned in October, 1761, although the bitter pill was sweetened by the King granting him a pension of £3,000 per annum and his wife was allowed to take the title of Baroness Chatham. Further disagreements with Newcastle concerning the possible cost of a war with Spain meant that he too resigned at the end of May, 1762 enabling Lord Bute to become Prime Minister. Initially he was against accepting the position saying that he lacked the parliamentary skills of the man he replaced and when that failed, pleaded ill health. Eventually however, he was persuaded to become the King's first Minister but must have wondered why on earth he had agreed to it. The attacks from the press were disgraceful and even Lady Sarah Lennox said that the vilification of Bute, the King, and the King's mother, the Princess Dowager were the worst that she had ever seen. Given that if anyone had cause to have held a grudge against the King, Sarah Lennox had a possible case and this gives some idea of the severity of the treatment that she was talking about. The King was unhappy at all the attacks regardless as to who they were directed at, but it was the way his mother was treated that incensed him the most. The King told Bute:-

"They have also treated my mother in a cruel manner which I shall never forget nor forgive to the day of my death".

Besides the press, the King was none too forgiving of Henry Fox, later Lord Holland because Fox had tried to marry his sister-in-law, Sarah Lennox to the King and failing that, would have been reasonably content if she were merely his mistress. It was a cavalier way for a man to treat his sister-in-law but not only that, Henry Fox was considered a social climber and was not too bothered if he achieved his aims dishonestly. The King also felt that Fox was corrupt and 'devoid of all principles'. Henry Fox was not to be the last member of the Fox family that King George disliked intensely – later in life he would have quarrels with Henry Fox's son, Charles James (1749-1806), who became a brilliant Whig politician but was also a womaniser and a gambler. However, despite all of the faults that the elder Fox had, Bute only agreed to be Prime Minister if Henry Fox was Leader of the Commons and could give him the support that he felt he needed. This frustrated the King immensely but he consoled himself that the move would not be permanent.

King George did not have to wait too long but not before Lord Bute gave the King a scare by telling him that he wished to resign as he was now being physically attacked by mobs in the street and had to travel everywhere in disguise. However, not only did Bute want to resign, but to rub salt into the wound he suggested to the King that Henry Fox take over as Prime Minister, a situation that horrified King George. Fortunately for the King, Fox did not want to be Prime Minister but in exchange wanted the lucrative post of Paymaster General and be made Baron Holland of Foxley, Wiltshire. Fox suggested that George Grenville (1712-70), brother-in-law to William Pitt the Elder by virtue of being married to Pitt's sister Hester, take the top job which he did on 10th April 1763. The King was unhappy about this but still used his mentor Lord Bute for advice and support and even sent him a copy of Grenville's first King's speech for approval.

The King's escape from all these unwanted political intrigues was the happy family life he and Queen Charlotte had created. The King and Queen were good parents who made a point of spending a lot of time playing with their children unlike most members of the aristocracy, some of whom seemed to want to have as little as possible to do with their own offspring. George and Charlotte had fifteen children in all, nine sons and six girls. The first-born was George (1762-1830), the Prince of Wales and future King George IV, who was delivered on 12th August, 1762. The second was Frederick (1763-1827) who would become Duke of York, whilst the third was another son, William (1765-1837), later Duke of Clarence who reigned as William IV on the death of his brother in 1830 until his own death in 1837. It was then that the Hanoverian line ceased as William had no legitimate male heirs and so Queen Victoria took the throne as part of the Saxe-Coburg dynasty. George and Charlotte's fourth child was a girl named Charlotte after her mother and she lived from 1766 until 1828. The fifth child was Edward, future Duke of Kent (1767-1820) and father of the future Queen Victoria whilst the sixth was Augusta (1768-1840). Next came Elizabeth (1770-1840) and then Ernest, the future Duke of Cumberland and King of Hanover (1771-1851). There were seven still to be born and these were Augustus (1773-1843), later Duke of Sussex, Adolphus (1774-1850), the future Duke of Cambridge, and Mary (1776-1857), who married her cousin, William Frederick (1776-1834) the son of King George's brother William Henry, the Duke of Gloucester who died in 1805, passing the title to his son William

Frederick. Then came Sophia (1777-1848), Octavius (1779-83), Alfred (1780-82), and finally Amelia (1783-1810).

The King worked long hours on the nation's affairs, but he always had time for his children. He always attended their birthday parties and arranged little boat trips on the river. One family friend said that she had never seen more lovely children nor, 'a more pleasing sight than the King's fondness for them'. He kept a keen interest in their schoolwork and sent them notes of encouragement when they were doing well. Despite all this family happiness however, there would be sadness in the form of children dying early, which hardly any family, rich or poor could escape in the 18th century. The King and Queen lost two, the first one being Prince Alfred who died in 1782, not having reached the age of three years. If that was a blow, there was worse to come when Octavius died the following year, in 1783, having been born in 1779. The King was heartbroken and was reported to have said: "There will be no Heaven for me if Octavius is not there". There was some consolation for the Royal couple when Amelia was born the same year that Octavius died, but so far as the King was concerned, there was nothing that could make up for the loss of Octavius and as it turned out, Amelia was the last child that the King and Queen had.

Although the King was an indulgent father, he felt that he had no choice other than to adopt a stricter regime with the two older boys, George and Frederick. Their parents were often instilling the importance of leading a virtuous life to them but it was clear that George and Frederick were becoming harder to handle and so at the ages of eleven and ten respectively, the two boys started to be tutored separately from the other children at Kew Palace. With this in mind, the King placed the two boys in the care of Dr. William Markham, the Bishop of Chester who had to supervise a strict regime of rising at 6am, with the school lessons starting one hour later. Despite the tough nature of the timetable, the King decided that Markham was not strict enough and replaced him with Dr. Richard Hurd, Bishop of Lichfield and Coventry and a man who the King particularly liked. Prior to Dr. Hurd being appointed, the Prince's Sub-Preceptor was Cyril Jackson but he too was replaced by the Revd. William Arnold who was in fact Hurd's Chaplain. If the two Princes were sorry to see Markham replaced, then they were glad to see Jackson leave because he was in the habit of hitting the boys with a silver pencil-case, frequently drawing blood in the process.

It was at this time that problems first started showing between the King and his eldest son George. The timetable the two boys were forced to work to meant that they started at 7am and did not finish until 8pm, a very long day for anyone at the best of times but particularly hard on boys of that age. The King and Queen were constantly reminding the boys of their duty to lead a virtuous life and to fear God, but Prince George was beginning to think for himself and the feature of father and son of the Hanoverian line always seeming to dislike each other was beginning to show through now with George III and the future George IV. George III had been a good father and loved all his children when the boys were young but he now found it difficult to communicate with or even like the young George and started to became his severest critic. The two boys were sometimes beaten heavily for any misdemeanour, real or imagined and a combination of the King now away a great deal more on official duties than he had previously been coupled with the fact that the boys were getting older meant that the family relationships were changing. The Queen saw the elder boys on Friday and Saturday only and the King's absences meant that he saw the Queen less and was becoming unaware of some of her needs, although it has to be said, she coped well and the marriage remained happy.

The man who was Prime Minister at the commencement of the troubles with the colonies based in America was Lord Frederick North (1732-92), son of Francis, the 1st Earl of Guilford. Being the eldest son he was allowed to use the title of Lord North and still sit in the House of Commons which he entered in 1754 and being clever, soon was holding various offices of state until he became Prime Minister when the Duke of Grafton resigned in January, 1770. Lord North brought stability to the office as before him, there had been five Prime Ministers in the previous eight years whereas North was to remain in office for the next twelve years. He was also only the second Tory ever to be Prime Minister – the first being the King's favourite, Lord Bute, who had held the office from May, 1762 until April, 1763. Bute had never wanted the job and his tenure of office was the only time a Tory had held that post since Sir Robert Walpole became the first Prime Minister in 1721. Every other holder of the post including Walpole himself, had been a Whig.

Charles Townshend (1725-67) was the grandson of Charles, 2nd Viscount Townshend (1674-1738), an English statesman and amongst many other things, he had been one of the commissioners of the Union with Scotland in 1707. His grandson was Chancellor of the Exchequer in William Pitt the Elder's (Earl of Chatham) government until Townshend's own death in 1767. Prior to that, because of Chatham's own ill health it was almost certain that Townshend himself was going to form a government but he died before he was able. However, as Chancellor in Chatham's administration, he had done a lot of damage to Britain's relations with the thirteen colonies of America by imposing heavy taxes on goods that were sent there. This caused resentment in the Americas but that did not bother the British government too much as they held a rather paternal attitude to the colonies and treated them like ungrateful children. Much of the revenue raised by the taxes were to go in maintaining the redcoat soldiers that were there but the British government viewed the role of the soldiers in a very different way than the colonies did. Britain felt that the soldiers were protecting the states and keeping law and order whilst the people in the colonies saw them as an occupying army and this feeling of resentment was fuelled by the fact that they, the Americans, were being taxed but had no vote or say in the matter. It was these feelings that were to give rise to the later cry of 'No taxation without representation'.

The colonists were angry at the taxes and on 5th March, 1770 a confrontation occurred between a crowd of Boston residents and a contingent of redcoat soldiers that led to the soldiers firing into the crowd. The result of this was the instant death of three civilians plus a further two dying of their injuries later on. The soldiers were arrested and tried but against all odds given the negative feelings that the local people had against the British, they were acquitted. If anything, this verdict angered people even more and because of the fury felt by the people of the colonies towards the taxes levied by Townshend, the British government largely back-pedalled and reversed them all. All except one that is, and this tax concerned the importation of tea which the British government would not budge on. Matters came to a head on 16th March, 1773 when three ships each with a consignment of tea had docked in Boston Harbour. There were thousands of people at the docks and they decided that the ships should leave without any tax being paid but this led to a collision course when the Collector of Customs refused to let the ships leave without the tax being collected. As a result of this, approximately two hundred men marched to the wharf and threw the cargo of tea into Boston Harbour and this action later became known as the Boston Tea Party. Lord North's administration along with the King were furious at this act of insubordination and almost exactly one year later, in March, 1774, passed a series of acts called The Intolerable Acts.

The Impartial Administration of Justice Act allowed the Royal Governor to move trials to other colonies or even have them carried out in England if he thought the local juries would not be impartial and be able to judge a case fairly.

The Massachusetts Bay Regulating Act made all law officers subject to appointment by the Royal Governor and banned all town meetings that had not previously had the approval of the Royal Governor.

The Boston Port Act closed the port of Boston until the price of the tea that had been thrown overboard be recovered; it moved the capital of Massachusetts to Salem and made Marblehead the official port of entry for the colony at Massachusetts thus bypassing the town of Boston.

The Quartering Act allowed soldiers to stay in people's houses if barracks were not available or there were no empty houses that could be used, whilst the final act, The Quebec Act granted civil government and religious freedom to Catholics living in Quebec.

These acts, which were passed by Lord North's government but fully supported by the King had the opposite effect to that which was intended. Far from bringing the colonies into line, the acts merely antagonised them and caused them to dig their heels in.

The Regulating Act was to stop revolutionary meetings but citizens thought that it curtailed their freedoms. The Quartering Act was hated because not unnaturally, the colonists did not want redcoat soldiers, along with their often drunken ways, in their homes whilst the Quebec Act made the colonists feel they were lesser citizens than those who lived in Quebec as there was no way that King George wanted Catholics to have any positions of authority.

The actual prosecution of the war is dealt with in more detail in the chapter on the Prime Minister at the time, Lord North, but basically there were many people in the colonies during the first few years of argument that hoped there would be a peaceful outcome to the differences. Although the Americas were made up of thirteen individual states, in 1774 they achieved a unified Congress which tried to stay loyal to the British Parliament but eventually felt rightly or wrongly, that the King was indifferent to any views they had which caused a hardening of attitudes. In 1775, the revolutionaries gained control of each of the thirteen states and from this was born the Continental Army which was led by General George Washington (1732-99). The first fighting took place on 19th

April, 1775 and two months later on 17th June, 1775, the famous Battle of Bunker Hill was fought which was seen as a victory for the British, but nonetheless a hollow one as the British sustained far more casualties than the Americans.

Even at this stage, the Americans hoped that there could be peace and on 5th July 1775, three weeks after Bunker Hill, they adopted the Olive Branch Petition in which they expressed hope for a reconciliation with King George III but he wouldn't even read it. Instead he issued the Proclamation of Rebellion on 26th November, 1775 which took a bullying tone and instead of making the Americans step into line, merely hardened their attitudes and made war completely inevitable.

Although there were plenty of Americans who wanted to stay loyal to the British crown, there were also many people in Britain who understood and supported the American point of view, and one of these was the writer and political agitator, Thomas Paine (1737-1809). Paine supported them with actions as well as words and in January, 1776, he published a 50-page pamphlet entitled 'Common Sense' encouraging the thirteen colonies to declare their independence from Britain. He also served in the American Continental Army for a time. Paine went even further than supporting the American cause when he also criticised the whole concept of monarchy in general. He did this later on when the French revolution happened and in 1791, he published 'The Rights of Man', which was an answer to Edmund Burke's 'Reflection on the Revolution in France'. Burke (1729-97) was a respected statesman and philosopher whose 'Reflection...' encouraged the rulers of France to resist the revolution although this view put him at odds with many of his Whig colleagues including Charles James Fox.

On 11th June, 1776, a decision was made to set up a small committee to prepare a draft paper which would become the famous 'Declaration of Independence' and on 28th June, just over two weeks later, it was presented to the Second Congress by Thomas Jefferson, Benjamin Franklin, and John Adams. On the 2nd July, the Congress voted for the independence of the United States and two days later, on 4th July, 1776, the thirteen colonies voted for the 'Declaration of Independence' and now there was no going back. America had told the world that it was an independent country and the British government could either capitulate or fight. The King was never going to agree to the former, so war became inevitable. Although Franklin, Adams and Jefferson all had an input into the Declaration, it was mainly the work of the brilliant Thomas Jefferson (1743-1826) – born on 13th April, 1743, he was barely thirty three years of age when this document was drawn up.

The armed conflict effectively lasted until 17th October, 1781 when General Charles Cornwallis (1738-1805), the British Commander, surrendered at Yorktown to the combined French and American troops. When fighting had first broken out over six years before at Bunker Hill, the British were up against a people that had no one government and no army to speak of – it was made up of thirteen separate colonies, but by 1778, the Americans were supported by the French, and in the end, it became a war that Britain could not and did not win. The British Prime Minister, Lord North, was shattered and took the news of the

Yorktown surrender very badly, but the King seemed to be in complete denial that Britain had been defeated and wanted to continue the fighting.

The King's Speech was delivered at the opening of Parliament on 27th November, 1781 only two days after the news had reached London of Cornwallis's surrender. The speech was barely altered and the contents of it showed clearly that the King still thought it possible that his "deluded subjects in America would return to that happy and prosperous condition which they had formerly derived from a due obedience to the laws". In fact, if there had been any doubt, the surrender at Yorktown really finished the war and established America as an independent nation. Something else that the King found difficult to grasp was Lord North's determination to resign. Over the years Lord North had made it clear to the King that he wanted to leave the job but the King would not have it. However, this time he had no choice because it was clear that Parliament wanted North to go and after various motions of censure against the government, North resigned in March, 1782 but not before he had written a lengthy letter to the King explaining the necessity of his resignation. North explained to the King that "...the fate of the present Ministry is absolutely and irrevocably decided" and that because he had lost the support from Parliament that he needed to survive, resignation was the only possible outcome. The King wrote back a thoroughly ungracious letter which finished with the words:- "If you resign before I have decided what I will do, you will certainly for ever forfeit my regard". After so many years service to the King fighting the Americans along with the stability he brought to the position after there had been five Prime Ministers in the previous eight years before he took office, North did not deserve to receive such a letter. However, the King had to accept the position he was in and North got his way and resigned his office before Parliament could push him out.

The King was very bitter, both at Lord North's resignation and also the loss of the colonies and would admit to no fault on his part for the American defeat. In November, 1782, a year after the news of the defeat at Yorktown, the King wrote a letter to the Prime Minister, the Earl of Shelburne, where both his abdication of all responsibility along with his bitterness came through:-

"I cannot conclude without mentioning how sensibly I feel the dismemberment of America, and that I should be miserable indeed if I did not feel that no blame on that account can be laid at my door, and did I not know that knavery seems to be so much the striking feature of its inhabitants that it may not in the end be an evil that they become aliens to this kingdom".

The resignation of Lord North led to the ending of the period of government stability that the King had enjoyed between 1770 and 1782 and a period of instability followed for eighteen months when there were no less than three Prime Ministers during that period before the appointment of William Pitt the Younger (1759-1806) to the post at the age of twenty-four.

After the resignation of Lord North, the first Prime Minister was the Marquess of Rockingham who held the post from April 1782 until his death on 1st July, 1782. The second holder of the post was the Earl of Shelburne from July 1782 until March 1783, and the third Prime Minister in this period was the

Duke of Portland from April, 1783 until December 1783 when the young William Pitt took over.

After the resignation of Lord North, the King was faced with the problem of forming an administration with the Whigs and reluctantly appointed Charles Watson-Wentworth, the Marquess of Rockingham (1730-82) who had previously held the post in 1765-6 but in the event, his second tenure was even shorter as he died on 1st July, 1782, a mere four months after taking the job on. Rockingham's two Secretaries of State were William Petty-Fitzmaurice, the Earl of Shelburne (1737-1805) and Charles James Fox (1749-1806), the brilliant but unpredictable son of Henry Fox, the 1st Baron Holland and a man who hated the King and was hated *by* the King. The death of Rockingham led to the removal of Fox and the inclusion of William Pitt the Younger (1759-1806) as Chancellor of the Exchequer into the new government led by Shelburne from July, 1782. Fox being out of the government was a relief to the King but it was not to last, as less than a year later, in February, 1783, a coalition led by Fox and North voted down the Shelburne administration and they became Secretaries of State in the new administration led by William Henry Cavendish-Bentinck (1738-1809), the Duke of Portland from April, 1783. Portland had only become Prime Minister because the King refused point blank to appoint Fox to the position whilst Fox and North became the Secretaries of State. Fox was responsible for foreign affairs whilst North looked after the position at home. Whilst Portland was Prime Minister however, the government was always known as the Fox/North coalition and it was these two men who pulled the strings. The Fox/North coalition was brought down in December, 1783 by the King himself using a rather dubious method to get his own way.

The King was still unhappy as Charles James Fox was back in power, and he could not stomach the fact that what in effect was the post of Foreign Secretary was being held by a man whose sympathies had always been with the Americans during the War of Independence. The King had actually asked William Pitt the Younger to be Prime Minister before Portland had taken office but Pitt had refused. This time however, the King was determined to get his man and the way he did it was to wreck the bill that Fox was trying to get through Parliament concerning the running of the East India Company. A Select Committee had been set up in 1781 to examine the manner in which the East India Company was being administed. In 1773, Lord North had introduced a Regulating Act putting the company more in the hands of Parliament than the system before that which had produced corruption, a virtually bankrupt company, but also, that same company paying out huge dividends to shareholders. The 1773 act had put British possessions in India within political control, creating a Governor-General, a Council, and a Supreme Court. Unfortunately this did not work as the Council always seemed to have difficulty working harmoniously with Warren Hastings, the Governor-General, who would eventually return to Britain and face a lengthy trial on corruption charges. That was more than ten years away however, and something had to be done in the meantime. On 15th December, 1783, Charles James Fox introduced a Bill to the House of Lords reforming the way in which the company was run, and was extremely confident that he could get it passed. The East India Company was concerned that its power would be curtailed however and wrote to Parliament saying that Fox had misrepresented the company's finances, and in the process the company found that they were supported by many newspapers.

Although he was an extremely clever politician, Fox could not possibly have predicted what was going to happen next. The King wanted the company to be left alone, but he also wanted to be rid of Fox and to these ends, he did an extraordinary thing. Before the bill was due to go to the Lords, the King gave Lord Temple who until 1779 had been George Grenville (1753-1813), a card saying that:-

"His Majesty allowed Earl Temple to say, that whoever voted for the India Bill was not only not his friend, but would be considered by him as an enemy; and if these words were not strong enough, Earl Temple might use whatever words he might deem stronger and more to the purpose".

Even allowing for the period of time that this happened in, it was an extraordinary piece of royal interference but nevertheless, rightly or wrongly, the King achieved his aims. When the Bill reached the Lords for the final debate on 17th December, twenty-seven peers had wilted under the Royal pressure and switched their allegiance with the result that the bill was defeated by nineteen votes. Fox had been completely out manoeuvred by the King who acted quickly as a result of the Lords' vote. The very next day, 18th December, 1783, William Pitt the Younger had an audience with the King and was made Prime Minister at the extraordinarily young age of twenty-four. Fox was furious at losing office, the Bill being defeated, and the manner in which it was done, but consoled himself in the knowledge that he believed the appointment of a Prime Minister as young as Pitt was laughable and he would be lucky to stay in office more than a few weeks. In fact Pitt held office from 1783 until 1801 and again from 1804 until his death in 1806 – if William Pitt the Elder was seen as clever, his son, Pitt the Younger was if anything even more brilliant – the King had chosen well.

In October 1788, something happened that precipitated a constitutional crisis and would test the young Prime Minister, William Pitt, to the limit, although by this time, still not yet thirty, he had been in power for five years. The King had become very ill in both body and mind, and a small army of doctors did not know the cause. The illness had started the previous summer when he suffered painful stomach cramps and bilious attacks, and a number of doctors including Sir George Baker who was an authority on lead poisoning were called in. The doctors were all mystified as to the nature of the King's illness but collectively decided that the problem was gout, caused by the fact that his bile was not flowing correctly. However, the King showed no improvement as he refused to take the medicine they offered having a fairly low opinion of their skills, this despite the fact that Sir George Baker had been elected President of the College of Physicians no less than nine times. Another doctor called in was Dr. Anthony Addington who was the father of Henry Addington, Pitt's friend and the man who briefly succeeded him as Prime Minister between 1801 and 1804 before Pitt returned to the post. As it was Addington senior who once told William Pitt to drink plenty of port and it was this advice that almost certainly turned Pitt into an alcoholic, the King probably had a point. However, the King decided to visit the spa town of Cheltenham and after taking the waters, he seemed to improve somewhat. He visited several places in the west country to celebrate his recovery, and among these were the Abbey Church in Tewkesbury, Gloucester Cathedral, Croome Court which was home to the Earl of Coventry, and also Worcester Cathedral. However, when he was there, his behaviour started to become very eccentric and on one occasion in Worcester Cathedral when an orchestra was playing Handel's Messiah, the King pretended to conduct the musicians as they were performing the piece. His courtiers knew that Handel was the King's favourite composer and so did not seem too worried at first, but on his returning to Windsor Castle, he became very ill indeed. His illness was not constant, and his behaviour varied from being quite normal on occasions but on others, completely uncontrollable. He was naturally frightened because during his quieter moments he would show his anger towards the doctors who did not seem to understand what was happening to him nor did they have the ability to effect any sort of cure. It was during one of these calmer moments that he said to his son, the Duke of York:- "I wish to God I may die, for I am going to be mad".

The illness also put the government in danger because if the King's illness continued and he was unable to discharge his day to day duties, then the King's eldest son, George, the Prince of Wales, would become Regent and would be King in all but name. Whilst George III favoured William Pitt as Prime Minister, it was well known that the Prince of Wales would favour a Whig government headed by Charles James Fox (1749-1806), a man who the King loathed although it has to be said that the feeling was entirely mutual. The King had no time for Fox at all. He was the favourite son of Henry Fox, the 1st Baron Holland and as a child had been thoroughly spoiled and indulged. On one occasion he had been allowed to paddle in a huge bowl of cream during a dinner given by Fox and his wife, Lady Caroline and at the same dinner, had urinated on a joint of meat that was being prepared for the guests. As a young man, he drank a great deal, gambled recklessly, and didn't worry if he lost £30,000 in one night at Almack's (getting on for £2 million in today's terms) because he knew that his indulgent father would pay off his debts. As an adult, his appearance was slovenly, he was unwashed and unshaven, but set against that, he was a great orator, great company at dinner parties, and a consistent opponent of slavery. He was working towards ending this barbarism when he died in 1806, the year before Parliament made the trafficking in slavery illegal. However, there was history between Fox's family and the Royals going back a generation when Henry Fox (Lord Holland) had unsuccessfully tried to get his sister-in-law Sarah Lennox married to the young King George III.

After the King returned to Windsor on 16th August from his visit to the west country, he appeared to improve, but one night he suffered extreme stomach pains as he had before in June, and they hit him so violently that he was unable to speak for a few minutes. One of the surgeons, David Dundas, came to his bedside but was unable to form any opinion as to the cause of the problem although the other doctors did not stray from their earlier diagnosis of gout. Sir George Baker thought it was due to the fact that his Majesty, "had walked on the grass several hours; and, without having changed his stockings which were very wet went to St. James's and that at night he ate four large pears for supper".

The Prime Minister William Pitt was therefore desperate for the King to get better not just for his obvious wish for his Monarch's suffering to end, but also the fact that he wanted to stay in power and keep Fox and the Whigs in opposition. By this time there was an army of doctors looking after the King. These were Dr. William Heberden, a retired Physician who lived in Windsor; Dr. Richard Warren, a Fellow of the College of Physicians, and after him came Dr. Henry Revell Reynolds who had once been a Physician at St. Thomas's Hospital and then the old Etonian, Sir Lucas Pepys, who would go on to be a future President of the College of Physicians. However, despite all these doctors treating the King, he showed no signs of getting better and once talked virtually non-stop for nineteen hours, most of it rambling and incoherent. A deeply religious man who had always been devoted to the Queen and completely faithful to her, he started talking about Lady Pembroke in a totally inappropriate way. Lady Pembroke had been at Court during King George's formative years and was described by someone at the King's Coronation as being 'the picture of majestic modesty'. Of all the doctors who were treating the King, it is Warren who was trusted least of all by the Queen because of the fact that he had also treated the Prince of Wales, Charles James Fox and a number of other Whigs who were mistrusted by the Royal family. The treatments he prescribed the King were horrific – he wanted his shaven scalp to be blistered to draw out the poisonous matters from his brain. His legs were also blistered with plasters of cantharides and mustard and leeches were attached to his forehead. He was also given strong purges and then sedatives and Warren finished this barbaric treatment by ordering the King's room to be unheated. It was so cold that people other than the King could hardly bear to stay there. Eventually in December 1788, the Queen called in Dr. Francis Willis (1717-1807), a man who claimed to have had a long and successful career in treating mental disorders. He lived in and ran a private asylum at Greatford Hall, Lincolnshire and was completely confident in his ability to effect a cure. He appeared before a Commons Committee on 4th December along with several other doctors, but it was Willis who was the most insistent that he could return the King to his previous good health. The other doctors did not trust Willis. They thought that his qualifications were suspect as he was not a member of the Royal College of Physicians and the King who by now was feeling better, did not welcome the attentions of Willis either.

The King knew that Willis had previously been a clergyman, and when he first met Willis the King said:- "Sir, you have quitted a profession I have always loved, and you have embraced one I most heartily detest". However, the attitude that Willis had towards people with a mental illness and the methods that he used to treat his patients show a kindly disposition compared to most people at the time. His patients were dressed smartly so that they did not stand out from other people as having a mental condition and Dr. Willis actually got them to carry out certain jobs at the asylum to give them a sense of purpose and normality. However, Willis, along with his son John, did not hesitate to use fairly severe methods if patients were unruly or uncooperative and often would use a straitjacket. The King was to be no exception to this rule and often found himself a victim of the straitjacket when Dr. Willis found it necessary. Having said that, the King, who never seemed to trust physicians, seemed if not to actually like, certainly respected Dr. Willis more than he respected the other doctors although that wasn't necessarily difficult, as he didn't trust any of them at all, especially Dr. Warren. Meanwhile, the Prime Minister, William Pitt was desperately trying to fend off attempts by the Prince of Wales and Charles James Fox to take power for the Whig party along with giving the Prince of Wales the power of being Regent. To this end, on 10th December, 1788, Pitt made a brilliant speech in the House asking for another committee to be formed to discuss the issue of any precedents that would help them in the present situation, a speech that infuriated Fox and the other Whigs who knew only too well that Pitt was merely trying to buy time before the situation became completely impossible to manage.

Meanwhile the Queen, who spent her whole married life being devoted to the King, was completely distraught about the situation. Unable to help her husband she was almost afraid of speaking to him and his illness frightened her but that did not stop her loving him and wanting to help him, it's just that she did not know how. Both the King and Queen spoke to Fanny Burney about the situation. Fanny had joined the Royal household in June, 1786 and before as well as during her employment at Court, she had kept a diary, faithfully recording each day's events as she saw them. She was very attached to the Queen and could see how distressed the terrible situation she found herself in made her. It is probably worth quoting directly from the diary to see at first hand just how badly the King's illness affected the Queen which in turn caused Fanny distress. On the 3rd November, 1788, Fanny had written:-

"...we are all here in a most uneasy state. The King is better and worse so frequently, and changes so, daily, backwards and forwards, that everything is to be apprehended, if his nerves are not some way quieted. I dreadfully fear he is on the eve of some severe fever. The Queen is almost overpowered with some secret terror. I am affected beyond all expression in her presence, to see what struggles she makes to support serenity. Today, she gave up the conflict when I was alone with her, and burst into a violent fit of tears. It was very, very terrible to see!"

And the following day, Fanny wrote:

"...Oh my dear friends, what a history! The King, at dinner, had broken forth into positive delirium, which long had been menacing all who saw him most closely; and the Queen was so overpowered as to fall into violent hysterics. All the Princesses were in misery, and the Prince of Wales had burst into tears..."

These are just two partial entries from page after page giving vivid descriptions by a skilled diarist and writer who was involved to the highest degree in the life of the family and the horror of what they were all suffering. They were also written approximately five weeks before Pitt's speech on 10th December when he was trying to buy time by asking for an extra committee to be formed to discuss possible precedents. No-one knew how long this situation would go on for and not only was the King suffering badly, but also the Queen, their children, friends of the Royal family, and for different reasons, the Prime Minister, William Pitt along with everybody at Court who genuinely loved the

King and Queen. By the time Pitt made his speech to the Committee, the King's illness had been going on for several months and understandably the family's nerves were in shreds.

Prior to Dr. Willis being called in, there had been no lasting improvement in the King's illness, but certainly after Willis had been treating him for a few weeks, the King's condition seemed to improve, although Warren refused to believe it and it was often difficult to get the doctors to agree to a joint statement being released concerning the King's condition at any given moment. Although his condition improved somewhat under the care of Willis, it was not a gradual improvement, but was haphazard, showing an improvement one day followed by a relapse the next, but gradually the bad days were becoming fewer although the Queen had told all the ladies who waited on her that they must have no contact with the King. On one occasion that is recorded in Fanny Burney's diary, she speaks of the 2nd February 1789 when she was walking in Kew Gardens, having previously been told that the King was in Richmond. Whilst she was walking, she saw three figures who she did not recognise heading towards her but thinking they were gardeners thought little of it. In fact it was the King along with Dr. Willis and his son John, and the sight of them filled Fanny with terror and she simply ran away as fast as she could. The King kept on calling her name as he chased her so that Fanny was in a panic, on the one hand being told not to have any contact with the King and on the other not wishing to distress the King by ignoring his calls for her to stop. In the event, she didn't run fast enough and eventually she found herself facing the King wondering how angry he would be by ignoring his calls to her and her continuing to run. The two doctors had got the King between them whilst there were three attendants hovering about the scene. Fanny was terrified but the King merely put his arms round her and gently kissed her on the cheek. Despite reservations from other people at Court, Fanny liked Dr. Willis and his son, and they quietly retreated from the scene and encouraged the King to walk with Fanny whereupon he talked incessantly to her. She wrote in her diary:-

"...Everything that came uppermost in his mind he mentioned: he seemed to have just such remains of his flightiness as heated his imagination without deranging his reason, and robbed him of all control over his speech, though nearly in his perfect state of mind as to his opinions. What did he not say! He opened his whole heart to me – expounded all his sentiments, and acquainted me with all his intentions."

Despite the fact that Pitt had been quite brilliant in stalling Fox and the Whigs who had been aching to take power, he had no option other than to prepare a Regency Bill which he did and presented to the House of Commons on 5th February 1789, and again to the Lords on 16th February. By now despite his impatience at Pitt's stalling tactics, Fox was now convinced that power was in his grasp. However, on the very next day, the 17th, a bulletin was put out by the doctors saying that the King was fully recovered and able to resume his duties. Pitt had been within 24 hours of losing power and Fox was 24 hours from gaining it, but the extraordinary timing of the medical bulletin made Pitt more powerful than ever and the King more popular as there was great rejoicing amongst the whole population, rich and poor, once the good news had spread. The following day, 18th February 1789, Fanny Burney wrote in her diary:-

"The King I have seen again – in the Queen's dressing room. On opening the door, there he stood! He smiled at my start, and saying he had waited on purpose to see me added: 'I am quite well now - I was nearly so when I saw you before – but I could overtake you better now!' And then he left the room. I was quite melted with joy and thankfulness at this so entire restoration." Her next entry was:-

"End of February, 1789. Dieu Merci!"

It was accepted that the King was completely well again and the Regency Bill was withdrawn. Fanny Burney, who had gone to work for the Royal Family with great reluctance had found herself right in the middle of this constitutional crisis, having had both the King and Queen confiding in her at different times. The Queen gave their trusted friend a copy of the '*Prayer of Thanksgiving upon the King's Recovery*' which would eventually be given to every church in the country. In March, 1782, the King and the then Prime Minister, Lord North, were two of the most unpopular people in the country as they were blamed for losing the American War of Independence; now the King found himself the most loved man in the land. There was great joy at the news of the King's recovery and there were parties and balls all over London – it seemed the whole country rejoiced.

The doctors who attended the King were well rewarded financially speaking, especially Dr. Francis Willis and his son, Dr. John. The elder Willis was given the handsome sum of £1,000 per annum for twenty years which given his age of seventy-two at the time of the King's illness was effectively a pension for life. His son, Dr. John Willis, was granted a sum of £500 per annum for life.

On 23rd April, 1789 which was in fact St. George's Day, there was a service of Thanksgiving held in St. Paul's Cathedral and whilst there was great joy in the Royal household that it was to be taking place, there was concern that it was a little too soon and he may yet not be quite ready for it. However, his wit shone through and convinced those around him that he would in fact be able to cope. The Archbishop of Canterbury had suggested to him that the service was possibly a little too soon, whereupon the King replied:- "My Lord, I have twice read over the evidence of the physicians on my case, and if I can stand that, I can stand anything." Given his views on members of the medical profession, he probably held the view that he recovered his health despite the doctors' treatment rather than because of it, and as modern thinking supports the view that he was not insane but probably had suffered from porphyria, he could well have been right.

On the day of the service, crowds lined the street, singing the National Anthem with great gusto and shouting huzzas to the Royal Couple when their coach passed various points on the way to St. Paul's. The Prime Minister, William Pitt, who had worked so hard to delay the Regency Bill, was also given a rousing reception, but there was one person who wasn't, and that was Charles James Fox. Once so certain that he was soon to be heading a Whig government, and in fact was very close to it, he was now vilified, and in the short term at least, a spent force and seemingly out of touch with the public mood.

The King's health steadied over the next few years, but another problem was looming which would trouble the Pitt government, and that was the situation in France. Revolution was in the air, but it was a different kind than the one that had occurred in America who were fighting Britain as a united country. The trouble that occurred in France was internal and in the end, led to the execution of the King, Louis XVI, and the Queen, Marie Antoinette which in turn led to the abolition of the Royal family. There was a great deal of tension in the country from 1788 and the French King's early popularity was gradually eroded when he dissolved all Parliaments in May 1788. However, things became worse when the following August he decreed that all cash payments should cease apart from those to his troops. A National Assembly was formed and it was decided to produce a new constitution and the Constituent Assembly was formed. On 12th July 1789 there was a huge outbreak of violence and two days later, the Bastille was stormed. The Royal Family were imprisoned before the Assembly dissolved itself in December 1792 and was replaced by the National Convention. France had now become a Republic and if all this wasn't enough for George III's nerves, the news that the French King had been brought to trial on charges of treason and executed by guillotine on 23rd January 1793 brought shock waves which spread to every country that had a Monarchy. France was joined by Spain and Portugal in a coalition and declared war on Britain and the Netherlands on 1st February 1793.

Britain was practically bankrupt after the American War of Independence which had lasted six years, and the country had only enjoyed ten years of peace, and so William Pitt felt that the only way the war with France could be financed was by a form of income tax. The bloodshed that had happened in France followed by the cruel removal of the Royal family horrified King George and could well have helped bring on his illness again in 1804, fearing as he did that the same fate could happen to him.

Apart from a temporary peace which lasted for fourteen months when the Treaty of Amiens was signed on 25th March 1802, the war with France lasted from 1st February, 1793 until 18th June, 1815 when the Duke of Wellington beat the French army at Waterloo, the French troops being led by the brilliant Corsican General, Napoleon Bonaparte (1769-1821). People had first taken notice of Napoleon in 1795 when he helped defeat supporters of the counter-revolution in Paris with the famous 'whiff of grapeshot' against the mob at Tuileries followed by his being appointed to command the army of Italy in 1796. Despite the Battle of Waterloo virtually ending the war with France, the individual battle that is most famous is the sea battle between Britain's fleet commanded by Admiral Lord Nelson which beat the combined French and Spanish fleets at Trafalgar on 21st October 1805. That battle had produced mixed feelings in the country, because whilst the nation rejoiced at the great victory, it was the battle that cost Nelson his life and plunged the country into a collective grief. Although the battle did not end the war, it put paid to any hopes that Bonaparte had of invading Britain and reminded people of the brilliant comment made before Trafalgar by the ever confident Admiral John Jervis (1735-1823), the Earl St. Vincent who had been First Lord of the Admiralty between 1801 and 1804. He had said:- "I do not say the French cannot come. I only say they cannot come by sea." The war with France itself was to last another ten years until Waterloo.

However, before the triumph of Trafalgar, the King's doctors feared that the stress of the war would bring the King's illness back but he seemed to relish the fight. The King wrote to his friend Bishop Hurd:-

"We are here in daily expectation that Bonaparte will attempt his threatened invasion... Should his troops effect a landing, I shall certainly put myself at the head of mine, and my other armed subjects, to repel them."

However, this fighting talk notwithstanding, the King did become ill again and this may have been brought on by the war, or the Prime Minister's wish for Catholic emancipation or both. There had been a lull in the fighting between 1801 and 1802 and Pitt wanted to take advantage of this break by introducing some legislation that would give Catholics a measure of freedom. The King had nothing against Catholics individually and would always treat anyone, Catholic or Anglican, with equal courtesy, but he felt that it was totally against his Coronation Oath to let Catholic emancipation happen. In late February 1801, George became unwell again and once more, Doctor Willis was sent for. However, he was now eighty-two years old and had retired but Dr. John Willis along with his brother, the Reverend Thomas Willis went to the King with yet another brother, Robert Darling Willis. Meanwhile, Pitt had no wish to distress the King by continuing with this legislation and this, along with his own feelings of tiredness having been Premier for eighteen years, caused him to tender his resignation on 5th February 1801, just a few weeks before the King had become unwell again. Pitt was succeeded by the Speaker, Henry Addington (1757-1844) son of the Doctor Addington who had advised Pitt many years before to drink plenty of port, advice that almost certainly turned Pitt into an alcoholic.

On 21st February, 1801, the King became very unwell, and confided to Dr. Willis that he thought it was due to the Catholic question although once again, Willis expressed his confidence that he could make the King well as he and his father had done before. The King's illness was difficult to bear and so were the so-called 'cures' that were used by the Doctors Willis. Hot vinegar was applied to his feet, blisters to his head, he was given musk and quinine along with tartar emetics and a pillow of warm hops was placed under his head to calm him down and help him sleep. The King's fear that the illness was brought on by his agitation over the Catholic question caused Pitt to send a message to the King saying that he would drop the subject completely. Although the King's illness was severe, he seemed to recover more quickly than after the first bout thirteen years earlier and by 5th March he was sitting up in bed and eating his meals properly and without help. However, if he recovered more quickly than the first time he was ill, he was told by Willis that this time he would have to convalesce for a longer period. During this enforced rest he slept badly, had lost a lot of weight to the point that he looked emaciated and generally looked thoroughly strained. After three months he looked no better but urged by ministers, made a number of appearances at St. James' Palace – each appearance causing him to undergo the usual horrific treatment by the Willis's beforehand which in the event fooled no-one as everybody could see how ill he was.

The relationship between the Willis's and the King were strained. George III felt he didn't want the doctors to have control over him any more whilst they were determined to treat him for as long as was necessary. Whilst he was at the White House at Kew, they entered his room and told the King that they were removing him by force to which the King replied:- "Sir, I will never forgive you whilst I live". This battle of wills continued until the end of June, 1801, when the King seemed to improve to such an extent that the doctors felt that he could go to Weymouth and finish his convalescence by the sea. With him were the Queen, the Princesses, and Prince Adolphus, (1774-1850), later the Duke of Cambridge.

Gradually the King got better and in October 1801, Lord Chichester (1728-1805) saw the King and felt he was in good health both physically and mentally. Lord Chichester was Thomas Pelham and his political pedigree was excellent. He was the first cousin once removed of both Henry Pelham (1695-1754) who had been Prime Minister from 1743 until his sudden death in 1754 and also his elder brother Thomas Pelham Holles (1693-1768) who was Prime Minister twice, succeeding his brother from 1754 until 1756, and then being Prime Minister again from 1757 until 1762 when he was succeeded by the King's favourite, Lord Bute.

The fact that the King became well again may have had something to do with Britain and France signing the Treaty of Amiens in March, 1802 which would have lessened the stress that he would have been suffering. However, it was an uneasy peace and Britain declared war on France again in May, 1803 due to the French annexing Piedmont, occupying Parma and interfering in Swiss internal affairs. In the short term, the resuming of hostilities did not seem to hinder the progress of the King, not even when it was clear that Napoleon intended to invade Britain. The King even said that he would lead the troops in battle against Bonaparte saying to a German officer at Weymouth;- "I should like to fight Boney single handed - I'm sure I should. I should give him a good hiding. I'm sure I should. I'm sure of it." Even if he was being a little deluded, it certainly showed that his old spirit had returned and certainly the doctors were happy that he had recovered once more.

There had been a tendency amongst Hanoverian Kings for fathers and sons to not get on well and George III and his son, the Prince of Wales were no exception to that rule. George III was a man with high morals who was entirely faithful to his wife, Queen Charlotte and he also possessed a sense of duty to his country which he took very seriously. The Prince of Wales, who would be the future George IV, could not have been more different than his father. When Britain went to war with France, it was hoped by many that the King and his son would get on better with each other. After the dreadful execution of Louis XVI and France becoming a Republic, there was a common enemy as it was in the interest of both father and son that nothing like it should be allowed to happen to the British monarchy. However, it was not to be. The Prince of Wales loved to gamble, to have numerous sexual affairs, was a complete glutton when it came to food, and owed thousands of pounds in unpaid debts. When the King was ill in the late 1780's, the Prince's main concern was becoming Regent and changing the government from the Tories led by William Pitt to the Whigs with

Charles James Fox as Prime Minister. In the end, it didn't happen, but it was a close run thing.

In the 18th century, cartoonists were much less respectful of the monarchy, and the Prince of Wales gave them plenty of ammunition. Probably the most cutting of all the cartoonists was James Gillray (1757-1815), born in London but the son of a Lanark trooper. Gillray was insane for the last four years of his life and this surprises no-one who saw his work. In July 1792, his most famous caricature was issued under the title of 'A Voluptuary under the Horrors of Digestion', which depicts the Prince being incredibly fat, lounging back in a chair and picking his teeth with a fork – there is even a suggestion of venereal disease. Gillray never took sides with his cartoons, he simply lampooned everybody, so despite the fact that the King was completely different from his son he was still caricatured. A few weeks after the cartoon of the Prince of Wales, Gillray took a swipe at the King and Queen with a cartoon of them in the act of enjoying a frugal meal of boiled eggs and salad in a sparse room and with no fire in the grate. The Queen was also depicted as being a frightfully ugly woman with half her teeth missing.

Although the Prince of Wales was a womaniser, he did fall in love, the lady in question being a widow six years older than himself. Her name was Mrs. Maria Fitzherbert but it posed a problem for the Prince as she was a Catholic. She took her faith seriously and so she made it plain that she would not be the King's mistress. Mary Anne Smythe (1756-1837) as she was, although she always called herself Maria, had married Edward Weld in 1775 but he had died within a year. In 1778 she was married again, this time to Thomas Fitzherbert but he too died in 1781 leaving her a twice married widow. That, along with the fact that she was a Roman Catholic made a legal marriage between herself and the Prince of Wales out of the question as the Royal Marriages Act of 1772 along with the 1701 Act of Settlement forbade anyone who married a Catholic from taking the throne. Lord North and his government had put the Royal Marriages Act of 1772 through although a surprise opponent of the Bill was Charles James Fox who, whilst he did not wish the country to have a Royal Family, nonetheless felt that individuals within that family should marry who they like.

The Prince of Wales had expressed his passionate love for Maria, and whilst she was flattered, she had been warned of the Prince's wild ways and was not at all sure that she wanted to marry him. She therefore decided to go abroad in an effort to escape his attentions but getting wind of her plans, the Prince became even more excitable and staged a dramatic suicide bid. This could have been a genuine attempt to take his own life but was more than likely a way of getting Mrs. Fitzherbert to stay. If it was the former, it didn't work, but if the latter, it worked well and she was shocked when she went to his bedside and found him covered in blood. He asked her to marry him saying that if she did not consent, he could see no reason for living and not knowing what to do, she agreed. However, she was in no fit state to make a decision like that and after some serious thought, realised that she couldn't go through with it and sailed to the Continent to escape the situation. The King forbade his son to go after her and so the Prince bombarded her with lengthy passionate love letters. The first one he sent was eighteen pages long, but getting ever more desperate, the last one was forty-two pages. This went on for a year and Mrs. Fitzherbert, finally tiring of being away from England and equally tired of being bombarded with the Prince's letters, returned home and agreed to marry him. An Anglican parson was found who agreed to perform the marriage service in Mrs. Fitzherbert's drawing room on 15th December, 1785 although the Prince was completely aware that this marriage was illegal. Because of this, the Prince promptly denied the fact that he had married Mrs. Fitzherbert to his friend, Charles James Fox who believed him to such an extent that he made an announcement in the House of Commons that the couple were not married. He also added that he had the full authority from the Prince himself to make this statement. Mrs. Fitzherbert, annoyed and hurt that the Prince could agree to this statement left him again and refused to see him at all which led to even more letters to Mrs. Fitzherbert begging her to return to him, and eventually once more she did.

The relationship between the King and his son improved somewhat when an effort was made to clear the Prince's colossal debts. It was Parliament who came to his rescue. They granted £161,000 to help him become solvent, along with £60,000 towards the completion of Carlton House which by now he had left to settle in Brighton with his new wife. The Prince already received £50,000 a year anyway and a further £10,000 was added from the Civil list plus £13,000 from the Duchy of Lancaster giving him a total of £73,000 per annum.

Despite the above sums that were paid to the Prince, ten years or so later, in 1794, his debts had once again reached colossal proportions and he realised that the patience of both Parliament and the King had long since run out. The only way that he could see to rectify the situation was to marry legally, and with that thought in mind, he cruelly ended the illegal marriage with Maria Fitzherbert which made him free to enter 'a more creditable line of life'. The person chosen to be his bride was his cousin, Princess Caroline, who was the daughter of Princess Augusta, the King's sister and her husband, Charles William Ferdinand, the Duke of Brunswick. The Prince accepted her with no enthusiasm whatsoever, and she was certainly a person who was hard to like. The Prince of Wales was a fat, gluttonous man who thought nothing of sponging off friends but he did have charm and certainly no-one could accuse the dirty, sullen Princess Caroline of having that. The Queen didn't like Princess Caroline and strongly disapproved of the match but unlike the Queen and the Prince, the King was happy with it and the wedding duly took place in the Chapel Royal at St. James's Palace on 8th April 1795. The wedding ceremony was in the evening and the Prince was so unhappy that he was drunk throughout. Repulsed by her and still drunk, he ignored her on their wedding night although recovered enough to do his duty in the morning and make her pregnant. Nine months later, on 7th January, 1796, their daughter, Princess Charlotte was born. It is quite possible that that was the only occasion the couple slept together.

The marriage was a disaster from the beginning and within a few short months, both parties wanted to be rid of each other. The Prince begged his father to be allowed to get out of the union, and also begged his mother to talk to his father about the situation. Everybody but the person the Prince needed most disliked Princess Caroline but the King would not budge and refused his son's wishes reminding him that he was not a private citizen and both the public and Parliament would know of the failure of the marriage. The Prince was very annoyed and frustrated at the King's attitude and made the mistake of having all correspondence between father and son published in various newspapers. This did him no good whatsoever and all of his family encouraged the Prince to make his peace with the King but the only way to do this was for the two men to meet. Eventually the Prince agreed, writing to his mother to that effect on 4th July, 1804.

There was a complication however. The Prince became worried because he had been warned that the King had been unwell since the beginning of the year and he wondered what reception he would receive. The usual symptoms had come back of gout, and agitation amongst others and on the 14th February he had run a high fever and talked non-stop for five hours. Three days later the government decided that his condition was so bad that the Willises were called in but on arrival were refused access to the King. When he had recovered from the previous illness the King had extracted a promise that they would not be summoned should he fall ill again, and both the Dukes of Cumberland and Kent agreed that the King would be agitated if he saw them. Henry Addington, the Prime Minister sent for Dr. Samuel Foart Simmons who was a specialist in mental illness, and was based at St. Luke's Hospital for Lunaticks. However, his treatment may not have been very different from that of Willis, as Simmons quickly used the dreaded straitjacket on the King. Fortunately however, it did not have to be used for any length of time because on the 26th February, the Prime Minister, Henry Addington, announced to the House of Commons that the King was completely well and was able to resume his normal constitutional matters again. A few weeks later, Addington, knowing he was not really up to the job of Prime Minister handed in his seals of office to the King, and in May 1804, William Pitt was summoned by the King and asked to form a government again. Pitt found the King perfectly normal during the meeting but the King's recovery was a fragile one because after another audience only two days later, Pitt remarked that the King was again talking for long periods and in a hurried state. Another bad sign was that the King was speaking ill of the Queen again, something he only did when he was unwell.

Soon it was clear the statement that Addington had made to the House the previous February saying that the King was well had been very premature as it was clear that he wasn't. Rumours abounded that he had told the Queen that he would take a mistress as she would not sleep with him anymore. His mind once more returned to Lady Pembroke but if she would not succumb, he would see the Duchess of Rutland or Lady Georgiana Buckley. There were other stories that he had made indecent advances to ladies whilst in Weymouth, and that he had also behaved in an indecent and obscene manner when back at Windsor. Although some of these stories may have been untrue, there was enough substance in them for those around him to be alarmed. Apart from his behaviour, he had physical signs of his illness that could not be doubted; he was irritable and impatient, and according to Prince William, the King would have ridden his horse into a church if he had not been stopped by an equerry.

A few months earlier, members of the Royal Family had urged the Prince of Wales to make peace with his father which he had eventually agreed to the previous July, 1804 but the suggested meeting had never taken place because to insiders the King was clearly still unwell, and any meeting might well have made the situation between the two men worse than it already was. However, to the outside world the King was well and there was no talk of a Regency as there had been in 1788 during his first illness, because the King was clearly better than he had been at that time. At last a date for a meeting between father and son was agreed and on 12th November, a nervous Prince of Wales arrived at Windsor and was greeted warmly by the Queen and the Princesses but whilst the King acknowledged him, it was done with no warmth and the minimum of talk. Apart from the King's strange mindset at this time, another reason that would hinder a reconciliation was the fact that he was still visiting his daughter-in-law, Princess Caroline at Blackheath.

William Pitt, the Prime Minister was now in charge of the King's health which came as a relief to the Queen who with the situation as it was, had become worried and agitated, although she kept the Willises informed of what was going on, even though they were no longer involved in the King's treatment. In the summer of 1805 he had lost much of his sight but apart from that he was much better. The Royal Family had moved from the Queens House to Windsor Castle itself and there was a celebration by way of a concert with the music of Handel, the King's favourite composer, being played followed by a banquet grander than the one that celebrated the King's recovery in 1789. The King and the Prince of Wales barely spoke a word to each other so the meeting the previous year between the two had obviously not brought about an improvement in their relationship. Not only that, but members of the Royal Family along with the staff were unhappy with the move to Windsor because the rooms in the castle were freezing, and the Queen and Princesses along with many of the servants, hated it. Later on after the banquet was over, the crowds were let in and the King watched them from an upstairs window, and although improved in health, he was slightly agitated at the sight of all the people grabbing at everything they could.

The King never really fully recovered after that illness, but as he grew older and more infirm, his popularity increased. The cartoonists no longer showed him as a buffoon and he was treated with a great deal more sympathy and respect. His upright morals were appreciated and he was compared favourably to his sons. The two sons that would eventually take the throne were the Prince of Wales in 1820 until his death in 1830, and not having an heir, the succession moved sideways to his brother the Duke of Clarence who took the throne as William 1V and who reigned from 1830 until 1837. The Prince of Wales' daughter, Charlotte who had been born in January, 1796 had married Leopold of Saxe-Coburg-Saalfeld but she died on 6th November, 1817 after giving birth to a still-born son after a difficult and painful labour. After Charlotte had died, King George III was left with twelve children but no legitimate grandchildren. This produced a rather unromantic and unseemly rush by the King's sons to produce marriages in order to secure the line of succession. Like the Prince of Wales, his brother, the Duke of Clarence had no legitimate heir because he was unmarried, although he had lived with an attractive Irish actress by the name of Dora Jordan and they produced ten illegitimate children, five sons and five daughters. When Parliament promised William that they would pay off his debts if he married, he left Dora Jordan in a rather sudden and callous way in order that he could try to find a bride so that the order of the line of succession could be continued. However, he did not have a large choice of suitable women to choose from although eventually a marriage was arranged between himself and Princess Adelaide of Saxe-Coburg-Meiningen and they were married on 11th July, 1818 at Kew Palace. In fact it was a double marriage as his brother, Edward, the Duke of Kent, married Mary Louisa Victoria, Princess of Saxe-Coburg-Saalfeld and they were the parents of the future Queen Victoria who was born in 1819. When William died on 20th June, 1837, he had produced no children who had lived to adulthood and so the succession again became a problem. It would normally have gone to William's brother, Edward, the Duke of Kent, but he had died in 1820, and so his daughter, Victoria became Queen, ruling from 1837 until her death in 1901.

Meanwhile, George III, although still unwell, managed to read the King's speech in 1804 and again the following year, although it had to be printed in huge letters. He seemed happy enough and even spoke of the Prince of Wales with affection added to which his daughters were very supportive and loving, although often feeling a deep frustration that their lives were very restricted. The King's daily routine at Windsor suited him and made no demands on him. After rising at 7.30am, he would attend morning service at the Chapel after which he would go for a ride with his equerries and two or three daughters. After an afternoon of limited public business with his private secretary, he would spend the evening with the Queen before retiring to bed at 11pm. One day followed another like this but the daily predictable tranquillity was shattered when he learned that his much loved daughter, Princess Amelia had been struck down with pulmonary tuberculosis which was almost certainly going to be fatal. Added to that was the fact that she was in agony whenever the doctors tried to drain her lungs which had become swollen. Born in 1783, Amelia was only twenty-seven years old when she was struck down with this illness and the thought of her threatened loss caused the King huge anguish which both his mental and physical state could not cope with. The King had great problems with all his sons, except possibly his favourite, Frederick, the Duke of York, but his daughters had rarely given him problems that he knew about and he loved them all, but it was Amelia that he loved the best. Whenever he visited her, the scenes were deeply distressing for everybody concerned – the King, whilst barely able to see his daughter with his failing eyesight, would weep at her bedside a great deal. When he was not with Amelia, the King would ask his physician, Sir Henry Halford, for bulletins on her three times a day. Sir Henry (1766-1844) was a respected physician and was President of the Royal College of Physicians for an unprecedented 24 years. He was physician to no less than four reigning monarchs and also had many famous patients including Georgiana, the Duchess of Devonshire. It was Sir Henry who accurately diagnosed that she was suffering from a liver abscess which none of the other doctors attending her managed to do. It was also Sir Henry who had to relay to the King the sad news that his beloved Amelia passed away on 2nd November, 1810. She was buried on 13th November in the Royal Vault at St. George's Chapel in the evening whilst the King was asleep and was unaware of what was going on. Princess Amelia had known for a while that she was going to die, and when she was certain of it, she arranged for Rundell and Bridges, jewellers to the Royal Family, to have a valuable stone put into the ring along with a locket of her hair to remind the King of her. The King collapsed in tears when he saw what it was and what it signified, and although he tried to write her a letter expressing his feelings to her, the writing was so bad that it was impossible to read.

The King's health deteriorated on the death of his precious daughter but improved slightly at the beginning of December, just a month after Amelia had died. However, he went downhill again almost straight away and the succession of doctors who were treating him, including Robert and John Willis thought that he was close to death. The Prime Minister at this time was Spencer Perceval (1762-1812). There had been two Prime Ministers since William Pitt had died four years earlier in 1806, but Perceval was trusted by the King because of his anti-Catholic views which Pitt certainly would never have agreed with had he lived longer. Perceval was shot by an assassin in 1812 when entering the lobby of the House of Commons, the only Prime Minister who has died in this manner. However, in early 1811 when Perceval was still the First Minister, the King seem to rally and when the Prime Minister spoke to the King about the need for a Regency, the King took the news quite calmly. The Prince of Wales was sworn in as Regent on 6th February, 1811, and took everyone by surprise because he kept the present government in power rather than sacking Perceval and allowing the Whigs to form an administration, although this time, there was no Charles James Fox to lead it as like Pitt, he had died in 1806. The Prince did it because he said that he was merely acting for his father, but it was certainly a different reaction to the one he would no doubt have had if he'd taken over as Regent in 1789, the first time that the King had been ill. However, the sad irony of the situation was that whilst Spencer Perceval would not have liked being thrown out of office, if he had been it may well have saved him from the assassin's bullet the following year.

A committee of advisors and the Queen were now responsible for the King's welfare and she went to see the King on 8th February, 1811, the first time for quite a while. She was surprised to see how well the King looked, in fact there was now the ironic situation whereby the Regent had fallen ill and was in fact in a worse state than the King. However, the King, although outwardly well, was still muddled about events and people and sometimes seemed convinced that Amelia was still alive and happily married, and was living in Hanover. Also, his thoughts yet again turned to Lady Pembroke and he was sometimes convinced that he was actually married to her. This upset the Queen who for nearly fifty years had been devoted to the King but was now permanently irritated by him and less than sympathetic to his plight. It was a sad situation because the King was one of the few 18th century husbands who moved in that social circle who was always completely faithful to his wife. This once happy couple, so close for so many years, were now barely able to communicate with one another and this situation would go on for many years before their deaths, hers in 1818, and his in 1820. The Queen's impatience was so bad that Princess Elizabeth approached Sir Henry Halford to ask the Queen to be more patient with the King especially when he was having one of his calmer moments and was aware of what was going on around him. However, with respect to her daughter's wishes regarding her treatment of the King, it should be borne in mind that the situation had made the Queen ill herself - her hair had turned grey and after once being so heavy that one spectator who saw her walk on the terrace at Windsor said that she looked pregnant, she was now very thin and didn't seem well at all.

When George III was younger and he and the Queen were creating a family, they were viewed as great parents, with the King often eschewing any kind of formality with the children and constantly playing with them whilst working on the country's affairs. Any person seeing him then would probably say he was the perfect father. However, both the King and Queen were possessive with the daughters to such an extent that when they became adults, the daughters referred to themselves as 'The Nunnery'. The only men they were ever likely to meet were the King's equerries and servants. Princess Elizabeth (1770-1840) herself was longing to have her own family and expressed a wish to marry Louis Phillipe, duc d'Orleans, but the Queen put a stop to this without even mentioning it to the King as she knew what his reaction would be to one of his daughters marrying a penniless Roman Catholic. Elizabeth did marry eventually just as she was turning thirty-eight years old, her husband being Friederich Joseph Louis of Hesse-Homburg (1769-1829) who became Landgrave on the death of his father.

The King's favourite daughter, Princess Amelia, (1783-1810) fell passionately in love with Major-General the Hon. Charles Fitzroy and although twenty years older than Amelia and considered rather dull, there was no doubting the strength of her feelings as upon her death, she left him all her possessions. The Queen had known about Amelia's feelings since 1803, but kept them from the King as she knew how upset he would be. Amelia had desperately hoped that she would be able to marry Fitzroy when her brother would take the throne as George IV, but her early sad death made it an impossibility, although she never completely gave up hope until the day she died.

Another sister, Princess Sophia, (1777-1848), had an affair with General Thomas Garth (1744-1829). Whereas Amelia's lover Fitzroy was considered good looking, he was also considered a rather boring character, interested only in his career, whilst General Garth, although tubby, thirty-three years older than Sophia and possessing a face that had an unsightly birthmark on it, was far more witty and he had a great deal of charm. Unfortunately, Sophia became pregnant and to keep the news from the King, she was taken to Weymouth where in August, 1800, she gave birth to a boy she called Thomas who was eventually adopted by General Garth himself.

Of the remaining three daughters, Charlotte (1766-1828), married the very overweight King Frederick of Wurttemberg in 1797 at the age of thirty, and although his first wife died under strange circumstances, she considered herself lucky to escape the nunnery.

Augusta (1768-1840), had fallen deeply in love with Sir Brent Spencer, one of the King's equerries and tried hard to marry him, asking the Prince Regent for his permission, but in the end she failed and died at the age of 72 in 1840, three years after Queen Victoria's reign had started. Augusta had not only lived through her father's reign, but also those of her two brothers, George IV (1820-30) and William IV (1830-37).

The last daughter Mary, wed her first cousin, William Frederick, the Duke of Gloucester (1776-1834), known as 'Silly Billy' but who was something of a tyrant. He was also considered boring and dense, but nonetheless, Mary was very fond of him and seemed completely content.

The King's relationships with his sons gave him more trouble as he had been able to have control over his daughters until he was too ill to really know what was going on, but his sons were a different problem entirely and ever since they had become young men they caused the King trouble. The first and obvious one was George, the Prince of Wales (1762-1830). As already mentioned, they didn't get on with each other at all, and the Prince ran up enormous debts with gambling and womanising. He went through a completely illegal marriage when he married Maria Fitzherbert in 1785 and his subsequent marriage to Caroline of Brunswick ten years later was an abject failure. One of his best friends was the Whig politician, Charles James Fox, who was also a womaniser and a gambler and who the King loathed.

Frederick, the Duke of York (1763-1827) was the King's favourite son although it is a little difficult to understand why as he pursued the same extravagant life style of his brothers, he too being a womaniser and a gambler. He had joined the army and in 1798 had been promoted to Commander-in-Chief where despite his lack of ability in the field of battle, he had done well as an administrator and showed an interest in reforming the army. He had had a mistress named Mrs. Mary Anne Clarke who had a fairly wild streak but he did not marry her, and in 1791 chose instead Princess Frederica of Prussia of whom the King approved.

The next son was William, the Duke of Clarence (1765-1837) who would eventually rule as William IV after his elder brother George died in 1830. William was King until 1837 when his niece Victoria (daughter of William and George's brother Edward, the Duke of Kent who had died in 1820, the same year as his father, George III) took the throne. George III sent his son to sea when William was only thirteen years old and he left with his father's advice ringing in his ears that he should always study hard and be polite to superior officers and not to put on any airs and graces because of who he was. It seemed that he took little notice of the advice, but although he was quite a good seaman, he was a bully and behaved stupidly on occasions earning little respect from anyone except perhaps people like Captain Horatio Nelson. There were certain people who thought of royalty with great reverence, thinking of them almost in a God-like fashion, Fanny Burney's father Charles Burney the musician being one of them whilst Nelson was another. When Nelson met Clarence, he said that he was potentially "an ornament to our Service… superior to near two thirds of the List". In fact, William was a womaniser, was always picking up girls from different ports, and frequenting brothels which meant that on more than one occasion, he contracted a venereal disease. As an officer, he was not shy about using the lash for seamen who he thought had stepped out of line. However, despite all that, the reports he received as a naval officer were better than those he received concerning his studies which showed that he had absolutely no interest in learning Latin.

In fairness to him, it has to be said that he genuinely wanted to serve against the French but his father would not allow it. As mentioned before, although in his fifties, he had never married but had fathered ten illegitimate children none of whom were eligible to take the throne as the mother was a Mrs. Jordan, who the Prince had lived with since 1791. However, in an attempt to sire a legitimate heir to the throne, he married Princess Adelaide of Saxe-Coburg-Meiningen (1792-1849) on 11th July, 1818 at Kew Palace. They had two daughters but both died in infancy which meant that on William's death in 1837, the crown transferred to his neice, Victoria (1819-1901), the daughter of William's late brother, the Duke of Kent (1767-1820) and his widow, Mary Louisa Victoria (1786-1861), the Duchess of Kent.

The same could be said for Edward, the Duke of Kent (1767-1820). He had been sent to Hanover but had spent rather more money than he had coming in and had been sent to Geneva with a very strict tutor named Colonel Baron Von Wangenheim. He hated Geneva and constantly wrote to his father requesting permission to come home and also to be given enough money to settle his debts. His father never answered his letters; in fact he never wrote to Edward at all whilst he was abroad and so Edward decided to come back anyway. After a quick meeting with the King, he was then sent to Gibraltar which he hated even more than Geneva. He became a commanding officer of the Royal Fusiliers but whatever his father said to him during their brief meeting made no difference to his attitude concerning money and he again completely overspent running up further debts. He was moved on again, this time to Quebec, which like all the other places he had been to, he hated. Up until now, the King thought less of Edward than any of his sons, but in January, 1794, he was placed on the staff of the Commander in Chief in the West Indies and at last pleased his father by being mentioned in dispatches. Parliament granted him £12,000 per year when he became Duke of Kent and eventually he was brought home but to the consternation of his parents, also brought home his mistress, Therese-Bernardine Mongenet. After a brief spell in England, in 1802 he was made Governor of Gibraltar but his overstrict method of command caused a mutiny and recalled in disgrace, he was never again given a posting.

Ernest, the Duke of Cumberland (1771-1851) was exactly like his other brothers in as much as he found no favour with his father. He was sent to the University of Gottingen when he was fifteen and here he found that the curriculum had a distinct military base to it and in 1792, at the age of twenty-one, he was still abroad training with the Hanoverian Army. Like his brothers, he wanted to come home but when he asked permission he was also given the same negative reply from the King. The Prince then served with the 9th Hanoverian Hussars in the field of battle and after another request to return home had been refused, he was eventually allowed back to England in 1794. He had lost the use of an arm and an eye in military action, and on hearing this, the

King relented. He also granted his sons request for an increase in his allowance but the pleasure Ernest received from being home was soon outweighed by the fact that he was forced to accompany the King and Queen to Weymouth. The King was cheerful enough; he usually was when he was at Weymouth but his long illness had taken its toll of the Queen who was unsmiling, unhappy and sullen. Either way, the mood that Ernest's parents were in meant little to him as he was simply bored stiff in Weymouth, obviously believing that he would be enjoying the London nightlife when he was home. However, he was soon sent back to the Continent but was extremely unhappy when told that he was not allowed to go on holiday to Hanover but was ordered to stay with his regiment. In 1795, he was once again allowed to return home but was still unhappy as he wasn't given the military command he thought he deserved.

Eventually, in 1799, he was made Lieutenant-General in the British Army and became the Duke of Cumberland. It was not only the King who didn't like Cumberland too much; his brothers seemed to share the same opinion. He was cruel with his humour and also a womaniser, supposed to be one of the many lovers that the Princess of Wales took. One of the most damaging rumours however, was that it was he, rather than General Thomas Garth who was the father of his sister Sophia's baby that she gave birth to when in Weymouth in 1800. Not too many people gave this credence however and it was far more likely that her baby's father was in fact Garth, especially as he brought the child up.

Augustus, the Duke of Sussex (1773-1843) was sent to Gottingen University as Cumberland had been and Adolphus, the Duke of Cambridge was to go. He did not serve in the army as he was not fit enough having a weak chest. He lived in Switzerland and Italy but was very homesick as not only was he physically unfit, but mentally he wasn't strong either. Like most of his brothers, he had written to his father several times requesting permission to return home, and like his brothers did not receive a reply. The family dynamics seemed to have changed rapidly over the years, as the doting father they had as children had disappeared and there seemed little communication between father and sons.

George III thought it advantageous to his son's health for him to live abroad and wouldn't budge, so Augustus wrote to the Prince of Wales which did him no good at all when the King found out that Augustus had married Lady Augusta Murray, a lady ten years older than himself. Much worse than that however was the fact that the marriage had taken place in Rome and whilst he didn't marry her in order to get home, that is in fact what happened. The King ordered Augustus back to England immediately but was not too pleased when Augustus brought his pregnant wife with him. In order to legitimise the marriage in the eyes of his father, Augustus married his wife again at St. George's, London on 5th December, 1793 and soon after the ceremony she gave birth to a son followed eight years later by a daughter. It cut no ice with the King however who forbade the Prince ever to see Lady Augusta again, Augustus being sent abroad once more whilst his wife stayed in England. Eventually, after initially refusing the King's instructions for the couple to stop being together as man and wife, Augustus agreed on a separation and in return the King looked after Lady Augusta and her children financially. The Prince lived his life out in a rather meaningless fashion after his request to have some sort of military appointment was refused – it was clear that he was totally unsuitable for such an appointment.

Prince Adolphus, (1774-1850) had become the Duke of Cambridge in 1801 and seemed to have given the King and Queen less trouble than any of his brothers, although Frederick, the Duke of York, remained the King's favourite son. The only thing Adolphus seems to have had in common with his brothers, the Dukes of Sussex and Cumberland was that he attended Gottingen University as unlike his brothers, he was neither in debt nor was he a womaniser. In fact he seems quite conventional having expressed a wish to marry his cousin, Frederica of Mecklenburg-Strelitz, the young widow of Prince Frederick of Prussia. The King agreed, but wanted the wedding delayed until the war with France was over. Adolphus duly obliged, but his honourable sacrifice rebounded on him because Frederica fell in love with and married the Prince of Solms-Braunfels and shortly afterwards had a child by him. However, the unkindest cut of all happened when Frederica's second husband died and in 1815, she married Adolphus's brother, Ernest, the Duke of Cumberland. Adolphus eventually married Princess Augusta of Hesse-Cassel who would one day be the grandmother of Princess May of Teck who was Queen of Great Britain when George V reigned as King between 1910 and 1936. It was the death of George V in 1936 that caused a constitutional crisis when his eldest son, Edward VIII abdicated in order to marry Wallis Simpson.

Octavius and Alfred did not live to adulthood, Octavius living between 1779 and 1783 and Alfred living for just two years between 1780 and 1782. Octavius had been the King's favourite son and he had been grief stricken when Octavius died – it was probably the birth of Amelia in 1783 that possibly stopped the King becoming ill sooner than he did when he eventually succumbed in 1788.

It is a shame that after being such a wonderful father when his children were very young, that the relationships broke down when they became adults. It does seem that he was too strict and whilst he was more able to have control over his daughters, most of his sons simply rebelled against the King's puritanical ways and spent their lives doing exactly the opposite of what their father wanted. It seems to be a regular occurrence over the years that in both the House of Hanover and then later on, the House of Windsor that the sons were very different from their fathers.

In later years, rumours were always going round about the King's health – some were true and some not. In late May, 1811, the rumour spread in Windsor that the King was better and indeed he did manage to make a public appearance although he was practically blind. He rode through the Little Park to the Great Park but was back behind the castle walls within an hour. However, that was the last time he ventured out and he was never seen outside the castle by the populace again.

The last few years of the King's life were sad. He was blind, deaf and completely deluded. He lived in his own world which was a totally confused one. He spoke of people long since dead as if they were still alive, and people who were living as if they were dead and would often refer to himself in the third person as if he was somebody else. The Queen went to see him briefly in

June, 1812, but after all those years as a devoted couple, she never saw him again although she lived for a further six years. It is difficult to understand why this happened. Perhaps the sight of the man she had loved for so many years in the situation that he was in was too distressing for her. Maybe she thought that there was no point as the King would probably be unaware of who she was but maybe she simply wasn't thinking logically. The Queen had also retreated from the world but in a different way as she knew what was going on and was not ill in the way that the King was. She became more and more difficult to get along with and quarrelled with just about everybody, including her daughters. This once loved Queen was a sad person in her twilight years who made herself completely unloved by the time she died in August, 1818 at Kew and the King, who was in his own twilight world, was not even aware of her death. She was buried at Saint George's Chapel in Windsor where she would be joined eighteen months later by her husband. He never recovered from his last illness and the Prince of Wales had ruled as Regent from 1811 until the King himself died on 29th January, 1820 at Windsor whereupon his son succeeded him as George IV. The King's favourite son, Frederick, the Duke of York, was with him when he passed away. He was laid to rest after his funeral on 16th February, 1820, and on that day there was national mourning on a huge scale, 30,000 people travelling into Windsor on the day.

George III has gone down in history as the mad King who lost Britain the Americas but this is a grotesque simplification of his reign and one that does him no justice. Advances in modern medicine have enabled the medical profession to be fairly certain that he was not insane, but as already mentioned, suffering from porphyria, a genetic disorder that causes abdominal pain, discoloured urine, weakness of the limbs, paranoia, schizophrenia, and a mental derangement that causes the sufferer to speak for hours on end in a hurried and rambling fashion. With regard to the Americas, he certainly adopted a confrontational attitude to the colonies and ignored their Olive Branch Petition of 5th July, 1775 in which they expressed a desire to be reconciled with the King. Not only that, but his Proclamation of Rebellion on 26th November of the same year merely antagonised the Americans and caused them to dig their heels in. Despite this however, it seemed that the rebels were determined to go their own way and in so far as he had much influence over the way that the war with America was conducted, the final outcome would almost certainly have been the same. Military historians and even people at the time, felt that given the distance between America and Britain, it was a war that simply could not be won whoever the Monarch was and whoever was Prime Minister at the time. America notwithstanding, his legacy is a better one than many people imagine. He was the first Hanoverian King who considered himself English and who spoke the language and who loved the country that he was born in. He was a talented architect who championed both the arts and the sciences. He was so keen on astronomy that he had his own observatory at Kew and was great friends with the German born British astronomer, Sir William Herschel (1738-1822).

Herschel was originally a musician but later took up astronomy, and in 1773 he made a reflecting telescope which enabled him to discover a new planet in

1781 which he named 'Georgium Sidus' after the King although we know it now as Uranus. On inheriting the throne on the death of his grandfather, George II in 1760, he was determined to set a high moral standard which he did and never wavered from. He was always faithful to the Queen and when they were younger, was a good father to his children, often playing with them during the day as opposed to merely seeing them for a few minutes before bedtime that most moneyed people in the 18th century did. He had a great interest in agriculture and indeed the British Agricultural Revolution had reached its peak and he was often seen talking to farm labourers about their work which gave him the not unkindly meant nickname of 'Farmer George'. During his reign the country also experienced the Industrial Revolution and trade and commerce made huge strides with the value of imports and exports increasing fourfold during his reign. There was an explosion of inventions that produced easy ways of weaving cotton; steam engines were being built along with better roads and canals and the Agricultural Revolution made farming methods more efficient. For many years in his reign, Britain was fighting the French which must have put a strain on his constitution, but fortunately the country had a powerful navy and a well drilled army. Although wars are not won by individuals, their input to individual battles cannot be overestimated and Britain was blessed with a brilliant naval officer in Admiral Lord Horatio Nelson who beat the combined Spanish and French fleet on 21st October, 1805 at the Battle of Trafalgar although it cost Nelson his life. The country also had a brilliant general in the Duke of Wellington who beat the French at the Battle of Waterloo on 18th June, 1815, effectively ending the war with Napoleon Bonaparte. Wellington went on to be Prime Minister from January, 1828 until November, 1830 during the reign of George IV. After reigning for sixty years until 1820 over all these events, it is a pity that King George III's last years were painful, both physically and mentally, and also long drawn out and unhappy years. He and the Queen had always put duty before pleasure and neither of them deserved the unhappiness and pain that they had to endure during the latter part of their lives. Modern historians have tended to assess King George III more kindly than he has been judged until now and that is the least that he deserves.

-oOOo-

18

Olaudah Equiano
(1745-1797)

African slave who beat the system and ended up a wealthy English gentleman.

The story of Olaudah Equiano tells of the amazing events whereby an African boy of eleven years old was taken from his family, made a slave and despite having to suffer the cruelties of the slave trade was eventually able to make his escape and beat this barbaric system. He managed to free himself, educate himself and become in effect, an English gentleman, even to the stage whereby he wrote his autobiography and married a white woman, a marriage that would have been an unusual occurrence in the 18th century, and many years before Parliament passed a bill in 1807 outlawing the slave trade.

Equiano was born in 1745 in Essaka, a small village in the kingdom of Benin in Nigeria and lived with his parents, along with five brothers and one sister. Equiano was the youngest of the brothers whilst his sister was younger than he. It was in 1756 when he was just eleven years old, that Equiano, along with his sister, was taken from the rest of their family, being dragged away by African slave traders. It happened during the day when the rest of the family were at work and there was just Equiano and his sister looking after the house.

Their captors gagged them so that they could not cry out, and also bound their hands. They travelled across country and stopped at a house where their captors had a meal, and although Equiano and his sister were offered some of the food, they were too distressed to eat and fell asleep in each other's arms. The first night, completely frightened and unaware of who their captors were or what was going to happen to them, Equiano and his sister clung to each other all night for support wishing they were back home with their parents. However, even worse was to come the next day when their captors separated them leaving each of them to face their futures alone. During this early period of captivity, the bewildered and frightened Equiano had a series of what he called masters, some of whom were not unkind to him, and at one point he thought that one family in particular who took charge of him were so kind that he thought that they were going to adopt him and let him live permanently with them. Sadly, this did not happen and he was moved on to someone else with whom he travelled although he did not have any idea of what the destination was. At one time after having several masters, he was staying at the house of one of them for two or three days when a wealthy woman with her young son came to visit.

The lady's son was about the same age and size as Equiano and both the boy and his mother took a liking to Equiano with the result that they purchased him from the merchant and went back to her home. Both her house and surrounding gardens looked beautiful to Equiano and he was amazed and grateful as to how well the family treated him. The day after arriving, Equiano was washed and perfumed and then taken to the room where the lady and her son were to dine. To Equiano's surprise, he was treated as one of the family and he was allowed to dine before the lady's son because he, Equiano, was older than the son and it was customary for the eldest to eat first. The family had slaves but as Equiano was treated as one of the family he did not have to perform any duties at all but was allowed to play with the boy just as he had done with his own siblings in the past. After about two months, Equiano was beginning to come to terms with the fact that he wouldn't see his birth family again, and was as happy as he could be where he was and felt that this would be his permanent home. Sadly for Equiano however, his dreams of a happy life were shattered as early one morning when his master and wife were asleep, he was captured and was taken from this family who had been kind to him. He was now with a group of people who were very different from those that he had just been with, and he was made to travel to the coast with these people who he did not know, who fought amongst themselves and treated the Africans with undue cruelty. After travelling some time they eventually arrived at the coast where Equiano was to see his first slave ship and witness some of the cruelties that took place first hand. They were now at the mercy of others who were operating slavery in the so-called triangular route which had been operating for many years.

Before we look at Equiano's life in particular, it is worth spending a little time at looking how the slave trade operated generally which will allow the reader to see just how great Olaudah's triumph was in eventually breaking free from this barbaric practice. The triangular route consisted of sailing from Britain to the African coast with manufactured goods, purchasing slaves like those of Equiano and his sister, who were dragged from their homes and taken to the coast. They were then bought with the produce that had been brought over from Britain, and then taken to the West Indies where they were sold to work on plantations. The slaves produced goods such as cotton, sugar and tobacco and these were shipped back to England. The conditions in which the slaves were transported were absolutely horrific and they were shackled together in the hold of the ship with no space between them and no way of moving. When the captives were first taken on board ships, they were often terrified that they were going to be eaten. When writing many years later in his autobiography about his feelings at the time of capture, Equiano said:- "When I saw a large furnace of copper boiling and a multitude of black people, of every description, chained together, every one of their countenances expressing dejection and sorrow, I no longer doubted of my fate". The men lay in a space no bigger and possibly even smaller than a coffin and they were kept like that for as long as the journey took, which would often be about three months. They lay in their own urine and excrement and were barely fed. Sometimes they were so hungry that if a person lying next to them died, they would attempt to keep it a secret in order to have that person's food ration. The stench in the hold was dreadful and made it almost impossible for crew members to spend more than a few minutes down there at any one time. Deaths from various diseases were commonplace and every day several slaves would die from smallpox, measles or worms. When this happened, the dead people were simply thrown overboard as food for the sharks.

Sailors have often said that they could smell a slave ship from a mile away so deeply had the stench penetrated and William Wilberforce (1759-1833), the man who probably did more than any other to end the slave trade in 1807, said that:- "Never can so much misery be found condensed into so small a space as in a slave-ship during the Middle Passage".

Some of the slaves literally went mad during the voyages and for that they were taken up on board deck and severely flogged. If that didn't cure them, which of course most of the time it didn't, they were simply thrown overboard although for some of them, even this cruel death must have been seen as a blessed release from the horrors that they were suffering. Some of them would attempt suicide in any case, and one ship's surgeon wrote:- "He put his head down under water but lifted his hands up, and thus went down as if exulting he had got away". The same happened to slaves that fell ill. They were brought on deck and examined by the ship's doctor, and if their wounds and sores were considered incurable, the Captain would simply have them thrown overboard, although so great was their misery, most of them went cheerfully.

On some ships the slaves were brought up on deck whilst the holds were cleaned with vinegar and whilst this was happening they were made to dance and if the crew did not think that they were putting enough effort into it they were flogged with no mercy shown. The music was produced by very basic instruments, and Equiano noted to his surprise that they were of a very rudimentary nature, in fact he felt that they were very much like the ones used by the Africans themselves. However, come the night, a very different sound was heard which was a dreadful howling of the African captives which horrified Equiano. The slaves were crying for the lives that they had lost and moaning in fear of their unknown future which they knew that in all probability would be too awful to contemplate. Equiano was later to write:- "...the shrieks of the women and the groans of the dying which rendered the whole scene of horror almost inconceivable". Both sexes were treated abominably but it is a shocking truth that the women were treated more badly than the men. One officer noted that:- "The officers are permitted to indulge their passions with them at pleasure and sometimes are guilty of such brutal excesses as disgrace human nature". John Newton, once a slave ship captain who was to eventually see the error of his ways, wrote of it saying that when the women slaves who:- "naked, trembling and terrified, perhaps almost exhausted", came on board, they were watched by the crew and "in imagination, the prey is divided, upon the spot, and only reserved until opportunity offers". If a woman refused a crew member, she was almost always flogged but if she gave in to the man's advances, she was spared and sometimes given a few beads and accomodation that was more comfortable than the other slaves had to endure. However, it did not always happen that the woman was given improved quarters and the inevitable result of the crew member's behaviour was that many of the women fell pregnant. They would often give birth chained to a slave who was next to her and who could well be dead or dying. Another barbaric form of treatment was meted out to the slaves if they refused food, either because it was bad or they were attempting to starve themselves to death. Two men would force the slave to his or her knees and deliberately burn the slave's lips with hot coal. When the slave cried out and his mouth inevitably opened, the member of the crew shovelled food, such as it was, down the throat of the slave and whipped the victim's Adam's Apple to ensure that the food was swallowed. Apart from flogging, thumb screws were used to punish what the crew felt was insubordination. Newton, referring to flogging said:- "I have seen them sentenced to unmerciful whippings, continued till the poor creatures have not the power to groan under their misery, and hardly a sign of life has remained". With regard to the thumb screws, Newton went on to say:- "I have seen them agonizing for hours, I believe for days together, under the torture of the thumb screws, which if the screw be turned by an unrelenting hand can give intolerable anguish". John Newton (1725-1807), was once a Captain of a slave ship but in 1748 repented although it was not until the 1760's that he renounced the slave trade completely and worked for the abolitionist's cause. He eventually took Holy Orders and became a Curate in a church in Buckinghamshire later becoming Rector of a church in central London. However, in the 1750's he was still involved in the slave trade and whilst not defending the conditions that the slaves were kept under, pointed out that the crews of the slave ships were hardly treated any better, the reason being that they were probably more expendable than the slaves. Newton wrote:- "I suppose there is no trade in which seamen are treated with so little humanity. I have myself seen them when sick, beaten for being lazy till they died under the blows". Whilst realising that this treatment was wrong, he excused it by saying:- "without strict discipline, the common sailors would be unmanageable since they were for the most part the refuse and dregs of the nation". Other slaves, once they had been sold to someone in Virginia, were also treated with dreadful cruelty, and often had to wear the dreaded 'iron muzzle' which was clamped round their mouth making it virtually impossible for them to either speak or eat. However, although suffering inhuman treatment, the reason that slaves were not always that much worse off than the crew was due to the fact that slaves when sold, would bring in money, whilst members of the crew didn't. Should crewmembers die, they were simply replaced by the Press Gangs making the crew members expendable. However, the whole trade was barbaric in every way and in later years Newton would completely repent and worked with William Wilberforce in the latter's determination to bring the whole business to an end.

It says much for Olaudah's bravery and tenacity that he eventually escaped the captivity and the utter cruelty of it all. However, that was many years away. After his initial capture, he was transported across Africa to Virginia which was ruled by the British at the time. It was whilst he was on the slave ship that he was transported in that he became acutely aware of the cruelty that was prevalent. He had never seen European sailors before and was astounded by their different complexions as well as the way they behaved. He was not long on the ship when he was suffered to go down to the hold where the stench was almost unbearable. He was feeling so ill that he was completely unable to eat, but on refusing food when it was offered, he was tied to the windlass and flogged so severely that he wished for death. Had he been able to jump overboard and allow himself to drown, he would have done, but he was unable to because of the netting that went round the ship, and also due to the fact that the crew watched over all the slaves carefully. Olaudah, like many of his countrymen, were often flogged in this manner which was routinely carried out every hour. Much to Olaudah's surprise, he saw white men, in other words, members of the crew, treated in the same manner. There was one particular European he saw that was flogged so heavily that he died and afterwards was simply thrown overboard.

The stench from the hold was unbearable, but luckily Equiano was sometimes allowed to remain on deck, but such was his misery that he still wished for death as a release from the position he was in. Every day, people were brought up to the deck in a state of near death, and every day Equiano wished that his own life would quickly end giving him relief from the miserable position that he was in. Once, several crew members caught a large number of fish and after eating until they were full, threw the remainder back in the sea.

The pleas from Equiano and some of the other slaves to be able to eat the remainder went unheeded and after some of them tried to take the left over fish when they thought crew members were not watching, resulted in them being severely flogged. It was obvious that the position on board was intolerable for the Africans and three of them attempted suicide by jumping overboard, somehow managing to get over the nets and into the sea. The crew, quickly alerted to what was going on, forced Equiano and the others to stay in the hold of the ship with its disgustingly putrid smell and then they got into one of the boats and tried to retrieve the slaves from the water. Two of them had died, but the other had survived and he was dragged back into the ship and flogged without any mercy being shown.

Eventually they arrived in Barbados and from there shipped to North America. It has to be said that they were treated more kindly on this voyage and were also fed properly on rice and pork. They landed at Virginia where Olaudah spent a few weeks on a plantation weeding grass and collecting stones whilst all the other people that he knew had disappeared until there was no-one for him to converse with. Again, surrounded by people who could talk to each other but not to him, he became so miserable that he wished for death. Eventually he was taken from this place when a Lieutenant Michael Pascal, an officer in the Royal Navy and the Captain of a ship named the *Industrious Bee* visited the plantation, liked the look of Equiano and duly purchased him. Pascal promptly re-named him Gustavus Vassa, which was a Latin derivation of Gustav Vasa, a Swedish nobleman.

Compared to the dreadful sufferings that other slaves went through, Olaudah was treated quite well. He virtually became a member of the crew and gained a partial knowledge of English which enabled him to converse with others. All the crew members seemed kind and he was treated well by everybody and he enjoyed the fact that he was getting good food.

After a few days on the ship, they set sail for England, and whilst all the crew were good to him there was a particular crew member named Richard Baker who was a few years older than Olaudah but who was serving on board for the first time. Baker took Olaudah under his wing and befriended him. Olaudah's new friend was American and seemed to be very well educated. Olaudah was surprised at the way his friend treated him as an equal and as both were new to seamanship, they often literally clung to each other for comfort.

Sadly, Baker was to die in 1759 and in his later autobiography, Olaudah described the loss of Baker:- "...as I lost at once a kind interpreter, an agreeable companion, and a faithful friend; who, at the age of fifteen, discovered a mind superior to prejudice; and who was not ashamed to notice, to associate with, and to be a friend and instructor of one who was ignorant, a stranger, of a different complexion, and a slave!"

However, that is jumping ahead two years but at this time Olaudah and Baker were enjoying each other's company on the ship commanded by Lieutenant Pascal and were heading to England. After a voyage lasting thirteen weeks they arrived in Falmouth in the spring of 1757 where they stocked up with fresh food because the stocks on board had got low in both quality as well as quantity. Olaudah was completely overawed by the streets and buildings of Falmouth which was a strange new land to him and one morning when he went on deck he found that it was covered in snow although he had never seen snow before and had no idea what it was, thinking that it could be salt. After asking one of the crew members he was told that it was snow and that, as well as the rain that followed it, was confusing to him. When he asked, he was told that it was made by a great man in the heavens who was called God, and this great man had created everything.

Soon after this, he went to church, but again it confused him and when he asked what the service was about, he was told that it was to worship God, the man who had created all things on earth. Everything Olaudah saw was new to him – the worshipping of God, the fact that they did not buy and sell each other, the white women who were slimmer than the Africans, and the fact that they never washed their hands before eating. His grasp of English was still limited but his friend Richard Baker was always pleased to answer his questions, even though they were delivered in halting English. There were so many things happening to him that he had not witnessed before and one of these were books which he had never even seen, much less read. He had seen his friend reading and Equiano picked a book up and started to talk to it and then put it to his ear, being surprised when there was no answer.

Lieutenant Pascal along with Equiano lodged with a gentleman and his family in Falmouth who treated him with great kindness but after a little while they returned to the ship and headed off for Guernsey where Olaudah and his friend Richard were placed with a family that Lieutenant Pascal knew whilst he sailed for England. The family had a little daughter called Mary who was aged about five or six years who Olaudah grew very attached to. He was still clearly confused about his ethnicity because he noticed that when Mary's mother washed the little girl's face, it went a very rosy colour whilst his did not, however hard he scrubbed. This left him frustrated and puzzled as he wanted to be the same colour as the family that had looked after him so well. During the summer of 1757, Pascal sent for Equiano and Baker and they boarded a sloop that sailed for England so that the Lieutenant could join his new ship the *Roebuck*. As they sailed up to the Nore to join the new ship, a Man-of-War came alongside the sloop which caused everybody to hide so Equiano did the same, not quite knowing why. They were hiding from the dreaded Press Gang who boarded the sloop heavily armed with swords and proceeded to take men away.

Equiano was discovered, but whilst they made sport with him, laughing at his fear, they let him stay on the sloop, much to his relief and eventually, Lieutenant Pascal came on board to take them to the *Roebuck*, much to Equiano's joy. Further to his joy at seeing his master again, he found that there were several boys of his own age to play with and he stayed on this ship some considerable time, visiting various places, one of which was Holland, where the ship went twice.

On one of the voyages from Holland, they brought back some gentlemen of 'distinction' as Olaudah called them, and the crew paired all the young boys off with each other and made them fight each other for the amusement of the guests that they had on the ship. These fights had no time limit and on one occasion Equiano thought he had fought another boy for something like an hour before both boys were too exhausted to carry on. The gentlemen who the ship were transporting gave the boys who had fought for them between five and nine shillings each and this so-called sport was encouraged by both the captain and the crew.

Eventually the ship reached the Orkneys and from there took on a large company of soldiers and joining a fleet, left there to sail for England. Apart from meeting a ship on the way that they originally took to be a French frigate, but was in fact British, the trip to Portsmouth was uneventful much to Olaudah's disappointment as he was hoping to get involved in action against the French. When they arrived in Portsmouth, the Captain was sent to London as he had been given promotion whilst Equiano and Baker were transferred to the *Savage* and after that sent ashore in Deal where they stayed until Lieutenant Pascal sent for them to go to London, a place that Equiano was desperate to see. When they arrived they were met by a Mr. Guerin who was a relation of Pascal. Mr. Guerin had two sisters who were very kind to Equiano and looked after him almost as soon as he had arrived there. However, just as he was settling in he became very ill and was sent to St. George's Hospital where he became so ill that the doctors thought it would be necessary to amputate his left leg in order that his life could be saved. Equiano refused to allow the operation to go ahead however, and amazingly made a full recovery. At this point in time, Equiano seemed to be leading a charmed life as he then caught smallpox, which was a dreadful disease that killed millions all over the world, but again he made a full recovery. This was very unusual as it was to be nearly forty years before Dr. Edward Jenner, the modest country doctor from Berkeley in Gloucestershire, made his first attempts at finding a cure for this appalling illness.

It was during this period that Pascal had been promoted to 1st Lieutenant on the *Preston*, a new Man of War that was moored at Deptford, and he sent for Equiano and Richard Baker to join him and once again they sailed to Holland to bring back some minor royal. Pascal was then transferred to the *Royal George* and initially wanted Equiano to stay on board the *Preston,* but Equiano, who had by this time become very attached to Pascal, begged him to take him on board the *Royal George* which Pascal agreed to, although he insisted on Baker staying on board the *Preston.* The two friends were heartbroken but there was no changing Pascal's mind, and the two young friends embraced for one last time, parting company and destined never to see each other again.

Equiano was miserable on the *Royal George* without his friend and he had no one person to talk to in the way he could with Richard. Before long however, there was another change taking place as Pascal was made sixth Lieutenant on the *Namur* which was at Spithead being prepared for action. The crew of the *Royal George* were all transferred to her so at least Equiano was not taken from his master at this point in time. The expedition that the *Namur* was joining was set up to mount a force to take the town of Louisburgh and was led by Vice-Admiral Boscawen and they were joined by another fleet under Admiral Cornish in the *Lennox* who was heading for the East Indies. The two fleets set sail together but parted company after a few days.

Equiano was certainly serving with the naval elite when he was being led by someone like Vice-Admiral Edward Boscawen (1711-61). The third son of Viscount Falmouth, he was known as Old Dreadnought. He acquitted himself brilliantly when he took Porto Bello in 1739 and also at the siege of Cartagena two years later and in 1744, whilst in command of the *Dreadnought*, he captured the French *Medee,* taking 800 prisoners in the process. In 1755, he intercepted the French fleet off Newfoundland, capturing two 64-gun ships and this time taking no less than 1,500 prisoners.

In the summer of 1758, Boscawen's fleet sailed to Cape Breton where the soldiers that were on board were landed in order that they might fight the French at Louisbough. The French at Cape Breton resisted the British troops for a long time whilst the sea battle was equally ferocious before the British were at last successful in taking Louisbough although there were large casualties on both sides. The British sailors were often ashore after that and the French Governor and his wife came aboard ship and dined with the British officers. Although the fighting was fierce, there was always a mutual respect in the 18th century for the enemy and so the friendliness between the British and French officers was by no means unusual. Eventually, a small fleet was left in port at Louisbough whilst Vice-Admiral Boscawen and the remainder of the fleet sailed for home and arrived at Spithead at the beginning of 1759 and from there sailed to Portsmouth Harbour to re-fit. Equiano and his master, Lieutenant Pascal followed Boscawen to London where a Press Gang was formed in order to complement the crews that had returned. Thus did Equiano get his first taste of action – he was to be involved in many more.

Equiano now spoke English well – he had been away from England nearly three years but had learned the language on board ship and could certainly understand everything that was being said to him. He liked the Europeans and no longer was in awe of them as he was when he first came across them. He certainly felt that they were superior to his own people but in such a way that he thought he could emulate as he was desperate to be like them in speech, manners, and religion. Whilst in London with his master, Lieutenant Pascal, he was sent to the Guerin sisters who were relatives of Pascal, and who had been so kind to him before. Olaudah was keen to become a Christian, and on hearing from one of the other servants that you would not go to Heaven when you died if you had not first been baptized, he asked the Guerin sisters whether he could in fact go through that process.

The elder one agreed at once and in February, 1759, he was baptized in St. Margaret's Church, Westminster, which as it turned out, was quite a famous church being the place where many eminent politicians such as Winston Churchill were married.

After spending some time with the Guerin sisters it was time to move on again which meant a sad parting between Equiano and the two ladies who had been so kind to him. Lieutenant Pascal was ordered back to the *Namur* and he took Equiano with him. Their orders were to sail to the Mediterranean along with a large fleet and soon after setting sail from England they arrived in Gibraltar in August, 1759 which Equiano liked because he was allowed to go on shore. Whilst he was in Gibraltar however, Olaudah heard some news that saddened him greatly. He had previously left his best friend, Richard Baker on board the *Preston* and was overjoyed when she joined them at Gibraltar. However, joy quickly turned to utter despair when he was told that his young friend had died. The crew brought Baker's chest which was full of his possessions and gave them to Lieutenant Pascal who then gave them to Equiano, who kept the belongings, "as a memorial to my friend, whom I loved, and grieved for, as a brother". After a short time, they sailed to Barcelona and after taking in supplies, sailed again to Toulon, where they took part in a blockade to fight the French fleet should they make an appearance.

Equiano made friends with a man of about forty years of age called Daniel Queen who took Olaudah under his wing teaching him many things such as shaving and cutting hair, and probably most important of all, he taught him how to read using the Bible. Equiano served with distinction during the seven years war and in 1763, when it was over, he assumed that because of his bravery during the war when his life was constantly in danger, his promotion to Able Seaman and the fact that he had been baptised, he would be released by his master as a free man, but he was completely wrong. Pascal, who Equiano had served so loyally over the years had completely deceived him, had kept all his wages and prize money and wanted to sell him to a Captain James Doran. Equiano argued with Doran that he was entitled to his freedom but to no avail and Doran duly purchased him from Pascal. Olaudah was owed a huge amount of money but received nothing from Pascal. He did have nine guineas (£9.45p), which had been able to acquire by buying and selling small goods when he was ashore but kept that a secret from Pascal in case he took that money as well. He was taken back to the West Indies where he feared that he would be back to where he started many years before.

Equiano was told by a messenger that he was to go ashore and his future would be made quite clear very soon. Equiano was very nervous but he had no option other than to do what he was told and go ashore where he met the Captain who was with a man called Robert King. The Captain told Equiano that his present master, Doran, and his previous master, Michael Pascal, both assured the Captain of Olaudah's good character and the Captain told Equiano that he would like to take him to England, but felt he couldn't as he thought that Equiano was likely to escape. He assured Equiano however, that his new Master was the best and the kindest of masters that anyone could wish to have. Equiano was deeply upset by now but his new Master, Robert King tried to reassure him. Robert

King was a Quaker, and Quakers had a core belief that all men and women were born equal and so the idea of owning a slave did not sit well in their belief system. Also, the Quakers were good traders but the iron that they sold was used to chain the slaves together and the confectionery they also sold was manufactured with the aid of the sugar plantation that was worked by the slaves. Robert King was a kindly man, and he had problems trying to justify his religion with his actions to himself, let alone other people. However, he told Equiano that he was going to take him to Philadelphia and would put him through school and also give Equiano the job of being King's Clerk. Equiano was relieved but still sad when his ship parted the next day and it was a long time before he got over this latest upheaval. However, it turned out that King was very much the kindly man that he was portrayed as. Equiano described him as, "possessing a most amiable disposition and temper, and was very charitable and humane. If any of his slaves behaved amiss he did not beat them or use them ill, but parted with them". King told Equiano that he would not treat him as other slaves were treated, even the lucky ones who had him for a master. King asked Equiano what he knew and Equiano told him that he had learned seamanship, knew how to shave people and dress hair, that he could refine wines, read and write and was able to calculate arithmetical problems. If Equiano had to be a slave, then he was lucky to be with a man such as Robert King. He treated his slaves better than any other master and would often give slaves who were not his extra food, as he felt that they never received enough. You did not need to own land to be a slave owner and it was common practice in slavery that a person without any land would buy a slave and let them out to plantation owners at so much a day and then give their slaves what they chose to give for each days work. Often it simply wasn't enough but Equiano had witnessed slaves being beaten simply for asking for more than the starvation allowances that they were receiving.

Equiano served Robert King well, and his master was very pleased with him. He worked on King's ships, and worked as a clerk delivering and receiving cargoes to the ships, and would often shave and dress his master and look after his horses. King openly acknowledged that Equiano had saved him a lot of money that he would otherwise have had to pay a clerk. King not only treated Equiano well, he offered him hope of an escape route out of the slave trade. King promised Equiano that he could buy his freedom from King if he, Equiano, could pay him the £40 that King had originally paid for him. When Equiano sailed from the West Indies to America he decided that he would raise the £40 to buy his way out of the system. He only had a small amount of money but he went ashore and traded with small items until his money gradually started to build up. He watched other traders carefully and learned well as he went along until in the end, he became a good trader himself. In the meantime however, although he was treated well along with Robert King's other slaves, Equiano was witness to many cruel acts against them. He tells of other clerks along with other white men gratifying their sexual urges on little African girls who would have been terrified as to what was going to happen to them anyway. He tells tales of men who called themselves Christians raping girls as young as ten years old and although sickened by what he saw, he could do nothing to prevent it. He also saw an African man staked to the ground, and cut very badly over his body and then having to suffer his ears being cut off bit by bit because he'd been having sex with a white woman. The woman in question was a prostitute and had in fact consented to the act. Equiano was not at all bothered that the lady in question was a prostitute, but it was the fact that an African man was being severely punished for having sex with a white woman and was therefore committing an offence and yet it was deemed acceptable for a white man to commit sexual horrors on very young African girls. The injustice of it all confused him completely. Some plantation owners often travelled away for weeks or months at a time and left the management of their slaves to men who Equiano called 'Human Butchers'. These men took full advantage of the situation beating and starving their charges into submission. There were a few good masters and Robert King was one of them. Apart from being a naturally kind man, he also thought it only sensible to look after his slaves well because they would produce more work if they were happier and healthy, and that would result in more profit for the owners. Equiano also found out that one plantation owner had several children of mixed race working for him as slaves, and that he, the plantation owner, was the father. Although they were his children he considered them no more worthy because he was the father and they were treated equally badly as the other slaves, presumably because their mother was African.

In 1763, after Equiano had been away from his original home for seven years, luck seemed to turn in his favour. Being in charge of a sloop belonging to his master was Captain Thomas Farmer, an English naval officer and had taken a liking to Equiano because of his hard work and reliability not to mention the bravery he had shown in the seven years war against the French. Farmer was a very capable commander and Equiano's master had made a great deal of money as a result of the captain's efficiency. Many of the sloop's crew were unreliable and often got drunk resulting in them deserting their positions thus making Farmer short on crew members. As a result, Farmer asked Equiano's master, Robert King, if he, Farmer, could have Equiano as a proper crew member as opposed to a slave. King was unwilling to let Equiano go but Captain Farmer persisted, and said that having Equiano on board would be better than any three white men that he currently had. In the event, Farmer wore King down and to Equiano's delight, asked him if he wanted to go to sea or to stay ashore and look after Mr. King's stores. Equiano, thinking that by travelling, he was more likely to make some money chose to go to sea with Captain Farmer. He also thought that by being a proper member of the crew, he would be better fed as he was still on limited rations and always hungry. However, he still belonged to King, and whenever the ship was in port, King always had jobs that he wanted Equiano to do, so he got little rest and was always tired, but at least he was well thought of by the people that mattered.

After some time sailing with his captain, Equiano thought that he would try his hand at buying and selling items in order to make some money. All he had was the equivalent of three old pence but when he was in a Dutch island called St. Eustatia he bought a glass tumbler for that amount and sold it in Montserrat for double the amount, six old pence. For a while, the ship went back and forth between St. Eustatia and Montserrat and on his next trip Equiano bought two more tumblers with his six pence and again sold these for double that amount. The sloop travelled around to many different islands and in each one, Equiano bought and sold at a profit until he had a full dollar, which to an ex-slave in the 18th century, was a lot of money. Despite the fact that to all intents and purposes he was an ordinary member of the crew, he was still ill treated by white men and at one stage had his possessions that he was buying and selling stolen from him. However, he was ever resilient and managed to earn himself money once more and with the proceeds bought a bible.

Despite the fact that life wasn't looking too bad for Equiano, he was still witnessing the horrors of the way Africans were treated, and even if he ever won his freedom, he wondered whether it would actually mean anything. One day, the ship was in Monserrat waiting to set sail for Philadelphia when a shocking thing happened which Equiano was witness to. On board there was a member of the crew named Joseph Clipson who was a gentleman of mixed race and who had been with the ship a long time. The Captain and mate plus members of the crew saw him as a free man and many of them had known him since he was a child. One day, the captain of a ship bound for Bermuda came on board and told Clipson that he was not free and that he, the captain, had received orders from Clipson's master that he be apprehended and taken to Bermuda. Clipson showed the captain a certificate that confirmed he had been born a free man in St. Kitts but they took no notice, and their numbers being heavy, were able to apprehend Clipson and remove him from Equiano's ship. He asked if he could be taken to the magistrates so that they could confirm that he was speaking the truth and he was told that they would do that.

However, as soon as the poor man was off the ship they went back on their word and took him on board their own ship where he lay for a night before being forcibly kept on the ship that sailed the next day. He wasn't even allowed to say goodbye to his wife and child and it is almost certain that he never saw them again. This made Equiano wonder whether freedom was worth obtaining for his race as he was witness to other examples of this nature. He felt that it was almost worse being a free African rather than a slave who was reasonably well treated, because as a free black person, you were always living in fear of being captured and taken away. Certainly in the West Indies, the law courts did not recognise that a black man had any rights at all, so it was almost worse than useless to try and get redress there. Despite this, Equiano was still determined to get his freedom but wished to claim it in the correct manner because even though he had opportunities to escape over the months and years, he was extremely fond of his master, Robert King, and was determined to legitimately buy his freedom even if it took years to do. King had already promised Equiano that if he raised the sum of £40 which is what King paid for him, he, Equiano, could have his freedom. They soon sailed for Philadelphia where Equiano was able to trade again, making good profits on the goods that he was selling so that one day he could take his master at his word.

Whilst the ship was in Montserrat, Equiano was told of a woman named Mrs. Davis who told people's fortunes but he did not believe that any human being would have the ability to do such a thing and he completely dismissed it from his mind. However, that night, he dreamt of this woman, although he had never previously seen her. Try as he might, the next day Equiano was unable to get this dream out of his mind and after his previous indifference, was now determined to see her. He found out her address and went to see her, where to his astonishment, she was wearing the same dress that had appeared on her the previous night in the dream. She further astonished Equiano when she told him that he had dreamt of her the previous night and sat him down and gave him a reading. She told him of many incidents that had previously happened to him with great accuracy and also said that he would not be a slave for long. She also said that he would twice be in great danger of his life, but if he escaped death, he would go on to have his freedom and enjoy a good life. Whether she was a charlatan or a genuine medium we will never know, but certainly Equiano was convinced by the things that she had told him.

Equiano continued to sail with the captain that he liked so much but was not pleased with what the ship was doing, as it was picking up slaves from Montserrat and transporting them to Georgia and Charlestown. This did not sit well with him but although well treated, he was still a slave and there was little he could do about it. Whilst at Charleston, he continued to trade but was deceived by a white man who, whilst buying his goods, gave him money that was supposed to be dollars but were in fact worthless. When Equiano tried to pass them on during further trading, he was about to be beaten up but luckily made his escape and found his way back to the ship but was nevertheless uneasy until the ship had sailed. However, he was not so fortunate when the ship arrived at Georgia. One Sunday night, he was with some other Africans in the yard of their master, Doctor Perkins, who as it happened was a very cruel man who treated his slaves badly, often being drunk. For some reason he was not best pleased when he saw Equiano with his slaves and along with another white man, beat Equiano up so badly he was near death, and they then dumped him at the local jail. The Captain, knowing that Equiano was very reliable was very concerned that he had not returned to the ship that night and so made enquiries as to his whereabouts. Eventually he found him and horror struck at Equiano's condition, immediately summoned several of the best doctors, all of whom initially expressed the view that Equiano could not survive such a beating and that he would die. The Captain sought Dr. Perkins, the man who had hurt Equiano so badly, out and challenged him to a fight, but the cowardly Perkins refused. Equiano was nursed back to health by a Doctor Brady with his master constantly in attendance, and eventually Equiano was fit to work again when the ship set sail for Montserrat. No action was taken against Dr. Perkins showing once again that slaves had no redress through the courts. The year was 1764 and the ship stayed in Montserrat until the beginning of 1765.

At the beginning of 1766, Robert King, Equiano's master, purchased another ship called the *Nancy* and this was the largest ship that Equiano had seen. He was very pleased at King's choice as it meant that he could store more items that he bought so that he could make more money. The more items he was able to buy and store, the more money he could make. Much as he liked Robert King, Equiano was determined to purchase his freedom and without realising it, King was helping him to do just that by buying a larger ship. When they arrived in Philadelphia, Equiano started trading as quickly as he could, and he found the

Quakers more honest than any of the previous people he had dealt with and so mainly traded with them.

Equiano was by now very interested in finding religion. He longed to be part of the white person's world and they all seemed to be Christians so he tried to find out more about it. There was a particular Sunday morning when he was going to church that he went past a meeting house that was full of Quakers. He entered the house, and was astonished to see a woman standing in the middle of this large group of people talking to them all in a loud voice that he could hear. At the end of the meeting, Equiano asked several of the people who were present what it was that the woman was saying but everyone seemed reluctant to tell him. At this he lost interest and left to find a church which he eventually managed to do but this too puzzled him. He had been in churches before but had never seen one with so many people inside such as this one had. The church was completely full, and so was the churchyard and there were even people who had climbed ladders and were looking in through the windows. When Equiano asked why it was so crowded, he was told that the Revd. George Whitefield was preaching. Equiano had heard of Whitefield but this was the first time that he had ever seen him preaching and he was anxious to hear what it was that Whitefield was speaking about that caused so many people to go and see him preach. What he saw and heard fascinated him. Equiano wrote of Whitefield in his book:- "When I got into the church I saw this pious man exhorting the people with the greatest fervour and earnestness, and sweating as much as I ever did while in slavery on Montserrat beach".

He added a few lines later:- "… I thought it strange I had never seen divines exert themselves in this manner before, and I was no longer at a loss to account for the thin congregations they preached to".

George Whitefield (1714-1770) was one of the most famous speakers of his day, if not *the* most famous. He was born in Gloucester, the son of a widow who kept an inn in the town and was educated at the Crypt School, Gloucester and then Pembroke College, Oxford. He preached his first sermon in the Crypt Church in his home town but in 1738, at the age of twenty-four, he went to America where he preached that year in Georgia. He founded the Bethesda Orphanage which is still running today. Curiously, he supported slavery and in fact kept slaves himself who worked at the orphanage. Slaves were originally prohibited in Georgia but in 1749 there was a movement to allow the practice there, a movement which he supported. He was one of the first speakers to preach in the open air and some of his sermons attracted thousands of people. Along with John and Charles Wesley, he helped to found the Methodist movement although he fell out with them over the doctrine of predestination in 1741. He went to America seven times altogether and left England for America for the last time in 1769 and died in Boston the following year.

Returning to the life of Equiano, eventually, after three years, he had made enough money to pay King and purchase the freedom that he cherished so much but he asked the Captain how he should go about broaching the subject to his master. This was because promises made to him in the past had been reneged upon and he was nervous that it would happen again, kind as King had always been. The Captain told Equiano to come with him one morning at breakfast to talk to King and this they did. King was amazed that Equiano had raised the money and said that he would not have made the promise if he had thought Equiano would have raised the money so quickly. However, with a little bit of pushing from the Captain, Robert King was as good as his word and agreed to sign the necessary forms declaring that Equiano was a free man. Olaudah was overjoyed and rushed to the Registry Office where he was congratulated by the staff there and given the necessary papers which he took back to King who duly signed. Olaudah raced outside running everywhere overjoyed at what he thought was the happiest day of his life.

Given how much this meant to Equiano, or Gustavus Vassa as he was often known, it is probably worth quoting the full text here:-

"Montserrat – To all men under whom these presents shall come: I Robert King, of the parish of St. Anthony in the said island, merchant, send greeting: Know ye, that I the aforesaid Robert King, for and in consideration of the sum of seventy pounds current money of the said island, to me in hand paid, and to the intent that a negro man-slave, named Gustavus Vassa, shall and may become free, have manumitted, emancipated, enfranchised, and set free, and by these presents do manumit, emancipate, enfranchise, and set free, the aforesaid negro man-slave, named Gustavus Vassa, for ever, hereby giving, granting, and releasing unto him, the said Gustavus Vassa, all right, title, dominion, sovereignity, and property, which, as lord and master over the aforesaid Gustavus Vassa, I had, or now I have, or by any means whatsoever I may or can hereafter possibly have over him the aforesaid negro, for ever. In witness whereof I the above said Robert King have unto these presents set my hand and seal, this tenth day of July, in the year of our Lord one thousand seven hundred and sixty-six.

ROBERT KING

Signed, sealed and delivered in the presence of Terrylegay, Montserrat.

Registered the within manumission at full length, this eleventh day of July, 1766, in liber D.

TERRYLEGAY, Register."

It was 1766 and Equiano was a freeman and now keen to travel to London which he had not seen for four years. He loved London – it felt like home to him and there were many black people living there who were not slaves but had been accepted in all walks of society. However, Equiano knew that freedom could not be gained merely by having a piece of paper, he also needed money. London was full of trading opportunities and Equiano turned the skills that he had already learned to try his hand at making some money. He also decided to look up friends that he had met there when he had been in London four years previously. He called on the Guerin sisters who had always been kind to him and they were delighted to see him and receive the news that he was a free man. The sisters arranged for him to lodge at a hairdressers shop in the Haymarket which also enabled him to have an apprenticeship there. Added to this was the fact that he also paid for lessons in playing the French horn and for studying mathematics which meant that he was becoming a member of the British society that he had wished to be for so long.

After a while however, he realised that he simply was not successful at making the money that he hoped for and felt that the only way he could improve his finances was to go back to sea again, although not as a slave, but as a merchant adventurer. He sailed round the Mediterranean and renewed old friendships. Equiano enjoyed being back at sea because he felt free being a sailor and was well fed but he was unaware of the danger that lay ahead of him. An African man who was a friend of his and was also a free man was captured and made a slave. Equiano was frightened at this and feared that the same thing would happen to him and sadly it did. One day whilst he was on route for Jamaica, he was talking to a Master of a small ship who asked Equiano whether he would join him but Equiano refused. The man was persistent but Equiano was equally determined that he would not go, but without any warning, the Master turned nasty, attacked Equiano when he wasn't expecting it and Equiano was bound and gagged and seemingly right back to where he had been as a slave years before. The papers that he had giving him his freedom were taken from him and without them, he had no proof that he was a free man. He had no comeback anyway, as the Courts in the West Indies would always side with the Master, so that in effect, there was no such thing as a free African. After all that he had achieved in educating himself over a period of years and saving up enough of his honestly earned money to buy his freedom from Robert King, he found himself bound tightly in the rigging of the ship that he was on and a slave once more.

However, eventually Equiano's luck changed and he managed to escape and once more went back to being an adventurer, a way of life that he happily embraced. He carried on like this until May, 1773 when seeing the chance of fame, he joined an expedition that was to go to the North Pole. The purpose of this trip was to find the notorious North West Passage across the top of the earth and had it succeeded would have given Equiano both fame and fortune. The expedition was headed by Captain Constantine John Phipps (1744-92) who was an officer in the Royal Navy as well as an explorer, his trip setting off in June 1773. Captain Cook (1728-79) also tried to find this route a few years later when he set off with two ships, the *Resolution* and the *Discovery* in 1776 but it ended in disaster on 14th February 1779 with Cook's death after a scuffle with the local people in Hawaii. Like Cook, Phipps set off with two ships, the *Racehorse* which he commanded and the *Carcass*, the Captain being Skeffington Lutwidge and on this ship was a nineteen-year-old Midshipman named Horatio Nelson. This is the trip where Nelson had his famous encounter with a polar bear which almost killed him. Given the extraordinary successes that Nelson would later have in his career against the French in the Battle of the Nile (1798) and the Battle of Trafalgar (1805), it is possible that the war with Napoleon Bonaparte could well have had a different ending had this young midshipman not survived this particular fight.

Amongst the people that Phipps took on the voyage was a Dr. Charles Irving who acted as the naturalist. Equiano had met Dr. Irving a few years earlier in 1768 when he was in fact employed by Irving. Irving had achieved fame of sorts by being able to successfully distil sea water and make it fresh. Another person taken on the trip was Israel Lyons (1739-75) who acted as Astronomer. Sadly, this trip was unsuccessful as the ships had to turn back and return home due to their inability to find a way through the ice, again something that Cook and many others before him as well as Phipps had not been able to achieve.

However, there was one small consolation which was that it gave Equiano the distinction of being the first black person to go to the North Pole.

Despite his achievements, Equiano could find no peace of mind. He was happy doing what he was doing but felt that there was a spiritual aspect to his life that was missing. He felt that he would never be completely free on earth all the while he was in danger of being captured again, and so he started looking around for a spiritual freedom. He started visiting churches but he found no comfort. He attended Quaker meetings but they had no preacher so he gleaned nothing from that, and for whatever reason, although he tried the Catholic faith, that did nothing for him either. What did make him find a faith was an incident off Cadiz, Spain in 1774. Equiano was a steward in a ship called the *Hope,* the man in charge being a Captain Richard Strange. One day Equiano stood at the stern of the ship, depressed and thinking that he might drown himself, although he also had this mournful fear of death which he spoke to many people about. He was persuaded not to do it but was unhappy at being on the ship with so many of the crew not having the Christian faith. On the morning of 6th October,1774, Equiano had a strange feeling that he was about to witness something supernatural – he didn't know what it would be, he just sensed that something was about to happen. In the evening of the same day, something *did* happen and these were the words that Equiano himself used to describe it:- "…not knowing whether salvation was to be had partly for our own good deeds, or solely as the sovereign gift of God; in this deep consternation the Lord was pleased to break in upon my soul with his bright beams of heavenly light; and in an instant as it were, removing the veil, and letting light into a dark place…". A few paragraphs later in his book he says:- "The amazing things of that hour can never be told – it was the joy in the Holy Ghost! I felt an astonishing change; the burden of sin, the gaping jaws of hell, and the fears of death, that weighed me down before, now lost their horror; indeed, I thought death would now be the best earthly friend I ever had. Such were my grief and joy as I believe are seldom experienced. I was bathed in tears, and said, "What am I that God should thus look on me the vilest of sinners?" Then:- "…I viewed the unconverted people of the world in a very awful state, being without God and without hope". Equiano thought that his life must have a purpose and it was not long before he realised what it should be. He felt that he was put on the earth because he had a mission to help other people generally, but more specifically to help save his own people from the barbaric cruelty of slavery. However, his conversion gave him a huge challenge, which was to question the very thing that the Christian society based it's way of life and economic success on, the barbaric use of fellow human beings as slaves, and the utter cruelty that went with it. Inevitably, he was drawn to the abolitionist cause that was headed by William Wilberforce (1759-1833), and which included many dedicated people such as Thomas Clarkson (1760-1846), Hannah More (1745-1833), and the Prime Minister,

William Pitt the Younger (1759-1806). However, the original decision to campaign relentlessly against slavery until its abolition was taken by three friends and colleagues on 12th May, 1787 under an oak tree in Pitt's estate in Holwood. The three young men were William Pitt, William Wilberforce, and Pitt's cousin, William Grenville (1759-1834), who was Prime Minister in 1807, the year that the trafficking of slaves was made illegal and the year following Pitt's early death in 1806. They shared the same Christian name as well as being born in the same year, but the most important thing they shared was their hatred of slavery.

Although that famous meeting between the three friends under the tree on Pitt's estate was the start of a long Parliamentary campaign against slavery, there was a man who wanted desperately to tackle the problem years before and his name was Granville Sharp (1735-1813), and like many important things, his involvement came by pure chance. William Wilberforce's name has deservedly gone down in history more than any other when the issue of the abolishment of slavery is mentioned, but to many, Granville Sharp is known as the father of the abolition movement. Sharp was born on 10th November, 1735 and was the son of an Archdeacon. Granville was one of thirteen brothers and sisters and they were all devoted to music, Granville playing the flute and oboe. Indeed, there were so many of them that played a musical instrument that they formed an orchestra together and Granville delighted in the fact that his Christian name, surname, and love of music enabled him to engrave his instruments G#.

His involvement with the abolitionist movement began one day in 1765 when he was walking down Mincing Lane in London, having just left his brother's surgery. His brother was a doctor and also a kindly man who often gave free treatment to the poor and when Granville came across an African man lying badly injured in the gutter, he took him back to see his brother in order that he may receive much needed medical treatment. His name was Jonathan Strong and he told Granville that his Master was a West Indian planter called David Lisle. One day Lisle got very drunk and flogged Strong so badly that he could barely walk and was blinded temporarily. He also threw Strong out of his house and quite how he managed to end up near Doctor Sharp's surgery is not known, but it started a chain of events that began the abolitionist movement. Granville's brother thought Strong's injuries so bad that he had him admitted to St. Bartholomew's Hospital where he remained for four months.

Granville's eyes had been opened to the horrors of the slave trade and he wanted to bring about some constructive action that would help end it but in this he found that he had to be patient. However, his chance came in 1772 when a slave called James Somersett escaped from his Master's custody whilst in England but had been recaptured and was being held in captivity before being shipped off to the West Indies. Sharp decided to dispute the case taking the view that the man's detention in England was illegal. The case was brought before a Judge Mansfield who ruled that:- "the state of slavery is so odious that nothing can be suffered to support it but positive law, and there is no law". He ordered Somersett's immediate discharge. This ruling lead to the release of some ten thousand slaves who were in England but in fact Judge Mansfield's ruling had been misinterpreted. He was actually ruling that until legislation explicitly covering the status of slaves in England was passed by Parliament and made law, a Master's colonial rights could not be used in Britain and at the time of Somersett's case, there was no law. However, that case began the abolitionist movement but although the pioneer of it, Sharp handed over the leading of the cause to Thomas Clarkson who worked so hard for it over the years that he made himself very ill and he had to take a break from it to give himself time to recover - indeed he had worn himself out so badly that some of his colleagues thought he might never return. However, he did return and once William Wilberforce, along with Pitt and Grenville had made their promise to each other under the oak tree in May, 1787, there proceeded a relentless campaign in and out of Parliament for the abolition of the trade which was passed twenty years later in 1807, although slavery itself was not made illegal until 1833, the year that Wilberforce died, although he lived just long enough to see it.

From that moment under the tree on Pitt's estate in 1787, William Wilberforce campaigned relentlessly for the abolition of the slave trade and his was the parliamentary voice, but Olaudah Equiano worked hard outside parliament writing many letters to the press that not only brought the public's attention to the barbaric trade, but also shattered the myth that all black people were ignorant illiterate savages as letter after letter was printed in the papers of the day. In this, he was fighting an uphill battle because a few years earlier, a court case showed that that was exactly how Africans were seen, not only as ignorant illiterate savages but even worse, inanimate goods and chattel.

In 1781, a slave ship, the *Zong*, captained by Luke Collingwood set sail from Liverpool to Africa in order to pick up slaves with a view to taking them to Jamaica to sell. However, tragedy was to follow as the incompetent and cruel Collingwood had taken on board more slaves than he could transport with any safety. They had left Africa on 6th September, 1781 but there was a bad case of dysentery on board and by the 29th November seven of the crew were dead along with sixty slaves. The dead were in the hold of the ship and Collingwood knew that he would not be able to claim on the insurance if they arrived in Jamaica with the bodies still on board so he gave the order for them to be thrown overboard. Along with the slaves that were already dead he added many more who were sick and a total of 122 slaves, many of whom were still alive, were jettisoned. By so doing, Collingwood claimed £30 per head on each of the dead slaves on behalf of the owners of the *Zong* and this was duly paid by the insurers. The journey had been delayed through Collingwood's useless navigation which made the journey much longer than would have been necessary and he cited lack of water as the reason he had to get rid of the sick and dying. The shipowners won the case despite the fact that there was indeed plenty of water but lost the Appeal to the insurers for the same reason, that there was plenty of water which may have kept the prisoners alive. It was during this period that both Olaudah Equiano and Granville Sharp became involved in the case. On the 19th March, 1783, Equiano had visited Granville Sharp and told him the story of the killings on board the *Zong* and it reunited Sharp and Lord Chief Justice Mansfield who had been involved with Sharp a decade earlier in the case of James Somersett. The Appeal concerning the *Zong* was presided over by Lord Chief Justice Lord Mansfield and having won the Appeal, the door was now open for murder charges to be brought against Collingwood and his crew but for reasons that are unclear this simply didn't happen. Despite the fact that Judge Mansfield had described it as 'a very shocking case' it appeared that not everyone took his view. One of the horrifying judgements that came out of this dreadful incident was that Mr. John Lee, the Solicitor-General, said that: "Blacks are goods and chattels' and refused to accept that any murders had taken place. He said that: "The case was the same as if horses had been thrown overboard" and as a result no officers were prosecuted for murder as in Lee's view, the slaves were no more than inanimate objects. Indeed, that thinking was the basis of the original insurance policy which stated that it was insurance against jettisoning 'goods and of part to save the residue'. By jettisoning the 122 weakest slaves, Collingwood had hoped to save the health of the remaining Africans, not for compassionate reasons, but merely so that they could be sold in Jamaica.

Returning to Wilberforce, he was going to present what would be the first of many bills to the House of Commons when he was taken ill in January, 1788 and was unable to do it. In fact he was very ill, and some thought he may not recover but in the meantime it was William Pitt the Prime Minister who stepped in and started the discussions in Parliament about how to be rid of slavery. It was at this time that Olaudah Equiano was writing his book, *'The Interesting Narrative of the Life of Olaudah Equiano, or Gustavus Vassa the African written by Himself'*, which was printed in 1789. Equiano had raised his profile by writing to the papers about slavery and he used the fact that people knew of him by writing a book about his life generally and the slave trade in particular. He had been round the world as a seaman and was knowledgeable about African societies as well as plantation societies which was essential if his book was to have credibility. Equiano knew that he had to face the inevitable criticism that the British economy was based on the slave trade operating as it did and that he would have to come up with a viable alternative. He argued that Britain should enter into a free trade with Africa which would benefit the African nations and would replace the revenue brought in by the slave trade. He also said that not only would no revenue be lost but that Britain would be better off socially and morally. It was customary in the 18th century when writing a book to arrange for subscribers to pay in advance so that publishing the first edition would be financed. Because of his already high profile, the first subscriber named was the Prince of Wales, followed by the Dukes of York and Cumberland along with members of the aristocracy, churches, and leading abolitionists. In order for him to achieve large sales he had to appeal to the largest audience possible so he was aiming for a wide readership. To do this he described the slave trade in some detail, but he also needed to make himself a positive role model for African people, so in the front of the book there was a portrait of Equiano dressed in the clothes of a wealthy Englishman and at the same time holding a bible. The book became an instant best seller, making the author extremely wealthy and raising the profile of the slave trade by describing in detail its horrors to a general public that for the most part were unaware of just what was going on and how slaves were treated.

However, there were too many vested interests for the slavery issue to be handled in any meaningful way and far too much opposition for any bill on the subject to be successful, but it did mean that the abolishment movement had put down a marker and would not give up until they won the day. Wilberforce and Equiano had support from many influential people and one of these was the famous pottery maker, Josiah Wedgewood (1730-95). He produced unglazed blue jasper ware and these included an image of a slave kneeling with the words:- "Am I not a man and a Brother?" which he also had engraved on medallions. The medallions sold in huge amounts to the wealthy and almost became a fashion accessory – no matter, they raised the profile of the slavery issue amongst the rich and powerful. This image was very effective and also caught the attention of the masses, some men having snuff boxes engraved and these too sold in huge amounts. It took twenty gruelling years of Wilberforce's and other people's lives, but eventually on 23rd February, 1807, Wilberforce succeeded in getting the bill to abolish the slave trade through the House of Commons by the huge margin of 283 votes for and a mere 16 against.

However, in the meantime, after writing his book and publishing it in 1789, Equiano had re-invented himself and become a very rich English gentleman, something he had wanted for himself for a very long time. After all his travel over many years, Equiano decided to settle in Britain which he did, and married a local girl named Susannah Cullen on 7th April, 1792 in St. Andrews Church, Soham, Cambridgeshire. The couple lived in the area and had two daughters, Anna Maria, who was born on 16th October, 1793 and Joanna, born on 11th April, 1795.

Equiano was extremely popular and now because of the book, extremely rich and when that happens, there is almost always a backlash against that person. This happened to Equiano because there was a pro-slavery lobby which met under the name of the West India Committee. They started to question Equiano's version of how he was born and claimed that he was not born in Africa as he said, but born into slavery in South Carolina in America. They said that this meant he could not have experienced the horrors of the middle passage although they had to concede that everything else could be true.

However, it seemed to be a legitimate question to ask because they found their information by looking up Equiano's baptism record and also his naval records. With regard to his baptism records, that could be countered by saying it was misinformation by slave owners but the naval records are harder to explain away. By the time he was serving in the navy, he was an adult and under no pressure to falsify his records, although again, it's quite possible that Equiano simply told the clerk at the time to put that down as he did not feel it important. Perhaps by the time he was in the navy, he was simply wanting to forget his painful past, but the truth is, we probably will never know the answer. What is undisputed however, is the fact that the unanswered question of his birth had not affected his book sales in any way. It is also certain that wherever he was born, this would not have any affect as to the validity of the facts written by Equiano concerning slavery, but if he was seen to lie about the way he was taken from his parents and then after that his sister, it would nullify the first chapter of the book and undermine the contents of the rest of it.

Whatever his origins, Olaudah Equiano has earned his place in history and deserves to be remembered with respect and affection. There is no doubt that he suffered badly by the hands of slave owners and yet seems to bear little or no grudge against any of these owners who perpetuated this horror on fellow human beings. He deserves gratitude and affection also because of the millions of African lives that along with others, he helped to change for the better. His wife Susannah died in February 1796, aged just thirty-four years, whilst Equiano died the following year on 31st March, 1797 aged fifty-one. It is sad that he never saw that the slave trade was eventually abolished because it was another ten years after his death before that was achieved, but his name will live on as one of those few who took up the cause of getting rid of slavery, and refused to give up even when the odds seemed impossible.

-oOOo-